D1105824

HUMAN
BODY
COMPOSITION

Alex F. Roche, MD, PhD, DSc
Wright State University
Yellow Springs, Ohio

Steven B. Heymsfield, MD
St. Luke's Roosevelt Hospital
New York, New York

Timothy G. Lohman, PhD
University of Arizona
Tuscon, Arizona

Editors

Human Kinetics

To

Gilbert B. Forbes

in appreciation of his outstanding lifelong achievements

Library of Congress Cataloging-in-Publication-Data

Human body composition / Alex F. Roche, Steven B. Heymsfield, Timothy
G. Lohman, editors.
  p. cm.
  Includes bibliographical references and index.
  ISBN 0-87322-638-0
  1. Body composition. 2. Body composition--Measurement.
3. Anthropometry. I. Roche, Alex F., 1921-   . II. Heymsfield,
Steven, 1944-   . III. Lohman, Timothy G., 1940-   .
QP33.5.H85   1996
612--dc20   95-21397
                                                    CIP

ISBN: 0-87322-638-0

Copyright © 1996 by Alex F. Roche, Steven B. Heymsfield, and Timothy G. Lohman

All rights reserved. Except for use in a review, the reproduction or utilization of this work in any form or by any electronic, mechanical, or other means, now known or hereafter invented, including xerography, photocopying, and recording, and in any information storage and retrieval system, is forbidden without the written permission of the publisher.

Acquisitions Editor: Richard A. Washburn, PhD; **Developmental Editor:** Marni Basic; **Assistant Editors:** Susan Moore and Ed Giles; **Editorial Assistants:** Alecia Mapes Walk and Jennifer J. Hemphill; **Copyeditor:** Karl Stull; **Proofreader:** Dawn Barker; **Typesetting and Text Layout:** Yvonne Winsor; **Layout Artist:** Tara Welsch; **Text Designer:** Judy Henderson; **Cover Designer:** Jack Davis; **Illustrators:** Craig Ronto and Jennifer Delmotte; **Printer:** Braun-Brumfield

Printed in the United States of America   10 9 8 7 6 5 4 3 2 1

Human Kinetics
P.O. Box 5076, Champaign, IL 61825-5076
1-800-747-4457

Canada: Human Kinetics, Box 24040, Windsor, ON N8Y 4Y9
1-800-465-7301 (in Canada only)

Europe: Human Kinetics, P.O. Box IW14, Leeds LS16 6TR, United Kingdom
(44) 1132 781708

Australia: Human Kinetics, 2 Ingrid Street, Clapham 5062, South Australia
(08) 371 3755

New Zealand: Human Kinetics, P.O. Box 105-231, Auckland 1
(09) 523 3462

Contents

Contributors

Douglas L. Ballor, PhD
Human Development Studies
University of Vermont
210 Patrick Gym
Burlington, VT 05405-0001, USA

Richard N. Baumgartner, PhD
Clinical Nutrition Research Center
Surge Building, Room 215
University of New Mexico
School of Medicine
Albuquerque, NM 87131-5666, USA

Per Björntorp, MD, PhD
Dept. Heart & Lung Diseases
Sahlgren's Hospital
University of Göteborg
S-413 45 Göteborg, Sweden

Claude Bouchard, PhD
Physical Activity Sciences Laboratory
PEPS, Laval University
Quebec City, Quebec, Canada G1K 7P4

Wm. Cameron Chumlea, PhD
Division of Human Biology
Wright State University
1005 Xenia Avenue
Yellow Springs, OH 45387-1695, USA

Jean-Pierre Després, PhD
Lipid Research Centre
Laval University
Medical Research Centre
2705 Laurier Boulevard
Ste-Foy, Quebec, Canada, G1V 4G2

Staffan Edén, MD, PhD
Department of Physiology
Medicinaregatan II
University of Göteborg
S-413 90 Göteborg, Sweden

Kenneth J. Ellis, PhD
USDA/ARS Children's Nutrition Research
   Center
Department of Pediatrics
Baylor College of Medicine
Texas Children's Hospital
1100 Bates Street
Houston, TX 77030-2600, USA

Scott B. Going, PhD
Department of Physiology
University of Arizona
Ina E. Gittings Building
Tucson, AZ 85721, USA

Shumei S. Guo, PhD
Division of Human Biology
Wright State University
1005 Xenia Avenue
Yellow Springs, OH 45387-1695, USA

Steven B. Heymsfield, MD
Obesity Research Center
St. Luke's Roosevelt Hospital
1090 Amsterdam Avenue
New York, NY 10025, USA

Khursheed N. Jeejeebhoy, PhD
St. Michael's Hospital
Division of Gastroenterology
30 Bond Street, 3F-372
Toronto, Ontario, Canada M5B 1W8

Simone Lemieux, MSc, RD
Le Centre Hospitalier de l'Université Laval
2705 Boulevard Laurier
Ste-Foy, Quebec, Canada, G1V 4G2

Timothy G. Lohman, PhD
Department of Exercise and Sport Sciences
University of Arizona
Ina E. Gittings Building
Tucson, AZ 85721, USA

Henry C. Lukaski, PhD
USDA/ARS
University Station
Grand Forks Human Nutrition Research Center
P.O. Box 9034
Grand Forks, ND 58202-9034, USA

Robert M. Malina, PhD
Institute for the Study of Youth Sports
213 I.M. Sports Circle
Michigan State University
East Lansing, MI 48824-1049

Alex F. Roche, MD, PhD, DSc
Division of Human Biology
Wright State University
1005 Xenia Avenue
Yellow Springs, OH 45387-1695, USA

Robert Ross, PhD
School of Physical and Health Education
Queen's University
Kingston, Ontario, Canada, K7L 3N6

Dale A. Schoeller, PhD
The University of Chicago
Division of the Biological Sciences
5841 S. Maryland Avenue
MC 4080
Chicago, IL 60637, USA

Jacob C. Seidell, PhD
National Institute of Public Health
Dept. Chronic Disease & Environmental
  Epidemiology
Postbus 1, Antonie Van Leeuwhoeklaan 9
NL-3720 BA Bilthoven
The Netherlands

Wayne E. Sinning, PhD
Applied Physiology Research Laboratory
School of Exercise, Leisure and Sport
Kent State University
Kent, OH 44242-0001, USA

Marta D. Van Loan, PhD
Western Human Nutrition Research Center
U.S. Department of Agriculture
P.O. Box 29997
Presidio of San Francisco, CA 94129, USA

Zi-Mian Wang, MS
Obesity Research Center
St. Luke's Roosevelt Hospital
1090 Amsterdam Avenue
New York, NY 10025, USA

Robert T. Withers, PhD
Exercise Physiology Laboratory
School of Education
The Flinders University of South Australia
GPO Box 2100, Adelaide 5001, Australia

Preface

This book has been written because we considered it necessary to present, in a single publication, details of the methods used in the study of human body composition and the results that have been obtained. To date, the descriptions of methods in the literature have often been incomplete. Furthermore, inappropriate methods have been applied in some studies, and the interpretation of the results is not always correct. One should not blame the research workers involved because it is almost impossible for any individual to be familiar with the enormous literature on body composition methods, particularly when the literature is scattered in a wide variety of journals.

The chapters in this volume are grouped into parts according to our editorial aims. Part I provides comprehensive evaluative reviews by leading research workers that address the underlying concepts of methods for the measurement of body composition, the validity of the assumptions that are made, and details of their application. In these reviews, every effort has been made to provide accurate information that will be useful to the readers. The chapters in Part II address reported results for general populations and particular groups. These results were selected from many publications, taking into account the methods used to obtain the data and the size and nature of the groups studied. The chapters in Part III give attention to the relationships between body composition and risk factors for cardiovascular and selected metabolic diseases and some factors that influence body composition. Finally, information is provided in the Appendix about sources of equipment and supplies.

Reported data for the precision (replicability) and validity (accuracy) of body composition methods describe the situation when the methods are applied with the attention to detail that is usual in research laboratories. It is expected that all can achieve these levels of precision and validity if the instructions and guidelines in this book are followed. Otherwise, the errors of the measurements are likely to be larger than those reported from research laboratories and the interpretation of the data will be less certain.

The editors wish to express their thanks to the authors for their efficiency and enthusiasm and to the staff of Human Kinetics, particularly Marni Basic, for help and encouragement. Thanks are due also to many others, including Joan Hunter and Terry Graham.

Editing this book has been enjoyable and instructive for us; we hope the readers will have similar experiences.

Alex Roche
Steve Heymsfield
Tim Lohman

Measurement
and
Prediction Methods

1

Densitometry

Scott B. Going

The term *densitometry* refers to the general procedure of estimating body composition from body density. Although several methods can be used to estimate body density, densitometry has become virtually synonymous with underwater weighing, also called *hydrostatic weighing* or *hydrodensitometry*. Because of its widespread application, the main focus of this chapter will be on measurement issues related to underwater weighing, although an overview of other methods will be given. The discussion of the limitations and potential errors associated with the assumptions underlying the derivation of composition from density applies to all densitometric techniques.

The density of the human body (D_b), like any material, is equivalent to the ratio of its mass (MA) and volume (V):

$$D_b = MA/V. \qquad (1.1)$$

Body mass estimated from body weight is relatively easy to measure, and recommendations for accurately measuring weight have been given (Lohman, Roche, & Martorell, 1988). Thus, the primary requirement for accurately estimating body density is to obtain an accurate measure of body volume. Indeed, most methods commonly considered to be densitometric techniques are, in fact, methods for estimating body volume. Once volume is known, density can be calculated from Equation 1.1, and composition can then be estimated as outlined below.

Long considered the "gold standard," hydrodensitometry often has been used as the criterion method in validation studies of new body composition assessment methods. The findings from recent studies, however, using both anatomical (Clarys, Martin, & Drinkwater, 1984) and chemical (Heymsfield, Wang, & Kehayias, 1989; Lohman & Going, 1993; Williams et al., 1993) models of body composition, have emphasized the limitations of densitometry, especially when applied across a wide age range without adjustments for the changes that occur with growth and maturation (Lohman, 1986) and aging (Going, Williams, Lohman, & Hewitt, 1994). Although density can be estimated with acceptable precision and accuracy in most groups, the assumption of an invariant fat-free composition, commonly used to convert density to composition, may not be valid for many individuals. Indeed, it is the magnitude of the deviation from the assumed fat-free composition, more than measurement errors in body density, that ultimately determines the accuracy of densitometric estimates of body composition for any individual or group.

Body Composition Models

The density of any material is a function of the proportions and densities of its components. In the classic two-component (2C) model of body composition, body weight is divided into fat (F) and fat-free fractions (FFM). Thus,

$$1/D_b = F/d_F + FFM/d_{FFM} \qquad (1.2)$$

where $1/D_b$ equals body mass, set equal to unity, divided by body density (D_b), and F/d_F and FFM/d_{FFM} are the proportions of the fat and fat-free masses divided by their respective densities. The fat-free mass is a heterogeneous compartment that can be further divided into its primary constituents of water (W), protein (P), and mineral (M). Thus a four-component (4C) model of body composition can be derived:

$$1/D_b = F/d_F + W/d_W + P/d_P + M/d_M \qquad (1.3)$$

where W/d_W, P/d_P, and M/d_M are the fractions of water, protein, and mineral divided by their respective densities. Three-component (3C) models can also be derived by combining two constituents of the FFM into one component. For example, if the protein and mineral fractions of FFM are combined, then

$$1/D_b = F/d_F + W/d_W + S/d_S \qquad (1.4)$$

where S/d_S represents the nonaqueous (solids) fraction of FFM divided by its density. Similarly, if water and protein are combined to form the lean soft tissue (LST) fraction of FFM, then

$$1/D_b = F/d_F + M/d_M + LST/d_{LST}. \qquad (1.5)$$

A third 3C model can be derived by combining the water and mineral fractions of FFM; however, the protein fraction is difficult to measure, and this approach is not commonly used.

On the basis of limited data from chemical analyses of animal carcasses and human cadavers (Brožek et al., 1963; Keys & Brožek, 1953), d_F, W, P, and M have been estimated, and an estimate of d_{FFM} has been derived (Table 1.1). Using these values and solving for F, it is possible to simplify Equations 1.2 through 1.5 to derive formulas for calculating percent body fat from body density based on 2C, 3C, and 4C models of body composition (Table 1.2). The Siri (1956) and Brožek et al. (1963) equations, both based on the 2C model, represent the simplest and most common fat estimating formulas. Unlike the Siri equation, which is based on fat-free mass, the Brožek equation utilizes the concept of a reference body of specified density and composition and avoids estimating the d_{FFM}. Variation from the reference body density (Table 1.1) is assumed to be due to gain or loss of "obesity

Table 1.1   Composition and Density of Fat-Free Mass and Reference Body

Component	Density (g/ml)	Fat-free mass (%)	Reference body (%)
Water (W)	0.9937	73.8	62.4
Protein (P)	1.34	19.4	16.4
Mineral (M)	3.038	6.8	5.9
Osseous	2.982	5.6	4.8
Nonosseous	3.317	1.2	1.1
Fat (F)	0.9007		15.3
Fat-free mass (FFM)	1.100	100	84.7
Total reference body	1.064		100

Densities are at 36 °C.
Adapted from "Densitometric Analysis of Body Composition: Revision of Some Quantitative Assumptions," by J. Brožek, F. Grande, J.T. Anderson, and A. Keys, 1963, *Annals of the New York Academy of Sciences,* **110**, pp. 113-140. Copyright 1963 by New York Academy of Sciences. Adapted with permission.

tissue" whereas variation in body fat (triglyceride) is assumed to explain variations in density when the FFM model (Siri equation) is used. Within density units of 1.09 g/ml and 1.03 g/ml, the two formulas give highly correlated ($r = 0.999$, $SEE = 0.3$ kg) (Wilmore & Behnke, 1968) and nearly identical (0.5 to 1% fat) estimates of fat. For subjects over 30% fat, however, the Siri equation gives increasingly higher values than the Brožek equation (Lohman, 1981). Thus, except for the very lean and obese, for whom the Brožek equation is better suited, the two equations give similar results.

Assumptions and Their Validity

The validity of the estimation of body fat from body density depends on the following assumptions:

1. The separate densities of the body components are additive.
2. The densities of the constituents of the body are relatively constant from person to person.
3. The proportions of the constituents other than fat (or adipose tissue in the case of the Brožek equation) are relatively constant from person to person.

Table 1.2 Equations for Estimating % Fat Based on 2-, 3-, and 4-Component Models of Body Composition

Model	Equation	Reference
2C	$\% \text{ Fat} = (\frac{4.95}{D_b} - 4.50)\,100$	Siri, 1956
	$\% \text{ Fat} = (\frac{4.570}{D_b} - 4.142)\,100$	Brožek et al., 1963
3C	$\% \text{ Fat} = (\frac{2.118}{D_b} - 0.78W - 1.354)\,100$	Siri, 1961
	$\% \text{ Fat} = (\frac{6.386}{D_b} - 3.96M - 6.090)\,100$	Lohman, 1986
4C	$\% \text{ Fat} = (\frac{2.747}{D_b} - 0.714W + 1.146B - 2.0503)\,100$	Selinger, 1977

D_b = body density, W = total body water as a fraction of body weight, M = mineral (osseous + nonosseous) as a fraction of body weight, B = osseous mineral as a fraction of body weight.

4. The person being measured differs from a standard reference body only in the amount of body fat (triglyceride) (Siri, 1956) or adipose tissue (Brožek et al., 1963).

It follows then that the application of the 2C equations depends on the assumption that the human body can be considered a two-component model with constant density of fat (0.90 g/ml) and constant proportions and densities of FFM constituents. Although the studies of Fidanza, Keys, and Anderson (1953) indicate remarkable uniformity in the density of human fat irrespective of body site, it is unlikely that the ether-extractable lipid portion of the body has constant density of 0.90 g/ml across individuals. Nonetheless, the assumption of 0.90 g/ml for the average density of all body fat would propagate a relatively small error in the density formulae with the possible exception of very lean subjects. The assumption of an invariant nonfat compartment is more critical. A variety of studies based on chemical and anatomical models have demonstrated considerable variation in FFM composition and density due to growth and maturation (Lohman, 1986), specialized training (Bunt et al., 1990), and aging (Deurenberg, Weststrate, & van der Kooy, 1989a; Heymsfield et al., 1989). Gender and racial differences also exist (Côté & Adams, 1993; Schutte et al., 1984), and even within a population there is considerable interindividual

variation that challenges the assumption of FFM "chemical constancy."

Variation in FFM Composition and Percent Fat Estimation Errors

It would be a misleading simplification to assume that the accuracy with which body composition can be estimated is dependent solely on the accuracy of the estimate of body density. Even if experimental errors were non-existent, there would remain a substantial residual uncertainty (standard deviation) related to individual deviations from the standard or reference body, which constitute an irreducible biological variability when the 2C model is applied.

Several investigators have presented theoretical or empirical analyses of the errors associated with biological variability in FFM composition when percent fat is estimated by densitometry (Table 1.3). In his pioneering work leading to the development of the 3C equation based on density and body water (equation 4), Siri estimated that a 2% variation in body water in the general population would lead to a 2.7% error (standard deviation) in percent fat. Moreover, variability in the protein-to-mineral ratio would lead to a 2.1% error (Siri, 1956). Siri also estimated the error related to variation in the composition of adipose tissue to be ~1.9%. Assuming each of these sources of variation is independent of the others, the total error (σ_T)

can be estimated, using the so-called "law of propagation of errors," by taking the square root of the sum of the squares of the individual sources of error. Thus,

$$(\sigma_T) = \sqrt{(2.7^2) + (2.1^2) + (1.9^2)} = 3.9\%.$$

The total error of 3.9% is equivalent to a biological variation of ~0.0084 g/ml in d_{FFM} (Table 1.3).

The errors in fat estimates from body density have also been examined in relation to variation in the anatomical and chemical components of the lean body mass, which includes a small amount of essential fat. Bakker and Struikenkamp (1977), using estimates of the variation in body water, the fraction and density of osseous minerals, and the fat-free adipose tissue fraction of FFM, derived an estimate of the error in percent fat associated with variability in FFM composition in the general population that is similar to the estimate made by Siri (1956). Given this magnitude of error, densitometry is not recommended as a criterion method in a heterogeneous group of subjects differing, for example, in age, activity levels, and ethnicity, unless appropriate corrections are made for variation in the water and mineral fractions of FFM.

It is impossible to know exactly the degree to which the variability in the constituents of the FFM in the general population is reduced in a more homogeneous population of similar age, gender,

Table 1.3 Theoretical Variation in Body Density and Calculated % Body Fat Due to Variation in the Composition of FFM

Source of variation	General population[1]		Specific population[2]	
	Density (g/ml)	% body fat	Density (g/ml)	% body fat
Water content	.0057	2.7	.0040	1.9
Protein/mineral ratio	.0046	2.1	.0033	1.5
Mean fat content of adipose tissue	.0039	1.8	.0028	1.3
Adipose tissue density	.0011	0.5	.0008	0.35
Average fat content of Reference Man	.0011	0.5	.0008	0.35
Total	.0084	3.9	.0060	2.8

[1]Data from Siri, 1956, 1961. [2]Data from Lohman, 1981.

and ethnicity. For some homogeneous populations—for example, young men—the reduction may be considerable whereas for others, such as prepubescent children, the reduction may not be as great. Lohman (1992) has speculated that one-half the variability in the general population may be found in a specific population. If that is true, then the combined effect of the major sources of variation would lead to a percent fat error of 2.8%, and a variation in the density of the FFM of 0.0060 g/ml (Table 1.3). Following the suggestion of Womersley and Durnin (1977) that one-half of the variation between body density from skinfolds and values from densitometry be assigned to each method, and using 0.0070 g/ml as the average standard error of estimate for predicting body density from skinfolds (Lohman, 1981), an estimate of 0.0049 g/ml can be derived for the variation in body density at a given body fat. Thus, this indirect empirical analysis, attributing the variation between two methods to variation in d_{FFM}, gives a reasonably similar result that supports the more theoretical analyses (Bakker & Struikenkamp, 1977; Lohman, 1992; Siri, 1961).

Two strategies are possible to minimize the potential errors in estimates of percent fat associated with variability in FFM composition. The ideal procedure is to combine measures of body density with measures of body water and bone mineral and estimate body composition using Equation 1.3 based on the 4C model. This approach eliminates the need for assumptions regarding the proportionalities among the constituents of the FFM. Alternatively, body density can be combined with measures of body water (Equation 1.4) or bone mineral (Equation 1.5) and estimates of body fat based on a 3C model can be derived. Although presumably more accurate than the 2C equations, these equations assume a constant protein-to-mineral (Equation 1.4) or protein-to-water (Equation 1.5) ratio, and individual deviations from the assumed ratios introduce error, albeit less than in the 2C model. Whether Equation 1.4 or Equation 1.5 is preferable depends on which constituent is likely to vary most within the population being studied. Equation 1.5 is useful when variability in the mineral fraction of FFM (M_{FFM}) exceeds variability in the water fraction (W_{FFM}), as may occur in perimenopausal women (Williams et al., 1993) and young adult black males (Schutte et al., 1984), and Equation 1.4 is useful when variability in W_{FFM} exceeds variability in M_{FFM}, as when serial measurements are made throughout the menstrual cycle (Bunt, Lohman, & Boileau, 1989; Byrd & Thomas, 1983).

Although the multicomponent (3C or 4C) approach is preferred, it is commonly not possible to measure water and mineral due to lack of equipment, time constraints, or expense. In this situation, percent fat can be estimated from density alone using modifications of the Siri equation (Siri, 1956) derived from estimates of FFM composition in the population of interest. Estimates of FFM fractional composition and d_{FFM} have been published for black and white children and young adults (Foman, Haschke, Ziegler, & Nelson, 1982; Haschke, 1983; Haschke, Foman, & Ziegler, 1981; Lohman, 1986), obese persons (Deurenberg, Leenen, van der Kooy, & Hautvast, 1989b), and older white men and women (Deurenberg et al., 1989a), although only limited data are available in the latter three groups. Using average estimates of W_{FFM} and M_{FFM} for a given age to estimate d_{FFM}, Lohman (1989) has derived 2C equations for use in children and adolescents (Table 1.4). These equations make it possible to use densitometry as a criterion method in children although it is important to note that, at any age, children and adolescents of the same gender differ to some extent in W_{FFM} and M_{FFM}, which leads to increased errors in percent fat estimation when these group-specific values are used.

Available data suggest that the density of the FFM in elderly females and in obese individuals may be lower than the assumed 1.100 g/ml, and in black men it may be higher. Using published estimates of d_{FFM} for elderly females (d_{FFM} = 1.0919 g/ml; Deurenberg et al., 1989a), obese individuals (d_{FFM} = 1.0932 g/ml at ≈38% fat; Deurenberg et al., 1989b), or black males (d_{FFM} = 1.113 g/ml; Schutte et al., 1984), and following the procedures outlined in Table 1.5, modified equations can be derived for these groups or any other group for whom valid estimates of d_{FFM} are available. At present, however, little direct evidence is available to confirm estimates of d_{FFM} in these or other groups and, until d_{FFM} is better established, multiple component equations represent the best approach.

Estimation of Body Volume by Underwater Weighing

Early studies by Behnke, Feen, and Welham (1942) demonstrated that body volume could be

Table 1.4 Equations for Estimating % Fat From Body Density Based on Age and Gender

Age (yrs)	Males		Females	
	C_1	C_2	C_1	C_2
1	5.72	5.36	5.69	5.33
1-2	5.64	5.26	5.65	5.26
3-4	5.53	5.14	5.58	5.20
5-6	5.43	5.03	5.53	5.14
7-8	5.38	4.97	5.43	5.03
9-10	5.30	4.89	5.35	4.95
11-12	5.23	4.81	5.25	4.84
13-14	5.07	4.64	5.12	4.69
15-16	5.03	4.59	5.07	4.64
18	4.95	4.50	5.05	4.62

Note. C_1 and C_2 are the terms in percent fat equation to substitute in the Siri (1956) equation for the calculation of percent fat:

$$\% \text{ BF} = [C_1/D_b - C_2] \cdot 100.$$

Reprinted from "Assessment of Body Composition in Children," by T.G. Lohman, 1989, *Pediatric Exercise Science*, **1**(1), pp. 19-30. Copyright 1989 by Human Kinetics. Reprinted with permission.

Table 1.5 Derivation of Equations to Estimate % Body Fat (BF) Using Specific Densities of the Fat-Free Mass

Basic equation for estimating % BF from body density (D_b):

$$\% \text{ BF} = [\frac{1}{D_b} \times \frac{D_{FFM} \times D_F}{D_{FFM} - D_F} - \frac{D_F}{D_{FFM} - D_F}] \times 100$$

where D_{FFM} = density of the fat-free mass; D_F = density of the fat mass.

For 70-year-old women:

Using D_{FFM} = 1.0919 g/ml and D_F = 0.901 g/ml,

$$\% \text{ BF} = [\frac{1}{D_b} \times \frac{1.0919 \times 0.901}{1.0919 - 0.901} - \frac{0.901}{1.0919 - 0.901}] \times 100$$

$$= [\frac{5.15}{D_b} - 4.72] \times 100.$$

With a D_b = 1.05 g/ml, the Siri equation estimates % BF = 21.4%, whereas the new equation gives % BF = 18.5%.

For 20-year-old black males:

Using D_{FFM} = 1.113 g/ml and D_F = 0.901,

$$\% \text{ BF} = [\frac{1}{D_b} \times \frac{1.113 \times 0.901}{1.113 - 0.901} - \frac{0.901}{1.113 - 0.901}] \times 100$$

$$= [\frac{4.73}{D_b} - 4.25] \times 100.$$

With a D_b = 1.07 g/ml, the Siri equation estimates % BF = 12.6%, whereas the new equation gives % BF = 17.1%.

Adapted from *Exercise in Health and Disease* (p. 54), by M.L. Pollock and J.H. Wilmore, 1990, Philadelphia: W.B. Saunders. Copyright 1990 by W.B. Saunders Company. Adapted with permission.

accurately estimated by underwater weighing. This approach utilizes Archimedes' basic principle that a body immersed in a fluid is acted on by a buoyancy force, which is evidenced by a "loss" of weight equal to the weight of the displaced fluid. Thus, when a subject is submerged in water, body volume is equal to the loss of weight in water, corrected for the density of water (D_w) corresponding to the temperature of the water at the time of the submersion:

$$V = (W_a - W_w)/D_w \qquad (1.6)$$

where W_a and W_w are the subject's weight in air and water respectively. Air in the lungs and flatus in the gastrointestinal tract at the time of measurement are two extraneous volumes included in total body volume that must be reconciled in the final calculation. Usually, the underwater weight is measured after a maximal expiration, and a correction for the residual lung volume (RV) is made, although other volumes have been used. The residual volume makes a sizable contribution to the estimate of total body volume (1 to 2 L), and, since residual volume is highly variable, it is essential to obtain an accurate estimate of the individual's residual volume at the time of weighing. The volume of flatus is considerably smaller and is not measured. Buskirk (1961) has proposed the use of a constant correction of 100 ml to approximate the volume of gas in the gastrointestinal tract. With the corrections for residual volume (RV) and GI tract gas volume, the calculation of body density becomes:

$$D_b = \frac{W_a}{\dfrac{(W_a - W_w)}{D_w} - (RV + 100)} . \qquad (1.7)$$

Equipment

The accurate estimation of body volume from underwater weight requires an appropriate site and the equipment to make precise and accurate measurements of body weight, underwater weight, air in the lungs, expired gas, water and ambient temperatures, and barometric pressure. The equipment needed to make these measurements depends on whether an autopsy (spring) scale or transducer system is used to measure underwater weight and whether residual volume is measured with the subject in the water at the time of weighing or outside the tank, before or after weighing. In addition, in most situations, a heater,

water circulator, and filter appropriate for the size of the tank are also needed.

Measurement Site

The underwater weight of most subjects can be measured in almost any body of fresh water that is at least 2.3 meters deep. Underwater weight can be measured in the field at poolside, using a portable autopsy scale suspended from a stanchion or from a low diving board. Water turbulence, which can make poolside measurements difficult, can be decreased by weighing subjects inside a small framed crib placed within the pool (Katch, 1968). A redwood tub (or its equivalent) or a stainless-steel or plexiglass reinforced tank is recommended for laboratory use. A tank no smaller than 3 m × 3 m × 3 m is suitable to accommodate a range of subject sizes (a 4 m depth is helpful for subjects taller than 200 cm). The tank should have an easily accessible emergency water drainage system. In addition, a water heater and filtering system are recommended. For subject comfort and to promote compliance, water temperatures close to skin temperature (≈32 to 35 °C) are desirable. Water quality must be maintained through filtering and regular chemical treatments to maintain chlorine levels at the manufacturer's recommended levels for spas. Water pH must be maintained between 7.4 and 7.6.

A primary concern is the ease of entry and exit from the tank. A recessed tank with steps or ladder leading into the water is ideal for use with all subjects. A wooden platform with steps and railing facilitates entry into an above-ground tank. The platform should be built up on at least one side of the tank so that the top of the tank is no higher than waist level. Then, if an autopsy scale is used, the scale is approximately at eye level. Although ladders mounted on the outside and inside of the tank can be used to enter and exit tanks that are above ground, access for many subjects (e.g., elderly adults and physically challenged individuals) will be restricted. No matter what site is used, the surrounding floor and deck surfaces and the surfaces of ladder rungs and steps should be covered with a nonslip carpet or textured paint.

Underwater Weight

Typically underwater weight is measured with the subject seated on a chair assembly suspended from a spring-loaded autopsy scale (Figure 1.1) or with the subject seated or kneeling on a weighing platform supported from four force transducers (Figure 1.2)

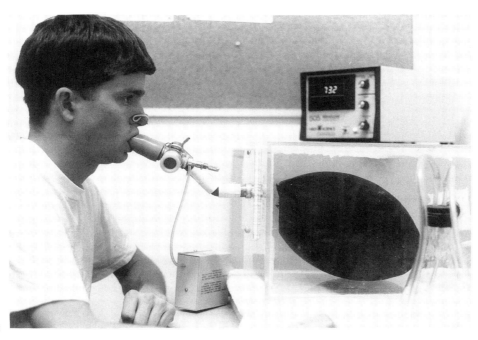

Figure 1.1   Redwood tank and spring-loaded autopsy scales for underwater weighing. The weighing chair is constructed from 3.81 cm (inner diameter) PVC pipe (a). Residual volume is measured on land prior to underwater weighing (b).

Figure 1.2 Underwater weighing using a force transducer system with residual volume measured simultaneously with underwater weight. Weight is obtained from three waterproof force transducers mounted in a triangular arrangement under the weighing chair.

Reprinted from "An Automated Real Time Underwater Weighing System," by L.W. Organ, A.D. Eklund, and J.D. Ledbetter, 1994, *Medicine and Science in Sports and Exercise,* **26,** pp. 383-391. Copyright 1994 by Williams & Wilkins. Reprinted with permission.

with digital or analog display. A 9 kg × 10 g Chatillon autopsy scale, or an equivalent scale, is adequate for most subjects, although a 15 kg × 25 g scale may be necessary for very large individuals with low body fat. For permanent installations, the scales are usually suspended securely above the tank, mounted to a ceiling beam and, if possible, attached to a quarter-ton hoist, which is helpful in adjusting the seat height for variations in the sitting height of subjects. Scale oscillations caused by underwater movements limit the accuracy of autopsy scales for measuring underwater weight. Although interpolation within 20 to 60 g is often possible, for some subjects "swing averaging" can be grossly inaccurate (>100 g). A stable, comfortable chair assembly, such as can be constructed from 2 in. plastic pipe and nylon webbing, aids in minimizing subject motion underwater.

Using a strain gauge or load cell that is directly attached to an analog recorder, a digital readout, or a microcomputer is a more sophisticated technique for measuring underwater weight. The underwater weighing system originally described by Goldman and Buskirk (1961), and later refined by Akers and Buskirk (1969), has gained widespread use. This system uses a rectangular weighing platform made from 1 in. aluminum pipe and galvanized hardware cloth of 1/2 in. mesh suspended from four load cells mounted on a 2 in. rim surrounding the top of a welded aluminum (1/4 in. stock) tank. Alternatively, the weighing platform can be set on load cells that are sealed and mounted under the water on the bottom of the tank, which eliminates the need for an elaborate support system but makes the load cells less accessible for calibration and repair. Although fewer load cells might be used, four load cells mounted at the corners of a rectangular weighing platform give maximum stability. If the extreme range of underwater weights is ±10 kg, then transducers of ±0.1% accuracy and repeatability and a linear range of 20 kg are adequate to accommodate the weight of the subject and weighing platform and to measure underwater weight with the same accuracy with which subjects can be weighed in air (±20 g, Akers & Buskirk). Although the additional instrumentation (force transducers, signal conditioner for integrating the transducer outputs, and analog recorder or digital display) makes force transducer systems more expensive, they have several important advantages over autopsy scales including greater stability, less motion underwater/fewer fluctuations in underwater weight, a permanent record of the weight, and more objective and accurate measurements. Although autopsy scales and force transducer systems may give comparable results on average in a group of subjects, significant individual differences occur. When the objective is to obtain accurate individual results or to detect small changes in underwater weight, a force transducer system should be used whereas the autopsy scale is adequate for large-scale screening and measurements in field settings.

Residual Volume

Residual volume is commonly measured using either the closed-circuit approach, where there is a dilution and eventual equilibration of an inert tracer or indicator gas such as nitrogen, oxygen, or helium, or the open circuit approach where nitrogen is "washed-out" of the lungs during a specified period of oxygen breathing. Both approaches yield precise estimates of residual volume and with appropriate equipment and procedural modifications can be used to estimate residual volume with the subject either inside the tank (simultaneously with underwater weighing) or outside the tank.

The closed-circuit oxygen dilution technique described by Wilmore (1969a) has the advantage of being very rapid (6 to 10 breaths), making it suitable for multiple measurements in a reasonable amount of time; hence, it has gained widespread use. This technique entails having the subject breathe in and out of a spirometer filled with a known volume ($\approx$80 to 90% of vital capacity) and concentration (medical grade) of oxygen until the nitrogen concentration in the lungs and spirometer has equilibrated. The spirometer should be modified to reduce dead space as described by Wilmore, which enables a faster clearance of nitrogen from the system prior to testing and increases accuracy by decreasing the total volume of the system. A nitrogen gas analyzer in the stream of respired air is used for continuous electronic gas analysis for nitrogen concentration. Depending on the analyzer used, respired gases are sampled either with a remote sampling head placed at the distal end of the system between the two-way breathing valve and mouthpiece or with a needle valve seated in the breathing valve. A digital display or analog recorder is used to monitor and record nitrogen concentration. Wearing nose clips and with the mouthpiece comfortably in the mouth, the subject makes 4 to 5 normal respirations of room air and

then inhales and exhales maximally, signaling when maximal expiration is reached. At this point, the breathing valve is switched and the subject breathes in and out of the spirometer at approximately two-thirds of vital capacity at a rate of one respiration every 3 seconds until nitrogen equilibrium is reached. Once equilibrium is attained, usually within 5 to 8 breaths, the subject inspires maximally, then expires maximally, and the breathing valve is switched back to room air when the maximal expiration is complete. Measurements of fractional nitrogen concentration are made at the termination of the initial maximal expiration (Ai_{N_2}), which is assumed to represent the initial alveolar nitrogen concentration, at equilibrium (E_{N_2}), and at the endpoint of the final maximal expiration, which represents the final alveolar concentration (Af_{N_2}). Residual volume (RV; ml) is calculated as follows:

$$RV = \left[\frac{VO_2 \, (E_{N_2} - I_{N_2})}{(Ai_{N_2} - Af_{N_2})} - DS \right] \times BTPS \text{ factor}$$

(1.8)

where VO_2 is the initial volume of O_2 in the spirometer system, including the dead space between the breathing valve and spirometer bell; E_{N_2} is the fractional percentage of nitrogen at the point of equilibrium; I_{N_2} is the fractional percentage of nitrogen initially in VO_2 (impurity); Ai_{N_2} is the fractional percentage of nitrogen in alveolar air initially when breathing room air; Af_{N_2} is the fractional percentage of nitrogen in alveolar air at termination of the test; DS is the dead space of the mouthpiece, sensing element of the nitrogen analyzer (if one is used), and breathing valve; and BTPS factor is the correction of volume using body temperature, ambient pressure, and spirometer temperature. The widespread availability of microcomputers has greatly simplified data processing: Calculations of RV as well as D_b, FFM, and percent fat are generally done via computer algorithms.

Because of its simplicity and the minimal time involved, the O_2 dilution technique is particularly appealing for measuring RV at the time of underwater weighing. For this procedure, 3/4 in. diameter plastiflex tubing is used to deliver respiratory gases to the subject so that the rebreathing procedure can be done while the subject is in the tank. Shorter lengths of tubing (~25 in.) can be used if the tubing is brought through the side of the tank rather than from above, and this reduces the dead space. Bringing the tubing through the side of the tank also facilitates adjustment for the buoyancy of the tubing which, if left uncorrected, results in an underestimation of underwater weight. The mouthpiece is connected directly to the tubing, which is fitted inside the tank to a 2 in. length of 3/4 in. diameter aluminum pipe welded to the tank so that 1 in. of pipe protrudes on both the inside and outside of the tank. A pneumatic three-port breathing valve with nitrogen-sensor assembly or needle valve is connected directly to the pipe on the outside of the tank. A 5 liter rubber rebreathing (anesthesia) bag, which replaces the spirometer, is attached to the second port, and the third port is used to deliver oxygen to the bag.

To measure residual volume, the bag is first flushed three times and then filled with 3 to 5 liters (~80 to 90% of vital capacity) of 100% oxygen. Modifying the breathing valve so that it can be connected to a vacuum pump (capacity 125 L/min) speeds the emptying of the bag. While in the water and on the weighing platform, the subject takes 4 to 5 breaths of room air and then exhales maximally while bending forward and submerging the head and shoulders. The subject remains submerged at the end of expiration until the underwater weight is obtained. The breathing valve is then switched from room air to the bag and the subject breathes in and out of the bag of oxygen until nitrogen equilibrium is reached. Constants are used because the remote location of the nitrogen sensor away from the mouth makes it impossible to measure Ai_{N_2} and Af_{N_2} accurately. Thus, Equation 1.8 for calculating residual volume becomes

$$RV = \left[\frac{VO_2 (E_{N_2} - I_{N_2})}{(0.80 - Af_{N_2})} - DS \right] \times BTPS \text{ factor}$$

(1.9)

where 0.80 is Ai_{N_2}, assumed constant at 80%; Af_{N_2} is the fractional percentage of nitrogen in alveolar air at the end of the test, assumed to be 0.2% N_2 higher than the equilibrium percentage (i.e., E_{N_2} + 0.2% N_2); and DS is the dead space in the mouthpiece, plastiflex hose, and breathing valve. Wilmore et al. (1980) have shown good average agreement (8 ml) and a high correlation ($r = 0.92$) between this simplified approach and the more complex procedure originally described by Wilmore (1969a).

Direct comparisons between the closed-circuit oxygen dilution technique and the open-circuit nitrogen washout technique have shown the two procedures are very reliable ($r \geq 0.97$, mean differences = 5 ml) and give very similar (mean difference = 26 ml) and highly correlated ($r = 0.96$) estimates of residual volume in healthy men and

women (Cournand, Baldwin, Darling, & Richards, 1941; Darling, Cournand, & Richards, 1940; Wilmore, 1969a). In addition, the excellent reliability ($r = 0.99$; $SEE = 28$ to 30 ml) of the O_2 dilution technique was confirmed in additional samples of young men ($n = 195$) and young women ($n = 102$) by Wilmore. Thus, for normal healthy adults, the closed-circuit technique gives valid, reliable, and accurate estimates of residual volume and, because of its rapidity, is useful for multiple determinations of residual volume obtained simultaneously with measurements of underwater weight. Whether similar results are possible in older individuals and patients with impaired pulmonary function has not been established. Hence, in these populations the open-circuit nitrogen washout procedure may be a better technique.

To estimate residual volume using the nitrogen washout technique, a breathing system comprising a metered source of oxygen, a three-port breathing valve and hose assembly, and a collecting spirometer is used. In the system described by Akers and Buskirk (1969), oxygen is fed from a cylinder into a small spirometer, which acts as a demand-breathing system for the subject, and a 150 L chain-compensated Tissot spirometer is used to collect expired gases. The inspired and expired gases flow through plastiflex tubing brought in through the side of the tank to facilitate measurements with the subject in the tank. While on the weighing platform, the subject breathes room air normally and then exhales maximally and submerges for the measurement of underwater weight. As soon as the underwater weight is obtained, the breathing valve is switched and the subject surfaces and inspires oxygen and expires into the collecting spirometer. The nitrogen in the subject's lungs is flushed into the spirometer during a 4 to 7 min "washout" period. The volume of expired nitrogen is determined from the volume of collected gas and the nitrogen concentration measured with a nitrogen gas analyzer. Residual volume is then calculated as follows:

$$RV = \frac{(V + DS) N_{2T} - DS \times N_{2DS}}{N_{2i} - N_{2f}}$$

(1.10)

where V is the volume of air expired into the collecting spirometer during the washout; DS is the dead space of the collecting spirometer; N_{2T} is the fraction of nitrogen in the collecting spirometer at the completion of the washout period; N_{2DS} is the fraction of nitrogen in the dead space prior to the washout period; N_{2i} is the fraction of nitrogen in the end alveolar air at the point of maximal expiration, just prior to the start of the washout period;

N_{2f} is the fraction of nitrogen in the end alveolar sample at the point of maximal expiration at the completion of the washout period. Although the extended washout period makes it difficult to accomplish more than one or two trials using this technique, the nitrogen washout technique may be less affected by incomplete mixing of gases in the lungs and thus provide more accurate estimates of residual volume, particularly in people with impaired pulmonary function.

Although used less frequently, the closed-circuit helium dilution technique can be used to obtain estimates of RV that are comparable to estimates obtained using the oxygen dilution and nitrogen washout techniques (Motley, 1957). The conceptual basis is the same; lung volume is estimated from the dilution of a tracer gas, in this case, helium. The subject is connected to a spirometer containing a known concentration of helium, which is virtually insoluble in blood. After a period of breathing at tidal volume, lasting typically 1 to 2 minutes and sometimes as long as 5 minutes, the helium concentration in the spirometer and lungs becomes the same. Since there is no loss of helium, the amount of helium present before equilibrium (concentration × volume) is $C_1 \times V_1$ and equals the amount after equilibration, $C_2 \times (V_1 + V_2)$. From this, $V_2 = V_1(C_1 - C_2)/C_2$, and V_2 is equal to lung volume. In practice, oxygen is added to the spirometer during equilibration to make up for the oxygen consumed by the subject, and carbon dioxide is absorbed.

Automated Real Time System

Organ et al. (1994) have recently described an automated real time underwater weighing system using a weighing chair mounted on three waterproof force transducers positioned in a triangular arrangement to measure underwater weight combined with simultaneous measurement of RV by the oxygen dilution technique. The instrumentation for data acquisition consists of a custom I/O (input/output) module with an Intel 80C196KB 16-bit microcontroller that serves as a strain gauge signal and amplifier and performs 10-bit analog-to-digital signal conversion for the analog outputs from the spirometer, nitrogen analyzer, and the summed output from the force transducers (Figure 1.3). The digital signals are read by a microcomputer over serial RS232 communications lines and a custom program for data acquisition, analysis, and display is used to enter subject information and system deadspace, control calibration, record

and display underwater weight and nitrogen concentration, and calculate and display body density, FFM, and percent fat. The real time display of data and immediate results provided by this system make it possible to use percent fat as the criterion for selecting trials for averaging rather than maximum underwater weight, which depends on accurate measurements of residual volume. Accuracy of percent fat requires only that the corresponding values of underwater weight and lung volume be known, without the necessity that the weight be maximum or the lung volume truly residual. Thus, the number of trials is likely reduced since each trial is potentially useful regardless of the magnitude of underwater weight. Also, the graphical display of underwater weight can be reviewed with the subject to reinforce instructions and facilitate learning the procedure.

Methodological Issues

There are several methodological issues to consider when estimating body volume from underwater weight. These include subject position, residual volume, number of trials and selection criteria, alternative lung volumes, and head placement. Description of these methodological issues is given here.

Subject Position

Weighing a subject underwater is usually accomplished with the subject completely submerged—sitting, kneeling, or prone—after a maximal expiration. Alternatively, other positions and lung volumes have been used, and sometimes subjects have been measured with the head above water. The specifications for tank size depend on which positions are likely to be used. Subject position should be chosen with subject comfort and flexibility and stability and reproducibility of the data as determining factors. If residual volume is measured with the subject outside the tank, it is important that the position for weighing and RV measurements be as similar as possible. The seated position is generally used when weight is measured with an autopsy scale whereas seated or kneeling positions are used with weighing platforms. For many older persons and subjects with arthritic knees, a sitting position on the weighing platform may be most comfortable. Young children and shorter adults may be more at ease in the water when in a kneeling position. Likewise,

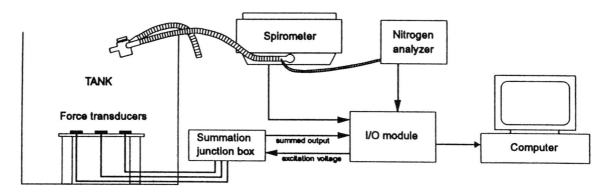

Figure 1.3 Instrumentation and data flow for a real time underwater weighing system.
Reprinted from "An Automated Real Time Underwater Weighing System," by L.W. Organ, A.D. Eklund, and J.D. Ledbetter, 1994, *Medicine and Science in Sports and Exercise, **26**,* pp. 383-391. Copyright 1994 by Williams & Wilkins. Reprinted with permission.

subjects with protruding abdomens and subjects with limited low back flexibility may find it easier to bend forward and submerge their head and shoulders when kneeling as compared to sitting in the water.

Residual Volume

The residual volume can be measured using either the open-circuit or closed-circuit technique on land before underwater weighing or simultaneously with underwater weighing with the subject in the tank. Although it is slightly more complex to set up the equipment for simultaneous measurements, with this approach it is not necessary to assume that subjects are able to match accurately maximal exhalations on land and in the water since the actual volume of air in the lungs at the time of underwater weighing is measured. Measurement inside the tank has two other advantages: (1) the error due to the compressive force of water on the thoracic cavity, which reduces the residual volume in water compared to land (Girandola et al., 1977), is avoided (although its effect on computed body fat is small), and (2) fewer trials are needed to obtain a reliable and accurate estimate of density. Thus, measurement of residual volume at the time of underwater weighing is time-efficient, is easier on subjects for whom multiple trials are burdensome, and contributes to more valid estimates of body density. Nevertheless, good agreement between average measurements of residual volume on land and in the water is possible (Wilmore, 1969a), and measurements outside the tank are adequate when a group description (average) is the primary goal. It is important to note, however,

that comparisons have been limited to measurements in healthy young adults measured by experienced investigators, and even under optimal conditions some significant individual differences (≥ 200 ml) occurred. Whether similar agreement would be found in other groups—for example, children and the elderly—is doubtful. For these groups, and when detection of individual differences or changes in serial measurements is of primary importance, measurements at the time of underwater weighing are required.

Although not recommended for research purposes, in situations where direct measurements of residual volume are not possible, body density has been calculated using a constant age- and sex-specific average residual volume or estimates of residual volume predicted from other more readily measured lung volumes or easily measured physical characteristics. The following equations, developed by Goldman and Becklake (1959), have been recommended (Pollock and Wilmore, 1990) for estimating residual volume from stature:

Men: RV = 0.017 (age in years)
　　　　+ 0.06858 (stature in inches) − 3.477

Women: RV = 0.009 (age in years)
　　　　　+ 0.08128 (stature in inches) − 3.9

Alternatively, residual volume can be estimated as a constant fraction of vital capacity (0.24 in males and 0.28 in females), which is more readily measured than residual volume (Wilmore, 1969b). Wilmore also showed that the mean difference in body densities calculated using actual and predicted residual volumes is less than 0.001 g/ml.

Nevertheless, significant individual differences were evident with more than 50% of the subjects having deviations in density values ranging from ±0.003 to greater than ±0.0099 g/ml (percent fat deviations ranging from 1 to 4%). The significance of this finding is evident when one considers that changes in body density with physical training are sometimes less than 0.003 g/ml. Thus, for screening purposes or measuring large groups, acceptable results can be obtained using an estimated residual volume, but when maximum accuracy is required it is crucial that residual volume be measured.

Number of Trials and Selection Criteria

Variation in body density of 0.0015 to 0.0020 g/ml is characteristic of the expected trial-to-trial variation within a day, reflecting the combined measurement error from several sources. This degree of agreement is easily accomplished with the combination of a force transducer system for measuring underwater weight and with residual volume measured at the time of underwater weighing. Generally one or two practice trials are sufficient to acquaint the subject with the procedure, followed by three additional trials, which are averaged to obtain the criterion estimate of body density. An on-line microcomputer system programmed for immediate calculation is ideal for monitoring trial-to-trial variation in underwater weight, residual volume, and body density. In many settings immediate calculation of body density is not feasible, making it necessary to monitor digital or analog recordings and the covariance in underwater weight and equilibrium nitrogen concentration to determine qualitatively whether the system is functioning appropriately. For example, when the O_2 dilution technique is used to measure residual volume and the same initial volume of oxygen is used for each trial, then a decrease in equilibrium nitrogen concentration should correspond to an increase in underwater weight, and vice versa. Trial-to-trial variation in underwater weight typically will not exceed ±100 g, reflecting variance in the volume of expired air; larger differences may indicate poor subject compliance.

The possibility of a "practice curve" associated with successive trials of underwater weighing may make it necessary to use more trials when residual volume is measured outside the tank. Katch (1969) has demonstrated a progressive increase in underwater weight, suggesting that subjects learn to expel more air from their lungs with each additional trial. His data support the use of the average of the eighth, ninth, and tenth trials to obtain the best estimate of the "true" underwater weight. Behnke and Wilmore (1974) also advocate the use of ten trials but recommend different selection criteria. They select

1. the highest weight obtained if it appears more than twice,
2. the second highest weight if it is observed more than once and the first criterion is not satisfied, or
3. the third highest weight if neither the first nor second criteria is met.

This method of selecting trials was adopted to reduce the possibility of underestimating the actual underwater weight in subjects who attained the highest weights during early trials. In practice, for many subjects, it is likely that the two procedures give very similar results. The selection of any single trial (Criterion 3) from a series of trials may not yield the most accurate or reliable score because it may contain a variable and unknown source of error. The chance of error is compounded when weight is measured using an autopsy scale and "swing averaging." Therefore, the average of three trials is the recommended criterion score for underwater weight.

In a more recent study, Bonge and Donnelly (1989) did not show a practice curve. In their data there was a range of only 25 g across Trials 2 through 10. Adjacent trial correlations were $r = 0.98$ or higher for Trials 2 through 10, and higher underwater weights were observed more frequently (64%) during Trials 1 through 5 than Trials 6 through 10. Moreover, estimates of body density and % BF derived from

1. the average of Trials 8 to 10,
2. the average of the first three consecutive trials having a range of 100 g or less, and
3. the average of the first three nonconsecutive trials having a range of 100 g or less

were found to be virtually identical and highly correlated ($r = 0.99$). Criteria 2 and 3 were satisfied within four trials and demonstrated slightly smaller intraindividual variation than the average of Trials 8 through 10. These results suggest four or five trials and use of the average of three trials agreeing within 100 g is an acceptable alternative in subjects for whom 10 trials is burdensome. For others, given the conflicting results, it would seem prudent to conduct sufficient trials to establish a plateau in underwater weight until more definitive research is done.

Alternative Lung Volumes

Residual volume has been the lung volume used most widely during underwater weighing because it is the volume least affected by hydrostatic pressure (Welch & Crisp, 1958) and may be the most precise. Concern regarding the subject's ability to accurately and reliably reproduce land residual volume underwater has led some investigators to determine body density at other lung volumes, most notably, functional residual capacity (Thomas & Etheridge, 1980), a constant fraction of vital capacity (Welch & Crisp), and total lung capacity (TLC; Timson & Coffman, 1984; Weltman & Katch, 1981). For some subjects, determining body density at lung volumes other than residual volume is more comfortable, which may improve subject compliance. In particular, measurements at TLC may be advantageous since subjects may be more at ease and able to stay submerged longer, allowing more time for the scale to steady and thus reduce scale oscillations when underwater weight is read. Other potential advantages include minimizing the problem of air-trapping due to airway closure (Thomas & Etheridge), absence of a "practice curve," and easement of the burden for subjects who are unable to perform the novel task of maximal exhalation while underwater.

Whether more precise and accurate estimates of body density are possible at TLC remains to be resolved. The results of one study (Weltman & Katch, 1981) suggest that body density values measured at RV and TLC (both measured on land) are the same for practical purposes. However, the lung volumes were measured on land and Timson and Coffman (1984) found significant differences between density and percent fat calculated using TLC measured on land and in the water. The difference between TLC measured in and out of the water is quite variable, ranging from 1 to 13% when the subject is submerged to the neck. The error in density due to the reduction in TLC when measured in the water is directly related to the weight of the subject and inversely related to the percent reduction in TLC. Timson and Coffman have also shown that a 6% reduction in TLC for a 70 kg man with a land-measured TLC of 6 L would result in a body density error of 0.0056 g/ml and a percent fat error of 2.5%. Thus, measurement of TLC in the water appears essential to reduce the error in density associated with error in lung volume measurement. Timson and Coffman have shown that mean body densities at TLC and RV are not significantly different when lung volumes are measured in the water, suggesting underwater weighing at TLC measured in the water may be an acceptable alternative to RV. The question of which lung volume to measure is moot, however, when lung volume is measured simultaneously with underwater weighing (Goldman & Buskirk, 1961; Thomas & Etheridge, 1980) as long as a stable measurement is obtained since the actual lung volume at the time of weighing is measured.

Head Placement

In an attempt to enhance subject compliance and broaden the application of underwater weighing, some investigators have estimated body density using underwater weighing without head submersion (Donnelly et al., 1988). Although potentially advantageous in some subjects who are unaccustomed or unable to submerge their heads, an unknown and variable, albeit relatively small, error is introduced. Moreover, there is the potential for additional error unless care is taken to ensure subject position in the water is consistent. Donnelly et al. have described a method for standardizing subject position and head placement using a spirit level to draw a horizontal line from the angle of the mandible to a site on the neck inferior to the ear lobe to be used as a reference level. A winch attached to the autopsy scale is used to raise or lower the subject to the desired depth and the subject flexes or extends his/her neck, following the investigator's instructions, so that the water just touches the inferior surface of the chin and the horizontal reference mark. The test-retest reliability of body density at TLC using this technique was good ($r = 0.98$) with a mean difference of 0.0008 g/ml. Nevertheless, body density at TLC with the head above the water was only moderately related to body density measured at RV while the subject was fully submerged ($r = 0.88$, $SEE = 0.0067$ g/ml in males and $r = 0.85$, $SEE = 0.0061$ g/ml in females). Although further work is needed to refine this technique, it may be useful for serial measurements aimed at detecting changes in composition if care is taken to standardize subject position in the water. The technique may have special utility in clinical work or for subjects who are obese, elderly, very young, or either mentally or physically handicapped.

Technical Errors

Technical errors in the measurement of body density are well documented. Measurement errors are evident in the variation in density observed from trial to trial, which reflects primarily technical errors, and in the variation observed in repeated measurements over several days, caused by both technical errors and biological variation. A third source of error relates to whether the residual volume is measured in the water simultaneously with underwater weight or with the subject outside of the water. Akers and Buskirk (1969) have estimated the combined technical and biological error in the measurement of body density to be 0.0017 g/ml in an 80 kg man. Siri (1956) has estimated the measurement error to be slightly higher at 0.0025 g/ml, and in the laboratory situation the error was found to be 0.0020 g/ml (Buskirk, 1961).

Akers and Buskirk (1969) have carefully analyzed the sources of error in body density and shown errors in residual volume to be the major source of variation. The variations in body weight, underwater weight, and water temperature at the time of weighing have much smaller effects leading to a combined error of 0.0006 g/ml if body weight is measured within 0.02 kg, underwater weight within 0.02 kg, and water temperature within 0.0005 °C. The combined error from residual volume, when RV is measured within 100 ml (0.00139 g/ml variation in density), plus the above errors, is 0.0017 g/ml or ~0.8% fat. Variation in body density of 0.0015 to 0.0020 g/ml is characteristic of the trial-to-trial variation within a day, reflecting the combined measurement error inherent in most underwater weighing systems. Within-subject variation greater than 0.0020 g/ml reflects larger measurement errors in one or more of the components of body density and indicates a need to improve measurement precision. Lohman (1992) has suggested periodic estimates of within-subject variation using at least 10 subjects each measured three or more times as an important quality control procedure.

The technical error for repeated estimates of body density over several days, estimated to be 0.0030 g/ml (Jackson et al., 1988) or 1.1% fat in men and 1.2% fat in women, is somewhat larger than the error associated with repeated trials within a day. The source of the additional variation is likely to be fluctuation in body water and variation in gastrointestinal flatus, which is assumed constant at 100 ml. Despite the additional variation in day-to-day measurements, it is clear that the technical errors associated with both within-subject variation within a day and between days are quite small when residual volume is measured and that % BF can be estimated with a precision of ≤ 1%. The error is inflated when residual volume is

estimated, for example, from age, sex, and stature, which can easily lead to errors in RV of 300 to 400 ml in a given subject.

The accuracy of the estimate of body density depends on carefully calibrated systems for measuring body weight, underwater weight, temperature, and residual volume. Lohman (1992) has reported interlaboratory comparisons of two subjects measured in six different laboratories by experienced investigators to identify systematic differences among laboratories associated with calibration errors. The results confirmed previous analyses and demonstrated that interlaboratory variation (standard deviation) should not exceed 0.0015 g/ml.

Total Error of Estimating Fat Content From Underwater Weighing

The total error associated with the estimation of % BF from body density using the underwater weighing technique can be estimated from the combined errors due to biological variability in FFM composition and d_{FFM}, discussed previously, and the measurement errors associated with estimation of body density. Given a variation in d_{FFM} of 0.0059 g/ml in a specific population and a technical error of 0.0020 g/ml, the combined error is estimated to be 0.0062 g/ml or the equivalent of ~2% fat. This estimate represents the theoretical limit of accuracy when other techniques are used to estimate density due to the inherent limitations in the underwater weighing technique.

The impact of measurement errors in body weight, underwater weight, residual volume, and water temperature on estimates of body density and percent fat are illustrated in Table 1.6. As indicated in the foregoing discussion, inaccuracies in residual volume represent a major source of error in body density and percent fat. As shown in the table, for every 100 ml error in residual volume or 100 g error in underwater weight, percent fat will be in error by ~0.7 percent fat units. Typically the error in underwater weight will be less than 100 g, although larger errors may occur when an autopsy scale is used to measure subjects having difficulty remaining motionless underwater. In contrast, discrepancies of 100 to 200 ml (0.7 to 1.4% fat units) can easily occur when residual volume is measured on land rather than simultaneously with underwater weight, and larger errors (300 to 400 ml) are likely when residual volume is estimated rather than measured directly. Relatively large errors in

Table 1.6   Effect of Errors in Residual Volume, Underwater Weight, Body Weight, and Water Temperature on Body Density and % Fat

Measure	Actual	Errors		
		1	2	3
Residual volume (L)	1.200	1.300	1.6000	2.200
D_b (g/ml)	1.0645	1.0661	1.0710	1.0809
% BF	15.0	14.3	12.2	8.0
Underwater weight (kg)	3.36	3.38	3.41	3.46
D_b (g/ml)	1.0645	1.0648	1.0653	1.0661
% BF	15.0	14.9	14.6	14.3
Body weight (kg)	70.0	70.1	70.5	71.0
D_b (g/ml)	1.0645	1.0643	1.0639	1.0634
% BF	15.0	15.1	15.3	15.5
Water temperature (°C)	36.0	36.1	36.5	37.0
D_b (g/ml)	1.0645	1.0644	1.0643	1.0641
% BF	15.0	15.1	15.1	15.2

The error attributed to each variable was calculated individually with the other variables held constant at the actual values.

water temperature and body weight in air have relatively minor effects on body density and % BF; nevertheless all variables must be measured as accurately as possible to minimize the combined total error.

Calibration Procedures

It is essential that all components of the underwater weighing system be calibrated prior to each testing session to avoid introducing constant errors. Standard weights covering the possible range of underwater weights should be used to test the performance of the load cells and of the recorder used to measure underwater weight. The digital or analog recorder is first zeroed, usually with the weighing platform in place, and then the recorder gain is adjusted so the appropriate readings are displayed. It is imperative to use a series of weights hung from the scale to calibrate autopsy scales since their performance deteriorates over time. Regression analysis is then used to derive a calibration line (underwater weight = $b_0 \times$ (scale weight) $- b_1$) to convert scale weight to "true" underwater weight. Inaccurate estimates of residual volume are a major source of error that can only be minimized by careful calibration of the gas analyzer used to measure nitrogen concentration and the

spirometer used to measure initial gas (oxygen) volume. Typically, nitrogen analyzers are zeroed and then calibrated against room air. Using this procedure introduces a small, variable error since the nitrogen concentration of room air will vary with percent humidity; a better approach is to first humidify the air to 100% saturation. Certified gases with known nitrogen concentrations, verified by Scholander analysis (Scholander, 1947), should be used to verify accuracy in the expected range. A 3 L calibrated syringe is used to calibrate spirometer volume.

Other Methods for Estimating Body Volume

There are several other methods for estimating body volume, including water displacement with a whole-body volumeter, gas dilution, whole-body plethysmography, and the buoyancy method. A brief description of these methods is given here. These methods are not used commonly for body composition assessment, due either to expense or to the difficulty of obtaining precise and accurate estimates of volume.

Water Displacement

The water displacement method is similar to the underwater weighing method except that the actual volume of water displaced by the subject is measured rather than the loss of weight in water. The water displacement is measured by submerging the subject and then measuring the rise in the water level using a fine-bore burette connected to the tank, which has been previously calibrated by placing small objects or water of known volumes into the tank and noting the corresponding readings. It is also necessary to measure the residual lung volume to account for its effect on the final determination of body density. Body density is then calculated as follows:

$$D_b = \frac{\text{body weight}}{\text{volume}/D_w - (RV + 100 \text{ ml})}. \quad (1.11)$$

This technique is less precise than underwater weighing or the helium dilution technique because of difficulties inherent in measuring changes in the volume in the tank with sufficient accuracy to detect small differences in body volume.

Gas Dilution

Body volume can be estimated from gas dilution using an inert gas such as helium as a tracer. To do so, a known volume of helium (V_{He}) is allowed to mix freely with the air in a small closed chamber of constant volume (V_c) in which the subject is enclosed. The concentration of helium at the point of equilibrium (C_{He}) is measured and applied to the subsequent calculation of body volume. The volume actually being estimated is the difference (Δ_V) between the chamber and subject volumes:

$$\Delta_V = \frac{V_{He}\,(1 - C_{He})}{d \times C_{He}} \qquad (1.12)$$

where d is the ratio of the absolute temperature of the helium to the chamber air measured just prior to mixing the two volumes. Substituting $V_C - V_S$ for Δ_V and solving for V_S gives

$$V_S = V_C - \frac{V_{He}\,(1 - C_{He})}{d \times C_{He}}. \qquad (1.13)$$

This technique has the advantage of not requiring a measurement of residual lung volume since the lungs comprise a part of Δ_V. Also, helium dilution is applicable to individuals from infancy through old age, whether healthy or ambulatory, and it requires relatively little subject cooperation and effort. However, the technique is more complex than others, has a relatively high initial cost, and requires continuous calibration checks and very precise measurements of helium concentrations to discriminate between subjects of varying volumes.

Plethysmography

Body volume can be estimated using a plethysmograph, which eliminates the need for total immersion of the subject (Garrow et al., 1979). This method uses a closed vessel in which the subject stands in water up to neck level; the volume of the subject is determined by measuring pressure changes produced by a pump of known stroke volume. This method requires an apparatus more complex than underwater weighing, but it does not require the instrumentation for residual volume determinations. Thus, total body volume can be determined with minimal subject cooperation and good precision (< 0.3 kg fat), and the technique may be useful in subjects apprehensive about complete submersion. Further work is needed to establish the precision and accuracy of this technique across the range of potential subjects.

Bottle Buoyancy

An inexpensive and simple method for estimating body volume reported by Katch, Hortobagyi, and Denahan (1989) eliminates the need for a scale or other measurement device to record the underwater weight. The procedure involves the direct measurement of water volume and application of the fact that 1 L of displaced water has a buoyancy force exerted upon it that equals 9.81 N of weight at 4 °C. With this technique, the subject holds a prefilled (5 to 6 L) plastic bottle (7.57 L capacity) against his/her chest, exhales maximally, then submerges underwater to determine whether he/she sinks or floats. A series of trials is conducted with water added or removed from the bottle to create a state of neutral buoyancy (submerged and suspended just below the surface of the water). Once the neutral buoyant state is reached, the water in the bottle is carefully measured using a graduated cylinder accurate to ±5 ml. The volume of water necessary to overcome the buoyancy of the bottle must also be determined and added as a constant to the water volume for each subject. The volume of water measured by the bottle procedure is a substitution for the weighing scale because 1 g = 1 ml water at 4 °C. Body volume is calculated according to equation 1.14, in which the symbols are the same as previously defined:

$$\text{Volume} = \frac{[W_a - (W_w \cdot D_w) + \text{bottle buoyancy}]}{D_w} - (RV + 100). \qquad (1.14)$$

Using a constant fraction (25%) of vital capacity to estimate RV, Katch et al. (1989) have shown high test-retest correlation coefficients ($r > 0.99$) and small mean differences (~85 ml) between repeat tests. When volume from the bottle buoyancy technique and the traditional autopsy scale were used to calculate density, the mean difference was 0.001 density units ($r = 0.998$). Thus, the bottle buoyancy technique seems to be suitable for densitometric analysis for screening purposes without the need for specialized or expensive equipment. The use of estimated RV, however, is an important source of error, and for research or individual counseling, RV must be measured using appropriate methods.

Recommended Procedures

Based on considerations of expense and the precision and accuracy of measurement, the underwater weighing technique continues to be the most widespread and useful method for estimating body volume leading to the assessment of body composition. It is applicable in most groups except for very young children and individuals who cannot or will not be submerged. The most precise and accurate estimates of body volume and density are derived using a force transducer system to measure underwater weight, with simultaneous measurement of residual volume by either the oxygen dilution or nitrogen washout techniques. The O_2 dilution technique with its rapid equilibration times is particularly suited for multiple determinations along with underwater weight whereas the nitrogen washout technique may be more accurate in individuals with impaired lung function. An autopsy scale, with residual volume measured inside the tank (preferably) or outside the tank, can be used when screening or describing a group is the goal; however, when individual counseling or detecting small changes across serial measurements is of concern, estimation of residual volume at the time of underwater weighing is mandatory.

Subject Preparation

Ideally, underwater weight should be measured with the subject having fasted at least four hours and having refrained from strenuous exercise and other situations that can cause unusual dehydration or overhydration. The subject should avoid gas-producing foods for at least 12 hours and there should be no smoking for at least 3 hours prior to weighing. Prior to weighing, subjects are instructed to void the bladder and defecate. Subjects should be weighed nude or wearing lightweight, tight-fitting nylon swimsuits or their equivalent to minimize trapped air. Bathing caps should not be worn since they trap air bubbles. If possible, subjects should shower prior to entering the tank to remove organic wastes such as perspiration and body oils that tend to cloud the water.

Body Weight

Body weight on land should be measured to the nearest 25 to 50 g after evacuating the bladder and bowels and prior to showering, with the subject nude or clothed in the same attire (swimsuit) that will be worn when the subject is weighed underwater.

Underwater Weighing With Simultaneous Residual Volume

Once the subject is in the water, he/she should slowly rub the hands over the entire body to eliminate air bubbles attached to the skin. This should be done while attempting to stir the water as little as possible. Gently tugging the top and bottom of the swimsuit, and submerging the head and running the fingers through the hair, helps to release any trapped air. The tare weight is then obtained. The tare weight is simply the weight of the weighing platform or chair measured with the subject in the water. If a weight belt is used to help the subject submerge, it should be attached to the platform (chair) so that it is included in the tare weight. Also, if a system of hoses is used to deliver respiratory gases to the subject while in the water, the mouthpiece should be removed and the hoses plugged and fastened to the platform while the tare weight is measured to adjust for the "buoyancy effect" on the underwater weight. The tare weight should be measured with the subject submerged, without touching the weighing platform. For calculation of "true" underwater weight, the tare weight is subtracted from the total weight underwater, and volume is then estimated according to Equation 1.6.

Once the tare weight is obtained, the subject is instructed to move onto the weighing platform and assume a comfortable position. The weight belt, if one is used, should be secured around the waist, the hoses unfastened from the weighing platform, and the mouthpiece connected to the breathing hose. The total procedure should then be explained to the subject and then, with the breathing valve turned to room air, the subject should be allowed to practice while being talked through the procedure. The subject is instructed to do the following:

1. Take 5 to 6 normal breaths, then exhale while in the upright position.
2. Continue to exhale, and slowly lower the head under the water until the shoulders and top of the head are completely submerged. The subject must submerge slowly so as not to create undue water movement, which would increase the time needed to obtain the underwater weight. If the head is not completely submerged, the technician should lightly tap the top of the subject's head until it clears the surface.
3. Continue to exhale until air can no longer be expelled from the lungs; that is, until residual volume is reached. Then relax and

remain motionless underwater until the underwater weight is determined. Subjects who are apprehensive may be more at ease if reminded that they can breathe underwater through the mouthpiece and breathing hoses if they must, or they may lift their heads out of the water. The trial is simply aborted and another trial is done. Allowing the subject to submerge and practice breathing underwater is also helpful.

4. Once the underwater weight is determined, begin breathing through the mouthpiece and hoses, then slowly lift the head back out of the water while continuing to breathe. A knock on the side of the tank can be used as a signal to surface although usually the subject will be able to hear loud verbal instructions while under the water.

Adequate practice should be given until the subject is comfortable with the procedure. For most subjects, one or two trials will be sufficient although children and individuals apprehensive in the water may need additional practice. Once the subject has learned the procedure, the water temperature is recorded and the breathing system is flushed with oxygen several times until the initial nitrogen concentration is close to zero. The spirometer or breathing bag is then filled with oxygen and the initial volume and concentration are recorded. The subject then exhales and submerges, and the underwater weight is obtained as outlined above. The breathing valve should be switched to oxygen before the signal to surface is given; the subject then surfaces and respires into the bag until nitrogen equilibration is reached. The nitrogen concentration at equilibrium and gas temperature in the bag are recorded, and then the system is readied for the next trial. The subject should rest quietly between trials and avoid creating water movement. The subject should wear nose clips during the procedure but can remove them between trials if they desire. Because the residual volume is measured at the time of underwater weight, three trials are generally adequate to estimate body density, and the average of the values from three trials is the recommended criterion score.

References

Akers, R., & Buskirk, E.R. (1969). An underwater weighing system utilizing "force cube" transducers. *Journal of Applied Physiology, 26,* 649-652.

Bakker, H.K., & Struikenkamp, R.S. (1977). Biological variability and lean body mass estimates. *Human Biology, 49,* 187-202.

Behnke, A.R., Feen, B.G., & Welham, W.C. (1942). The specific gravity of healthy men. *Journal of the American Medical Association, 118,* 495-498.

Behnke, A.R., & Wilmore, J.H. (1974). *Evaluation and regulation of body build and composition.* Englewood Cliffs, NJ: Prentice Hall.

Bonge, D., & Donnelly, J.E. (1989). Trials to criteria for hydrostatic weighing at residual volume. *Research Quarterly for Exercise and Sport, 60,* 176-179.

Brožek, J., Grande, F., Anderson, J.T., et al. (1963). Densitometric analysis of body composition: Revision of some quantitative assumptions. *Annals of the New York Academy of Sciences, 110,* 113-140.

Bunt, J.C., Going, S.B., Lohman, T.G., et al. (1990). Variation in bone mineral content and estimated body fat in young adult females. *Medicine and Science in Sports & Exercise, 22,* 564-569.

Bunt, J.C., Lohman, T.G., & Boileau, R.A. (1989). Impact of total body water fluctuation on estimating of body fat from body density. *Medicine and Science in Sports & Exercise, 21,* 96-100.

Buskirk, E.R. (1961). Underwater weighing and body density: A review of procedures. In J. Brožek & A. Henschel (Eds.), *Techniques for Measuring Body Composition* (pp. 90-105). Washington, D.C.: National Academy of Sciences, National Research Council.

Byrd, P.J., & Thomas, T.R. (1983). Hydrostatic weighing during different stages of the menstrual cycle. *Research Quarterly, 54,* 296-298.

Clarys, J.P., Martin, A.D., & Drinkwater, D.T. (1984). Gross tissue weights in the human body by cadaver dissection. *Human Biology, 56,* 459-473.

Côté, K.D., & Adams, W.C. (1993). Effect of bone density on body composition estimates in young adult black and white women. *Medicine and Science in Sports & Exercise, 25,* 290-296.

Cournand, A., Baldwin, E.D., Darling, R.C., & Richards, D.W. (1941). Studies on intrapulmonary mixture of gases, [Part] IV: The significance of the pulmonary emptying rate and a simplified open circuit measurement of residual air. *Journal of Clinical Investigation, 20,* 681-689.

Darling, R.C., Cournand, A., & Richards, D.W. (1940). Studies on the intrapulmonary mixture of gases, III: An open-circuit method for measuring residual air. *Journal of Clinical Investigation, 19,* 609-618.

Deurenberg, P., Leenen, R., van der Kooy, K., & Hautvast, J.G.A.J. (1989b). In obese subjects the body fat percentage calculated with Siri's formula is an overestimate. *European Journal of Clinical Nutrition, 43,* 569-575.

Deurenberg, P., Weststrate, J.A., & van der Kooy, K. (1989a). Is an adaptation of Siri's formula for the calculation of body fat percentage from body density in the elderly necessary? *European Journal of Clinical Nutrition, 43,* 559-568.

Donnelly, J.E., Brown, T.E., Israel, R.G., et al. (1988). Hydrostatic weighing without head submersion: Description of a method. *Medicine and Science in Sports & Exercise, 20,* 66-69.

Fidanza, F., Keys, A., & Anderson, J.T. (1953). Density of body fat in man and other mammals. *Journal of Applied Physiology, 6,* 252-256.

Foman, S.J., Haschke, F., Ziegler, E.E., & Nelson, S.E. (1982). Body composition of reference children from birth to age 10 years. *American Journal of Clinical Nutrition, 35,* 1169-1175.

Garrow, J.S., Stally, S., Diethielm, R., et al. (1979). A new method for measuring the body density of obese adults. *British Journal of Nutrition, 42,* 173-183.

Girandola, R.N., Wiswell, R.A., Mohler, J.G., et al. (1977). Effects of water immersion on lung volumes: Implications for body composition analysis. *Journal of Applied Physiology, 43,* 276-279.

Going, S.B., Williams, D.P., Lohman, T.G., & Hewitt, M.J. (1994). Aging, body composition, and physical activity: A review. *Journal of Aging and Physical Activity, 2,* 38-66.

Goldman, H.I., & Becklake, M.R. (1959). Respiratory function tests: Normal values at medium altitudes and the prediction of normal results. *American Review of Tuberculosis and Respiratory Diseases, 79,* 457-467.

Goldman, R.F., & Buskirk, E.R. (1961). Body volume measurement by under-water weighing: Description of a method. In J. Brožek & A. Henschel (Eds.), Techniques for measuring body composition (pp. 78-89). Washington, DC: National Academy of Sciences, National Research Council.

Haschke, F. (1983). Body composition of adolescent males, Part 2: Body composition of male reference adolescents. *Acta Paediatrica Scandinavica, 307* (suppl), 13-23.

Haschke, F., Foman, S.J., & Ziegler, E.E. (1981). Body composition of a nine-year-old reference boy. *Pediatric Research, 15,* 847-849.

Heymsfield, S.B., Wang, J., Kehayias, J., et al. (1989). Chemical determination of human body density in vivo: Relevance to hydrodensitometry. *American Journal of Clinical Nutrition, 50,* 1282-1289.

Heymsfield, S.B., Wang, J., Lichtman, et al. (1989). Body composition in elderly subjects: A critical appraisal of clinical methodology. *American Journal of Clinical Nutrition, 50,* 1167-1175.

Jackson, A.S., Pollock, M.L., Graves, J., et al. (1988). Reliability and validity of bioelectrical impedance in determining body composition. *Journal of Applied Physiology, 64,* 529-534.

Katch, F.I. (1968). Apparent body density and variability during underwater weighing. *Research Quarterly, 39,* 993-999.

Katch, F.I. (1969). Practice curves and errors of measurement in estimating underwater weight by hydrostatic weighing. *Medicine and Science in Sports, 1,* 212-216.

Katch, F.I., Hortobagyi, T., & Denahan, T. (1989). Reliability and validity of a new method for the measurement of total body volume. *Research Quarterly for Exercise & Sport, 60,* 286-291.

Keys, A., & Brožek, J. (1953). Body fat in adult man. *Physiological Research, 33,* 245-345.

Lohman, T.G. (1981). Skinfolds and body density and their relation to body fatness: A review. *Human Biology, 53,* 181-225.

Lohman, T.G. (1986). Applicability of body composition techniques and constants for children and youth. *Exercise and Sport Sciences Reviews, 14,* 325-357.

Lohman, T.G. (1989). Assessment of body composition in children. *Pediatric Exercise Science, 1,* 19-30.

Lohman, T.G. (1992). *Advances in Body Composition Assessment.* Champaign, IL: Human Kinetics.

Lohman, T.G., & Going, S.B. (1993). Multicomponent models in body composition research: Opportunities and pitfalls. In K. Ellis & J. Eastman (Eds.), *Human body composition: In vivo methods, models and assessment* (pp. 53-58). New York: Plenum.

Lohman, T.G., Going, S.B., Slaughter, M.H., & Boileau, R.A. (1989). Concept of chemical immaturity in body composition estimates: Implications for estimating the prevalence of obesity in childhood and youth. *American Journal of Human Biology, 1,* 201-204.

Lohman, T.G., Roche, A.F., & Martorell, R. (Eds.) (1988). *Anthropometric standardization reference manual.* Champaign, IL: Human Kinetics.

Motley, H.L. (1957). Comparison of a simple helium closed with the oxygen open-circuit method for measuring residual air. *American Review of Tuberculosis and Pulmonary Diseases, 76,* 701-715.

Organ, L.W., Eklund, A.D., & Ledbetter, J.D. (1994). An automated real time underwater weighing system. *Medicine and Science in Sports and Exercise, 26,* 383-391.

Pollock, M.L., & Wilmore, J.H. (1990). *Exercise in health and disease*. Philadelphia: Saunders.

Scholander, P.F. (1947). Analyzer for accurate estimation of respiratory gases in one-half cubic centimeter samples. *Journal of Biological Chemistry*, **167**, 235-250.

Schutte, J.E., Townsend, E.J., Hugg, J., et al. (1984). Density of lean body mass is greater in blacks than in whites. *Journal of Applied Physiology*, **56**, 1647-1649.

Selinger, A. (1977). *The body as a three component system*. Unpublished doctoral dissertation, University of Illinois, Urbana, IL.

Siri, W.E. (1956). The gross composition of the body. In C.A. Tobias & J.H. Lawrence (Eds.), *Advances in biological and medical physics* (Vol. 4, pp. 239-280). New York: Academic.

Siri, W.E. (1961). Body composition from fluid spaces and density: Analysis of methods. In J. Brožek & A. Henschel (Eds.), *Techniques for measuring body composition* (pp. 223-224). Washington, DC: National Academy of Sciences, National Research Council.

Thomas, T.R., & Etheridge, G.L. (1980). Hydrostatic weighing at residual volume and functional residual capacity. *Journal of Applied Physiology*, **49**, 157-159.

Timson, B.F., & Coffman, J.L. (1984). Body composition by hydrostatic weighing at total lung capacity and residual volume. *Medicine and Science in Sports & Exercise*, **16**, 411-414.

Welch, B.D., & Crisp, C.E. (1958). Effect of level of expiration on body density measurement. *Journal of Applied Physiology*, **12**, 399-402.

Weltman, A., & Katch, V. (1981). Comparison of hydrostatic weighing at residual volume and total lung capacity. *Medicine and Science in Sports & Exercise*, **13**, 210-213.

Williams, D.P., Going, S.B., Massett, M.P., et al. (1993). Aqueous and mineral fractions of the fat-free body and their relation to body fat estimates in men and women aged 49-82 years. In K. Ellis & J. Eastman (Eds.), *Human body composition: In vivo methods, models and assessment* (pp. 109-113). New York: Plenum.

Wilmore, J.H. (1969a). A simplified method for determination of residual lung volumes. *Journal of Applied Physiology*, **27**, 96-100.

Wilmore, J.H. (1969b). The use of actual, predicted and constant residual volumes in the assessment of body composition by underwater weighing. *Medicine and Science in Sports*, **1**, 87-90.

Wilmore, J.H., & Behnke, A.R. (1968). Predictability of lean body weight through anthropometric assessment in college men. *Journal of Applied Physiology*, **25**, 349-355.

Wilmore, J.H., Vodak, P.A., Parr, R.B., et al. (1980). Further simplification of a method for determination of residual lung volume. *Medicine and Science in Sports & Exercise*, **12**, 216-218.

Womersley, J., & Durnin, J.V.G.A. (1977). A comparison of the skinfold method with extent of overweight and various weight-height relationships in the assessment of obesity. *British Journal of Nutrition*, **38**, 271-284.

CHAPTER

2

Hydrometry

Dale A. Schoeller

Water is by far the most abundant of the constituents of the body (Forbes, 1962; Keys & Brožek, 1953; Moore et al., 1963). The percentage of body weight as water varies from 70 to 75% at birth to less than 40% in obese adults. Water is essential for life, serving as a solvent for biochemical reactions and as a transport media. Despite being the most abundant constituent of the body, it is often neglected because the volume of body water is well regulated in health. Indeed, a 15% decrease in body water due to dehydration is life threatening. Even a small change in total body water (TBW), however, can produce a measurable change in body weight and thus a determination of TBW is central to measuring body composition.

Water is an important constituent at the molecular, cellular, and tissue levels of models describing body composition (Wang, Pierson, & Heymsfield, 1992). At the molecular level, water constitutes a single and well defined component. Unlike the other components of the body at the molecular level, the water compartment is comprised of a single molecular species, hydrogen oxide. This uniqueness of molecular structure simplifies the task of measurement, and thus TBW has been a common method for the assessment of body composition at the molecular level. At the cellular level, water can no longer be viewed as a single entity. It is found in two compartments: the body cell mass, which is about 73% water and 27% solids (Moore et al., 1963), and the extracellular fluid compartment, which is about 94% water and 6%

solids (Wang et al., 1992). Finally, on a tissue or anatomical level, water is viewed as being in five compartments. These are intracellular water, which is found in the cytosol of every tissue in the body; plasma water; interstitial water, which is the water in the lymphatic system; dense connective tissue water, which includes the water found in bone, cartilage, and other dense connective tissues; and transcellular water, which is a diverse collection of largely excretory extracellular fluids such as bile, gastrointestinal secretions, mucuses, cerebrospinal fluids, and other minor components (Edelman & Leibman, 1959). The distribution of water at each of the levels for the reference male is summarized in Table 2.1.

As noted in the preceding text, water, unlike other components of the body viewed at the molecular level, comprises a single molecular species. This property lends itself well to the use of the dilution principle, which in its simplest form states that the volume of the compartment is equal to the amount of tracer added to the compartment divided by the concentration of the tracer in that compartment (Edelman et al., 1952). This can be illustrated by the analogy of measuring the amount of water in a beaker by adding a known amount of dye. For a given dose of dye added to the beaker, the intensity of the color will be inversely proportional to the volume of water in the beaker; thus by measuring the intensity of the color or concentration of the dye, the exact volume of water can be determined. Admittedly,

Table 2.1 Approximate Distribution of Water in the Young Male

Model	Compartment	Kg	% TBW
Molecular	Total body water (TBW)	40	100
Cellular	Intracellular	23	57
	Extracellular	17	43
Tissue	Intracellular	23	57
	Plasma	2.8	7
	Interstitial	8.0	20
	Bone	2.8	7
	Dense connective tissue	2.8	7
	Transcellular	1.6	4

Adapted from *Report of the Task Force on Reference Man* (p. 28), by International Commission on Radiologic Protection, 1975, Oxford, UK: Pergamon.

it would be faster to measure the dimensions of the beaker and calculate the volume; however, if the beaker were partially filled with insoluble solids, or if the beaker were of some unknown shape hidden below an opaque covering, then measurement of the simple dimensions of the container would not be possible.

Total Body Water (TBW)

As indicated above, total body water can be measured using the dilution principle. Application of the dilution principle in vivo, however, is more complex than in vitro. This complexity arises because the tracers used in the in vivo dilution do not behave in an ideal manner. Thus, measurement of total body water in vivo requires careful attention to these deviations from the basic assumptions underlying the dilution principle. In doing so, it is possible to design a protocol that will maximize the accuracy and precision of measuring total body water.

Assumptions and Their Validity

There are four assumptions in the measurement of total body water by dilution. These assumptions are basic to all applications of the dilution principle. The assumptions are:

1. the tracer is distributed only in body water,
2. the tracer is equally distributed in all anatomical water compartments,
3. the rate of equilibration of the tracer is rapid, and
4. neither the tracer nor body water is metabolized during the time of tracer equilibration.

The validity of these assumptions is dependent on the tracer used for the measurement of TBW by dilution. The list of tracers that have been used include antipyrine, ethanol, urea, and isotopically labeled water. Although useful results can be obtained from the nonisotopic tracers, they and other water-soluble tracers are inferior to isotopically labeled water because of deviations with regard to these assumptions. Each of these nonisotopic tracers is rapidly metabolized, and thus significant elimination from the body occurs during the time for equilibration. In addition, antipyrine and urea are not equally distributed in body water, antipyrine because of a very small degree of plasma protein binding and urea because of significant two-compartment distribution. Because of this, the following discussion of these assumptions is limited to the isotopic tracers of water. These are the radioactive tracer tritium oxide and the two stable isotopic tracers deuterium oxide and oxygen-18 hydride.

Assumption 1. The Tracer Is Distributed Only in Body Water. None of the isotopic tracers is distributed only in body water. Each tracer exchanges to a small degree with nonaqueous molecules; thus the volume of distribution or dilution space of the isotope will be slightly greater than TBW. Until recently, however, there has been less than universal agreement about the extent of the overestimate because only tritium and deuterium oxide tracers were readily available and estimates of deuterium exchange were based on comparisons of the dilution space with TBW measured by desiccation in animal models. Estimates of hydrogen isotope exchange with nonaqueous molecules range from 0 to over 20% of TBW (Sheng & Huggins, 1979), although the majority of the comparisons indicate that the hydrogen exchange is between 2 and 6% (Table 2.2). Part of the controversy arises because it has been difficult to assess the fraction of the variation in these comparisons that is due to exchange and that due to measurement error. Both isotope dilution and desiccation are subject to systematic errors. Moreover, these errors tend to be in opposite directions and may lead to exaggerated estimates of exchange. For example, incomplete isotope administration results in an overestimate of the dilution space, while incomplete drying leads to an underestimate of total body water.

Table 2.2 Comparison of In Vivo Isotope Dilution Space With Total Body Water by Desiccation

Isotope	Species	No.	% Difference from desiccation (SD)		Reference
Tritium	Rat	10	6.6		Foy & Schneider, 1960
		32	12.0*		Tisavipat et al., 1974
		21	1.7	(2.4)	Culebras et al., 1977
		32	4.3		Rothwell & Stock, 1979
		—	2.1		Nagy & Costa, 1980
	Rabbit	—	3.1	(0.4)	Green & Dunsmore, 1978
	Gopher	12	9.2*		Gettinger, 1983
	Seal	4	4.0	(0.6)	Reilly & Fedak, 1990
Deuterium	Rat	16	6.4	(3.1)	Lifson et al., 1955
		24	3.4		Kanto & Clawson, 1980
	Pig	24	2.2		Houseman et al., 1973
	Seal	4	2.8	(0.9)	Reilly & Fedak, 1990
Oxygen-18	Rat	6	1.7	(1.4)	Lifson et al., 1955
		10	1.0	(2.7)	Nagy & Costa, 1980
	Pig	45	2.2	(0.1)	Whyte et al., 1985

Hydrogen mean (SD) 3.7 (1.7)
Oxygen mean (SD) 1.6 (0.6)
*Excluded from mean.

The recent increase in use of oxygen-18 hydride as a tracer for TBW provides an additional tool for the investigation of hydrogen isotope exchange. By simultaneously administering hydrogen- and oxygen-labeled waters, the increment in the hydrogen dilution space can be estimated from the differences in the dilution spaces without error from the desiccation method or from incomplete dosing, since both spaces are equally affected when the isotopes are mixed. Simultaneous determinations using both tracers have now been reported in more than 23 studies involving 270 subjects. These studies have demonstrated that the deuterium dilution space is 2.2% greater than that for oxygen in premature infants and 3.4% greater in infants and adults (Racette et al., 1994). The measured ratio is not constant between subjects, having a standard deviation of 1.5 to 2.0. It has been demonstrated, however, that over half the variance in the ratio of the dilution spaces is due to measurement error and that the physiological variation is therefore quite small (Racette et al.; Speakman, Nair, & Goran, 1993). Unless the deuterium and oxygen dilution spaces vary systematically, it can be inferred that the variation in deuterium exchange is only a small fraction of the TBW and thus the variability reported previously (Sheng & Huggins, 1979) is mostly due to measurement error.

The difference between premature infants and adults in the degree of exchange suggested by the smaller dilution space ratio in premature infants, however, appears to be physiological. Specifically, the extracellular fluid volume is expanded in premature infants, which leads to a large increase in the ratio of body water to protein. Because protein is the likely primary source of nonaqueous exchange (Culebras & Moore, 1977), the increase in the ratio of water to protein ratio from 3-to-1 in adults to 5-to-1 at birth (Fomon, Haschker, Ziegler, & Nelson, 1982) fully explains the difference in the relative dilution spaces between adults and premature infants.

Although the use of water containing both hydrogen and oxygen tracers has provided the much needed evidence indicating that the physiologic variation in hydrogen exchange is quite small in human beings, it does not provide an absolute measure of the exchange because oxygen is also subject to exchange. However, desiccation data (Table 2.2) indicate that the oxygen exchange is slightly more than 1% and that the deuterium/tritium exchange is slightly less than 4%. Theoretical considerations provide only slightly different values, with oxygen exchange estimated at slightly less than 1% (Schoeller et al., 1980) and maximal deuterium/tritium exchange calculated as 5% (Culebras & Moore, 1977). Taken together, these lines of evidence indicate that the oxygen exchange is 1% of TBW and that the deuterium (or tritium) exchange is 4% of TBW in adult human beings.

Assumption 2. The Tracer Is Equally Distributed in All Anatomical Water Compartments. Although isotopic tracers are almost identical to body water, differences in molecular weight can lead to isotopic fractionation, which is a change in the abundance of the isotopes in the product relative to that in the reactant, when a compound undergoes either a chemical or physical change. The phenomenon of isotopic fractionation includes both equilibrium isotope effects, which result from differences in the relative free energies of the isotopic species in the products and reactants, and kinetic isotope effects, which result from differences in reaction or distribution rates of the isotopic species under non-equilibrium conditions. Comparisons of the isotopic concentration in various anatomical water compartments has demonstrated that there is very little isotopic fractionation within the body. Plasma, urine, and sweat do not show fractionation (Schoeller, Leitch, & Brown, 1986a; Wong et al., 1988). Older studies, although slightly less precise, have also reported an absence of fractionation between water from plasma, liver, gastric fluid, and cisternal fluid (Edelman, 1952).

Isotopic fractionation, however, has been noted in water leaving the body by evaporation (Schoeller et al., 1986a; Wong et al., 1988). Isotopic fractionation between water vapor and liquid water is a well described physical property (Dansgaard, 1964) and thus not a surprise. The fractionation is greater for the hydrogen isotopes because of the differences in the hydrogen bonding energies of the three hydrogen isotopes. Water collected from exhaled breath is depleted in deuterium and oxygen-18 relative to body water. Similarly, transdermal evaporation loss, which is insensible water loss from the skin through routes other than the sweat glands, is isotopically fractionated (Schoeller et al., 1986a; Wong et al., 1988). These two data sets are in good agreement with regard to the values of the fractionation factors and, equally important, in good agreement with the values determined in vitro (Dansgaard, 1964). Saliva collected by spitting or similar methods is slightly enriched in deuterium and oxygen-18, because it is the residual after the lighter evaporative water loss is removed, but saliva collected by cannulation of the salivary gland is expected to be unfractionated. Similar in vivo measures are not available for tritium, but the fractionation factors between water and water vapor are known. These fractionation factors for all three isotopes, which are presented as the ratio

Table 2.3   Isotopic Fractionation Factors at 37 °C

System	^{18}O	^2H	^3H
H_2O_{vap}/H_2O_{liq}			
In vivo	0.990	0.945	0.92
In vitro	0.992	0.941	
CO_2/H_2O_{liq}			
In vivo	1.038		
In vitro	1.038		

Data from Haggarty et al., 1988; Schoeller et al., 1986a; & Wong et al., 1988.

of the heavy isotope concentration in water vapor divided by that in water, are presented in Table 2.3. It should be noted that these fractionation factors were determined in vitro, but they have been confirmed in vivo for deuterium and oxygen-18 prior to administration of any isotope (Schoeller et al., 1986a; Wong et al., 1988). There is concern, though not yet published, by some investigators that these fractionation factors do not apply after isotopic water is administered. It is difficult to invoke a physical mechanism for a change in the isotopic fractionation, although breath water may be subject to contamination during respiration, which may then become apparent after the isotopic administration increases the isotopic difference between body water and environmental water.

Assumption 3. The Rate of Equilibration of the Tracer Is Rapid. Obviously, equilibration is not instantaneous, and thus the practical question becomes: How long is the delay before equilibration occurs? The answer depends on the precision of the measurement method, since a more precise method requires a closer approach to equilibration. For this discussion, it will be assumed that the precision of the measurement is 1%. Schloerb et al. (1950) investigated the rate of equilibration as a function of route of deuterium oxide administration and found that equilibration was reached 2 hours after intravenous administration and 3 hours after subcutaneous or oral administration. Wong et al. (1988) also performed an extensive investigation of the time to equilibration after oral administration of labeled water to healthy subjects. In so doing, they demonstrated that the time to equilibration was less than 3 hours regardless of whether plasma, breath CO_2, breath water, saliva, or urine were sampled. The degree of error due to disequilibria did, however, differ between physiologic samples during the first one to two hours after the dose. Breath CO_2 demonstrated an initial 40% overestimate for ^{18}O relative to venous plasma water, and urine demonstrated a low isotopic enrichment for both stable isotopes of water relative to venous plasma water (Wong et al., 1988). The low enrichment of urine relative to plasma probably represents a memory effect in the bladder due to incomplete emptying of urine produced prior to isotope administration. This occurs despite a modest rate of isotope exchange across the wall of the bladder (Johnson, Cavert, Lifson, & Visscher, 1951). Because of this memory effect, it is also important to consider the number of voids, in addition to the time after the dose, when urine is sampled for the measurement of total body water. Three voids is recommended with the third void between 3 and 6 hours after the dose.

When the data from a large number of subjects are combined, a slight disequilibrium is still detectable at 3 hours after the dose. In 63 subjects receiving either deuterium or ^{18}O, we detected a 0.3% (±0.1%) smaller TBW at 3 hours than at 4 hours after oral isotope administration (Schoeller et al., 1985). While a third of this difference can be accounted for by water turnover (see discussion of Assumption 4), the 0.2% underestimate in measured TBW is probably due to a small continued mixing of the isotopes with poorly perfused body water compartments. This small underestimate, however, is negligible for most TBW measurements.

Even a small disequilibrium in healthy subjects raises concern about equilibration time in subjects with excess water in poorly vascularized compartments. Denne, Patel, and Kalhan (1990) measured the time to equilibration among pregnant women and found that pregnancy delayed equilibration by about one hour. Measurement of isotopic enrichments in amniotic fluid and plasma at 5 hours after oral administration of ^{18}O-labeled water indicated a slight, statistically insignificant, underenrichment of amniotic fluid (96% ± 5%). McCullough, Mullen, and Kalhan (1991) determined the equilibration time in patients with ascites and also noted a delay in equilibration, with the plateau not occurring until 4 hours after the dose. Because of these observations, equilibration times of 4 or 5 hours after oral isotope administration are suggested in patients with expanded extracellular water compartments.

Assumption 4. Neither the Tracer Nor Body Water Undergoes Metabolism During the Time of Tracer Equilibration. As indicated earlier, it is the inaccuracy of this assumption that causes water-soluble compounds like ethanol and antipyrine to be poor tracers for measuring TBW, but

even isotopically labeled water is not free of metabolic complications. Body water is in a constant state of flux. In temperate climates, the average fractional turnover rate in adults is 8% each day (Schoeller, 1988). In the reference male, this includes inputs of 1.5 L/d from beverages, 1 L/d from water of hydration in food, 0.2 L/d from metabolic water produced during the oxidation of fuels, and 0.2 L/d of exchange with atmospheric moisture. This is balanced by an output of 1.6 L/d in urine, 1.2 L/d of insensible losses as sweat, breath water, or transdermal evaporation, and 0.1 L/d in stool (National Research Council, 1989). Water turnover is 50 to 100% greater in tropical climates (Singh et al., 1989) due to increased insensible water loss.

This constant turnover has led to two approaches to the measurement of total body water (Figure 2.1). The first is the plateau method, which is the method discussed in the preceding paragraphs. When the plateau method is used, labeled water is administered and samples are collected for 3 to 5 hours, and TBW is calculated from the enrichment of the samples collected after the enrichment has reached a plateau or constant value. Because this plateau is not perfectly constant, due to the metabolism of water, a back-extrapolation or slope-intercept method has also been used (Coward, 1988). For this method, samples are collected for up to 14 days after the dose and the zero time intercept is calculated by back-extrapolation to the time of the dose.

Because of the continuous turnover of body water, one would expect the back-extrapolation method of calculating TBW to give a smaller and more accurate estimation. In general, however, both methods give very similar results. These methods require different approaches to the treatment of water flux. When the plateau method is used, efforts are made to reduce water intake during the equilibration period to minimize water turnover and thus flatten the plateau. With the back-extrapolation method, efforts are made during the first day and subsequent days to maintain constancy of the fractional turnover rate and thus ensure that the assumption of a log-linear elimination rate is met. The difficulty of maintaining constant turnover is the likely cause of the discrepancy between the plateau method and back-extrapolation method reported by Wong et al. (1989a). They found that TBW calculated from the 6 hour post-dose data in 10 lactating women averaged 0.6 kg more than the back-extrapolation values. Although they attributed this to failure of the 6 hour sample to equilibrate, it is more likely that it is due to

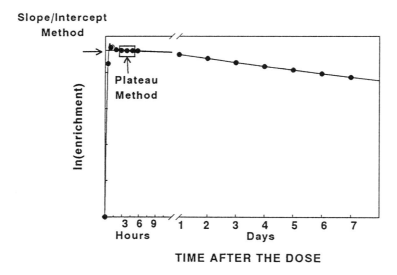

Figure 2.1 Graphic representation of the measurement of TBW by stable isotope dilution using the plateau method, in which the tracer enrichment is estimated from the value at a near steady state after equilibration, and the slope/intercept method, in which the enrichment is estimated from the zero time intercept. Note the change in time scale that was made for ease of viewing.

an overestimation of TBW by back-extrapolation. Failure to equilibrate results in high enrichment values and thus underestimates TBW in most fluids with the possible exception of urine. In contrast, a low turnover on the first day after the dose, due to a 6 hour period without water intake, results in a slightly high value of the intercept and hence an underestimate of TBW by back-extrapolation, which is what was observed.

Equipment

Labeled water for the measurement of TBW can be assayed using one of several methods. The choice of method is often one of convenience and depends on the local availability of instruments and expertise (Table 2.4). Although deuterium was the first tracer available to investigators for the measurement of TBW, its use was soon displaced by tritium because of the greater availability of scintillation counters and the simplicity of the assay, especially relative to the falling drop method (Schloerb et al., 1951), a technique that can best be described as an art form. The use of tritium, however, involves a small but finite radiation hazard. Because of this, the use of stable isotopic labels has again become common, especially for studies involving children and women of childbearing age. Of the two, deuterium is used more often than ^{18}O. Oxygen-18 has the advantage that its dilution

Table 2.4   Analytical Approaches to Measurement of Total Body Water

Method	Isotope	Representative citation
Scintillation counting	$^{3}H_2O$	Vaughan & Boling, 1961
Infrared spectrometry	$^{2}H_2O$	Lukaski & Johnson, 1985
Gas chromatography	$^{2}H_2O$	Nielson et al., 1971
Nuclear magnetic resonance	$^{2}H_2O$	Khaled et al., 1987
Mass spectrometry	$^{2}H_2O$	Wentzel et al., 1958
Isotope ratio mass spectrometry	$^{2}H_2O$ and $H_2{}^{18}O$	Schoeller et al., 1980

space more closely approximates TBW, but, as indicated previously, the reproducibility of the differences between the dilution spaces of deuterium and ^{18}O is such that the spaces can be mathematically interconverted with little error. The disadvantage of ^{18}O is that it can be adequately measured only by isotope ratio mass spectrometry and, even at the precisions offered by this instrumentation, the cost of ^{18}O-labeled water for measurement of TBW in an adult is more than $100 compared to $5 to $10 for deuterium.

Measurement Procedures

Attaining a precision of 1% in the measurement of TBW requires careful attention to detail. Each aspect of the measurement, including subject preparation, dosing, sample collection, and isotope analysis, must be controlled such that the systematic and random errors are less than 0.5%.

Subject preparation is somewhat dependent on the goals of the investigation. The most rigorous preparation is required for the extrapolation from TBW to body composition with additional measures of other body components. For this, the subject must be euvolemic. Overhydration or dehydration reduces the accuracy of the extrapolation. To establish euvolemia, the subject should have normal fluid and food intake the day before the measurement and avoid vigorous exercise after the final meal of the previous day to avoid dehydration or depletion of glycogen stores. Similarly, ambient conditions should be such that the subject does not sweat excessively after the last meal of the previous day. The final meal should be eaten between 12 and 15 hours prior to the dose to minimize the water content of the intestine. Lastly, the subject should not drink for several hours before the test to avoid overhydration. The measurement can be performed in the morning to minimize the discomfort of fasting.

The dose should be aliquoted by weight using a balance with a precision and accuracy such that the relative uncertainty in the dose of labeled water is less than 0.3%. Furthermore, the dose must be weighed and transported in a screw capped container to minimize evaporation. Although the dose can be given intravenously, which will reduce the equilibration time by about 1 hour, oral dosing is quite effective and is less invasive. Even for oral dosing, Millipore filtering is recommended. Syringe cap filters are generally adequate, but where extensive precautions are indicated or where the minor losses of costly ^{18}O are to be avoided, an online system can be used (Wong, Legg, Clark, & Klein, 1991). Intravenous or subcutaneous dosing requires that the dose be sterile and pyrogen free.

The dose should be given with the subject fasting to maximize the rate of absorption. Although isotopically labeled water will equilibrate with body water under conditions of reduced gastric emptying (Jones et al., 1987), studies have shown that absorption will be delayed (Scholer & Code, 1954).

Usually, when the plateau method is used, subjects are prevented from eating or drinking during the equilibration period. This minimizes the changes in the body pool size. In some subject groups, such as young children, the continued fast is stressful for all involved and a light meal can be given 1 hour after the dose. One hour is chosen on the assumption that the dose will have emptied from the stomach and yet there is still time for the water in the meal to mix with the body water pool during the equilibration period. The ingestion of large boluses (2 to 3% of the pool size) of fluid disturb the isotopic enrichment of plasma water for up to an hour after the bolus (Drews & Stein, 1992). The volumes of water in food and beverages should be carefully recorded so that they can be subtracted from the dilution space.

When the back-extrapolation method is used, meals should be delayed for one hour after the dose to permit isotope absorption, but then normal intakes should be instituted so that the isotopic elimination approximates the habitual value. The research group at the Dunn Nutrition Centre (Cambridge, UK) suggests that the subject be awakened at 4 a.m. to administer the labeled water so that a normal meal pattern can be established even on the day of dose administration (personal communication).

The dose should be administered with great care to avoid losses (Roberts, Fjeld, Westerterp, & Goran, 1990). When the dose is given orally, the container used for the dose should be washed with 20 to 50 ml of water and this should be drunk by the subject. Similarly, if the dose is administered via a naso-gastric tube, the tube should be flushed with water after the dose to rinse all the dose from the tube. If the undiluted volume is less than 10 ml, it is advisable to dilute the enriched dose waters before administration to minimize the effects of small losses. It is also advisable to have on hand a preweighed tissue and a sealed plastic bag. Should a small amount of the dose be spilled, the spill can be absorbed onto the tissue, the tissue resealed in the bag, and the tissue and bag reweighed to measure the loss.

Physiological samples must be collected over a period long enough to ensure equilibration. As indicated above, equilibration for the plateau method, defined as 99.5% of the final enrichment, is reached within 3 hours for subjects with normal water compartmentalization and 4 hours for subjects with expanded extracellular water volumes. Measurements of urine, however, require that a third void be produced to minimize the effects of incomplete emptying of the bladder. There is less certainty about recommendations for sample collection in the back-extrapolation method. Again, however, it appears prudent that the first sample should be collected within the 6 hour period after the dose and that the third void after the dose be measured. At least three additional samples should be collected on subsequent days at the same time of day to minimize the effects of diurnal variation on the elimination rate (Schoeller et al., 1986b).

Lest it be forgotten, physiological samples must also be collected prior to the dose, because each of the isotopes under consideration occurs naturally in the body. When isotope ratio mass spectrometry is used, it is important that the baseline sample be collected within 24 hours of the dose to minimize any day-to-day natural variation. This period must be shortened if the subjects are undergoing serial body composition measurements because isotope may still be present from the previous study. If the intervals between isotope doses are less than three biological half-lives (circa three weeks), then it may be advisable to collect a series of samples for 3 to 6 hours before the dose to estimate the rate of isotope elimination from the previous dose.

Sample size depends on the need for the assay, but samples smaller than 1 ml are generally not recommended. Small samples are subject to systematic error due to contamination with the moisture in air. All samples should be stored in airtight containers with minimal dead space within seconds after collection. Although these samples are quite stable during storage, refrigeration or freezing at $-10\ ^\circ C$ is recommended to minimize bacterial growth.

Generalized procedures for the isotopic analyses cannot be treated here because of the many types of assays that can be used (Table 2.4). It is, however, imperative that a sample of the dose be saved and analyzed for isotope enrichment using the same procedure used to analyze the physiological samples. This aliquot of the dose should be gravimetrically diluted with tap water so that the enrichment approximates that of the physiological samples to determine the exact concentration of the tracer. Use of the manufacturer's specifications regarding enrichment is not recommended because there may be systematic differences in the analytical procedures. It is recommended that the sample of diluted dose and diluting water be analyzed in the same batch as the physiological samples for maximal precision (Coward, 1990).

Calculation of Dilution Spaces

Under ideal conditions, the calculation of the isotope dilution space (N) involves the simple application of the dilution principle. Thus

$$N = d \cdot f \cdot E_{dose}/E_{bw} \qquad (2.1)$$

where d is the moles of water given in the dose, f is the fractionation factor for the physiological sample relative to body water, and E_{dose} and E_{bw} are the enrichments of the dose and body water, respectively. A limitation of this equation is that it often involves interconversion of the units with respect to both the dose (i.e., g to moles) and the various enrichment values to atom percent excess. A more user-friendly method is to measure both a sample of the diluted dose and the physiological samples during the same analytical run and to calculate dilution space from mass and instrumental units directly (Coward, 1990):

$$N = \frac{(WA/a)(S_a - S_t)f}{(S_s - S_p)} \qquad (2.2)$$

where N is expressed in grams, W is the mass of water used to dilute the dose, A is the dose administered to the subject, a is the mass of dose used in preparing the diluted dose, f is the fractionation factor for the physiological sample relative to body water, S_a is the measured value for the diluted dose, S_t is the value for the tap water used in the dilution, S_s is the value for the physiological sample, and S_p is the value for the pre-dose physiological sample.

The value of S_s can be obtained by the plateau method or back-extrapolation to the time of the dose. For the back-extrapolation technique, the isotope enrichment of each post-dose sample should be calculated relative to the isotope abundance in a sample collected prior to isotope administration and the zero time enrichments calculated by linear regression using the natural logarithms. Note that if samples are collected for more than two biological half-lives after the dose, this back-extrapolation may be inordinately affected by imprecise measurements at the latter time points (Schoeller et al., 1985). If excess isotope is not present in the subject from a previous measurement, then the enrichment may be used directly for calculating dilution spaces. If excess isotope is present, the enrichment relative to a physiological sample collected just prior to the second dosing must be calculated and used in the equations just given.

When the back-extrapolation method is used, the dilution space does not require correction for isotope loss in urine or insensible loss (Spears, Hyatt, Vogal, & Lang, 1974) nor for the addition of water to the pool because these factors are fully compensated for by the back-extrapolation, as long as the subject is in water balance and the turnover is constant. The plateau method, however, requires correction for water flux during the equilibration period. When the goal of the protocol is to measure dilution space at the time of the dose, any new water added to the pool from the dose, dietary intake, beverages, metabolic water, and atmospheric exchange in humid environments should be subtracted from the isotope dilution space. Estimates of these rates are presented in Table 2.5, and detailed equations are presented elsewhere (Fjeld, Brown, & Schoeller, 1988; Schoeller, 1991).

If the goal is to measure the dilution space at the time of sample collection (for example, in the morning after an isotope dose given the night before), the dose must be corrected for all isotope losses from the body water pool. These routes of loss include urine and insensible water loss, assuming that fecal losses are negligible (Spears et al., 1974). Although these corrections will be small and often negligible in studies of adults, where the subjects are not allowed to eat or drink during the equilibration period, the errors can be quite large in infants and children.

The final step in the determination of total body water from isotope dilution is to correct the above-calculated isotope dilution space for exchange with the nonaqueous compartment. As indicated, the bulk of the data suggests that tritium and deuterium overestimate the body water pool by 4% in adults and children and that deuterium overestimates the body water pool by 2% in premature infants. The overestimate for ^{18}O is smaller and estimated to be 1% in adults and 0.5% in premature infants.

Use of Body Water to Estimate Body Composition

As indicated in the introduction, body water can be used to estimate body composition on three

Table 2.5   Estimates of Average Daily Total Body Water (TBW) Flux in Young Adult Subjects Living in a Temperate Climate

Route	TBW turnover %/h	Absolute g/h
Urine	0.23	82
Breath	0.10	34
Sweat	0.02	6
Transdermal	0.02	8
Total	0.37	130

Calculated from data recorded in Chicago, Illinois (Schoeller et al., 1986a).

levels: molecular, cellular, and tissue. Because the cellular level requires an additional measurement to partition body water into an intracellular compartment, it will be discussed in the second section of this chapter. In the absence of measures other than weight, the most common and useful body composition model is the two-compartment model of fat and fat-free mass. This model is based on the knowledge that lipids are hydrophobic and thus free of water, which is therefore restricted to the fat-free compartment. The calculation of fat-free mass from body water depends on an assumption of constant hydration of fat-free mass—i.e., that the ratio of water to solids in fat-free mass is the same in all subjects. Clearly, this assumption is incorrect in subjects who are either dehydrated or who have abnormal water metabolism leading to edema. Among healthy subjects, however, hydration is relatively constant.

The most commonly used hydration constant is 0.73, which was first recommended by Pace and Rathbun (1945), who reviewed chemical analytic data from several small mammal species. Needless to say, the literature on the subject has expanded extensively since then, and this constant has been reinvestigated in a great number of animal species. Many of the chemical analyses of the hydration of fat-free mass were performed on eviscerated carcasses, including those reported by Pace and Rathbun, and thus do not necessarily apply to in vivo models. However, a review of the literature restricted to whole-animal analyses (Table 2.6) confirms the constant of 0.73 recommended by Pace and Rathbun (1945).

Although few adult human cadaver studies have been performed to determine the hydration constant (73.0 ± 2.7, n = 7), results are in excellent agreement with animal studies (Table 2.6), which is impressive considering that most of the subjects were quite ill prior to their death and analysis. An exception to constancy of hydration occurs in infancy when the hydration of fat-free mass is elevated relative to adult values in animals and humans. With regard to the humans, Fomon et al. (1982) have estimated the hydration constant for ages ranging from birth to 10 years; however, they assumed that deuterium oxide overestimated total body water by only 1.3%. These values have been recalculated assuming a 4% overestimate (Table 2.7).

The development of additional methods of measuring fat-free mass, such as neutron activation or water-independent measures such as xenon dilution, have provided investigators with the means to estimate the hydration constant in vivo. Studies to date indicate that there is no effect of aging

Table 2.6   Hydration of Fat-Free Mass (FFM) by Chemical Analysis of Whole Nonruminant Mammals

Species	No.	Sex	% Hydration FFM (SD)	Citation
Mouse	14	F	74.0 (1.4)	Annegers, 1954
	128		74.0	Dawson et al., 1972
	17		70.7 (1.0)	Holleman & Dieterich, 1975
Rat	16	F	72.2 (0.8)	Annegers, 1954
	7	M	73.0 (0.7)	Annegers, 1954
	112		71.4 (0.9)*	Babineau & Page, 1955
	16	F	72.3 (1.0)	Rothwell & Stock, 1979
	16	M	73.1 (1.0)	Rothwell & Stock, 1979
	72		73.0 (2.2)	Lesser et al., 1980
Lemming	5		73.7 (1.8)	Holleman & Dieterich, 1975
Vole	4		72.2 (0.3)	Holleman & Dieterich, 1975
Rabbit	3		76.3 (1.4)*	Harrison et al., 1936
Dog	2		74.4 (0.7)*	Harrison et al., 1936
Seal	4		72.2 (0.8)	Reilly & Fedak, 1990
Monkey	2		73.2 (0.3)*	Harrison et al., 1936
Human	4		72.9 (3.8)	Keys & Brožek, 1953
	1		73.7†	Moore et al., 1968
	2		72.8 (0.2)	Knight et al., 1986
Mean			73.1 (1.3)	

*Excludes intestines or intestinal contents. †Composition of viscera estimated from the literature.

through age 70 years (Schoeller, 1989). Further studies investigating the effects of gender, race, aging, and disease state on the hydration constant are being performed (Wang, J., personal communication, January 1994).

Despite the general agreement between various desiccation studies, the modest variation between investigations has raised some concern about the validity of the use of a hydration constant (Sheng & Huggins, 1979). It must be remembered, however, that chemical analysis is a very difficult procedure that is prone to errors. For example, underestimates of hydration can result from insensible water loss between the time of death and the time of analysis, or from incomplete desiccation. Errors that can lead to overestimates of the hydration constant include loss of tissues during dissection and loss of volatile solids during drying (Culebras et al., 1977). Without estimates of these measurement errors, it is not possible to estimate the true physiological variation in the hydration constant of healthy adults. However, taking 1% as the average measurement error and 1.1% as the average within-laboratory standard deviation of the in vivo

measure of hydration, then the physiological variation in the hydration constant can be estimated to be 0.5%, which is quite small. This constancy, however, does not apply to gross tissue wasting (Beddoe, Streat, & Hill, 1985) or to disease states that alter water metabolism; higher hydration constants have been measured in a grossly edematous male who died of endocarditis (Keys & Brožek, 1953).

Precision

The precision of the total body water measurement is dependent on the analytical method as well as the dose of tracer administered to the subject. In general, mass spectrometric methods have been the most precise. These methods, especially high-precision isotope ratio mass spectrometry, can detect very small excesses of deuterium or ^{18}O, and thus the investigator can administer a dose in which the increase in enrichment of body water exceeds the random measurement error by a factor of 200 to 500. Under these conditions, the precision

Table 2.7   Hydration of Fat-Free Mass (FFM) in Children

Age	Girls			Boys		
	Wt (g)	TBW (ml)	% FFM (g)	Wt (g)	TBW (ml)	% FFM (g)
Birth	3325	2280	80.6	3545	2467	80.6
1 m	4131	2716	80.1	4452	2966	80.1
2 m	4989	3071	79.7	5509	3450	79.8
3 m	5743	3407	79.5	6435	3848	79.6
6 m	7250	4124	78.9	8030	4646	79.2
9 m	8270	4777	78.6	9180	5392	78.9
1 y	9180	5374	78.3	10150	6050	78.6
2 y	11910	7215	77.7	12590	7713	77.7
3 y	14100	8721	77.4	14675	9134	77.0
4 y	15960	9995	77.3	16690	10534	76.6
5 y	17660	11112	77.1	18670	11893	76.1
6 y	19520	12301	77.0	20690	13300	75.8
7 y	21840	13699	76.9	22850	14733	75.5
8 y	24840	15436	76.8	25300	16215	75.2
9 y	28460	17464	76.6	28130	17919	74.9
10 y	32550	19656	76.5	31440	19843	74.6

Adapted from "Body Composition of Reference Children From Birth to Age 10 Years," by S.J. Fomon, F. Haschke, E.E. Ziegler, and S.E. Nelson, 1982, *American Journal of Clinical Nutrition*, **35**, pp. 1169-1175. Copyright 1982 by American Journal of Clinical Nutrition. Adapted with permission.

of the measurement as estimated from either repeat measurements (Schoeller et al., 1985; Speakman et al., 1993) or simultaneous measurements using two isotopes (Racette et al., 1994) is between 1 and 2%. Estimates of repeatability using other analytical methods are between 2 and 4% (Bartoli et al., 1993; Lukaski, 1987; Mendez et al., 1970; Wang, Pierson, & Kelly, 1973).

Accuracy

Unless there is bias due to failure to reach equilibrium, the accuracy of the isotope dilution method for the measurement of TBW is excellent. The accuracy depends only on the uncertainty of the estimate of nonaqueous exchange, which is about 1%. There is a further loss of accuracy in estimating fat-free mass due to uncertainty of the hydration constant, which is roughly estimated to be 0.5% in healthy adult subjects.

Recommended Standard Procedure for Measuring TBW

There is more than one standard procedure for the measurement of TBW, and these cannot all be detailed because of space limitations. What follows

is one recommended procedure for the measurement of TBW by the plateau method in adults.

- Subject should fast overnight and not drink fluids after midnight. The subject should also refrain from exercise after the previous meal and avoid excessive insensible water loss due to high ambient temperatures.
- Collect a baseline physiologic sample of saliva, plasma, urine, or breath water (with fractionation correction).
- Weigh the subject in a hospital gown or some other minimal weight clothing.
- Administer a weighed dose of isotope by mouth. Rinse the capped container with 50 ml of water and administer to the subject.
- Subject should not take anything by mouth during the sample collection period.
- If saliva, plasma, or breath water are sampled, post-dose samples should be collected at 3 and 4 hours after the dose. If there is excess extracellular water, samples should be collected at 4 and 5 hours after the dose.
- If urine is sampled, the subject should void once before the abovementioned times and this specimen should be discarded. Two specimens should then be collected at the prescribed times.

- Samples should be stored in airtight vessels until analysis.
- Enrichments of the two post-dose samples should agree within two standard deviations of the particular assay.

Summary

Water is the most abundant compound in the human body. The volume of water in the body can readily be measured by isotope dilution using tritium, deuterium, or ^{18}O-labeled water. These tracers are distributed rapidly within the body, but they are not perfect tracers. Equilibration after an oral dose requires 3 to 4 hours and corrections are required for exchange with nonaqueous hydrogen or oxygen. In addition, physiological samples that undergo a chemical or physical change require correction for isotope fractionation. With careful attention to detail, however, total body water can be measured with a precision and accuracy of 1 to 2%.

Intracellular Water (ICW) and Extracellular Water (ECW)

The volume of extracellular water can be measured in vivo using the dilution principle, a method similar to the measurement of total body water. The anatomy of extracellular water, however, is less defined than total body water. Furthermore the common tracers used in analysis of extracellular water by dilution are less ideal than those used for total body water. Because of this, the deviations from ideal dilution behavior can be significant, and they must be carefully considered in the design of the protocol to measure extracellular water volume.

Assumptions and Their Validity

Total body water can be divided into intracellular and extracellular water. Although intracellular water (ICW) is quite difficult to measure directly, extracellular water (ECW) can be measured by dilution and ICW calculated as the difference from TBW. The assumptions underlying the measurement of TBW by dilution are the same four assumptions underlying the measurement of ECW. The assumptions are:

1. the tracer is distributed only in ECW,
2. the tracer is evenly distributed in ECW,
3. the rate of equilibration of the tracer is rapid, and
4. neither the tracer nor ECW is metabolized during the time of tracer equilibration.

Investigators have proposed a number of tracers for the measurement of ECW including bromide, chloride, thiocyanate, thiosulfate, sulfate, inulin, sucrose, and mannitol. Each of these behaves differently with respect to the four assumptions, and a complete discussion of each would be quite lengthy. Previous reviews have indicated that the disaccharides fail to penetrate dense connective tissue and transcellular water and that thiosulfate and sulfate fail to penetrate transcellular water (Bell, 1985). Bromide and isotopic chloride dilution come the closest to approximating the extracellular space (Edelman & Leibman, 1959) and, with the advent of improved analytical techniques, bromine has become the most commonly used tracer. It should be remembered that neither bromine nor any other tracer used to date provides an exact measure of ECW because the physiological properties of the various compartments of ECW (i.e., plasma, interstitial, dense connective tissue, bone, and transcellular water) differ from one another. As such, dilution spaces may differ significantly between the various tracers, and comparisons must be made with caution.

Assumption 1. The Tracer Is Distributed Only in Extracellular Water. Bromine is found in the periodic table directly below chlorine. As such, its chemistry is very similar to chlorine and the bromide ion behaves similarly to the chloride ion. Thus, bromine will distribute within all the ECW compartments because all contain chloride, but bromide will overestimate ECW due to penetration into the intracellular space of erythrocytes and leukocytes as well as some cells within the testes and gastric mucosa (Edelman & Leibman, 1959). Based on chemical analyses and radiochlorine dilution studies, this intracellular penetration accounts for 10% of the fully equilibrated bromide dilution space, of which about half is due to erythrocytes (Edelman & Leibman). This assumption appears to break down even more so during disease where the bromide space appears enlarged relative to the expectation for ECW, possibly due to bromide penetrating the ICW (Schober, Lehr, & Hundeshagen, 1982).

Assumption 2. The Tracer Is Equally Distributed in All Extracellular Water Compartments. This assumption is examined on the basis of chloride distribution because the bromide concentrations in the various extracellular compartments mimic those of chloride. As such, partial failure of this assumption is anticipated because of differences in the concentration of chloride in plasma and filtrates of plasma. The differences, which are referred to as the Gibbs-Donnan effect (Donnan & Allmand, 1914), arise when a membrane-insoluble ionic material is present on one side of a membrane. When this occurs, the combined need to balance osmolality and charge leads to establishment of a concentration gradient of the membrane-soluble ion across that membrane. Interstitial-lymph fluids contain 1 to 3% more chloride per liter than plasma, while dense connective tissue contains 8 to 14% more chloride, an excess so great that it may also involve binding of chloride to extracellular proteins (Scatchard, Scheinberg, & Armstrong, 1950). The chloride concentration in bone water is very similar to that in plasma, while the transcellular chloride concentrations are less than those of plasma but quite variable (Edelman & Leibman, 1959). Taken together, the variation in concentration of chloride in these extracellular fluids, relative to plasma, means that the isotopic chloride and bromide dilution spaces will appear about 5% greater than the extracellular water space. As such, apparent bromide dilution must be corrected by 5%, which is the so called Donnan correction.

Assumption 3. The Rate of Equilibration of the Tracer Is Very Rapid. The equilibration of bromide has both a fast and a slow component. This is demonstrated by a low ratio of bromide to chloride in brain and cerebrospinal fluid relative to that in plasma (Dunning, Steele, & Berger, 1951; Gamble et al., 1953; Wallace & Brodie, 1939) for up to 24 hours after the administration of bromide.

Although the distribution kinetics of bromide and other halides does not reach a complete equilibrium plateau until 1 day after the dose, the changes are less than a few percent between 3 and 6 hours after the dose (McCullough et al., 1991) indicating that a relatively stable distribution has been reached. Furthermore, the ratio of bromide to chloride in most tissues is also stable 3 to 5 hours after the dose (Weir & Hastings, 1939). Thus, excepting cranial fluid, bromide equilibration time is similar to that of isotopic water—that is, 4 hours in normal individuals (Pierson, Price, Wang, & Jain, 1978). The equilibration time is extended to 6 hours or longer in subjects with expanded extracellular spaces due to ascites.

Assumption 4. Neither Bromine Nor ECW Is Metabolized During the Time of Tracer Equilibration. Bromide does not undergo biological alteration, but it is taken up by the kidney and excreted from the body. Fortunately, the rate of excretion is relatively slow and only 0.3% is excreted during 6 hours, if the subjects are not allowed either food or water (Spears et al., 1974). Longer-term losses are dependent on water and salt flux but typically average 4% or less in 12 hours (Cheek, 1953).

At the same time, the ECW volume may undergo changes. Many of these changes are similar to those of body water and reflect its dynamic nature. However, evaporative losses of water will not be accompanied by a loss of bromide. As such, these losses lead to a concentration of bromide in plasma and hence a decrease in measured ECW. In addition, however, the ratio of ECW to ICW can change if fluid redistributes within the body. Changes in posture, for example, can cause a shift from ECW to ICW over a period of several hours and thus the subject should be allowed to move about only briefly during equilibration or be required to assume a fixed posture during the period (Thompson & Yates, 1941; Thornton, Moore, & Pool, 1987).

Equipment

Interest in the quantification of bromine has lead to the development of many methods for measuring bromide. These include fluorimetry, ion chromatography, neutron activation, mass spectrometry, and beta counting for radiobromide. These techniques are summarized in Table 2.8. Most of these techniques require special instrumentation, but analytical developments during the last decade have increased the availability of methods for measuring bromide and increased the confidence in the results.

Table 2.8   Analytical Methods for the Measurement of Bromide

Method	Reference
Chromatography	Wong et al., 1989b
Rosaniline	Goodwin, 1971
Fluorescein	Trapp & Bell, 1989
Neutron activation	Vaisman et al., 1987
Radiobromide	Pierson et al., 1978
Inductively coupled mass spectrometry	Janghorbani et al., 1988

Measurement Procedures

The procedures for the measurement of bromide dilution are less standardized than those for TBW. This probably reflects less experience with the technique as well as a realization that the ultimate uncertainty in the calculation of the ECW from bromide dilution space is limited by imperfections of bromide as a tracer for ECW.

Subject preparation before the measurement is subject to the same considerations as for the measurement of TBW. The subject should be in a euvolemic state, unless, of course, the goals of the measurement are to document the effects of water imbalance on body composition. The subject should therefore have normal food and fluid intake the day before the measurement, avoid vigorous exercise, sweating, or diuretics, and the measurement should be performed in the morning between 12 and 15 hours after the previous meal.

The bromide should be given as the sodium salt. Because sodium bromide is hygroscopic, the salt must be stored in a desiccator. In humid areas, it is advisable to prepare the dose as a stock solution to avoid problems with moisture. In either case, the dose is given in water. Although oral administration is the least invasive and the most common means of administration, intravenous and subcutaneous administration have been used without a detectable difference in distribution time. When injected, sodium bromide is given as a sterile, pyrogen-free 2% solution. The optimal dose depends on the precision of the particular assay. Sodium bromide tastes salty and is toxic at high doses, but doses up to 25 mg/kg will not cause the concentration to exceed the pharmacological level (Basalt, 1980).

Sampling is limited to blood plasma, because bromide concentrations are not the same in all fluids (Brodie, Brand, & Leshin, 1939; Gamble et al., 1953). The concentration must be measured relative to pre-dose levels because bromide is normally present in plasma and because its concentration is variable depending on dietary intake.

Although the distribution kinetics of bromide include a slow terminal phase, the sampling interval in most subjects is similar to that for isotopes of water for TBW because this terminal phase represents a relatively small volume, of which a major portion may be exchange with bound chloride. Thus, sampling at 3 to 4 hours in normal individuals and 5 to 6 hours in subjects with expanded extracellular spaces is reasonable, although McCullough et al. (1991) noted that equilibration was only 88% complete in the peritoneal fluid of patients with appreciable ascites 6 hours after the dose.

The requirements and recommendations for ensuring quantitative administration of the dose and evaporation-free storage of the plasma samples for bromide are identical to those for labeled water. One additional requirement is that the plasma samples be obtained without hemolysis because bromide concentrations in erythrocytes are about 25% less than those in plasma (Weir & Hastings, 1939).

Calculation of the Bromide Dilution Space and ECW

The bromide dilution space (N_{Br}) is calculated from the dose of bromide and the increment of the concentration of bromide in plasma water using the dilution principle as already described for total body water.

$$N_{Br} = \frac{(WA/a)(S_a - S_t)c_1}{S_s - S_p} \qquad (2.3)$$

where W is the mass of water used to dilute the dose, A is the mass of bromide administered to the subject, a is the mass of dose used to make the diluted dose, S_a is the concentration of bromide in the diluted dose, S_t is the concentration of bromide in the water used to make the diluted dose, S_s is the concentration of bromide in the plasma sample, and S_p is the concentration of bromide in the pre-dose plasma sample. For maximal precision, concentrations are best measured per unit of specimen mass, and the correction c_1 is the weight fraction of water in plasma. This can be determined gravimetrically by drying a sample of plasma but is usually assumed to be 0.94. This correction will differ if the plasma is ultrafiltered, because of the removal of proteins, or if the subject is severely malnourished and levels of plasma proteins are reduced.

The bromide dilution space overestimates the extracellular water space due to the Gibbs-Donnan effect on the concentration of bromide in various extracellular fluids and because of the penetration of bromide in the intracellular space in erythrocytes, leukocytes, and secretory cells (Edelman & Leibman, 1959). Thus, extracellular water (ECW) is calculated as:

$$ECW = N_{Br}(c_2 c_3) \qquad (2.4)$$

where c_2 is the Gibbs-Donnan correction, and c_3 is the intracellular correction. The Gibbs-Donnan correction is generally assumed to be 0.95 and the intracellular correction is estimated to be 0.90. Intracellular water (ICW) is calculated as the difference between TBW and ECW:

$$ICW = TBW - ECW. \qquad (2.5)$$

Use of ECW and ICW in the Estimation of Body Composition

Both ECW and ICW are components of fat-free mass; however, the relationship between ICW and the metabolic properties of the body is much stronger than that of ECW or TBW (Barac-Nieto, 1979; Moore et al., 1963). By its very nature, ICW is valuable for estimating body composition at the cellular level (Moore et al.).

Precision

The relative precision of measuring the ECW by dilution is not as well characterized as that of TBW. Published distribution time curves of isotopes of both bromide and water show the residuals about the curves, which are assumed to represent random error, are about twice as large for bromide as for water. As with TBW, the precision of bromide dilution depends on the dose of tracer and the analytical method. Thomas, Van der Velde, and Schloerb (1991) suggest that relative precisions of 1% should be attainable, if the doses are carefully chosen for the particular analytical method.

The precision for the determination of ICW, when calculated by the difference between TBW and ECW, is worse because errors in both variables propagate through the calculation. Thus, even if TBW and ECW are determined with 1.5% relative precision (i.e., 0.6 and 0.2 kg, respectively), the precision of the ICW calculation will be 0.64 kg or about 2.5%. This propagation of error is usually the limiting factor in the usefulness of ICW measurements for the analysis of body composition, particularly on an individual basis.

Accuracy

The accuracy of the determination of ECW and ICW is unknown because direct chemical methods are not available to determine criterion values for these components of the body. The estimate of exchangeable chloride by in vivo bromide dilution, however, is within 1% of the chemically determined exchangeable chloride (Edelman & Leibman, 1959); thus the determination of ECW by

bromide in healthy subjects is probably accurate to 1%. The accuracy in subjects with atypical ECW spaces, however, is probably no better than 2 to 5% because of uncertainty in the correction constants for plasma water (c_1), Gibbs-Donnan equilibration (c_2), and penetration into the intracellular space (c_3) due to changes in plasma protein concentrations, hematocrit, and the relative distribution of the various extracellular fluids.

Recommended Standard Procedure for Measuring Bromide Dilution

There is more than one standard procedure for the measurement of bromide dilution. A representative procedure for adults is presented here that is purposefully similar to that for TBW so that the two components can be measured simultaneously.

- The subject should fast overnight and not drink fluids after midnight. The subject should also refrain from exercise after the previous meal and avoid excessive insensible water loss due to high ambient temperatures.
- Collect a baseline plasma sample.
- Weigh the subject in a hospital gown or some other minimal weight clothing.
- Administer a weighed dose of sodium bromide in 50 ml of water by mouth. Larger volumes may be used if the total dose exceeds 1 g. Rinse the capped container with 50 ml of water and administer to the subject.
- Subject should not take anything by mouth during the sample collection period.
- Collect post-dose plasma specimens at 3 and 4 hours after the dose, except when there is excess extracellular water, in which case specimens should be collected at 5 and 6 hours after the dose.
- Specimens should be stored in airtight vessels until analysis.
- Bromide concentrations of the two post-dose specimens should agree within two standard deviations of the particular assay.

Summary

Total body water can be further subdivided into intracellular and extracellular water. The ICW cannot be readily measured, but ECW can be closely approximated from bromide dilution. The bromide dilution can be performed simultaneously with isotope dilution for TBW, but plasma sampling is required. Relative precisions for ECW can approach that of TBW. The accuracy of the ECW determination is less clear, and significant (15%) corrections for unequal bromide concentrations in extracellular fluids and intracellular penetration are necessary. ICW is calculated by the difference between TBW and ECW with modest precision but good accuracy in groups of healthy subjects.

References

Annegers, J. (1954). Total body water in rats and in mice. *Proceedings of the Society for Experimental Biology and Medicine, 87*, 454-456.

Babineau, L.-M., & Page, E. (1955). On body fat and body water in rats. *Journal of Biochemistry & Physiology, 33*, 970-979.

Barac-Nieto, M., Spurr, G.B., Lotero, H., et al. (1979). Body composition during nutritional repletion of severely undernourished men. *American Journal of Clinical Nutrition, 32*, 981-991.

Bartoli, W.P., Davis, J.M., Pate, R.R., et al. (1993). Weekly variability in total body water using ^2H_2O dilution in college-age males. *Medicine and Science in Sports and Exercise, 25*, 1422-1428.

Basalt, R.C. (1980). *Analytical procedures for therapeutic drug monitoring and emerging toxicity.* Davis, CA: Biomedical.

Beddoe, A.H., Streat, S.J., & Hill, G.L. (1985). Hydration of fat-free body in protein-depleted patients. *American Journal of Physiology, 249*, E227-E233.

Bell, E.F. (1985). Body water in infancy. In A.F. Roche (Ed.), *Body composition assessments in youth and adults: Sixth Ross conferences on medical research* (pp. 30-33). Columbus, OH: Ross Laboratories.

Brodie, B.B., Brand, E., & Leshin, S. (1939). The use of bromide as a measure of extracellular fluid. *Journal of Biological Chemistry, 130*, 555-563.

Cheek, D.B. (1953). Estimation of the bromide space with a modification of Conway's method. *Journal of Applied Physiology, 5*, 639-645.

Coward, W.A. (1988). The doubly-labelled-water ($^2H_2^{18}O$) method: Principles and practice. *Proceedings of the Society for Nutrition, 47*, 209-218.

Coward, W.A. (1990). Calculation of pool sizes and flux rates. In A.M. Prentice (Ed.), *The doubly-labelled water method for measuring energy expenditure: Technical recommendations for use in humans (report)* (p. 48). Vienna: International Dietary Energy Consultancy Group.

Culebras, J.M., Fitzpatrick, G.F., Brennan, M.F., et al. (1977). Total body water and the exchangeable hydrogen, II: A review of comparative data from animals based on isotope dilution and desiccation, with a report of new data from the rat. *American Journal of Physiology, 232*, R60-R65.

Culebras, J.M., & Moore, F.D. (1977). Total body water and the exchangeable hydrogen, I: Theoretical calculation of nonaqueous exchangeable hydrogen in man. *American Journal of Physiology, 232*, R54-R59.

Dansgaard, W. (1964). Stable isotopes in precipitation. *Telus, 16*, 436-468.

Dawson, N.J., Stephenson, S.K., & Fredline, D.K. (1972). Body composition of mice subjected to genetic selection for different body proportions. *Comparative Biochemistry & Physiology, 42B*, 679-691.

Denne, S.C., Patel, D., & Kalhan, S.C. (1990). Total body water measurement in normal and diabetic pregnancy: Evidence for maternal and amniotic fluid equilibrium. *Biology Neonate, 57*, 284-291.

Donnan, F.G., & Allmand, A.J. (1914). Ionic equilibria across semi-permeable membranes. *Journal of Chemistry Society, 105*, 1941-1963.

Drews, D., & Stein, T.P. (1992). Effect of bolus fluid intake on energy expenditure values as determined by the doubly labeled water method. *Journal of Applied Physiology, 72*, 82-86.

Dunning, M.F., Steele, J.M., & Berger, E.Y. (1951). Measurement of total body chloride. *Proceedings for the Society for Experimental Biology & Medicine, 77*, 854-858.

Edelman, I.S. (1952). Exchange of water between blood and tissues: Characteristics of deuterium oxide equilibration in body water. *American Journal of Physiology, 171*, 279-296.

Edelman, I.S., & Leibman, J. (1959). Anatomy of body water and electrolytes. *American Journal of Medicine, 27*, 256-277.

Edelman, I.S., Olney, J.M., James, A.H., et al. (1952). Body composition: Studies in the human being by the dilution principle. *Science, 115*, 447-454.

Fjeld, C.R., Brown, K.H., & Schoeller, D.A. (1988). Validation of the deuterium oxide method for measuring average daily milk intake in infants. *American Journal of Clinical Nutrition, 48*, 671-679.

Fomon, S.J., Haschke, F., Ziegler, E.E., & Nelson, S.E. (1982). Body composition of reference children from birth to age 10 years. *American Journal of Clinical Nutrition, 35*, 1169-1175.

Forbes, G.B. (1962). Methods for determining composition of the human body. With a note on the effect of diet on body composition. *Pediatrics, 29*, 477-494.

Foy, J.M., & Schneider, H. (1960). Estimation of total body water (virtual tritium space) in the rat, cat, rabbit, guinea pig and man, and of the biological half-life of tritium in man. *Journal of Physiology (London), 154,* 169-176.

Gamble, J.L., Jr., Robertson, J.S., Hannigan, C.A., et al. (1953). Chloride, bromide, sodium and sucrose spaces in man. *Journal for Clinical Investigation, 32,* 483-487.

Gettinger, R.D. (1983). Use of doubly-labeled water ($^{3}HH^{18}O$) for determination of H_2O flux and CO_2 production by a mammal in a humid environment. *Oecologia (Berlin), 59,* 54-57.

Goodwin, J.F. (1971). Calorimetric measurement of serum bromide with a bromate-rosaniline method. *Clinical Chemistry, 17,* 544-547.

Green, B., & Dunsmore, J.D. (1978). Turnover of tritiated water and ^{22}sodium in captive rabbits (Oryctolagus cuniculus). *Journal of Mammalogy, 59,* 12-17.

Haggarty, P., McGaw, B.A., & Franklin, M.F. (1988). Measurement of fractionated water loss and CO^2 production using triply labelled water. *Journal of Theoretical Biology, 134,* 291-308.

Harrison, H.E., Darrow, D.C., & Yannet, H. (1936). The total electrolyte content of animals and its probable relation to the distribution of body water. *Journal of Biological Chemistry, 113,* 515-529.

Holleman, D.F., & Dieterich, R.A. (1975). An evaluation of the tritiated water method for estimating body water in small rodents. *Canadian Journal of Zoology, 53,* 1376-1378.

Houseman, R.A., McDonald, I., & Pennie, K. (1973). The measurement of total body water in living pigs by deuterium oxide dilution and its relation to body composition. *British Journal of Nutrition, 30,* 149-156.

International Commission on Radiologic Protection. (1975). *Report of the Task Force on Reference Man* (p. 28). Oxford, UK: Pergamon.

Janghorbani, M., Davis, T.A., & Ting, B.T.G. (1988). Measurement of stable isotopes of bromine in biological fluids with inductively coupled plasma mass spectrometry. *Analyst, 113,* 403-411.

Johnson, J.A., Cavert, H.M., Lifson, N., & Visscher, M.B. (1951). Permeability of the bladder to water studied by means of isotopes. *American Journal of Physiology, 165,* 87-92.

Jones, P.J.H., Winthrop, A.L., Schoeller, D.A., et al. (1987). Validation of doubly labeled water for assessing energy expenditure in infants. *Pediatric Research, 21,* 242-246.

Kanto, U., & Clawson, A.J. (1980). Use of deuterium oxide for the in vivo prediction of body composition in female rats in various physiological states. *Journal of Nutrition, 110,* 1840-1848.

Keys, A., & Brožek, J. (1953). Body fat in adult man. *Physiological Reviews, 33,* 245-325.

Khaled, M.A., Lukaski, H.C., & Watkins, C.L. (1987). Determination of total body water by deuterium NMR. *American Journal of Clinical Nutrition, 45,* 1-6.

Knight, G.S., Beddoe, A.H., Streat, S.J., & Hill, G.L. (1986). Body composition of two human cadavers by neutron activation and chemical analysis. *American Journal of Physiology, 250,* E179-E185.

Lesser, G.T., Deutsch, S., & Markofsky, J. (1980). Fat-free mass, total body water, and intracellular water in the aged rat. *American Journal of Physiology, 238,* R82-R90.

Lifson, N., Gordon, G.B., & McClintock, R. (1955). Measurement of total carbon dioxide production by means of $D_2{}^{18}O$. *Journal of Applied Physiology, 7,* 704-710.

Lukaski, H.C. (1987). Methods for the assessment of human body composition: Traditional and new. *American Journal of Clinical Nutrition, 46,* 537-556.

Lukaski, H.C., & Johnson, P.W. (1985). A simple, inexpensive method of determining total body water using a tracer dose of D_2O and infrared absorption of biological fluids. *American Journal of Clinical Nutrition, 41,* 363-370.

McCullough, A.J., Mullen, K.D., & Kalhan, S.C. (1991). Measurements of total body and extracellular water in cirrhotic patients with and without ascites. *Hepatology, 14,* 1102-1111.

Mendez, J., Prokop, E., Picon-Reategui, E., et al. (1970). Total body water by D_2O dilution using saliva samples and gas chromatography. *Journal of Applied Physiology, 28,* 354-357.

Moore, F.D., Lister, J., Boyden, C.M., et al. (1968). Skeleton as a feature of body composition. *Human Biology, 40,* 135-188.

Moore, F.D., Olesen, K.H., McMurray, J.D., et al. (1963). *The body cell mass and its supporting environment.* Philadelphia: W.B. Saunders.

Nagy, K.A., & Costa, D. (1980). Water flux in animals: Analysis of potential errors in the doubly labeled water method. *American Journal of Physiology, 238,* R454-R465

National Research Council and Subcommittee on the Tenth Edition. (1989). *Recommended daily allowances, tenth edition.* Water and electrolytes (pp. 247-249). Washington, DC: National Academy.

Nielson, W.C., Krzywicki, H.J., Johnson, H.L., & Consolazio, C.F. (1971). Use and evaluation of gas chromatography for determination of deuterium in body fluids. *Journal of Applied Physiology, 31,* 957-961.

Pace, N., & Rathbun, E.N. (1945). Studies on body composition, III: The body water and chemically combined nitrogen content in relation to fat content. *Journal of Biological Chemistry, 158,* 685-691.

Pierson, R.N., Jr., Price, D.C., Wang, J., & Jain, R.K. (1978). Extracellular water measurements: Organ tracer kinetics of bromide and sucrose in rats and man. *American Journal of Physiology, 235,* F254-F264.

Racette, S.B., Schoeller, D.A., Luke, A.H., et al. (1994). Relative dilution spaces of ^{2}H- and ^{18}O-labeled water in humans. *American Journal of Physiology, 267,* E585-E590.

Reilly, J.J., & Fedak, M.A. (1990). Measurement of the body composition of living gray seals by hydrogen isotope dilution. *Journal of Applied Physiology, 69,* 885-891.

Roberts, S., Fjeld, C., Westerterp, K., & Goran, M. (1990). Use of the doubly-labelled water method under difficult circumstances. In A.M. Prentice (Ed.), *The doubly-labelled water method for measuring energy expenditure: Technical recommendations for use in humans* (pp 251-263). Vienna: International Dietary Energy Consultancy Group.

Rothwell, N.J., & Stock, M.J. (1979). In vivo determination of body composition by tritium dilution in the rat. *British Journal of Nutrition, 4,* 625-628.

Scatchard, G., Scheinberg, I.H., & Armstrong, S.H., Jr. (1950). Physical chemistry of protein solutions, IV: The combination of human serum albumin with chloride ion. *Journal of American Chemistry Society, 72,* 535-540.

Schloerb, P.R., Friis-Hansen, B.J., Edelman, I.S., et al. (1950). The measurement of total body water in the human subject by deuterium oxide dilution. With a consideration of the dynamics of deuterium distribution. *Journal of Clinical Investigation, 29,* 1296-1310.

Schloerb, P.R., Friis-Hansen, B.J., Edelman, I.S., et al. (1951). The measurement of deuterium oxide in body fluids by the falling drop method. *Journal of Laboratory & Clinical Medicine, 37,* 653-662.

Schober, O., Lehr, L., & Hundeshagen, H. (1982). Bromide space, total body water and sick cell syndrome. *European Journal of Nuclear Medicine, 7,* 14-15.

Schoeller, D.A. (1988). Measurement of energy expenditure in free-living humans by using doubly labeled water. *Journal of Nutrition, 118,* 1278-1289.

Schoeller, D.A. (1989). Changes in total body water with age. *American Journal of Clinical Nutrition, 50,* 1176-1181.

Schoeller, D.A. (1991). Isotope dilution methods. In P. Bjorntorp & B.N. Brodoff (Eds.), *Obesity* (pp 80-88). New York: Lippincott.

Schoeller, D.A., Kushner, R.F., Taylor, P., et al. (1985). Measurement of total body water: Isotope dilutions techniques In A.F. Roche (Ed.), *Body composition assessments in youth and adults: Sixth Ross conferences on medical research* (pp. 124-129). Columbus, OH: Ross Laboratories.

Schoeller, D.A., Leitch, C.A., & Brown, C. (1986a). Doubly labeled water method: In vivo oxygen and hydrogen isotope fractionation. *American Journal of Physiology, 251,* R1137-R1143.

Schoeller, D.A., Ravussin, E., Schutz, Y., et al. (1986b). Energy expenditure by doubly labeled water: Validation in humans and proposed calculation. *American Journal of Physiology, 250,* R823-R830.

Schoeller, D.A., van Santen, E., Peterson, D.W., et al. (1980). Total body water measurement in humans with ^{18}O and ^{2}H labeled water. *American Journal of Clinical Nutrition, 33,* 2688-2693.

Scholer, J.F., & Code, C.F. (1954). Rate of absorption of water from stomach and small bowel of human beings. *American Journal of Physiology, 27,* 565-577.

Sheng, H-P., & Huggins, R.A. (1979). A review of body composition studies with emphasis on total body water and fat. *American Journal of Clinical Nutrition, 32,* 630-647.

Singh, J., Prentice, A.M., Diaz, E., et al. (1989). Energy expenditure of Gambian women during peak agricultural activity measured by the doubly-labelled water method. *British Journal of Nutrition, 62,* 315-329.

Speakman, J.R., Nair, K.S., & Goran, M.I. (1993). Revised equations for calculating CO_2 production from doubly labeled water in humans. *American Journal of Physiology, 264,* E912-E917.

Spears, C.P., Hyatt, K.H., Vogal, J.M., & Lang, F.H. (1974). Unified method for serial study of body fluid compartments. *Aerospace Medicine, 45,* 274-278.

Thomas, L.D., Van der Velde, D., & Schloerb, P.R. (1991). Optimum doses of deuterium oxide and sodium bromide for the determination of total body water and extracellular fluid. *Journal of Pharmaceutical Biomedical Analysis, 9,* 581-584.

Thompson, W.O., & Yates, B.J. (1941). Venous afferent elicited muscle pumping of a new orthostatic vasopressor mechanism. *Physiologist, 26* (Suppl), S74-S75.

Thornton, W.E., Moore, T.P., & Pool, S.L. (1987). Fluid shifts in weightlessness. *Aviation Space Environmental Medicine, 58,* A86-A90.

Tisavipat, A.S., Vibulsreth, H.P., Sheng, H.P., & Huggins, R.A. (1974). Total body water measured by desiccation and by tritiated water in adult rats. *Journal of Applied Physiology*, **37**, 699-701.

Trapp, S.A., & Bell, E.F. (1989). An improved spectrophotometric bromide assay for the estimation of extracellular water volume. *Clinica Chimica Acta*, **181**, 207-212.

Vaisman, N., Pencharz, P.B., & Koren, G. (1987). Comparison of oral and intravenous administration of sodium bromide for extracellular water measurements. *American Journal of Clinical Nutrition*, **46**, 1-4.

Vaughan, B.E., & Boling, E.A. (1961). Rapid assay procedure for tritium-labeled water in body fluids. *Journal of Laboratory & Clinical Medicine*, **57**, 159-164.

Wallace, G.W.B., & Brodie, B.B. (1939). The distribution of iodide, thiocyanate, bromide and chloride in the central nervous system and spinal fluid. *Journal of Pharmacology & Experimental Therapy*, **65**, 214-219.

Wang, J., Pierson, R.N., Jr., & Kelly, W.G. (1973). A rapid method for the determination of deuterium oxide in urine: Application to the measurement of total body water. *Journal of Laboratory & Clinical Medicine*, **82**, 170-178.

Wang, Z-M., Pierson, R.N., Jr., & Heymsfield, S.B. (1992). The five-level model: A new approach to organizing body-composition research. *American Journal of Clinical Nutrition*, **56**, 19-28.

Weir, E.G., & Hastings, A.B. (1939). The distribution of bromide and chloride in tissues and body fluids. *Journal of Biological Chemistry*, **129**, 547-558.

Wentzel, A.D., Iacono J.M., Allen T.H., & Roberts, J.E. (1958). Determination of heavy water (HDO) in body fluids by direct introduction of water with a mass spectrometer: Measurement of total body water. *Physiological & Medical Biology*, **3**, 1-6.

Whyte, R.K., Bayley, H.S., & Schwarcz, H.P. (1985). The measurement of whole body water by $H_2{}^{18}O$ dilution in newborn pigs. *American Journal of Clinical Nutrition*, **41**, 801-809.

Wong, W.W., Butte, N.F., Smith, E.O., et al. (1989a). Body composition of lactating women determined by anthropometry and deuterium dilution. *British Journal of Nutrition*, **61**, 25-33.

Wong, W.W., Cochran, W.J., Klish, W.J., et al. (1988). In vivo isotope-fractionation factors and the measurement of deuterium- and oxygen-18-dilution spaces from plasma, urine, saliva, respiratory water vapor, and carbon dioxide. *American Journal of Clinical Nutrition*, **47**, 1-6.

Wong, W.W., Legg, H.J.L., Clark, L.L., & Klein, P.D. (1991). Rapid preparation of pyrogen-free $^2H_2{}^{18}O$ for human nutrition studies. *American Journal of Clinical Nutrition*, **53**, 585-586.

Wong, W.W., Sheng, H-P., Morkenberg, J.C., et al. (1989b). Measurement of extracellular water volume by bromide ion chromatography. *American Journal of Clinical Nutrition*, **50**, 1290-1294.

3

Whole-Body Counting and Neutron Activation Analysis

Kenneth J. Ellis

Chemical analyses of tissues and fluids taken from the body, the launching of body composition examinations in humans, can be traced to the mid-19th century. As analytical chemical techniques evolved, biochemists would report new findings for humans. It was soon recognized that a certain degree of chemical normality exists within the body that could be altered with disease, malnutrition, or overfeeding. It is these analyses of the human fetus, and a very limited number of adult cadavers, over the next 100 years that form the fundamental basis of the chemical model of body composition. With the advent of nuclear chemistry in the mid-20th century, direct in vivo (nondestructive, noninvasive) chemical assays of the living human body became possible. The following sections in this chapter will describe several of these techniques.

Whole-Body Counting

The first-generation whole-body counters were mainly built in response to the need of health physics groups to monitor individuals for potential internal contamination by human-made radioactivity.

Health physics groups, which wanted these instruments available in case of a nuclear accident, were usually responsible for their design and operation. Accidents were rare, and interest developed in finding other uses for these costly instruments. As clinical procedures evolved for these counters, which were usually located at nuclear research facilities, it was recognized that compounds labeled with radiotracers would concentrate in selected organs. Nuclear medicine's origins can be traced, in part, to these efforts. In vivo measurements of body radioactivity, including the body's natural potassium, ^{40}K, can be traced to the development of scintillation detectors in the 1950s. A single individual or research group should not be credited with the development of these ideas. Nevertheless, the findings of Kulwich, Feinstein, and Anderson (1958) on the correlation of the natural potassium (^{40}K) concentration with fat-free mass (FFM), followed by those of Anderson and Langham (1959) and Forbes, Hursh, and Gallup (1961), offer some of the earliest investigations of total body potassium in relation to body composition in human beings. Although some universities and research centers also developed whole-body counters for the animal sciences, this chapter will focus only on measurements of human beings. By the 1970s, more than 180 whole-body counters had been built worldwide with about two-thirds of these performing body potassium measurements in human beings (International Atomic Energy Agency, 1970). There are an estimated 75 counters in the United States. In the last decade, two United States Department of Agriculture (USDA) human nutrition research centers, one major clinical/medical physics research center in New York, and one medical school in Texas have built multidetector whole-body counting instruments as part of their body composition laboratories.

Theoretical Basis of Whole-Body Counting

Potassium is naturally distributed in three isotopic states: 93.1% as ^{39}K, 6.9% as ^{41}K, and 0.0118% as ^{40}K. The isotope ^{40}K is radioactive, and for every gram of K there are 1.8×10^{18} radioactive atoms. The fundamental law of nuclear physics that describes the radioactivity decay of any isotope states that the number of disintegrations per unit time (dN/dt) is equal to λN, where N is the number of atoms and λ (the decay constant) is $\ln 2/t_{1/2}$ with $t_{1/2}$ being the physical half-life (1.3×10^9 years). Substitution of these values into the equation gives $dN/dt = 0.95 \times 10^9$ disintegrations per year per gram of K or about 1.8×10^3 disintegrations per minute (dpm). Of these events, 11% of the decays produce γ-rays or about 200 dpm per gram of K. These gammas from ^{40}K are high-energy gammas, many of which exit the body and can be easily detected by external counting. Because of the very long physical half-life of ^{40}K, corrections for physical decay are not necessary, and the rate per unit time per gram of K can be assumed constant.

The average total body potassium (TBK) content of an adult male is about 140 g (Forbes & Lewis, 1956) and contains about 15 mg (0.1 μCi) ^{40}K, which produces about 30,000 γ-rays per minute. An average woman's TBK is only about 100 g K, producing about 20,000 γ-rays per minute. The smaller the subject, the lower the ^{40}K content and thus the weaker the gamma signal; for pre-term infants (1 to 2 kg body weight), there are only about 350 to 700 dpm.

Assumptions and Their Validity

The basic assumptions of in vivo detection of radioactivity in human beings are well documented (International Atomic Energy Agency, 1970). The identification of the 1.46 MeV gamma from ^{40}K has a solid theoretical and experimental physics basis. Radiotracer counting is a recognized analytical chemistry technique based on the physical properties of an element. A further discussion of the conversion between TBK and body composition is included in the section on body composition calculations later in this chapter.

Applicability

Factors such as age, fitness, or restricted mobility due to surgery or illness do not tend to affect the precision of TBK measurements of subjects; minimum cooperation is required. Because the ^{40}K signal is natural and continuous, the measurement can be interrupted as necessary (e.g., to assist the subject) and resumed until the required counting time is completed. Anticlaustrophobic measures include the selection of bright colors for the shielded room and the installation of an intercom system with television, radio, or taped music. Toddlers (age 2 to 4 years) are the most difficult to measure unless they are asleep or have received a sedative, which probably explains why there is an almost complete lack of TBK data for this age group.

Equipment

There are three general equipment requirements when performing ^{40}K measurements in human beings:

1. efficient γ-ray detectors that can be placed close to the subject,
2. shielding for these detectors to reduce the natural background radiation levels (cosmic rays, radioactive contaminants in construction materials), and
3. computer-based instruments that enable identification of the unique γ-rays from ^{40}K (International Atomic Energy Agency, 1970).

The third requirement is especially critical because the human body contains several natural and human-made radioactive isotopes (radium, thorium, and cesium) in extremely small amounts. Their content is variable among subjects; thus failure to correct for their interference would significantly reduce the accuracy of the potassium measurement (Watson, 1987). To discriminate the γ-rays from these isotopes, one uses NaI(Tl) detectors with adequate energy resolution operated with multichannel pulse-height analyzers. The ^{40}K

photopeak detection procedure using plastic and liquid scintillation detectors has poor energy resolution, so interference from natural background isotopes cannot be completely resolved. The counter should not be located near any intense source of radiation such as medical therapy units, cyclotrons, or radiocobalt facilities. Nuclear medicine department personnel and patients who have recently received gamma-emitting radioisotopes should be carefully screened to reduce the risk of contamination of the counter.

A minimum whole-body counter design is the so-called "shadow-shield" counter (Figure 3.1). The subject is in a supine position on the bed, which is slowly moved beneath the Pb-shielded NaI(Tl) detector. The shielding is placed directly around the detector and along the sides of the bed and thus has the advantage of being much lighter in weight than a completely shielded room. There are, however, major disadvantages, including longer counting times with usually poorer precision and difficulty calibrating for differences in body size. Several designs are illustrated in the International Atomic Energy Agency's *Directory of Whole-Body Radioactivity Monitors* (International Atomic Energy Agency, 1970).

When the detector shielding is built into the room, it usually consists of an outer thick layer of concrete (0.5 to 1 m) and inner walls of steel (10 to 20 cm) finished with an inner liner (0.5 to 1 cm) of lead, aluminum, copper, and stainless steel. The construction materials for the shielding and fabrication of the detectors are optimally free of radioactive contaminants (International Atomic Energy Agency, 1970); the preferred material is pre-World War II steel. The room size is determined by the range of body sizes to be measured, the counting geometry (sitting, lying, or standing position), and the size and number of detectors. The door for the shielded room must be constructed of steel and kept closed during the counting procedure to reduce background levels. Adequate ventilation, lighting, and some form of voice communication with the subject are important factors. The detector

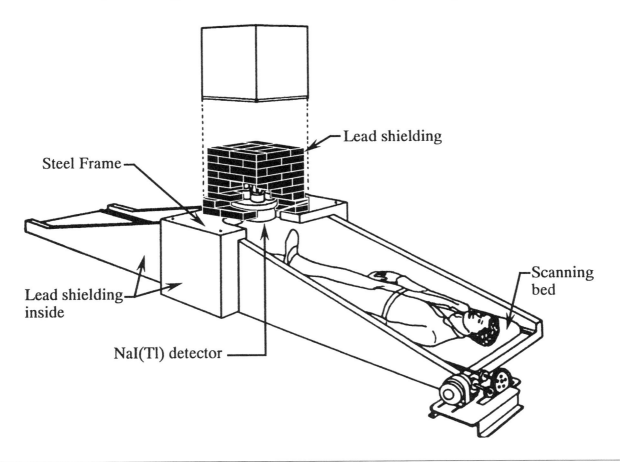

Figure 3.1 Basic design for a shadow-shield body counter. The subject is moved under the Pb-shielded NaI(Tl) detector on a motorized bed. Additional Pb-Fe shielding is placed along the sides of the bed to reduce the environmental background radiation.

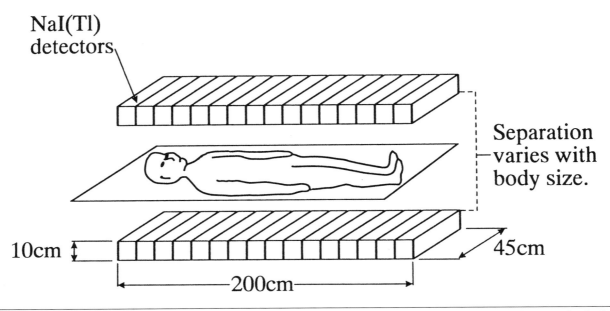

NaI(Tl) detectors

Separation varies with body size.

10cm

45cm

200cm

Figure 3.2 Basic design for a multidetector whole-body counter. The subject lies in a supine position on the bed with two fixed arrays of NaI(Tl) detectors above and below the bed. The counter is housed in a Fe-Pb shielded room.

arrangement for the Baylor College of Medicine whole-body counter (shown in Figure 3.2) is illustrative of the latest design (Ellis & Shypailo, 1993). The spacing between the upper and lower array is adjusted for body size while the number of detectors used in the count is determined by body length.

Measurement Procedures and Extraneous Variables

It is best to have subjects change from their street clothes since this clothing may contain dust particles with significant background contamination. Cotton pajamas or paper outfits are suitable. The subject should also remove jewelry (may have some trace radioactivity in the metal) before counting. There is no need to have the subject fast before the measurement, since most foods contain about the same potassium concentration as the whole body.

The ^{40}K technique is a noninvasive in vivo body composition procedure, which also can be considered nontraumatic with severe claustrophobia the one possible exception. Since the measurement procedure requires minimum cooperation from the subject, repeat assays can be performed to enhance the precision. The counting time varies with the design of the counter and size of the subject. For fixed-array counters, the counting times are typically less than 15 minutes. For shadow-shield

counters the time is about 40 minutes. The instrument's operation is automated so the counts within the energy region of the ^{40}K photopeak are integrated, corrected for background (previously recorded with the room empty), and converted to grams of K using the appropriate calibration factor (adjustments for body self-attenuation and size) within the time the subject has changed back to regular clothes.

Some centers have found it helpful, and occasionally necessary, to have the subject rest for several hours before the whole-body count. Lykken, Lukaski, Bolunchuk, and Sandstead (1983) reported the possibility of extraneous errors for the TBK measurement due to increased ^{214}Bi interference from the decay of inhaled radon following long-distance running or vigorous indoor exercise, but other centers have not observed changes in the potassium measurement under similar conditions (S.H. Cohn, 1973; K.J. Ellis, 1983, 1994; G.B. Forbes, 1990; R. Pierson, Jr., 1978; personal communications). Unexpected events, as illustrated dramatically by the Chernobyl accident, can release significant radioactivity into the environment producing transient background interference for the TBK measurement (Watson, 1987).

Calibration and Interlaboratory Comparisons of Whole-Body Counters

The net counts recorded in the ^{40}K energy region must be converted to grams of body K by the use of calibration factors. Models have been developed for checking the calibration of whole-body counters (Bewley, 1988), but the calibration factors are usually obtained by one of the following methods.

One approach is to monitor the gamma spectra for a series of normal subjects after they have received a known amount of ^{42}K, which has a gamma-ray energy very close to that of ^{40}K. The subjects are counted several times over 24 hours to allow for distribution of the radiotracer; urine is collected and counted to correct for loss from the body. The ratio of the detected counts to the administered activity provides a measure of the counter's detection efficiency for differences in body size. The alternate approach is to count a series of anthropomorphic-shaped phantoms constructed of ground meat that has been chemically assayed for its K content. In both approaches, a weight versus stature matrix of calibration factors (CF$_i$) for body size is established.

A third option, developed by Cohn, Dombrowski, Pate, and Robertson (1969) for use with fixed-array whole-body counters, is to determine the counts from a planar source positioned below the bed with and without the subject on the bed. The body's counting geometry and self-attenuation factors are based on the relative counts with and without the subject on the bed. In this case, the calibration factor is customized for the subject's body geometry. Although this approach has been found acceptable for subjects within a normal weight range, widely differing body sizes, as in severe obesity or wasting, have not been tested.

The only reported comparison of whole-body counters, recently performed in the United Kingdom, used a multinuclide anthropomorphic phantom (Fenwick, McKenzie, & Boddy, 1991). For the ten instruments compared, the results showed close agreement between the median estimate and the known activities in the phantom. Unfortunately, organized comparisons have not been achieved in the U.S.; several individuals (G.B. Forbes, personal communication, 1992) including the author have had TBK measurements at various counters.

Calculation of Body Potassium

The calculation of TBK from the ^{40}K count is straightforward. That is

$$TBK(g) = CF_i \times {}^{40}K \text{ counts} \qquad (3.1)$$

where the calibration factor (CF$_i$) is obtained as outlined in the previous section. For example, if

one uses a set of bottles to simulate body size (phantom) and administers a trace dose of ^{42}K to the subject, then the calibration factor becomes

$$CF_i = \left(\frac{g\ K_{bottles}}{{}^{40}K_{bottles}} \right) \times \left(\frac{{}^{42}K\ count_{bottles}}{{}^{42}K\ count_{subject}} \right). \qquad (3.2)$$

An alternate approach is to use the correction developed by Cohn et al. (1969) based on counting the subject with and without a broad-beam source below the bed of the counter, but Cohn's technique applies only to planar detector arrays and to a normal range of body sizes. For the extremely obese or wasted subject, the additional use of the intravenous infusion of a ^{42}K tracer can provide a more customized calibration. For this technique, it can be shown that the corrected total counts (C$_T$) for a subject using an array of 2n detectors is

$$C_T = 2 \sum_{i=1}^{n} A\ G\ (C_{iu}C_{il})^{0.5} \qquad (3.3)$$

where i denotes detector pairs in the upper (u) and lower (l) arrays, A is an absorption factor, and G is a geometry correction factor, each derived for the individual subject (Cohn et al., 1969). The corrected total counts obtained for the phantom are used to determine a single conversion value of corrected ^{40}K count per gram of K (CCF$_{phantom}$). Thus, body potassium in the subject becomes

$$TBK(g) = CCF_{phantom} \times C_{T,\ subject}. \qquad (3.4)$$

The third technique is to establish a calibration table, CF$_{w-s}$, for a range of body weights (W) and statures (S) using phantoms made of ground meat in which the K content has been measured by atomic absorption. For body sizes other than those used to construct the calibration table, extrapolation between adjacent elements in the table can be used. The value for body potassium becomes

$$TBK(g) = (CF_{w-s})_i \times {}^{40}K \text{ counts.} \qquad (3.5)$$

It should be obvious that the precision of the TBK value is governed by the ^{40}K counts, and accuracy is determined by the calibration technique.

Calculation of Body Composition Variables, Equations, and Constant

Francis Moore and his associates (1963) defined body cell mass (BCM) as "the working, energy-metabolizing portion of the human body in relation to its supporting structures." It consists of the cellular components of muscle, viscera, blood, and brain. For adults, they assumed an average K/N ratio of 3 mEq/g, and a 4% nitrogen content per gram of wet weight for the lean tissues. The resulting equation is:

$$BCM(kg) = 0.00833 \times K(mEq) . \qquad (3.6)$$

Infants have a higher water content in the lean tissues; thus Burmeister (1965) chose a lower K concentration for the body cell mass, the value being 92.5 mEq per kg.

The most used conversion factor to derive an estimate for the FFM has been that based on the pioneering work of Forbes and Lewis (1956). From cadaver data for only four adult males and one adult female, they derived a conversion factor of 68.1 mEq K/kg FFM. The reference models of growth and body composition later developed at the University of Iowa (Fomon, Haschke, Ziegler, & Nelson, 1982; Haschke, 1989; Ziegler, O'Donnell, Nelson, & Fomon, 1976) for fetuses, infants, and children have also provided tabulated estimates of the TBK/FFM conversion for each of these age groups.

Unfortunately, over the years, custom has enshrined some of these early estimates for the conversion factors between TBK and the body composition parameters of BCM and FFM. Many investigators have consistently indicated lower potassium concentrations for FFM: 54 to 59 mEq/kg for females, 59 to 62 mEq/kg for males (Cordain et al., 1989; Ellis, unpublished data). A summary of the TBK/FFM conversion factors for adults is provided in Table 3.1. Although the variations between investigators are small, they can become significant if one estimates the mass of body fat as the difference between body weight and FFM derived from the TBK measurement.

Clinically, BCM continues to be a useful concept (Pierson & Wang, 1988) as it represents those lean tissues most likely to be affected over relatively short intervals of time (days or weeks) by disease, nutrition, activity level, or treatment. Nevertheless, since BCM is simply TBK multiplied by a factor, changes in TBK or comparisons of TBK between individuals provide a direct measure of changes or differences in the BCM. Furthermore, as BCM is only about 50 to 60% of FFM, substantial changes can occur in FFM, which includes the extracellular fluid compartment, that are relatively independent of TBK. In fact, FFM and TBK can be uncoupled for short periods of time, one possibly decreasing while the other increases, or vice versa. TBK, therefore, best reflects the total FFM when the subject is in a steady-state (i.e., normal, healthy) condition.

Precision

The primary technical error for the whole-body counting procedure, governed by the random nature of radioactive decay, is described by Poisson statistics. In this special case, the error (SD) for a total count of N events is $N^{0.5}$. If the subject's gross count rate is separated into the subject's net count rate (N_i) and the empty room background (B_r) count, then the precision or percent counting error is calculated as follows:

$$\text{Precision (\%)} = \left(\left[\frac{N_i}{t_i} + \frac{B_r}{t_i} + \frac{B_r}{t_b} \right]^{0.5} \right) \times \left(\frac{100}{N_i} \right)$$
$$(3.7)$$

where t_i and t_b are the counting times for the subject and background, respectively. Increasing the counting times or the subject's net count rate, or decreasing the background rate, will improve the system's precision.

In general, the performance characteristics of most whole-body counters require 10 to 15 minute counting times, with precision in the range of 2 to 5% for adults (Cohn & Parr, 1985). This includes errors due to repositioning of the subject in the counter, which have been shown to be about 0.5 to 1.0%. Detailed descriptions and operating characteristics of many of the world's older whole-body counters can be found in the *Directory of Whole-Body Radioactivity Monitors* (International Atomic Energy Agency, 1970). The general performance of a modern system is represented by that of the Baylor College of Medicine whole-body counter (Ellis & Shypailo, 1992b, 1993), designed for body sizes starting with the pre-term infant and extending to the obese adult (Table 3.2).

Body potassium content is so small in infants and very young children that accurate measurements have been difficult until recently. Forbes (1968), for example, using a 4π plastic scintillator design, achieved precisions of only 8 to 12% for 15 to 40 minute count times with full-term newborn infants. The imprecisions of the TBK assays in infants reported by Rutledge et al. (1976) produced a range of TBK values that exceeded those of body weight. Improved NaI(T1) detector technology has helped to overcome these limitations.

Accuracy

While the precision of TBK measurement is well established, its accuracy is less firmly grounded. The

Table 3.1 Estimates of the Average Total Body Potassium (TBK) Content of the Fat-Free Mass (FFM) in Adult Human Beings

Race	Age	TBK/FFM (mEq/kg) Female	Male	Reference
White	25-70	68.1	68.1	Forbes & Lewis, 1956
	21-50*	57.8	67.8	Pierson et al., 1974
	20-79	57.9	64.5	Cohn et al., 1980
	> 20	60	65	Garrow & Webster, 1985
	24-56	62	—	Sjöström et al., 1986
	24-56	—	64.7	Kvist et al., 1988
	20-37	64	66	Hassager et al., 1989
	20-90*	66	66	Wang et al., 1992
	24-78*	56.6	—	Ortiz et al., 1992
	26-93*	52.0	60.0	Heymsfield et al., 1993
	18-37	—	63.7	Penn et al., 1994
	20-50	—	63.9	Gerace et al., 1994
Black	24-79	63.1	—	Ortiz et al., 1992
	20-60	—	62.3	Gerace et al., 1994

*TBK/FFM decreases with age.

Table 3.2 Performance Characteristics of the Whole-Body Counter at the USDA/ARS Children's Nutrition Research Center, Baylor College of Medicine

Age group	Detectors	Weight (kg)	Stature (cm)	CPS/gK*	Precision (%)	Time (min)
Very low birth weight 30 to 36 weeks[†]	3	0.5-3.0	25-50	0.41	3.3	30
Pre-term 36 to 44 weeks[†]	6	1.5-5.5	25-60	0.50	2.0	30
Infant < 9 months	12-16	2.5-10	45-70	0.41	2.5	15
Toddler < 3 years	16-20	5-15	60-100	0.35	2.1	15
Child 4 to 12 years	20-28	15-70	100-180	0.33	1.7	15
Adult > 13 years	30	40-130	150-200	0.25	0.8	15

*Counts per second per gram of K, a measure of counting sensitivity. [†]Gestational age.

ideal verification would be to compare the TBK values with results obtained for total body human cadavers analyzed chemically. The latter task would be difficult to complete and is not without its own substantial statistical inaccuracies. Unfortunately, the human cadavers analyzed by Forbes and Lewis (1956) for K content were not also counted in a whole-body counter. An alternate approach has been to administer the same amount of potassium radiotracer (^{42}K) to subjects with a wide range of body sizes, then show that the calibration corrections adjust for body size and self-attenuation of the gammas so the calculated activity equals the administered dose. When this technique was used in adults, the agreement was reported to be better than 4% (Cohn et al., 1969). For our infant counter, we obtained an average agreement of 6% between the absolute mass of TBK (via ^{40}K counting) and total carcass K analysis for 74 piglets in the weight range 1 to 40 kg (Ellis, unpublished data).

Once an accurate TBK value has been obtained, one is still left with decisions about conversions from the body's elemental content into a more physiological concept of body composition (see chapter 7). The conversion factors for TBK/FFM have been presented in Table 3.1. Pierson and Wang (1988) recently reviewed various measures of the lean tissue or fat-free mass, and reaffirmed the earlier conclusions of Moore and his co-workers (1963) that TBK provided the best index for the body's metabolically active tissues. TBK does not appear to provide the best measure of the total FFM, especially in very obese or extremely malnourished subjects where there can be significant alterations of the intracellular and extracellular fluid compartments.

Recommended Standard Procedure and Cost Aspects

Since the design for whole-body counters is not standardized, it is difficult to recommend a standard measurement procedure. There are, however, two basic designs, the fixed-array counter and the shadow-shield counter, for which the counting procedures are similar. In all ^{40}K measurements, it is recommended that the subject change into clothing already determined to be free of radioactivity. The subject should remove all jewelry when possible and not wear eye glasses during the count, which should be completed within a reasonable time, usually no longer than 30 minutes. In addition, the standard procedures should include provisions for testing the instrument's performance on a daily basis to ensure quality control for precision and accuracy. This can best be accomplished using phantoms with known concentrations of potassium.

The cost of a whole-body counter depends, in part, on the age range of the populations to be examined. For example, if only infants are to be examined, then fewer components [NaI(T1) detectors with compact shielding, electronics, PC-sized computer] are needed to construct the instrument. In general, the needed components include:

NaI(T1) detector plus its electronics ($6,800 each), interfaced ($1,500 per 8 detectors) with a PC-based computer ($1,500 to $4,000) containing a pulse-height analog-digital converter (ADC) board ($1,200). A compact infant counter using Pb and/or Fe shielding can be built for $5,000 to $10,000. The larger shadow-shield counter design has the additional expense of the scanning bed and motor, which would add about $10,000 to $15,000 to the cost. Each of these components, as well as several phantom models for calibration, are commercially available. The cost increases substantially when a shielded-room design is considered. These costs usually start at about $80,000 for a complete facility and increase with the amount of shielding, number of detectors, and the complexity of the computer-based analyzer system. As a rule of thumb, one can use the following cost estimates: $5,500 per NaI(T1) detector, $800 in electronics per detector, $2,000 to $4,000 per interface for up to 32 detectors, $10,000 for the computer-based analyzer unit with printer and mass storage components, and $10,000 per m^3 volume for a low-background shielded room. Several suppliers are listed in the Appendix who can provide individual components or completely integrated "turn-key" systems.

Neutron Activation Analysis

The basis for the chemical model of adult human body composition can be traced, in part, to the pioneering efforts of Forbes and Lewis (1956), who undertook the arduous task of total body carcass analyses of adult human cadavers using classical wet chemistry techniques. This fundamental approach to the study of human body composition continues today but is now replaced by the nondestructive direct elemental analyses offered by in vivo neutron activation analysis (IVNAA). Other nuclear-based techniques (radiography, magnetic resonance imaging, x-ray absorptiometry, and radiotracer or stable-tracer dilution) devised for the study of body composition provide information on tissue density or volume but not chemical content.

The first demonstration that neutron activation could be used for the in vivo measurement of body composition in human beings was reported 30 years ago at the University of Birmingham, England (Anderson et al., 1964). These researchers used a cyclotron to produce the neutrons and monitored activity induced in the body with a whole-body counter. Although the radiation exposures for these initial studies were relatively high, they are, nevertheless, comparable with many diagnostic radiographic techniques routinely used today. Since then, various research centers have built their own instruments focusing on clinical applications. Two International Atomic Energy Agency (IAEA) workshops (Cohn & Parr, 1985; Parr, 1973) extensively reviewed the technical aspects of IVNAA. Three international conferences within the last seven years focused on in vivo body composition studies, including presentations on state-of-the-art IVNAA facilities and their applications in human biology, physiology, and medicine (Ellis & Eastman, 1993; Ellis, Yasumura, & Morgan, 1987; Yasumura et al., 1990).

All atoms in the body have some probability of undergoing a nuclear reaction when exposed to neutrons. Our current measurement techniques, however, limit their in vivo detection (defined by acceptable accuracy and precision) for useful biological or clinical applications. Only IVNAA provides nondestructive analytical reporting of the total body content of the major body elements: calcium, sodium, chlorine, phosphorus, nitrogen, hydrogen, oxygen, and carbon. In addition, specialized partial-body IVNAA techniques have been developed for specific elements or organs in the body. These include in vivo measurements of cadmium, mercury, iron, iodine, aluminum, boron, lithium, and silicon in the kidneys, liver, brain, lungs, heart, and thyroid (Chettle & Fremlin, 1984; Cohn & Parr, 1985).

Delayed-Gamma Activation Analysis

When an atom captures a neutron, the atom is transformed to another nuclear state of the same chemical element. This new atom can be radioactive and decay with a known half-life. The following equation shows the general terms that relate the physical constants and experimental parameters that describe the activation and counting procedures for any facility to the induced activity for an element of mass M:

$$\text{Activity} = k \times M \times \varepsilon_1 \times \varepsilon_2 \times \phi$$
$$\times \text{Exp} \times \text{Delay} \times \text{Counting}. \quad (3.8)$$

The term k, defined as

$$k = \frac{(S \times N \times f_1 \times f_2)}{(A \times \lambda)} \quad (3.9)$$

combines the constants of nature for a particular element where S is the reaction cross-section, N is Avogadro's number, A is the atomic number, f_1 is

the isotopic abundance, f_2 is the gamma decay ratio, and λ is $\ln(2)/T_{1/2}$, the half-life of the induced activity.

The physical design of the neutron irradiator, the number of sources, and their type and position relative to the body will determine the value for the neutron fluence (ϕ). The type of detectors, their number, volume, and position relative to the body will define the values for the detection efficiency parameters: ε_1 is the energy efficiency (detector type and volume) and ε_2 is the geometry efficiency (number and position of detectors).

To correct for decay, the activation time (T_{act}), delay time (T_{delay}) between the end of activation and the start of counting, and the total counting time (T_{count}) are used in each of the exponential terms as follows:

Exposure term: $\text{Exp} = 1 - \exp[-\lambda \times T_{act}]$

Transfer term: $\text{Delay} = \exp[\lambda \times T_{delay}]^{-1}$

Counter term: $\text{Counting} = 1 - \exp[-\lambda \times T_{count}]$
$$(3.10)$$

The IVNAA techniques have been used mostly for independent research protocols for 30 years, but there is still minimum design standardization among centers (Chettle & Fremlin, 1984; Cohn & Parr, 1985). The designs often were influenced by availability of neutron sources and gamma counting systems. Thus, it has been necessary for each laboratory to establish its own empirical calibrations, generally using human-shaped phantoms filled with tissue-equivalent fluids. If the shape and size of the phantom parts are reasonable anthropomorphic approximations of the human body, and the elemental composition and spatial distributions within each phantom part are similar to those in the human body, then a comparative calibration technique can be used. That is, one can activate and count a phantom containing known amounts (M_i) of the target elements for a known exposure time (T_{act}), delay time (T_{delay}), and counting time (T_{count}). The net counts in the photopeak ($C_{i,net}$) generated under these conditions for a given element of mass, M, produce a phantom calibration factor (CF_i):

$$CF_i = Q_{phantom} \times (\text{Mass}/C_{i,net}) \quad (3.11)$$

where the k, ε_1, ε_2, ϕ, Exp, Delay, and Counting terms are constants and combined into the single value, $Q_{phantom}$. As long as the phantom used for calibration is a good model of the range of subject sizes to be measured, one can obtain an accurate or "absolute" calibration. Once the initial calibration factors (CF_i) have been established for each element, the counts in the subject's spectra can be compared with the same elemental reference phantom library values as follows:

$$M_{i,\ subject} = CF_i \times (Net\ counts)_{i,\ subject}. \quad (3.12)$$

Although this calibration procedure is common to all neutron activation techniques, interchangeability of CF_i values between laboratories has not been practicable since each set of calibration factors varies with that center's instrument design. From a scientific perspective, direct chemical verification using human cadavers would be highly desirable. Most investigators recognize the analytical difficulties associated with this arduous task, not to mention its ethical uncertainties. Limited verifications using animal models have been reported (Ellis et al., 1992c).

Prompt-Gamma Activation Analysis

When a neutron is captured by a nucleus, the resulting nucleus can be stable or radioactive, but it is usually in an excited nuclear state due to the added energy provided by the neutron. The excited nucleus will last for only a fraction of a nanosecond and promptly returns to its lowest nuclear state, often with the emission of gamma-rays. Therefore, the major technical difference between the delayed-gamma technique described earlier and this application is that the induced gamma signal of interest must be measured at the same time as the neutron exposure. The basic equation that describes the prompt-gamma activation analysis (PGAA) technique is less complex, as the delay and counting terms are eliminated, and the total activity becomes directly proportional to the activation time (T_{act}). The basic PGAA equation is:

$$Counts = k \times \phi \times T_{act} \quad (3.13)$$

where the physical constants are grouped into the value of k as defined for the delayed-gamma procedure and ε_1 and ε_2 are determined by the detector type, volume, and geometry. Thus, for a given facility, the induced gamma signal is directly proportional to the intensity of the neutron flux and the total exposure time.

The first successful demonstration of the in vivo PGAA technique involved measurement of body hydrogen (Rundo & Bunce, 1966). At present, its major application is to measure body nitrogen, a chemical marker of body protein (Beddoe, Zuidmeer, & Hill, 1984; Biggin et al., 1972; Ellis, 1992c).

In about 15% of the $^{14}N(n, \gamma)^{15}N$ reactions in the body, the ^{15}N de-excitation produces a single gamma at 10.83 MeV. Since there is no environmental background signal at this energy level, it serves as a unique marker for nitrogen.

Vartsky and co-workers (1984) proposed that, for total body nitrogen (TBN) measurements, the hydrogen signal at 2.2 MeV also present in the PGAA could be used as an "internal normalization" for differences in body size. This approach overcomes the need for precise uniformity of the thermal neutron flux within the body. In this case, the determination of total body nitrogen (TBN) is based on the ratio of the nitrogen to hydrogen counts, an estimation of total body hydrogen (TBH), and a calibration factor (CF_i) derived using a phantom with known amounts of nitrogen and hydrogen. That is,

$$TBN = CF_i \times (N_{net}/H_{net})_{Counts} \times TBH. \quad (3.14)$$

A recent account of the theoretical basis and upgraded Brookhaven facility (Stamatelatos, Chettle, Green, & Scott, 1992; Stamatelatos et al., 1993) provides a detailed description of the type of calibration procedures required. Estimates of TBH can be based on a fixed percent of body weight or a more accurate model using the three major body compartments which contain: hydrogen, water, protein, and fat (Ellis, 1992; Sutcliffe, Smith, Barker, & Smith, 1993a).

The PGAA technique has gained acceptance for the measurement of body protein, assuming protein = 6.25 × nitrogen. Clinical facilities have been developed in a number of medical centers (Baur et al., 1991; Beddoe et al., 1984; Ellis et al., 1992c; Mackie, Cowen, & Hannan, 1990; Ryde et al., 1987; Stamatelatos et al., 1993; Vartsky et al., 1984). The accuracy and precision for the measurement of body nitrogen are reported to range from 2 to 6% using scanning times of 15 to 30 minutes at total body doses of about 0.3 mSv. An illustration of the Baylor College of Medicine facility is provided in Figure 3.3 to show the basic design components for a PGAA instrument.

Pulsed Activation Analysis

The pulsed activation technique (neutron inelastic scattering) needs further evaluation to determine its full potential for in vivo body composition studies. This system is still in the developmental stage. Only one center has investigated the technique for in vivo measurements of body carbon and oxygen in human beings (Kehayias, Ellis, Cohn, & Wein-

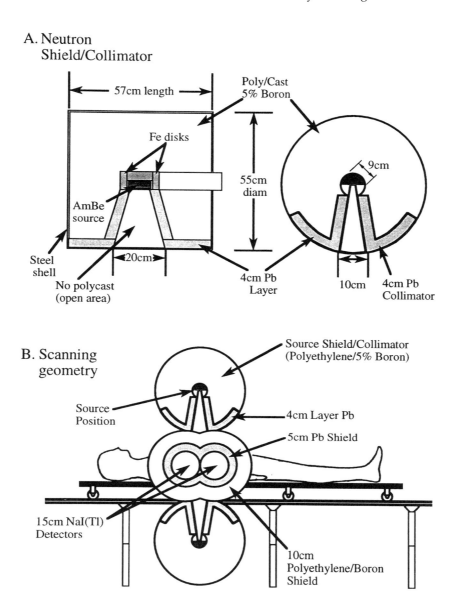

A. Neutron Shield/Collimator

57cm length

Poly/Cast 5% Boron

Fe disks

55cm diam

AmBe source

Steel shell

No polycast (open area)

20cm

4cm Pb Layer

9cm

10cm   4cm Pb Collimator

B. Scanning geometry

Source Shield/Collimator (Polyethylene/5% Boron)

Source Position

4cm Layer Pb

5cm Pb Shield

15cm NaI(Tl) Detectors

10cm Polyethylene/Boron Shield

Figure 3.3 Basic design for a prompt-gamma activation analysis facility. Panel A shows the boron-doped polyethylene shielding with the Pb collimator opening. Panel B shows the scanning geometry, in which the subject passes between the two collimated/shielded sources, while four NaI(Tl) detectors, with their shielding, are at the sides of the bed.

lein, 1987; Kehayias et al., 1991; Kyere et al., 1982). These analyses require high-energy neutrons that can only be produced by a (D,T) generator, which must be operated in a pulsed mode (4 to 10 kHz). Since the primary gamma signals are 4.44 MeV for carbon and 6.13 MeV for oxygen, large-volume detectors are required as for the PGAA technique. The basic neutron source-bed-detector configuration of the instrument is similar to that used for PGAA, but all the shielding components must be constructed of different (carbon-free) materials. In addition, the pulsed neutron source requires one

to use nuclear electronics that operate at high count rates during the neutron burst. Thus, the PGAA instrument is not suited for easy adaptation to the pulsed activation technique. Furthermore, Kehayias and Zhuang (1993) recently demonstrated that bismuth germanate (BGO) detectors offer a significant improvement over NaI(Tl) detectors for this application. Kehayias' instrument design remains the standard for this technique.

The potential body composition application is the measurement of body carbon as an accurate index of body fat. Longitudinal studies in progress are examining the relationship between in vivo changes in total body carbon and changes in body fat. The total body's carbon/oxygen ratio also has the potential to serve as a monitor for total energy expenditure in the individual (Kehayias & Zhuang, 1993).

Assumptions and Their Validity

The basic assumptions for the IVNAA procedures are solidly based on the chemical model of body composition (see chapter 7). It is estimated, for example, that more than 98% of total body calcium is in bone, that total body protein is 6.25 times total body nitrogen, and that no less than 95% of body carbon is in body fat (International Commission on Radiological Protection, 1984). Sutcliffe et al. (1993a, 1993b) reported theoretical analyses of the ways in which IVNAA data can be used to determine the total body content of water, protein, and fat. These investigators also derived simple equations, based on IVNAA elemental data, for the estimation of energy expenditure, fat stores, and body density.

Several limitations have impaired a broader use or acceptance of IVNAA measurements. In general, only the separate components required of each instrument are commercially available, so that no "turn-key" instruments for body composition analyses can be purchased "off the shelf." The assistance of an experienced highly trained investigator (usually a medical physicist) is commonly necessary to establish a new facility.

Another limitation to general unrestricted use of IVNAA is that any radiation exposure (including natural background levels of 1.0 to 1.7 mSv/yr) can be assigned some level of risk. For example, the delayed-gamma activation technique uses a dose of about 3.0 mSv. This dose is less than or comparable to that required for many routine diagnostic radiographic or nuclear medicine procedures, thus restricting its use in the general population. The prompt-gamma activation and pulsed activation techniques, however, use much lower doses, in the range of 0.1 to 0.3 mSv. This dose is within the variation of the natural background levels in the U.S. and is only about one-tenth that used for the delayed-gamma neutron activation procedures. Therefore, as with all procedures that involve radiation, it is essential to weigh the benefits of such measurements against the risks. To obtain a realistic perspective, some life experiences with risks comparable to that for the nitrogen measurement (prompt-gamma activation) are listed in Table 3.3. It is fundamental that

Table 3.3   Life Experiences With Comparable Risk (Probability of Death Estimated at 1 in 8 to 10 Million) to That for In Vivo Nitrogen Measurement by Prompt-Gamma Activation

Activity	Type of death
Travel options	
Air (150 miles)	Accident
Air (trans-Atlantic round trip)	Cancer (cosmic rays)
Car (15 miles)	Accident
Living conditions/location	
5,000 ft above sea level (3 months)	Cancer (cosmic rays)
Living in stone building (2 weeks)	Cancer (radon)
Employment conditions	
Working in average U.S. factory (3 days)	Accident
Working in U.S. coal mine (30 minutes)	Accident
Smoking (1 cigarette)	Cancer

we continue efforts to reduce the doses for all IVNAA procedures as much as reasonably possible without loss of precision or accuracy.

Equipment

There are three major components of a neutron activation system (Ellis, 1991). These are (1) the neutron sources for irradiator, (2) the gamma-detection system, and (3) the computer-based analyzer needed for data acquisition and spectra analysis. The design of each component is not totally independent of the other as irradiation and counting geometries will influence the overall accuracy and precision of the instrument.

Neutron Sources and Geometry. Neutron sources for delayed-gamma activation analysis (DGAA) or PGAA instruments are not standardized. The selection of a neutron source is based, in part, on the elements to be measured, the acceptable level of accuracy, and the allowable radiation dose (Ellis, 1991). The four types of neutron sources in use are ^{238}PuBe, ^{241}AmBe, ^{252}Cf, and the pulsed (D,T) generator. The number of sources varies with the institution; for example, Baylor College of Medicine uses 56 ^{241}AmBe sources, Brookhaven National Laboratory uses 14 ^{238}PuBe, while the

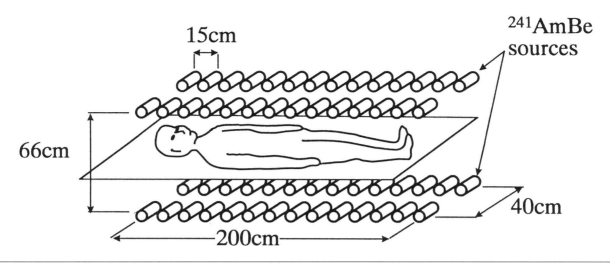

Figure 3.4   Basic design for a multisource irradiator for delayed-gamma activation analysis. The 56 sources are arranged in two 2 × 14 arrays above and below the subject bed. The vertical separation and horizontal spacing are fixed. The spacing of the two sources in each row can be adjusted to match the subject's body width.

University of Texas Medical Branch-Galveston plans to use 240 ^{241}AmBe. The Baylor facility (Ellis & Shypailo, 1992a) uses a biplanar geometry with sources positioned above and below the subject, who lies in a supine position on the bed for a 2 minute irradiation (Figure 3.4).

For PGAA, all four types of sources are in use. However, ^{252}Cf offers the important advantage of a lower dose for the same sensitivity (Stamatelatos et al., 1992). Most facilities use two sources in a bilateral scanning geometry in which the subject is moved past the collimated beam. A typical source-bed-detector geometry is shown in Figure 3.4.

Detection Systems.   For DGAA, the induced gamma spectrum of interest is between 1.0 MeV and 3.3 MeV; thus large-volume NaI(T1) detectors are needed. The detector systems routinely used for in vivo counting of ^{40}K are ideally suited for this IVNAA procedure. One does not need a low-background room, as required for the ^{40}K measurement, because the induced photopeaks in the spectrum from body calcium, sodium, and chlorine are well above the energy range of the natural environmental background. The last four whole-body counting facilities built for IVNAA in the U.S. have used 32 NaI(T1) detectors to provide a quasi-2 π counting geometry. The Baylor College of Medicine whole-body counter design has been described in this chapter.

Large-volume NaI(T1) detectors are also used for the PGAA technique. One major technical concern is their "pile-up" characteristics, produced when multiple neutron events occur within the detectors themselves. This increases the background under the nitrogen signal and reduces precision. Monte Carlo simulations have indicated that a larger number of smaller NaI(T1) detectors or BGO detectors may be more suited to this application (Chung, Wei, & Chen, 1993; Stamatelatos et al., 1992). For the pulsed activation technique, BGO detectors appear to be the best choice (Kehayias & Zhuang, 1993).

Computer/Analyzer Systems.   Complete "turnkey" instruments are available from several commercial suppliers, but all IVNAA instruments have been custom designed and assembled by the different research groups that use these techniques. The DGAA, PGAA, and pulsed activation facilities can be operated as independent, stand-alone instruments, or they can share a common multichannel analyzer system for data acquisition and analysis. These analyzers are desktop-size PC-based computers already loaded with commercial software for nuclear data acquisition, analysis, and storage. Some custom software, however, is required to match the unique design and calibration of each instrument. Standardization could be achieved and, for the most part, is in place for the PGAA instruments.

Measurement Procedures

Once the DGAA, PGAA, or pulsed activation facilities are constructed and calibrated, the measurement procedures are rather simple to perform. In each case, the subject lies in a supine position on a bed that is mechanically moved into the neutron beam area for a pre-set time. The DGAA procedure has an activation time of 2 to 5 minutes, then a delay of 1 to 3 minutes to transfer the subject to the whole-body counter, and a counting time of 15 minutes. With the PGAA technique, the subject also lies supine on a computer-controlled bed that moves across the collimated neutron beam area. As the body is scanned, the spectra are collected separately for 3 to 5 body sections. The measurement times are 100 to 300 seconds per section for a total time of 15 to 30 minutes. For the PGAA calculations, the thickness and width of each body section are measured to ± 0.5 cm and used to match that section with the appropriate size section of the calibration phantom. The results from all the sections are summed to give the total body estimates. The measurement procedures for the pulsed activation technique are the same as for the PGAA procedure.

Precision

Each technique's precision is defined by the basic equations presented earlier in this chapter. It is clear that precision is highly dependent on exposure time and detection efficiency. Repeated DGAA or PGAA measurements in the same person over a short time period have not been performed due to the cumulative dose required. As a result, each system's precision (reproducibility) has been based on multiple measurements of phantoms. For the DGAA technique, the reported precisions are ± 1% for calcium and ± 2 to 3% for body sodium and chlorine (Cohn & Dombrowski, 1971; Cohn & Parr, 1985). For the PGAA technique, the precision for body nitrogen is reported as ± 2.5 to 5.0%, while that for body carbon by this technique is ± 5 to 7% (Baur et al., 1991; Beddoe et al., 1984; Ellis et al., 1992c; Mackie et al., 1990; Stamatelatos et al., 1993; Vartsky et al., 1984). Body carbon by the pulsed activation technique has a reported precision of ± 3 to 5% at a dose of 0.1 mSv (Kehayias et al., 1991).

Accuracy

Each of these techniques provides a measure of the elemental content of the body. Thus, "true" accuracy can only be assessed against another analytical procedure that also measures chemical content. To date, the IVNAA results of two human cadavers have been compared directly with classical chemical analysis of the whole body (Knight, Beddoe, Streat, & Hill, 1986). For body nitrogen,

there was agreement within 4 to 40 g (0.7 to 2.7%) of the chemical estimate. For body chlorine, the agreement was within 2 to 3 g (2 to 9%) of the reference or chemical assay. For normal-size individuals, similar agreement for body calcium, sodium, and carbon could be expected. In vivo precisions for human beings, based on anthropometric-shaped phantoms, are reported at ± 5% (Cohn & Parr, 1985). Recent animal studies have confirmed this level of accuracy for the DGAA and PGAA procedures (Ellis et al., 1992c; Ellis, unpublished data), despite being limited by the accuracy of the animal carcass analyses. For IVNAA to achieve full status as a reference or standard method, one would prefer an accuracy of ± 2%, similar to that for the D_2O dilution technique.

Recommended Standard Procedure, and Cost Aspects

To recommend a single set of standard procedures for IVNAA in the absence of standardized instruments is difficult. It is clear, however, that all these instruments have been built to minimize the subject's discomfort and required level of participation, and the procedures are performed within 15 to 30 min at low doses. Any recommended operating procedures should conform to these general guidelines and include a quality-control component based on frequent phantom measurements to maintain performance characteristics.

Construction and calibration of these instruments tend to be highly technical, often requiring advanced expertise to achieve accurate and precise performance. Once installed, however, sufficient quality control can be established to ensure the measurement procedures are routine, with a minimum of staff training. If a whole-body counter using NaI(T1) detectors already exists, the addition of a DGAA irradiator can be achieved at relatively low cost. In the review by Cohn and Parr (1985), approximate cost estimates for the various types of IVNAA instruments are provided. These can range from $30,000 to $300,000 for DGAA facilities.

The PGAA instrument is the simplest to establish and operate. A basic PGAA or pulsed activation facility (shielding, scanning bed, detectors, electronics, and computer-based analyzer) can be assembled with an initial investment of about $75,000, excluding the cost of the neutron source. At present, ^{252}Cf sources for this application would typically cost $8,000 to $12,000; a pulsed (D,T) generator costs about $85,000.

Acknowledgment

I wish to thank L.A. Loddeke for her editorial assistance in completion of the manuscript. This work is a publication of the U.S. Department of Agriculture/Agricultural Research Service, Children's Nutrition Research Center, Houston, TX and was supported with funds from the USDA/ARS Cooperative Agreement NO. 58-7MN1-6-100. The contents of this publication do not necessarily reflect the views or policies of the USDA, nor does mention of trade names, commercial products, or organizations imply endorsement by the U.S. government.

References

Anderson, E.C., & Langham, W. (1959). Average potassium concentration of the human body as a function of age. *Science*, **130**, 713-714.

Anderson, J., Osborn, S.B., Newton, D., et al. (1964). Neutron activation analysis in man in vivo. A new technique in medical investigation. *Lancet*, 1201-1205.

Baur, L.A., Allen, B.J., Rose A., et al. (1991). A total body nitrogen facility for paediatric use. *Physics in Medicine and Biology*, **36**, 1363-1375.

Beddoe, A.H., Zuidmeer, H., & Hill, G.L. (1984). A prompt gamma in vivo neutron activation analysis facility for measurement of total body nitrogen in the critically ill. *Physics in Medicine and Biology*, **29**, 371-383.

Bewley, D.K. (1988). Anthropomorphic models for checking the calibration of whole body counters and activation analysis systems. *Physics in Medicine and Biology*, **33**, 805-813.

Biggin, H.C., Chen, C.S., Ettinger, K.V., et al. (1972). Determination of nitrogen in living patients, *Nature*, **236**, 187-189.

Burmeister, W. (1965). Potassium-40 content as a basis for the calculation of body cell mass in man. *Science*, **148**, 1336-1344.

Chettle, D.R., & Fremlin, J.H. (1984). Techniques of in vivo neutron activation analysis. *Physics in Medicine and Biology*, **29**, 1011-1043.

Chung, C., Wei, Y.Y., & Chen, Y.Y. (1993). Determination of whole body nitrogen and radiation assessment using in vivo prompt gamma activation technique. *International Journal of Applied Radiation and Isotopes*, **44**, 941-948.

Cohn, S.H., & Dombrowski, C.S. (1971). Measurement of total-body calcium, sodium, chlorine, nitrogen, and phosphorus in man by in-vivo neutron activation. *Journal of Nuclear Medicine*, **12**, 499-505.

Cohn, S.H., Dombrowski, C.S., Pate, H.R., & Robertson, J.S. (1969). A whole-body counter with an invariant response to radionuclide distribution and body size. *Physics in Medicine and Biology*, **14**, 645-658.

Cohn, S.H., & Parr, R.M. (1985). Nuclear-based techniques for the *in vivo* study of human body composition. *Clinical Physics and Physiological Measurement*, **6**, 275-301.

Cohn, S.H., Vartsky, D., Yasumura, S., et al. (1980) Compartmental body composition based on total-body nitrogen, potassium, and calcium. *American Journal of Physiology*, **239**, E524-E530.

Cordain, L., Johnson, J.E., Bainbridge, C.N., et al. (1989). Potassium content of the fat free body in children. *Journal of Sports Medicine and Physical Fitness*, **29**, 170-176.

Ellis, K.J. (1991). Planning *in vivo* body composition studies in humans. In K.S. Subramanian, K. Okamoto, G.V. Iyengar (Eds.), *Biological trace element research: Multidisciplinary perspectives* (pp. 25-39). Washington, DC: American Chemical Society.

Ellis, K.J. (1992). Measurement of whole-body protein content *in vivo*. In S. Nissen (Ed.), *Methods in protein nutrition and metabolism* (pp. 195-223). San Diego: Academic.

Ellis, K.J. (1994). [Testing the instrument calibration for absolute TBK mass]. Unpublished raw data.

Ellis, K.J., & Eastman, J. (Eds.) (1993). *Human body composition*: In vivo *methods, models and assessment*. New York: Plenum.

Ellis, K.J., & Shypailo, R.J. (1992a). Multi-geometry [241]AmBe neutron irradiator: Design and calibration for total-body neutron activation analysis. *Journal of Radioanalytical and Nuclear Chemistry*, **161**, 51-60.

Ellis, K.J., & Shypailo, R.J. (1992b). [40]K measurements in the infant. *Journal of Radioanalytical and Nuclear Chemistry*, **161**, 61-69.

Ellis, K.J., & Shypailo, R.J. (1993). Whole-body potassium measurements independent of body size. In K.J. Ellis & J.D. Eastman (Eds.), *Human body composition: In vivo methods, models, and assessment* (pp. 371-375). New York: Plenum.

Ellis, K.J., Shypailo, R.J., Sheng, H-P., & Pond, W.G. (1992c). In vivo measurements of nitrogen, hydrogen, and carbon in genetically obese and lean pigs. *Journal of Radioanalytical and Nuclear Chemistry*, **160**, 159-168.

Ellis, K.J., Yasumura, S., & Morgan, W.D. (Eds.) (1987). *In vivo body composition studies*. London: Institute of Physical Sciences in Medicine.

Fenwick, J.D., McKenzie, A.L., & Boddy, K. (1991). Intercomparison of whole-body counters using a multinuclide calibration phantom. *Physics in Medicine and Biology, 36,* 191-198.

Fomon, S.J., Haschke, F., Ziegler, E.E., & Nelson, S.E. (1982). Body composition of reference children from birth to age 10 years. *American Journal of Clinical Nutrition, 35,* 1169-1175.

Forbes, G.B. (1968). A 4π plastic scintillation detector. *International Journal of Applied Radiation and Isotopes, 19,* 535-541.

Forbes, G.B., Hursh. J., & Gallup. J. (1961) Estimation of total body fat from potassium-40 content. *Science, 133,* 101-102.

Forbes, G.B., & Lewis A. (1956). Total sodium, potassium, and chloride in adult man. *Journal of Clinical Investigation, 35,* 596-600.

Garrow, J.S., & Webster, J. (1985). Quetelet's index (W/H^2) as a measure of fatness. *International Journal of Obesity, 9,* 147-153.

Gerace. L., Aliprantis, A., Russell, M., et al. (1994). Skeletal differences between black and white men and their relevance to body composition estimates. *American Journal of Human Biology, 6,* 255-262.

Haschke, F. (1989). Body composition during adolescence. In W.J. Klish & N. Kretchner (Eds.), Body composition measurements in infants and children (pp. 76-82). 98th Ross Conference on Pediatric Research. Columbus, OH. Ross Laboratories.

Hassager, C., Sorensen, S.S., Nielsen, B., & Christiansen, C. (1989). Body composition measurement by dual photon absorptiometry: Comparison with body density and total body potassium measurements. *Clinical Physiology, 9,* 353-360.

Heymsfield, S.B., Wang, Z., Baumgartner, R.N., et al.. (1993). Body composition and aging: A study by in vivo neutron activation analysis. *Journal of Nutrition, 123,* 432-437.

International Atomic Energy Agency. (1970). *Directory of whole-body radioactivity monitors,* IAEA STI/PUB/213. Vienna: Author.

International Commission on Radiological Protection. (1984). *Report of the task group on reference man.* ICRP Report 23. New York: Pergamon.

Kehayias, J.J., Ellis, K.J., Cohn, S.H., & Weinlein, J.H. (1987). Use of a high-repetition rate neutron generator for in vivo body composition measurements via neutron inelastic scattering. *Nuclear Instruments and Methods in Physics Research,* **B24/25,** 1006-1009.

Kehayias, J.J., Heymsfield, S.B., LoMonte, A.F., et al. (1991). In vivo determination of body fat by measuring total body carbon. *American Journal of Clinical Nutriiton, 52,* 1339-1344.

Kehayias, J.J., & Zhuang, H. (1993). Measurement of regional body fat in vivo in humans by simultaneous detection of regional carbon and oxygen, using neutron inelastic scattering at low radiation exposure. In K.J. Ellis & J.D. Eastman (Eds.), *Human body composition: In vivo methods, models and assessment* (pp. 49-52). New York: Plenum.

Knight, G.S., Beddoe, A.H., Streat, S.J., & Hill, G.L. (1986). Body composition of two human cadavers by neutron activation and chemical analysis. *American Journal of Physiology, 250,* E179-E185.

Kulwich, R., Feinstein, L., & Anderson, E.C. (1958). Correlation of potassium-40 concentration and fat-free lean content of hams. *Science, 127,* 338-339.

Kvist, H., Chowdhury, B., Sjöström, L., et al. (1988). Adipose tissue volume determination in males by computed tomography and ^{40}K. *International Journal of Obesity, 12,* 249-266.

Kyere, K., Oldroyd, B., Oxby, C.B., et al. (1982). The feasibility of measuring total body carbon by counting neutron inelastic scatter gamma rays. *Physics in Medicine and Biology, 27,* 805-817.

Lykken, G.I., Lukaski, H.C., Bolonchuk, W.W., & Sandstead, H.H. (1983). Potential errors in body composition as estimated by whole body scintillation counting. *Journal of Laboratory and Clinical Medicine, 4,* 651-658.

Mackie, A., Cowen, S., & Hannan, J. (1990). Calibration of a prompt neutron activation facility for the measurement of total body protein. *Physics in Medicine and Biology, 35,* 613-624.

Moore, F.D., Olesen, K.H., McMurray, J.D., et al. (1963). *The body cell mass and its supporting environment.* Philadelphia: W.B. Saunders.

Ortiz, O., Russell. M., Daley, T.L., et al. (1992). Differences in skeletal muscle and bone mineral mass between black and white females and their relevance to estimates of body composition. *American Journal of Clinical Nutriiton, 55,* 8-13.

Parr, R.M. (Ed.) (1973). *In vivo neutron activation analysis.* Proceedings of IAEA Expert Panel. Vienna: International Atomic Energy Agency.

Penn, I-W., Wang, Z-M., Buhl, K.M., et al. (1994). Body composition and two-compartment model assumptions in male long distance runners. *Medicine and Science in Sports and Exercise, 26,* 392-397.

Pierson, R.N., Lin, D.H.Y., & Phillips, R.A. (1974). Total-body potassium in health: Effects of age, sex, height, and fat. *American Journal of Physiology, 226,* 206-212.

Pierson, R.N., & Wang, J. (1988). Body composition denominators for measurements of metabolism: What measurements can be believed? *Mayo Clinic Proceedings, 63,* 947-949.

Rundo, J., & Bunce, L.J. (1966). Estimation of total hydrogen content of the human body. *Nature,* **210,** 1023-1065.

Rutledge, M.M., Clark, J., Woodruff, C., et al. (1976). A longitudinal study of total body potassium in normal breast-fed and bottle-fed infants. *Pediatric Research, 10,* 114-117.

Ryde, S.J.S., Morgan, W.D., Sivyer, A., et al. (1987). A clinical instrument for multi-element in vivo analysis by prompt, delayed and cyclic neutron activation using ^{252}Cf. *Physics in Medicine and Biology, 32,* 1257-1271.

Sjöström, L., Kvist, H., Cederbland, A., & Tylen, U. (1986). Determination of total adipose tissue and body fat in women by computed tomography, ^{40}K, and tritium. *American Journal of Physiology,* **250,** E736-E745.

Stamatelatos, I.E.M., Chettle, D.R., Green, S., & Scott, M.C. (1992). Design studies related to an in vivo neutron activation analysis facility for measuring total body nitrogen. *Physics in Medicine and Biology, 37,* 1657-1674.

Stamatelatos, I.E., Dilmanian, F.A., Ma, R., et al. (1993). Calibration for measuring total body nitrogen with a newly upgraded prompt gamma neutron activation facility. *Physics in Medicine and Biology, 38,* 615-626.

Sutcliffe, J.F., Knight, G.S., Pinilla, J.C., & Hill, G. (1993b). New and simple equations to estimate the energy and fat contents and energy density of humans in sickness and health. *British Journal of Nutrition, 69,* 631-644.

Sutcliffe, J.F., Smith, A.H., Barker, M.C.J., & Smith, A. (1993a). A theoretical analysis using ratios of the major elements measured by neutron activation analysis to derive total body water, protein, and fat. *Physics in Medicine and Biology,* **20,** 1129-1134.

Vartsky, D., Ellis, K.J., Vaswani, A.N., et al. (1984). An improved calibration of in vivo determination of body nitrogen, hydrogen and fat. *Physics in Medicine and Biology, 29,* 209-218.

Wang, Z.R., Pierson, R.N., Jr., Heymsfield, S.B. (1992). The five-level model: A new approach to organizing body-composition research. *American Journal of Clinical Nutriiton, 56,* 19-28.

Watson, W.W. (1987). Total body potassium measurement: the effect of fallout from Chernobyl. *Clinical Physics and Physiological Measurement, 8,* 337-341.

Yasumura, S., Harrison, J.E., McNeill, K.G., et al. (Eds.) (1990). *In vivo body composition studies.* New York: Plenum.

Ziegler, E.E., O'Donnell, A.M., Nelson, S.E., & Fomon, S.J. (1976). Body composition of the reference fetus. *Growth, 40,* 329-341.

4

Dual Energy X-Ray Absorptiometry

Timothy G. Lohman

The widespread use of single and dual photon absorptiometry from 1963 to 1984 preceded the recent development of dual energy x-ray absorptiometry (DXA). The focus of this chapter is on the use of DXA to measure total body and regional body composition, including the estimation of bone mineral content, lean tissue mass, fat-free mass, and fat mass. Because of the lack of standardization in validation studies across investigators (including variation in criterion methods used, in type of DXA hardware and software instrumentation selected, and in sample characteristics), it is difficult at this time to present one standardized approach for these new methods. This chapter will deal with the key issues of underlying assumptions and their validity, applicability, hardware and software, measurement procedures, calibration, and precision and accuracy in the estimation of both total and regional body composition.

History and Development of Dual Energy X-Ray Absorptiometry (DXA)

Prior to the development of DXA, single (SPA) and dual photon (DPA) absorptiometry were used to estimate regional bone mineral content (BMC) (g/cm) and bone mineral density (BMD) (g/cm^2). The SPA technique was developed first and used iodine-125 as the photon source. This approach enabled bone mineral estimates of both distal and proximal sites for the radius and ulna. Validation, standardization, and normative data were developed by Cameron and Sorenson (1963) and by Mazess, Cameron, and Miller (1972).

The development, standardization, and validation of DPA, in which iodine-125 was replaced with gadolinium-153, which has gamma emissions at both 44 and 100 keV, was described by several authors (Gotfredsen, Borg, Christiansen, & Mazess, 1984; Mazess, Cameron, & Sorenson, 1970; Mazess, Peppler, Chestnut, et al., 1981; Peppler & Mazess, 1981; Witt & Mazess, 1978). The use of DPA allowed estimates of BMD for the lumbar vertebrae and parts of the femur and enabled estimates to be made of abdominal adipose tissue content (Going et al., 1990). This approach was extended to provide estimates of whole-body composition (Gotfredsen, Jensen, Borg, & Christiansen, 1986; Heymsfield et al., 1989; Mazess, Peppler, & Gibbons, 1984; Wang et al., 1989).

Limitations of DPA—due to the decay of the radioactive source over time leading to a lack of precision in estimating BMD changes in the same subject, and due to the assumed constant correction for the attenuation coefficient of soft tissue—led to the development of dual energy x-ray absorptiometry (DXA), in which the radioactive source is replaced by an x-ray tube with a filter to convert the polychromatic x-ray beam into low and high energy peaks. This new technique allows greater precision of measurement and estimation of soft tissue composition to correct for regional variation in fat content and thus provides better estimates of BMD and soft tissue composition. These advances led to the widespread use of DXA in the body composition field for estimates of fat, lean, and bone in human beings.

The acronyms for dual energy x-ray absorptiometry include DXA, DEXA, DRA, QDR, DER, and DEPR (Wilson, Collier, Carrera, & Jacobson, 1990). Wilson et al. proposed that DEXA, the acronym used most widely at that time, be replaced by DXA, omitting the *E* and allowing the *D* to represent "dual energy." This suggestion was supported by Gluer, Steiger, and Genant (1990) and is adopted in this chapter. It is proposed as the appropriate acronym for use in future research studies.

The acronyms for body composition components estimated from DXA include total body bone mineral (TBBM), total bone mineral density (TBMD), bone-free lean tissue mass (LTM), fat mass (FM), soft tissue mass (STM = LTM + FM), and fat-free mass (FFM = LTM + TBBM). To avoid confusion with TBBM, total body mass is expressed as FFM + FM. For consistency, it is recommended that these acronyms be used in future investigations. The printouts from DXA give percent body fat. These values should be interpreted with caution since, depending on the software used, the denominator may be body weight or STM.

Assumptions and Their Validity

The theoretical basis for DXA has been described for the estimation of soft tissue composition and bone mineral (Cullum, Ell, & Ryder, 1989; Johnson & Dawson-Hughes, 1991; Kelly, Slovik, Schoenfeld, & Neer, 1988; Mazess et al., 1989; Roubenoff, Kehayias, Dawson-Hughes, & Heymsfield, 1993).

Soft Tissue Composition

The estimation of the fat content in soft tissue (bone-free lean tissue) is derived from the assumed constant attenuation of pure fat (R_f) and of bone-free lean tissue (R_l). The R_f is 1.21 for pure fat using the x-ray energies of 40 kV and 70 kV (Mazess et al., 1989). Heymsfield et al. (1994) measured six chemical elements in 11 men by neutron activation. They reported a value of 1.18 for R_f, similar to the theoretical R_f calculated from various triglycerides. For lean tissue, the R_l calculated from the measured elements was $1.399 \pm .002$ (Heymsfield et al., 1994). Given the near constancy of these two values from subject to subject, it follows that the ratio of the attenuation at the lower energy relative to the higher energy in soft tissue (R_{st}), for the low and high energy x-rays, is a function of the proportion of fat (R_f) and lean (R_l) in each pixel. From the R_{st}, the fraction of soft tissue as lean is given by Gotfredsen et al. (1986):

$$R_{st} = \frac{(R_{st} - R_f)}{(R_l - R_f)} . \qquad (4.1)$$

Since DXA provides the proportion of fat and lean in each pixel, it estimates measures of fat rather than adipose tissue, unlike computed tomography (CT) and magnetic resonance imaging (MRI). Furthermore, CT and MRI differ from DXA in that pixels are allocated to adipose tissue, or to lean tissue depending on levels of Hounsfield units; pixels are not graded as mixtures of lean tissue and adipose tissue or fat.

The fat and lean content can be calculated by solving the two equations using known values of R_f and R_l. The constancy of R_f for subjects has not been contested by most researchers since the chemistry of fat and its density (about 0.9 g/cc) vary little among individuals. The constancy of R_l for soft tissue has been accepted by many, but it has been questioned by Roubenoff et al. (1993). These authors point out that the hydration of lean body mass varies from the assumed constant of 0.73 ml/ g, especially for some hospitalized patients and for the elderly. They state that a subject's hydration level can affect the R_l but add that the degree to which DXA measurements are sensitive to variation in hydration levels is unknown. One correction needs to be made to their argument. Although they are related, the water content of the bone-free lean tissue (LTM) is at issue rather than the water content of lean body mass, which includes bone mineral. Nord and Payne (1995a) have estimated that a 5% loss of water (% of body mass) causes a 2% decrease in body fatness estimated from DXA for a typical subject with a percent body fat of 35%. Their theoretical calculations are given in chart form but are not explained in detail.

The sensitivity of DXA to changes in hydration level has been tested by Going et al. (1993), who conducted a study in which the subjects intentionally dehydrated during a 24 hour period and the variations in DXA estimates were recorded. It was found that 98% of the change in weight with dehydration could be attributed to changes in LTM from DXA. The correlation between change in weight and change in LTM was 0.70, compared to a correlation of 0.90 between weight and the change in total soft tissue mass. Assuming that the change in body weight reflected only water changes during the 24 hour period, these results indicate only small losses in accuracy of the DXA measurements with water losses of 1 to 3 kg.

A second assumption underlying the use of DXA is that the measurements are not affected by the anteroposterior thickness of the body. While this appears to be the case for subject thicknesses less than 20 cm, thicknesses larger than 25 cm may have an effect. The influence of subject thickness has been investigated by Laskey, Lyttle, Flarman, and Barber (1992) using Lunar DPX (software version 3.1) and by Jebb, Goldberg, and Marinos (1993) using the Hologic QDR-1000/W (software version not reported) to analyze phantoms. Both studies used in vitro simulations to document systematic effects of increasing tissue thicknesses by increasing the thickness of water (to represent fat-free soft tissue) at varying levels of fatness (oil or lard were used to represent fat). Laskey et al. concluded that for body thicknesses less than 20 cm, fat is overestimated by only 4% or less and fat-free soft tissue is overestimated by 2% or less. When the body thicknesses exceed 20 cm, the errors and the imprecision of the estimates increase. Jebb et al. reported that fat mass is overestimated for both thin and thick tissue layers with the greater effect at higher than lower thickness. In both studies, thicknesses between 20 and 25 cm had significant effects on the estimates of fat and bone. Subject size is one limitation of the DXA method. Its use in all populations is not appropriate as discussed later in the section on applicability of DXA.

A third assumption of DXA is related to the area of the body analyzed to obtain composition data and the degree to which the fat content of the area analyzed is associated with the fat content of the area that is not analyzed. It has been estimated that 40 to 45% of the 21,000 pixels in a typical whole-body scan contain bone in addition to soft tissue, and these pixels therefore are excluded from the calculation of values for soft tissues. Thus, the extent to which the composition in the excluded area differs from the considered area in a given population is a source of systematic error for that population. In addition, individual variation in composition between the two areas is a further source of error in the estimation of total composition. Related to this problem in the estimation of total body composition by DXA is the assumption that the composition of each body region is equally represented, per unit volume, in the calculated total body values. The influence of the arm and thorax on the total body composition estimates may be under-represented because of the relatively large areas of bone in these regions. As a result, proportionately fewer pixels are used to estimate soft tissue composition in these regions than in the lower extremities and the abdomen (Roubenoff et al., 1993).

Bone Mineral Assessment

Estimation of bone mineral mass (g), bone mineral content (g/cm), and bone mineral area density (g/cm^2) can be obtained from DXA. In these calculations, the measurements expressed in relation to cm or cm^2 are adjusted for the widths or areas, respectively, of the parts of the skeleton that are scanned. The theoretical basis for the dual energy assessment of bone mineral measurements has been described (Heymsfield et al., 1989; Mazess et al., 1984; Peppler & Mazess, 1981). Investigations have established a higher precision and accuracy for DXA than for DPA (Kelly et al., 1988; Mazess et al., 1989; Mazess, Barden, Bisek, & Hanson, 1990). Early work on the validation of the dual energy approach using neutron activation analysis for total body calcium established a close relationship between the two methods. The calibration of one DXA instrument (Lunar DPX) is described by Mazess et al. (1991) using samples of calcium hydroxyapatite and an aluminum spine phantom within a water bath covered with different thicknesses of lard, paraffin, and plastic.

The effect of subject thickness on BMD estimates was investigated by Laskey et al. (1992) and Jebb et al. (1993) using phantoms as previously described. Both studies showed an increase of about 2% in BMD with an increase in subject thickness up to 28 cm. For Lunar DPX, a manual adjustment of bone edges was required to maintain accuracy when local tissue thicknesses were greater than 22 cm. Tothill & Avenell (1994) studied the effect of soft tissue thickness in four spinal models with Lunar DPX (software version 3.4), Hologic QDR (4.47p), and Norland XR-26 (2.23). The BMD values were affected by thickness, machine, and the spinal phantom used for calibration, but the magnitude of the effects of increasing thickness generally was less than 3%. Going et al. (1993) have shown that small changes in the hydration of the FFM do not affect BMD estimates.

Applicability of DXA

The general applicability of DXA in human populations of all ages results from the low radiation exposure. The exposure for a whole-body scan ranges from 0.05 mrem to 1.5 mrem depending on the instrument and the scan speed. Because this exposure is less than that during one transcontinental flight across the U.S. (4 to 6 mrems), less than the 10 to 15 mrem from DPA, and much less than the typical radiation exposure with conventional x-rays of 25 to 270 mrem (chest x-ray, CT scan), DXA is used widely for subjects of all ages. Since some radiation is involved, DXA is not recommended for use with pregnant women, and a pregnancy test is necessary before DXA measurements are made in women of childbearing age. Special software (version 5.61, Hologic, Inc.) that assumes a higher hydration of lean tissue and, therefore, a different attenuation coefficient is used for infants. Special pediatric software is also available from Lunar. Systematic error in estimating body composition in piglets and premature infants indicates the need for further validation studies in this population (Brunton, Bayley, & Atkinson, 1993; Svendsen, Haarbo, Hassager, & Christiansen, 1993a, 1993b). There are only small effects from food intake and fluid intake on DXA estimates of body composition (Horber et al., 1992). Similarly when 1 to 4 kg of salt-containing fluid were removed by hemodialysis, the estimates of lean mass decreased, as expected, with little change in bone mineral content or fat mass (Horber et al.).

Large subjects may not be measured accurately by DXA. For subjects taller than 193 cm or wider than the scan area (58 to 65 cm), a whole-body scan cannot be obtained because part of the body will be outside the scan area. Also, for thicker subjects, for those heavier than 100 kg, or for those with a value for $\sqrt{W/S}$ greater than 0.72, where W is weight (kg) and S is stature (cm), the accuracy of the body composition estimates may be reduced due to the dependency of the attenuation coefficients for soft tissue and bone mineral on subject thickness, as noted earlier. Furthermore, increased variability in body composition estimates can occur in thick regions of the body due to increased attenuation and, therefore, decreased radiation counts. Recent hardware and software versions developed by the manufacturers (Hologic, Lunar, and Norland) have attempted to deal with these factors, but a comprehensive study comparing different instruments and software in subjects of varying thickness has not been completed.

An interesting approach to the problem of large subjects has recently been reported by Tataranni and Ravussin (personal communication) who used DXA to compare the composition of right and left sides in obese subjects. Because of the high association between values from the two sides, the authors recommend that, in studies of subjects wider than the scan area, scans be made of the right half of the body and that total body composition be estimated assuming bilateral symmetry. Errors would be introduced with this approach because some bilateral asymmetry occurs (see chapter 12) and because of errors in the identification of the midline.

The preceding statements address biological aspects of the application of DXA to the assessment of body composition. At present, DXA has not been approved for the clinical assessment of body composition in the U.S. although it can be used for this purpose in approved research studies.

Equipment: Hardware

There are three commercial versions of DXA. Each version is based on a different configuration of hardware and software, but all assess bone mineral and fat and lean tissue masses. The three manufacturers refer to their instruments as QDR (Hologic, Waltham, MA), DPX (Lunar Radiation, Madison, WI), and XR (Norland, Fort Atkinson, WI). A description of each commercial version is provided in the following sections.

Hologic QDR

The Hologic QDR systems were first described by Kelly et al. (1988). Two x-ray beams of different energies (70 and 140 kVp) are pulsed alternately. The resulting spectra have maximum photon energies at 45 keV and 100 keV. The QDR utilizes an internal calibration system with a rotating filter wheel composed of two sections of epoxy-resin-based material. At each measurement location, the beam passes through the calibration system to provide continuous internal calibration. The QDR-1000 allows for regional BMD measurements of the spine, hip, and forearm. The QDR-1000/W adds whole-body scanning to the regional assessment and allows for both BMD and body composition assessments. Each pixel covers a 1 × 1 mm area. A total body scan requires about 4 minutes and the radiation exposure is 1.5 mrems. The QDR-2000 has both pencil beam and fan beam configurations. The fan beam provides better resolution and precision, shorter scanning time, and the ability to make lateral scans of the spine. Consequently, it is recommended over the pencil beam configuration although it has not been fully evaluated. Recent comparisons among the 1000/W, 2000 pencil, and 2000 fan configurations show excellent agreement among these scanner modes with low SEE and comparable mean BMD values (Faulkner, Gluer, Engelke, & Genant, 1992; Harper, Lobaugh, King, & Drezner, 1992). If a change is made from QDR-1000 to QDR-2000 pencil or to QDR-2000 fan, cross-calibration should be completed using a series of phantom and patient scans on both scanners (Faulkner et al.).

Lunar DPX

The Lunar DPX system was described by Mazess et al. (1990). This instrument uses a constant potential x-ray source and a K-edge filter to achieve an x-ray beam of stable energy radiation of 38 and 70 keV. The x-rays are emitted from a source below the subject and pass through the subject, who lies in a supine position on a table. The total scan area is 60 by 200 cm. The attenuated x-rays, after passing through the subject, are measured with an energy-discriminating detector situated above the subject on the scanning arm. The DPX instrument makes transverse scans of the body at 1 cm intervals from head to toe. For each transverse scan, about 120 pixel elements yield data on the attenuation ratio with each pixel covering a 5 × 10 mm area for the fast and medium mode (10 and 20 minutes) and a 5 × 5 mm area for the detail mode (20 minutes). The radiation exposure varies from 0.02 mrems (fast mode) to 0.06 mrems (detail mode). Recent developments in the system hardware and software allow for lateral spinal scans in addition to anteroposterior scans (DPX-L) and forearm scans (DPX-∂). Lunar has also developed an instrument, known as the EXPERT, that has increased resolution, but the available software allows only the measurement of bone mineral in the lumbar spine and the proximal end of the femur.

Norland XR

The Norland XR system, described by Clark, Kuta, and Sullivan (1993) and by Nord and Payne (1995c), uses a K-edge filter (samarium) to produce two photon peaks at 44 and 100 keV. For the XR-26 model, the pixel size is 6 × 13 mm and the total body scan is made in about 20 minutes with a radiation exposure of 0.05 mrem. Both total body and regional BMD can be obtained. The XR-36 DXA system includes a unique feature called "dynamic filtration," which varies the x-ray intensity by patient thickness. Thus, the hardware of this instrument compensates for the effects of tissue thickness on the precision and accuracy of the measurements. There is a need to evaluate this approach to compensating for tissue thickness in comparison with the software of other instruments that has been updated to achieve a similar purpose. The XR-36 DXA system has a scanning area of 193 cm × 64 cm and allows analyses of total bone mineral and body composition, regional BMC, forearm BMD, and small subject scanning. Regional body composition analyses can also be made using software versions 2.4 and 2.5.

Equipment: Software

The software versions for each commercial unit have been upgraded many times during the past five years. Each software version is based on specific assumptions to estimate BMD and body composition for the total body and for body regions. It is essential that researchers include the software versions used in their studies to facilitate evaluation of the findings and to allow judgments regarding the performance of the upgrades. The most recent Lunar (3.6), Hologic (5.64), and Norland (2.5) software versions are presently being evaluated by many research laboratories. In longitudinal studies, it may be important to repeat the analyses with the most recent software versions. The following paragraphs briefly describe the software updates for each company (Table 4.1).

The Hologic software versions 5.0 to 5.64 have undergone several changes to increase the precision and accuracy of body composition analysis. In addition, Hologic has developed a Standard Whole Body Analysis and an Enhanced Whole Body Analysis for recent software versions (5.53 to 5.64). Hologic recommends using the Enhanced Whole Body Analysis for subjects with large changes in body mass. All the Hologic fan beam whole-body

Table 4.1   Software Versions for DXA Instruments

Lunar	Hologic (whole-body or enhanced whole-body)	Norland
3.0 Original version.	**5.39 to 5.47** Early version of body composition.	**2.2 & 2.3** Whole-body composition; regional BMD.
3.1 Corrected for artifacts; provides BMD in thin tissue.	**5.48 to 5.54** Whole-body and enhanced whole-body; corrected for tissue thickness and large weight change.	**2.4 & 2.5** Recalibrated fat-lean system; regional body composition added with flexible cuts (released March 1993).
3.2 Further corrections for artifacts and anomalous points.	**5.55** Rats: whole-body.	
3.4 Changes for spine and femur.	**5.56** Infant: whole-body.	
3.4R Corrections for tissue thickness, high density metal.	**5.57** Whole-body analysis.	
3.5 Updated version of 3.4 and 3.4R.	**5.60** Forearm analysis.	
3.6 (1.3y) Flexible cuts for different regions, high resolution mode, tissue thickness corrections, forearm and lateral spine analysis (released August 1992).	**5.61** Infant: whole-body. **5.64** Enhanced whole-body analysis (released May 1993). **5.65 to 5.67** No changes in body composition.	

measurements use the Enhanced Analysis. Hologic recommends the Standard analysis for scanning pigs, dogs, and certain whole-body phantoms. While mean differences between the two versions (Standard and Enhanced) are fairly small (1 to 4%), regional differences and individual differences may be larger. For new studies, version 5.64 should be used, and the selection of Standard or Enhanced Whole Body Analysis must be made by the investigator depending on the particular experimental situation.

Lunar software versions 3.1 through 3.6 provide similar mean body composition values (Going, personal communication, May 1994) (Table 4.2). The more recent software versions (3.4 to 3.6), however, provide different body composition estimates for amenorrheic subjects and obese subjects with body thicknesses greater than 20 cm. The most recent version (3.6) also allows for more flexible boundaries for regional analysis of body composition.

Norland's earlier software versions 2.2 and 2.3 allowed for whole-body composition and total and

Table 4.2   Comparison of Mean Percent Body Fat From Two Versions of Lunar Software

Sample	DPX (3.1)		DPX (3.6)	
	Mean	SD	Mean	SD
Men	23.5	5.2	23.4	5.4
Women	37.3	7.6	37.2	7.9

Data from Going, personal communication, May 1994.

regional BMD measurements (Table 4.1). The software versions 2.4 and 2.5 were recalibrated for fat and lean with a new set of standards (Nord & Payne, 1995c). A new fat distribution model was used and options were introduced to allow regional analysis of body composition. In this model, the amount of fat near the bone is assumed to be greater than that farther from the bone and, consequently, it is weighted more heavily in the regression model (Nord & Payne).

Measurement Procedures

The measurement procedures for assessing bone mineral and body composition are similar for each instrument (Hologic, Lunar, Norland). In general, all body composition measurements are made in the anteroposterior position. A series of transverse scans is made from head to toe of the subject at 0.6 to 1.0 cm intervals over the entire scan area. The whole-body scan takes 5 to 30 minutes depending on the instrument. Special subject preparation and requirements for measurements in the fasting state are not needed to obtain accurate results.

Careful positioning is essential to achieve reproducible regional bone mineral assessments. For precise measurements of regional BMD, separate scans of the spine (anteroposterior or lateral), femur, and forearm are conducted. The anteroposterior spine scan is considerably more precise than the lateral scan (Blake, Jagathesan, Herd, & Fogelman, 1994; Larnack et al., 1992; Lilley et al., 1994). BMD of the distal or ultradistal radius shaft can be measured by DXA using Hologic QDR, Lunar DPX, or Norland XR. There is a close relationship between SPA measurements and DPX measurements of BMD (Faulkner et al., 1994; Ilich et al., 1994; Nelson, Feingold, Mascha, & Kleerekoper, 1992; Nieves, Cosman, Mars, & Lindsay, 1992).

Training in the operation, positioning of subjects, and data management is essential to obtain precise and accurate data from DXA and is provided by each company along with a standard operating manual. In some American states, DXA measurements must be made by a licensed x-ray technician.

Calibration Procedures

The calibration of DXA involves the use of different standards and assumptions depending on the company and software version that is applied. Mazess et al. (1989) used water, lard, Delrin, and mixtures of water and isopropyl alcohol to simulate various mixtures of fat and lean tissues. Also comparisons were made with DPA, which had been calibrated with a series of graded mixtures of lean beef and fat (Nuti et al., 1991; Wang et al., 1989). The calibration procedure for bone mineral is described by Mazess et al. (1991). The calibration resulted in the following formula: % fat DXA = 500 (1.40 − R_{st}) (Hansen et al., 1993). Heymsfield et al (1994) reported theoretical and empirical evidence to support this equation with fat having an R_f of 1.18 (compared to 1.20 in the equation) and fat-free mass an R_f of 1.40, as derived in the equation.

The equations used by Hologic and Norland have not been published. Both companies used a mixture of 0.6% NaCl in water solution and stearic acid to simulate pure lean tissue and fat respectively (Nord & Payne, 1995c). Using mixtures of these substances, any DXA instrument can be calibrated to derive an equation relating R_{st} to percent fat. Mazess et al. (1991) proposed using plastic (Delrin, equivalent to 40% fat) and water in a phantom with a simulated composition of 5% fat and 95% lean. Goodsitt (1992) evaluated the Nord and Payne approach using Hologic QDR-1000, Lunar DPX, and Norland XR-26 data. The authors found equivalent results for the three instruments when 0.8% NaCl was used.

Precision of Total and Regional Composition Estimates

The precision of total and regional body composition estimates from DXA can be evaluated over the short term (within and between days) and long term (during months within individuals) for bone mineral, body fat, and lean soft tissue. Precision is somewhat greater for regional body composition assessment than for whole-body assessments.

Total Body Precision

The short-term precision of total body composition assessments by DXA is usually evaluated by repeated scans of subjects and calculating an intraindividual standard deviation for each subject. The standard deviations are then pooled to obtain a more reliable estimate. The results for TBBM, TBMD, LTM, and percent fat from several short-term studies are summarized in Table 4.3. In general, the standard deviation is about 1.0% for percent fat, which is comparable with the precision of other methods (e.g., body density and bioelectric impedance). The coefficient of variation (standard deviation/mean × 100) can be affected by the mean fat content. In the study by Mazess et al. (1990), for which the mean fat content was about 21%, the coefficient of variation was 6.9%, whereas Hansen et al. (1993), in a study of subjects with a mean fat content of 31%, reported a coefficient of variation of 3.8% (Table 4.3).

In general, it is recommended that percent fat be included in future studies of the precision of DXA hardware and software and that both the

Table 4.3　Short-Term Precision of Total Body Composition by DXA

Study	TBBM (g) SD	TBBM (g) CV	TBMD (g/cm²) SD	TBMD (g/cm²) CV	LTM (kg) SD	LTM (kg) CV	Fat (%) SD	Fat (%) CV
Fuller et al., 1992 (n = 28)	—	—	.03	0.9	.42	0.8	—	—
Hansen et al., 1993 (N = 104)	—	—	.006	—	.50	—	1.2	3.8
Jensen et al., 1993 (n = 12)	—	—	—	—	—	—	0.5	2.0
Johnson & Dawson-Hughes, 1991 (n = 6)	—	—	—	0.7	—	1.1	—	—
Mazess et al., 1990 (n = 12)	39	1.5	.007	0.6	.76	1.6	1.2	6.9
Russell-Aulet et al., 1991 (n = 6)	—	—	—	—	—	—	0.8	—

Table 4.4　Long-Term Precision of Total Body Composition by DXA

Study	Interval (mo)	TBBM SD	TBBM CV	BMD SD	BMD CV	LTM SD	LTM CV	FTM SD	FTM CV	% Fat SD	% Fat CV
Haarbo et al., 1991 (n = 6)	6	.03	1.2	—	—	1.4	3.1	1.1	6.4	1.6	5.7
Johnson & Dawson-Hughes, 1991 (n = 6)	9	—	—	—	0.6	—	1.0	—	—	—	—

standard deviation and coefficient of variation be reported. For TBBM, TBMD, and LTM coefficients of variation for short-term precision vary from 0.6 to 1.6%, with about 1% being a representative value for each of these variables (Table 4.3).

To determine long-term precision, Haarbo, Gotfredson, Hassajer, and Christiansen (1991) remeasured six individuals after a six-month interval, and Johnson and Dawson-Hughes (1991) remeasured six individuals after a nine-month interval (Table 4.4). Haarbo et al. found long-term precision comparable to short-term precision for all variables except LTM (CV = 3.1% for long term, in contrast with 0.8 to 1.6% for short term, as shown in Table 4.3). Johnson and Dawson-Hughes found variations for TBMD and LTM to be similar over the long term and short term. For variation among Lunar scanners used with a phantom, Mazess et al. (1990) found a CV for TBMD of 1.0% and CV values for regional BMD ranging from 1.3 to 2.5%. The estimates were somewhat higher among scanners than within scanners for both TBMD and regional BMD.

Regional Body Precision

Regional body composition assessments are somewhat more precise than whole-body assessments.

Studies by Mazess et al. (1990) and Fuller et al. (1992) indicate that the CV for fat is larger than that for lean mass and BMD (Table 4.5). While there is good agreement between these reports in the precision found for fat, lean mass, and BMD in most regions, the fat CV for Fuller et al. is considerably less than for Mazess et al. for legs and trunk but not for the arm(s) (both used Lunar DPX).

Accuracy of DXA for the Measurement of Fatness

The prediction of body fatness from DXA can be evaluated in several ways. First, there may be systematic errors in comparing DXA estimates with those from another reference method, and the magnitude of these systematic errors may vary with different populations and with different DXA instruments. The systematic error may be due to inaccuracy of the reference method or inaccuracies of the DXA estimates or a combination of these. Secondly, the SEE for percent fat should be less than 3% for a new method to be accepted as accurate. Errors exceeding 4% show too much variability and errors between 3 and 4% show limited validity (Lohman, 1992). Many methods tend to

Table 4.5 Short-Term Precision of Regional Body Composition and Bone Mineral Density by DXA

| | Coefficients of Variation (%) | | | | | |
| | Mazess et al., 1990[1] | | | Fuller et al., 1992[2] | | |
Region	Fat	Lean mass	BMD	Fat	Lean mass	BMD
Arms	9.2	2.7	1.5	9.0	2.8	2.0
Legs	7.0	1.9	0.8	3.4	1.2	1.4
Trunk	7.1	1.9	1.1	4.1	1.2	2.0

[1]Data from five scans for each subject during five to seven days. The within-subject standard deviation was pooled over 12 subjects (Lunar DPX).

[2]Data from the differences between repeated DXA scans obtained from the estimates of component masses for 28 subjects (Lunar DPX).

overestimate fatness in lean populations and underestimate fatness in the obese. This characteristic may be reflected in a smaller standard deviation of the new method or in a slope of the regression of percent fat from the reference method on percent fat from DXA that differs from unity. Animal studies allow validation of a new method against chemical analyses of carcasses. Finally, new software has to be tested to determine if the prediction of fatness is improved.

Human Validation Studies

To examine the extent of systematic error for DXA, this section will deal with recent Hologic, Lunar, and Norland software as described previously. Snead, Birge, and Kohrt (1993) reported excellent agreement between percent fat from body density and values from DXA using the Hologic QDR-1000/W (software version 5.4) in young men and women, but percent fat DXA underestimated the mean fat content by 6.1% in older men and 5.4% in older women (Table 4.6). This underestimation could not be explained by the lower BMD in older populations (4.7% bone mineral in FFM for young men as compared to 4.6% for older men and 5.2 and 4.5% for younger and older women, respectively). For example, when adjustments were made for the lower BMD in women, percent fat from body density was reduced only slightly from 39.9% to 38.7% as compared to 34.5% for DXA. The authors found that adding 2 kg strips of fat to the thigh was almost completely detected by DXA

(96%); however, strips of fat added to the trunk were only partially measured (55%; Snead et al.). Thus, the discrepancy between methods could be accounted for by additional truncal fat in older populations that is not detected by DXA. For the two methods to agree, trunk fat would have to be underestimated by 22% and thus there would be 25 kg of fat rather than 22.3 kg in this area. In an experiment similar to that by Snead et al., Milliken, Going, and Lohman (1994) using Lunar DPX (software version 3.6) found that only 50% of fat added to the trunk could be detected, compared to 92% for fat added to the thigh. These results contrast with those from a study by Svendsen, Hassager, Bergman, and Christiansen (1993b), who used Lunar software version 3.2. In this study, they added 8.8 kg of lard to the anterior surface of the trunk in six women. This did not affect the assessments of fat or lean tissue.

Boileau et al. (1994) presented data obtained with a Hologic QDR-2000/W (software version 5.54) in young and older adults. These authors used a multicomponent body composition model that incorporated bone mineral and body water as the reference method and found good agreement (within 2%) for young and older men and women (Table 4.6). Their use of a more recent software version than that available to Snead et al. (1993) may explain the differences between the results from these two studies. With the development of further versions of the Hologic software, 5.56, 5.57, and 5.64, much of the underestimation of truncal fat may be eliminated, but further evaluation is needed in older populations.

To examine further the possible systematic errors between DXA and body density assessments, two studies using Lunar DPX are reviewed (Going, personal communication, May 1994; Wellens et al., 1994). In older men and women, Going and his associates found DXA percent fat (Lunar DPX, software version 3.6) was 7.5% less than that from a four-component body density model for men and 4.5% less for women (calculations from body density gave percent fat as 30.9% and 41.7% for men and women, respectively). As mentioned previously, these authors did not find a difference between the mean DXA of body fat from Lunar software versions 3.1 and 3.6 (Table 4.2). Wellens et al., using Lunar DPX (3.4) found good agreement between values from DXA and those from a four-component body density model in men and women aged 18 to 67 years; the discrepancies between methods increased with age in men but not in women. Since men may add more truncal fat with age than women, these results, along with

Table 4.6 Comparison of Methods for Estimating Percent Fat in Young and Older Adults

| | | Hologic QDR-1000/W Snead et al., 1993 | | | | | Hologic QDR-2000/W Boileau et al., 1994 | | | |
| | | % Fat—D | | % Fat DXA | | | % Fat—4C | | % Fat DXA | |
	Age	Mean	SD	Mean	SD	Age	Mean	SD	Mean	SD
Young adults										
Men	29.3	13.7	6.1	12.7	5.3	35.7	17.7	8.0	17.0	8.2
Women	29.1	21.8	5.7	22.7	5.3	26.6	21.3	6.1	23.2	6.3
Older adults										
Men	68.1	27.4	7.2	21.3	6.3	63.4	23.0	6.2	21.7	7.1
Women	66.3	39.9	6.3	34.5	6.6	63.5	35.3	5.7	36.7	7.1

% Fat—D = percent body fat from body density; % Fat—4C = percent body fat from a multicomponent model (density, water, and bone mineral).

those of Going suggest that Lunar DPX may underestimate truncal fat in older subjects.

The slope of the regression of percent fat from reference methods on percent fat DXA is an aspect of validation that needs examination. If the two methods have construct validity and are calibrated correctly to estimate percent fat, then the regression line relating the values from the two methods should have a slope equal to 1.0. A slope that deviates markedly from unity shows that a unit change in the DXA value does not correspond to a unit change in the reference value. In premenopausal women, the slope of the regression line for percent fat (body density) on percent fat DXA was 0.77 (Hansen et al., 1993). The SEE was low (2.4%) and the mean agreement between methods was excellent (% fat body density = 29.9% and % fat DXA = 29.7%). Furthermore, the means for the leanest (20.3% vs. 22.0%) and for the fattest (44.0% vs. 42.5%) five subjects agreed well between methods.

Clark et al. (1993) compared percent fat from DXA (Norland XR-26, 2.2) with values from body density and from two skinfold equations in 35 young white men. There was a high correlation ($r = 0.91$) between the values from DXA and those from body density with a fairly low SEE (3.0% fat). The mean percent fat for DXA was significantly higher than the means from the other three methods. The authors suggest that this discrepancy could be due to the assumptions used in the development of DXA software for Norland. The calibration standard phantom for this software is based on hydroxyapatite for bone mineral, 0.6% NaCl water solution for lean tissue, and stearic acid for fat. The 4% difference between percent fat from body density and percent fat DXA could also be related to the bone mineral content of the FFM. If this were larger in this sample than assumed for young men, the two-component model body density method would underestimate percent fat. The values predicted from the skinfold equations were more in agreement with those from body density than with those from DXA, suggesting that the density of FFM was close to the expected value. The Norland software has been modified since the study by Clark et al. The latest versions (2.4 and 2.5) use new material standards, a new fat distribution model, and new regional estimates. Evaluations of this software have not been reported. Nord and Payne (1995a, 1995b) suggest that the observed difference between data from DXA Lunar and DXA Norland (software versions unidentified) is related to the assumed composition of reference man. They derived a density of the FFM for young men of 1.109 g/cc and for women of 1.118 g/cc and developed new density-fat equations. Using these equations, they found good agreement between body density percent fat and DXA percent fat.

Animal Validation Studies

Several animal validation studies have been published using Hologic and Lunar instruments. Svendsen et al. (1993a), using Lunar DPX (3.2) in seven pig carcasses ranging in weight from 35 to 95 kg, found a mean difference in fat content of 2.2% between carcass chemical analysis and DXA. The SEE for the regression analysis was 2.9%.

Brunton et al. (1993) used Hologic QDR-1000/W and the pediatric whole-body software (6.01) in small piglets (mean weight 1.6 kg). In comparison with chemical analyses of carcasses, DXA overestimated fat by 100%; lean estimates were within 6% agreement, and bone mineral was underestimated by 30%. In larger piglets (mean weight 6.0 kg), DXA overestimated fat by 36%, but there was excellent agreement for lean mass and bone mineral. The authors concluded that additional work was needed on the hydration of lean tissue before accurate estimates of body composition could be obtained from DXA. Lohman (1989) estimated that the hydration of FFM changes from more than 80% in young infants and 79% at one year of age to 73.5% for young adults. Thus consideration of the hydration of the FFM is essential for assessments of body composition by DXA at young ages.

Accuracy of DXA Estimates of Body Composition Changes

Larger than expected changes in total body and spine bone mineral content with weight loss have been reported (Jensen, Quaade, & Sorenson, 1994; Lukaski, Siders, & Gallager, 1992). This raises concern about the accuracy with which DXA can estimate changes in body composition. The measurement of changes in body composition in obese subjects who lose weight is difficult because there is a loss of body water with weight loss from dieting, surgery, or hemodialysis. This again directs attention to the hydration level of FFM and its influence on DXA body composition estimates before and after weight loss. Lukaski et al., using Hologic (5.39), reported a decrease of 8% in TBBM during three months in women who lost 7 kg body weight. Reanalysis of the same data using the enhanced software version 5.64 showed only a 1.5% decrease (Lukaski, personal communication, February 1994). Jensen et al. (1994) using Hologic QDR reported a 6% decrease in TBBM with a 12 kg weight loss. Svendsen et al. (1993a) found DXA measures of TBBM were increased by 7% when 8.8 kg lard was added to the anterior aspects of the bodies of six adults (Lunar DPX, 3.2). The same authors reported a decrease of only 1 to 2% in TBBM in older women who lost about 10 kg body weight during 12 weeks of dieting or diet and exercise (Svendsen et al., 1993d).

From a theoretical standpoint, a decrease in the hydration level should increase the elemental content, leading to a higher molecular weight of the LTM and changing its attenuation coefficient. Thus, if a subject were to lose 1.5 kg of water,

there should be a slight bias in the estimates of the dehydrated subjects due to the application of the same attenuation formula both before and after the dehydration. In the study by Going et al. (1993), body weight decreased 1.5 kg due to dehydration. They found 98% of the change in weight with dehydration was measured by DXA. The measures of bone mineral and fat were unaffected by changes in hydration in this study. Thus, normal variations in hydration (1 to 3% of body weight) have little effect on the ability of DXA to detect body composition changes. The standard deviation of the difference between measures in the two states (hydration, dehydration) was, however, increased from 0.62 kg for total mass and 0.94 kg for LTM. Dividing 0.94 kg by the square root of 2 yields 0.66 kg for an estimate of the precision of LTM estimates that compares well with the estimate of 0.76 kg by Mazess et al. (1989) and suggests that changes in hydration do not add to the measurement error. The precision of LTM measures is, however, less than that for total body mass (Going et al.).

Accuracy of Regional Body Composition Assessments

Validation studies of regional body composition are scarce. Some idea of the accuracy of the regional values can be obtained by comparing the results from different methods. Schlemmer, Hassager, Haarbo, and Christiansen (1990) assessed abdominal fat by DPA and correlated it with measures of percent body fat by DPA and body circumferences. Waist circumferences correlated better than waist-to-hip ratio with various measures of abdominal fatness and about the same as overall percent body fat. Going et al. (1990) also assessed abdominal fat by DPA at L2-4 combined with an abdominal skinfold thickness and found higher correlations between DPA-estimated abdominal fat and truncal skinfold thicknesses than for extremity skinfold thicknesses. These authors also reported high precision for abdominal fat from DPA.

Lohman (1992) suggested that the use of DXA abdominal fat, in combination with skinfold thicknesses, could be used to estimate intra-abdominal fat. DXA estimates of abdominal fat have been validated using CT as a reference method by Svendsen et al. (1993c). They found that DXA measures of abdominal fat accounted for 80% of the variance in intra-abdominal fat by CT and that the combination of trunk skinfold thicknesses and abdominal fat by DXA accounted for 91% of the variation ($CV = 14.8\%$) in CT intra-abdominal fat.

Limb composition measures from DXA have been validated. Fuller et al. (1992) reported moderate correlations between anthropometric estimates of limb composition and volume and estimates from DXA. There was a considerable difference between the mean values for leg volume, but not for arm volume, between DXA estimates and direct measures. Heymsfield et al. (1990) used DPA to estimate extremity skeletal muscle mass and compared these estimates with those from anthropometry and estimates of whole-body skeletal muscle from total body potassium and nitrogen. Anthropometric indices of extremity muscle mass and total body potassium had the highest correlations with DPA estimates of extremity skeletal muscle. Somewhat lower correlations were found between the DPA estimates and total body nitrogen. The authors concluded that the DPA approach was a practical method to quantify human skeletal muscle in the limbs.

Steps Toward Standardization of DXA

Recently, Van Loan et al. (1994) compared results from a Hologic QDR-2000 (pencil) using software version 5.54 and a Lunar DPX using software version 3.6 in a sample of women (Table 4.7). They

Table 4.7 Ratios of Tissue Masses in a Sample of Women: Hologic QDR-2000 Version 5.54/Lunar DPX Version 3.6

Region	Fat mass	Lean mass	Bone mineral content	Bone density
Arm	0.97	0.84	0.96	0.94
Leg	0.97	0.93	0.99	0.95
Trunk	0.87	1.13	—	—
Pelvis	—	—	0.83	0.90
Spine	—	—	0.76	0.83
Total	0.93	1.07	0.97	0.96

Reprinted from "Comparison of Bone Mineral Content (BMC), Bone Mineral Density, Lean and Fat Measurements From Two Different Bone Densitometers," by M.D. Van Loan, J. Thompson, G. Butterfield, et al., 1994, *Medicine and Science in Sports and Exercise*, **26**, p. S40. Reprinted with permission of M.D. Van Loan.

found systematic differences between instruments in bone mineral and other aspects of body composition. The largest differences were in the regional content of bone mineral and fat. The Lunar measures of percent body fat (mean = 39.7%) were larger than the Hologic measures (mean = 36.5%). There were differences also for LTM, with means of 37.3 kg for Lunar and 39.8 kg for Hologic measures, for TBBM, with means of 2.27 kg for Lunar and 2.15 kg for Hologic. Part of the observed difference between instruments is due to different boundaries being used for the same region, depending on the software version and company. Comparisons are needed among the Hologic, Lunar, and Norland instruments, with different populations and using the most recent software. Documenting these differences, and validating the results against data from a multicomponent model, could lead to standardization of software among the instruments.

Summary

Several aspects of DXA methodology have been reviewed in this chapter. There is general agreement that DXA offers a precise method to estimate aspects of body composition, including TBBM, TBMD, STM, LTM, FM, and FFM. Regional body composition can also be estimated using DXA with adequate precision, though somewhat less than in total body composition.

The accuracy of DXA for estimating LTM, FM, and TBMD has not been established. When percent body fat from DXA is used to predict percent body fat obtained by a reference method, the SEE values are generally similar or lower than those when values from other traditional methods are used to predict values from a reference method. When DXA percent fat is compared against percent body fat from body density using a multicomponent method, the *SEE* values typically range from 2.5 to 3.5%.

Factors in determining the accuracy of DXA include subject thickness, subject size, calibration procedures, software version, and instrument company and model. Because each company uses different methods to derive the relationship between x-ray attenuation of the body and body composition, different results have been obtained by each instrument and software version. Recent changes by Hologic (software version 5.64), Lunar (version 3.6), and Norland (versions 2.4 and 2.5) have dealt with some confounding factors but each uses different assumptions and models. Until these approaches are validated in the same sample against data from a multicomponent model, it is difficult to recommend a standard procedure, approach, or instrument. Validation studies are needed to determine the accuracy of each approach in the same samples.

Hydration level needs more attention. Because of variation in hydration level, especially in selected diseased states, in infants, and in the elderly, the effects on body composition estimates need to be established for theoretical and empirical reasons. Knowledge of these effects would improve regional and whole-body estimates of body composition from DXA.

Each company uses a different approach to estimate the distribution of fat in pixels that include bone. The fat in such pixels must be estimated since it cannot be measured. These approaches have not been described in detail in the literature. Accurate estimates of the fat content of these pixels is essential to obtain accurate DXA measures of LTM and FM. Since more than 40% of the pixels that contain body composition information include bone, it is essential that the associated fat and lean volumes be estimated accurately. If these estimates are inaccurate, the DXA measures for the whole body and for regions will be inaccurate. Also, because of the widespread use of DXA to estimate body composition changes with age, exercise, and diet, it is essential that changes in fat distribution not affect the accuracy of the estimates. The adding of fat to the surface of the body has been used as a model to observe the effect of changes in fat distribution and has led to recent improvements in software. Further studies are needed with all instruments, using the most recent software, to determine the effects of changes in fat distribution on whole-body and regional estimates.

In conclusion, DXA offers precise estimates of body composition. It can be used in a multicomponent approach, most commonly by providing a measure of TBBM, or by itself to yield estimates of bone mineral, lean tissue, and fat mass for regional and total body composition. With additional research as suggested in this chapter, DXA may become a reference method to estimate body composition. Future studies are likely to clarify the present limitations to its accuracy and lead to a more standardized approach.

References

Blake, G.M., Jagathesan, T., Herd, R.J.M., & Fogelman, I. (1994). A longitudinal study of supine lateral dual x-ray absorptiometry in peri- and post-menopausal women. In E.F.J. Ring, D.M. Eloins, & A.K. Bhalla (Eds.), *Current research in osteoporosis and bone mineral measurement III* (pp. 55-61). London: British Institute of Radiology.

Boileau, R., Slaughter, M., Stillman, R., et al. (1994). Precision of fat and fat-free body (FFB) composition estimates: Comparison of four methods. *Federation of American Societies for Experimental Biology,* **8** (part 1), A179.

Brunton, J.A., Bayley, H.S., & Atkinson, S.A. (1993). Validation and application of dual-energy x-ray absorptiometry to measure bone mass and body composition in small infants. *American Journal of Clinical Nutrition,* **58**, 839-845.

Cameron, J.R., & Sorenson, J.A. (1963). Measurement of bone mineral in vivo: An improved method. *Science,* **142**, 230-232.

Clark, R.R., Kuta, J.M., & Sullivan, J.C. (1993). Prediction of percent body fat in adult males using dual-energy x-ray absorptiometry, skinfolds, and hydrostatic weighing. *Medicine and Science in Sports and Exercise,* **25**, 528-535.

Cullum, I.D., Ell, P.J., & Ryder, J.R. (1989). X-ray dual photon absorptiometry: A new method for the measurement of bone density. *British Journal of Radiology,* **62**, 587-592.

Faulkner, K.G., Gluer, C.C., Engelke, K., & Genant, H.K. (1992). Cross calibration of QDR-1000/W and QDR-2000 scanners. *Journal of Bone Mineral Research,* **7**, 518S.

Faulkner, K.G., McClung, M.R., Schmeer, M.S., et al. (1994). Densitometry of the radius using single and dual energy absorptiometry. *Calcified Tissue International,* **54**, 208-211.

Fuller, N.J., Laskey, M.A., & Elia, M. (1992). Assessment of the composition of major body regions by dual-energy x-ray absorptiometry (DEXA) with special reference to limb muscle mass. *Clinical Physiology,* **12**, 253-266.

Gluer, C.C., Steiger, P., & Genant, H.K. (1990). Letter to the editor. *Radiology,* **176**, 875-876.

Going, S.B., Massett, M.P., Hall, M.C., et al. (1993). Detection of small changes in body composition by dual-energy x-ray absorptiometry. *American Journal of Clinical Nutrition,* **57**, 845-850.

Going, S.B., Pamenter, R.W., Lohman, T.G., et al. (1990). Estimation of total body composition by regional dual photon absorptiometry. *American Journal of Human Biology,* **2**, 703-710.

Goodsitt, M.M. (1992). Evaluation of a new set of calibration standards for the measurement of fat content via DPA and DXA. *Medical Physics,* **19**, 35-44.

Gotfredsen, A., Borg, J., Christiansen, C., & Mazess, R.B. (1984). Total body bone mineral in vivo by photon absorptiometry, II: Accuracy. *Clinical Physiology, 4*, 357-362.

Gotfredsen, A., Jensen, J., Borg, J., & Christiansen, C. (1986). Measurement of lean body mass and total body fat using dual photon absorptiometry. *Metabolism, 35*, 88-93.

Haarbo, J., Gotfredsen, A., Hassajer, C., & Christiansen, C. (1991). Validation of body composition by dual energy x-ray absorptiometry (DEXA). *Clinical Physiology, 11*, 331-341.

Hansen, N.J., Lohman, T.G., Going, S.B., et al. (1993). Prediction of body composition in premenopausal females from dual-energy x-ray absorptiometry. *Journal of Applied Physiology, 75*, 1637-1641.

Harper, K.D., Lobaugh, K., King, S.T., & Drezner, M.K. (1992). Upgrading dual-energy x-ray absorptiometry scanners: Do new models provide equivalent methods? *Journal of Bone Mineral Research, 7*, S191.

Heymsfield, S.B., Smith, R., Aulet, M., et al. (1990). Appendicular skeletal muscle mass: measured by dual-photon absorptiometry. *American Journal of Clinical Nutrition, 52*, 214-218.

Heymsfield, S.B., Wang, J., Heshka, S., et al. (1989). Dual photon absorptiometry: Comparison of bone mineral and soft tissue mass measurements in vivo with established methods. *American Journal of Clinical Nutrition, 49*, 1283-1289.

Heymsfield, S.B., Wang, Z., Wang, J., et al. (1994). Theoretical foundation of dual energy x-ray absorptiometry (DEXA) soft tissue estimates: Validation in situ and in vivo. *Federation of American Societies for Experimental Biology, 8* (part 1), A278.

Horber, F.F., Thomi, F., Casez, J.P., et al. (1992). Impact of hydration status on body composition as measured by dual-energy x-ray absorptiometry in normal volunteers and patients on haemodialysis. *British Journal of Radiology, 65*, 895-900.

Ilich, J.Z., Hsiel, L.C., Tzagournis, M.A., et al. (1994). A comparison of single photon and dual x-ray absorptiometry of the forearm in children and adults. *Bone, 15*, 187-191.

Jebb, S.A., Goldberg, G.R., & Marinos, E. (1993). DXA measurements of fat and bone mineral density in relation to depth and adiposity. In K.J. Ellis & J.D. Eastman (Eds.), *Human body composition* (pp. 115-119). New York: Plenum.

Jensen, L.B., Quaade, F., & Sorenson, O.H. (1994). Bone loss accompanying voluntary weight loss in obese humans. *Journal of Bone Mineral Research, 9*, 459-463.

Jensen, M.D., Kamaley, J.A., Roust, L.R., et al. (1993). Assessment of body composition with use of dual-energy x-ray absorptiometry: Evaluation and comparison with other methods. *Mayo Clinical Proceedings, 68*, 867-873.

Johnson, J., & Dawson-Hughes, B. (1991). Precision and stability of dual-energy x-ray absorptiometry measurements. *Calcified Tissue International, 49*, 174-178.

Kelly, T.L., Slovik, D.M., Schoenfeld, D.A., & Neer, R.M. (1988). Quantitative digital radiography versus dual photon absorptiometry of the lumbar spine. *Journal of Clinical Endocrinology Metabolism, 67*, 839-844.

Larnach, T.A., Boyd, S.J., Smart, R.C., et al. (1992). Reproducibility of lateral spine scans using dual-energy x-ray absorptiometry. *Calcified Tissue International, 51*, 255-258.

Laskey, M.A., Lyttle, K.D., Flarman, M.E., & Barber, R.W. (1992). The influence of tissue depth and composition on the performance of the Lunar dual energy x-ray absorptiometer whole body scanning mode. *European Journal of Clinical Nutrition, 46*, 39-45.

Lilley, J., Eyre, S., Walters, B., et al. (1994). An investigation of spinal bone mineral density measured laterally: A normal range for U.K. women. *British Journal of Radiology, 67*, 157-161.

Lohman, T.G. (1989). Assessment of body composition in children. *Pediatric Exercise Science, 1*, 19-30.

Lohman, T.G. (1992). Advances in body composition assessment. Champaign, IL: Human Kinetics.

Lukaski, H.C., Siders, W.A., & Gallager, S.K. (1992). Decreased bone mineral status assessed by dual-energy x-ray absorptiometry (DXA) in obese women during weight loss. *American Journal of Clinical Nutrition, 55* (Suppl 1), 82.

Mazess, R.B., Barden, H.S., Bisek, J.P., & Hanson, J. (1990). Dual-energy x-ray absorptiometry for total-body and regional bone-mineral and soft-tissue composition. *American Journal of Clinical Nutrition, 51*, 1106-1112.

Mazess, R.B., Cameron, J.R., & Miller, H. (1972). Direct readout of bone mineral content using radiomuclide absorptiometry. *International Journal of Applied Radiation Isotopes, 23*, 471-479.

Mazess, R.B., Cameron, J.R., & Sorenson, J.A. (1970). Determining body composition by radiation absorption spectrometry. *Nature, 228*, 771-772.

Mazess, R., Collick, B., Trempe, J., et al. (1989). Performance evaluation of a dual-energy x-ray bone densitometer. *Calcified Tissue International*, **44**, 228-232.

Mazess, R.B., Peppler, W.W., Chestnut, C.H., III, et al. (1981). Total body bone mineral and lean body mass by dual-photon absorptiometry, II: Comparison with total body calcium by neutron activation analysis. *Calcified Tissue International*, **33**, 361-363.

Mazess, R.B., Peppler, W.W., & Gibbons, M. (1984). Total body composition by dual-photon (153Gd) absorptiometry. *American Journal of Clinical Nutrition*, **40**, 834-839.

Mazess, R.B., Trempe, J.A., Bisek, J.P., et al. (1991). Calibration of dual-energy x-ray absorptiometry for bone density. *Journal of Bone and Mineral Research*, **6**, 799-806.

Milliken, L.A., Going, S.B., & Lohman, T.G. (1994). Accuracy of the Lunar dual-energy x-ray absorptiometer when packets of lard, water, and lean meat are placed upon human subjects. (Submitted for publication).

Nelson, D., Feingold, M., Mascha, E., & Kleerekoper, M. (1992). Comparison of single-photon and dual-energy x-ray absorptiometry of the radius. *Bone Mineral*, **18**, 77-83.

Nieves, J.W., Cosman, F., Mars, C., & Lindsay, R. (1992). Comparative assessment of bone mineral density of the forearm single-photon dual x-ray absorptiometry. *Calcified Tissue International*, **51**, 352-355.

Nord, R.H., & Payne, R.K. (1995a). DXA vs. underwater weighing: Comparison of strengths and weaknesses. *Asia Pacific Journal of Clinical Nutrition*, **4**, 173-175.

Nord, R.H., & Payne, R.K. (1995b). A new equation for converting body density to percent fat. *Asia Pacific Journal of Clinical Nutrition*, **4**, 177-179.

Nord, R.H., & Payne, R.K. (1995c). Body composition by DXA: A review of technology. *Asia Pacific Journal of Clinical Nutrition*, **4**, 167-171.

Nuti, R., Martine, G., Richi, G., et al. (1991). Comparison of total body measurements by dual-energy x-ray absorptiometry and dual-photon absorptiometry. *Journal of Bone and Mineral Research*, **6**, 681-687.

Peppler, W.W., & Mazess, R.B. (1981). Total body bone mineral and lean body mass by dual-photon absorptiometry, I: Theory and measurement procedure. *Calcified Tissue International*, **33**, 353-359.

Roubenoff, R., Kehayias, J.J., Dawson-Hughes, B., & Heymsfield, S.B. (1993). Use of dual-energy x-ray absorptiometry in body composition studies: Not yet a "gold standard." *American Journal of Clinical Nutrition*, **58**, 589-591.

Russell-Aulet, M., Wang, J., Thornton, J., & Pierson, R.N., Jr. (1991). Comparison of dual-photon absorptiometry systems for total body bone and soft tissue measurements: Dual-energy x-rays versus Gadolinium153. *Journal of Bone Mineral Research*, **6**, 411-415.

Schlemmer, A., Hassager, C., Haarbo, J., & Christiansen, C. (1990). Direct measurement of abdominal fat by dual photon absorptiometry. *International Journal of Obesity*, **14**, 603-611.

Snead, D.B., Birge, S.J., & Kohrt, W.M. (1993). Age-related differences in body composition by hydrodensitometry and dual-energy x-ray absorptiometry. *Journal of Applied Physiology*, **74**, 770-775.

Svendsen, O.L., Haarbo, J., Hassager, C., & Christiansen, C. (1993a). Accuracy of measurements of total-body soft-tissue composition by dual energy x-ray absorptiometry in vivo. *American Journal of Clinical Nutrition*, **57**, 605-608.

Svendsen, O.L., Haarbo, J., Hassager, C., & Christiansen, C. (1993b). Accuracy of measurements of total-body soft-tissue composition by dual energy x-ray absorptiometry in vivo. In K.J. Ellis & J.D. Eastman (Eds.), *Human body composition* (pp. 381-383). New York: Plenum.

Svendsen, O.L., Hassager, C., Bergmann, I., & Christiansen, C. (1993c). Measurement of abdominal and intra-abdominal fat in postmenopausal women by dual-energy x-ray absorptiometry and anthropometry: Comparison with computerized tomography. *International Journal of Obesity*, **17**, 45-51.

Svendsen, O.L., Hassager, C., & Christiansen, C. (1993d). Effect of an energy-restrictive diet, with or without exercise, on lean tissue mass, resting metabolic rate, cardiovascular risk factors, and bone in overweight postmenopausal women. *American Journal of Medicine*, **95**, 131-140.

Tothill, P., & Avenell, A. (1994). Errors in dual-energy x-ray absorptiometry of the lumbar spine owing to fat distribution and soft tissue thickness during weight change. *British Journal of Radiology*, **67**, 71-75.

Van Loan, M.D., Thompson, J., Butterfield, G., et al. (1994). Comparison of bone mineral content (BMC), bone mineral density, lean and fat measurements from two different bone densitometers. *Medicine and Science in Sports and Exercise*, **26**, S40.

Wang, J., Heymsfield, S. B., Aulet, M., et al. (1989). Body fat from body density: Underwater weighing vs. dual-photon absorptiometry. *American Journal of Physiology*, **256**, E829-E834.

Wellens, R., Chumlea, W.C., Guo, S., et al. (1994). Body composition in white adults by dual-energy x-ray absorptiometry, densitometry, and total body water. *American Journal of Clinical Nutrition*, **59**, 547-555.

Wilson, C.R., Collier, B.D., Carrera, G.F., & Jacobson, D.R. (1990). Acronym for dual-energy x-ray absorptiometry. *Radiology*, **176**, 875.

Witt, R.M., & Mazess, R.B. (1978). Photon absorptiometry of soft-tissue and fluid content: The method and its precision and accuracy. *Physical Medicinal Biology*, **23**, 620-629.

5

Electrical Impedance and Total Body Electrical Conductivity

Richard N. Baumgartner

In the last decade, the use of bioelectric impedance and conductivity methods for the prediction of body composition has grown rapidly. Bioelectric impedance is now regarded as either a substitute or supplement to conventional anthropometry in field studies. A variety of approaches has been developed, including bipolar and tetrapolar electrode, single and multifrequency, whole body and segmental methods. As the use of bioelectric impedance becomes more widespread, other approaches are likely to develop. Two conferences have been held recently with the goal of standardizing methods. The use of total body electrical conductivity (TOBEC) has been more limited, due to the high cost and cumbersome equipment. Presently, TOBEC is rarely used outside of clinical pediatric and small animal studies.

Electrical Impedance

Although studies of the conduction of electrical currents in biological tissues date to the turn of the century, the specific use of electrical impedance to quantify various aspects of body composition is relatively recent (Baumgartner et al, 1991; Kushner, 1992). Nyboer's monograph in 1959 on the use of bioelectric impedance to study various aspects of human physiology such as blood flow stimulated several other investigators to explore its use in quantifying body composition. A French physiologist, A.J. Thomasset, first demonstrated that total body water could be estimated from whole body impedance with a fixed-frequency, alternating electric current using a two-needle electrode approach in 1962. Thomasset and his associates later demonstrated the use of impedance measurements at different frequencies for separating extracellular fluid from total body water (Ducrot et al., 1970; Jenin et al., 1975). Hoffer and associates showed that a technique with four surface electrodes, adapted from blood flow studies, could be used to estimate total body water also (Hoffer et al., 1969). This approach was subsequently extended by Nyboer to estimating fat-free mass and percent body fat (1981).

Much of the early work using bioelectric impedance was limited by technological problems. While there was a variety of devices for research purposes, commercially available, affordable single-frequency bioelectric impedance devices for body composition analysis were first introduced in the mid-1980s by RJL, Inc. (Detroit, MI). Several investigators evaluated the RJL device for estimating total body water, fat-free mass, body cell mass, and percent body fat (Guo et al., 1987; Kushner & Schoeller, 1986; Lukaski, Johnson, Bolunchuk, & Lykken, 1985; McDougall & Shizgall, 1986; Segal et al., 1985). Other manufacturers subsequently introduced bioelectric impedance devices for body composition analysis (see appendix). A large volume of research followed on various technical, physiological, and environmental factors affecting bioelectric impedance body composition analysis (see Baumgartner et al., 1990). Lukaski and Bolonchuk (1988) showed that the resistance and reactance components of impedance could be used separately to estimate total body water and extracellular fluid, and Segal et al. (1991) used a three-frequency device to estimate separate body water components. Xitron Technologies (San Diego, CA) introduced the first commercially available, affordable, multifrequency instrument for body composition analysis in 1991.

Assumptions

The use of bioelectric impedance analysis (BIA) to estimate body composition is based on the different conductive and dielectric properties of various biological tissues at various frequencies of current. Tissues that contain a lot of water and electrolytes such as cerebrospinal fluid, blood, or muscle are highly conductive whereas fat, bone, and air-filled spaces such as lung are highly resistive or dielectric tissues. An applied electric current always follows the path of least resistance, and in the human body this will include extracellular fluid, blood, muscle, and other conductive tissues that comprise the majority of the fat-free mass. The volume of these tissues can be deduced from measurements of their combined resistances. A basic knowledge of electrophysiological theory is necessary for the appropriate application of the standard BIA single-frequency approach to body composition analysis. A more sophisticated understanding is needed for the more complex multifrequency method of analyzing body fluid distribution. Assumptions are made in both approaches that do not apply perfectly to the human body as a conductor, and it is important to understand these limitations when using BIA to estimate body composition. Ackmann

and Seitz (1984) provide a highly technical overview of the theory of conduction of electric currents in biological tissues and methods of bioelectric impedance measurement and analysis. Baumgartner et al. (1990) and Kushner (1992) provide reviews of how this theory relates specifically to body composition analysis. The following paragraphs present a simplified overview of the principles with a minimum of technical details.

Impedance (Z) is the frequency-dependent opposition of a conductor to the flow of an alternating electric current and is composed of two components, resistance (R) and reactance (Xc). Resistance is the pure opposition of the conductor to the flow of the current and is the reciprocal of conductance. Reactance is an additional "imaginary" opposition and is defined as the reciprocal of capacitance, or the storage of an electrical charge by a condenser for a brief moment in time. Impedance is defined as the square root of the sum of the squares of R and Xc, or $Z = (R^2 + Xc^2)^{1/2}$. Biological conductors contain both resistive and reactive elements. In the BIA literature, Z and R are often used interchangeably because Xc is ordinarily very small relative to Z (< 4%). In certain contexts, however, the role of Xc, and consequently the distinction between Z and R, is very important. This is particularly true for multifrequency BIA analysis.

The resistance between any two points in a conductor is defined by Ohm's Law as $R = E/I$, where E is the potential difference in volts between the two points, I is the current in amperes, and R is measured in volts per ampere, or *ohms* (Ω). For a cylindrical, isotropic conductor such as a wire, R is directly proportional to its length (L, cm) and inversely proportional to its cross-sectional area (A, cm²), or $R = \rho L/A$, where ρ (ohm · cm) is a proportionality constant known as the *specific resistivity* and is the reciprocal of conductivity. Since volume (V) equals L × A, algebraic rearrangement shows that $V = \rho L^2/R$. Hence, the volume of a conductor can be deduced from measurements of its length and resistance. Electrical conduction in biological tissues is mainly ionic: that is, electric charges are transferred between ionized salts, bases, and acids dissolved in the body fluids (Ackmann and Seitz, 1984; Kushner, 1992). Thus, in a biological ionic conductor, specific resistivity is directly proportional to fluid volume (V) and inversely proportional to the number of free, electrolytic ions (N_e), or $\rho = kV/N_e$ (Khaled et al., 1988). Resistivity is inversely related to temperature also (Geddes & Baker, 1967). In sum, changes in volume, "geometry" (L/A), electrolyte concentration (N_e/V), or body temperature can alter bioelectric resistance. When an alternating current is used, impedance is inversely related to frequency. Over the range of frequencies used in BIA (e.g., 5 kHz to 1 MHz), this relationship can be described by a negative logarithmic function and is attributed to the appearance and disappearance of capacitative effects as the frequency increases. This phenomenon is referred to as "β-dispersion" or the "structural relaxation" of tissues following excitation by the applied current (Kanai et al., 1987).

A capacitor in a circuit conducting an alternating electric current stores some of the electric charge for a brief moment in time and causes the sinusoidal signal for the voltage to be out of phase with that for the current. Specifically, the voltage is said to *lag* behind the current. Because reactance is defined as the reciprocal of capacitance, this *phase shift* can be quantified geometrically as the arc tangent of the ratio of reactance to the resistance (arctan(Xc/R)), or the *phase angle* (ϕ), which can range from zero to 90 degrees. If the circuit is purely resistive, ϕ will equal zero; if it is purely capacitive, ϕ will equal 90 degrees. In the human body ϕ varies generally between 8 and 15 degrees (Baumgartner et al., 1988). Most BIA analyzers are equipped with systems that measure resistance and the amount of phase shift or angle in a conductor due to capacitative effects, and these measurements are used to compute reactance and impedance. Like resistance, reactance is quantified in ohms and is frequency-dependent. The different relationships of resistance and reactance to frequency are illustrated in Figure 5.1.

Capacitance or reactance in biological conductors may be associated with a variety of charge-storage or polarization processes. The dominant mechanism, over the range of frequencies used in BIA, is most likely to be *interfacial polarization* (Ackmann and Seitz, 1984). Interfacial polarization occurs in heterogeneous materials in which discrete regions of highly conductive material are separated by regions of low conductivity. A simple biological model would consist of cells suspended in extracellular fluid. The highly conductive intracellular and extracellular materials are separated by cell membranes that consist of insulating layers of polar proteins and lipids. Thus, in biological conductors, cell membranes, and probably tissue interfaces, act as capacitors and produce reactance.

Beginning with the work of Fricke (1925), a variety of "circuit-equivalent models" have been developed to describe the nature of electrical conduction and capacitance in biological tissues

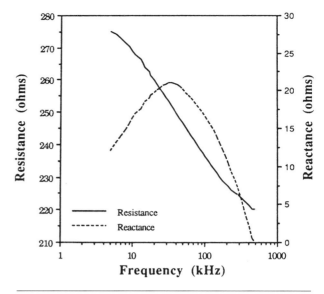

Figure 5.1 Whole-body resistances and reactances over frequencies of current from 5 to 500 kHz in a white, elderly male.

(Ackmann and Seitz, 1984). A commonly accepted, simplified model is shown in Figure 5.2. The tissue is modeled minimally in terms of two parallel conductive paths. The resistances Re and Ri represent the resistances of extracellular and intracellular compartments, respectively. The capacitive effect of the cell membrane is indicated by Cm. A somewhat more realistic model would include Re with a large number of interconnected parallel Ri-Cm elements representing all the cells within the conductive pathway (Cole and Cole, 1941; Kanai et al., 1987). Because cells vary in size, orientation, and concentration within various tissues and because cell membranes are imperfect capacitors, the intracellular resistance and capacitance values in this model are distributed continuously with mean and variance values (Cornish, Thomas, & Ward, 1993; Kanai et al., 1987; Pethig, 1979). This model is important for understanding the basic bioelectric behavior of the body when fluid and electrolyte shifts occur between intra- and extracellular compartments and/or the frequency of the alternating current is varied, and the model is considered essential for the proper application and interpretation of BIA in body composition analysis.

The complex relationships among R, Xc, Z, and ϕ for the simplified, biological circuit-equivalent model when the frequency of current is varied are shown in Figure 5.3. In this *impedance locus plot*, Resistance (R) is shown on the abscissa and Reactance (Xc) on the ordinate. Impedance (Z) is defined by the vector from the origin to points along

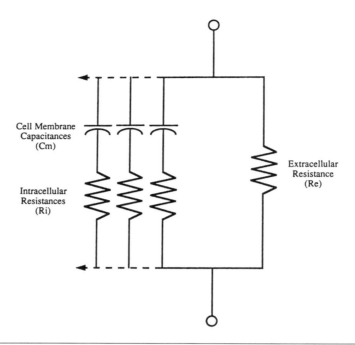

Figure 5.2 A circuit-equivalent model for conduction of an alternating electric current in a suspension of cells in extracellular fluid matrix; a series of parallel capacitor-resistor (Cm-Ri) circuits for multiple cells is shown.

the semicircle that is described by changes in Xc relative to R as the frequency of the current is varied. At low frequencies, cell membranes completely block the flow of the current through the intracellular pathway and there is no measurable reactance. The measured impedance is therefore purely resistive and represents that of the extracellular compartment only (i.e., Re). As the frequency is increased, the electric charge is transmitted increasingly across the cell membranes following a capacitive time delay and Xc increases in proportion to R. In other words, phase angle (ϕ) increases as the capacitive effects of the cell membranes cause the voltage to lag increasingly behind the current. Reactance and phase angle increase up to maximum values at a *characteristic frequency* (ω_c) above which they decrease as the capacitive effects of the cell membranes are increasingly short-circuited at higher frequencies. At very high frequencies the impedance is again purely resistive and reflects the combined resistances of both the extracellular (Re) and intracellular (Ri) media. More detailed, technical presentations of the impedance locus plot shown in Figure 5.3 and of the underlying mathematical relationships among Z, R, and Xc as the frequency of the current is varied can be found in Ackmann and Seitz (1984) and in Cornish, Thomas, and Ward (1993).

The preceding paragraphs have presented a basic background against which some of the underlying assumptions of the single-frequency BIA approach to body composition analysis can be addressed, as well as to help explain the newer multifrequency approach that is referred to increasingly as bioelectric impedance *spectroscopy* (BIS). The single-frequency BIA approach is based on the assumption that the relationship $V = \rho L^2 / R$ is applicable to the human body. The conventional approach is to measure "whole body" resistance or impedance between the wrist and the ipsilateral ankle and to use stature (S) as an index of the length of the conductor. Thus, S^2/R or S^2/Z is the basic variable used in BIA equations for predicting total body water or fat-free mass. Several limitations to this assumption are immediately apparent. Geometrically, the body is not a cylinder with uniform cross-sectional area but is better represented as five cylinders (two arms, two legs, and a trunk) connected in series that have large differences in their cross-sectional areas. When such a set of conductors is connected in series, the conductor with the smallest cross-sectional area (i.e., the arm) will determine most of the resistance of the series. Thus, whereas an arm is about 4% and a leg about 17% of body weight, they account for about 47% and 50%, respectively, of whole-body resistance: conversely, the trunk comprises about 46% of body weight but may have little if any influence on whole body resistance when measured conventionally from the right ankle to the right wrist

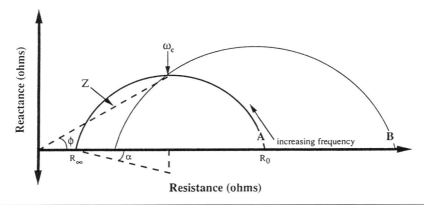

Figure 5.3 Impedance locus plot. Reactance increases with increasing frequency as resistance decreases to a characteristic frequency (ω_c) after which reactance decreases. At low frequencies, the measured resistance (R_0) is mainly determined by extracellular fluid. At high frequencies, R_∞ is a combination of intracellular and extracellular resistivities. Impedance (Z) is the vector described by changes in reactance relative to resistance. Phase angle (ϕ) and depression angle (α) are shown. Curve A represents the impedance locus found for normal volume and ionic equilibrium. Curve B illustrates the change that may occur when extracellular volume is increased or, conversely, ionic concentration is decreased (see Sasser, Gerth, & Wu, 1993).

(Baumgartner, Chumlea, & Roche, 1989; Patterson, Ranganathan, Engel, & Berkseth, 1988).

Differences in the structure as well as the relative proportions of the trunk versus the limbs also affect the conduction of the current. The relationship $V = \rho L^2/R$ assumes that the conduction of the current within the volume is isotropic so that the measurement of resistance will be the same regardless of direction. This clearly is not true in the human body, which is highly anisotropic. Skeletal muscle is composed of elongated fibers, and resistance measured transversely to the fiber direction is considerably greater than resistance measured longitudinally (Rush, Abildskov, & McFee, 1963). Skeletal muscle fibers generally run parallel to the long axis in the limbs, but the trunk contains muscles that are oriented in a variety of directions as well as organs, lungs, and adipose tissue deposits. Whereas the specific resistivity (ρ) of the limbs can be modeled crudely in terms of concentric cylinders of fat, muscle, and bone, such a model is not possible for the trunk, for which the specific resistivities are 2 to 3 times more variable (Baumgartner et al., 1990; Chumlea, Baumgartner, & Guo, 1993a; Chumlea, Baumgartner, & Roche, 1988; Rush, Abildskov, & McFee, 1963). Fuller and Elia (1989) found that the specific resistivity of the trunk was significantly greater in obese than nonobese subjects. Chumlea et al. (1993a) also reported that the specific resistivity for the trunk was correlated significantly with body fatness even after adjustment for proportional differences in size between the trunk and the limbs. In sum, several

studies suggest that relative differences among individuals in the proportions and structure of the body segments, including the size and orientation of muscle fibers as well as presumed dielectric bodies such as lung and intra-abdominal fat, result in varying amounts of anisotropy and effects on specific resistivities. As a result, the assumption that whole-body resistance is linearly related to the conductive volume and its electrolyte concentration may not be strictly true. Notably, some have reported that BIA predicts fat-free mass less well at the extremes of body fatness (Gray, Bray, Gemayel, & Kaplan, 1989; Hodgdon & Fitzgerald, 1987; Segal et al., 1988).

Nonetheless, S^2/R has been shown empirically to be correlated highly ($rs > 0.90$) and consistently across groups with total body water and fat-free mass (Baumgartner et al., 1990; Cordain, Whicker, & Johnson, 1988; Kushner, Schoeller, Fjeld, & Danford, 1992). The coefficient of variation (CV) among the slopes of regressions of total body water on S^2/R reported by Kushner (1992) for five independent studies is 5.4%. For slopes of regressions of fat-free mass on S^2/R, the CV for seven independent studies reported by Kushner (1992) is about 3%. These low CVs indicate very similar findings for relationships between total body water and fat-free mass and S^2/R by a variety of investigators and support the empirical stability of the method. It is important to note that correlations for total body water and fat-free mass with S^2/R are only marginally better than those obtained when using arm length^2/arm resistance (Baumgartner et al., 1989). Thus, the prediction of total body water or fat-free mass using the conventional "whole body" BIA approach is dependent to a large extent on their strong associations with the mass and bioelectric characteristics of the appendicular skeletal muscle.

This does not mean that the trunk has no importance in BIA body composition analysis. Individuals who deviate markedly from the norm for the size of the trunk in proportion to the limbs are more likely to have erroneous estimates. This might explain the reported improvement in prediction associated with proximal electrode placements that reduce the influence of the distal parts of the limbs (Lukaski, 1993). Impedance measurements of the trunk alone have been shown to have value in relation to fluid distribution and body composition. Trunk reactance increases disproportionately to resistance in patients undergoing treatment with diuretics or dialysis, presumably due to fluid and electrolyte shifts and changes in cell membrane properties affecting capacitance (Spence, Baliga, Nyboer, & Bhatia, 1979; Subramanyan, Manchanda, Nyboer, & Bhatia, 1980). The result was a significant increase in the phase angle for the trunk. In contrast, investigators using whole-body measurements have reported generally that single-frequency BIA is insensitive to fluid changes in the trunk associated with peritoneal dialysis or paracentesis (Guglielmi et al., 1991; Kurtin, Shapiro, Tomita, & Raisman, 1990; Zillikens, van den Berg, Wilson, & Swart, 1992). Kushner (1992) suggested that segmental methods (trunk measurements in particular) might be preferred for detecting changes in thoracic and abdominal fluid volumes as occur in congestive heart failure, ascites, or peritoneal dialysis.

Studies of changes in body composition during weight loss have relied exclusively on whole-body measurements and have generally indicated a limited ability to quantify changes accurately (Deurenberg, Weststrate, & Hautvast, 1989c; Deurenberg, Weststrate, & van der Kooy, 1989d; Gray, 1988; Kushner et al., 1990; Paijmans, Wilmore, & Wilmore, 1992; Ross, Leger, Martin, & Roche, 1989; van der Kooy et al., 1992; Vazquez & Janosky, 1991). The underlying assumptions in these studies are: (1) that the weight loss will consist of fairly predictable losses in fat-free relative to fat components, (2) body fluid distribution will not change, and (3) the changes will be distributed proportionately between the trunk and the limbs. The ability of the whole-body BIA technique to detect changes may be limited in part by the validity of these assumptions (van der Kooy et al.). Baumgartner et al. (1988) showed that the

phase angle for the trunk was significantly lower in obese than non-obese individuals and correlated significantly with percent body fat, suggesting that obese subjects have more extracellular water in the trunk than leaner subjects. If so, the whole body method may be insensitive to short-term changes in body composition during weight loss in obese patients, if these are associated largely with fluid loss from the trunk. Patterson and associates (1988) suggested that combined segmental measurements could track changes in body composition with weight loss better than whole-body measurements. The benefit, however, could depend on whether the type of obesity or fat distribution is associated with regional differences in fat-free mass or fluid distribution.

Most single frequency BIA analyzers operate at a frequency of 50 kHz. This frequency was chosen partly for engineering and safety considerations but also because it represents the mean characteristic frequency of muscle tissue (Geddes & Baker, 1967; Settle, Foster, Epstein, & Mullen, 1980). Muscle characteristic frequencies (ω_m), however, may range widely among individuals from 30 to more than 100 kHz (Baumgartner, unpublished data; Cornish et al., 1993; Geddes & Baker, 1967). This has led some investigators to question whether the current is conducted completely by the intracellular path in some individuals when a 50 kHz frequency is used (Baumgartner et al., 1990; Cornish et al.; Deurenberg, 1993; Settle et al.). In other words, body composition may be estimated with greater error in individuals who deviate significantly from the assumed mean value for ω_m. Variation in ω_m may depend on a variety of factors, but it is likely that the ratio of extracellular fluid (ECF) to intracellular fluid (ICF) has the greatest impact (Deurenberg, 1993; Deurenberg & Schouten, 1992). Variations in ECF/ICF within and between individuals may explain, in part, the observed sex and age differences in the associations of body composition and impedance and the inability to predict changes in obese or sick individuals with abnormal ECF/ICF ratios when using measurements at 50 kHz.

Cornish et al. (1993) reported that the use of impedance measured for each individual's muscle characteristic frequency in the denominator of the impedance-volume index (i.e., $S^2/Z\omega_m$) improved significantly the estimation of total body water in rats. This suggests that impedance analyzers can be "tuned" to the frequencies that optimally predict body composition in individuals. Similar results, however, have not been reported from studies of human beings. A simplified approach would be to use an arbitrary high frequency for which impedance measurements are not confounded by differences among individuals for maximum reactance or characteristic frequency (e.g., 250 kHz). A few recent studies have reported that the use of high frequency impedance measurements does not improve significantly the prediction of body composition in human beings compared to impedance at 50 kHz (Chumlea, Guo, Baumgartner, & Siervogel, 1993b; Deurenberg et al., 1994; Deurenberg & Schouten, 1992). Experimental studies with animals indicate that the size as well as the location of the frequency-dependent impedance plot changes with alterations in fluid volume and electrolyte balance between intracellular and extracellular spaces (Sasser et al., 1993). Specifically, perfusion with a hypotonic solution shifts the impedance locus curve to the right (see Figure 5.3), increases reactance relative to resistance, and greatly decreases the characteristic frequency at which reactance and phase angle are at their maxima. Kanai et al. (1987) reported similar findings for men following exercise-induced dehydration. These studies suggest that the changes in impedance due to changes in fluid or hydration status are more complex than they appear using the single-frequency approach.

Applicability

The bioelectric impedance method of estimating body composition is best suited to epidemiologic studies. In this context it can improve population estimates of obesity and can be used to supplement other field methods in assessing levels of protein-energy malnutrition (Deurenberg, Smit, & Kusters, 1989a; Vettorazzi et al., 1989). Various aspects of measurement standardization and choice of predictive equations, however, must be observed carefully (Baumgartner et al., 1990; Roche & Guo, 1993). BIA can be used also in clinical settings to quantify body composition (Pullicino, Coward, Stubbs, & Elia, 1990; Tagliabue et al., 1992). The accuracy of the estimated variables in this context is complicated by factors that may produce shifts in body fluids or electrolytes (Deurenberg, 1993; Gleichauf & Roe, 1989). The ability of BIA to detect small changes in body composition has practical limitations as well (Deurenberg et al., 1989c, 1989d; Forbes, Simon, & Amatruda, 1992; Gray, 1988; Kushner et al., 1990; Ross et al., 1989; van der Kooy et al., 1992). New techniques are being developed using multifrequency impedance that could allow

rapid qualitative rather than quantitative assessments of abnormalities in fluid distribution or electrolyte concentrations that may have considerable clinical utility (Deurenberg, et al., 1993; DeVries, 1993; Sasser et al., 1993).

The BIA method is applicable technically to all subjects regardless of age, sex, ethnicity, or health status. Although some authors have reported its use with neonatal patients (Mayfield, Vauy, & Waidelich, 1991), there may be some question as to whether impedance is measured reliably or accurately in this application (Gartner et al., 1993). In very small subjects, it is possible technically for the electrodes to be spaced too close together and cause either electrode polarization or surface conduction. In the tetrapolar technique, the paired source and receiving electrodes must be separated by at least 5 cm to avoid interaction. Barillas-Mury, Vettorazzi, Molina, and Pineda (1987) were able to separate the electrodes sufficiently to stabilize the measurement of resistance on the feet but not the hands of children aged 3 to 10 years. The uniformity of the electrical field or "current density distribution" within the body, and therefore the accuracy of the measurement of impedance, increases theoretically with the ratio of length to cross-sectional area (L/A) when surface spot-electrodes are used (Baker, 1987). If the source electrodes are too close, the electrical field will be nonuniform and the measurement of impedance can be distorted. The source electrodes in the tetrapolar technique must be separated by a sufficient distance for deep conduction of the current also. Neonatal subjects have a low L/A compared to older children or adults; thus, impedance measurements could be somewhat less accurate. Segmental measurements of neonates may not be possible using conventional surface electrodes. Most experimental studies with small animals report the use of needle electrodes (Cornish et al., 1993; Sasser et al., 1993). Rapid changes in body fluids occur in newborn infants that may confound BIA and are different in those who are small versus those appropriate for gestational age (Gartner et al., 1993). In adults, another possible physical limitation to accurate impedance measurements could be extreme obesity (Gray et al., 1989). The potential insulating effect of a thick layer of subcutaneous fat on deep conduction of the current and accurate measurement of impedance in obese subjects has not been examined.

The main limitation to the general applicability of BIA is the availability of appropriately calibrated, cross-validated predictive equations. It is most important to make a careful selection of equations that were developed from a sample that is similar in age, sex, ethnicity, and health status to the subjects under study (Baumgartner et al., 1990; Deurenberg et al., 1989a; Roche & Guo, 1993). As noted, resistance is inversely proportional to the volume of total body water and the concentration of free electrolytes. Thus, factors that affect the distribution of fluids and electrolyte concentrations between intra- and extracellular compartments can be expected to affect resistance (Deurenberg, 1993). Because these changes affect cell membrane permeability also, they will affect the reactive component of impedance. Thus, it may be useful to select equations that include reactance as a predictor variable if abnormalities in fluid distribution are expected to be prevalent in the sample under study (Baumgartner et al., 1990). Most published equations for predicting total body water have been developed from healthy subjects who can be assumed to be in normal fluid and electrolyte equilibrium. These equations may produce unpredictable errors when applied to sick patients who are in abnormal or rapidly changing states of fluid and electrolyte balance. Similarly, factors that have acute, temporary effects on fluid and electrolyte equilibrium in healthy subjects, such as exercise, need to be controlled or significant errors may result. Pregnancy and menstruation may affect fluid balance and the accuracy of BIA predictions of body composition also (Gleichauf & Roe, 1989). Children and elderly adults are reported to have systematically increased amounts of extracellular fluid, relative to intracellular fluid, compared to young and middle-aged adults (Moore et al., 1963). Whether or not this results in significant error when BIA equations for predicting total body water in young and middle-aged adults are applied to these age groups has been not been studied. Until this issue is resolved, the use of equations for predicting total body water that are specific to children or elderly adults are recommended (Baumgartner et al., 1991; Deurenberg, Kusters, & Smit, 1990a; Deurenberg, van der Kooy, Evers, & Hulshof, 1990b; Guo, Roche, & Houtkooper, 1990).

The prediction of fat-free mass using BIA is subject to additional complications that may limit applicability over and above those noted so far. The most important is considered to be variation in the concentration of water within the fat-free mass, or the ratio of total body water to fat-free mass (TBW/FFM). In normal, healthy adults this ratio is generally considered to average about 0.732 with a fairly narrow range of variation from 0.69 to 0.77 (Streat,

Beddoe, & Hill, 1985). Although small, this variability in TBW/FFM, or "hydration," will increase the error of prediction of FFM using BIA. Results from studies of normal healthy adults in whom both total body water and fat-free mass were measured by independent methods help to illustrate this point. Lukaski et al. (1985) estimated fat-free mass by hydrodensitometry and total body water by deuterium dilution in 37 healthy men aged 28.8 ± 7.1 years. The regression of total body water on S^2/R resulted in the regression equation $y = 2.03 + 0.63 \times S^2/R$ with a standard error of estimate of 2.08 kg total body water. If one divides the slope of this equation by the normally assumed TBW/FFM ratio, or 0.63/0.732, the result, 0.86, could be considered the expected slope for the regression of FFM on S^2/R if hydration did not vary among subjects. The actual regression equation found for FFM was $y = 3.04 + 0.85 \times S^2/R$ with a standard error of estimate of 2.61 kg. Clearly, in this sample of healthy young men the mean TBW/FFM was very close to the expected value with a narrow range of variation resulting in only a small increase in the error of prediction of FFM compared to TBW. This situation, however, cannot be assumed to hold for samples including children, women, the elderly, or sick patients who may have different mean levels as well as greater variability for TBW/FFM. Equations that are specific for these groups are recommended. The inclusion of additional predictors such as age, sex, body circumferences, or weight in these equations may indirectly account for some of the variation in TBW/FFM, as well as in body shape or "geometry," and improve prediction accuracy. Some equations have been calibrated against estimates from multicompartmental models that control for variation in the composition of the fat-free mass (Baumgartner et al., 1991; Guo et al., 1990). These are recommended for groups for which the mean TBW/FFM is believed to differ systematically from the assumed normal adult value, as in children or the elderly. Studies of the effects of alterations in fluid distribution, hydration, and other physiologic factors on the reliability and accuracy of the BIA method are reviewed in greater detail later in this chapter.

Equipment

All BIA devices consist essentially of: (1) an alternating electrical current source, (2) cables and electrodes for introducing the current into the body and for sensing the voltage drop due to impedance, and (3) a system for measuring impedance and, optionally, the phase shift due to capacitance. Two very different approaches have been used: two-electrode and four-electrode techniques. Each approach has specific advantages and disadvantages. Ackmann and Seitz (1984) discuss these from a highly technical perspective; Boulier, Fricker, Thomasset, and Apfelbaum (1990) provide a simplified overview.

In the two-electrode bridge technique, the electrodes that sense the voltage drop are the same as those that introduce the current. The main advantages of this approach are that highly accurate measurements can be obtained with a very low amplitude current and that electromagnetic leakage toward nearby metallic objects is minimal. There are two major disadvantages to this method. First, the impedance measured reflects both the impedance of the body as well as that due to electrode polarization, which may be high at low frequencies (Ackmann and Seitz, 1984). Various approaches have been developed to overcome this problem, which has been suspected of causing nonreproducible total impedance measurements (Boulier et al., 1990; Settle et al., 1980). Second, needle electrodes must be used to avoid the high impedance of the skin. These must be inserted subcutaneously in a standardized fashion and may result in minor pain and local tissue trauma that reduce both the acceptability and the accuracy of the impedance measurements. In addition, it is difficult to determine reproducibility in vivo when using needle electrodes since repeated insertion increases the risk of tissue trauma. Moreover, segmental measurements are difficult to make using needle electrodes, especially of the trunk, due to absence of acceptable insertion sites. The two-electrode approach was perfected by Thomasset (1962), who demonstrated its use for quantifying fluid distribution (Jenin et al., 1975). Boulier et al. reported the use of a two-electrode device to predict fat-free mass. This device (IMP BO 1, l'Impulsion, Caën, France) measures impedance with a 50 μA alternating current at 5 kHz and 1 MHz.

The four surface-electrode technique overcomes the main disadvantages of the two-electrode approach (Ackmann and Seitz, 1984; Lukaski, 1991). In this method, the current is applied with one pair of electrodes located distally while a second pair located proximally measures the electrical potential across a segment of the conductor (Figure 5.4). Because the electrodes that inject the current are separate from those that detect the potential, impedance due to electrode polarization can be eliminated. The use of spot or band electrodes that are attached to the surface of the skin, rather than

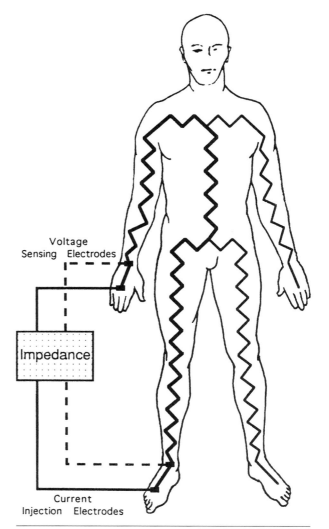

Figure 5.4 Standard placement of electrodes for whole-body impedance measurements.

penetrating it, avoids problems associated with pain and tissue trauma. The high cutaneous impedance is overcome by using currents with higher amplitudes (500 μA to 1 mA). The two main disadvantages are considered to be the control of stray capacitances produced by the paired wires and electromagnetic leakage to external metallic objects when very high frequencies of current are used (Boulier et al., 1990).

A variety of single frequency, four-electrode BIA devices are commercially available. (A listing of manufacturers is provided in the appendix). Most operate at a fixed frequency of 50 kHz but at different amplitudes of current. The two most commonly used single-frequency devices are the RJL BIA 101, which operates at 800 μA, and the Valhalla 1990B, which operates at 500 μA. Both devices use phase-sensitive detectors and provide separate measurements of resistance and reactance. When using these instruments to predict body composition, it is most important to select the device that was used in the development of the predictive equation to be applied (Deurenberg et al., 1989a; Graves et al., 1989). Cables and electrodes are carefully tuned to particular devices by the manufacturers to minimize stray capacitances and should not be interchanged between different brands or models.

There are currently few choices of commercially available multifrequency BIS devices. The Xitron 4000 (Xitron Technologies, San Diego, CA) is the only one for which studies of human beings have been reported (Deurenberg et al., 1994; Deurenberg & Schouten, 1992; Van Loan & Mayclin, 1992). The Xitron 4000 multifrequency analyzer uses a tetrapolar surface electrode arrangement with phase-sensitive electronics to measure impedance to a nominal 250 µA current over frequencies from 1 kHz to 1.35 MHz (or 5 kHz to 1 MHz with the 4000B model). Several different options are available for selecting up to 50 frequencies randomly or nonrandomly at either arithmetically or logarithmically spaced intervals, and the instrument can monitor changes in impedance over time at either one or two frequencies.

Segal et al. (1991) reported the use of a three-frequency instrument (TVI-10) manufactured by Danninger Medical Technology (Columbus, OH), but this specially built device is not available commercially. Sasser et al. (1993) studied in vivo fluid shifts in rats using a Solartron 1260 impedance analyzer (Schlumberger Technologies, Farnborough, UK). The Solartron system uses a tetrapolar electrode arrangement, 500 mA current, and measures impedance at 25 discrete frequencies from 3.5 to 250 kHz. Cornish et al. (1993) reported the use of an instrument manufactured by SEAC (Brisbane, Australia) to measure impedance in rats. This tetrapolar device injects a 100 mA alternating current and measures impedance and phase at six frequencies from 1 to 100 kHz. Each of these systems requires a microcomputer and specialized software for analysis of the complex, spectral impedance data.

Measurement Procedures

It is very important to adhere to standardized measurement procedures when using BIA (Deurenberg, 1994). Bioelectric impedance is measured in a standard fashion while the subject lies supine on a flat, nonconductive bed, cot, or couch. (Hospital beds often have highly conductive metallic frames that can distort impedance measurements.) The arms are abducted slightly so that they do not touch the sides of the trunk. The legs are separated so that the ankles are at least 20 cm apart and, ideally, the thighs do not touch. Complete separation of the thighs may be difficult to attain in extremely obese subjects. The head should be flat against the bed or elevated minimally with a thin pillow. It is very important to adhere to this standard body positioning, which has been used in virtually all calibration studies, because deviations produce large differences in the measured impedance (Roos, Westendorp, Frölich, & Meinders, 1992). The subject may wear clothing, with the exception of shoes and socks, and must not wear metallic jewelry. Generally, care should be taken to ensure that the subject and the impedance analyzer are isolated from all metallic objects and other electronic devices by a distance of at least 50 cm. This is particularly important when measuring impedance at high frequencies using multifrequency devices.

For whole-body measurements of adults using the four-electrode technique, the electrodes are attached in the standard fashion to the dorsal surface of the hand and anterior surface of the ipsilateral foot. One voltage-sensing electrode is attached to the wrist midway between the styloid processes; the other is attached to the ankle midway between the malleoli. The electrodes for introducing the current (source electrodes) are attached to the foot and hand at least 5 cm distal to the sensing electrodes: generally on the third metatarso-phalangeal and third metacarpo-phalangeal joints, respectively. The skin should be lightly washed with alcohol before attaching the electrodes. The electrodes should have a surface area of at least 5 cm^2 to avoid effects of skin resistivity, especially when making measurements at frequencies less than 50 kHz. Spot or band electrodes may be used; those recommended by the manufacturer of the particular analyzer are preferred. The paired cables from the analyzer to the electrodes are usually color-coded (e.g., black for source and red for sensing) and cannot be crossed between the pairs of source and sensing electrodes on the hand and foot. Figure 5.4 illustrates the standard four-electrode placement. This standard arrangement applies regardless of whether single-frequency or multifrequency measurements are to be made.

Some alternative schemes for electrode placement have been suggested for the four-electrode technique. The side of the body to which the electrodes are attached does not usually have a significant effect on impedance measurements in healthy subjects. Subjects who have experienced stroke, trauma, or other factors that result in atrophy of one side of the body are obvious exceptions. The side of the body on which measurements are made should be clearly noted. Contralateral placement (e.g., right hand/left foot) results in a small effect (< 1.7%; Lukaski et al., 1985). Some recent studies have indicated that a more proximal placement of the sensing electrodes on the extremities increases the replicability of measurements, possibly because this arrangement is less sensitive to fluid redistribution in the distal limbs following movement from a standing to supine position (Gudivaka, Kushner, & Schoeller, 1993; Lukaski, 1993). A more proximal placement of the sensing electrodes may be necessary in infants and small children to ensure that the source and sensing electrodes are separated sufficiently to avoid interaction. A standardized method for the more proximal location of sensing electrodes has not yet been recognized. A tentatively recommended procedure would be to place the sensing electrodes over the soft tissue on the forearm at a point midway between the radial styloid process and the olecranon of the ulna and on the leg at a point midway between the lateral malleolus and the head of the fibula. Electrode placements for the separate measurement of the major body segments (arm, leg, trunk) have been described (Chumlea et al., 1988; Fuller & Elia, 1989), but a standardized procedure has not been recognized (Deurenberg, 1994). An exact description should be given of the landmarks and methods used to define electrode placements whenever nonstandard proximal or segmental measurements are made.

The two-electrode approach is used rarely outside of France, and methods of electrode placement and impedance measurement for it will not be discussed. In general, the two needle electrodes are inserted subcutaneously on the dorsal surface of the hand and anterior surface of the ipsilateral foot. A more thorough description can be found in Boulier et al. (1990).

Impedance measurements should be taken after a minimum 2 hour fast and at least 8 to 12 hours after any strenuous exercise, alcohol, or other factors that may alter hydration (Kushner, 1992). It is recommended that the stage of the menstrual cycle be recorded in longitudinal studies of premenopausal females (Deurenberg, 1994; Gleichauf & Roe, 1989), although some investigators have not found effects of menstruation on impedance measurements (Roche, Chumlea, & Guo, 1986). Although few studies have demonstrated significant effects, it is recommended that the subject void the bladder completely immediately prior to measurement. Room temperature should always be noted, but body temperature should be measured only if the subject appears to have a fever. The subject should not move during the measurement and respiration should be normal. To minimize changes in impedance due to gravity-induced fluid shifts in healthy subjects, it is recommended that impedance measurements be taken within 5 to 10 minutes after lying down (Gudivaka et al., 1993). For bedfast patients, measurements should be taken after the subject has been lying supine with the head at the same level as the feet for at least 45 to 60 minutes (Deurenberg, 1994).

Precision

The reliability of measurements of impedance, resistance, and reactance with most impedance analyzers is generally very high, although some exceptions have been noted (Deurenberg, van der Kooy, & Leenen, 1989b). The precision of most BIA instruments when measuring test objects is reported to be less than 0.5% (0.5 to 3 ohms) depending on frequency. Errors tend to increase at low (< 10 kHz) and very high (> 500 kHz) frequencies. Variations in the correct placement and replacement of the electrodes result in additional errors of up to 1% (Roche et al., 1986). Day to day variability in impedance in weight-stable subjects is reported to be 1 to 2% (3 to 10 ohms; Lukaski et al., 1985; Roche et al., 1986).

Careful standardization of procedures is necessary to reduce the effects of multiple factors that can decrease precision (Deurenberg, 1994). In healthy subjects, factors that can influence fluid status such as recent exercise, liquid intake, or stage of menstrual cycle should be controlled (see Baumgartner et al., 1990). Bioelectric impedance is temperature-dependent, and large variations within and between subjects in environmental and body temperature will affect the reproducibility and accuracy of the predicted values (Caton, Molé, Adams, & Heustis, 1988). Measurements should not be made in extremely hot or cold environments, and variations in ambient temperature should be minimized (e.g., ± 2 °C). It may be desirable to cover the subject with a light blanket if serial measurements are to be made over a time period longer than 10 minutes (Baumgartner et al., 1990). Impedance measurements will be reduced systematically in patients with fever. Recent strenuous exercise will decrease resistance also (Khaled et al., 1988). Body position has important effects.

Measurements should be taken with the subject lying supine on a nonconductive surface. The time spent lying supine before measurements are taken must be standardized, since gravitational effects result in movement of body fluids from the limbs toward the trunk and, perhaps, from extracellular to intracellular spaces. This fluid redistribution can change impedance measurements by 1 to 2% within the first 10 minutes and by 4 to 9% during 1 to 4 hours (Gudivaka et al., 1993). Abduction of the arms from the sides from 30 to 90° while the subject is recumbent alters the effective conductor length and can result in a 2% increase in resistance (Schell & Gross, 1987). Deep respiration can alter measurements of trunk impedance by 4 to 5% (Baumgartner et al., 1988).

Accuracy

The accuracy of body composition estimates provided by the BIA method depends on the accuracy and precision of the impedance measurements, the accuracy and precision of any additional variables recorded such as stature, weight, or body circumferences, and the appropriateness of the predictive equation selected for the sample or individual under study. The prediction errors reported for equations developed in various studies should be regarded as "ideal" or "minimum" errors. Actual errors are likely to be greater but will be unknown unless a cross-validation study is performed. The reported prediction errors for total body water range from 1.5 to 2.5 kg; for extracellular water, 1.0 to 1.5 kg; for fat-free mass, 2.0 to 3.5 kg; and for percent body fat, 3.5 to 5.0%. Selected published predictive equations are tabulated in Table 5.1 for TBW and Table 5.2 for FFM, with notations regarding sample composition (age, sex, ethnicity), methods used for calibration, expected prediction errors, and cross-validation. Table 5.3 shows equations published recently for predicting ECF as well as TBW using multifrequency methods. The use of these equations is recommended generally over those provided by the manufacturers of the various BIA instruments: Many of these equations are undocumented and most have not been cross-validated.

Several studies have examined the accuracy of estimated changes in body composition from BIA. Kushner (1992) reviewed several of these studies in relation to the detection of acute (within-day), short-term (1 to 2 days), and long-term (1+ week) changes and concluded that BIA was best suited for quantifying group changes and could only detect relatively large changes in individuals (e.g., 2 to 5 L TBW, or 8 to 10%), as would occur in either extreme or long-term interventions. If an intervention alters ECF/ICF significantly, the relationship of impedance to body composition will be altered (Deurenberg, 1993). Thus, the equation used to predict body composition at baseline may not be appropriate after intervention and the estimated change in body composition will be erroneous. To date, equations have not been reported in which change in body composition is the dependent variable. The detection of changes in fat-free mass or percent body fat is complicated additionally by their variability among individuals. Moreover, conventional criterion methods such as body density or total body water are subject to considerable error when used to estimate changes in fat or fat-free mass (van der Kooy et al., 1992). Some have argued that changes in impedance contribute little to prediction in BIA equations that include weight as an independent variable (Forbes et al., 1992). As noted earlier, it is possible that the future application of segmental and/or multifrequency techniques could improve the prediction of changes in body composition.

Calculations

Once an appropriate predictive equation has been selected, the bioelectric impedance and anthropometric data can be used to estimate body composition. Field applications will require a portable computer or programmable calculator. Some BIA devices come with portable computers; otherwise data can be stored and analyzed later. When using published equations, it is important to adhere closely to the methods used by the authors and not to round off multiplication coefficients, since rounding can translate into substantial errors in the predicted values. In some circumstances, it may be desirable to apply two or more published predictive equations and to average the results. This may be most appropriate when the sample is unusual with regard to ethnicity, hydration of the fat-free mass, level of body fatness, or some other factor that is suspected to influence impedance.

If predictive equations are to be developed, it is important to apply appropriate statistical techniques and to cross-validate the equation in either an independent sample or a randomly selected sub-sample (see chapter 10). Ideally, the sample should be selected to be representative of a well defined target population. Techniques used in surveys to select representative samples have rarely been used in the development of BIA predictive

Table 5.1   Selected Single-Frequency BIA Equations for Predicting Total Body Water

Study	Reference method*	N†	Age	Equation§	R^2	SEE	Comments
Children							
Davies et al., 1988	^{18}O	12 M, 14 F	5-18 y	$0.60 (S^2/R) - 0.50$	0.97	1.69	Sample included sick children
Fjeld et al., 1990	^{18}O	65	0.4-3 y	$0.67(S^2/Z) + 0.48$	0.98	0.36	
Mayfield et al., 1991	^{18}O	17	4-7 d	$235.8(WL^2/R) + 567$	0.96	0.76	L = crown-heel length
Adults							
Heitman, 1990	^{3}H	72 M, 67 F	35-65 y	$0.24(S^2/R) + 0.172(W)$ $+ 0.039(Sex \cdot W)$ $+ 0.165(S) - 17.577$	0.92	3.47	Danish sample, split-sample cross-validation
Kushner & Schoeller, 1986	^{2}H	20 M, 20 F	19-65 y	$0.556(S^2/R) + 0.096(W) + 1.73$	0.99	1.75	Cross-validated in 18 M and F
Lukaski et al., 1985	^{2}H	37 M	19-42 y	$0.63(S^2/R) + 2.03$	0.95	2.03	
Lukaski & Bolonchuk, 1988	^{2}H	25 M, 28 F	20-73 y	$0.372(S^2/R) + 3.05(Sex)$ $+ 0.142(W) - 0.069(Age)$	0.97	1.61	Cross-validated in 57 M and F
Zillikens & Conway, 1991	^{2}H	88 M, 20 F	19-61 y	$0.484(S^2/R) + 0.144(W)$ $+ 1.356(Sex) + 0.105(Xc)$ $- 0.057(Age)$	0.98	1.53	Black sample

*^{2}H, deuterium dilution; ^{3}H, tritium dilution; ^{18}O, oxygen-18 dilution. †M, male; F, female. §R, resistance; S, stature; W, body weight; Xc, reactance; Z, impedance.

Table 5.2   Selected Single-Frequency BIA Equations for Predicting Fat-Free Mass

Study	Reference method*	N[†]	Age	Equation[§]	R^2	SEE	Comments
Children							
Deurenberg et al., 1991	D_b	166	7-15	$0.406(S^2/R) + 0.36(W) + 5.58(S) + 0.56(Sex) - 6.48$	0.97	1.68	Split-sample cross-validation FFM by age-adjusted D_b equations
Guo et al., 1987	D_b	140 M	7-25	$0.646(W) - 0.116(LC) - 0.375(Mx) + 0.475(AC) + 0.156(S^2/R) - 2.932$	0.98	2.31	FFM by age-adjusted D_b equations; cross-validated in 94 white children by Houtkooper et al., 1989
		110 F	7-25	$0.682(W) - 0.185(LC) - 0.244(T) - 0.202(SS) + 0.182(S^2/R) + 4.338$	0.95	2.23	
Houtkooper et al., 1989	3C	53 M, 41 F	10-14	$0.83(S^2/R) + 4.43$	0.88	2.60	Model based on deuterium dilution and D_b
Adults							
Baumgartner et al., 1991	4C	35 M, 63 F	65-94	$0.28(S^2/R) + 0.27(W) + 4.5(Sex) + 0.31(Thigh\ C) - 1.732$	0.91	2.47	Model based on tritium dilution, D_b, and dual photon absorptiometry; elderly-specific equation
Deurenberg et al., 1990b	D_b	35 M, 37 F	65-83	$0.36(S^2/R) + 0.359(W) + 4.5(Sex) - 0.20(Thigh\ C) + 7.0$	0.96	2.50	Elderly-specific equation (Dutch)
Deurenberg et al., 1991	D_b	661	16-83	$0.34(S^2/R) - 0.127(Age) + 0.273(W) + 4.56(Sex) + 15.34(S) - 12.44$	0.93	2.63	Split-sample cross-validation
Lohman, 1992	D_b	153 M, 153 F	"Young adults"	$0.485(S^2/R) + 0.338(W) + 5.32$; $0.475(S^2/R) + 0.295(W) + 5.49$		2.90 ; 2.10	Cross-validated across five labs
Lukaski et al., 1986	D_b	84 M, 67 F	18-50	$0.756(S^2/R) + 0.11(W) + 0.107(Xc) - 5.463$	0.98	2.06	Split-sample cross-validation
Segal et al., 1985	3C	34 M, 41 F	17-59	$0.363(S^2/R) + 0.214(S) + 0.133(W) - 5.619(Sex)$	0.96	3.06	3C model based on tritium dilution and D_b
Segal et al., 1988	D_b ; D_b	1,069 M ; 498 F	17-62	$0.0013(S^2) - 0.044(R) + 0.305(W) - 0.168(Age) + 22.668$; $0.0011(S^2) - 0.021(R) + 0.232(W) - 0.068(Age) + 14.595$	0.89 ; 0.89	3.61 ; 2.43	Cross-validated across four labs ; Cross-validated by Gray et al., 1989

*D_b, body density; 3C, 4C, three- and four-component models, respectively. [†]M, male; F, female. [§]AC, arm circumference; LC, lateral calf skinfold; Mx, midaxillary skinfold; R, resistance; S, stature; SS, subscapular skinfold; T, triceps skinfold; Thigh C, thigh circumference; W, body weight; Xc, reactance.

Table 5.3 Multifrequency BIA Equations for Predicting Extracellular Fluid (ECF) and Total Body Water (TBW) Volume

Study	Dependent variable	N*	Age	Equation[†]	R^2	SEE	Comments[§]
Deurenberg et al., 1994	ECF	33 M, 27 F	19-52	$0.229(S^2/Z_1) + 4.5$	0.78	1.14	ECF by Br; TBW by ^{2}H; Xitron 4000
	TBW	33 M, 27 F	19-52	$0.483(S^2/Z_{100}) + 8.4$	0.89	2.27	
Segal et al., 1991	ECF	36 M	19-64	$0.284(S^2/R_5) + 0.112(W) - 6.115$	0.93	1.94	ECF by RS; TBW by ^{3}H; Danninger analyzer
	TBW	36 M	19-64	$0.455(S^2/R_{100}) + 0.14(W) + 3.43$	0.95	2.64	
Van Loan & Mayclin, 1992	ECF	40 M, 20 F	19-65	$0.099(S^2/R_{224}) + 0.093(W)$ $- 1.396(Sex) - 5.178$	0.92	1.06	Split sample cross-validation; ECF by Br; TBW by ^{2}H; Xitron 4000
	TBW	40 M, 20 F	19-65	$0.297(S^2/R_{224}) + 0.147(W)$ $- 3.637(Sex) + 14.017$	0.86	3.58	

*M, male; F, female. [†]R, resistance; S, stature; W, body weight; Z, impedance. Subscripts to R_s indicate current frequencies (e.g., f = 1, 5, 100, 224). [§]Br, bromide dilution; ^{2}H, deuterium dilution; ^{3}H, tritium dilution; RS, radiosulfate dilution.

equations. Caution is warranted, however, given the evidence of very limited generalizability of many anthropometric predictive equations developed from small, selected samples (Roche & Guo, 1993). There has been no clear analysis to date, however, of how much the issue of sample representativeness affects generalizability. Generalizability will be increased if there is a wide range of values for the prediction variables in the sample. The predictive equation should include as few variables as possible, and these should be selected with regard to statistical independence as well as biological considerations or correlation with the dependent variable, since the use of many, highly correlated predictors can result in unstable, highly sample-specific equations (see chapter 10). It may be desirable to include resistance measurements, taken either with proximal electrode placements or for body segments (e.g., the trunk), and reactance or multifrequency values as independent variables when variability in body proportions or fluid distribution in the sample is expected to be large (Baumgartner et al., 1990). A variety of statistical methods are reviewed in chapter 10 for assessing the effects of multicollinearity among predictors, for reducing these effects, and for evaluating the accuracy of a predictive equation during cross-validation.

Recommended Standard Procedure

In 1993, a standardization consensus conference was held in Rome, Italy to develop guidelines for the use of bioelectric impedance across studies to ensure comparability of data. At present, the standard positioning and procedures described earlier in this chapter are recommended. If unconventional positioning or electrode placements are to be used, these should be described concisely. When additional anthropometric variables are to be collected, these should be taken using recommended standardized procedures and equipment (Lohman, Roche, & Martorell, 1988). All measurements should be taken in a standard fashion two or more times by two independent observers for at least a randomly selected subsample to assess the technical errors of the measurements. These are useful in relation to evaluations of the accuracy and sources of error of different predictive equations.

Summary

Single frequency bioelectric impedance analysis is a useful adjunct to anthropometry for assessing body composition in field studies. It is appropriate for quick, bedside assessments in clinical settings in which moderate inaccuracy is tolerable. It should not be used to predict changes in body composition during treatment unless these are expected to be large and/or the duration of follow-up is long. The current single-frequency BIA method has insufficient sensitivity to quantify accurately small or short-term changes. Segmental and multifrequency bioelectric impedance techniques have considerable promise as clinical tools for assessing abnormal fluid distribution associated with chronic illnesses, malnutrition, or certain injuries. The use of BIS in this context currently appears to be limited to detecting qualitative differences, since difficulties remain in distinguishing changes in fluid volume from changes in electrolyte concentrations. At present, BIS has not been shown to result in any significant improvement in the prediction of body composition over single-frequency BIA in field studies.

Total Body Electrical Conductivity

The total body electrical conductivity (TOBEC) method of body composition analysis was first introduced as an in vivo method of estimating the lean mass of hogs by Wesley Harker in 1973 (Fiorotto, 1991; Funk, Kerekes, & Lanphier, 1993). This application was not successful commercially: the method was not considered to be sufficiently accurate due to complex problems associated with animal geometry and movement and with correct calibration. Devices referred to as "electronic meat measuring equipment" (EMME) continued to be produced for lean/fat compositional analysis of packaged meat products. Prototype instruments for in vivo analysis of human body composition in adults and infants were introduced in 1981-1982 by Dickey-john Medical Instrument Corporation (Auburn, IL). The initial testing of these prototypes was promising (Harrison & Van Itallie, 1982; Klish, Forbes, Gordon, & Cochran, 1984; Presta et al., 1983a, 1983b), and improved devices were released commercially in 1985, including new instruments using a "scanning" approach to measurement (Van Loan & Mayclin, 1987). The technology was purchased in 1988 by EM-SCAN Inc. (Springfield, IL), and several different types of TOBEC devices were made available for small animal, pediatric, and adult human body composition analysis. In 1994, EM-SCAN discontinued the manufacture of

TOBEC devices for these purposes. Some researchers, however, may continue to use previously purchased TOBEC models so a thorough review of this method remains useful.

The underlying principle in TOBEC is the same as in bioelectric impedance analysis (BIA): The conductivity (1/resistivity) of a tissue is dependent on its water and free electrolyte concentration, temperature, and the frequency of the current. Lean tissues (with the exception of bone) have about 20 times the conductivity of fat (Geddes & Baker, 1967; Pethig, 1979). Thus, total body electrical conductivity is directly proportional to the volume of the fat- and bone-free body mass. The approach to measurement in TOBEC, however, is completely different from that in BIA. In TOBEC an electric current is induced in the body using an electromagnetic field without physical contact, rather than by injecting a current using electrodes as in BIA. This is accomplished by inserting the body into a large electric coil, or solenoid, that is generating an electromagnetic field. The magnetic field is perpendicular to the flow of the current and parallel to the long axis of the coil, as illustrated in Figure 5.5. When a body or other conductor is inserted into the magnetic field within the coil, an "eddy current" is induced in the conductive part of the body. This current is perpendicular to the magnetic field with a direction of flow opposite to that of the current in the coil. The magnitude of the induced current depends on the strength of

the magnetic field and the impedance and cross-sectional area of the conductive part of the body (Funk et al., 1993).

Technically, TOBEC does not measure conductivity or impedance per se (Funk et al., 1993). When a current is induced in the conductive part of the body, a small amount of energy (~500 μW) is absorbed that is dissipated as heat. The amount of energy absorbed is a function of the strength of the current and the conductivity and length of the conductor. For a cylindrical conductor of uniform length and homogenous composition, the amount of energy absorbed is determined by the formula:

$$E = k \cdot B \cdot \sigma \cdot A^2 \cdot L \qquad (5.1)$$

where E is energy absorbed, k is a constant reflecting physical factors related to coil geometry and frequency of current, B is the magnetic field strength, σ is the specific conductivity of the material, and A and L are the cross-sectional area and length, respectively, of the cylinder. Since the volume (V) of a cylinder is equal to A · L, it is readily seen that

$$E = c_1 \cdot V^2 / L \qquad (5.2)$$

and, by rearrangement,

$$V = c_2 \cdot (E \cdot L)^{1/2}$$

where c_1 represents the consolidation of k, B, and σ, and c_2 equals $1/\sqrt{c_1}$. E is referred to commonly

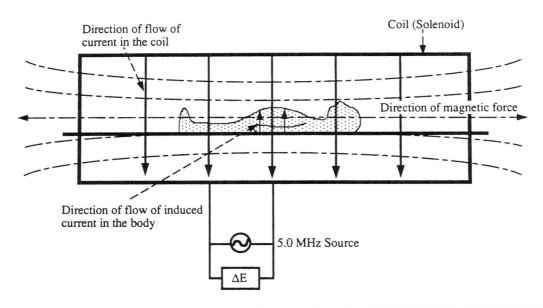

Direction of flow of current in the coil

Coil (Solenoid)

Direction of magnetic force

Direction of flow of induced current in the body

5.0 MHz Source

ΔE

Figure 5.5 The basic design of the original TOBEC. The subject lies stationary within the large solenoid. Alternating current in the solenoid creates a magnetic field that induces an opposing current within the body. Energy is absorbed by the body and released as heat. The absorbed energy is measured by a decrease in coil impedance.

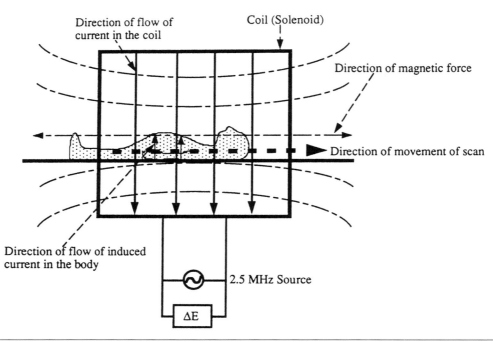

Figure 5.6 The basic design of a scanning TOBEC device. The subject is drawn through the uniform part of the electromagnetic field generated by a shortened coil and scanned in segments.

in the literature as the "TOBEC number." Thus, the volume of the conductor is proportional to the square root of the product of its length and TOBEC number.

An important engineering consideration in estimating conductive volume using this formula is the uniformity of the magnetic field, which is necessary for accurate measurements (Funk et al., 1993). The lines of magnetic force in a coil or solenoid are relatively parallel (uniform field) throughout most of its length but diverge at both ends (nonuniform field). Thus, to enclose the subject completely within the uniform part of the field, the coil has to be somewhat longer than the subject (see Figure 5.5). This requirement is easily satisfied for shorter subjects: the present-day small animal (SA-2) and human pediatric (HP-2) devices have this design. The prototype adult human TOBEC instrument had this design also, but its length was considered to be an awkward and undesirable feature. The current adult human device (HA-2) uses a "scanning" approach in which the subject is passed through the uniform part of the magnetic field of a shorter coil and measured in 64 segments or "slices." Figure 5.6 illustrates the somewhat different configuration of the shorter, scanning design. The results from such a scan can be viewed as a plot of detector output by subject position in the coil, as shown in Figure 5.7.

In the original instruments, the detector was not designed to separate capacitative from conductive effects and the output (TOBEC number) reflected both. This was considered undesirable because the capacitative component was highly dependent on the shape of the subject and difficult to predict (Fiorotto, 1991). A solution used in the nonscanning devices was to redefine detector output in terms of "phase change," or the difference in the impedance of the coil between the empty and occupied states, which is less confounded by capacitative effects. In the scanning instruments, however, the phase readings still contained capacitative effects due to interaction between the dielectric components of the body and the nonuniform parts of the field as the subject was drawn through the coil. These interactions occur mainly at entry and exit from the field and affect the coil amplitude. As shown in Figure 5.7, the result is an asymmetric bimodal curve when phase is plotted by subject position in the coil (Van Itallie, Segal, & Funk, 1987). Van Loan and Mayclin (1987) showed that Fourier analysis could be used to analyze this convoluted curve into separate coefficients describing the average phase value across the curve (FC0), the shape and position of the primary unimodal curve (FC1), and the shape and position of the underlying, secondary bimodal curve (FC2). The first coefficient, FC0, or the "average phase," provides a number closely similar to the older TOBEC

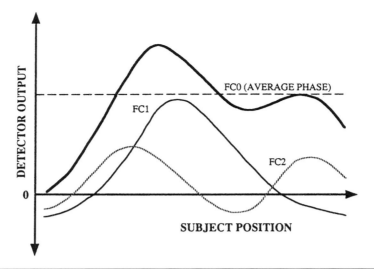

Figure 5.7 Output from a TOBEC scan.

number. FC1 reflects the interaction of the conductive volume of the body as it moves through the field, while FC2 reflects the interaction of the dielectric, capacitive elements. Van Itallie et al. described FC1 and FC2 as "raw conductivity" and "raw amplitude" plots, respectively. Since 1988, however, TOBEC scanning instruments have been made with "balanced" coils that dampen the amplitude changes associated with dielectric interactive effects at the ends of the magnetic field. As a result, the phase-by-position plots are generally unimodal, primarily reflecting conductance. It is believed that this refinement should provide more accurate estimates (Fiorotto, 1991).

Assumptions

The analysis of body composition by TOBEC is subject to many of the same limiting assumptions that apply to BIA, as well as others that are specific to this approach. The fundamental relationship described in the TOBEC equation applies exactly only to a homogenous cylindrical conductor that has uniform conductivity, constant cross-sectional area, and known length. Additionally, it is assumed that the magnetic field is of uniform direction and intensity, there is no conduction in "nonconductive" components of the body, and that energy absorption or phase change is measured accurately (Funk et al., 1993). TOBEC scans of the human body do not fully satisfy all these criteria.

Careful engineering has solved many problems associated with uniformity of the magnetic field and accurate measurement of E, or phase change,

so long as positioning is standardized and clothing (i.e., no metal jewelry) and body movement restrictions are followed carefully (see section on measurement procedure). At the frequencies of current used (5 MHz in nonscanning and 2.5 MHz in scanning instruments), the assumptions of no conduction by fat or bone and of uniform conduction within the fat-free mass appear to be reasonably valid.

Klish and associates (1984) tested the ability of TOBEC to correctly quantify volumes of electrolyte solutions containing varying concentrations of lipid (5 to 40%). The TOBEC number was correlated highly with the volume of electrolyte solution and was independent of the concentration of lipid. In this experiment, however, the lipid was emulsified using a detergent and distributed evenly throughout the electrolyte volume. This in vitro model does not correspond well to the human body, in which fat is localized anatomically in subcutaneous and intra-abdominal depots and significantly alters body geometry. Increased subcutaneous and intra-abdominal adipose tissue expands considerably the cross-sectional areas of the limbs and trunk and thereby could affect conductance. In this regard, Segal and coworkers (1985) reported that residual errors after the regression of TOBEC measurements on fat-free mass from underwater weighing were not correlated with level of body fatness in adults ranging from 5 to 55% fat. In contrast to BIA, there is little evidence for increased error of prediction of fat-free mass at higher levels of adiposity (Gray et al., 1989; Hodgdon & Fitzgerald, 1987). The effect of body fat distribution on TOBEC determinations of fat-free mass has not been studied.

Bone presents a problem in that it is nonconductive at the frequencies of current used in TOBEC but is part of the fat-free mass. Variation in bone mineral density influences the derivation of fat-free mass from hydrodensitometry but does not affect conductivity. The two-compartment hydrodensitometric model, which does not adjust for variation in bone mineral density, has been the most common method used to calibrate TOBEC predictive equations. Boileau (1988) showed that adjusting for variation in bone mineral density resulted in a slight reduction (about 7% or 200 g) in the standard error of estimate of fat-free mass from TOBEC. Horswill and associates (1989) reported that correlations of TOBEC estimates of fat-free mass with fat-free mass from hydrodensitometry and with muscle mass from 3-methylhistidine excretion were nearly identical ($R^2 = 0.95$). Fiorotto (1991) has argued that the TOBEC measurement includes bone indirectly because the skeleton increases the cross-sectional area of the non-bone fat-free mass and thereby increases the signal from the non-bone lean mass "almost proportionally" to the area occupied by the bone. If this were true, however, intra-abdominal adipose tissue would have a similar effect on the TOBEC signal from the trunk. It seems more likely that the range of variation among subjects for skeletal volume as a fraction of total fat-free volume has been too narrow to have detectable effects on TOBEC predictions in most studies. The accuracy of TOBEC in patients with severe wasting diseases, such as anorexia nervosa or marasmus, in whom there is an extreme loss of muscle tissue and subsequent expansion of skeletal volume as a fraction of fat-free volume, has not been reported.

In BIA an important issue has been the effect of abnormal distributions of fluids and electrolytes between the intra- and extracellular compartments on electrical conductivity and measurements of impedance (Deurenberg, 1993). These alterations affect the assumption of uniform conductivity within the fat-free mass. It has been argued by Funk et al. (1993) that this should not pose a significant problem in TOBEC because the frequency of the current is very high compared to BIA (2.5 to 5 MHz versus 50 kHz). Several TOBEC investigators have tested this issue by experimentally altering fluid distribution or electrolyte concentrations. Klish and coworkers (1984) demonstrated in vitro that equivalent volumes with different electrolyte concentrations had markedly different TOBEC signals. Cunningham, Molnar, Meara, and Bode (1986), however, reported that experimentally induced changes in fluid and electrolyte status do not have significant effects on TOBEC predictions of total body water in Sprague-Dawley rats. Fiorotto, Cochran, and Klish (1987) compared TOBEC predictions of total body water in infant miniature pigs and mature rabbits. The pigs had significantly greater hydration of the fat-free mass than the rabbits (80 vs. 74%), and a significantly greater fraction of the body water was extracellular (37 vs. 27%). The slopes of the regressions of total body water on the TOBEC index [(TOBEC number · L)$^{0.5}$] were not significantly different. Finally, Cochran, Fiorotto, Sheng, and Klish (1989) injected 11 miniature piglets with physiological saline producing a 12 to 34% increase in extracellular fluid volume without alteration of electrolyte concentration. The slopes of the regressions of total body water and fat-free mass on the TOBEC index after injection were not significantly different from those before injection, indicating that TOBEC accurately tracked the increase in lean volume without confounding due to the altered distribution of fluid between intra- and extracellular spaces. Thus, at the frequencies of current used in TOBEC, the assumption of uniform conductivity within the fat-free mass seems to be valid.

The main problem, as in BIA, appears to be the complex geometry of the body, particularly the large changes in cross-sectional areas of the lean, conductive volumes between the trunk and the limbs. Conduction is much less (i.e., resistivity is higher) in the limbs than in the trunk due to their smaller cross-sectional areas. In BIA, whole body resistance is dominated by the resistance of the arm, which has the smallest cross-sectional area (Baumgartner et al., 1989). The relative influence of the trunk compared to the limbs on total body conductivity cannot be examined using TOBEC because the instrument has not been designed to measure body segments separately. The inclusion of variables such as sex, age, and stature or weight/stature^2 in some TOBEC predictive equations may adjust in part for some of the variation among individuals in "geometry." In sum, TOBEC is an indirect method and the predictive equations are subject to many of the same statistical limitations that apply to those for BIA.

Applicability

The TOBEC method is applicable generally to normal, healthy subjects from infancy through old age (Boileau, 1988; Cochran, Klish, Wong, & Klein, 1986; Klish, 1993; Van Loan, 1990; Van Loan & Koehler, 1990). Although originally presented as an approach that could be useful in population surveys (Presta et al., 1983b), TOBEC instruments have been recognized subsequently as far too cumbersome and expensive for field use and their main application appears to be limited to laboratory and clinical investigations. As noted above, TOBEC seems to be relatively insensitive to shifts of fluid and/or electrolytes between intra- and extracellular compartments that may occur in various diseases or accompany acute weight changes (Cochran et al., 1989; Fiorotto et al., 1987). Because these shifts are suspected to confound the ability of single-frequency BIA to quantify accurately small changes in body composition (Deurenberg, 1993), TOBEC may be somewhat more accurate than BIA for quantifying the small changes in TBW or FFM that occur, for example, in diet/exercise weight loss studies (Van Loan, Belko, Mayclin, & Barbieri, 1987a; Van Loan, Keim, & Phinney, 1993; Vazquez & Janosky, 1991). On the other hand, TOBEC will not be able to differentiate whether the small changes occur in the extracellular rather than the intracellular compartment as may be discerned with multifrequency BIS. It may be important to note that studies have not been reported validating the ability of TOBEC to quantify accurately changes in body composition in sick patients undergoing treatments such as dialysis.

Some alternative approaches to the use of TOBEC have been suggested. Van Itallie and associates (1987) noted that, based on the same principles that underlie the use of multifrequency BIA, TOBEC measurements at two or more frequencies might be used to quantify separately extracellular and intracellular fluid volumes or to derive body cell mass. Funk and associates (1993) presented some preliminary data that would appear to support this new application; however, this approach has not been developed further and it has not been validated experimentally by any independent investigators. Funk et al. also described a method by which the information provided by a TOBEC scan could be used to produce a "lean profile" for an individual. It was suggested that this information might be used to derive body fat distribution, which is of considerable interest with regard to risk for some chronic diseases, but reports of this application are lacking. The further development of these applications appears unlikely unless EM-SCAN or another manufacturer chooses to resume production of TOBEC devices.

Equipment

Three models of TOBEC devices exist: a small animal analyzer (SA-2), and pediatric (HP-2) and adult (HA-2) analyzers. The HP-2 instrument operates at 5 MHz in a nonscanning mode and is essentially a downsized version of the original HA-1 adult analyzer. The HP-2 is 3.56 m long, 71 cm wide, and 1.22 m high and weighs about 477 kg. About half the length is composed of the electromagnetic coil, which has a diameter of about 37 cm. The HP-2 can accommodate infants and children between 1.5 and 18 kg body weight and less than 110 cm in recumbent length: This effectively limits its use to children less than 6 years of age.

The original HA-1 adult TOBEC analyzer was massive: The coil was approximately 3.6 m long and 56 cm in diameter, and the subject entry carriage basically doubled this length. The extreme awkwardness of this instrument was undoubtedly one factor leading to the development of the TOBEC scanning approach. The HA-2 scanning analyzer is still relatively large: 5.94 m long, 1.22 m wide, 1.52 m high and about 900 kg in weight, including the subject loading section. The electromagnetic coil is about 2.1 m long and 75 cm in diameter. The HA-2 can accommodate subjects between 14 and 180 kg in weight. Body length is of less importance than in the nonscanning designs because the subjects are measured in segments as they pass through the uniform part of the magnetic field.

Measurement Procedures

Subjects wear clothes, excluding shoes or metal jewelry, which may form intermittent connections between the limbs and the body (Funk et al., 1993), and lie supine on a sled or loading carriage that is inserted into the coil. Infants must be swaddled to restrict movement and to help standardize their shape (Klish et al., 1984). In the HP-2 analyzer, the subject remains within the center of the coil while a minimum of three consecutive readings is made, each lasting approximately 1 second (Klish, 1993). A typical analysis takes about 2 minutes, including data entry and processing time. In the HA-2 analyzer, the subject is drawn head first through the magnetic field at a fixed rate, and conductivity is measured for 64 "slices" or segments. Each scan takes approximately 30 seconds, and two to five repeated scans are recommended (Lukaski, 1992). If additional anthropometric measurements are required, these should be taken using standardized procedures and properly calibrated equipment by well trained observers (Lohman, Roche, & Martorell, 1988).

Precision

TOBEC measurements are highly precise, in terms of repeatability. Coefficients of variation for repeated measurements in human subjects ranged from 2 to 6% for the older, nonscanning HA-1 devices (Presta et al., 1983a; Segal et al., 1985). The newer devices, which have more sophisticated electronics and operate at a lower current frequency (2.5 vs 5.0 MHz), are reported to have higher precisions of 0.5 to 1% (Fiorotto, 1991).

To maintain high precision, close attention must be paid to several factors that can affect the repeatability of measurements. The most important include machine calibration and the control of body movement and of variations in temperature and humidity. Instrument drift may occur over time. As a result, both nonscanning and scanning instruments must be calibrated daily using a standard device that produces a constant, known signal (Lukaski, 1992). This device generally consists of a precision resistor in series with several loops of copper wire wound around a nonconductive frame (Presta et al., 1983a; Van Loan & Mayclin, 1987). In nonscanning instruments, the standard device is placed in the center of the magnetic field with the wire loops coaxial to the coil; in scanning instruments, it is drawn through the coil in the same manner as an actual subject. The gain of the instrument is adjusted until the signal from the calibration device is within ± 1% tolerance of the known, standard value. Body movements, including deep breathing, can seriously affect measurements and must be minimized. When measuring infants, it is recommended that the operator observe the infant carefully and obtain measurements between breaths or cries (Klish, 1993). Ambient room temperature should be relatively constant, varying no more than ± 8 °C, and there should not be any strong drafts. Subjects should have normal body temperature, although the effect of increased temperature, as in fever, is considered to be highly predictable and appropriate corrections can be made (Fiorotto, 1991). Relative humidity should be less than 60%. The subject's body and his or her clothing should be dry at the time of measurement. It is most desirable to measure subjects after a 6 hour fast and with the bladder empty.

Accuracy

Multiple factors affect the accuracy of TOBEC predictions of body composition. Clearly, careful attention must be paid to the factors already noted that can affect the precision or repeatability of the TOBEC measurements of conductivity. If predictive equations that include anthropometric variables are to be used, these must be recorded reliably using methods that match those used in the development of the equation because measurement errors in the predictor variables will be propagated to the dependent body composition estimates.

Of possibly greater importance is the correct calibration of predictive equations against dependent measurements of known accuracy. Most TOBEC equations for predicting percent body fat or fat-free mass have been calibrated against estimates from body density by underwater weighing. The technical error of measurement of body density by underwater weighing has been estimated to be about ± 0.0063 g/ml in healthy, young adults, which translates into an error of about ± 2.5% body fat or about ± 1 kg fat-free mass (Lohman 1992). This could be considered the theoretical minimum or "inescapable" error associated with the TOBEC method if all independent predictors were measured without error. The error associated with underwater weighing, however, is likely to be considerably greater in children, the elderly, and frail or sick patients. Moreover, in these groups additional "biological error" will be introduced if traditional two-compartment equations (e.g., the Siri equation or Keys-Brožek equation) are applied to convert body density into estimates of percent body fat or fat-free mass, as explained in chapter 1. For these special groups, it is desirable to use predictive equations that have been calibrated against estimates from multicompartment models or from methods known to be unaffected by age, sex, ethnicity, obesity, or health-related alterations in body composition. Currently, few such equations are available for either BIA or TOBEC. It is important to note also that equations for predicting infant body composition have been calibrated against animal models (miniature pigs) believed to be representative of normal human infants (Fiorotto, 1991; Fiorotto & Klish, 1991).

Table 5.4 lists published TOBEC equations for predicting various aspects of body composition, their reported errors, and information on the size and composition of the samples used to calibrate the equations. Generally, TOBEC can be considered to be slightly more accurate in most applications than BIA. The standard errors of estimate reported for cross-sectional studies, as well as of changes in body composition, range from 1.43 to 2.86 kg for fat-free mass and 0.68 to 1.57 L for total

Table 5.4   Selected TOBEC Equations for Predicting Fat-Free Mass (FFM) and Total Body Water (TBW)

Study	Dependent variable	N*	Age	Equation†	R^2	SEE	Comments§
Children							
Boileau, 1988	FFM	17	8-12	$0.03(FC_1^{0.5} \cdot S) - 0.018(FC_2^{0.5} \cdot S) + 9.603$	0.96	1.26	FFM by D_b
	FFM	11	13-18	$0.03(FC_1^{0.5} \cdot S) - 0.015(FC_2^{0.5} \cdot S) + 6.832$	0.97	1.60	
Van Loan, 1990	FFM	33 M, 17 F	11-19	$0.102(FC_0) + 0.062(FC_1) - 0.291(FC_2) + 22.999$	0.98	1.43	FFM by ^2H and D_b
Adults							
Boileau, 1988	FFM	62	19-35	$0.028(FC_1^{0.5} \cdot S) - 0.010(FC_2^{0.5} \cdot S) + 1.545$	0.98	2.86	FFM by D_b
	FFM	100	> 35	$0.024(FC_1^{0.5} \cdot S) - 0.011(FC_2^{0.5} \cdot S) - 3.195(Sex) + 12.61$	0.94	2.72	
Cochran et al., 1988	TBW	10 M, 10 F	23-58	$0.072(FC_0) - 0.221(FC_2) + 0.039(Age) + 9.2(S \cdot AC) + 10.8$	0.99	0.68	TBW by ^{18}O
Segal et al., 1985	FFM	34 M, 41 F	17-59	$2.324(TB^{0.5} \cdot S^2) - 5.759(Sex) + 27.986$	0.97	2.53	FFM by ^3H and D_b
Van Loan & Mayclin, 1987	TBW	20 M, 20 F	19-35	$0.054(FC_0) + 0.070(FC_1) - 0.137(FC_2) + 14.299$	0.96	1.57	TBW by ^2H
	FFM	20 M, 20 F	19-35	$0.089(FC_0) + 0.074(FC_1) - 0.228(FC_2) + 20.694$	0.98	1.66	FFM by ^2H and D_b
Van Loan et al., 1987b	FFM	157	18-35	$0.012(FC_1^{0.5} \cdot S) + 12.347(FC_2^{0.5}) + 0.063(FC_0) - 0.923(FC_2) - 1.324(Sex) - 36.41$	0.96	2.17	FFM by D_b; cross-validated in two samples

*M, male; F, female. †AC, average circumference; FC_0, zero-order Fourier coefficient or "offset"; FC_1, first Fourier coefficient; FC_2, second Fourier coefficient; S, stature; TB, TOBEC#. §D_b, body density; ^2H, deuterium dilution; ^3H, tritium dilution; ^{18}O, oxygen-18 dilution.

body water (Table 5.4). These values are marginally better than those reported for BIA, for which errors typically range from 1.68 to 3.61 kg fat-free mass and 1.53 to 3.47 L for total body water (see Tables 5.1 and 5.2). Thus, on average, TOBEC may be considered to be marginally more accurate than BIA. The much greater cost of TOBEC compared to BIA (10- to 12-fold) must be considered, however, in relation to the small increase in accuracy. The high cost as well as the size and weight of TOBEC devices has greatly limited the application of this method of analyzing body composition.

Calculations

The use of most published TOBEC equations for predicting TBW and FFM is complicated somewhat by the need to perform preliminary Fourier analyses of the raw conductivity data. Fortunately, software for this purpose has been provided by the manufacturer for the newer devices. Once the Fourier coefficients have been calculated, it is necessary to select an age- and sex-appropriate predictive equation. As with BIA, it is desirable to select one that has been derived from a sample closely matching the individuals under study and to adhere closely to the methods used by the author. It is important not to round off multiplication coefficients, since rounding can translate into substantial errors in the predicted values.

Since the manufacture of TOBEC devices has been discontinued, it seems unlikely that many investigators will produce new predictive equations in the near future. In any event, the statistical methods discussed by Roche and Guo (1993) and in chapter 10 are recommended. In brief, these include issues related to sampling, control of measurement errors, appropriate selection of variables, reduction of multicollinearity among predictors, and measuring the stability of equations through appropriate cross-validation.

Recommended Standard Procedure

The scanning procedure recommended by the manufacturer should be followed closely. Care should be taken to minimize the effects of the factors noted that can affect precision and accuracy. The most important of these may be body movements and temperature. The averaging of the results of several scans is recommended (Lukaski, 1992). Any additional anthropometric data should be recorded carefully with regard to recommended standard procedures (Lohman et al., 1988).

Summary

TOBEC is considered to be a highly reliable and relatively accurate means of estimating total body water and fat-free mass. For this purpose it is marginally superior to BIA, but the comparatively high cost of the instrumentation generally erodes this benefit in most applications. Moreover, TOBEC measurements do not provide information on the composition of the fat-free mass as do other methods that are comparable in cost, such as dual energy x-ray absorptiometry. The manufacture of TOBEC devices was most likely discontinued for these as well as other reasons. This review has been provided in part as an historical anecdote on this alternative electromagnetic method of body composition analysis but also for current users who may need a summary of TOBEC methods and in the event that the development and commercial production of these devices is resumed.

References

Ackmann, J.J., & Seitz, M.A. (1984). Methods of complex impedance measurements in biologic tissue. *Critical Reviews in Biomedical Engineering,* **11**, 281-311.

Baker, L.E. (1987). Principles of the impedance technique. *IEEE Engineering in Medicine & Biology,* **3**, 15-20.

Barillas-Mury, C., Vettorazzi, C., Molina, S., & Pineda, O. (1987). Experience with bioelectric impedance analysis in young children: Sources of variability. In K.J. Ellis, S. Yasumura, & W.D. Morgan (Eds.), *In vivo body composition studies* (pp. 87-90). London: Institute of Physical Sciences in Medicine.

Baumgartner, R.N., Chumlea, W.C., & Roche, A.F. (1988). Bioelectric impedance phase angle and body composition. *American Journal of Clinical Nutrition,* **48**, 16-23.

Baumgartner, R.N., Chumlea, W.C., & Roche, A.F. (1989). Estimation of body composition from segmental impedance. *American Journal of Clinical Nutrition,* **50**, 221-225.

Baumgartner, R.N., Chumlea, W.C., & Roche, A.F. (1990). Bioelectric impedance for body composition. *Exercise and Sport Sciences Reviews,* **18**, 193-224.

Baumgartner, R.N., Heymsfield, S.B., Lichtman, S., et al. (1991). Body composition in elderly people: Effect of criterion estimates on predictive equations. *American Journal of Clinical Nutrition,* **53**, 1345-1349.

Boileau, R.A. (1988). Utilization of total body electrical conductivity in determining body composition. In National Research Council, *Designing foods: Animal product options in the marketplace* (pp. 251-257). Washington, DC: National Academy.

Boulier, A., Fricker, J., Thomasset, A., & Apfelbaum, M. (1990). Fat-free mass estimation by the two-electrode impedance method. *American Journal of Clinical Nutrition, 52*, 581-585.

Caton, J.R., Molé, P.A., Adams, W.C., & Heustis, D.S. (1988). Body composition analysis by bioelectric impedance: Effect of skin temperature. *Medicine and Science in Sports and Exercise, 20*, 489-491.

Chumlea, W.C., Baumgartner, R.N., & Guo, S. (1993a). Segmental bioelectric impedance, subcutaneous adipose tissue, and fat patterns in adults. In J.G. Kral & T.B. Van Itallie (Eds.), *Recent developments in body composition analysis: Methods and applications* (pp. 49-60). London: Smith-Gordon.

Chumlea, W.C., Baumgartner, R.N., & Roche, A.F. (1988). The use of specific resistivity to estimate fat-free mass from segmental body measures of bioelectric impedance. *American Journal of Clinical Nutrition, 48*, 7-15.

Chumlea, W.C., Guo, S., Baumgartner, R.N., & Siervogel, R.M. (1993b). Determination of body fluid compartments with multiple frequency bioelectric impedance. In K.J. Ellis & J.D. Eastman (Eds.), *Human body composition* (pp. 23-26). New York: Plenum.

Cochran, W.J., Fiorotto, M.L., Sheng, H.P., & Klish, W.J. (1989). Reliability of fat-free mass estimates derived from total body electrical conductivity measurements as influenced by changes in extracellular fluid volume. *American Journal of Clinical Nutrition, 49*, 29-32.

Cochran, W.J., Klish, W.J., Wong, W., & Klein, P.D. (1986). Total body electrical conductivity used to determine body composition in infants. *Pediatric Research, 20*, 561-564.

Cochran, W.J., Wong, W.W., Fiorotto, M.L., et al. (1988). Total body water estimated by measuring total-body electrical conductivity. *American Journal of Clinical Nutrition, 48*, 946-950.

Cole, K.S., & Cole, R.H. (1941). Dispersion and absorption in dielectrics, I: Alternating current characteristics. *Journal of Chemical Physics, 9*, 341-351.

Cordain, L, Whicker, R.E., & Johnson, J.E. (1988). Body composition determination in children using bioelectric impedance. *Growth, Development, and Aging, 52*, 37-40.

Cornish, B.H., Thomas, B.J., & Ward, L.C. (1993). Improved prediction of extracellular and total body water using impedance loci generated by multiple frequency bioelectrical impedance analysis. *Physics in Medicine and Biology, 38*, 337-346.

Cunningham, J.J., Molnar, J.A., Meara, P.A., & Bode, H.H. (1986). In vivo total body electrical conductivity following perturbations of body fluid compartments in rats. *Metabolism, 35*, 572-575.

Davies, P.S.W., Preece, M.A., Hicks, C.J., et al. (1988). The prediction of total body water using bioelectrical impedance in children and adolescents. *Annals of Human Biology, 15*, 237-240.

Deurenberg, P. (1993). The dependency of bioelectrical impedance on intra- and extracellular water distribution. In J.G. Kral & T.B. Van Itallie (Eds.), *Recent developments in body composition analysis: Methods and applications* (pp. 43-48). London: Smith-Gordon.

Deurenberg, P. (1994). International consensus conference on impedance in body composition. *Age & Nutrition, 5*, 142-145.

Deurenberg, P., Broekhoff, C., Andreoli, A., deLorenzo, A. (1994). The use of multifrequency impedance in assessing changes in body water compartments. *Age & Nutrition, 5*, 137-141.

Deurenberg, P., Kusters, C.S.L., & Smit, H.E. (1990a). Assessment of body composition by bioelectric impedance in children and young adults is strongly age-dependent. *European Journal of Clinical Nutrition, 44*, 261-268.

Deurenberg, P., & Schouten, F.J.M. (1992). Loss of total body water and extracellular water assessed by multifrequency impedance. *European Journal of Clinical Nutrition, 46*, 247-255.

Deurenberg, P., Smit, H.E., & Kusters, C.S.L. (1989a). Is the bioelectric impedance method suitable for epidemiologic field studies? *European Journal of Clinical Nutrition, 43*, 647-654.

Deurenberg, P., van der Kooy, K., Evers, P., & Hulshof, T. (1990b). Assessment of body composition by bioelectrical impedance in a population aged > 60 y. *American Journal of Clinical Nutrition, 51*, 3-6.

Deurenberg, P., van der Kooy, K., & Leenen, R. (1989b). Differences in body impedance when measured with different instruments. *European Journal of Clinical Nutrition, 43*, 885-886.

Deurenberg, P., van der Kooy, K., Leenen, R., et al. (1991). Sex and age specific prediction formulas for estimating body composition from bioelectrical impedance: A cross-validation study. *International Journal of Obesity, 15*, 17-25.

Deurenberg, P., Weststrate, J.A., & Hautvast, J.G. (1989c). Changes in fat-free mass during weight loss measured by bioelectrical impedance and densitometry. *American Journal of Clinical Nutrition*, **49**, 33-36.

Deurenberg, P., Weststrate, J.A., & van der Kooy, K. (1989d). Body composition changes assessed by bioelectrical impedance measurements. *American Journal of Clinical Nutrition*, **49**, 401-433.

DeVries, P.M.J.M., Kouw, P.M., Olthof, C.G., Meijer, J.H., DeVries, J.P.M.M., Oe, L.P., Donker, J.M. (1994). A segmental multifrequency conductivity technique to measure dynamic body fluid changes. *Age & Nutrition*, **5**, 118-122.

Ducrot, H., Thomasset, A., Joly, R., et al. (1970). Détermination du volume des liquids extracellulaires chez l'homme par la mesure de l'impedance corporelle totale [Determination of extracellular fluid volumes in humans by the measurement of total body impedance]. *Presse Médicale*, **78**, 2269-2272.

Fiorotto, M.L. (1991). Measurements of total body electrical conductivity for the estimation of fat and fat-free mass. In R.G. Whitehead & A. Prentice (Eds.), *New techniques in nutritional research* (pp. 281-302). San Diego, CA: Academic.

Fiorotto, M.L., Cochran, W.J., & Klish, W.J. (1987). Fat-free mass and total body water of infants estimated from total body electrical conductivity measurements. *Pediatric Research*, **22**, 417-421.

Fiorotto, M.L., & Klish, W.J. (1991). Total body electrical conductivity measurements in the neonate. *Clinics in Perinatology*, **18**, 611-627.

Fjeld, C.R., Freundt-Thurne, J., & Schoeller, D.A. (1990). Total body water measured by ^{18}O dilution and bioelectrical impedance in well and malnourished children. *Pediatric Research*, **27**, 98-102.

Forbes, G.B., Simon, W., & Amatruda, J.M. (1992). Is bioimpedance a good predictor of body-composition change? *American Journal of Clinical Nutrition*, **56**, 4-6.

Fricke, H. (1925). Mathematical treatment of the electric conductivity and capacity of disperse systems. *Physical Reviews*, **26**, 678-681.

Fuller, N.J., & Elia, M. (1989). Potential use of bioelectrical impedance of the "whole body" and of body segments for the assessment of body composition: Comparison with densitometry and anthropometry. *European Journal of Clinical Nutrition*, **43**, 779-791.

Funk, R.C., Kerekes, B.F., & Lanphier, R.C. (1993). Total body electrical conductivity: New developments and expanded applications In J.G. Kral & T.B. Van Itallie (Eds.), *Recent developments in body composition analysis: Methods and applications* (pp. 61-74). London: Smith-Gordon.

Gartner, A., Maire, B., Delpeuch, C.P. et al. (1993). The use of bioelectrical impedance analysis (BIA) in newborns: The need for standardization. In K.J. Ellis & J.D. Eastman (Eds.), *Human body composition* (pp. 165-168). New York: Plenum.

Geddes, L.A., & Baker, L.E. (1967). The specific resistance of biological material: A compendium of data for the biomedical engineer and physiologist. *Medical and Biological Engineering and Computing*, **5**, 271-293.

Gleichauf, C.N., & Roe, D.A. (1989). The menstrual cycle's effect on the reliability of bioimpedance measurements for assessing body composition. *American Journal of Clinical Nutrition*, **50**, 903-907.

Graves, J.E., Pollock, M.L., Colvin, A.B., et al.. (1989). Comparison of different bioelectrical impedance analyzers in the prediction of body composition. *American Journal of Human Biology*, **1**, 603-612.

Gray, D.S. (1988). Changes in bioelectrical impedance during fasting. *American Journal of Clinical Nutrition*, **48**, 1184-1187.

Gray, D.S., Bray, G.A., Gemayel, N., & Kaplan, K. (1989). Effect of obesity on bioelectrical impedance. *American Journal of Clinical Nutrition*, **50**, 255-260.

Gudivaka, R., Schoeller, D., Ho, T., Spiegel, D., Kushner, R. (1994). Effect of body position, electrode placement and time on prediction of total body water by multifrequency bioelectrical impedance analysis. *Age & Nutrition*, **5**, 111-117.

Guglielmi, F.W., Contento, F., Laddaga, L., et al. (1991). Bioelectric impedance analysis: Experience with male patients with cirrhosis. *Hepatology*, **13**, 892-895.

Guo, S., Roche, A.F., Chumlea, W.C. et al. (1987). Body composition predictions from bioelectric impedance. *Human Biology*, **59**, 221-234.

Guo, S., Roche, A.F., & Houtkooper, L. (1990). Fat-free mass in children and young adults predicted from bioelectric impedance and anthropometric variables. *American Journal of Clinical Nutrition*, **50**, 435-443.

Harrison, G.G., & Van Itallie, T.B. (1982). Estimation of body composition: A new approach based on electromagnetic principles. *American Journal of Clinical Nutrition*, **35**, 1176-1179.

Heitmann, B.L. (1990). Prediction of body water and fat in adult Danes from measurements of electrical impedance. *International Journal of Obesity*, **14**, 789-802.

Hodgdon, J.A., & Fitzgerald, P.I. (1987). Validity of impedance predictions at various levels of fatness. *Human Biology*, **59**, 281-298.

Hoffer, E.C., Meador, C., & Simpson, D.C. (1969). Correlation of whole-body impedance with total body water volume. *Journal of Applied Physiology*, **27**, 531-534.

Horswill, C.A., Geeseman, R., Boileau, R.A., et al. (1989). Total-body electrical conductivity (TO-BEC): Relationship to estimates of muscle mass, fat-free weight, and lean body mass. *American Journal of Clinical Nutrition*, **49**, 593-598.

Houtkooper, L.B., Lohman, T.G., Going, S.B., & Hall, M.C. (1989). Validity of bioelectrical impedance for body composition assessment in children. *Journal of Applied Physiology*, **66**, 814-821.

Jenin, P., Lenoir, J., Roullet, C., et al. (1975). Determination of body fluid compartments by electrical impedance measurements. *Aviation Space and Environmental Medicine*, **46**, 152-155.

Kanai, H., Haeno, M., & Sakamoto, K. (1987). Electrical measurement of fluid distribution in legs and arms. *Medical Progress Through Technology*, **12**, 159-170.

Khaled, M.A., McCutcheon, M.J., Reddy, S., et al. (1988). Electrical impedance in assessing human body composition: The BIA method. *American Journal of Clinical Nutrition*, **47**, 789-792.

Klish, W.J. (1993). Use of the TOBEC instrument in the measurement of body composition in children. In J.G. Kral & T.B. Van Itallie (Eds.), *Recent developments in body composition analysis: Methods and applications* (pp. 111-120). London: Smith-Gordon.

Klish, W.J., Forbes, G.B., Gordon, A., & Cochran, W.J. (1984). New method for the estimation of lean body mass in infants (EEME Instrument): Validation in nonhuman models. *Journal of Pediatric Gastroenterology and Nutrition*, **3**, 199-204.

Kurtin, P.S., Shapiro, A.C., Tomita, H., & Raisman, D. (1990). Volume status and body composition of chronic dialysis patients: Utility of bioelectrical impedance plethysmography. *American Journal of Nephrology*, **10**, 363-367.

Kushner, R.F. (1992). Bioelectric impedance analysis: A review of principles and applications. *Journal of the American College of Nutrition*, **11**, 199-209.

Kushner, R.F., Kunigk, A., Alspaugh, M., et al. (1990). Validation of bioelectrical impedance analysis as a measurement of changes in body composition in obesity. *American Journal of Clinical Nutrition*, **52**, 219-223.

Kushner, R.F., & Schoeller, D.A. (1986). Estimation of total body water by bioelectrical impedance analysis. *American Journal of Clinical Nutrition*, **44**, 417-424.

Kushner, R.F., Schoeller, D.A., Fjeld, C.R., & Danford, L. (1992). Is the impedance index (ht2/R) significant in predicting total body water? *American Journal of Clinical Nutrition*, **56**, 835-839.

Lohman, T.G. (1992). *Advances in body composition assessment*. Champaign, IL: Human Kinetics.

Lohman, T.G., Roche, A.F., & Martorell, R. (Eds). (1988). *Anthropometric standardization reference manual*. Champaign, IL: Human Kinetics.

Lukaski, H.C. (1991). Assessment of body composition using tetrapolar bioelectrical impedance analysis. In R.G. Whitehead & A. Prentice (Eds.), *New techniques in nutritional research* (pp. 303-317). San Diego, CA: Academic.

Lukaski, H.C. (1992). Body composition assessment using impedance methods. In P. Björntorp & B.N. Brodoff (Eds.), *Obesity* (pp. 67-79). Philadelphia: J.B. Lippincott.

Lukaski, H.C. (1993). Comparison of proximal and distal placements of electrodes to assess human body composition by bioelectrical impedance. In K.J. Ellis & J.D. Eastman (Eds.), *Human body composition* (pp. 39-44). New York: Plenum.

Lukaski, H.C., & Bolonchuk, W.W. (1988). Estimation of body fluid volumes using tetrapolar bioelectrical impedance measurements. *Aviation Space and Environmental Medicine*, **59**, 1163-1169.

Lukaski, H.C., Bolonchuk, W.W., Hall, C.B., & Siders, W.A (1986). Validation of tetrapolar bioelectrical impedance method to assess human body composition. *Journal of Applied Physiology*, **60**, 1327-1332.

Lukaski, H.C., Johnson, P.E., Bolonchuk, W.W., & Lykken, G.I. (1985). Assessment of fat free mass using bioelectric impedance measurements of the human body. *American Journal of Clinical Nutrition*, **41**, 810-817.

Mayfield, S.R., Vauy, R., & Waidelich, D. (1991). Body composition of low-birth-weight infants determined by using bioelectric resistance and reactance. *American Journal of Clinical Nutrition*, **54**, 296-303.

McDougall, D., & Shizgall, H.M. (1986). Body composition measurements from whole body resistance and reactance. *Surgical Forum*, **36**, 42-44.

Moore, F.D., Olesen, K.H., McMurrey, J.D., et al. (1963). *The body cell mass and its supporting environment in body composition in health and disease*. Philadelphia: W.B. Saunders.

Nyboer, J. (1959). *Electrical impedance plethysmography: The electrical resistive measure of the blood pulse volume*. Springfield, IL: CC Thomas.

Nyboer J. (1981). Percent body fat by four terminal bio-electrical impedance and body density in college freshmen. In *Proceedings of the Vth International Conference on Electrical Bio-Impedance*. Distributed by Business for Academic Societies, Japan.

Paijmans, I.J.M., Wilmore, K.M., & Wilmore, J.H. (1992). Use of skinfolds and bioelectrical impedance for body composition assessment after weight reduction. *Journal of the American College of Nutrition, 11*, 145-151.

Patterson, R., Ranganathan, C., Engel, R., & Berkseth, R. (1988). Measurement of body fluid volume change using multiple impedance measurements. *Medical and Biological Engineering and Computing, 26*, 33-37.

Pethig, R. (1979). *Dielectric and electronic properties of biological materials*. Chichester, UK: Wiley.

Presta, E., Segal, K.R., Gutin, B., et al. (1983a). Comparison in man of total body electrical conductivity and lean body mass derived from body density: Validation of a new body composition method. *Metabolism, 32*, 524-527.

Presta, E., Wang, J., Harrison, G.G., et al. (1983b). Measurement of total body electrical conductivity: A new method for estimation of body composition. *American Journal of Clinical Nutrition, 37*, 735-739.

Pullicino, E., Coward, W.A., Stubbs, R.J., & Elia, M. (1990). Bedside and field methods for assessing body composition: Comparison with deuterium dilution technique. *European Journal of Clinical Nutrition, 44*, 753-762.

Roche, A.F., Chumlea, W.C., & Guo, S. (1986). *Identification and validation of new anthropometric techniques for quantifying body composition*. Natick, MA: US Army Research and Development Center.

Roche, A.F., & Guo, S. (1993). Development, testing and use of predictive equations for body composition measures. In J.G. Kral & T.B. Van Itallie (Eds.), *Recent developments in body composition analysis: Methods and applications* (pp. 1-16). London: Smith-Gordon.

Roos, A.N., Westendorp, R.G.J., Frölich, M., & Meinders, A.E. (1992). Tetrapolar body impedance is influenced by body position and plasma sodium concentration. *European Journal of Clinical Nutrition, 46*, 53-60.

Ross, R., Leger, L., Martin, P., & Roch, R. (1989). Sensitivity of bioelectrical impedance to detect changes in human body composition. *Journal of Applied Physiology, 67*, 1643-1648.

Rush, S., Abildskov, J.A., & McFee, R. (1963). Resistivity of body tissues at low frequencies. *Circulation Research, 12*, 40-50.

Sasser, D.C., Gerth, W.A., & Wu, Y-C. (1993). Monitoring of segmental intra- and extracellular volume changes using electric impedance spectroscopy. *Journal of Applied Physiology, 74*, 2180-2187.

Schell, B., & Gross, R. (1987). The reliability of bioelectrical impedance measurements in the assessment of body composition in healthy subjects. *Nutrition Reports International, 36*, 449-459.

Segal, K.R., Burastero, S., Chun, A., et al. (1991). Estimation of extracellular and total body water by multiple-frequency bioelectrical impedance measurement. *American Journal of Clinical Nutrition, 54*, 26-29.

Segal, K.R., Gutin, B., Presta, E., et al. (1985). Estimation of human body composition by electrical impedance methods: A comparative study. *Journal of Applied Physiology, 58*, 1565-1571.

Segal, K.R., Van Loan, M.D., Fitzgerald, P.I., et al. (1988). Lean body mass estimated by bioelectrical impedance analysis: A four site cross validation study. *American Journal of Clinical Nutrition, 47*, 7-14.

Settle, R.G., Foster, K.R., Epstein, B.R., & Mullen, J.L. (1980). Nutritional assessment: Whole body impedance and body fluid compartments. *Nutrition and Cancer, 2*, 72-80.

Spence, J.A., Baliga, R, Nyboer, J., & Bhatia, M.L. (1979). Changes during heomdialysis in total body water, cardiac output and chest fluid as detected by bioelectrical impedance analysis. *Transactions: American Society for Artificial Internal Organs, 25*, 51-55.

Streat, S.J., Beddoe, A.H., & Hill, G.L. (1985). Measurement of body fat and hydration of the fat-free body in health and disease. *Metabolism, 34*, 509-518.

Subramanyan, R., Manchanda, S.C., Nyboer, J., & Bhatia, M.L. (1980). Total body water in congestive heart failure. A pre and post treatment study. *Journal of the Association of Physicians of India, 28*, 257-262.

Tagliabue, A., Cena, H., Trentani, C., et al. (1992). How reliable is bio-electrical impedance analysis for individual patients? *International Journal of Obesity, 16*, 649-652.

Thomasset, A. (1962). Bio-electrical properties of tissue impedance measurements. *Lyon Medical, 207*, 107-118.

van der Kooy, K., Leenen, R., Deurenberg, P., et al. (1992). Changes in fat-free mass in obese subjects after weight loss: A comparison of body composition measures. *International Journal of Obesity, 16*, 675-684.

Van Itallie, T.B., Segal, K.R., & Funk, R.C. (1987). Measurement of total body electrical conductivity: A new method for the rapid estimation of human body composition. *American Institute of Nutrition, Symposium Proceedings, Nutrition '87* (pp. 82-87). Bethesda, MD: American Institute of Nutrition.

Van Loan, M.D. (1990). Assessment of fat-free mass in teen-agers: Use of TOBEC methodology. *American Journal of Clinical Nutrition, 52,* 586-590.

Van Loan, M.D., Belko, A.Z., Mayclin, P.L., & Barbieri, T.F. (1987a). Use of total-body electrical conductivity for monitoring body composition changes during weight reduction. *American Journal of Clinical Nutrition, 46,* 5-8.

Van Loan, M.D., Keim, N.L., & Phinney, S.D. (1993). Use of bioelectric techniques to monitor composition of weight loss in obese individuals during weight reduction. In J.G. Kral & T.B. Van Itallie (Eds.), *Recent developments in body composition analysis: Methods and applications* (pp. 157-168). London: Smith-Gordon.

Van Loan, M.D., & Koehler, L.S. (1990). Use of total-body electrical conductivity for the assessment of body composition in middle-aged and elderly individuals. *American Journal of Clinical Nutrition, 51,* 548-552.

Van Loan, M., & Mayclin, P. (1987). A new TOBEC instrument and procedure for the assessment of body composition: Use of Fourier coefficients to predict lean body mass and total body water. *American Journal of Clinical Nutrition, 45,* 131-137.

Van Loan, M.D., & Mayclin, P. (1992). Use of multi-frequency bioelectrical impedance analysis for the estimation of extracellular fluid. *European Journal of Clinical Nutrition, 46,* 117-124.

Van Loan, M.D., Segal, K.R., Bracco, E.F., et al. (1987b). TOBEC methodology for body composition assessment: A cross-validation study. *American Journal of Clinical Nutrition, 46,* 9-12.

Vazquez, J.A., & Janosky, J.E. (1991). Validity of bioelectrical-impedance analysis in measuring changes in lean body mass during weight reduction. *American Journal of Clinical Nutrition, 54,* 970-975.

Vettorazzi, C., Molina, S., Santizo, M.C., et al. (1989). Bioelectrical impedance indices in protein-energy malnourished children as an indicator of total body water status. In S. Yasumura, J.E. Harrison, K.G. McNeil, et al. (Eds.), *In vivo body composition studies: Recent advances* (pp. 45-50). New York: Plenum.

Zillikens, M.C., & Conway, J.M. (1991). The estimation of total body water by bioelectrical impedance in blacks. *American Journal of Human Biology, 3,* 25-32.

Zillikens, M.C., van den Berg, J.W.O., Wilson, J.H.P., & Swart, R.G. (1992). Whole-body and segmental bioelectrical-impedance analysis in patients with cirrhosis of the liver: Changes after treatment of ascites. *American Journal of Clinical Nutrition, 55,* 621-625.

6

Estimation of Muscle Mass

Henry C. Lukaski

Methods for the assessment of human body composition emphasize the estimation of body fat with limited availability of approaches and techniques to assess muscle mass (Forbes, 1987; Lukaski, 1987). This emphasis reflects, in part, the demands of the scientific community to estimate a compositional variable (i.e., percent body fat) that might be a potentially useful predictor of risk of future development of chronic disease, particularly ischemic heart disease. More recently, however, an increased awareness of the significance of the development and maintenance of skeletal muscle mass has stimulated a reappraisal of available approaches for the in vivo assessment of skeletal muscle mass.

In the body, muscle is present in three distinct forms: skeletal, smooth, and cardiac. Skeletal, also known as voluntary or striated, muscle represents approximately 30% of the body weight of a healthy 58 kg woman or 40% of the body weight of a 70 kg man (International Commission on Radiological Protection, 1975). In an adult, the majority of skeletal muscle is found in the legs with lesser amounts in the head, trunk, and arms.

The need for methods to estimate either whole-body or regional muscle mass is compelling and reflects multidisciplinary interests. One application of such methods is to monitor changes in muscle mass in relation to growth and development of infants and children and to establish normative data for use in medicine and clinical investigations.

There are additional applications in physiology, nutrition and medicine. Because skeletal muscle is required for movement, exercise scientists are interested in relating estimates of muscle mass to various types of aerobic and anaerobic athletic performance and to the effects of physical training on work capacity and physical performance. Clinicians require estimates of muscle mass to evaluate the progression of catabolic disease and to evaluate the efficacy of therapeutic interventions on prognosis. Currently, geriatricians seek longitudinal assessments of muscle mass to monitor the effects of aging on muscular development and function, to evaluate the efficacy of strength-building exercise programs to maintain and improve functional capacity and ambulation of the elderly, and thus to improve the quality of life for elders.

One limitation to the general availability of a useful technique of assessing skeletal muscle mass is the relative lack of direct data on anatomical tissue masses. As discussed by Martin, Spenst, Drinkwater, and Clarys (1990), skeletal muscle masses determined by dissection and body masses are known for only 25 men. Therefore, development and validation of most current methods of assessment of muscle mass are limited by the use of indirect reference methods relying on some biochemical or physical characteristic of skeletal muscle.

This article will describe available methods for the estimation of human skeletal muscle mass in vivo. Emphasis will be placed on the biological and physical basis of each approach, and the application and the limitations of the methods.

Anthropometric Indicators of Muscle Mass

The use of anthropometry to estimate muscle mass requires the selection of some body measurements that are predictive of muscle mass. In general, a muscle group is selected with the assumptions that site-specific physical measurements reflect the mass of that muscle, and the mass of the estimated muscle group is directly proportional to the whole-body skeletal muscle mass.

Estimation of Regional Muscle Mass

Historically, the use of anthropometric values from the upper arm to estimate muscle mass has dominated the literature (Jelliffe & Jelliffe, 1969). Estimates of upper arm muscle circumference have served as a functional index of protein-energy malnutrition (Jelliffe, 1966). Measurements of the lower leg also have been used but only infrequently (Heymsfield, Olafson, Kutner, & Nixon, 1979).

The common variables for the upper arm include arm circumference (C_A), corrected for subcutaneous adipose tissue thickness, and muscle cross-sectional area estimated from the corrected circumference (Figure 6.1). The tissue boundaries in the arm cross-section are assumed to be circular and concentric. If the skin plus adipose tissue thickness is defined as d, then the arm muscle circumference (C_M) is given as $C_M = C_A - 2\pi d$. Since the skinfold measurement includes two thickness of adipose tissue, and if 2d is represented by S, then $C_M = C_A - \pi S$.

Because it was realized that estimates of arm circumference represent a unidimensional approximation and muscle mass is a three-dimensional quantity, the estimation of muscle area has taken prominence as an index of nutritional assessment (Frisancho, 1974; Heymsfield, McMannus, Stevens, & Smith, 1982a). The basic assumptions of this index include: (1) the mid-arm is circular, (2) the triceps skinfold thickness is twice the average adipose tissue rim diameter at the middle of the upper arm, (3) the mid-arm muscle compartment is circular, and (4) bone responds similarly to muscle and adipose tissue during growth and caloric deprivation (Gurney & Jelliffe, 1973; Jelliffe, 1966).

The validity of the anthropometric estimation of upper arm circumference has been examined. Heymsfield et al. (1979) reported that each of the assumptions was in error to some degree. In a sample of adults with body weights ranging from 60 to 120% ideal body weight, anthropometric mid-arm muscle area was overestimated 15 to 25% as compared to reference values determined by computed axial tomography. Subsequently, gender-specific equations were derived to account for errors in each of the four assumptions (Heymsfield et al., 1982b). The revised equations, containing corrections for bone contributions to anthropometric values, resulted in an average intraindividual error of 7 to 8% in the calculated mid-arm muscle

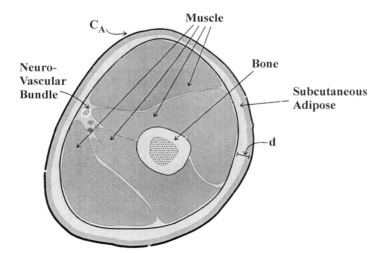

Figure 6.1 Diagram of the anthropometric variables for the determination of mid-arm muscle circumference. The measurements include arm circumference (C_A) and skinfold plus skin thickness (d).

area. However, in the subjects whose ideal body weight was greater than 150%, the mid-arm muscle area was in error by more than 50% even after the revised equations were used.

Estimation of Whole-Body Muscle Mass

A few attempts have been made to use anthropometric values to estimate whole-body, as compared to regional, muscle mass. All the proposed models are similar because they rely on measurements of regional body circumferences and skinfold thicknesses, but they differ because of the reference methods used to derive and validate the prediction models.

In 1921, Mateiga proposed a model based on the circumferences of the forearm, upper arm, thigh, and calf, corrected for the corresponding skinfold thicknesses, to derive an average value for limb muscle radius. This value was squared, multiplied by stature, and then multiplied by the "constant" of 6.5. This hypothetical model was neither validated by Mateiga nor examined by subsequent investigators.

Using anthropometric estimates of arm muscle area corrected for bone in combination with stature, Heymsfield et al. (1982a) attempted to predict whole-body muscle mass values estimated from urinary creatinine excretion. It was assumed that each gram of creatinine excreted in the urine per day was equivalent to 20 kg of muscle mass. The error of the predicted values ranged from 5 to 9%, with an average error of about 8%.

These approaches have some general limitations. The use of a single, regional measurement promotes errors in the estimation of whole-body muscle mass because of interindividual variability in the distributions of muscle mass, adipose tissue, and bone thickness. The validity of this approach is poor in individuals with excess adipose tissue in the upper extremities. Thus, this approach provides only a qualitative index of whole-body muscle mass.

Brussels Cadaver Study

In contrast to the studies considered earlier, the Brussels cadaver study utilized anthropometric values and tissue mass determinations in the same subjects (Clarys, Martin, & Drinkwater, 1984). These data were used to develop regression models for the estimation of whole-body muscle mass (Martin et al., 1990).

Twenty-five cadavers were studied: 12 were embalmed (6 men and 6 women) and 13 were unembalmed (6 men and 7 women). The anthropometric variables included skinfold thicknesses (triceps, subscapular, biceps, anterior thigh, and medial calf) and circumferences (forearm, mid upper-arm, mid anterior thigh, and calf). Limb muscle girths were estimated by correcting limb girths for skinfold thicknesses. Data from the six unembalmed cadavers were used to develop a regression model, and the data from five embalmed cadavers were used for validation. Data from one embalmed cadaver were not used for the validation study because of atrophy of muscle and bone in one leg.

Regional anthropometric values were strong predictors of total dissected muscle mass (Table 6.1). Because skinfold thickness of the forearm is measured infrequently and the correlation coefficient of the uncorrected forearm circumference with total dissected muscle mass was very strong, Martin et al. (1990) derived the following predictive equation for men:

$$MM = STAT\,(0.0546\;CTG^2 + 0.119\;FG^2 + 0.0256\;CCG^2) - 2980 \qquad (6.1)$$

where MM is total skeletal muscle mass (g), STAT is stature (cm), CTG is thigh circumference corrected for anterior thigh circumference (cm), FG is uncorrected forearm circumference (cm), and CCG is calf circumference corrected for skinfold thickness (cm).

Comparison of predicted and dissected total skeletal muscle mass in five unembalmed male

Table 6.1 Relationships of Limb Girths to Total Dissected Skeletal Muscle Mass in Six Unembalmed Male Cadavers

| Site | Correlation coefficients | |
	Basic girth	Girth corrected for skinfold thickness
Arm	0.824	0.896
Forearm	0.963	0.998
Thigh	0.942	0.990
Calf	0.836	0.911

Adapted from "Anthropometric Estimation of Muscle Mass," by A.D. Martin, L.F. Spenst, D.T. Drinkwater, and J.P. Clarys, 1990, *Medicine and Science in Sports and Exercise*, **22**, pp. 729-733. Copyright 1990 by Williams & Wilkins. Adapted with permission.

cadavers indicated a relationship similar to the line of identity with $R^2 = 0.93$ and $SEE = 1.58$ kg.

The authors proposed that because the SEE values between the derived model (1.56 kg) and the validation comparison (1.58 kg) were similar, a combined model for men should be generated. This model is:

$$MM = STAT\ (0.0553\ CTG^2 + 0.0987\ FG^2 + 0.0331\ CCG^2) - 2445. \qquad (6.2)$$

For this model, $SEE = 1.53$ kg and $R^2 = 0.97$. The validity of the derived model was examined also in relation to values predicted from the models of Heymsfield et al. (1982b) and Mateiga (1921). Estimated error (calculated as the estimated minus the dissected value) for five embalmed cadavers was evaluated as a function of dissected muscle mass. The model derived by Martin et al. (1990) had a random and substantially reduced error (approximately ± 2 kg) compared to the other prediction models, which consistently underestimated muscle mass by amounts ranging from 5 to more than 10 kg.

Limitations to the Use of Anthropometric Estimates of Muscle Mass

In general, the use of anthropometric values, typically combined circumference and skinfold thickness measurements, to predict both regional and total muscle masses yields qualitative assessments. At present, however, it is not known if anthropometric estimations are either sufficiently accurate or sensitive to monitor small changes in muscle mass associated with weight loss or gain in an individual. Some of this limitation may be explained by the use of four independent variables (limb circumferences adjusted for skinfold thicknesses) plus an intercept to model muscle mass based on a very small sample size ($n = 6$). This overparamaterized model may be highly sample-specific and not adequately robust for general utilization.

Muscle Metabolites

The hypothesis that endogenous components or metabolites of skeletal muscle metabolism may be used to estimate skeletal muscle mass is established on some basic premises. The assumptions are that the chemical marker is found only in skeletal muscle, the size of the pool of the marker is

constant, the rate of turnover is relatively unchanged over long periods of time, and the compound is not further metabolized after release into the circulation. Two metabolites specific to skeletal muscle have been used as indices of skeletal muscle mass.

Creatinine

The origin of endogenous creatinine is found in the synthesis of its precursor, creatine, in the liver and kidney (Figure 6.2). Although many tissues and organs take up creatine, the vast majority (98%) of it is found in skeletal muscle, principally in the form of creatine phosphate (Borsook & Dubnoff, 1947). Creatinine is formed by the nonenzymatic hydrolysis of free creatine that is liberated during the dephosphorylation of creatine phosphate (Borsook & Dubnoff).

Since Folin (1905) hypothesized that urinary creatinine was a qualitative indicator of body composition and Hoberman, Sims, & Peters (1948) demonstrated the direct proportionality of body creatine to the daily urinary creatinine output using nitrogen-15 isotopic dilution, it has been acknowledged generally that urinary creatinine excretion is related to fat-free mass (FFM) and skeletal muscle mass (Cheek, 1968; Forbes & Bruining, 1976; Talbot, 1938).

Estimation of skeletal muscle mass from daily urinary creatinine excretion presumes a constant relation between these variables. Talbot (1938) estimated that 1 g of creatinine excreted during a 24 hour period was derived from approximately 18 kg of muscle mass. Cheek et al. (1968), however, suggested that each gram of creatinine excreted daily was derived from 20 kg of muscle tissue. This difference between the studies probably reflects discrepancies in muscle sampling and variations in methods between the studies.

Although the appeal of implementing urinary creatinine excretion as an indicator of muscle mass has generated its considerable use in clinical investigations (Forbes, 1987), some factors have been identified that affect the validity of this approach. One limitation is the relatively large intraindividual variability in daily urinary creatinine excretion. The mean within-individual coefficient of variation (100% × standard deviation/mean) of daily urinary creatinine output ranges from 11 to 30% for individuals consuming self-selected diets (Bleiler & Schedl, 1962; Greenblatt et al., 1976; Lykken, Jacob, Munoz, & Sandstead, 1980; Ransil, Greenblatt, & Koch-Weser, 1977). This variability

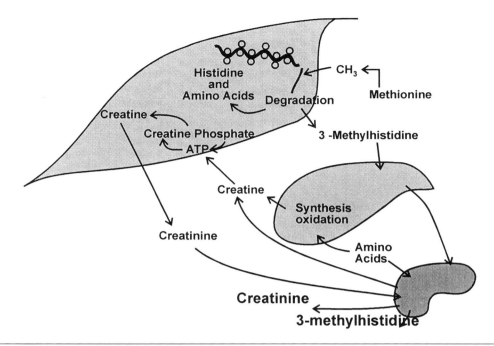

Figure 6.2 Schematic representation of the metabolism of creatinine and 3-methylhistidine in human beings.

can be reduced to less than 5% if meat-free diets are consumed (Lukaski & Mendez, 1980; Lykken et. al.).

Diet influences the daily urinary creatinine excretion. Significant reductions (10 to 20%) in excretion occur in healthy men consuming meat-free diets for several weeks (Bleiler & Schedl, 1962; Calloway & Margen, 1971). Changes in urinary creatinine output are related directly to daily creatine intake. Among healthy young men consecutively fed 0.23 g creatine per day for 9 days, 10 g creatine per day for 10 days, and then a creatine-free diet for 71 days, urinary creatinine excretion increased with creatine feeding, then decreased with the creatine-free diet (Crim, Calloway, & Margen, 1975). Nitrogen balance was positive during all diet periods. Similarly, Lykken et al. (1980), on the basis of his experimental findings, derived a mathematical model with feedback controls that describes the creatinine pool size and creatinine excretion as a function of time and of changes in the amount of creatine and protein consumed. These findings suggest that the body creatinine pool size is not under strict metabolic control and that urinary creatinine excretion may be, to some degree, independent of body composition.

Other factors affecting the validity of the use of urinary creatinine relate to the renal handling of creatinine and the timing of urine collection. It has been reported that creatinine is filtered and secreted within the glomerulus (Materson, 1971).

In addition, the need for accurately timed urine collections is critical. Forbes & Bruining (1976) have demonstrated that an error as small as 15 minutes in the duration of a collection period represents an error of 1% in the determination of 24 hour urinary creatinine excretion. Thus, it has been advised to make three consecutive 24 hour urine collections to reduce intraindividual variation in daily urinary creatinine excretion (Forbes & Bruining).

The critical question of the constancy of the ratio of one gram of urinary endogenous creatinine excretion to a unit of muscle mass or even FFM has been addressed. Based on their evaluation of the positive intercepts of the relationships between endogenous urinary creatinine output and FFM in children and adults, Forbes & Bruining (1976) proposed that urinary creatinine excretion does not represent a constant fraction of either muscle or FFM. They concluded that it is inappropriate to use a constant ratio of creatinine to muscle unless factors such as age, gender, maturity, physical training, and metabolic state are controlled.

Schutte et al. (1981) proposed the use of total circulating creatinine as an index of skeletal muscle mass. A strong relationship ($r = 0.82$, $p < 0.001$) was reported between total plasma creatinine (plasma volume × plasma creatinine concentration) and 24 hour urinary creatinine excretion in 24 healthy men. Muscle mass was calculated from urinary creatinine excretion using the conversion factors of Cheek (1968) and Talbot (1938). Schutte et al. estimated that each milligram of total plasma creatinine would account for 0.9 to 1.0 kg skeletal muscle. This empirical relationship was subsequently evaluated by direct dissection of skeletal muscle and determination of total plasma creatinine in dogs. It was determined that each milligram of total plasma creatinine was equivalent to about 0.9 kg skeletal muscle. A mean error of about 4% (range 0.5 to 10%) was found between the predicted and measured values.

3-Methylhistidine

The endogenous excretion of the amino acid 3-methylhistidine (3-MH) has been suggested as a measure of muscle protein breakdown (Young & Munro, 1978). This unique amino acid is located principally in skeletal muscle (Figure 6.2). Elia, Carter, and Smith (1979) reported a comprehensive series of measurements of tissues taken postmortem from five adults aged 43 to 63 years at death. They found that skeletal muscles had the greatest 3-MH concentration (3.31 ± 0.05 µmol/g fat-free dry weight, mean ± SE) with intermediate concentrations in cardiac and some smooth muscle tissues (1 to 2 µmol/g) and low values (< 1 µmol/g) in tissues, such as spleen, liver, and kidney.

The 3-MH concentration of human muscle is relatively constant with age. Tomas, Ballard, & Pope (1979) measured the 3-MH content in muscle biopsy samples from the vastus lateralis of human beings aged 2 days to 65 years. They reported that the 3-MH concentration was relatively constant (3.63 ± 0.06 µmol/g) between the ages of 4 to 65 years. Urinary excretion of 3-MH decreased with age. This observation was interpreted to indicate that 3-MH turnover decreased with age. It is reasonable to suggest, however, that the reduction in urinary 3-MH output might reflect a decreased muscle mass with age, a general trend in the population (Cohn et al., 1980b).

In addition to its unique distribution in skeletal muscle, some other metabolic characteristics of 3-MH suggest that it may be a useful index of muscle mass. Experimental evidence indicates that specific histidine residues are methylated after the formation of the peptide chains of actin of all muscle fibers and the myosin of white muscle fibers (Asatoor & Armstrong, 1967; Hardy & Perry, 1969; Johnson, Harris, & Perry, 1967; Reporter, 1973). During catabolism of the myofibrillar proteins, the released 3-MH is neither reutilized for protein synthesis (Young, Baliga, Alexis, & Munro, 1970) nor

metabolized oxidatively (Long et al., 1975) but is excreted in the urine (Long et al., 1977).

Few investigations have attempted to establish the relationship between endogenous 3-MH excretion and human body composition. In a study of 16 healthy men consuming a meat-free diet for three days, 24 hour urinary 3-MH output was well correlated ($r = 0.90$, $p < 0.001$) with FFM (Lukaski & Mendez, 1980). Urinary creatinine excretion also was correlated ($r = 0.67$, $p < 0.01$) with FFM. Subsequently, a strong relationship ($r = 0.91$, $p < 0.001$) between muscle mass—assessed from determinations of total body potassium (TBK) and nitrogen (TBN) and by using the models of Burkinshaw, Hill, and Morgan (1978)—and endogenous 3-MH was determined in 14 athletic men fed a meat-free diet for seven days (Lukaski, Mendez, Buskirk, & Cohn, 1981a). Only a weak ($r = 0.33$) correlation between endogenous 3-MH excretion and nonmuscle protein mass was observed. Urinary creatinine excretion was correlated ($r = 0.79$, $p < 0.01$) with muscle mass.

Because creatine and 3-MH share a similar site of origin in muscle, there was an interest in determining the relationship between urinary endogenous creatinine and 3-MH excretions. Tomas et al. (1979) studied two men and two women aged 19 to 38 years who consumed a meat-free diet for three days. Urine from each micturition was collected and analyzed for these muscle metabolites. A significant relationship ($r = 0.96$) was found. The variability in predicting 3-MH excretion from urinary creatinine excretion was less than 0.001 µmol/ml within the range of 0.05 to 0.7 µmol/ml. A similar, although more variable, relationship ($r = 0.87$) was found in daily urinary 3-MH and creatinine excretions from 14 men consuming isonitrogenous meat-containing and meat-free diets (Lukaski et al., 1981a).

The use of 3-MH as a marker of muscle mass has been criticized because of the potential influence of nonskeletal muscle protein turnover on its excretion rate (Rennie & Millward, 1983). Studies in rats indicated a significant contribution of smooth muscle protein turnover from the skin and gastrointestinal tract to the urinary output of 3-MH (Millward et al., 1980; Wassner & Li, 1982). Harris (1981) challenged the findings of Millward et al. (1980) on the basis that the assumption of an equal rate of myofibrillar degradation and fractional rate of synthesis within each of the tissues studied was incorrect. This problem has not been examined in detail in human beings for whom simultaneous determinations of myofibrillar protein synthetic and degradation rates have been assessed. In addition, the relative rates of muscle to nonmuscle protein synthesis and turnover are greater for the adult human being than for the rat (37 vs 12%, respectively; Millward & Bates, 1983). Furthermore, skeletal muscle may be the more important source of endogenous 3-MH in urine in human beings, whereas the intestines and skin may be more important contributors in the rat.

The quantitative contribution of creatinine and 3-MH from muscle has been addressed indirectly by Afting, Bernhardt, Janzen, and Rothig (1981). In a paralyzed patient, about 1.2 μmol 3-MH/kg body weight was excreted daily. Urinary creatinine excretion was 35 μmol/kg body weight per day. The patient did not have either macroscopically or microscopically detectable skeletal muscle tissue in the limbs. Therefore, these findings indicate that both creatinine and 3-MH can be derived from nonskeletal muscle sources. Comparison of data from healthy control subjects indicated that about 25% of the 3-MH was from nonskeletal muscle sources. Thus, the findings of Afting et al. agree with the conclusion of Harris (1981) that about 75% of the excreted 3-MH in human beings is derived from skeletal muscle.

The general use of urinary 3-MH excretion as a marker of muscle mass may be reasonable in conditions of severe sepsis or significant physical trauma in which accelerated rates of protein degradation occur, especially in skeletal muscle (Cannon et al., 1991; Clowes, George, Ville, & Saravis, 1983). This is in contrast with clinical conditions in which significant muscle depletion has already occurred or in which prior inadequate nutritional intake has resulted in a diminished state of health (Rennie et al., 1983). In the latter examples, reduction of protein synthesis, in contrast to increased protein degradation, is the basis for the loss of muscle mass.

Limitations to the Use of Muscle Metabolites to Index Muscle Mass

Although creatinine and 3-MH arise primarily from muscle, their relationship to skeletal muscle mass needs further examination with respect to factors that affect their pool sizes and turnover rates. Additional study is required in human beings to discern the significance of contributions of nonskeletal muscle sources of these metabolites to daily endogenous excretion. The routine use of total plasma creatinine is hampered by the requirement for determination of plasma volume. This limits the use of this approach to laboratory studies.

Two additional factors limit the general use of urinary excretion of endogenous metabolites to predict muscle mass in vivo. There is a need to consume a meat-free diet that is adequate in protein content to eliminate exogenous sources of creatine, creatinine, and 3-MH (Lukaski et al., 1981a). Additionally, accurately timed urine collections are necessary to estimate endogenous excretion of creatinine and 3-MH.

Radiographic Methods

In contrast to other methods that indirectly assess muscle mass, radiographic techniques offer unique opportunities for direct visualization and measurement of compositional variables, including adipose tissue, bone, and muscle. These methods rely on the differing responses among tissues, based on their chemical composition, as the tissue interacts with electromagnetic energy. Thus, these techniques facilitate the regional measurement and, in some cases, whole-body assessment of body composition.

Three radiographic techniques currently utilized in body composition research are computed tomography (CT), magnetic resonance imaging (MRI), and dual x-ray absorptiometry (DXA). Although the principal use of CT and MRI in body composition research has been the determination of regional adipose tissue, both subcutaneous and visceral (Fuller, Fowler, McNeill, & Foster, 1994), these methods can measure muscle mass. Essentially the same compositional information that is available from CT is also available from MRI. The DXA technique also has the capability to assess bone mineral, fat, and fat-free tissues. Whereas CT and MRI provide cross-sectional anatomical images that can be used to calculate volumes, DXA provides two-dimensional representations of body structures, usually in a posteroanterior plane. These methods are discussed fully in relation to the measurement of body composition generally in chapters 4 and 8. The present account will include brief descriptions of these methods and will describe more fully their application to the measurement of muscle mass.

Computed Tomography

Computed tomography (CT) requires the placement of a patient on a bed between a collimated x-ray source (0.1 to 0.2 A, 60 to 120 kVp) and detectors aligned at opposite poles of a gantry. As x-rays pass through tissues of the body, the x-rays are attenuated. The induced attenuations in x-ray intensity are related to differences in the physical density of the tissues examined. This physical effect is expressed quantitatively as the linear attenuation coefficient or CT number. The CT number, expressed in Hounsfield units, is a measure of the tissue attenuation relative to that of water. For example, air, adipose tissue, and muscle have average CT numbers of −1000, −70, and +20, respectively.

The attenuation of the x-ray beam, and thus the CT number, depends on some physical effects of each tissue: coherent scattering, photoelectric absorption, and Compton interactions (Haus, 1979). The principal determinants of these effects are the physical density of the tissue and the atomic numbers of its chemical components. In general, there is a linear relationship between tissue density and CT number.

Each CT image is reconstructed from picture elements, or pixels, which are usually 1 mm × 1 mm (length × width) in dimension. A third dimension is slice thickness. Each pixel or voxel, a volume element derived from pixel dimensions and slice thickness, has a corresponding CT number. Thus, the reconstructed picture represents not the image at the surface of a tissue slice, but rather an average representing the full thickness of the slice. The CT method provides high image contrast and clear separation of adipose tissue from other soft tissues (Figure 6.3). The differing attenuation of adipose tissue and skeletal muscle permits visual and mathematical separation of image components.

Different approaches have been used with CT to assess body composition (Heymsfield, 1987). The structure of interest is traced directly on the viewing console with a cursor. The cross-sectional area of the tissue of interest (adipose tissue, bone, muscle, etc.) then can be determined. Since the slice thickness is known, one can calculate the volume occupied by the tissue or organ in the reconstructed picture. This technique has been used to obtain reference values for skeletal muscle area for use in the development of anthropometric models for estimating mid-arm muscle area and for the assessment of arm muscle area in malnutrition and obesity (Heymsfield et al., 1982b).

Another CT technique is used when the boundaries between structures are not sharp, but the tissues differ markedly in radiographic density. The pixels in successive slices are plotted as a function of physical density in a histogram separating the pixels into adipose and fat-free tissues (Figure 6.3). The volume of each pixel can be calculated and the volumes of skeletal muscle and adipose tissue in each slice can be determined from the number of pixels identified as adipose tissue or muscle.

Although the CT method offers considerable promise as a method to assess muscle mass, data are limited regarding comparisons between CT estimates and those from other methods. In an abstract, Wang et al. (1993) compared estimates of skeletal muscle mass derived from 22 CT images with other predictions from indirect methods, including anthropometry, endogenous creatinine and 3-MH excretions, and DXA. They did not find differences between the estimates derived from CT and those from anthropometry, whereas those from the other techniques differed from the CT estimates. Because CT is a more direct method than the others, the authors concluded that the indirect methods require further refinement to yield accurate estimates of muscle mass.

Recently, Ma et al. (1994) compared estimates of muscle mass from 16 healthy men and 8 men with AIDS determined with CT, DXA, and in vivo neutron activation analysis of TBN together with whole-body counting of potassium-40 according to the model of Burkinshaw, Hedge, King, and Cohn (1990). The correlation between CT and DXA estimates of skeletal muscle was strong ($r = 0.86$, $p < 0.001$); the correlation was similar between CT estimates and assessments from the combined nitrogen-potassium model ($r = 0.82$, $p < 0.001$). The nitrogen-potassium model (24.9 ± 7.6 kg) underestimated skeletal muscle mass relative to the CT method (31.7 ± 6.4 kg). It was suggested that the nitrogen-potassium model of estimating skeletal muscle mass requires modification.

The use of CT has provided unique measurements of change in regional body composition of human beings. In a strength-training study of nonagenarians, Fiatarone et al. (1990) used regional CT scans to show significant changes in mid-thigh muscle area with marked increases in quadriceps (9%) and hamstring and adductor areas (8.4%) in response to strength training. The changes in subcutaneous or intramuscular adipose tissue were not significant. These impressive gains in muscle area were not paralleled with a measurable increase in FFM, indicating the need to conduct regional, as compared to whole-body, assessment of body composition to document structural adaptation in response to physical training of a limb. Another example is the use of CT to characterize a significant increase in skeletal muscle mass (2.4 kg) in 10 adults with complete pituitary deficiency after undergoing recombinant human growth hormone treatment (Lonn et al., 1993).

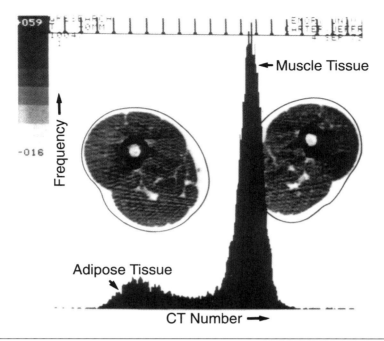

Figure 6.3 Cross-sectional CT image of the mid-thigh area of a healthy adult and a histogram of the image pixels.
Reprinted from "Human Body Composition: Analysis by Computerized Axial Tomography and Nuclear Magnetic Resonance," by S.B. Heymsfield. In *AIN symposium proceedings: Nutrition '87* (pp. 92-96) by O.E. Levander (Ed.), 1987, Bethesda, MD: American Institute of Nutrition. Copyright 1987 by Journal of Nutrition. Reprinted with permission.

Some caution is needed with regard to the use of CT to assess muscle. There is a wide variation in the attenuation of normal muscle, from +30 to +80 Hounsfield units, depending on which muscle group is examined (Bulcke, Termote, Palmers, & Crolla, 1979; Mategrano et al., 1977). Although the cross-sectional area of a muscle can be measured, the sizes or volumes of muscles on contralateral sides of the body may differ. Because of the wide normal variation in muscle size associated with physical activity (i.e., increased size) and poor nutritional status (i.e., decreased size), generalized reductions in muscle size are difficult to diagnose in the early stages of disease without baseline reference data. The most common type of muscle disorder identified by CT is atrophy, in which the muscle diminishes in size and, because of infiltration by fat, shows reduced attenuation. In gross atrophy, for example, the muscle fibers may be replaced, for the most part, with material characterized by fatty attenuation and yield negative Hounsfield unit values (Dixon, 1991).

Magnetic Resonance Imaging

Nuclear magnetic resonance (NMR) is a powerful technique that can present both images (MRI) and chemical composition of tissues (NMR spectroscopy); an NMR instrument can perform either imaging or spectroscopy but not both functions. As with CT, MRI can be used to assess regional and, by calculation, whole-body composition.

The basis of NMR is the fact that atomic nuclei can behave like magnets. The application of an external magnetic field across a segment of the body causes each nucleus in the segment to attempt to align with the field. When a radio-frequency electromagnetic wave is directed into body tissues, some nuclei absorb energy from the magnetic field. When the radio wave is turned off, the activated nuclei emit the radio signal that they absorbed. A computer uses the emitted signal to develop an image of the chemical composition of the tissue.

Elements with dipole nuclei, such as hydrogen-1, phosphorus-31, carbon-13, and sodium-23, have been examined with NMR. Each of these nuclei has an angular momentum, or spin, with dipole momentum arising from its inherent nuclear characteristics. Because these nuclei have electrical charges, the spin generates a dipole moment. In response to an external magnetic field, these nuclei align themselves either parallel or antiparallel to the lines of induction from the field. A resonant radio-frequency pulse is used to rotate the nuclei 90° relative to the magnetic field. After the radio-frequency signal is stopped, the nuclei re-align themselves by a process termed relaxation. The absorbed energy is dissipated into the environment.

Instruments used for clinical investigation surround the patient with a magnetic coil that has a 5- to 30-mm wavelength (60 to 110 MHz) radio-frequency signal. The signal produced when the nuclei relax is collected by the NMR receiver and stored for analysis.

In contrast to the dependency of conventional x-ray radiographic and CT images on electron density, MRI depends on the density of hydrogen nuclei and the physical state of the tissue as reflected in the relaxation times to evaluate body compositional variables, particularly adipose tissue and muscle. Anatomical information has been verified by comparing MRI images and corresponding frozen sections of animals (Hansen, Crooks, & Margulis, 1980). In addition, proton MRI has been used to estimate total body water of baboons (Lewis, Rollwitz, Bertrand, & Masoro, 1986). The hydrogen associated with body water was measured as the amplitude of the free-induction decay voltage. Body water was calculated as the product of peak amplitude by the experimentally determined constant for a water standard. Values for total body water were similar whether calculated from MRI or by the gravimetric method.

Recently, MRI has been used to assess FFM in human beings (Ross et al., 1994). Transverse slices of 10 mm thickness were acquired at each 50 mm distance from the head to the foot. The areas of the tissue regions in each slice were computed automatically by summing the pixels for each tissue and multiplying by the pixel surface area. The volumes of the fat-free and adipose regions in each slice were calculated by multiplying the tissue area by the slice thickness. The total fat-free and adipose volumes were calculated by adding the volumes of truncated pyramids defined by pairs of consecutive slices (Ross et al., 1992). Comparison with anthropometric predictions of FFM had a variability of 3.6 and 6.5% for men and women, respectively. To date, proton MRI has not been used to estimate total skeletal muscle mass in vivo.

Dual X-Ray Absorptiometry

Another radiographic technique that is used for body composition assessment is dual x-ray absorptiometry (DXA). Although originally developed for regional assessment of bone mineral content (BMC) and bone area density, this technique has been refined for the assessment of soft tissue composition (Lukaski, 1993).

As with CT, DXA exposes the patient to x-rays, although the amount of radiation exposure is substantially less with DXA (Kellie, 1992; Lang et al., 1991). The attenuation of an x-ray beam as it passes through a region of the body depends on the composition of the region, its thickness, and the energy of the x-rays. Specifically, soft tissues, which contain principally water and organic compounds, cause much less attenuation than bone.

The DXA scanning systems include a source that emits x-rays, which are collimated into a beam that can be turned on and off by a shutter mechanism. The beam passes in a posteroanterior direction through bone and soft tissue, continues upward, and enters the detector. The system's components are mechanically connected so as to scan the body in a rectilinear pattern.

Although a variety of software algorithms are available, a general pattern for analysis of x-ray attenuation is used (Lukaski, 1993). First, the attenuation due to bone is determined, then attenuation due to soft tissue composition is assessed. Soft tissue composition (fat and fat-free) is calculated from the ratio of beam attenuation at the lower energy relative to that at the higher energy. In this manner, regional and whole-body estimates of BMC and bone area density, together with assessment of fat and bone-free lean tissue masses (LTM), are performed with appropriate computer software.

The DXA scan can distinguish compositional differences between individuals with the same stature and body weight (Figure 6.4). As shown in Table 6.2, marked differences in BMC, body fatness, and LTM are evident despite similar body masses and stature.

This method additionally permits regional body composition assessment, with a particular emphasis on appendicular muscle mass. Heymsfield et al. (1990) related estimates of appendicular muscle mass in healthy men and women assessed with dual photon absorptiometry, a method similar to DXA, to measurements of TBK and TBN and anthropometric assessments of regional muscle mass. The variability of repeated measurements in a subsample of four volunteers was 7, 2.4, and 3% for arm, leg, and combined appendicular muscle mass, respectively. Significant correlations were found between appendicular muscle mass and TBK ($r = 0.94$), TBN ($r = 0.78$), and upper arm ($r = 0.82$) and thigh ($r = 0.88$) muscle-plus-bone areas

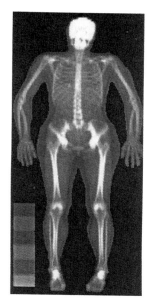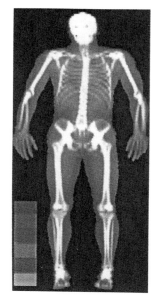

Woman   Man

Figure 6.4 Whole-body dual x-ray absorptiometric scan images of a man and a woman of similar age, body weight, and stature.

Table 6.2 Whole-Body and Regional Dual X-Ray Absorptiometric Assessment (Hologic 2000/W, Enhanced Whole-Body Version 5.54) of Bone Mineral Content and Soft Tissue Composition of a Man and Woman of Similar Age, Body Weight, and Stature

	Man	Woman
Weight (kg)	70.5	70.0
Stature (cm)	174.0	172.6
BMI (kg/m^2)	23.3	23.5
BMC (g)	2761	2230
Fat (kg)	7.1	24.6
Fat (%)	9.9	35.5
LTM (kg)	61.1	42.5

BMI = body mass index, BMC = bone mineral content, LTM = bone-free lean tissue (mainly muscle and vital organs).

from anthropometry. These findings indicate the potential use of DXA to assess regional muscle mass, at least in healthy individuals.

One concern about the use of DXA in the clinical assessment of muscle mass is the potential interference from fluid accumulation. Because DXA cannot differentiate between body water and fat-free mass (Nord & Payne, 1990), Horber et al. (1992) examined the effect of food consumption and hemodialysis on DXA estimates of body composition. The ingestion of fluid volumes ranging from 0.5 to 2.4 L one hour before a DXA scan did not affect DXA estimates of BMC or fat mass but did result in significant increases in LTM, as expected. Ingestion of small fluid volumes (less than 500 ml) did not bias estimates of body composition.

Studies of the effects of hemodialysis on DXA estimates of body composition revealed some important findings (Horber et al., 1992). Following dialytic treatment, body weight decreased 0.9 to 4.4 kg in six patients. The DXA estimates of whole-body BMC and fat did not change despite removal of water and salts. In contrast, a significant decrease in LTM mass was observed, which accounted for about 95% of the change in body weight as a consequence of the dialytic therapy. The amount of weight lost and the change in LTM observed during therapy were correlated ($r = 0.94$; $p < 0.006$). There were no changes in BMC or fat content with dialysis within body regions (e.g., trunk, arms, legs, etc.), but the post-dialytic decrease in LTM was disproportionally attributed to the trunk (61%), legs (30%), arms (5.5%), and remainder of the body (3.5%). These findings suggest that areas of the body that accumulate excess water and salts in patients with end-stage renal disease are the regions in which decreases in LTM occur with dialytic therapy.

The ingestion of fluid and regional accumulation of water and salts, which increase in the extracellular fluid volume, are monitored by DXA as changes in LTM. The DXA technique is unable to distinguish between intra- and extracellular fluids.

Limitations to the Use of Radiographic Methods

Optimism for the application of CT and MRI to muscle mass assessment is tempered by practical considerations. The high cost of the instrumentation and the cost per study limit the availability of CT and MRI to major medical centers and thus restrict the routine use of these instruments for muscle mass determinations of healthy individuals. Because of the exposure to ionizing radiation, use of CT for routine scans or multiple scans of the same individual and scans of pregnant women and children are unrealistic. In contrast, MRI does not use ionizing radiation and hence may be presumed to be a safe alternative to CT for determination of muscle mass in various segments of the population. The limited use of MRI in body composition studies may be attributed to the difficulty of access to these instruments, cost, and the time required for a whole-body scan (about 45 minutes). In addition, studies determining the validity of CT and MRI to assess body composition, including muscle mass, have yet to be performed.

The DXA method offers a reasonable alternative to CT and MRI for assessments of muscle mass, bone, and fat. Cost, however, is a limiting factor for routine assessment of body composition. Although ionizing radiation is used with DXA, the patient is exposed to far less than with CT. Also, the time needed for a DXA scan is less than that required for MRI scans (20 vs 45 minutes). The sensitivity of DXA to changes in extracellular fluid accumulation does not affect estimates of bone or fat but predictably influences estimates of whole-body and appendicular FFM and muscle mass.

Nuclear Techniques

Knowledge of the physical characteristics and biological distribution of the elements potassium and nitrogen has promoted the development of techniques to measure these elements and the derivation of models to estimate muscle in the body. This approach has proven useful in the study of body composition in health and disease (Cohn et al., 1980a, 1980b).

Total Body Potassium

Chemical analyses have shown that potassium is essentially an intracellular cation that is not present in stored triglyceride. In addition, potassium-40, which emits a characteristic gamma ray at 1.46 MeV, exists in the body at a known natural abundance (0.012%) with a very long physical half-life (1.3 billion years). These facts have promoted the estimation of body cell mass and FFM in animals and humans by external counting of potassium-40.

Estimation of total body potassium (TBK) by external counting of potassium-40 has three basic requirements. A heavily shielded room for counting is needed to minimize natural background radiation from cosmic and terrestrial sources. Detection of gamma rays requires a sensitive detector system positioned in direct proximity to the patient and a data acquisition system capable of absolute discrimination of the 1.46 MeV gamma ray from other body burdens of contaminant gamma-emitting radioisotopes.

Once accurate and reproducible measurements of TBK are available, the challenge is to translate the data into estimates of body composition. As discussed by Forbes (1987), the potassium content of the fat-free mass is "reasonably consistent" in a variety of species.

In human beings the potassium content of FFM has been reported to be quite consistent. Chemical analyses of a limited number of human cadavers yielded values of 2.66 and 2.50 g potassium/kg FFM in men and women, respectively (Forbes, 1987). Less direct approaches using whole-body counting and determinations of total body water (2.5 and 2.31 g/kg for men and women, respectively) and densitometry (2.46 and 2.28 g/kg for men and women, respectively) have yielded remarkably similar estimates (Boling, Taylor, Entenman, & Behnke, 1962; Lukaski, Mendez, Buskirk, & Cohn, 1981b).

The accuracy of the estimation of muscle mass from TBK measurements is limited because other components of the fat-free mass contain appreciable amounts of potassium (Forbes, 1987). Although the potassium content of skeletal muscle is high (3.1 to 3.5 g/kg) and that of bone is negligible (0.2 g/kg), other organs and tissues have variable amounts of potassium (liver, 3.0 g/kg; adipose tissue, 1.9 g/kg; skin, 0.8 g/kg). Thus, use of TBK measurements to estimate muscle mass is prone to significant error because of the lack of sensitivity of potassium to differentiate muscle from the other components of the fat-free mass.

Total Body Nitrogen

Because of its unique role as an essential component of body protein, the assessment of body nitrogen has been used as an index of whole-body protein mass. The development of neutron activation techniques permitted the in vivo measurement of total body nitrogen (TBN). Whole-body neutron activation systems designed for in vivo studies deliver a moderated beam of fast neutrons to the subject. Capture of those neutrons by atoms of the target elements in the body creates unstable isotopes. The induced unstable isotopes revert to a stable condition by the emission of one or more gamma rays of characteristic energy. Radiation from the irradiated subject is determined from the radiospectrum of the emissions. The energy levels of the emissions identify the activated elements, and the levels of activity indicate their abundance in the body.

The first nuclear methods for direct in vivo determination of TBN in humans used the $^{14}N(n, 2n)^{13}N$ reaction (Boddy, Holloway, & Elliot, 1973; Cohn & Dombrowski, 1971). This approach suffered from a lack of specificity because of interference by positron emissions from other elements in the body. The later development of the prompt-gamma techniques (Vartsky, Ellis, & Cohn, 1979; Vartsky, Ellis, Vaswani et al., 1984) using the reaction $^{14}N(n, \gamma)^{15}N$ led to the clinical usefulness of TBN measurements in body composition assessments in health and disease.

The prompt-gamma technique uses a plutonium-238 beryllium source to provide fast neutrons that are slowed by passage through a deuterium oxide moderator before contacting the subject, who is irradiated bilaterally. This method quantitates TBN absolutely by using total body hydrogen as an internal standard (Vartsky et al., 1979, 1984). By using thermal neutron capture, the nitrogen and hydrogen molecules interact with the moderated or slow neutrons to produce transiently (10^{-15} s) induced nuclides, ^{15}N and ^{2}H, emitting gamma rays of characteristic energy levels (10.83 and 2.23 MeV, respectively) that are quantitated simultaneously during the neutron irradiation. This procedure requires a 20 minute neutron irradiation. The advantage of this technique over the conventional method of analysis is that errors in counting resulting from differences in irradiation and detection conditions and from differences in size and shape of patients are

reduced considerably. These are important considerations for clinical studies of patients with varying degrees of body habitus.

Nitrogen-Potassium Models

With the advent of neutron activation techniques to measure TBN, the calculation to total body protein became quite easy (TBN × 6.25). Clinical investigators, however, soon became interested in fractionating the body protein mass into its muscle and nonmuscle protein components. Two conceptual models were proposed; both require measurements of TBN and TBK and depend on differences in the relative concentrations of nitrogen and potassium in different tissues and fluid compartments of the body.

The Leeds model was developed from the proposal by Burkinshaw et al. (1978) that the body protein mass could be partitioned into muscle and nonmuscle protein fractions of the FFM on the basis of differences in the distribution of potassium and nitrogen in these components of FFM. The assumed concentrations of potassium and nitrogen in muscle and nonmuscle protein are listed in Table 6.3. Based on these assumed values, one can calculate muscle (M_m) and nonmuscle (NM_m) masses:

$$M_m = [19.25 \, (TBK) - TBN] / 38.34$$
$$NM_m = [TBN - 8.45 \, (TBK)] / 20.20 \quad (6.3)$$

where M_m and NM_m are in kg, and TBK and TBN are in g.

Although this approach has been used to document differences in human body composition in health and disease (Cohn et al., 1980a, 1980b), there have been few attempts to examine the validity of

Table 6.3 Assumed Potassium (K) and Nitrogen (N) in the Muscle and Nonmuscle Mass of the Fat-Free Body

	K (g/kg)	N (g/kg)	N/K
Muscle	3.55	30	8.45
Nonmuscle	1.87	36	19.25

Adapted from "Assessment of the Distribution of Protein in the Human Body by In Vivo Neutron Activation Analysis," by L. Burkinshaw, G.L. Hill, and D.B. Morgan. In *Nuclear activation techniques in the life sciences* (pp. 787-798), 1979, Vienna, Austria: International Atomic Energy Agency. Copyright 1979 by International Atomic Energy Agency. Adapted with permission.

the Leeds model. The principal reason has been the lack of appropriate reference values required for comparison. Furthermore, evaluation by comparison with less direct reference data has not been attempted.

Burkinshaw (1987) compared estimates of muscle mass from more than 200 healthy adults with published data on muscle mass obtained by dissection (International Commission on Radiological Protection, 1975). The results suggested that the Leeds model may underestimate muscle mass in healthy men and women aged 20 to 80 years by about 5 kg or approximately 25% of muscle mass.

Another approach was to examine the predicted muscle mass with the endogenous excretion of 3-MH (Lukaski et al., 1981a). In a sample of 14 healthy men, a significant relationship ($r = 0.91$) was found between muscle mass, estimated with the Leeds model, and 3-MH (Lukaski et al., 1981a). The strong correlation coefficient reflects a general relationship; it does not indicate the accuracy of the prediction of muscle mass.

Finally, the model was tested by using it to predict the muscle mass of 87 healthy volunteers and comparing the results with predictions based on extrapolations from anthropometric cross-sectional muscle areas of the upper arm. The correlation coefficients ($r = 0.25$ and 0.33 for men and women, respectively) were not statistically significant (Burkinshaw, 1987). This finding was not unexpected because the approximate error in estimating whole-body muscle mass from anthropometric upper arm values is about 8% (Heymsfield et al., 1982b). The results of these diverse, indirect attempts to examine the validity of the Leeds model led Burkinshaw et al. (1990) to conclude that the Leeds model is "at best only approximately correct" (p. 21).

The doubtful accuracy of the Leeds model may be related to the relative inconsistency of the potassium/nitrogen ratio in the muscle and nonmuscle protein parts of the FFM. Review of the basic data used by Burkinshaw et al. (1978) indicates considerable variation of the assumed chemical composition of protein components of the FFM (Lukaski, 1992). The variability in the potassium content of muscle is about 39% depending on the different muscles examined. In contrast, the variability of the nitrogen concentration is relatively small, about 10%. In addition, calculation of the total error associated with the variability in the TBK (4%) and TBN (6%) measurements performed by Burkinshaw et al. (1978) suggests large errors in the estimation of muscle (17%) and nonmuscle (19%) protein masses (Forbes, 1987).

Burkinshaw et al. (1990) acknowledged these limitations and proposed a revision of the original model. The revised model is based on the premise that nutritional imbalance and disease cause changes in the fat, protein, water, and mineral content of the body, and measurement of the absolute elemental composition of the body is needed. The investigators proposed a model based on measurements of total body water by isotopic dilution and of total body protein and minerals by neutron activation analysis. This model awaits evaluation in patients with wasting disease and obesity.

An alternative, the Birmingham model, has been proposed by James et al. (1984). These workers suggested the division of the body protein mass into intra- and extracellular components assuming that all TBK is intracellular. Unfortunately, the validity of this model cannot be evaluated because of the lack of independent estimates of intra- and extracellular protein.

Limitations to the Use of Nitrogen-Potassium Models

Nuclear techniques for the determination of TBK and TBN provide the only noninvasive approaches for the estimation of body cell mass and protein. The use of the potassium/nitrogen ratio as an index of protein distribution in the body, however, should be viewed with caution because of the variation of this ratio in the muscle component of the FFM. The cost of whole-body counters and neutron activation analysis systems limits their use to a few highly specialized research centers.

Bioelectrical Impedance

Another approach for the assessment of regional muscle mass is bioelectrical impedance analysis (BI). This method relies on the conduction of an applied electrical current to an index conductor volume (Lukaski, 1991). Because skeletal muscle in the upper arm is the dominant conductor in that region, and because the upper arm musculature has been used as an index of nutritional status, an adaptation of the BI method has been proposed for the noninvasive assessment of upper arm composition.

Brown, Karatzas, Nakielny, & Clark (1988) used a tetrapolar electrode arrangement of band electrodes and a 1 mA current at 50 kHz to measure the longitudinal resistance of the upper arm of 20 healthy volunteers. A parallel resistance model was used as an equivalent circuit assuming the resistivity of muscle, fat, and bone were 1.18, 16, and > 100 ohm · m, respectively. Reference compositional data were derived from anthropometric assessment (Heymsfield et al., 1982b) and CT measurements of muscle and adipose tissue areas.

The areas of adipose tissue and muscle in the upper arm from CT were related to those estimated by anthropometry and BI (Table 6.4). The areas of muscle and fat estimated by BI were significantly correlated with CT measurements. The mean differences between BI and CT estimates of muscle and adipose tissue areas were not significantly different from zero. Anthropometric estimates of muscle and adipose tissue areas were also significantly related to CT measurements. The BI method accounted for more of the variance in muscle and adipose tissue areas (96 and 89%, respectively) than did anthropometry (89 and 77%, respectively). The mean differences between the CT and anthropometric values for muscle and adipose tissue areas were significantly greater ($p < 0.01$) than zero. These findings indicate the potential of bioelectrical impedance measurements to assess upper arm muscle and adipose tissue areas.

Limitations to the Use of Bioelectrical Impedance

There is a strong potential for routine use of this technique to assess regional composition due to the ease of measurement and the availability of the instrument. Some caution is needed because additional factors require further investigation.

Table 6.4 Correlation Coefficients (r) and Errors or Mean Differences (cm²) Between Estimates of Upper Arm Skeletal Muscle and Adipose Tissue Areas Determined by Computed Tomography (CT) and Estimated by Anthropometric (ANT) and Bioelectrical Impedance (BI) Measurements

	Muscle area		Adipose tissue area	
	r	Error	r	Error
CT vs BI	0.981	0.22	0.945	0.73
CT vs ANT	0.943	−2.62	0.876	2.61

Adapted from "Determination of Upper Arm Muscle and Fat Areas Using Electrical Impedance Measurements," by B.H. Brown, T. Karatzas, R. Nakielny, and R.G. Clark, 1988, *Clinical Physics and Physiological Measurement*, 9, pp. 47-55. Copyright 1988 by Institute of Physics. Adapted with permission.

The type of electrodes, spot or circumferential, and their placement have not been defined in reference to minimizing the error of this technique. In addition, the potential advantage of using a multifrequency, as compared to a single-frequency, analyzer to assess regional composition has not been examined. Finally, the effect of edema on the bioelectrical impedance measurements, and hence the estimation of muscle mass, requires investigation.

High Frequency Energy Absorption

High frequency energy absorption (HFEA) relies on the absorption of electromagnetic energy by a conductor in a biological specimen to estimate its chemical composition. Two basic assumptions are required. The distribution of water and electrolytes between the intra- and extracellular spaces is relatively constant, and electrolytes are not present in bone or fat. If these premises are correct, then one can estimate the volume of the biological conductor of a limb, and perhaps the whole body.

Michaelsen et al. (1993) developed a portable induction coil powered by a 9 V battery for determination of regional HFEA. The HFEA is measured as the difference in voltage from when the induction coil is empty to when it encircles an object. In a calibration study, the HFEA readings of beakers increased in relation to circumference and salt (NaCl) concentrations of the beakers. The HFEA technique was also evaluated in six volunteers who underwent two determinations of HFEA of the calf and thigh. The coefficients of variation for repeated HFEA measurements ranged from 4 to 8%.

In a second trial, MRI sections of the calf and thigh and HFEA measurements were made in 12 men and 12 women aged 8 to 61 years. Muscle values were expressed as a fraction of the limb volume. HFEA was measured at the same site as the MRI and expressed relative to HFEA of normal saline at the same circumference of the limb. There were significant sex effects in the prediction of calf HFEA measurements; 80% of the variation of calf HFEA was explained by MRI and sex. In the thigh, 74% of the variance in HFEA was attributed to MRI and coil circumference. The standard error was 6 to 7% for calf and thigh HFEA measurements, respectively.

These preliminary data suggest the potential value of HFEA measurements to assess regional muscle volume as an index of nutritional status.

The advantage of this approach is its portability for use at the bedside and outside a laboratory. Because of the reliance on the assumption of a normal distribution of electrolytes and fluids in the intra- and extracellular compartments, additional investigation is needed to ascertain the validity of the technique in patients with altered fluid status and acid-base balance.

Summary

Clinical investigators and practitioners seek methods for the reliable and accurate assessment of regional and whole-body muscle mass. These methods need to be available at costs, both in terms of time and money, that facilitate their routine use in clinics and outside of laboratories. The availability of such a method, or methods, remains to be established.

Table 6.5 compares the characteristics of the methods described in this presentation for in vivo assessment of muscle mass. In general, the techniques with the greatest precision tend to be the most expensive, although acceptable precision is available from the less costly techniques, such as BI and HFEA. Accuracy has not been established for all these methods. Based on indirect comparisons among these techniques, it appears that the radiographic methods, along with BI and HFEA, can be considered to have acceptable levels of accuracy ($\pm$ 5% of reference value).

Table 6.5 Ranking of Methods for Assessment of Skeletal Muscle Mass in Human Beings

Method	Site	Precision	Accuracy	Utility	Cost
Anthropometry	R, WB	3	?	4	1
Creatinine	WB	2	2	1	3
3-MH	WB	2	2	1	4
CT	R, WB	5	4	4	5
MRI	R, WB	5	4	4	5
DXA	R, WB	5	4	4	4
TBK-TBN	WB	4	2	1	5
BI	R	4	?	4	1
HFEA	R	4	3	3	3

Ranking system: ascending scale, 1 = least and 5 = greatest.
R = regional and WB = whole-body assessment.

The ease with which a technique is employed is an important practical issue. Generally, all the methods, with the exception of the urinary metabolites of muscle metabolism and the measurement of TBK and TBN, can be performed with minimal technical expertise. The limitation of the use of urinary creatinine and 3-MH is the need for consumption of a meat-free diet and timed urine collections, in addition to the required analytical instrumentation. Although many of the techniques have the potential for whole-body assessments, the routine use is to measure selected regions of the body.

Selection of a method may depend on the resources available and the experimental question. For example, if radiographic instrumentation is available, then it could be used for either regional or whole-body assessments of muscle. In addition, if an experimental intervention is hypothesized to affect a specific region of the body, then any method, with the exception of the urinary metabolites and potassium-nitrogen model, would appear to be adequate.

Evaluation of the available methods for assessment suggests the need for the development of portable, inexpensive, safe, and convenient methods for general use. Although sophisticated radiographic techniques are available, factors such as cost, access, and, in some cases, exposure to radiation make it necessary to investigate further the development of BI and HFEA for future applications.

Within the limitations described in this presentation, methods are available for assessment of human muscle mass. The selection of a technique depends on an understanding of the practical considerations and limitations of each method in relation to the experimental hypotheses being evaluated.

Notes

U.S. Department of Agriculture, Agricultural Research Service, Northern Plains Area, is an equal opportunity/affirmative action employer and all agency services are available without discrimination.

Mention of a trademark or proprietary product does not constitute a guarantee or warranty of the product by the United States Department of Agriculture and does not imply its approval to the exclusion of other products that may also be suitable.

References

Afting, E.G., Bernhardt, W., Janzen, R.W.C., & Rothig, H.J. (1981). Quantitative importance of non-skeletal muscle N-methylhistidine and creatinine in human urine. *Biochemistry Journal, 200*, 449-452.

Asatoor, A.M., & Armstrong, M.D. (1967). 3-methylhistidine, a component of actin. *Biochemical and Biophysical Research Communications, 26*, 168-174.

Bleiler, R.E., & Schedl, H.P. (1962). Creatinine excretion: Variability and relationship to diet and body size. *Journal of Laboratory and Clinical Medicine, 59*, 945-955.

Boddy, K., Holloway, I., & Elliot, A. (1973). A simple facility for total body in vivo neutron activation analysis. *International Journal of Applied Radiation and Isotopes, 24*, 428-430.

Boling, E.A., Taylor, W.L., Entenman, C., & Behnke, A.R. (1962). Total exchangeable potassium and chloride, and total body water in healthy men of varying fat content. *Journal of Clinical Investigation, 41*, 1840-1849.

Borsook, H., & Dubnoff, J.W. (1947). The hydrolysis of phosphocreatine and the origin of urinary creatinine. *Journal of Biological Chemistry, 168*, 493-510.

Brown, B.H., Karatzas, T., Nakielny, R., & Clark, R.G. (1988). Determination of upper arm muscle and fat areas using electrical impedance measurements. *Clinical Physics and Physiological Measurement, 9*, 47-55.

Bulcke, J.A.L., Termote, J.-L., Palmers, Y., & Crolla, D. (1979). Computed tomography of the human skeletal muscular system. *Neuroradiology, 17*, 127-136.

Burkinshaw, L. (1987). Models of the distribution of protein in the human body. In K.J. Ellis, S. Yasumura, & W.D. Morgan (Eds.), *In vivo body composition studies* (pp. 15-24). London: Institute of Physical Sciences in Medicine.

Burkinshaw, L., Hedge, A.P., King, R.F.J.G., & Cohn, S.H. (1990). Models of the distribution of protein, water and electrolytes in the human body. *Infusiontherapie, 17* (Suppl 3), 21-25.

Burkinshaw, L., Hill, G.L., & Morgan, D.B. (1978). Assessment of the distribution of protein in the human body by in vivo neutron activation analysis. In *International symposium on nuclear activation techniques in the life sciences* (pp. 787-798). Vienna: International Atomic Energy Association.

Calloway, D.H., & Margen, S. (1971). Variation in endogenous nitrogen excretion and dietary nitrogen utilization as determinants of human protein requirement. *Journal of Nutrition, 101*, 205-216.

Cannon, J.G., Meydani, S.N., Fielding, R.A., et al. (1991). Acute phase response in exercise, II: Associations between vitamin E, cytokines and muscle protein degradation. *American Journal of Physiology, 29*, R1235-R1240.

Cheek, D.B. (1968). Human growth: Body composition, cell growth, energy and intelligence. In D.B. Cheek (Ed.), *Human growth* (pp. 31-47). Philadelphia: Lea & Febiger.

Clarys, J.P., Martin, A.D., & Drinkwater, D.T. (1984). Gross tissue weights in the human body by cadaver dissection. *Human Biology, 56*, 459-473.

Clowes, G.H.A., George, B.C., Ville, C.A., & Saravis, C.A. (1983). Muscle proteolysis induced by a circulating peptide in septic and traumatized patients. *New England Journal of Medicine, 308*, 545-552.

Cohn, S.H., & Dombrowski, C.S. (1971). Measurement of total body calcium, sodium, chlorine, nitrogen, and phosphorus in man by neutron activation analysis. *Journal of Nuclear Medicine, 12*, 499-505.

Cohn, S.H., Gartenhaus, W., Sawitsky, A., et al. (1980a). Compartmental body composition of cancer patients by measurement of total body nitrogen, potassium and water. *Metabolism, 30*, 222-229.

Cohn, S.H., Vartsky, D., Yasumura, S., et al. (1980b). Compartmental body composition based on total body nitrogen, potassium and calcium. *American Journal of Physiology, 239*, E524-E530.

Crim, M.C., Calloway, D.H., & Margen, S. (1975). Creatine metabolism in men: Urinary creatine and creatinine excretions with creatine feedings. *Journal of Nutrition, 105*, 428-438.

Dixon, A.K. (1991). Imaging techniques in nutrition and the assessment of bone status: computed tomography. In R.G. Whitehead & A. Prentice (Eds.), *New techniques in nutritional research* (pp. 361-377). San Diego: Academic.

Elia, M., Carter, A., & Smith, R. (1979). The 3-methylhistidine content of human tissues. *British Journal of Nutrition, 42*, 567-570.

Fiatarone, M.A., Marks, E.C., Ryan, N.D., Meredith, C.N., et al. (1990). High-intensity strength training in nonagenarians. *Journal of the American Medical Association, 263*, 3029-3034.

Folin, O. (1905). Laws governing the chemical composition of urine. *American Journal of Physiology,* **13**, 66-115.

Forbes, G.B. (1987). *Human body composition.* New York: Springer-Verlag.

Forbes, G.B., & Bruining, G.J. (1976). Urinary creatinine excretion and lean body mass. *American Journal of Clinical Nutrition,* **29**, 1359-1366.

Frisancho, A.R. (1974). New standards of weight and upper arm muscle size for assessment of nutritional status. *American Journal of Clinical Nutrition,* **27**, 1052-1058.

Fuller, M.F., Fowler, P.A., McNeill, G., & Foster, M.A. (1994). Imaging techniques for the assessment of body composition. *Journal of Nutrition,* **124**, 1546S-15450S.

Greenblatt, D.C., Ransil, B.J., Harmatz, J.S., et al. (1976). Variability of 24-hr urinary creatinine excretion by normal subjects. *Journal of Clinical Pharmacology,* **16**, 321-328.

Gurney, L.M., & Jelliffe, D.B. (1973). Arm anthropometry in nutritional assessment: Nomogram for rapid calculation of muscle circumference and cross-sectional muscle and fat areas. *American Journal of Clinical Nutrition,* **26**, 912-915.

Hansen, G., Crooks, L.E., & Marguilis, A.R. (1980). In vivo imaging of the rat with nuclear magnetic resonance, *Radiology,* **136**, 695-700.

Hardy, M.F., & Perry, S.V. (1969). In vitro methylation of muscle proteins. *Nature,* **223**, 300-302.

Harris, C.I. (1981). Reappraisal of the quantitative importance of non-skeletal-muscle source of N τ-methylhistidine in urine. *Biochemical Journal,* **194**, 1011-1014.

Haus, A.G. (1979). *The physics of medical imaging: Recording system measurements and techniques.* New York: American Institute of Physics.

Heymsfield, S.B. (1987). Human body composition: Analysis by computerized axial tomography and nuclear magnetic resonance. In O.E. Levander (Ed.), *AIN symposium proceedings: Nutrition '87* (pp. 92-96). Bethesda, MD: American Institute of Nutrition.

Heymsfield, S.B., McMannus, C., Smith, J., et al. (1982b). Anthropometric measurements of muscle mass: Revised equations for calculating bone-free arm muscle area. *American Journal of Clinical Nutrition,* **36**, 680-690.

Heymsfield, S.B., McMannus, C., Stevens, V., & Smith, J. (1982a). Muscle mass: Reliable indicator of protein energy malnutrition severity and outcome. *American Journal of Clinical Nutrition,* **35**, 1192-1199.

Heymsfield, S.B., Olafson, R.P., Kutner, M.H., & Nixon, D.W. (1979). A radiographic method of quantifying protein-calorie undernutrition. *American Journal of Clinical Nutrition,* **32**, 693-702.

Heymsfield, S.B., Smith, R., Aulet, M., et al. (1990). Appendicular skeletal muscle mass: Measurement by dual-photon absorptiometry. *American Journal of Clinical Nutrition,* **52**, 214-218.

Hoberman, H.D., Sims, E.A.H., & Peters, J.H. (1948). Creatine and creatinine metabolism in the normal male studied with the aid of isotopic nitrogen. *Journal of Biological Chemistry,* **172**, 45-58.

Horber, F.F., Thomi, F., Casez, J.P., et al. (1992). Impact of hydration status on body composition as measured by dual energy x-ray absorptiometry in normal volunteers and patients on haemodialysis. *British Journal of Radiology,* **65**, 895-900.

International Commission on Radiological Protection. (1975). *Report of the task group on reference man* (pp. 108-112). Oxford: Pergamon.

James, H.M., Dabek, J.T., Chettle, D.R., et al. (1984). Whole body cellular and collagen nitrogen in healthy and wasted men. *Clinical Science,* **67**, 73-82.

Jelliffe, D.B. (1966). *The assessment of the nutritional status of the community.* WHO monograph series no. 53. Geneva: World Health Organization.

Jelliffe, E.F.P., & Jelliffe, D.B. (1969). The arm circumference as a public health index of protein-calorie malnutrition of early childhood. *Journal of Tropical Pediatrics,* **15**, 225-230.

Johnson, P., Harris, C.I., & Perry, S.V. (1967). 3-Methylhistidine in actin and other muscle proteins. *Biochemical Journal,* **105**, 361-370.

Kellie, S.E. (1992). Measurement of bone density with dual-energy x-ray absorptiometry (DXA). *Journal of the American Medical Association,* **267**, 286-294.

Lang, P., Steiger, P., Faulkner, K., et al. (1991) Osteoporosis: Current techniques and recent developments in quantitative bone densitometry. *Radiologic Clinics of North America,* **29**, 49-76.

Lewis, D.S., Rollwitz, W.L., Bertrand, H.A., & Masoro, E.J. (1986). Use of NMR for measurement of total body water and fat. *Journal of Applied Physiology,* **60**, 836-840.

Long, C.L., Haverberg, L.N., Young, V.R., et al. (1975). Metabolism of 3-methylhistidine in man. *Metabolism,* **24**, 929-935.

Long, C.L., Schiller, W.R., Blakemeore, W.S., et al. (1977). Muscle protein catabolism in the septic patient as measured by 3-methylhistidine excretion. *American Journal of Clinical Nutrition,* **30**, 1349-1352.

Lonn, L., Kvist, H., Grangard, U., et al. (1993). CT-determined body composition changes with recombinant human growth hormone treatment. In K.J. Ellis & J.D. Eastman (Eds.), *Human body composition: In vivo methods, models and assessment* (pp. 229-231). New York: Plenum.

Lukaski, H.C. (1987). Methods for the assessment of human body composition: Traditional and new. *American Journal of Clinical Nutrition*, **46**, 537-556.

Lukaski, H.C. (1991). Assessment of body composition using tetrapolar bioelectrical impedance analysis. In R.G. Whitehead & A. Prentice (Eds.), *New techniques in nutritional research* (pp. 303-315). San Diego: Academic.

Lukaski, H.C. (1992). Methodology of body composition studies. In J.C. Watkins, R. Roubenoff, & I.H. Rosenberg (Eds.), *Body composition: The measure and meaning of changes with aging* (pp. 13-24). Boston: Foundation for Nutritional Advancement.

Lukaski, H.C. (1993). Soft tissue composition and bone mineral status: Evaluation by dual energy x-ray absorptiometry. *Journal of Nutrition*, **123**, 438-443.

Lukaski, H.C., & Mendez, J. (1980). Relationship between fat-free weight and urinary 3-methylhistidine in man. *Metabolism*, **29**, 758-761.

Lukaski, H.C., Mendez, J., Buskirk, E.R., & Cohn, S.H. (1981a). Relationship between endogenous 3-methylhistidine excretion and body composition. *American Journal of Physiology*, **240**, E302.

Lukaski, H.C., Mendez, J., Buskirk, E.R., & Cohn, S.H. (1981b). A comparison of methods of assessment of body composition including neutron activation analysis of total body nitrogen. *Metabolism*, **30**, 777-782.

Lykken, G.I., Jacob, R.A., Munoz, J.M., & Sandstead, H.H. (1980). A mathematical model of creatine metabolism in normal males: Comparison between theory and experiment. *American Journal of Clinical Nutrition*, **33**, 2674-2685.

Ma, R., Wang, Z., Gallagher, D., et al. (1994). Measurement of skeletal muscle in vivo: Comparison of results from radiographic and neutron activation methods. *Federation of American Societies for Experimental Biology Journal*, **8**, A279 (abstract #1611).

Martin, A.D., Spenst, L.F., Drinkwater, D.T., & Clarys, J.P. (1990). Anthropometric estimation of muscle mass. *Medicine and Science in Sports and Exercise*, **22**, 729-733.

Mategrano, V.C., Petasnick, J.P., Clark, J.W., et al. (1977). Attenuation values in computed tomography of the abdomen. *Radiology*, **125**, 135-140.

Mateiga, J. (1921). The testing of physical efficiency. *American Journal of Physical Anthropology*, **4**, 223-230.

Materson, B.J. (1971). Measurement of glomerular filtration rate. *CRC Critical Reviews in Clinical Laboratory Sciences*, **2**, 1-44.

Michaelsen, K.F., Wellens, R., Roche, A.F., et al. (1993). The use of high frequency energy absorption to measure limb musculature. In K. J. Ellis & J. D. Eastman (Eds.), *Human body composition: In vivo methods, models and assessment* (pp. 359-362). New York: Plenum.

Millward, D.J., & Bates, P.C. (1983). 3-methylhistidine turnover in the whole-body and the contribution of skeletal muscle and intestine to urinary 3-methylhistidine excretion in the adult rat. *Biochemical Journal*, **214**, 607-615.

Millward, D.J., Bates, P.C., Grimble, G.K., et al. (1980). Quantitative importance of non-skeletal muscle sources of N τ-methylhistidine sources in urine. *Biochemical Journal*, **190**, 225-228.

Nord, R.H., & Payne, R.K. (1990). Standards for body composition calibration in DEXA. In E.F.J. Ring (Ed), *Current research in osteoporosis and bone mineral measurement* (pp. 27-28). London: British Institute of Radiology.

Ransil, B.J., Greenblatt, D.J., & Koch-Weser, J. (1977). Evidence for systematic temporal variation in 24-hr urinary creatinine excretion. *Journal of Clinical Pharmacology*, **17**, 108-119.

Rennie, M.J., Edwards, R.H.T., Emery, R.W., Halliday, D., et al. (1983). Depressed protein synthesis is the dominant characteristic of muscle wasting and cachexia. *Clinical Physiology*, **3**, 387-398.

Rennie, M.J., & Millward, D.J. (1983). 3-methylhistidine excretion and the urinary 3-methylhistidine/creatinine ratio are poor indicators of skeletal muscle protein breakdown. *Clinical Science*, **65**, 217-225.

Reporter, M. (1973). Protein synthesis in cultured cells: Methylation of nascent proteins. *Archives of Biochemistry and Biophysics*, **158**, 577-585.

Ross, R., Leger, L., Morris, D., et al. (1992). Quantification of adipose tissue by MRI: Relationship with anthropometric variables. *Journal of Applied Physiology*, **72**, 787-795.

Ross, R., Shaw, K.D., Rissanen, J., et al. (1994). Sex differences in lean and adipose tissue distribution by magnetic resonance imaging: Anthropometric relationships. *American Journal of Clinical Nutrition*, **59**, 1277-1285.

Schutte, J.E., Longhurst, J.C., Gaffney, F.A., et al. (1981). Total plasma creatinine: An accurate measure of total striated muscle mass. *American Journal of Physiology*, **239**, E524-E530.

Talbot, N.B. (1938). Measurement of obesity by the creatinine coefficient. *American Journal of Diseases of Children, 55, 42-50.*

Tomas, F.M., Ballard, F.J., & Pope, L.M. (1979). Age-dependent changes in the rate of myofibrillar protein degradation in humans as assessed by 3-methylhistidine and creatinine excretion. *Clinical Science, 56, 341-346.*

Vartsky, D., Ellis, K.J., & Cohn, S.H. (1979). In vivo measurement of body nitrogen by analysis of prompt gamma from neutron capture. *Journal of Nuclear Medicine, 20, 1158-1165.*

Vartsky, D., Ellis, K.J., Vaswani, A.N., et al. (1984). An improved calibration for the in vivo determination of body nitrogen, hydrogen, and fat. *Physics in Medicine and Biology, 29, 209-218.*

Wang, Z., Elam, R., Ma, R., et al. (1993). Validation of indirect skeletal muscle mass methods by computerized axial tomography. *Federation of American Societies for Experimental Biology Journal, 7, A83 (abstract #477).*

Wassner, S.J., & Li, J.B. (1982). N τ-methylhistidine release: Contributions of rat skeletal muscle, GI tract, and skin. *American Journal of Physiology, 243, E293-E297.*

Young, V.R., Baliga, B.S., Alexis, S.D., & Munro, H.N. (1970). Lack of in vitro binding of 3-methylhistidine to transfer RNA by aminoacyl ligases from skeletal muscle. *Biochimica et Biophysica Acta, 199, 297-300.*

Young, V.R., & Munro, H.N. (1978). N τ-methylhistidine (3-methylhistidine) and muscle protein turnover: An overview. *Federation Proceedings, 37, 2291-2300.*

7

Multicomponent Molecular Level Models of Body Composition Analysis

Steven B. Heymsfield, Zi-Mian Wang, and Robert T. Withers

At present, most body composition research is performed using the two-component model. The classic two-component model describes the human body as the sum of fat and fat-free body mass (Brožek, Grande, Anderson, & Keys, 1963; Heymsfield & Waki, 1991; Siri, 1961). Other two-component models are recognized, but this one is widely used and refers to the molecular level of body composition (Wang, Pierson, & Heymsfield, 1992). In this review, we have concentrated our discussion on body composition models that expand this two-component model. Specifically, our focus is on multicomponent models in which the human body is divided into three or more molecular level components.

Our discussion of multicomponent models begins with an overview of body composition models. We then describe the main underlying theories of body composition methods in order to demonstrate the concepts that lead to the construction of

multicomponent models. In the section that follows, we review in detail representative published molecular level multicomponent models. The concluding section presents an overview of areas in need of further investigation.

Five-Level Body Composition Model

The term *body composition model* is used in a variety of contexts, but in this section we concentrate specifically on the five level model. The five level model characterizes the human body in terms of five increasingly complex levels: atomic, molecular, cellular, tissue-system, and whole-body (Figure 7.1) (Wang et al., 1992). Each of these levels is distinct; they do not overlap. At each level, the sum of all components is equivalent to body weight. Representative body composition models are

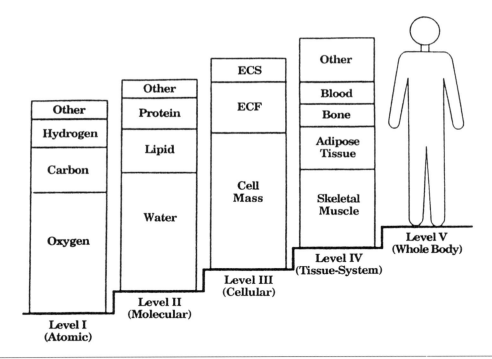

Figure 7.1   The five level model of human body composition. ECF and ECS are extracellular fluid and solids, respectively.
Adapted from "The Five Level Model: A New Approach to Organizing Body Composition Research," by Z.M. Wang, R.N. Pierson, Jr., and S.B. Heymsfield, 1992, *American Journal of Clinical Nutrition, 56*, pp. 19-28. Copyright 1992 by American Journal of Clinical Nutrition. Adapted with permission.

Table 7.1   Representative Multicomponent Models at Four of the Five Body Composition Levels

Level	Body composition model	No. components
I. Atomic	BW = H + O + N + C + Na + K + Cl + P + Ca + Mg + S	11
II. Molecular	BW = FM + W + Pro + Mc + TBBM + G	6
	BW = FM + W + Pro + M	4
	BW = FM + W + nonfat solids	3
	BW = FM + TBBM + residual	3
	BW = FM + FFM	2
III. Cellular	BW = CM + ECF + ECS	
	BW = FM + BCM + ECF + ECS	
IV. Tissue-system	BW = AT + SM + bone + other tissues	

Abbreviations: AT, adipose tissue; BCM, body cell mass; BW, body weight; CM, cell mass; ECF, extracellular fluid; ECS, extracellular solids; FFM, fat-free body mass; FM, fat mass; G, glycogen; M, mineral; Mc, soft tissue mineral; Pro, protein; SM, skeletal muscle; TBBM, total body bone mineral; W, water.

shown for the first four levels of body composition in Table 7.1. Our emphasis is on the three-, four-, and six-component models at the molecular level.

The major molecular level components and models are shown in Figure 7.2. The classical cadaver analysis consists of five main components: fat, total body water (TBW), bone minerals, nonbone (soft tissue) minerals, and protein. A sixth component, glycogen, is not considered in cadaver studies because of its relatively small amount (~300 to 500 g) and rapid postmortem autolysis. Some multicomponent models include glycogen estimates based on in

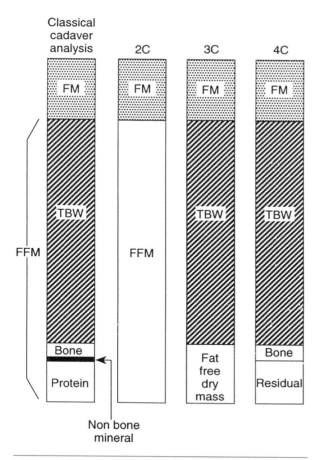

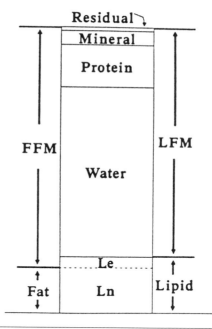

Figure 7.3 Components at the molecular level of body composition that demonstrate the distinction between fat-free body mass (FFM) and lipid-free body mass (LFM). Le and Ln are essential and nonessential lipids, respectively.

Adapted from "The Five Level Model: A New Approach to Organizing Body Composition Research," by Z.M. Wang, R.N. Pierson, Jr., and S.B. Heymsfield, 1992, *American Journal of Clinical Nutrition*, **56**, pp. 19-28. Copyright 1992 by American Journal of Clinical Nutrition. Adapted with permission.

Figure 7.2 Some of the widely used molecular level models and their respective components. *Abbreviations*: bone, bone mineral; C, component; FFM, fat-free body mass; FM, fat mass; TBW, total body water.

vivo biopsy studies. Fat-free mass (FFM) is considered the sum of total body water, bone minerals, soft tissue minerals, protein, and glycogen; alternatively, FFM = body weight – fat mass (FM). Representative two- (2C), three- (3C), and four-component (4C) molecular level models are shown in Figure 7.2.

A source of confusion with respect to molecular level components is the terminology related to the lipid component. The term *lipid* refers to chemical compounds that are insoluble in water and very soluble in organic solvents such as diethyl ether (Gurr & Harwood, 1991). About 50 different lipids are found in human tissues, such as triglycerides, phospholipids, sphingolipids, and steroids.

Lipids can be classified physiologically into essential and non-essential (Figure 7.3). Essential lipids, such as sphingomyelin and phospholipids, serve indispensable functions such as forming cell membranes. Non-essential lipids, mainly in the form of triglycerides, provide thermal insulation

and a storage depot of available fuel. In the reference man, about 10% of total body lipids is essential, and the remaining 90% is non-essential (Snyder et al., 1975). The non-essential component is synonymous with the term *fat* as it consists almost entirely of triglycerides. Therefore, although the terms fat and lipid are often confused, fat is clearly a subcategory of total lipid. The small essential lipid component is usually ignored in body composition research or grouped into a miscellaneous or residual mass component.

An important characteristic of the five levels of body composition is that a steady state exists between some components at the same or different levels during periods of weight equilibrium. This important concept implies that when a steady state is present, characteristic constant or relatively constant relationships exist between components that can be exploited in developing multicomponent models. For example, with reference to fat, the carbon content of triglycerides is constant in adult humans at 77% of weight (Kehayias et al., 1991). These stable and quantifiable relationships allow the development of multicomponent body composition methods as described in later sections.

General Concepts of Body Composition Methods

There are more than 30 major components at the five levels of body composition (Table 7.2). Methods of quantifying these components in vivo can be organized as suggested by the general formula

$$C = f(Q) \qquad (7.1)$$

where C represents an unknown component, Q a measurable quantity, and f a mathematical function relating Q to C (Wang et al., 1995).

The quantity portion (Q) of formula 7.1 can be classified into three categories. The first is a measurable *property*, such as body volume, decay profiles of specific isotopes, or electrical resistance. For example, total body water can be measured from the dilution of tritiated water as described in chapter 2. The measurable property in this example is the 0.018 MeV β-decay of tritium. About one-half of the body composition components can now be quantified using property-based methods (Figure 7.4).

The second category of quantity that can be used with general formula 7.1 is a known *component*. With component-based methods the known component must be quantified first using a property-based method. An example is the calculation of fat-free body mass from total body water. A property-based method, such as tritiated water dilution, must first be used to quantify total body water.

Finally, a third *combined* category exists in which the measurable quantities used in general formula 7.1 are both property and component. An example

is the calculation of total body fat from two measurable properties (body volume and body weight) and a measurable component (total body water) (Siri, 1961).

The mathematical function in general formula 7.1 can be one of two types. The first, which we refer to as *type I*, is developed using a reference method and regression analysis of experimental data to derive the predictive equation (chapter 10). Typically a reference method is used to measure the "unknown" component (C) in a group of subjects with well defined characteristics. The measurable quantity (Q; i.e., property and/or the known component), as defined in formula 7.1, is also estimated in the subjects. Regression analysis is then used to establish the mathematical function (f) and thus develop the equation that predicts the unknown component from the measurable property and/or the known component.

The second type of mathematical function, which we refer to as *type II*, is based on a well established model. These models usually represent ratios or proportions of measurable quantities to components that are assumed constant both within and between subjects. For example, the ratio of total body water (TBW) to fat-free body mass is assumed constant (0.73) and can be used to develop a type II method for estimating fat-free body mass as $1.37 \times TBW$ (Pace & Rathbun 1945; Sheng & Huggins, 1979).

An important feature of type II methods is that assumptions are needed in their development. For example, a classic type II method is the measurement of total body protein (TBPro) from total body nitrogen (TBN) as $TBPro = 6.25 \times TBN$ (Cunningham, 1994). There are two assumptions in this method: that "all" the total body nitrogen is in protein and that average human proteins are 16% nitrogen. According to these assumptions, the ratio TBN/TBPro is constant, or relatively constant,

Table 7.2   Main Body Composition Components at the Five Levels of Human Body Composition

	Atomic	Molecular	Cellular	Tissue-system	Whole-body
Commonly used components	O, C, H, N, Ca, P, S, K, Na, Cl, Mg	Fat, essential lipids, water, protein, bone mineral, soft-tissue mineral, glycogen, fat-free body mass, fat-free solids	Fat cells, cell mass, intracellular fluid, extracellular fluid, extracellular solids, body cell mass	Adipose tissue (AT), subcutaneous AT, visceral AT, bone, skeletal muscle, skeleton	Head, neck, arms, trunk, legs
No. components	11	9	6	6	5

within and between subjects at 0.16. All multicomponent methods described in later sections are related to type II methods and, therefore, are based on well established models. A focus of our review is a critical analysis of the assumptions that form the basis of these type II models.

A useful step in understanding this methodological classification, and the multicomponent methods that follow, is to analyze three classic two-component approaches for measuring the molecular level components fat and fat-free mass. These methods are reviewed in detail in other chapters. Our aim here is to describe the basis of these methods as an introduction to the more complex multicomponent methods that are described later.

Two-Component Hydrodensitometry Method

The two-component hydrodensitometry method was originally proposed by Behnke, Feen, and Welham (1942). This method was derived from two models at the molecular level, the body weight (BW, kg) model (BW = FM + FFM) and the body volume (BV, L) model (BV = FM/0.9007 + FFM/1.100). The body weight model does not involve any assumptions. The body volume model is based on two assumptions, that at 36 °C the density of fat is constant at 0.9007 kg/L and that the density of fat-free body mass is constant at 1.100 kg/L.

Combining the body weight model with the body volume model, there are two unknown components (FM and FFM) and two measurable quantities (BW and BV). The body weight and body volume simultaneous equations can then be solved for the unknown components as:

$$FM \ (kg) = 4.971 \times BV \ (L) - 4.519 \times BW \ (kg),$$

and

$$FFM \ (kg) = 5.519 \times BW \ (kg) - 4.971 \times BV \ (L). \tag{7.2}$$

The FM equation can be rewritten to express FM as a fraction of body weight,

$$FM/BW \ (kg/kg) = 4.971 \times BV \ (L)/BW \ (kg) - 4.519,$$

or

$$FM/BW \ (kg/kg) = 4.971/D_b - 4.519 \tag{7.3}$$

where D_b is body density (kg/L).

The hydrodensitometry method, according to the classification system outlined in Figure 7.4, is a property-based type II method. The two properties are body weight and body volume. The main assumptions are that fat and fat-free body mass have constant densities within and between subjects. Body weight is measured using a scale and, in the original Behnke method (1942), body volume was measured using a hydrodensitometry system.

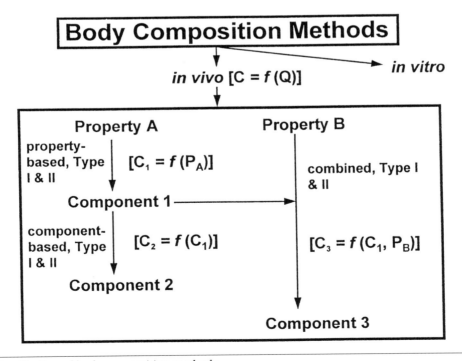

Figure 7.4 Classification of body composition methods.

Two-Component Total Body Water Method

The total body water (TBW) approach is a traditional two-component method that consists of three separate steps. The first is to administer a known amount of tritium-labeled water, which emits a 0.018 MeV β-ray. Other labeled isotopes of water (e.g., ^2H_2O or $H_2^{18}O$) can also be used (chapter 2). There is a known constant ratio of β-ray counts to tritium that allows measurement of tritium dilution volume based on the dilution model. Total body water can then be calculated from tritium dilution volume using a correction of the tritium space for proton exchange and the known density of water at average body temperature. According to this approach, measurement of TBW is a property-based type II method. The measurable property is a specific isotope decay profile (0.018 MeV β-ray) and the mathematical function is based on the dilution model.

The next step is formulated on the well established stable ratio between TBW and FFM (Forbes, 1987; Pace & Rathbun, 1945; Sheng & Huggins, 1979). Assuming the hydration of FFM is relatively stable (TBW/FFM = 0.73) both within and between subjects, FFM can be calculated from TBW as FFM = $1.37 \times$ TBW. This is a component-based type II method in which water is the known component and the assumed constant ratio of water to FFM (0.73) is used to create the mathematical function.

Finally, a combined type II method, which involves a measurable property (body weight) and a known component (FFM), is used to solve for total body fat. The equation (FM = body weight – FFM) is derived from a two-component body composition model (see Table 7.1). This example reveals that measuring total body fat by tritiated water dilution incorporates three separate methods: a property-based method, a component-based method, and a combined method. These type II methods are shown in Figure 7.5.

Two-Component Total Body Potassium Method

The third classic approach for measuring total body fat is the *total body potassium* (TBK) approach,

which also includes three type II methods. The first stage is to measure the γ-ray decay (1.46 MeV) of natural ^{40}K found in human tissues. Because there are known constant ratios between the γ-ray counts and ^{40}K, and between ^{40}K and TBK (^{40}K/TBK=0.000118) (Forbes, 1987), the mass of TBK can be measured by using a property-based type II method.

The next stage is the calculation of fat-free body mass from TBK. A relatively stable ratio exists between TBK and FFM (TBK/FFM = 68.1 mmol/kg = 0.00266 kg/kg). Accordingly, FFM (kg) = 376 × TBK (kg). This is a component-based type II method where TBK is the known component. The final step in the calculation of FM is the same as for the total body water method. The three stages in the estimation of total body fat from TBK are shown in Figure 7.6.

Component-Based Type II Methods and Relationship Types

Models based on stable or relatively stable relationships between components are central to type II component-based methods. The component-based type II TBW method involves a model formulated on the relatively stable relationship that exists between water and FFM. Similarly, the TBK method is formulated on the relatively stable ratio of potassium to FFM. Some component pairs are more suitable for developing models than others and, in contrast, not all component pairs are appropriate for developing models. The study of relationships that exist between components gives important information related to the development of multicomponent models.

Component interactions can be classified into six relationship types based on their dependency relationships and combination characteristics (Wang et al., 1995). Dependency relations describe the quantitative associations between components as subordinate (e.g., water and FFM), separate (e.g., sulfur and nitrogen), or overlapping. A subordinate component pair is defined as the presence of > 98% of a smaller component within a larger

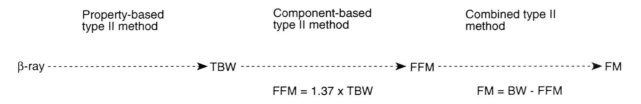

Property-based type II method	Component-based type II method	Combined type II method

β-ray ----------------------------►TBW ----------------------------► FFM ----------------------------► FM

FFM = 1.37 x TBW   FM = BW - FFM

Figure 7.5 Pathway summarizing the three stages in the estimation of total body fat from TBW.

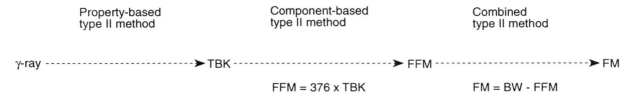

Property-based type II method	Component-based type II method	Combined type II method

γ-ray - ➤ TBK - ➤ FFM - ➤ FM

FFM = 376 x TBK   FM = BW - FFM

Figure 7.6 Pathway summarizing the three stages in the estimation of total body fat from TBK.

component. An example of overlapping components is the relationship between total body carbon and fat. A portion of carbon is incorporated into fat molecules, but carbon is also contained in protein, glycogen, and bone minerals. Similarly, the molecular structure of fat includes hydrogen and oxygen in addition to carbon.

Combination characteristics are of two main types, chemical (e.g., N covalently bound to amino acids in protein) and nonchemical (e.g., water and FFM). The three dependency relations and two combination characteristics result in six types of component-pair interactions.

The six component-pair interactions and some models developed from them are shown in Table 7.3. Generalizations can be made that describe types of component-pair relationships. First, chemical relationships tend to be very stable and are population-general as they vary little across all populations or with disease. Only a few nonchemical associations are relatively stable and thus useful in body composition methods. Most models developed from nonchemical component pairs, because of the physiological nature of their associations, may be population-specific and not population-general as are the chemical component pair models. This is because nonchemical physiological linkages are more flexible associations than are chemical relationships. For example, the TBW/FFM ratio varies throughout the lifespan and is higher in infants and children than in adults. Second, subordinate and separate dependency relations are suitable for developing monocomponent methods (Table 7.3). Monocomponent methods are those in which one component is predicted from another component. Overlapping relations, on the other hand, are appropriate for developing multicomponent models in which two or more components are used to predict an unknown component. There are no stable or relatively stable component-pairs that are classified as nonchemical separate types. Nonchemical separate relationship types can only approximately estimate the mass of a component, such as glycogen from nitrogen or soft

tissue mineral from bone mineral (Table 7.3). An in-depth review of these concepts is presented in Wang et al. (1995).

Errors in Component Measurements

Our organization of body composition methods provides an opportunity to systematically evaluate errors in component measurements. Our intent here is not to be exhaustive but rather to highlight the main types of error involved in assessing the mass of a component. Other reviews, including chapters 1 to 6 and 8 and 9 in this volume, provide a comprehensive assessment of errors in body composition methodology (Lohman, 1992; Lohman & Going, 1993; Mueller & Martorell, 1988).

The first category involves errors in measuring the quantity term (Q) of formula 7.1. Each of the measurement errors can be evaluated separately in complex methods such as the use of TBW and TBK for estimating total body fat. Additionally, there are measurement errors that occur between observers, instruments, laboratories, and over time. Only rarely have body composition studies included a comprehensive evaluation of the many sources of measurement error.

The second group of errors involves the mathematical function term (f) of formula 7.1. With type I methods there are errors related to the reference method for assessing the unknown component. Predictive equations also have characteristic errors (chapter 10). The errors in type II methods are related to the various assumptions that ultimately determine the "stability" of models within and between subjects.

Multicomponent Molecular Level Body Composition Methods

The purpose of using multicomponent methods to study body composition is twofold. First, these methods allow analysis of three or more molecular level components rather than the two traditional

Table 7.3　Component Relationship Types and Some Representative Models

Combination characteristics	Dependency relationships		
	Subordinate	Separate	Overlapping
Chemical	TBN = 0.161 · TBPro	TBS = 0.062 · TBN	TBC = 0.759 · fat + 0.532 · TBPro + 0.444 · glycogen + 0.180 · TBBM
	TBCa = 0.34 · TBBM		TBH = 0.122 · fat + 0.111 · TBW + 0.070 · TBPro
Nonchemical	TBW = 0.73 · FFM	Glycogen = 0.275 · TBN	TBK = 0.00469 · BCM + 0.00016 · ECF
	TBK = 0.00266 · FFM	ST mineral = 0.235 · TBBM	TBC = 0.640 · AT + 0.107 · SM + 0.148 · bone + 0.121 · other tissues
Model type	Monocomponent	Monocomponent	Multicomponent

Note. All units are in kg. *Abbreviations*: ASM, appendicular skeletal muscle; AT, adipose tissue; BCM, body cell mass; ECF, extracellular fluid; FFM; fat-free body mass; SM, total body skeletal muscle; ST, soft tissue; TB, total body elements C, Ca, H, K, N, and S; TBBM, total body bone mineral; TBPro, total body protein; TBW, total body water.

fat and FFM components. There are many biological conditions in which the study of these multiple components are of interest. Second, measuring multiple components often reduces the errors of the assumptions in type II methods. The two-component hydrodensitometry method is formulated on the assumption that the proportions of FFM as water, protein, and mineral are constant. Adding a measurement of TBW to the method reduces the error in fat and FFM estimates due to individual differences in hydration. Multicomponent methods are therefore important in biological investigations and in body composition research.

In the sections that follow, we give a brief historical overview, a description of some of the various models and their assumptions, a review of the measurements involved, and lastly we discuss errors for several of the methods. Our primary intent is to describe the process and underlying theoretical basis upon which multicomponent methods are developed.

Methods that comprise three or more molecular level components are of two main types, component-based and combined. All multicomponent methods are based on type II mathematical functions.

Component-Based Methods

All component-based type II methods are founded on the formula, $C_u = f(C_k)$, where C_u and C_k are unknown and known components, respectively. With multicomponent methods there are more than two known components.

Total Body Carbon (TBC) Method. Almost all body carbon is incorporated into three organic chemical components: fat, protein, and glycogen (Snyder et al., 1975). Small amounts of carbon are also found in bone mineral and to a lesser extent in other molecular species such as essential lipids. Kyere et al. (1982) first proposed a model in which fat could be calculated from TBC measured by neutron activation analysis. Kehayias et al. (1991) and Heymsfield (1991) and their respective colleagues at Brookhaven National Laboratory later refined the TBC model, which is as follows: TBC = $0.77 \times$ FM + $0.532 \times$ protein + $0.444 \times$ glycogen + $0.20 \times$ carbonate in bone mineral + $0.197 \times HCO_3^-$ in extracellular fluid, where all units are in kg. The equation can be rearranged to solve for FM:

$$FM = 1.29 \times [TBC - (3.37 \times TBN) + (0.052 \times TBCa) + (0.085 \times TBCl)]$$

(7.4)

where TB prefixed to an element symbol is the total body quantity for that element. The four remaining unknown components can be measured (protein from TBN, bone mineral from TBCa, and HCO_3^- from TBCl) or approximated (glycogen from TBN). This is a component-based type II multicomponent method based on overlapping chemical relationships. Because the model is developed using highly stable chemical proportions, the TBC method of measuring fat is assumed to be population-general.

The main assumptions of the method are twofold: that TBC is distributed in fat, protein, glycogen, bone minerals, and electrolytes, and that the proportion of carbon in each of these molecular level components is known and constant. The total body carbon method provides an excellent example of the various assumptions that are incorporated into most type II component-based methods.

At present, protein cannot be measured in vivo using property-based methods. Instead, nitrogen is typically measured by neutron activation analysis (Dilmanian et al., 1990; Vartsky, Ellis, & Cohn, 1979) and converted to protein using a type II component-based method: protein = 6.25 × TBN. As noted earlier, this approach assumes a constant TBN/protein ratio (0.16) and complete incorporation of TBN into protein.

Nitrogen and protein components exist in a chemical subordinate relationship that is generally assumed to be relatively stable within and between subjects (Wang et al., 1995). Mulder, who first introduced the term protein in 1838, is credited with suggesting two chemical formulas for protein ($C_{40}H_{31}N_5O_{12}$ and $C_{48}H_{36}N_6O_{14}$) (Cunningham, 1994). Today the general formula for meat protein is assumed to be $C_{100}H_{159}N_{26}O_{32}S_{0.7}$ with N/protein equal to 0.16 (Kleiber, 1975; Snyder et al., 1975). It is clear, however, that the nitrogen content of specific proteins differs from 16%. Knight, Beddoe, Streat, & Hill (1986) reported N/protein ratios of 0.172, 0.159, and 0.137 for collagen, actinomyosin, and albumin, respectively. Nevertheless, their chemical analyses of two persons who died of cancer yielded whole-body N/protein ratios of 0.158 and 0.156. They concluded that these data did not justify a change in the assumed N/protein ratio of 0.16.

Under normal circumstances > 99% of total body nitrogen (TBN) is incorporated into protein (Diem, 1962; Snyder et al., 1975). Nonprotein sources of nitrogen include urea, creatine, creatinine, uric acid, free amino acids, and several other compounds. When serious disease is present, such as renal failure or congestive heart failure, total body levels of nitrogenous nonprotein compounds can increase substantially, although the impact on the N/protein ratio is not large even in these extreme circumstances. For example, in renal failure, blood urea nitrogen concentration can increase from a normal level of 0.1 g/L to 1.0 g/L. Assuming a TBW of 42 L, total body urea nitrogen would increase with renal failure from 4.2 g to 42 g. TBN is approximately 1800 g in the Reference Man (Snyder et al.), so urea nitrogen would increase from 0.23% to 2.3% of total body nitrogen. If we assume that 99.77% of total body nitrogen is in protein in healthy subjects (i.e., TBN − urea N), our protein estimate using 6.25 × TBN would be 11.2 kg. If

instead 2.3% of TBN were urea nitrogen, then our protein estimate would be 11.0 kg. Hence the classical assumption that all body nitrogen is in the form of protein is subject to a systematic error of 2 to 3% with serious renal disease and other states in which nitrogen accumulates. Alternatively, corrections in TBN could be made for urea nitrogen and other nitrogenous nonprotein compounds using blood levels of these compounds along with TBW estimates to evaluate total body amounts as in our approximate calculations.

Glycogen, which is present mainly in liver, skeletal muscle, and heart, comprises about 1% of FFM in weight-stable adults. The concentration of glycogen in these tissues varies with fasting and feeding, so that the amount present is at a minimum of < 300 to 500 g for the total body early in the morning (Diem, 1962; Snyder et al., 1975). This is the time of day that body composition measurements are usually made and, because of its small amount, glycogen is not considered in most body composition models. In the TBC method for estimating fat, it is assumed that the glycogen to protein ratio is 0.044 (Kehayias et al., 1991), but this must be considered a very approximate estimate. It is based on a nonchemical separate relationship between two components which, as we described earlier, will not tend to form a ratio that is stable within and between subjects. The total amount of carbon in glycogen is small (~0.2 kg), and measurement errors in this portion of the model have only a small impact on fat estimates. There is a small amount of carbon in the carbonate component of bone mineral (Brožek et al., 1963) and in the anion HCO_3^- which is distributed mainly in extracellular fluid.

The TBC method of estimating fat assumes that all body calcium is in bone mineral and that the bone carbon to calcium ratio is constant at 0.05 (Kehayias et al., 1991; Snyder et al., 1975). Under most conditions, almost all body calcium is incorporated into bone mineral. This is a chemical subordinate relationship that is assumed to be very stable in vivo. The carbon/calcium ratio is an approximation (Biltz & Pellegrino, 1969; Brožek et al, 1963), but, as with glycogen, the errors have only small impacts on fat estimates.

The small amount of carbon in extracellular fluid as HCO_3^- is estimated by assuming a constant ratio of bicarbonate to chlorine; the latter is found almost entirely in extracellular fluid. This is a nonchemical separate relationship type and thus only an approximation of bicarbonate is possible from total body chlorine. The method assumes that fat is 77%

carbon. Triglycerides extracted from human tissues vary in fatty acid composition and the carbon/triglyceride ratio of 0.77 represents an average based on the Reference Man (Snyder et al., 1975). Table 7.4 gives representative formulas for long-chain triglycerides found in human beings and their carbon/triglyceride ratio (C/TG). As can be seen from the various stoichiometries, carbon only varies slightly as a fraction of these representative triglycerides (0.76 to 0.77).

Thus many assumptions of varying quality form the basis of the TBC method of estimating total body fat. Nevertheless, the main assumptions are highly stable and the method is thus valuable as a research tool for measuring fat mass independent of other conventional approaches.

The Kehayias TBC method requires measurement of TBC, TBN, TBCa, and TBCl. TBC is measured by neutron inelastic scattering, which is based on the reaction $^{12}C + n \rightarrow {}^{12}C^* + n' \rightarrow {}^{12}C + n' + \gamma$ (4.44 MeV). The source of 14 MeV neutrons in our laboratory is a small sealed deuterium-tritium generator that is pulsed at 4 to 10 kHz (Kehayias et al., 1987). Carbon is detected by counting the 4.44 MeV γ-rays from the inelastic scattering of fast neutrons from ^{12}C nuclei. Sodium iodide detectors detect carbon's 4.44 MeV γ-rays from carbon.

TBN is measured using prompt-γ neutron activation analysis and is based on the reaction $^{14}N + n \rightarrow {}^{15}N^* \rightarrow {}^{15}N + \gamma$ (10.83 MeV). The system used in our laboratory has a ^{238}Pu-Be neutron source (85 Ci), and the high energy prompt 10.83 MeV γ-rays from nitrogen are simultaneously detected by NaI crystals with radiation (Dilmanian et al., 1990).

Delayed-γ neutron activation is used to measure total body calcium and chlorine based on the reactions $^{48}Ca + n \rightarrow {}^{49}Ca^* \rightarrow {}^{49}Ca + \gamma$ (3.10 MeV) and $^{37}Cl + n \rightarrow {}^{38}Cl^* \rightarrow {}^{38}Cl + \gamma$ (2.17 MeV). There are two parts to this system, an irradiation facility and

a shielded whole-body γ-ray counter (Dilmanian et al., 1990). The irradiation system uses an array of ^{238}Pu-Be moderated neutron sources. Following neutron exposure, the subjects are rapidly transported to the whole-body counter where the induced γ-rays emitted from neutron capture activation of calcium and chlorine are counted.

The between-measurement coefficients of variation (CV) for total body carbon, nitrogen, calcium, and chlorine are shown in Table 7.5. The propagated error in the TBC method of estimating total body fat is 3.4 to 4% (Heymsfield et al., 1991; Kehayias et al., 1991). The table also gives the radiation exposure for representative neutron activation measurements.

The importance of the TBC method for quantifying total body fat is that it provides values that are independent of the classical two-component methods described earlier. The method is primarily based on highly stable chemical models that are not known to be influenced to an appreciable degree by age, gender, or ethnicity. Since only a few centers in the world have the necessary neutron activation systems, the TBC method has limited applicability.

Four- and Six-Component Neutron Activation Methods. Cohn and his colleagues (1984) at Brookhaven National Laboratory originally proposed a four-component method based on measurement of tritiated water dilution volume (L), TBN (kg), TBCa (kg), and body weight (kg). The method is designed to provide measurements of four components (in kg): total body fat, water, protein, and minerals. The equations are as follows:

FM = BW − (TBPro + TBW + TBA)

TBPro = 6.25 × TBN

TBW = 0.95 × 0.994 × tritium dilution volume

TBA = TBCa/0.34

$$(7.5)$$

where TBA is total body bone ash.

Our group, also working at Brookhaven, expanded Cohn's model (Heymsfield et al., 1991) to six components:

FM = BW − (TBPro + TBW + bone mineral + soft tissue mineral + glycogen + unmeasured residuals)

TBPro = 6.25 × TBN

TBW = 0.95 × 0.994 × tritium dilution volume

bone mineral = TBCa / 0.364

Table 7.4   Carbon/Triglyceride Ratio for Representative Long-Chain Triglycerides

Formula	C/TG
$C_{57}H_{104}O_6$	0.7737
$C_{51}H_{98}O_6$	0.7593
$C_{55}H_{102}O_6$	0.7692
$C_{55}H_{104}O_6$	0.7674
Average	0.7674

C/TG, carbon to triglyceride ratio.

Table 7.5 Representative Errors and Radiation Exposure for Multicomponent Molecular Level Methods

Quantity	Measurement method	Errors (CV, %)*	Radiation exposure (mSv)	Reference
1. Components				
Total body nitrogen	PGNA	3.6		Dutton, 1991
		2.7	0.26	Pierson et al., 1990
		4.1		Beddoe et al., 1984
		3.0	0.26	Mernagh et al., 1977
Total body hydrogen	PGNA	0.4	0.26	Dutton, 1991
Total body potassium	WBC	1.5	0.00	Pierson et al., 1990
Total body carbon	INS	4.2		Dutton, 1991
		3.0	0.16	Pierson et al., 1990
Total body calcium	DGNA	2.6		Dutton, 1991
		0.8	2.50	Pierson et al., 1990
Total body phosphorus	DGNA	5.1		Dutton, 1991
		3.0	2.50	Pierson et al., 1990
Total body sodium	DGNA	2.5	2.50	Pierson et al., 1990
Total body chlorine	DGNA	1.5		Dutton, 1991
		2.5	2.50	Pierson et al., 1990
Total body water	^3H_2O dilution	1.5	0.12	Wang et al., 1973
	^2H_2O dilution	1.5	0.00	Pierson et al., 1990
		4.0		Bartoli et al., 1993
	$H_2^{18}O$ dilution	2.0	0.00	Schoeller et al., 1980
Total body fat	TBC	—	3.06	Kehayias et al., 1991 Heymsfield et al., 1991
	3C-UWW	—	0.00	
	4C-IVNA	—	2.88	Cohn et al., 1984
	4C-UWW	—	< 0.01	
	6C-IVNA	—	3.04	Heymsfield et al., 1991
Bone mineral	DXA	1.28	< 0.01	Heymsfield et al., 1990
2. Properties				
Body weight	Scale	< 1%	0.00	Heymsfield, 1991
Body volume/density	Hydro-densitometry	0.5%BF	0.00	Withers, unpublished data
Stature	Stadiometer	0.2	0.00	Heymsfield et al., 1991

Abbreviations: BF, body fat; C, component; CV, coefficient of variation; DXA, dual energy x-ray absorptiometry; DGNA, delayed-γ neutron activation analysis; INS, inelastic neutron scattering; IVNA, in vivo neutron activation analysis; PGNA, prompt-γ neutron activation analysis; TBC, total body carbon; UWW, underwater weighing; WBC, ^{40}K whole-body counting.

*CVs represent between-measurement variation in phantoms or humans on the same or different days. Measurement errors for total body fat estimates are discussed in the text.

soft tissue mineral = 2.76 × TBK + 1.00 × TBNa +
    1.43 × TBCl − 0.038 × TBCa

glycogen = 0.275 × TBN

(7.6)

Fat mass is determined by the TBC method described earlier.

The Swansea (UK) and Auckland (NZ) groups have each developed models based on the analysis of total body elements (Beddoe et al., 1984; Ryde et al., 1993). All the neutron activation/whole-body counting models share common characteristics. In addition to the assumptions related to estimates of fat from carbon and of protein from nitrogen described earlier, the main assumptions are as follows:

- **Glycogen**. The highly variable and rapidly changing glycogen component is estimated in most methods or is ignored due to the relatively small amount of total body glycogen. In the six-component model, as with the TBC method, the glycogen-to-protein ratio is assumed constant at 0.044. Beddoe et al. (1984) assumed that glycogen is 0.91% of FFM. Of importance to multicomponent methods, glycogen can now be measured in vivo using ^{13}C nuclear magnetic resonance spectroscopy and the results agree well with chemical analysis of skeletal muscle biopsies (Jue et al., 1989; Taylor et al., 1992). This new ability to quantitate glycogen in vivo should allow development of improved glycogen models in the future.

- **Water**. TBW is measured using tritium or deuterium dilution and in some laboratories by ^{18}O labeled water (chapter 2). Each isotope measures a specific dilution volume, and the volume measured for all three isotopes is larger than the actual TBW volume. For tritium and deuterium, the dilution volume is larger than TBW because the labeled hydrogen atoms exchange with hydrogen atoms associated with carboxyl, hydroxyl, and amino groups (Culebras & Moore, 1977; Heymsfield & Matthews, 1994). Similarly, ^{18}O exchanges with labile oxygen atoms in carboxyl and phosphate groups (Schoeller et al., 1980; Wong et al., 1988). The exchange of labeled atoms with unlabeled atoms from labile molecular components probably varies with a number of factors (Goran, Poehlman, Nair, & Danforth, 1992; Heymsfield & Matthews), but most workers assume a constant exchange rate that approximates 4 to 5% for tritium and deuterium and 0 to 1% for ^{18}O (Culebras & Moore; Forbes, 1987; Schoeller & Jones, 1980). To calculate TBW, the isotope dilution volume is multiplied, to account for isotope exchange, by a correction factor such as 0.95 to 0.96 for ^3H_2O and ^2H_2O dilution volume and 0.98 to 0.99 for $H_2^{18}O$ dilution volume. Some workers assume that ^{18}O exchange is negligible. These corrections are extremely important because water is the largest component of FFM, and even small relative errors in its estimation have an impact on the various models as a whole. Nevertheless, at present, there does not appear to be an improved method of estimating isotope exchange. The density of water in this model (0.994 g/cm^3) is assumed constant at 36 °C. We discuss this assumption in more detail later.

- **Bone mineral**. The ratio of calcium to bone mineral is assumed constant at 0.364 (Heymsfield et al., 1991). Bone mineral ash is the remaining noncombustible matter after heating bone to a high temperature (> 500 °C) (Woodward, 1962). The organic matter, mainly proteins such as collagen, are volatilized during the ashing process (Snyder et al., 1975; Woodward, 1964). The main mineral in bone is calcium hydroxyapatite. Calcium, oxygen, and phosphorus are the abundant elements in bone mineral, with smaller amounts of sodium, potassium, and magnesium. The ratio of calcium to bone mineral (0.364) is close to the proportion of calcium in calcium hydroxyapatite (0.398) (Woodward, 1964). This ratio appears relatively stable across men and women and in normal and osteoporotic women (Burnell et al., 1982) and may even be similar across different species (Biltz & Pellegrino, 1969).

Calcium is found at a concentration of 3 and 3 to 5 mmol/kg in intracellular and extracellular fluid, respectively. Only small deviations from these concentrations are observed in various disease states. The total non-osseous calcium is less than 14 g, whereas there is 1000 g of bone calcium in the Reference Man (Snyder et al., 1975). The assumption that calcium is a chemical subordinate component of bone mineral is therefore appropriate.

- **Soft tissue mineral**. Soft tissue minerals occur in many forms and their total amount in vivo is relatively small (~0.4 kg in the Reference Man, Snyder et al., 1975). Brožek and colleagues (1963) were the first to attempt a systematic analysis of soft tissue minerals and to estimate their combined density in vivo. Two approaches are now used in estimating soft tissue minerals. First, they can be assumed to be present in a constant amount relative to another component such as bone mineral (Heymsfield et al., 1990). This is a component-based type II method and a nonchemical separate relationship type. Accordingly, soft tissue mineral estimates using this approach are approximate.

The alternative is to estimate soft tissue minerals separately. For example, in our six-component model, we measure total body sodium and calcium with delayed-γ neutron activation analysis. Sodium is found as a cation in several soft tissue minerals and is also bound to the crystalline matrix of bone mineral (Woodward, 1962, 1964). The ratio of sodium to calcium in bone mineral is known (Woodward, 1962), and a component-based type II method can therefore be used to estimate bone mineral sodium from total body calcium [Na in bone mineral (g) = 0.038 × TBCa (g)]. Sodium in soft tissues can then be calculated as the difference between total body sodium and sodium in bone mineral. Using similar approaches, six main soft tissue minerals/electrolytes (Na^+, K^+, Mg^{++}, Cl^-, $H_2PO_4^-$, HCO_3^-) can be estimated from four measurable elements (Na, K, Cl, Ca) and then summed for total soft tissue mineral mass.

Elements are measured by the neutron activation whole-body counting methods described earlier. Total body sodium is measured along with Ca and Cl using delayed-γ neutron activation (Dilmanian et al., 1990) with the reaction $^{23}Na + n \rightarrow ^{24}Na^* \rightarrow ^{24}Na + \gamma$ (2.75 MeV). TBW is measured using either deuterium or tritium dilution as described in chapter 2. The CVs for elemental measurements are shown in Table 7.5. The propagated errors for estimating total body fat by the four- and six-component methods are 2.7% and 3.4%, respectively.

Combined Methods

All combined methods have the general form $C_u = f(P, C_k)$, where C_u and C_k are unknown and known components, respectively, and P is the measurable property. Multicomponent methods are all based on type II methods.

Behnke's two-component hydrodensitometry method assumes known and constant proportions of FFM as water, protein, and mineral (1942). It was from these assumed proportions, and the density of each chemical component, that the total density of FFM was derived (Brožek et al., 1963). This led ultimately to the development of various hydrodensitometry-based two-component methods (Brožek et al.; Siri, 1961).

It is obvious that deviations from the assumed chemical component proportions are possible with conditions that alter body composition such as aging, pregnancy, weight reduction in the obese, and various disease states. A more desirable approach in these conditions would be to make fewer assumptions by measuring more components/properties in addition to body volume. Over the several decades following Behnke's milestone research, the two-component method was expanded to three components and more recently to four components by adding water and mineral estimates.

Siri (1961) suggested a three-component model (Table 7.1) in which there are three measurable quantities, body weight, body volume, and TBW. The measurement of TBW eliminates the errors in Behnke's two-component method (Behnke et al., 1942) related to individual differences in hydration. Siri's three-component model still assumes,

however, that the ratio of protein to mineral remains constant (Table 7.6). Protein and mineral form a nonchemical separate relationship type (see Table 7.3); the protein/mineral ratio is inherently unstable, but it has value as an approximation.

Lohman (1986) used the same conceptual framework as Siri (1961) to derive a three-component (fat, bone mineral, and residual) model (see Table 7.1). This model assumes fat, mineral, and protein + water densities of 0.9007, 3.037, and 1.0486 g/cm^3, respectively (Lohman). The advantage of this model over the two-component hydrodensitometry model is that it accounts for biological variability in bone mineral, which has a relatively high density and comprises 5 to 6% of FFM.

Later investigators expanded Siri's classic three-component model by adding bone mineral (TBBM) measurements to eliminate errors related to individual differences in bone mineral content of FFM (Baumgartner et al., 1991; Friedl, DeLuca, Marchitelli, & Vogel, 1992; Fuller, Jebb, Laskey, & Coward, 1992; Heymsfield et al., 1990; Selinger 1977). In these type II models, four quantities are measured: body volume, TBW, bone mineral, and body weight. Representative four-compartment methods are shown in Table 7.6. Two main strategies are used in developing these methods. All share assumed densities for fat, water, and bone mineral. In one approach, the remainder of body weight after the subtraction of fat, water, and bone mineral is assumed to be protein and soft tissue minerals of known densities. In the other approach, the remainder is assumed to represent a combined residual mass (protein, soft tissue minerals, and other) of known density.

A useful exercise is to examine the simultaneous equations upon which four-component hydrodensitometry methods are developed. The body weight model for this method is

$$BW = FM + water + bone\ mineral + residual \tag{7.7}$$

where all units are in kg. Residual mass includes protein, soft tissue minerals, glycogen, and other substances that are present in very small amounts such as nucleic acids. The body volume model for this method is

$$BV = FM/0.9007 + water/0.99371 \\ + TBBM/2.982 + residual/1.404. \tag{7.8}$$

This model assumes known and constant densities for each of the four components: fat, 0.9007 kg/L and water, 0.99371 kg/L at 36 °C; bone mineral,

Table 7.6 Some Type II Combined Methods for Measuring Total Body Fat

Author	Measurable property	Known component(s)	Simultaneous models	Type II combined method
Siri, 1961	BW, BV	Water	BW = FM + water + protein + mineral BV = FM/0.900 + water/0.994 + protein/1.34 + mineral/3.04 Protein = 2.40 × mineral	FM = 2.057 × BV − 0.786 × water − 1.286 × BW
Lohman, 1986	BW, BV	Mineral	BW = FM + water + protein + mineral BV = FM/0.9007 + water/0.994 + protein/1.34 + mineral/3.04 Water = 4.00 × protein	FM = 6.386 × BV + 3.961 × mineral − 6.09 × BW
Baumgartner et al., 1991	BW, BV	Water, mineral	BW = FM + water + protein + TBBM + Ms BV = FM/0.9007 + water/0.994 + protein/1.34 + TBBM/2.982 + Ms/3.317 Soft tissue mineral = 0.235 × TBBM	FM = 2.75 × BV − 0.714 × water + 1.148 × mineral − 2.05 × BW
Selinger, 1977	BW, BV	Water, TBBM	BW = FM + water + protein + TBBM + Ms BV = FM/0.9007 + water/0.994 + protein/1.34 + TBBM/2.982 + Ms/3.317 Ms = 0.0105 × BW	FM = 2.75 × BV − 0.714 × water + 1.129 × TBBM − 2.037 × BW
This review	BW, BV	Water, TBBM	BW = FM + water + TBBM + residual BV = FM/0.9007 + water/0.99371 + TBBM/2.982 + residual/1.404	FM = 2.513 × BV − 0.739 × water + 0.947 × TBBM − 1.79 × BW

Abbreviations: BV, body volume (L); BW, body weight (kg); FM, fat mass (kg); Ms, soft tissue mineral (kg); TBBM, ashed bone (kg) from DXA × 1.0436.

2.982 kg/L; and residual mass, 1.404 kg/L for animals and human beings at 37 °C (Allen, Krzywicki, & Roberts, 1959). Combining the body weight and body volume equations, fat mass can then be derived as follows:

$$FM = 2.513 \times BV - 0.739 \times \text{water} + 0.947 \times TBBM - 1.79 \times BW.$$

(7.9)

Most four-component hydrodensitometry methods give very similar estimates for total body fat, since they are based on closely related models and assumptions. We now review these assumptions in detail:

• **Body temperature**. The density of components at the molecular level of body composition is closely related to body temperature. This has been a source of much confusion in the body composition literature. Obviously, the body temperature varies from core to skin in a predictable

manner. It is usual to assume a single representative average body temperature, although structures near the skin, such as subcutaneous adipose tissue, are at a lower temperature than those located deep in the viscera.

The two-component models of Brožek et al. (1963) and Siri (1961) assume respective mean body temperatures of 36 °C and 37 °C. The temperature of 37 °C is representative of core temperature, which is measured in the rectum, esophagus, or at the tympanic membrane. The average body temperature under basal resting conditions and in a comfortable environment is likely to be 1 to 2 °C lower than the core temperature of ~37 °C. If it is assumed that the rectal and mean skin temperatures are 37 °C and 34 °C, respectively, in a thermoneutral environment, then the formula of Burton (1935) yields the theoretical mean body temperature of 36 °C, which was used by Brožek et al. The average body temperature would also probably be 36 °C during underwater weighing when water temperature is maintained at 35 °C.

While 36 °C appears to be the best estimate of mean body temperature, it is interesting to speculate whether fat and other molecular level components have different mean temperatures. For example, a case could be made for a lower temperature for fat since a high proportion of this component is subcutaneous and it has low levels of vascular perfusion. Conversely, it can be argued that water has a higher mean temperature since skin and subcutaneous adipose tissue contain only a small proportion of TBW. However, mathematical modeling of the human thermal system by Werner and Buse (1988) emphasizes that specific tissues have a range of temperatures in vivo. It is therefore virtually impossible to specify a mean temperature for fat and each of the molecular level components. The best estimate of average body temperature under controlled laboratory conditions thus appears to be about 36 °C.

- **Lipid density**. Lipids can be divided into essential and non-essential according to distribution, function, and solubility characteristics (Gurr & Harwood, 1991; Wang et al., 1992). Hydrodensitometry models usually consider only non-essential lipids, which consist almost entirely of triglycerides. Essential lipids are included in the FFM component. There are 1500 g of essential lipid in the 70 kg Reference Man (Snyder et al., 1975). Mendez et al. (1960) suggested the lipids in the adult nervous system amount to 200 to 300 g.

Fidanza, Keys, and Anderson (1953) reported that the density of 20 ether extractable lipid samples from the intra-abdominal and subcutaneous adipose tissue of 5 subjects was ($\bar{x} \pm$ SD) 0.9007 $\pm$ 0.00068 g/cm^3 at 36 °C with a coefficient of thermal expansion of 0.00074 g/(cm$^3 \cdot$ °C) over the range of 15 to 37 °C. The small between-subject coefficient of variation of 0.08% supports the use of a "constant" fat density (0.9007 g/cm^3) in body composition models.

Although the preceding analyses were conducted on ether extracts of adipose tissue, this should not introduce major errors into the assumed density of triglyceride. Cholesterol (density = 1.067 g/cm^3) and phospholipids (density = 1.035 g/cm^3) comprise only 1% of the ether-extractable lipid from rabbit adipose tissue (Mendez et al., 1960). Triglyceride or "fat" is therefore assumed to account for 99% of the ether-extractable lipid (Wang et al., 1992). These considerations therefore lead us to conclude that the assumed density of fat (0.9007 g/cm^3) at 36 °C is reasonably accurate and stable between subjects.

- **Water density**. Water measurement and isotope exchange were discussed earlier. The densities of water at either 36 °C or 37 °C are used in three-and four-component models to convert water volume to water mass.

- **Protein density**. The densities of most proteins in the dry crystalline state are close to 1.27 g/cm^3 (Haurowitz, 1963). However, proteins are the principal water-binding substances in human beings and the resultant hydration is accompanied by a volume contraction of both the solute and the solvent. The specific volume of hydrated protein therefore decreases until the apparent density is 1.34 g/cm^3, which appears to be the best available estimate for hydrated protein in the living cell. Specific proteins differ, however, in density. For example, collagen, which is found mainly in bone and skin, has an average dry density of 1.36 g/cm^3 and comprises 25 to 30% of total body protein (Hulmes & Miller, 1979). The density used for total body protein is thus more tenuous than those used for fat and water.

- **Glycogen density**. Glycogen has a density of 1.52 g/cm^3 at 37 °C. Hydrodensitometry four-component methods either pool the small glycogen mass with protein or include it in residual mass. In either case, the estimates of glycogen in the various models are so approximate that glycogen must be considered a source of model error.

- **Mineral density**. The density of bone mineral of 2.982 g/cm^3 is based on the mean of only four samples (Mendez et al., 1960) isolated from the long bones of animals (cow tibia at 36 °C: 2.9930 and 3.0066 g/cm^3; dog femur and tibia at 36.7 °C: 2.9624 and 2.9667 g/cm^3). Brožek et al. (1963) further verified this value against that of the stoichiometry for the prototype mineral hydroxyapatite after allowance for water of crystallization and CO_2. Mendez et al. also cited earlier work by Dallemagne and Melon (1945), who reported the densities of bone and dental mineral to be 2.99 and 3.0 g/cm^3, respectively.

The density of soft tissue minerals was estimated as follows. The classical cadaver analyses assumed that all calcium was contained within bone and that it was accompanied by the same amounts of phosphorus, sodium, and magnesium as observed in bone ash. This is a reasonable assumption since extra skeletal calcium represents less than 0.4% of total body calcium (Snyder et al., 1975). The excess was then assigned to nonbone mineral and the density of this was determined by measuring the apparent specific volume occupied by 1 g of each of five salts, which represented the nonbone mineral. The apparent densities (reciprocal of apparent specific volume), which ranged from 3.07 g/cm^3 for potassium bicarbonate to 4.99 g/cm^3 for magnesium chloride (all at 40 °C), were then multiplied by their relative contributions to nonbone mineral to yield an overall density of 3.317 g/cm^3.

Some four-component hydrodensitometry methods assume a constant ratio of soft tissue minerals (Ms) to either body weight or to bone mineral (Table 7.6). These must be considered very approximate estimates; soft tissue minerals are not directly proportional to body weight and thus the Ms/BW ratio is not constant; moreover, Ms/TBBM is based on a nonchemical separate relationship type and is thus not a stable ratio within and between subjects. Soft tissue minerals are a small fraction of body weight and errors introduced into fat estimates using the various assumptions and models associated with soft tissue minerals are unlikely to be very large.

The density of residual mass in animals and human beings, 1.404 g/cm^3, was measured by Allen et al. (1959) at 37 °C. The two largest components of residual mass are protein (density 1.34 g/cm^3) and glycogen (density 1.52 g/cm^3). Soft tissue minerals (density 3.317 g/cm^3) and other miscellaneous chemical components constitute the remainder.

Detailed reviews of the densitometry, total body water, and bone mineral methods are presented in chapters 1, 2, and 4, respectively. The measurement errors for these methods are presented in Table 7.5. As can be gathered from the preceding discussion, the calculation of errors in three- and four-component hydrodensitometry methods is complex and involves many uncertainties related to assumption and measurement errors. While greater validity should be associated with the measurement of more components, there is some concern that the resultant greater control over the biological variability of FFM may be offset somewhat by the propagation of measurement errors associated with the determination of body density, TBW, and bone mineral. A worst case scenario for this propagation of errors can be calculated by assuming that the squared errors or error variances (SEE^2; or TEM^2, the standard error of a single determination) are independent and additive:

$$SD \text{ of total error} = [SEE^2 \text{ for underwater weighing } \% \text{ fat} \\ + SEE^2 \text{ for TBW } \% \text{ fat} \\ + SEE^2 \text{ for effect of bone mineral on } \% \text{ fat}]^{0.5}.$$

(7.10)

Test-retest reliability data collected at the Flinders University of South Australia are given in Table 7.7. From Table 7.7.:

$$SD \text{ of total error} = [0.43^2 + 0.71^2 + 0.05^2]^{0.5} \\ = 0.9 \% \text{ body fat from SEE values}$$

or

$$= [0.28^2 + 0.48^2 + 0.04^2]^{0.5} \\ = 0.6 \% \text{ body fat from TEM values.}$$

(7.11)

The test-retest reliability data thus yield a value of about 1% body fat units.

Friedl and colleagues (1992) investigated the reliability of fat estimates from multicomponent methods in 10 soldiers studied three times each. These investigators found the greatest sources of error in their four-component method was in the underwater weighing procedure (~1% of body weight), followed by TBW estimates (~0.5 L). They observed reliability coefficients of 0.991 and 0.994, and within-subjects standard deviations of ± 1.0 and ± 1.1 for percent body fat estimates using two- and four-component models, respectively.

Siri (1961) suggested that variability in the density of FFM resulted in an error with a standard deviation of 3.8% body fat units (~0.00084 g/cm^3) when percent body fat was estimated from body density alone. Lohman (1981) suggested that this error decreases to 2.7% body fat for specific populations. Neither estimate includes the technical error associated with body density measurement. Siri further suggested that the error could be reduced to 1.5% body fat units with a three-component method, if the error in measuring TBW could be maintained at about 1% of body weight; Friedl and colleagues (1992) found an error in total body water of about 1% of body weight. Thse observations suggest that the additive measurement errors in three- and four-component methods do not offset the improved accuracy in estimating fat over that of the traditional two-component underwater weighing method.

Table 7.7　Test-Retest Reliability Data

Test	SEE (% fat)	TEM (% fat)
Underwater weighing	0.43	0.28
Total body water	0.71	0.48
Bone mineral	0.05	0.04

Conclusion

The aim of this overview of multicomponent molecular level models was to examine in depth the theoretical basis of multicomponent methods and then to demonstrate these concepts with a few specific examples. The concepts presented should allow the development of methods suited to the research needs and resources of each investigator. The possibility exists to prepare many different multicomponent methods with a firm understanding of the process by which such methods are developed.

There are many future research possibilities related to the development of multicomponent methods. As is clear from this review, innumerable assumptions are required in developing multicomponent methods. Many of these assumptions are extremely tenuous and would benefit from probing studies in the future. Our review only touched on the area of multicomponent method errors; far more work is needed in this area. Finally, powerful new methods are now being introduced that promise to expand measurement possibilities to such previously unmeasured components as skeletal muscle and liver glycogen.

The area of multicomponent method research includes other body composition levels that are not reviewed in this report but which share identical underlying concepts. The study of multicomponent body composition methods thus offers a vast potential area for future research.

Acknowledgment

Supported by National Institutes of Health grants POI-DK 42618 and ROI-AG-13021.

References

Allen T.H., Krzywicki H.J., & Roberts, J.E. (1959). Density, fat, water and solids in freshly isolated tissues. *Journal of Applied Physiology, 14*, 1005-1008.

Bartoli, W.P., Davis, J.M., Pate, R.R., et al. (1993). Weekly variability in total body water using ^2H_2O dilution in college-age males. *Medicine and Science in Sports and Exercise, 25*, 1422-1428.

Baumgartner, R.N., Heymsfield, S.B., Lichtman, S., et al. (1991). Body composition in elderly people: Effect of criterion estimates on predictive equations. *American Journal of Clinical Nutrition, 53*, 1345-1353.

Beddoe, A.H., Streat, S.J., & Hill, G.L. (1984). Evaluation of an in vivo prompt gamma neutron activation facility for body composition studies in critically ill intensive care patients: Results on 41 normals. *Metabolism, 33*, 270-280.

Behnke, A.R., Jr., Feen, B.G., & Welham, W.C. (1942). The specific gravity of healthy men. *Journal of the American Medical Association, 118*, 495-498.

Biltz, R.M., & Pellegrino, E.D. (1969). The chemical anatomy of bone. *The Journal of Bone and Joint Surgery [AM], 51A*, 456-466.

Brožek, J., Grande, F., Anderson, J.T., & Keys, A. (1963). Densitometric analysis of body composition: Revision of some quantitative assumptions. *Annals of the New York Academy of Sciences, 110*, 113-140.

Burnell, J.M., Baylink, D.J., Chestnut, C.H., III, et al. (1982). Bone matrix and mineral abnormalities in postmenopausal osteoporosis. *Metabolism, Clinical and Experimental, 31*, 1113-1120.

Burton, A.C. (1935). Human calorimetry, II: The average temperature of the tissues of the body. *Journal of Nutrition, 9*, 261-280.

Cohn, S.H., Vaswani, A.N., Yasumura, S., et al. (1984). Improved model for determination of body fat by in vivo neutron activation. *American Journal of Clinical Nutrition, 40*, 255-259.

Culebras, J.M., & Moore, F.D. (1977). Total body water and the exchangeable hydrogen, 1: Theoretical calculation of nonaqueous exchangeable hydrogen in man. *American Journal of Physiology (Regulatory, Integrative & Comparitive Physiology), 232*, R54-R59.

Cunningham, J. (1994). N × 6.25: Recognizing a bivariate expression for protein balance in hospitalized patients. *Nutrition, 10*, 124-127.

Dallemagne, M.J., & Melon, J. (1945). Le poids spécifique et l'indice de réfraction de l'os, de l'émail, de la dentine et du cément. *Bulletin de la Société de chimie biologique, 27*, 85-89.

Diem, K. (Ed.) (1962). *Documenta Geigy Scientific Tables*. Ardsley, NY: Geigy Pharmaceuticals.

Dilmanian, F.A., Weber, D.A., Yasumura, S., et al. (1990). Performance of the delayed- and prompt-gamma and neutron activation systems at Brookhaven National Laboratory. In S.Yasumura, J.E. Harrison, K.G. McNeill, et al. (Eds.), *Advances in in vivo body composition studies* (pp. 309-315). New York: Plenum.

Dutton, J. (1991). *In vivo* analysis of body elements and body composition. *University of Wales Science and Technology Review, 8*, 19-30.

Fidanza, F., Keys, A., & Anderson, J.T. (1953). Density of body fat in man and other mammals. *Journal of Applied Physiology, 6,* 252-256.

Forbes, G.B. (1987). *Human body composition: Growth, aging, nutrition and activity.* New York: Springer-Verlag.

Friedl, K.E., DeLuca, J.P., Marchitelli, L.J., & Vogel, J.A. (1992). Reliability of body-fat estimations from a four-compartment model by using density, body water, and bone mineral measurements. *American Journal of Clinical Nutrition, 55,* 764-770.

Fuller, N.J., Jebb, S.A., Laskey, M.A., et al. (1992). Four component model for the assessment of body composition in humans: Comparison with alternative methods, and evaluation of the density and hydration of the fat-free mass. *Clinical Science, 82,* 687-693.

Goran, M.I., Poehlman, E.T., Nair, K.S., & Danforth, E., Jr. (1992). Effect of gender, body composition, and equilibration time on the ^{3}H-to-^{18}O dilution space ratio. *American Journal of Physiology (Endocrinology & Metabolism), 263,* E1119-E1124.

Gurr, M.I., & Harwood, J.L. (1991). *Lipid biochemistry.* 4th Ed. London: Chapman and Hall.

Haurowitz, F. (1963). *The chemistry and function of proteins.* New York: Academic (p. 119).

Heymsfield, S.B., Lichtman, S., Baumgartner, R.N., et al. (1990). Body composition of humans: Comparison of two improved four-compartment models that differ in expense, technical complexity, and radiation exposure. *American Journal of Clinical Nutrition, 52,* 52-58.

Heymsfield, S.B., & Matthews, D. (1994). Body composition: Research and clinical advances. *Journal of Parenteral and Enteral Nutrition, 18,* 91-103.

Heymsfield, S.B., & Waki, M. (1991). Body composition in humans: Advances in the development of multicompartment chemical models. *Nutrition Reviews, 49,* 97-108.

Heymsfield, S.B., Waki, M., Kehayias, J., et al. (1991). Chemical and elemental analysis of humans in vivo using improved body composition models. *American Journal of Physiology (Endocrinology & Metabolism), 261,* E190-E198.

Hulmes, D.J.S., & Miller, A. (1979). Quasi-hexagonal molecular packing in collagen fibrils. *Nature, 282,* 878-880.

Jue, T., Rothman, D.L., Shulman, G.I., et al. (1989). Direct observation of glycogen synthesis in human muscle with ^{13}C NMR. *Proceedings of the National Academy of Science USA, 86,* 4489-4491.

Kehayias, J.J., Ellis, K.J., Cohn, S.H., et al. (1987). Use of a pulsed neutron generator for in vivo measurement of body carbon. In K.J. Ellis, S. Yasumura, & W.D. Morgan (Eds.), *In vivo body composition studies.* (pp. 427-435). London: Institute of Physical Sciences in Medicine.

Kehayias, J.J., Heymsfield, S.B., LoMonte, A.F., et al. (1991). In vivo determination of body fat by measuring total body carbon. *American Journal of Clinical Nutrition, 53,* 1339-1344.

Kleiber, M. (1975). *The Fire of Life.* Huntington, NY: Krieger (pp. 60-93).

Knight, G.S., Beddoe, A.H., Streat, S.J., & Hill, G.L. (1986). Body composition of two human cadavers by neutron activation and chemical analysis. *American Journal of Physiology (Endocrinology & Metabolism), 250,* E179-E185.

Kyere, K., Oldroyd, B., Oxby, C.B., et al. (1982). The feasibility of measuring total body carbon by counting neutron inelastic scatter gamma rays. *Physics in Medicine and Biology, 27,* 805-817.

Lohman, T.G. (1981). Skinfolds and body density and their relation to body fatness: A review. *Human Biology, 53,* 181-225.

Lohman, T.G. (1986). Applicability of body composition techniques and constants for children and youths. *Exercise and Sport Sciences Reviews, 14,* 325-357.

Lohman, T.G. (1992). *Advances in body composition assessment.* Champaign, IL: Human Kinetics.

Lohman, T.G., & Going, S.B. (1993). Multicomponent models in body composition research: Opportunities and pitfalls. In K.J. Ellis & J.D. Eastman (Eds.), *Human body composition* (pp. 53-58). New York.: Plenum.

Méndez, J., Keys, A., Anderson, J.T., & Grande, F. (1960). Density of fat and bone mineral of the mammalian body. *Metabolism, 9,* 472-477.

Mernagh, J.R., Harrison, J.E., & McNeill, K.G. (1977). *In vivo* determination of nitrogen using Pu-Be sources. *Physical Medicine and Biology, 22,* 831-835.

Mueller, W.H., & Martorell, R. (1988). Reliability and accuracy of measurement. In T.B. Lohman, A.F. Roche, & R. Martorell (Eds.), *Anthropometric standardization reference manual* (pp. 83-86). Champaign, IL: Human Kinetics.

Pace, N., & Rathbun, E.N. (1945). Studies on body composition, III: The body water and chemically combined nitrogen content in relation to fat content. *Journal of Biological Chemistry, 158,* 685-691.

Pierson, R.N., Jr., Wang, J., Heymsfield, S.B., et al. (1990). High precision in-vivo neutron activation analysis: A new era for compartmental analysis on body composition. In S. Yasumura, J.E. Harrison, K.G. McNeill, et al. (Eds.), *Advances in in vivo body composition studies* (pp. 317-325). New York: Plenum.

Ryde, S.J.S., Birks, J.L., Morgan, W.D., et al. (1993). A five-compartment model of body composition of healthy subjects assessed using *in vivo* neutron activation analysis. *European Journal of Clinical Nutrition, 47,* 863-874.

Schoeller, D.A., & Jones, P.J.H. (1987). Measurement of total body water by isotope dilution: A unified approach to calculations. In K.J. Ellis, S. Yasumura, & W.D. Morgan (Eds.), *In vivo body composition studies* (pp. 131-137). London: Institute of Physical Sciences in Medicine.

Schoeller, D.A., Van Santen, E., Peterson, D.W., et al. (1980). Total body water measurement in humans with ^{18}O and ^{2}H labeled water. *American Journal of Clinical Nutrition, 33,* 2686-2693.

Selinger, A. (1977). The body as a three component system. Unpublished doctoral dissertation, University of Illinois, Urbana, IL.

Sheng, H.P., & Huggins, R.A. (1979). A review of body composition studies with emphasis on total body water and fat. *American Journal of Clinical Nutrition, 32,* 630-647.

Siri, W.E. (1961). Body composition from fluid spaces and density: Analysis of methods. In J. Brožek & A. Henschel (Eds.), *Techniques for measuring body composition* (pp. 223-244). Washington, DC: National Academy of Sciences/National Research Council.

Snyder, W.S., Cook, M.J., Nasset, E.S., et al. (1975). *Report of the task group on reference man.* Elmsford, NY: Pergamon.

Taylor, R., Price, T.B., Rothman, D.L., et al. (1992). Validation of ^{13}C NMR measurement of human skeletal muscle glycogen by direct biochemical assay of needle biopsy samples. *Magnetic Resonance in Medicine, 27,* 13-20.

Vartsky, D., Ellis, K.J., & Cohn, S.H. (1979). In vivo measurement of body nitrogen by analysis of prompt gammas from neutron capture. *Journal of Nuclear Medicine, 20,* 1158-1165.

Wang, J., Pierson, R.N., & Kelly, W.G. (1973). A rapid method for the determination of deuterium oxide in urine: Application to the measurement of total body water. *Journal of Laboratory and Clinical Medicine, 82,* 170-178.

Wang, Z.M., Heshka, S., Pierson, R.N., & Heymsfield, S.B. (1995). Systematic organization of body composition methodology: An overview with emphasis on component-based methods. *American Journal of Clinical Nutrition, 61,* 457-465.

Wang, Z.M., Pierson, R.N., Jr., & Heymsfield, S.B. (1992). The five level model: A new approach to organizing body composition research. *American Journal of Clinical Nutrition, 56,* 19-28.

Werner, J., & Buse, M. (1988). Temperature profiles with respect to inhomogeneity and geometry of the human body. *Journal of Applied Physiology, 65,* 1110-1118.

Wong, W.W., Cochran, W.J., Klish, W.J., et al. (1988). *In vivo* isotope-fractionation factors and the measurement of deuterium and oxygen-18 dilution spaces from plasma, urine, saliva, respiratory water vapor, and carbon dioxide. *American Journal of Clinical Nutrition, 47,* 1-6.

Woodard, H.Q. (1962). The elementary composition of human cortical bone. *Health Physics, 8,* 513-517.

Woodard, H.Q. (1964). The composition of human cortical bone. *Clinical Orthopedics, 37,* 187-193.

8

Imaging Techniques Applied to the Measurement of Human Body Composition

Jean-Pierre Després, Robert Ross, and Simone Lemieux

Among the more important recent advances in the field of human body composition assessment has been the introduction of computed tomography (CT) and magnetic resonance imaging (MRI). The ability to generate images of human anatomy with these techniques has allowed researchers to measure body composition in ways that were impossible. The measurement of regional as well as total adipose tissue (AT) distribution (Kvist et al., 1988a; Ross et al., 1992), quantification of lean tissue and its principal constituent, which is skeletal muscle (Ross et al., 1994), and the assessment of intra-abdominal or visceral adipose tissue (VAT) (Kvist et al., 1988a; Seidell et al., 1987) are among the advantages unique to both CT and MRI. Indeed, the ability to quantify VAT has provided the researcher with significant insights into the complex relationships between body composition and health risk (Björntorp, 1990; Després et al., 1990).

The first objective of this chapter is to describe briefly the technical aspects of the use of CT and MRI. Secondly, the measurement of total and regional AT distribution by these techniques will be examined. Where appropriate, consideration will be given to the associations between measures of AT from CT or MRI and various metabolic aberrations. Finally, current knowledge with respect to the anthropometric prediction of body composition values from CT or MRI will be considered.

Computed Tomography

Computed tomography (CT) is a radiological technique that is commonly used for diagnostic purposes. Studies conducted in the 1980s have indicated that this technique is suitable for the measurement of body composition, since cross-sectional areas of AT, muscle, and bone can be easily measured in CT scans at any body site (Borkan et al., 1983; Sjöström, Kvist, Cederblad, & Tylén, 1986; Tokunaga et al., 1983).

Acquisition of CT Images: Basic Principles

Briefly, an x-ray tube and detectors are located at opposite poles of a large ring. The x-ray tube rotates around a table on which the subject lies with arms stretched above the head; this table is placed at a standardized position relative to the tube. The detectors allow the rapid measurement of the intensity of many attenuated x-ray beams as they pass through the subject. The computer then generates an image from the attenuated beams that allows the separate recognition of bone, AT, and lean tissues. Indeed, differences in the distribution of attenuation values between these three tissues allow the use of CT as a means to assess body composition (Foster, Fowler, Fuller, & Knight, 1988; Rössner et al., 1990; van der Kooy & Seidell, 1993). The attenuation scores, measured in Hounsfield units (HU) for CT, which depend upon the level of absorption of emitted x-ray beams, vary from −1000 (air) to +1000 (bone). It has been established that the attenuation values for AT vary between −190 to −30 HU (Kvist et al., 1988a; Sjöström et al., 1986), but slightly different intervals have been used by other investigators (Enzi et al., 1986; Koester et al., 1992; Seidell et al.; 1988). The use of these slightly different attenuation intervals has only minor influences on the adipose tissue areas derived by CT (Rössner et al., 1990; van der Kooy & Seidell, 1993).

Accuracy and Precision of CT Images

Perhaps due to its high cost and the associated ionizing radiation, few validation studies of CT have been performed. Rössner et al. (1990) compared the AT cross-sectional areas from 21 abdominal CT slices on two cadavers with the corresponding values obtained using direct planimetry. High correlation coefficients were found between CT and planimetry for both total ($r = 0.94$) and intra-abdominal ($r = 0.83$) AT areas. Janssens et al. (1994) attempted to assess the relationships between AT volumes measured by CT and corresponding volumes obtained by dissection of unembalmed frozen cadavers. Unfortunately, problems inherent to the CT imaging of frozen cadavers limited the observations of AT, but the CT and dissection values for muscle volumes did not differ. Ross, Léger, Guardo, de Guise, & Pike (1991) reported that whole body AT mass from CT correlated highly ($r = 0.98$) with chemically extracted lipid mass in a group of rats varying in adiposity. The

precision of CT measurements of AT is high. Kvist et al. (1988a) reported that the difference between repeated measurements of total AT volume in eight subjects was about 0.6%.

Magnetic Resonance Imaging (MRI)

Magnetic resonance imaging is based on the interaction between nuclei of hydrogen atoms, which are abundant in all biological tissues, and the magnetic fields generated and controlled by the instrumentation of the MRI system. Hydrogen nuclei, or protons, behave like tiny magnets, because they have a nonzero magnetic moment. In the weak magnetic field of the earth, these magnetic moments are oriented randomly and thus tend to cancel each other.

Acquisition of MR Images: Basic Principles

When a subject is placed inside the magnetic field of an MR imager, where the field strength is typically 10,000 times stronger than that of the earth, the magnetic moments of the protons tend to align with the magnetic field. Having aligned the hydrogen protons in a known direction, a pulsed radiofrequency (RF) field is applied to the body tissues causing many hydrogen protons to flip, or absorb energy. When the RF field is turned off, the protons gradually return to their original positions, and they release the energy they absorbed in the form of an RF signal. This signal is used to generate the MRI images by computer.

To increase the contrast between AT and skeletal muscle, MRI data acquisition can be programmed to take advantage of the specific proton density and relaxation times (the rate at which the absorbed energy is released) of the various types of tissues. This is accomplished by varying what are known as the time parameters. These are the time to repeat (TR) and the time to echo (TE) of the RF pulse. Manipulation of the TR and TE times varies the RF *pulse sequence*. When using one such sequence called *spin-echo*, the TR parameter can be adjusted to exploit the difference in T1 relaxation times of AT and muscle, which provides the tissue contrast required for high quality MR images. With few exceptions, the spin-echo pulse sequence has been selected to acquire AT data from MRI.

Fast MR Imaging

One limitation associated with the acquisition of body composition data from MRI is the time required to obtain quality images. For example, for the spin-echo pulse sequences, approximately 8 minutes are required to obtain quality MR images of the abdominal region (Ross et al., 1992). As a result, motion artifacts caused by respiration and cardiac motion tend to decrease the image quality. Consequently, MR pulse sequences have been developed that require less time. Known as FLASH (Fast Low Angle Shot) or GRASS (Gradient Recalled Acquisition at Steady State), these RF pulse sequences manipulate the time parameters (TR and TE) so that quality MR images can be obtained in seconds. Using these procedures, MRI data from the abdominal region can now be obtained during a normal breath-hold (i.e., less than 20 seconds). While it remains to be determined whether the accuracy or precision of MRI will be improved by using fast imaging techniques, there is little doubt that they will allow the acquisition of MRI data in relatively short periods of time.

Quantification of MR Data

Once an MR image is acquired, the next step involves quantifying the tissue of interest by subjecting the MRI data to various segmentation techniques similar to those described for CT. Unfortunately, the quantification of AT data from MRI is not straightforward. Usually the MR image matrix consists of 256 rows by 256 columns; each resulting square is termed a pixel. Unlike CT, where pixel values consistently represent specific tissues regardless of slice position or individual being assessed, MRI pixel values for a given tissue (the emitted RF signal of the protons within a pixel) may vary from slice to slice or between individuals. This is partially due to the fact that pixel values in MR images are dependent on the excitation pulse sequences and a combination of proton density and tissue relaxation values, which may vary between individuals. More important, however, is the variation in signal intensities that may occur for the same tissue within a single study or acquisition. This variation may result from heterogeneities in the magnetic field or other system imperfections (e.g., variations in slice profile, main or gradient field heterogeneities) (Ross et al., 1992). The principal result of heterogeneities in the magnetic field is the occurrence of random variations in pixel intensities for a given tissue within and/or between images. An example of this phenomenon

is illustrated in Figure 8.1. The arrow in Panel B indicates a region in the subcutaneous AT that appears as a shadow; this is sometimes referred to as "ghosting." The pixels in this region have a lower intensity value than the other subcutaneous AT (SAT) pixels. Thus, when the SAT is quantified by using a single threshold for AT, the pixels in the affected area will not be counted, resulting in an underestimation of the true AT area.

Recent improvements to MRI hardware and computer software have improved the quality of MR images and substantially reduced the frequency of MRI artifacts. Nevertheless, their occurrence suggests that quantification of a given tissue on MR images requires image analysis software that permits visual verification of the segmentation result. In other words, the researcher must manually correct for AT areas that are not counted by the initial threshold selection. While these procedures can be accomplished using straightforward image analysis techniques, they add a degree of subjectivity to the quantification of tissues on an MR image that is not required when quantifying a given tissue using CT. It is necessary to emphasize that the quantification of AT on MR images cannot be accomplished by simply identifying an AT threshold and using software to count the pixels with HU above or below that threshold, without manual correction of the segmented MR images.

Accuracy of MRI

Foster, Hutchison, Mallard, and Fuller (1984) were among the first to demonstrate that MRI could measure AT accurately. They reported that a T1 weighted inversion recovery pulse sequence yielded a very high contrast between adipose tissue and adjacent muscle on the MRI image and, as a consequence, any AT thickness could be obtained by MRI. These observations were validated using both carcass and cadaver data. In the same study, it was observed that the tissue thicknesses determined by MRI did not differ from those determined by direct physical measurement.

Subsequently, using a rat model, Ross et al. (1991) found that whole-carcass chemically extracted lipid was highly correlated with AT mass from MRI ($r = 0.97$, p < 0.01) and that the standard error of estimate was 10.5%. Fowler et al. (1992) compared AT from MRI measurements to those obtained by dissection in lean and obese pigs. The authors observed that the AT from MRI correlated strongly with AT by dissection ($r = 0.98$), and that the mean square error was 2.1%.

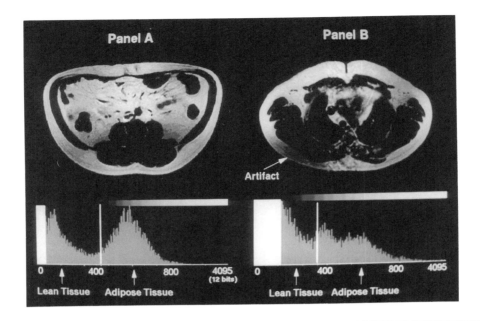

Figure 8.1 Two transverse MR images of the lower (Panel A) and upper (Panel B) abdomen. For the MR image in Panel A, the adipose tissue pixel intensities are uniform and thus the related histogram (below the image) reveals two unique pixel intensity peaks for lean and adipose tissue, respectively. The area indicated by the arrow in Panel B is the consequence of randomly occurring MRI artifacts, which, as illustrated in the associated histogram, result in poorly defined thresholds for lean and adipose tissue.

At this point, there is only one report that has compared MRI measurements of AT with those derived by dissection of human cadavers. Abate et al. (1994) compared MRI measures of abdominal subcutaneous and visceral AT to those obtained by direct weighing of the same AT compartments after dissection of three human cadavers. In this study, the authors subdivided visceral AT into intraperitoneal and retroperitoneal depots. For the various compartments, the mean difference between the two methods was 0.075 kg (~6%). Thus, although additional data comparing MRI and human cadaver derived estimates of AT would be useful, these preliminary observations provide evidence in support of the accuracy of MRI estimates of human adiposity.

Further attempts to validate MRI have been made by comparing MRI measurements of AT to those obtained by CT using both animal (Ross et al., 1991) and human (Seidell et al., 1990) models (Table 8.1). In human beings, evaluation of the relationships between the two methods has generally been performed by comparing measurements of SAT and VAT areas obtained from a single abdominal image. The data in Table 8.1 reveal that, in general, the correlations obtained between MRI and CT areas are quite high for SAT. Furthermore, given that measurements of the extremities are unaffected by the motion artifacts previously described, it is likely that the coefficient of variation

(CV) between MRI and CT measures of SAT in the limbs is substantially less than the 5 to 12% reported for the abdominal region.

While the differences between measures from CT and from MRI are generally low for SAT, the CV for VAT is higher, ranging from 13 to 20% (Table 8.1). In addition, it has been observed that the relationship between MRI and CT measures of VAT improves with increasing visceral adiposity (Seidell et al., 1990). This is probably due to the increased signal to noise (motion artifacts) ratio associated with increasing quantities of VAT. Thus the ability of MRI to predict CT measures of VAT in lean subjects is suspect due to the decreased signal to noise ratio. Unfortunately, data are not available that would indicate the lower limit of values for VAT areas below which substantial differences occur between MRI and CT measures. The use of fast imaging protocols that avoid the problems associated with motion artifacts may enhance tissue contrast and, thus, improve the ability of MRI to measure VAT in lean subjects.

In summary, by comparison to limited cadaver and animal data, it appears that MRI measures total AT with a *SEE* in the range of 2 to 10%. Comparison with CT suggest that MRI provides images of the abdomen with similar anatomic detail, with *CV* for SAT and VAT in the order of 5 and 15%, respectively.

Table 8.1   MRI Validation Studies, Comparisons With CT

Reference	Subject (N)	IV	Correlation (SEE, %)		
			SAT	VAT	TAT
Seidell et al., 1990	Human beings (7)	CT mid-abdomen	0.79 (4.9)	0.79 (12.8)	0.99 (4.4)
Sobel et al., 1991	Human beings (11)	Umbilicus	0.98 (8)	0.93 (21)	—
Ross et al., 1991	Rats (21)	Whole body	0.98 (12)	0.98 (13.6)	0.99 (8.7)

Abbreviations: IV, independent variable; SAT, subcutaneous adipose tissue; VAT, visceral adipose tissue; TAT, total adipose tissue.

Table 8.2   MRI Precision

Reference	Subject (N)	T	MRI sequence	Anatomical position	CV (%)		
					SAT	VAT	TAT
Staten et al., 1989	Human beings (6)	0.5	SE	Mid-abdomen	5.0	10.0	3.0
Seidell et al., 1990	Human beings (7)	1.5	IR	Umbilicus	10.1	10.6	5.4
Gerard et al., 1991	Human beings (4)	1.5	SE	Abdominal images (6)	3.0	9.0	—
Ross et al., 1991	Rats (11)	1.5	SE	Whole body	—	—	4.3
Ross et al., 1993	Human beings (3)	1.5	SE	L4-L5	1.1	5.5	—
				Whole body	—	—	2.5
Sohlström et al., 1993	Human beings (3)	0.02	SR	Whole body	1.7	5.3*	1.5

*Reported as nonsubcutaneous AT.

Abbreviations: T, strength of magnet in Tesla units; SAT, subcutaneous adipose tissue; VAT, visceral adipose tissue; TAT, total adipose tissue; SE, spin-echo; IR, inverse recovery; SR, saturation recovery.

Precision of MRI

Adipose Tissue.   Several studies have evaluated whether MRI measurements of SAT and VAT are reproducible. The results in Table 8.2 show that, for a single MR image in the abdominal region, the *CV* for repeated measures of SAT ranges from 1.1 to 10.1%. For VAT, the *CV* for repeated measurements ranges from 5.3 to 10.6%. Taken together, these data suggest that when MRI is used the expected error for measurement of VAT areas is approximately 10%, but it is lower for SAT areas.

Lean Tissue.   As described previously, MRI can discriminate between lean tissue and AT. This is particularly true in the limbs because the principal tissues (skeletal muscle and AT) are discriminated easily based upon pixel intensity values. In the abdominal region, however, discrimination between them is ambiguous because the pixel intensity values of all lean tissues (skeletal muscle, organs) fall within a small range. Therefore measurements of lean tissue by MRI, in particular skeletal muscle, are restricted to the limbs.

Unfortunately there is little evidence regarding the precision of MRI measures of lean tissue. Ross et al. (1994) reported that, for a single MR image of the proximal thigh, the *CV* for repeated measurements of lean tissue (skeletal muscle and bone combined) is 1.2%. In addition, these authors reported that the *CV* is 3.9%. for lean tissue volume in the leg derived from 15 images. While the precision of MRI measures of lean tissues requires further investigation, these preliminary results are encouraging. Given the importance of skeletal muscle in the development of insulin resistance and glucose intolerance, the availability of a noninvasive method for measuring lean tissue, without the approximations of anthropometric techniques, would be a significant advance. The results in Table 8.2 suggest that MRI may serve as a criterion method for skeletal muscle measurement, thereby providing reference data for anthropometric comparisons.

CT and Body Composition

Two groups of investigators have used CT to assess whole-body composition. Tokunaga et al. (1983) measured the areas in multiple scans and the distances between adjacent scans and the areas in these scans. They calculated total and regional AT volumes from these data. Sjöström and Kvist (1988) made 22 consecutive scans covering the whole body. They found that the AT volume from CT is highly correlated with fat mass estimated by the tritiated water, ^{40}K, or hydrostatic weighing techniques (Kvist et al., 1988b; Sjöström et al., 1986). Thus, it appears that CT is an accurate technique for the assessment of body composition, and it does not rely on assumptions such as the constancy of either the density or the water content of fat-free mass. A clear distinction between AT and lean tissue can be obtained with CT, but, since this method involves exposure to radiation, scans at many levels cannot be used in serial studies. It has been shown, however, that nine scans can provide essentially the same information as 22 scans for the assessment of total AT volume (Sjöström, 1988). Furthermore, we have reported that a partial AT volume obtained from the measurement of three scans (Th8-Th9, L4-L5, and mid-thigh), and the assumption of cylindrical shapes, is highly correlated with the fat mass determined by hydrostatic weighing in premenopausal obese women (Ferland et al., 1989). Furthermore, we and others have shown that the total cross-sectional AT area at the abdominal (L4-L5) level is highly correlated with total AT mass in men and women (Després et al., 1991; Ferland et al., 1989; Koester et al., 1992;

Lemieux et al., 1993) (Figures 8.2 and 8.3). Thus, a single abdominal scan can be used not only to obtain critical information on the level of atherogenic VAT, but also to estimate total AT mass.

The most important application of CT in the field of body composition has been to the measurement of abdominal VAT. Indeed, by drawing a line within the muscle wall delineating the abdominal cavity at L4-L5 and by providing the computer with the attenuation values of AT (−190 to −30 HU), the VAT area can be calculated (Figure 8.4). The cross-sectional VAT area at L4-L5 is highly correlated with the VAT volume from

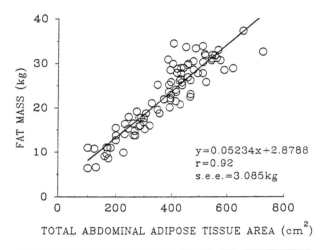

Figure 8.2 Relation of total cross-sectional abdominal adipose tissue area measured by computed tomography to body fat mass assessed by hydrostatic weighing in a sample of 89 men.

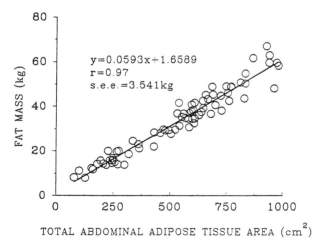

Figure 8.3 Relation of total cross-sectional abdominal adipose tissue area measured by computed tomography to body fat mass assessed by hydrostatic weighing in a sample of 75 premenopausal women.

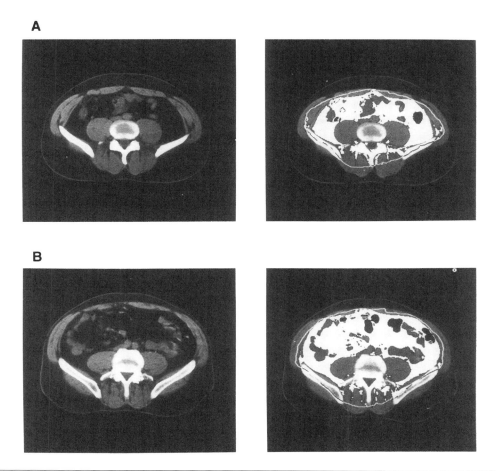

Figure 8.4 Cross-sectional images of the abdomen obtained by computed tomography at L4-L5 in a young man (A) and in a middle aged man (B) matched for total body fat mass (19.8 kg). The visceral adipose tissue area (96 cm² for the young man and 115 cm² for the middle aged man), which is delineated by drawing a line within the muscle wall surrounding the abdominal cavity, is highlighted in the images on the right.

multiple abdominal scans (Kvist et al., 1988a). Thus, the use of one abdominal scan appears to be sufficient to assess VAT accumulation and to identify those individuals who are at risk for the development of diabetes mellitus and some cardiovascular diseases. It is not clear, however, whether more than one abdominal scan should be recommended in intervention studies in which the effects of diet and/or exercise would be examined.

Regarding the assessment of risk, we have reported that the level of VAT measured by CT is the best correlate of glucose tolerance and plasma insulin levels in both men and women and that these associations are independent from concomitant variation in the level of total body fat (Després et al., 1989b; Pouliot et al., 1992). To further assess the independent contributions of obesity and of VAT accumulation to disturbances in plasma glucose-insulin homeostasis, we compared two groups of subjects individually matched for age and total adiposity, but with either low or high levels of VAT, to a group of lean subjects. We performed these analyses in men and women separately. Obese subjects with low levels of VAT showed marginally higher plasma insulin levels than did lean controls, yet the glycemic response to an oral glucose challenge was similar between groups. Obesity in the presence of elevated levels of VAT was associated, however, with a higher glycemic response in the presence of marked hyperinsulinemia, indicating the occurrence of an insulin resistance state (Figures 8.5 and 8.6). It is clear that the measurement of total adiposity alone would mislead an investigator or clinician interested in assessing the risk associated with obesity. We have also performed these group comparisons for plasma lipoprotein-lipid levels and reached similar conclusions; the level of VAT is the critical correlate of the dyslipidemic profile frequently observed in obese patients (Figure 8.7) (Després et al., 1989a; Després, 1993; Pouliot et al., 1992) .

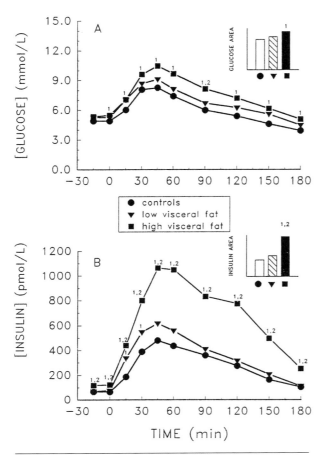

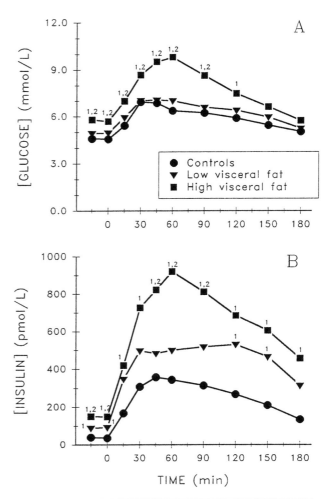

Figure 8.5 Plasma glucose (A), and insulin (B) levels during a 75 g oral glucose tolerance test in lean control men (●) and in obese men with either low (▼) or high (■) levels of visceral adipose tissue. Differences in age among the three groups were not significant. Mean ± *SD* percent body fat values were 19.7 ± 4.7% in the lean men, 31.3 ± 2.3% in the obese men with low levels of visceral adipose tissue, and 32.2 ± 3.3% in the obese men with high levels of visceral adipose tissue (difference not significant between the two obese groups). Whereas differences in the waist-to-hip ratio and in the subcutaneous abdominal adipose tissue measured by computed tomography were not significant among the two groups of obese men, the obese men with high levels of visceral adipose tissue had almost twice the amount of VAT (area: 212.2 ± 23.7 cm²) than the obese men with low levels of VAT (area: 109.9 ± 14.0 cm²). The VAT areas in both groups of obese men were significantly different from those in the control men and the difference between the two groups of obese men was also statistically significant. Number 1 indicates that plasma glucose and insulin levels are significantly different ($p < 0.05$) from the control men values, whereas number 2 indicates a significant difference ($p < 0.05$) from values found in obese men with low VAT areas. Adapted from "Visceral Obesity in Men. Associations With Glucose Tolerance, Plasma Insulin, and Lipoprotein Levels," by M.C. Pouliot, J.P. Després, A. Nadeau, et al., 1992, *Diabetes*, **41**, pp. 826-834. Copyright 1992 by American Diabetes Association, Inc. Adapted with permission.

Figure 8.6 Plasma glucose (A) and insulin (B) in fasting state (−15 and 0 minutes) and during an oral glucose tolerance test in obese women with high (■) or low (▼) levels of visceral adipose tissue ($n = 10$ subjects/group) and in a sample of lean women (●) ($n = 25$) . Number 1 indicates that plasma glucose and insulin levels are significantly different ($p < 0.05$) from the control women values, whereas number 2 indicates a significant difference ($p < 0.05$) from values found in obese women with low VAT areas. Adapted from "Abdominal Obesity as Important Component of Insulin-Resistance Syndrome," by J.P. Després, 1993, *Nutrition*, **9**, pp. 452-459. Copyright 1993 by Elsevier Science. Adapted with permission.

MRI and Body Composition

Because multiple images can be obtained without any known health risks to the subject, MRI is well suited for assessment of whole-body AT distribution. One principal benefit of multislice acquisitions is that the volumes of various AT depots

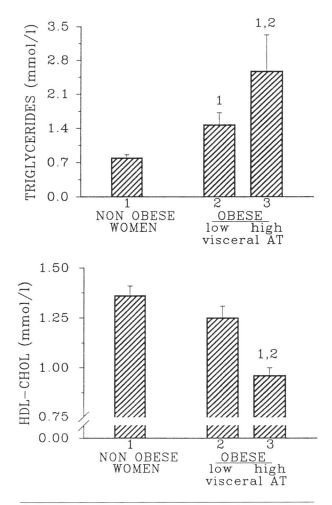

Figure 8.7 Plasma triglyceride and high-density lipoprotein (HDL) cholesterol levels in lean women and in two subgroups of obese women with either low or high levels of VAT. Number 1 indicates a significant difference (p < 0.05) from the control women values, whereas number 2 indicates a significant difference (p < 0.05) from values found in obese women with low VAT areas. For further details on subject characteristics, see legend to Fig. 8.6.
Adapted from "Abdominal Obesity as Important Component of Insulin-Resistance Syndrome," by J.P. Després, 1993, *Nutrition, 9*, pp. 452-459. Copyright 1993 by Elsevier Science. Adapted with permission.

can be derived (Figure 8.8). Therefore, regional or segmental analysis of AT is possible that permits evaluation of regional AT distribution. (Ross et al. 1994). This protocol is particularly useful when evaluating the efficacy of interventions that may induce changes in AT distribution (Ross et al., in press).

Four groups have employed a multislice MRI protocol to evaluate whole body AT distribution in human subjects. Fowler et al. (1991) acquired 28 MR images over the entire body, while Ross et al. (1992,1993) used 41 images to measure AT and lean tissue distribution in normal male and obese female subjects. Sohlström et al. (1993) have recently described AT distribution in normal, healthy women using a 30-image protocol.

One principal concern with multislice protocols is the high cost associated with obtaining multiple images. As a result, attempts have been made to establish the minimal number of images required for accurate measurements of the whole-body AT. For example, Fowler et al., (1991) reported that as few as four properly positioned MR slices can accurately predict whole-body AT volume derived using 28 slices. Furthermore, Ross et al. (1992) have shown that cross-sectional AT area measured by MRI at the L4-L5 level is highly correlated ($r = 0.96$) with the total AT volume obtained from 41 images. These results suggest that in cross-sectional studies, where a rapid estimate of total adipose tissue is required, the measurement of AT area at the L4-L5 level could be useful.

It is important to note, however, that the practical or physiological value of substantially reducing the number of images required to derive whole-body AT volume from MRI is limited. For CT, a reduction in the number of images acquired to calculate AT volume has the practical advantage of reducing the exposure of the subjects to ionizing radiation. Since MRI is not subject to such restrictions, a reduction in data acquisition has no practical advantage. Furthermore, a reduction in the number of images acquired would not substantially decrease the time required to gather the data since most MRI systems can acquire data for several body slices in the same time it takes to acquire a single slice. Therefore, if MRI is to be used as a reference method to assess AT distribution, it is recommended that, within feasible and reasonable limits, the maximum number of images be acquired.

MRI is also useful for discriminating between VAT and SAT accumulation. To obtain a volume of VAT using MRI, Ross et al. (1992) performed seven abdominal scans (two distal to L4-L5, one at L4-L5, and four proximal to L4-L5) in a sample of men. Their results indicated that the VAT area at L4-L5 is the strongest correlate of total VAT volume from seven scans ($r = 0.95$). Therefore, one image at the L4-L5 level can adequately identify subjects with excess VAT accumulation. Since, however, multiple slices are possible with MRI, the measurement of VAT volume using multiple images is suggested, especially in intervention

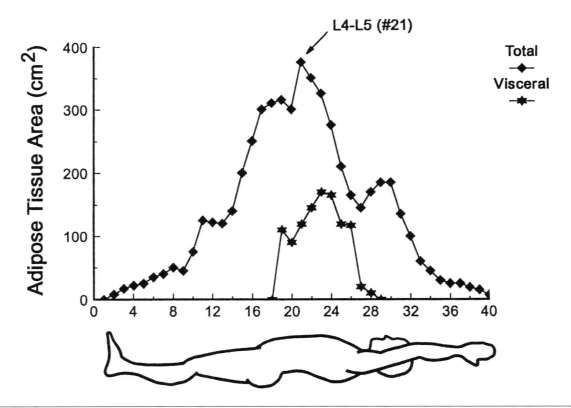

Figure 8.8   Distribution of MRI-measured cross-sectional adipose tissue areas. Image 1 (x-axis) is at the level of the foot; image 41 is at the level of the hands. In general, images 1-17 represent the lower limbs, 19-26 the abdomen, and 28-41 the upper torso and upper extremities.

Adapted from "Quantification of Adipose Tissue by MRI: Relationship With Anthropometric Variables," by R. Ross, L. Leger, D. Morris, et al., 1992, *Journal of Applied Physiology*, **72**, pp. 787-795. Adapted with permission of American Physiological Society.

studies where small changes in VAT volume are expected. Finally, as with CT, efforts to discriminate between retroperitoneal and intraperitoneal AT must be viewed with caution since the relevant methods have not been fully validated (Ross et al., 1994; Rössner et al., 1990; Seidell et al., 1990).

Studies that have assessed VAT accumulation by MRI have shown that the VAT area at the L4-L5 level is a strong correlate of the metabolic complications of obesity (Gray et al., 1991; Leenen, van der Kooy, Seidell, & Deurenberg, 1992). Indeed, Leenen et al. demonstrated that women with a large VAT area at the L4-L5 level measured with MRI are characterized by higher triglycerides and lower HDL-cholesterol, even after adjustment for age and percent body fat. In men, however, the association between a large VAT area and a dyslipidemic state disappeared when corresponding adjustments were made. Since age is positively associated with VAT accumulation, control for age may have eliminated the effect of the concomitant increase in VAT.

Anthropometric Estimation of CT and MRI Measures of Body Composition

Due to the high cost and restricted availability associated with both CT and MRI, attempts have been made to estimate CT and MRI body composition values using anthropometry. Effective predictive equations would be useful in epidemiological and clinical situations.

Whole-Body Lean Tissue

There have been few attempts to establish the relationships between CT or MRI measured lean tissue, or, more important perhaps, skeletal muscle, and anthropometric variables. Ross et al. (1994) have reported that whole-body lean tissue from MRI in obese men and women can be predicted from anthropometric data with an accuracy of 3.6% and 6.5%, respectively (Table 8.3).

Table 8.3 Multiple Regression Equation for Predicting Lean Tissue Volume Measured by MRI in Obese Women and Men From Anthropometric Measurements

Predictors	R^2	SEE (L)	SEE (%)	P
Women[1]				
X_1 Weight (kg)	0.50	3.3	7.77	< 0.001
X_2 Hip circumference (cm)	0.62	2.8	6.5	< 0.001
Men[2]				
X_1 Weight (kg)	0.57	4.1	7.0	< 0.001
X_2 Waist circumference (cm)	0.66	3.6	6.2	< 0.001
X_3 Thigh circumference (cm)	0.89	2.1	3.6	< 0.001

[1]Lean tissue volume (L) = 0.501 X_1 − 0.379 X_2 + 43.01

[2]Lean tissue volume (L) = 0.990 X_1 − .542 − 0.881 X_3 + 73.12

Adapted from "Sex Differences in Lean and Adipose Tissue Distribution by Magnetic Resonance Imaging: Anthropometric Relationships," by R. Ross, K.D. Shaw, J. Rissanen, et al., 1994, *American Journal of Clinical Nutrition,* **59**, pp. 1277-1285. Copyright 1994 by *American Journal of Clinical Nutrition.* Reprinted with permission.

Table 8.4 Multiple Regression Equation for Predicting Total Adipose Tissue Volume Measured by MRI in Obese Women and Men From Anthropometric Measurements

Predictors	R^2	SEE (L)	SEE (%)	P
Women[1]				
X_1 Hip circumference (cm)	0.90	3.9	9.1	< 0.001
X_2 Waist circumference (cm)	0.93	3.3	7.7	< 0.001
Men[2]				
X_1 Thigh circumference (cm)	0.58	4.8	13.3	< 0.001
X_2 Waist circumference (cm)	0.80	1.1	9.1	< 0.001
X_3 Hip circumference (cm)	0.87	2.7	7.5	< 0.001

[1]Total AT volume (L) = 0.355 X_1 + 0.717 X_2 − 78.56

[2]Total AT volume (L) = 1.41 X_1 + .501 − 0.750 X_3 − 26.65

Adapted from "Sex Differences in Lean and Adipose Tissue Distribution by Magnetic Resonance Imaging: Anthropometric Relationships," by R. Ross, K.D. Shaw, J. Rissanen, et al., 1994, *American Journal of Clinical Nutrition,* **59**, pp. 1277-1285. Copyright 1994 by *American Journal of Clinical Nutrition.* Reprinted with permission.

Whole-Body AT

Kvist et al. (1988a) measured whole-body (total) AT volume by CT in a group of men and women differing in adiposity and reported *SEE* of less than 11% when predicting total AT volume from anthropometry. Among the anthropometric variables tested, the best predictors were weight, hip circumference, and weight/stature. These observations are similar to those reported by Ross et al. (1994) for obese men and women. These workers observed that weight, hip circumference, and body mass index (BMI) were the best single predictors. In a stepwise regression model, the combination of waist and hip circumferences in women, and these variables with the addition of thigh circumference for men, predicted total AT volume from MRI with an accuracy of ~8% (Table 8.4). Taken together, these reports suggest that the maximum precision for anthropometrical predictions of total AT volume is ~8 to 10%.

Visceral Adipose Tissue

Because it is hypothesized that the VAT depot conveys the greatest health risk (Després et al., 1990),

and it is the parameter uniquely measured by CT and MRI, numerous studies have examined the relationship between VAT and anthropometric variables. Skinfold thicknesses, body circumferences, and diameters have been studied as potential correlates of VAT accumulation. The heterogeneity of body fatness in the samples that have been studied has markedly influenced the strength of the associations reported between anthropometric variables and VAT. In fact, when a sample with large variation in total adiposity was studied, numerous anthropometric variables were significantly associated with abdominal VAT accumulation (Després et al., 1991) (Table 8.5).

Among the various skinfold thicknesses assessed, those measured on the trunk, and more specifically the abdomen, are most closely associated with the accumulation of abdominal VAT (Després et al., 1991; Koester et al., 1992). The mean adiposity level of the study sample may affect the relationships between skinfold thicknesses and VAT accumulation. It has been demonstrated that although the correlation between trunk skinfold thicknesses and VAT is significant in a subsample

Table 8.5   Correlation Coefficients for the Associations Between Abdominal Adipose Tissue Areas From CT and Anthropometric Variables in 110 Men

Variable	Adipose tissue		
	Total	Visceral	Subcutaneous
Age	0.50	0.63	0.40
Weight	0.90	0.68	0.91
Body mass index (BMI)	0.92	0.79	0.89
Fat mass	0.95	0.76	0.95
Sum of skinfold thicknesses	0.77	0.48	0.83
Waist circumference	0.97	0.82	0.94
Hip circumference	0.91	0.71	0.91
Waist-hip-ratio (WHR)	0.81	0.76	0.75
Sagittal diameter (CT abdominal scan)	0.95	0.85	0.91

All correlations are significant at $P < 0.0001$.

of men with BMI values less than 28 kg/m², this association is not present in men with BMI values greater than 28 kg/m² (Després et al., 1991).

Waist and hip circumferences and the waist-to-hip ratio (WHR) have also been studied as potential predictors of VAT accumulation. The WHR has been used widely to investigate the relationship between regional adipose tissue distribution and metabolic profiles (Björntorp, 1988; Kissebah & Peiris, 1989; Lapidus et al., 1984; Larsson et al., 1984). Indeed, it has been considered that the relationship between WHR and health risk was due to its ability to predict the accumulation of VAT, but the WHR is only moderately related to the amount of abdominal VAT (Ferland et al., 1989; Ross et al. 1992; Seidell et al., 1988; Sjöström, 1988). Some have reported that the waist circumference alone is more closely associated to the amount of abdominal VAT and related metabolic disturbances than the WHR (Borkan et al., 1983; Després et al., 1991; Ferland et al., 1989; Pouliot et al., 1994; Ross et al., 1994; Seidell et al., 1988) (Figures 8.9 and 8.10). Therefore, it has been suggested that waist circumference may be particularly useful in the assessment of the health hazard of obesity,

since this measure is a good correlate of both VAT accumulation and total adiposity.

Transverse and sagittal abdominal diameters have been used to predict VAT accumulation (Kvist et al., 1988a; Sjöström 1988). Indeed, Sjöström (1991) suggested that a large accumulation of VAT would maintain the sagittal (anteroposterior) diameter of the abdomen, in supine subjects while abdominal subcutaneous AT would decrease the sagittal diameter due to gravity. Furthermore, it has been reported that the abdominal sagittal diameter has correlations with the VAT area that are similar in magnitude to those for waist circumference (Després et al., 1991; Kvist et al., 1988a; Pouliot et al., 1994; Ross et al., 1994). In most of these studies, the sagittal diameters were measured directly on CT or MRI images. In those studies that have compared anthropometrically assessed sagittal diameters to those obtained on CT or MRI images, the correlation coefficients were greater than 0.8 (Koester et al., 1992; van der Kooy et al., 1993b), but these studies were of small samples; thus further study of these relationships is warranted.

Predictive Equations for the Estimation of VAT

Considering the associations between anthropometric variables and VAT accumulation, attempts have been made to develop equations that would predict the amount of abdominal VAT (Després et al., 1991; Ferland et al., 1989; Ross et al., 1994; Seidell et al., 1987, 1988; Weits, van der Beek, Wedel, & ter Haar Romeny, 1988). In this regard, we have shown that in premenopausal women weight, abdominal and subscapular skinfold thickness, WHR, and age in combination can explain up to 74% of the variance in abdominal VAT area (Ferland et al., 1989). We have also reported, from a study of 110 men, that 74% of the variance in abdominal VAT accumulation can be explained by a combination of waist circumference and age. Other equations developed with skinfold thicknesses and circumferences yielded similar results with an explained variance of about 70 to 80% (Després et al., 1991). Moreover, Kvist and collaborators (1988a) have developed several predictive equations using diameters as independent variables, but were unable to explain more than 80% of the variance in VAT accumulation.

Few studies have cross-validated equations developed to predict VAT. Kvist et al. (1988a) tested their predictive equations on small cross-validation groups (7 men, 9 women). The mean difference between VAT areas from CT and predicted

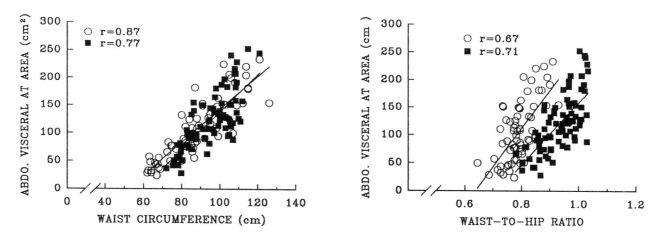

Figure 8.9 Relation of waist circumference and the waist-to-hip ratio to abdominal visceral adipose tissue areas measured by computed tomography in men and women.
Adapted from "Waist Circumference and Abdominal Sagittal Diameter: Best Simple Anthropometric Indexes of Abdominal Visceral Adipose Tissue Accumulation and Related Cardiovascular Risk in Men and Women," by M.C. Pouliot, J.P. Després, S. Lemieux, et al., 1994, *American Journal of Cardiology*, **73**(7), pp. 460-468. Adapted with permission from *American Journal of Cardiology*.

values ranged from 8.4 to 11.5% in males and from 18.4 to 27.3% in females depending upon the equation used. Koester et al. (1992) also cross-validated equations developed by their group and by others with a cross-validation sample of 21 men. They compared VAT areas from CT to the predicted values and found that most of the differences were significant by t-test. In fact, only studies from validation groups with sample characteristics similar to those in the cross-validation group reported satisfactory results, indicating the importance of covariates such as age, sex, adiposity, and health status in the estimation of VAT accumulation.

We cross-validated a predictive equation developed in a sample of 110 men, with a mean age of 31 years, on two samples. One sample was of middle-aged men (*n* = 34, mean age 55 years) and the other was of young men (*n* = 41, mean age 25 years). In the middle-aged men, a correlation coefficient of 0.86 was found between the measured and the predicted values with a standard error of estimate of 33.3 cm² (22.5%). In the young men, the correlation was 0.66 with a standard error of estimate of 29.3 cm² (42.6%) (Després et al., unpublished data). These results provide further evidence that accurate predictions of VAT accumulation from anthropometry alone are not possible. Therefore it is recommended that attempts to predict VAT should take age and gender

into account. The obvious gender differences in AT distribution may lead to gender differences in the relation of total body fat to VAT accumulation. In this regard, we examined the relation of total body fat to VAT accumulation in young men and women (Lemieux et al., 1993). Although positive correlations between body fat mass and VAT area were noted in each gender, the regression slope was steeper in men than in women, indicating that obesity in men was associated with a greater VAT accumulation than in women (Figure 8.11). Furthermore, there is a larger accumulation of VAT in the elderly than in young adults, even after control for concomitant variation in total fatness (Enzi et al., 1986; Kotani et al., 1994; Seidell et al., 1988) (see Figure 8.4). This phenomenon is observed in men and women. Furthermore, menopause is associated with an increase in VAT accumulation, particularly in the absence of estrogen replacement therapy (Haarbo, Marslew, Gotfredson, & Christiansen, 1991; Ley, Lees, & Stevenson, 1992). Thus, it is important to consider gender and age in the prediction of VAT from anthropometry. It has been shown, however, that the inclusion of total body fat in the model does not significantly improve the percentage of variance in VAT area that is explained (Koester et al., 1992).

In summary, anthropometric data cannot provide accurate predictions of VAT. This is not surprising since it has been reported from weight gain

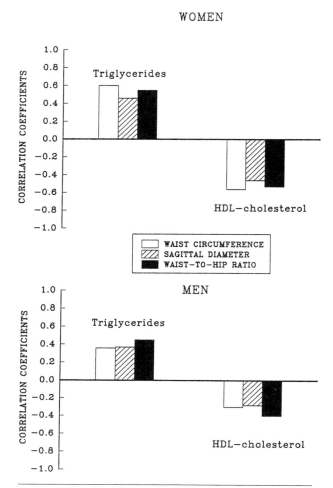

Figure 8.10 Correlation coefficients between waist circumference, abdominal sagittal diameter, and waist-to-hip ratio, with metabolic variables that have been associated with regional adipose tissue distribution and cardiovascular disease risk factors. All correlation coefficients were significant at $P < 0.01$. HDL = high-density lipoprotein.

Adapted from "Waist Circumference and Abdominal Sagittal Diameter: Best Simple Anthropometric Indexes of Abdominal Visceral Adipose Tissue Accumulation and Related Cardiovascular Risk in Men and Women," by M.C. Pouliot, J.P. Després, S. Lemieux, et al., 1994, *American Journal of Cardiology*, **73**(7), pp. 460-468. Adapted with permission from *American Journal of Cardiology*.

Are CT and MRI Reference Techniques for the Measurement of Body Fat?

Although MRI and CT are not widely available, these modalities might serve as reference techniques for the validation of other methods of body composition assessment. Of principal interest is whether MRI data can be used to calibrate field methods of body fat assessment. Two key issues must be resolved in order to measure body fat by MRI or CT. The principal issue relates to the conversion of AT volume to lipid mass (body fat). This requires knowledge of AT density and its lipid fraction: AT lipid mass = AT volume × AT density × adipose lipid fraction. The normal physiological range for AT density and AT lipid fraction is 0.91 to 0.98 g/ml and 0.5 to 0.9, respectively (Martin, Daniel, Drinkwater, & Clarys, 1994). Thus the conversion of AT volume to AT lipid mass requires a factor that varies over the range of their product, approximately 0.5 to 0.8 g/ml. This considerable variation cannot be ignored; successful conversion requires a more accurate estimate of the value of this factor. There is a lack of in vivo methods for estimating either AT density or its lipid fraction. It has been shown, however, that these values are closely related to the degree of adiposity, with the highest AT densities and lowest lipid fractions occurring in the leanest individuals, and the lowest AT densities and highest lipid fractions occurring in the fattest individuals (Martin et al.). The second issue when using MRI or CT to estimate total body fat is that after AT lipid has been estimated, non-AT lipid must be added to this value to obtain total body lipid. The amount of non-AT lipid is variable and its estimation difficult.

These observations suggest that the error in the conversion of AT volumes from CT or MRI to lipid mass precludes its use as a reference measure of body fat. It is important to note, however, that the health implications of non-AT lipid are minimal. Therefore, the variable of interest with respect to health risk is AT lipid. As noted earlier, there are uncertainties in the calculation of total body lipid from CT or MRI data, but it may not be necessary to estimate total body lipid. Although, determination of AT lipid mass requires knowledge of the density and lipid fraction of AT, and these vary by site and among individuals, it may be possible to estimate them from measures of total adiposity. Future study related to the composition of human AT could help the application of this approach.

(Bouchard et al., 1990) and weight loss studies (van der Kooy et al., 1993a) that the change in subcutaneous SAT was a poor correlate of the change in VAT. Thus, only CT and MRI can accurately measure changes in cross-sectional VAT areas in intervention studies. When the use of imaging techniques is not practical, however, anthropometric variables such as the waist circumference may help identify individuals with a preferential accumulation of VAT and thus at increased risk of metabolic complications.

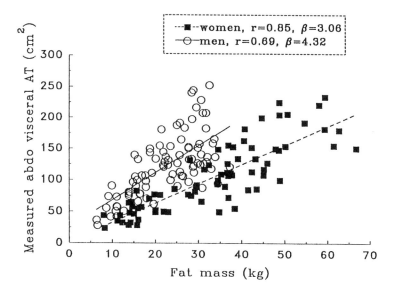

Figure 8.11 Relationship between total body fat calculated from body density and abdominal visceral adipose tissue (AT) area measured by CT in 89 men and 75 premenopausal women. Correlation coefficients were significant in men and in women, *P* < 0.0001.
Adapted from "Sex Differences in the Relation of Visceral Adipose Tissue Accumulation to Total Body Fatness," by S. Lemieux, D. Prud'homme, C. Bouchard, et al., 1993, *American Journal of Clinical Nutrition, 58*, pp. 463-467. Copyright 1993 by *American Journal of Clinical Nutrition*. Adapted with permission.

Conclusions

CT and MRI are exciting new tools that may become reference methods in the development of improved models for assessing human body composition. At this time, however, there is a need for further validation of both methods. Preliminary validation data demonstrate that CT and MRI are the methods of choice for the precise measurement of SAT and VAT. The assessment of VAT accumulation is critical in the assessment of the health risk since visceral obesity is closely associated with numerous metabolic alterations predictive of an increased risk of diabetes mellitus and cardiovascular diseases. Although the accurate prediction of VAT by anthropometry remains a problem, preliminary results suggest that waist circumference provides useful information in the assessment of the health risk associated with visceral obesity in each gender.

Acknowledgments

This research was supported by the Medical Research Council (MRC) of Canada, the Canadian Diabetes Association, the Heart and Stroke Foundation of Canada, the Natural Sciences and Engineering Research Council of Canada (NSERC), and by the Canadian Fitness and Lifestyle Research Institute. S. Lemieux is currently an MRC research fellow.

References

Abate, N., Burns, D., Peshock, R.M., et al. (1994). Estimation of adipose tissue mass by magnetic resonance imaging: Validation against dissection in human cadavers. *Journal of Lipid Research, 35*, 1490-1496.

Björntorp, P. (1988). Abdominal obesity and the development on non-insulin-dependent diabetes mellitus. *Diabetes/Metabolism Reviews, 4*, 615-622.

Björntorp P. (1990). "Portal" adipose tissue as a generator of risk factors for cardiovascular disease and diabetes. *Arteriosclerosis, 10*, 493-496.

Borkan, G.A., Hults, D.E., Gerzof, S.F. et al. (1983). Relationships between computed tomography tissue areas, thicknesses and total body composition. *Annals of Human Biology, 10*, 537-546.

Bouchard, C., Tremblay, A., Després, J.P., et al. (1990). The response to long-term overfeeding in identical twins. *New England Journal of Medicine, 322*, 1477-1482.

Després, J.P. (1993). Abdominal obesity as important component of insulin-resistance syndrome. *Nutrition, 9*, 452-459.

Després, J.P., Moorjani, S., Ferland, M., et al. (1989a). Adipose tissue distribution and plasma lipoprotein levels in obese women: Importance of intra-abdominal fat. *Arteriosclerosis*, **9**, 203-210.

Després, J.P., Moorjani, S., Lupien, P.J., et al. (1990). Regional distribution of body fat, plasma lipoproteins, and cardiovascular disease. *Arteriosclerosis*, **10**, 497-511.

Després, J.P., Nadeau, A., Tremblay, A., et al. (1989b). Role of deep abdominal fat in the association between regional adipose tissue distribution and glucose tolerance in obese women. *Diabetes*, **38**, 304-309.

Després, J.P., Prud'homme, D., Pouliot, M.C. et al. (1991). Estimation of deep abdominal adipose tissue anthropometric measurements in men. *American Journal of Clinical Nutrition*, **54**, 471-477.

Enzi, G., Gasparo, M., Biondetti, P.R., et al. (1986). Subcutaneous and visceral fat distribution according to sex, age, and overweight, evaluated by computed tomography. *American Journal of Clinical Nutrition*, **44**, 739-746.

Ferland, M., Després, J.P., Tremblay, A., et al. (1989). Assessment of adipose tissue distribution by computed axial tomography in obese women: Association with body density and anthropometric measurements. *British Journal of Nutrition*, **61**, 139-148.

Foster, M.A., Fowler, P.A., Fuller, M.F, & Knight, C.H. (1988). Non-invasive methods for assessment of body composition. *Proceedings of the Nutrition Society*, **47**, 375-385.

Foster, M.A., Hutchison, J.M.S., Mallard, J.R., & Fuller, M. (1984). Nuclear magnetic resonance pulse sequence and discrimination of high- and low-fat tissues. *Magnetic Resonance Imaging*, **2**, 187-192.

Fowler, P.A., Fuller, M.F., Glasbey, C.A., et al. (1991). Total and subcutaneous adipose tissue distribution in women: The measurement of distribution and accurate prediction of quantity by using magnetic resonance imaging. *American Journal of Clinical Nutrition*, **54**, 18-25.

Fowler, P.A., Fuller, M.F., Glasbey, C.A. et al. (1992). Validation of the in-vivo measurement of adipose tissue by magnetic resonance imaging of lean and obese pigs. *American Journal of Clinical Nutrition*, **56**, 7-13.

Gerard, E.L., Snow, R.C., Kennedy, D.N., et al. (1991). Overall body fat and regional fat distribution in young women: Quantification with MR imaging. *American Journal of Radiology*, **157**, 97-104.

Gray, D.S., Fujioka, K., Colletti, P.M., et al. (1991). Magnetic resonance imaging used for determining fat distribution in obesity and diabetes. *American Journal of Clinical Nutrition*, **54**, 623-627.

Haarbo, J., Marslew, J., Gotfredson, A., & Christiansen, C. (1991). Postmenopausal hormone replacement therapy prevents central distribution of body fat after menopause. *Metabolism*, **40**, 1323-1326.

Janssens, V., Thys, P., Clarys, J.P., et al. (1994). Post-mortem limitations of body composition analysis by computed tomography. *Ergonomics*, **37**, 207-216.

Kissebah, A.H., & Peiris, A.N. (1989). Biology of regional body fat distribution: Relationship to non-insulin-dependent diabetes mellitus. *Diabetes/Metabolism Reviews*, **5**, 83-109.

Koester, R.S., Hunter, G.R., Snyder, S., et al. (1992). Estimation of computerized tomography derived abdominal fat distribution. *International Journal of Obesity*, **16**, 543-554.

Kotani, K., Tokunaga, K., Fujioka, S., et al. (1994). Sexual dimorphism of age-related changes in whole-body fat distribution in the obese. *International Journal of Obesity*, **18**, 207-212.

Kvist, H., Chowdhury, B., Grangard, U., et al. (1988a). Total and visceral adipose tissue volumes derived from measurements with computed tomography in adult men and women: Predictive equations. *American Journal of Clinical Nutrition*, **48**, 1351-1361.

Kvist, H., Chowdhury, B., Sjöström, L., et al. (1988b). Adipose tissue volume determination in males by computed tomography and ^{40}K. *International Journal of Obesity*, **12**, 249-266.

Lapidus, L., Bengtsson, C., Larsson, B., et al. (1984). Distribution of adipose tissue and risk of cardiovascular disease and death: A 12-year follow-up of participants in the population study of women in Gothenburg, Sweden. *British Medical Journal*, **289**, 1261-1263.

Larsson, B., Svärdsudd, K., Welin, L., et al. (1984). Abdominal adipose tissue distribution obesity and risk of cardiovascular disease and death: 13-year follow-up of participants in the study of men born in 1913. *British Medical Journal*, **288**, 1401-1404.

Leenen, R., van der Kooy, K., Seidell, J.C., & Deurenberg, P. (1992). Visceral fat accumulation measured by magnetic resonance imaging in relation to serum lipids in obese men and women. *Atherosclerosis*, **94**, 171-181.

Lemieux, S., Prud'homme, D., Bouchard, C., et al. (1993). Sex differences in the relation of visceral adipose tissue accumulation to total body fatness. *American Journal of Clinical Nutrition, 58,* 463-467.

Ley, C.J., Lees, B., & Stevenson, J.C. (1992). Sex- and menopause-associated changes in body-fat distribution. *American Journal of Clinical Nutrition, 55,* 950-954.

Martin, A.D., Daniel, M.Z., Drinkwater, D.T., & Clarys, P. (1994). Adipose tissue density, estimated adipose lipid fraction and whole body adiposity in male cadavers. *International Journal of Obesity, 18,* 79-83.

Pouliot, M.C., Després, J.P., Lemieux, S., et al. (1994). Waist circumference and abdominal sagittal diameter: Best simple anthropometric indexes of abdominal visceral adipose tissue accumulation and related cardiovascular risk in men and women. *American Journal of Cardiology,* **73**(7), 460-468.

Pouliot, M.C., Després, J.P., Nadeau, A., et al. (1992). Visceral obesity in men: Associations with glucose tolerance, plasma insulin, and lipoprotein levels. *Diabetes, 41,* 826-834.

Ross, R., Léger L., Guardo, R., de Guise, J., & Pike, B.G. (1991). Adipose tissue volume measured by magnetic resonance imaging and computerized tomography in rats. *Journal of Applied Physiology,* **70,** 2164-2172.

Ross, R., Léger, L., Morris, D., et al. (1992). Quantification of adipose tissue by MRI: Relationship with anthropometric variables. *Journal of Applied Physiology,* **72,** 787-795.

Ross, R., & Rissanen, J. (1994). Mobilization of visceral and subcutaneous adipose tissue in response to caloric restriction and exercise. *American Journal of Clinical Nutrition, 60,* 695-703.

Ross, R., Shaw, K.D., Martel, Y., de Guise, J., & Avruch, L. (1993). Adipose tissue distribution measured by magnetic resonance imaging in obese women. *American Journal of Clinical Nutrition, 57,* 470-475.

Ross, R., Shaw, K.D., Rissanen, J., et al. (1994). Sex differences in lean and adipose tissue distribution by magnetic resonance imaging: Anthropometric relationships. *American Journal of Clinical Nutrition, 59,* 1277-1285.

Rössner, S., Bo, W.G., Hiltbrandt, E., et al. (1990). Adipose tissue determinations in cadavers: A comparison between cross-sectional planimetry and computed tomography. *International Journal of Obesity,* **14,** 839-902.

Seidell, J.C., Bakker, C.J.G., & van der Kooy, K. (1990). Imaging techniques for measuring adipose-tissue distribution: A comparison between computed tomography and 1.5-T magnetic resonance. *American Journal of Clinical Nutrition, 51,* 953-957.

Seidell, J.C., Oosterlee, A., Deurenberg, P., et al. (1988). Abdominal fat depots measured with computed tomography: Effects of degree of obesity, sex, and age. *European Journal of Clinical Nutrition, 42,* 805-815.

Seidell, J.C., Oosterlee, A., Thijssen, M.A.O., et al. (1987). Assessment of intra-abdominal and subcutaneous abdominal fat: Relation between anthropometry and computed tomography. *American Journal of Clinical Nutrition, 45,* 7-13.

Sjöström, L. (1988). Measurement of fat distribution. In C. Bouchard & F.E. Johnston (Eds.), *Fat distribution during growth and later health outcomes* (pp. 43-61). New York: Alan R. Liss.

Sjöström, L. (1991). A computer-tomography based multi-compartment body composition technique and anthropometric predictions of lean body mass, total and subcutaneous adipose tissue. *International Journal of Obesity, 15,* 19-30.

Sjöström, L. & Kvist, H. (1988). Regional body fat measurements with CT-scan and evaluation of anthropometric predictions. *Acta Medica Scandinavica Supplementum,* **723,** 169-177.

Sjöström, L., Kvist, H., Cederblad, A., & Tylén, U. (1986). Determination of total adipose tissue and body fat in women by computed tomography, ^{40}K, and tritium. *American Journal of Physiology,* **250,** E736-E745.

Sobel, W., Rossner, S., Hinson, B. et al. (1991). Evaluation of a new magnetic resonance imaging method for quantitating adipose tissue areas. *International Journal of Obesity,* **15,** 589-599.

Sohlström, A., Wahlund L.-O., & Forsum, E. (1993). Adipose tissue distribution as assessed by magnetic resonance imaging and total body fat by magnetic resonance imaging, underwater weighing, and body-water dilution in healthy women. *American Journal of Clinical Nutrition, 58,* 830-838.

Staten, M.A., Totty, W.G., & Kohrt, W.M. (1989). Measurement of fat distribution by magnetic resonance imaging. *Investigative Radiology, 24,* 345-349.

Tokunaga, K., Matsuzawa, Y., Ishikawa, K., et al. (1983). A novel technique for the determination of body fat by computed tomography. *International Journal of Obesity, 7,* 437-445.

van der Kooy, K., Leenen, R., Seidell, J.C., et al. (1993a) Waist-hip ratio is a poor predictor of changes in visceral fat. *American Journal of Clinical Nutrition, 57,* 327-333.

van der Kooy, K., Leenen, R., Seidell, J.C., et al. (1993b). Abdominal diameters as indicators of visceral fat: Comparison between magnetic resonance imaging and anthropometry. *British Journal of Nutrition*, **70**, 47-58.

van der Kooy, K., & Seidell, J.C. (1993). Techniques for the measurement of visceral fat: A practical guide. *International Journal of Obesity*, **17**, 187-196.

Weits, T., van der Beek, E.J., Wedel, M., & ter Haar Romeny, B.M. (1988). Computed tomography measurement of abdominal fat deposition in relation to anthropometry. *International Journal of Obesity*, **12**, 217-225.

9

Anthropometry and Ultrasound

Alex F. Roche

The scope of this chapter is restricted to the post-natal period; comprehensive data for fetal body composition have been reported by Singer, Sung, & Wigglesworth (1991), but little is known of the relationships between anthropometric variables and body composition during the fetal period. The major part of the chapter describes the relationships between anthropometric and body composition variables. The chapter also describes methods for the use of ultrasound and its application to the study of body composition.

Anthropometry

Anthropometry has considerable appeal since it can be applied in the laboratory and in rural or urban field situations. The instruments are portable and relatively cheap, but the portable equipment for measuring weight and stature may be less accurate than the fixed equipment used in a laboratory. Anthropometric procedures are noninvasive, and training can be provided "on the job" without prerequisite courses. Consequently, anthropometric methods are applicable to large samples and can provide national estimates and data for the analysis of secular changes.

Assumptions and Their Validity

In the interpretation of an anthropometric value, it is commonly assumed that the tissues included in the measurement are in a "standard" state, for example, that muscles are relaxed and that soft tissues are normally hydrated. If these conditions are not met, the interpretation may be invalid. Almost all anthropometric variables include a variety of tissues, and the separate influences of these tissues on the recorded values are not always clear. For example, variations in skin thicknesses among individuals affect the validity of skinfold thicknesses as measures of subcutaneous adipose tissue (SAT). This and the other abbreviations used in this chapter are listed in Table 9.1.

Lengths and breadths are interpreted as skeletal dimensions because they are made between bony landmarks. These distances are, however, influenced by the soft tissues that overlie the bony landmarks, and, therefore, while anthropometric skeletal breadths are highly correlated with radiographic breadths, the latter tend to be smaller (Young & Tensuan, 1963). The effects of soft tissues on recorded lengths and breadths can be reduced and made less variable by the use of recommended calipers and the application of firm pressure, but

167

Table 9.1 Abbreviations and Definitions

BMC = bone mineral content (g)

BMI = body mass index (weight/stature^2; kg/m^2)

CR = coefficient of reliability (%)

CT = computed tomography

DAT = deep adipose tissue: adipose tissue that is deep to the deep fascia

DXA = dual energy x-ray absorptiometry

FFM = fat-free mass (kg): mass of that part of the body that is free of extractable fat

MRI = magnetic resonance imaging

PE = pure error

RMSE = root mean square errors

SAT = subcutaneous adipose tissue: adipose tissue between the skin and the deep fascia

TBBM = total body bone mineral (g)

WHR = waist/hip circumference ratio

% BF = percent body fat: percentage of body weight (mass) that is fat

they remain considerable, especially for bi-iliac breadths.

Circumferences of the limbs are difficult to interpret because they include skin, SAT, muscle, bone, blood vessels, nerves, and small amounts of deep adipose tissue (DAT). It is even harder to interpret trunk circumferences, which include organs in addition to various tissues. Interpretation of buttocks (hip) circumference is uncertain because it includes large amounts of adipose tissue and muscle and it is affected by pelvic size and shape. Limb and trunk circumferences are measured with a tape measure while minimal tension is applied so that the soft tissues will not be compressed; therefore enlargement of muscle and SAT due to edema increases the recorded measurements. Even standing for 1 to 2 hours, or prolonged sitting, causes an accumulation of extracellular fluid in the lower limbs leading to increases in ankle and calf circumferences.

Trunk circumferences, particularly those of the abdomen, are difficult to measure in those who are markedly overweight, but high precision may be attained (Bray et al., 1978; Rasmussen et al., 1993). A natural waist may be lacking, and the umbilicus and the maximum anterior extension of the abdomen may be displaced from their usual vertebral levels. Consequently, measurements at the same nominal levels on the anterior surface of the abdomen (e.g., umbilicus), may be at different

vertebral levels in the lean and the overweight and may differ in the organs included. Sagging of the anterior wall on standing in the overweight is accompanied by movement of the small intestine and transverse colon to lower vertebral levels, but the other parts of the colon and the kidneys remain in the same locations.

As noted earlier, skinfolds include skin and SAT, the latter consisting of adipocytes that contain triglycerides and connective tissue that includes blood vessels and nerves. The thickness of a double layer of skin is about 1.8 mm, but this varies among individuals and systematically by site and with age (Bliznak & Staple, 1975; Edwards et al., 1955). The paucity of SAT in the lean can make it difficult to elevate a fold, and it is not easy to elevate skinfolds with parallel sides in those with large amounts of SAT. Consequently, skinfold thicknesses are less precise than circumferences in overweight individuals than in general populations (Bray et al., 1978), but skinfolds are less affected by edema than circumferences because caliper pressure reduces the fluid content of the SAT.

Skinfold thicknesses are affected by individual and regional differences in compressibility that vary with age, gender, and recent weight loss (Kuczmarski, Fanelli, & Koch, 1987; Weiss & Clark, 1987). When a skinfold thickness is measured, the pressure exerted by the calipers displaces some extracellular fluid. This displacement, and the corresponding compressibility, are marked in preterm infants soon after birth and in malnutrition when the extracellular fluid content of SAT is increased (Brans, Sumners, Dweck, & Cassady, 1974; Martin, Ross, Drinkwater, & Clarys, 1985). In addition, pressure from skinfold calipers may force some adipose tissue lobules to slide into areas of lesser pressure; this sliding may be more marked for thick skinfolds in which the adipose tissue contains little connective tissue. The conformist view is that intersite and intersubject differences in skinfold compressibility reduce the utility of skinfold thicknesses. If, however, variations in compressibility reflect differences in the fluid content of uncompressed skinfolds, the reduction of these differences by compression might increase the validity of skinfold thicknesses as measures of regional fatness.

The factors to be considered in the selection of skinfold sites for screening, or for possible inclusion in predictive equations, include accessibility in relation to undressing, precision, the availability of reference data, and the thickness of the fold, which is important in overweight subjects.

Anthropometry, when used in relation to body composition, is based on the assumption that tissue composition is independent of tissue size. This assumption may be violated. For example, the fat content of adipose tissue is positively related to SAT thicknesses within age groups (Pawan & Clode, 1960; Thomas, 1962), and the fat content becomes larger as SAT thicknesses increase during growth (Baker, 1969; Kabir & Forsum, 1993).

Applicability

The choice of anthropometric measures, and the procedures used, differ for some groups (Lohman, Roche, & Martorell, 1988). For example, the precise measurement of infants and preschool children requires that they be content; one cannot obtain precise measurements of hungry or thirsty children. Throughout this chapter, and throughout this volume, the term *precise* refers to repeatability judged from inter- or intraobserver differences, and the term *validity* refers to comparisons between observed measures and the true values. Disabled and elderly subjects who cannot stand erect must be measured recumbent to obtain precise and valid data (Chumlea et al., 1985a). It may be impossible to measure skinfold thicknesses at some sites in overweight subjects because the thicknesses may exceed the maximum jaw openings of the calipers (Harpenden, 55 mm; Holtain, 50 mm; Lange, 65 mm). As an alternative, measurements can be made at sites where there is little SAT (e.g., biceps), or ultrasound can be used to measure SAT thickness, but there are few reference data for unusual sites or for ultrasound values and few predictive equations based on them.

The utility and interpretation of anthropometric variables are related to their short-term variations. These variations may not be associated with changes in total body composition, but they could alter the values predicted from equations that include variables subject to short-term variations. There is a loss of stature and an increase in abdominal and calf circumferences with prolonged standing, and there is considerable day-to-day variability of weight due mainly to the intake and elimination of food and water (Edholm, Adam, & Best, 1974). These fluctuations in weight reflect alterations in extracellular water but are not otherwise related to changes in body composition. Because of these short-term fluctuations, it is recommended that relationships between anthropometric variables and body composition be determined from data recorded in the morning from fasting subjects after they have eliminated and that data not be collected in the week before a menstrual period or during a menstrual period, when there may be an increase in the fluid content of the fat-free mass (FFM) (Bunt, Lohman, & Boileau, 1989).

Measurements

Selected anthropometric variables that are relevant to body composition are listed in Table 9.2. Interobserver coefficients of reliability for many of these variables from a research study, are given in Table 9.3. Detailed procedures for the measurement of these variables are provided in Lohman et al. (1988), with the exception of knee height and abdominal depth. Knee height is measured on the left side with large sliding calipers while the subject is supine with the knee and ankle flexed to 90°. One blade of the caliper is placed under the heel and the other blade is placed on the anterior surface of the thigh just proximal to the patella with the caliper shaft parallel to the long axis of the tibia. Pressure is applied to compress the soft tissues and the measurement is recorded to the nearest 0.1 cm. Knee height can be used to predict stature in those unable to assume the standard position for the measurement of stature (Chumlea et al., 1985b). Alternatively, arm span, which is also little affected by aging, can be used in place of stature for elderly individuals who are unable to stand (Kwok & Whitelaw, 1991). Measured or predicted statures are used to calculate some indices of body composition, such as the body mass index (BMI; weight in kg/stature^2 in cm).

Abdominal depth is of interest because it is related to the amount of deep abdominal adipose tissue. The anthropometrist stands to the left of the subject and positions the stationary blade of a

Table 9.2 Selected Anthropometric Variables Relevant to Body Composition

Lengths: stature, recumbent length, arm span, knee height

Breadths: biacromial, bi-iliac, knee, ankle, elbow, wrist

Circumferences: waist, hip, thigh, calf, arm, wrist

Skinfold thicknesses: subscapular, midaxillary, paraumbilical, suprailiac, anterior thigh, medial calf, lateral calf, triceps, biceps

Other: weight, trunk depth

Table 9.3 Interobserver Coefficients of Reliability (CR; %) for Sexes Combined in the Fels Longitudinal Study (Roche, A.F., & Guo, S. [1993]. Unpublished data.)

Ages (yr)	0-4	4-8	8-18	18-40	> 40
No. of pairs	45	26-28	80-82	21-24	47-50
Breadths (cm)					
Biacromial	—	97.74	99.21	97.72	97.38
Bi-iliac	—	95.95	97.91	91.46	92.61
Knee	98.19	97.63	99.05	98.34	97.65
Elbow	94.64	95.55	98.20	96.89	95.76
Wrist	85.05	89.17	97.13	97.13	96.68
Circumferences (cm)					
Waist	97.71	99.26	99.81	99.76	99.64
Hip	97.83	99.38	99.87	99.50	99.68
Calf	98.95	99.78	99.95	99.78	99.81
Arm	98.13	99.74	99.95	99.83	99.80
Skinfold thicknesses (mm)					
Subscapular	83.41	94.96	98.68	96.51	91.38
Midaxillary	71.47	94.15	96.93	92.68	90.59
Suprailiac	77.47	87.82	97.38	96.79	97.60
Anterior thigh	—	97.90	97.88	96.50	96.61
Lateral calf	83.91	90.22	94.63	97.31	97.72
Triceps	66.13	94.01	97.22	98.04	95.14
Biceps	74.19	91.01	96.38	96.75	98.45
Other measurements (cm)					
Stature	—	99.90	99.97	99.98	99.95
Trunk depth	—	96.65	98.86	97.86	98.38

pair of spreading calipers in the midline posteriorly at the level of the maximum depth of the lumbar concavity. While the shaft of the caliper is held parallel to the floor, the moveable blade is brought into contact with the midline of the anterior abdominal wall and the measurement is read to the nearest mm.

Relationships Between Anthropometric Variables and Total Body Composition

In the discussion of the relationships between anthropometric variables and total body composition, some of the anthropometric variables are referred to as "indices" because they can be used to categorize individuals (e.g., lean, obese), but they do not provide metric values for aspects of body composition. It should also be noted that some variables that are indices of total body composition may be measures of regional body composition.

All reported relationships between anthropometric variables and total body composition understate the actual relationships because neither the anthropometric variables nor the body composition variables are measured with exact precision. The total body composition variables considered here are percent body fat (% BF), fat-free mass (FFM), total body muscle, and total body bone mineral (TBBM). Relationships of anthropometric values to % BF and to body density will be considered jointly because of their conceptual similarity. Some prefer body density to % BF as the dependent variable in predictive equations because the relationships with anthropometric values are not affected by the uncertain calculation of % BF or FFM from body density. This choice only delays the uncertainties. Almost always, after body density has been predicted, a body composition variable is calculated from it and these calculations are based on assumptions that may be inaccurate.

Lengths and Breadths. Stature is related to FFM with regression slopes of about 0.9 kg/cm for men and 0.5 kg/cm for women and with smaller slopes in children and the elderly (Forbes, 1974), but it is not an effective predictor of FFM when used alone (Slaughter & Lohman, 1980). Skeletal lengths and breadths have only low correlations with % BF, but breadths have correlations with FFM of about 0.6 that are reduced to about 0.3 when the effects of stature are removed (Himes, 1991; Sinning et al., 1985; Sinning & Wilson, 1984). The length, breadths, and depths of the skeleton can be combined conceptually as "frame size." Katch and Freedson (1982) developed a frame size model that included stature and the sum of biacromial and bitrochanteric breadths; stature is the main determinant of the frame size scores from this model. These scores are positively related to FFM and nearly independent of % BF.

Circumferences. Abdominal circumferences are correlated with body density ($r = -0.7$) (Pollock et al., 1975, 1976; Schlemmer, Hassager, Haarbo, Christiansen, 1990), and the correlations of limb circumferences with body density are about -0.4 (Wilmore & Behnke, 1969, 1970). The correlations of abdominal and limb circumferences with FFM are about 0.6 in each gender (Wilmore & Behnke, 1969, 1970).

Skinfold Thicknesses. Skinfold thicknesses have low correlations with FFM (about 0.2), but they are highly correlated with % BF ($r = 0.7$ to 0.9) and these correlations do not differ markedly among the common sites (Frerichs, Harsha, & Berenson, 1979; Lohman, Boileau, & Massey, 1975). Despite the relatively high correlations between skinfold thicknesses at single sites and % BF, no one skinfold thickness is an accurate predictor of % BF (Himes & Bouchard, 1989; Lohman, 1991). This reflects individual variation in the distribution of SAT and in the proportion of the total adipose tissue that is subcutaneous. Chin and cheek skinfold thicknesses are unlikely to be useful in the prediction of total body fatness because they are largely independent of thicknesses at other sites (Lohman et al., 1975; Shephard et al., 1969).

There are gender- and age-differences in the relationships of skinfold thicknesses to % BF (Lohman, 1981; Parízková, 1977). At a fixed body density, and presumably at a similar % BF, women have thinner skinfolds than men and the elderly have thinner skinfolds than young adults. This indicates that the proportion of adipose tissue that is deep, particularly that within and between muscles, may be larger in women and in the elderly.

Only three or four skinfold thicknesses are needed in predictive equations (Jackson & Pollock, 1978; Jackson, Pollock, & Ward, 1980). When skinfold thicknesses are included in such equations, the high correlations among most sites can make the regression coefficients unstable. This instability can be reduced by using the log of the sum of the skinfold thicknesses (Durnin & Womersley, 1974), but this gives greater weight to the thicker skinfolds. Other methods to reduce instability of regression coefficients due to intercorrelations (multicollinearity) among predictor variables are described in chapter 10.

In children, skinfold thicknesses are better predictors of body density than are circumferences (Boileau et al., 1981; Harsha, Frerichs, & Berenson, 1978). Some have found that circumferences are better than skinfold thicknesses as predictors of body density in adults, perhaps because of their greater precision (Mueller & Malina, 1987; Pollock et al., 1975), but others report little difference between the root mean square errors (RMSE) of equations using skinfold thicknesses and those using circumferences (Katch & McArdle, 1973; Lohman, 1988). In this chapter, the term RMSE is used instead of the standard error of the estimate to summarize the differences between observed and predicted values. These terms are mathematically the same, but the standard error of the estimate is ambiguous since it could refer to the estimation of the regression coefficients.

Pairs of Variables. There are no known pairs of variables that are good predictors of total body composition. Some pairs of these variables are used to screen for unusual body composition; the most common pairing is of weight and stature^2 as BMI. BMI values are moderately correlated with % BF (r about 0.6 to 0.8) (Fukagawa, Bandini, & Young, 1990; Roche, Siervogel, Chumlea, & Webb, 1981), but the RMSE of the prediction of % BF from BMI is about 3.5 to 5% BF (Deurenberg, van der Kooy, & Hautvast, 1990; Womersley & Durnin, 1977). Despite these errors, BMI has high specificity (recognition of true negatives) in screening for high % BF values (Himes & Bouchard, 1989). Other weight-stature indices are similar to BMI in their correlations with % BF and body density (Roche et al., 1981; Womersley & Durnin, 1973), and these correlations are increased only slightly by using fractional powers of weight and stature to maximize them (Abdel-Malek, Mukherjee, & Roche, 1985; Sjöström, 1987).

Limb circumference and a skinfold thickness at the same level can be used to calculate the cross-sectional areas of adipose tissue and of "muscle plus bone." The correlations between these adipose tissue areas and % BF are only slightly higher than those of skinfold thicknesses (Borkan et al., 1983; Himes, Roche, & Webb, 1980). The cross-sectional areas of muscle plus bone are correlated with FFM ($r = 0.7$) (Reid, Evans, & Ames, 1992).

Prediction of Percent Body Fat and Body Density. The statistical procedures to develop and cross-validate predictive equations, and guidelines for the application of such equations, are described in chapter 10. Predictive equations should be applied only after they have been successfully cross-validated for a population similar to the one that will be studied. In their application, the anthropometric procedures and instruments must match those that were used when the equations were developed. The sites for the measurement of skinfolds must match those in the validation study and the same calipers must be used (Lohman et al., 1984; Ruiz, Colley, & Hamilton, 1971). The importance of accurate site location for the measurement of skinfold thicknesses has been demonstrated by B-mode ultrasound images (Bellisari, 1993).

The present account is restricted to equations in which only anthropometric variables are used as predictors. Selected predictive equations for children and adolescents, young, middle-aged, and elderly adults, and the obese are considered. Equations that use combinations of anthropometric and impedance variables are discussed in chapter 5 and predictive equations for athletes are discussed in chapter 13. Few, if any, predictive equations can be recommended for individuals with major pathological conditions, partly because the assumptions underlying the calculation of body composition values from body density, total body water, or total body potassium are likely to be invalid. In theory, disease-specific equations could be developed using valid dependent variables, but it would be difficult to obtain large samples that are homogeneous in relation to the duration, severity, and treatment of the disease, and the effects of the disease may make it impossible to perform the procedures needed to obtain the dependent variable.

Almost all the equations considered were developed from validation samples larger than 50, the equations were cross-validated, and the RMSE for the validation group and the pure error (PE) for the cross-validation group were reported. The RMSE of a predictive equation is calculated as:

$$\text{RMSE} = \sqrt{\sum_{i=1}^{n} \frac{(y_i - \hat{y}_i)^2}{n - p - 1}} \qquad (9.1)$$

where y and $\hat{y}_i$ are the observed and predicted values for an individual, n is the number in the sample, and p is the number of predictor variables. The pure error (PE), which is derived from cross-validation data, is calculated as:

$$\text{PE} = \sqrt{\sum_{i=1}^{n} \frac{(y_i - \hat{y}_i)^2}{n}}. \qquad (9.2)$$

The need for cross-validation of predictive equations is demonstrated by the findings of Boileau et al. (1981), who reported systematic bias in predictions of body density when equations from one group of boys were applied to another group of similar age, size, and body density.

Errors in the dependent variable should be considered in evaluating the RMSE and PE of predictive equations. The random error in observed values for % BF in young adults is about 4% BF with the two-component model and about 2% BF with the four-component model (Bakker & Struikenkamp, 1977; Lohman, 1992). In addition, there are systematic errors in children and adolescents (Guo, Roche, & Houtkooper, 1989), and perhaps in the elderly and the obese, when a two-component model is used to calculate % BF from body density.

In reviewing the selected equations, the distributions of stature, weight, and skinfold thicknesses will be considered relative to U.S. national data (Najjar & Rowland, 1987) because this indicates the population to which they may be applicable. Most of the validation samples for the selected equations tended to be taller and lighter and to have thinner skinfolds than U.S. national samples.

The use of skinfold thicknesses to predict % BF from densitometry is based on implicit assumptions that (a) measurements of skinfold thicknesses at a few sites provide an adequate description of SAT and (b) there is a fixed relationship between SAT and DAT. The first assumption appears correct since there are generally high correlations between skinfold thicknesses at different sites, but there are age and gender differences in the relationships between SAT and DAT (Baumgartner et al., 1991; Durnin & Womersley, 1974). Equations developed by stepwise regression to predict % BF or body density commonly overestimate the low values and underestimate the high values, but this tendency is reduced if power terms are included (Jackson & Pollock, 1978). The inclusion of power terms in predictive equations that include skinfold thicknesses as predictors is conceptually desirable because there is a curvilinear relationship between skinfold thicknesses and body density (Boileau et al., 1981; Durnin & Womersley, 1974; Mayhew, Clark, McKeown, & Montaldi, 1985).

• **Children and adolescents.** Specific predictive equations are needed for children and adolescents because the distribution of adipose tissue and body proportions (e.g., leg length/stature) differs between children and adults. These differences can alter the relationships between anthropometric variables and body composition. In addition, if the dependent variable is obtained from densitometry a four-component model should be applied, as described in chapter 1, because of changes in the composition and the density of FFM with increasing age and maturity.

Boileau et al. (1981) developed linear equations to predict body density (BD) in a study of boys who were slightly taller and lighter than national U.S. samples, but similar in skinfold thicknesses and breadths. Nonlinear terms were excluded because they did not reduce the RMSE. The RMSE were 0.0054 to 0.0081 g/cc and the PE were about 20 to 80% larger than the RMSE. Consequently, the accuracy of these equations should be evaluated for the group to be studied before they are used.

- **Young adults**. The Jackson and Pollock (1978) equation to predict BD for young men was developed from a group that was slightly taller and lighter than U.S. national data (RMSE = 0.0077 g/cc). This equation was satisfactorily cross-validated (PE = 0.0077 g/cc) by Thorland et al. (1984) in a group that tended to be slightly taller and heavier than U.S. national data but had markedly smaller skinfold thicknesses. The Jackson and Pollock equation has also been satisfactorily cross-validated by Norgan and Ferro-Luzzi (1985) in a sample that was slightly shorter but markedly lighter than U.S. national data and had markedly thinner skinfolds.

When cross-validated by various workers, the PE for the equation of Sloan (1967) to predict body density in young men was about 20 to 40% larger than the RMSE for the validation group (0.0067 g/cc) except in the sample of Lohman (1981), for which the PE was approximately equal to the RMSE. Haisman (1970), using data from a sample that tended to be slightly shorter and markedly lighter than U.S. national data, cross-validated several equations and reported good results for the equations of Durnin and Womersley (1974) but not for those of Chinn and Allen (1960) and Steinkamp et al. (1965). Descriptive statistics were not provided by Chinn and Allen, but the Steinkamp sample tended to be taller and lighter than U.S. national data although similar for arm circumference.

The equation of Jackson et al. (1980) to predict body density for young women, which was developed from a group slightly taller and lighter than U.S. national data, had a RMSE of 0.0086 g/cc

which was equivalent to 3.9% BF in the validation group and a PE equivalent to 3.7% BF on cross-validation. Withers et al. (1987) cross-validated this and other equations in young Australian women who, in comparison with U.S. national data, were slightly taller and lighter and had markedly thinner skinfolds. The best results were for the equations of Wilmore and Behnke (1970), Katch and McArdle (1973), Katch & Michael (1968), Pollock et al. (1975), and Sloan, Burt, & Blyth (1962), each of which had PE ≤ 3.0% BF.

The log of the sum of four skinfold thicknesses (biceps, triceps, subscapular, suprailiac) has been used widely in age- and gender-specific equations to predict body density from which % BF can be calculated (Durnin & Womersley, 1974). In the Scottish sample from which Durnin and Womersley developed their equations, the statures were similar to U.S. national data but the weights tended to be smaller. The choice of a log function reduced the RMSE slightly for men and had irregular effects on the RMSE for various age groups of women. These equations performed poorly when applied to Italian men and to Indian and Australian women (Norgan & Ferro-Luzzi, 1985; Satwanti, Bharadwaj, & Singh, 1977; Withers et al., 1987). In comparison with the Durnin and Womersley validation groups, the Italian men were similar in stature and weight, the Indian women were shorter and lighter, and the Australian women were taller and lighter, but each of these cross-validation samples had thinner skinfolds than the Durnin and Womersley validation groups. These differences in skinfold thicknesses may have been a critical factor in the failure of cross-validation.

- **Middle-aged and elderly subjects**. Skinfold equations derived from young adults commonly underpredict % BF in the middle-aged and elderly (Pollock et al., 1976), perhaps because of changes with age in the density of FFM and in the relationship between SAT and DAT, including increases in the fat content of muscles (Baumgartner et al., 1993; Forsberg et al., 1991; Fülöp et al., 1985). There are few, if any, anthropometric equations for middle-aged and elderly subjects that predict body composition values derived from body density employing a four-component model. Therefore, while some equations have performed reasonably on cross-validation, there may be systematic errors in both the observed and the predicted values.

The skinfold equations of Durnin and Womersley (1974) for the elderly (50 to 72 years), which were derived from only 24 men and 37 women, give erroneously low values for body fatness (Cohn et al., 1981; Deurenberg, van der Kooy, Hulshof, & Evers, 1989). Vu Tran and Weltman (1988) reported an equation to predict % BF in middle-aged men using data from a group that was similar in stature but heavier than U.S. national samples. The equation, which was based on circumferences, had a RMSE of 3.6% BF in the validation group and a PE of 4.4% BF on cross-validation.

• **Obese adults**. In the obese, the proportion of total adipose tissue that is subcutaneous may be lower than in general populations and extracellular fluid is increased (Kral et al., 1993). Therefore, equations are needed that are specific for the obese (Segal et al., 1988; Teran et al., 1991). There is evidence that these equations should be based on circumferences rather than skinfold thicknesses (Fanelli, Kuczmarski, & Hirsch, 1988).

An equation has been developed to predict % BF calculated from body density using a two-component model in obese women aged 18 to 50 years (Teran et al., 1991). This equation uses the log sum of circumferences, the log sum of skinfolds, and forearm circumference. The forearm circumference was kept separate because, unlike the other circumferences, it was negatively correlated with % BF. The RMSE was 4.2% BF and the PE was 3.9% BF on cross-validation. This equation did not underestimate or overestimate at the lower or upper parts of the distributions of calculated % BF.

• **Ethnic groups**. Equations to predict % BF calculated from body density with a two-component model may be inaccurate in some ethnic groups because of differences from the general population in the density of FFM (Boileau et al., 1984; Russell-Aulet et al., 1991, 1993) and in body proportions (Malina, Brown, & Zavaleta, 1987). Ethnic differences in the density of FFM do not affect the accuracy of a four-component model (Côté & Adams, 1993), but ethnic-specific equations may still be needed because of different relationships between the independent and dependent variables in various ethnic groups.

Black and white children differ in the correlations between anthropometric variables and body density (Harsha et al., 1978). In addition, ethnic differences in the distribution of SAT indicate that skinfold equations are likely to perform poorly when applied to ethnic groups other than those from which they are derived (Hammer et al., 1991; Harsha, Voors, & Berenson, 1980). Such considerations have led to the development of equations that are specific for ethnic groups (Nagamine & Suzuki, 1964; Satwanti et al., 1977). Nevertheless, black/white ethnicity was not an important factor in one study to predict FFM in boys (Lohman et al., 1975).

In overview, it is emphasized that predicted values are less accurate than observed (calculated) values and that a predictive equation should not be applied to a group that is markedly different from the group used to develop the equation. Important group differences may relate to age, gender, ethnicity, and level of body fatness. While some anthropometric predictive equations have been successfully cross-validated, they may not perform well in all other groups.

Prediction of Fat-Free Mass. There is interest in the measurement and prediction of FFM because of its relationships to morbidity, mortality, physical performance, and caloric requirements. The major constituents of FFM are muscle, bone, vital organs, and extracellular fluid. *Fat-free mass* is the whole body except the mass of extractable fat, whereas *lean body mass* is an anatomical term that refers to the whole body other than the adipose tissue that is visible to the eye. The FFM excludes lipids in cell membranes, the central nervous system, and bone marrow, but some or all of these are typically included with lean body mass.

There is no advantage in predicting FFM in preference to % BF since a predicted value for either FFM or % BF can be used to calculate the other. Nevertheless, it is logical to predict FFM if bioelectric impedance values, circumferences, breadths, and lengths have been measured and to predict % BF if skinfold thicknesses dominate among the predictor variables. In judging equations to predict FFM, it should be recalled that the error in FFM values from body density is about 1.9 kg for men and 1.5 kg for women (Lohman, 1991).

Lohman et al. (1975) published equations to predict FFM in boys. The observed values for FFM were calculated from total body potassium employing constants derived from adults. These equations, which included weight and two skinfold thicknesses as predictors, had RMSE of 1.7 kg and PE of about 1.2 kg. The boys in the validation and cross-validation samples closely matched U.S. national data for stature and weight.

Fuchs, Theis, & Lancaster (1978), using a multicomponent model, obtained observed values for FFM from body density, total body water, and total body potassium in U.S. Air Force crewmen. Their predictive equation, which used stature and arm circumference, had a RMSE of 2.9 kg and a PE of 3.3 kg on cross-validation. Descriptive statistics for these samples were not reported. Crenier (1966) used data from a French sample of young men and women who were slightly shorter and considerably lighter than U.S. national data to develop equations that predicted FFM with an RMSE of 1.5 kg. On cross-validation, all the errors of the estimates for individuals were less than 1.3 kg in men and 1.4 kg in women, which is a remarkably good result. Jackson and Pollock (1976) reported predictive equations developed from a sample of young adults who tended to be taller and lighter and to have thinner skinfolds than the U.S. national data. These equations had RMSE of 3.2 kg for men and 2.3 kg for women, but the PE have not been reported. It is reasonable to conclude that the PE of anthropometric equations to predict FFM are about 1.2 kg in boys and 3.0 kg in young adults, although lower PE were reported by Crenier for French samples that were lighter than U.S. national data.

Equations designed to predict the minimal acceptable weight for high-school wrestlers predict FFM, to which 5 to 7% is added to allow for essential fat. These equations, which can be used to predict FFM in adolescent males, are considered in chapter 13. They may not be applicable to general populations.

Prediction of Total Body Muscle Mass. There is a lack of equations to predict total muscle mass because it is difficult to measure the dependent variable. The only methods for the measurement of total muscle mass in the living are serial wholebody CT or MRI scans, which are not applicable to large samples. Indices of muscle mass from creatinine excretion, labeled creatinine, or the potassium/nitrogen ratio are too uncertain to be used as the dependent variable (Heymsfield et al., 1983). Despite considerable independence among radiographic muscle thicknesses at different limb sites (Malina, 1986), limb cross-sectional areas of muscle plus bone from anthropometry predict limb muscle mass with RMSE = 1.8 kg, which is about 17% of the mean (Heymsfield et al., 1982, 1990). These predicted values are useful as indices of total muscle mass since skeletal muscle is more abundant than other types of muscle and about 74% of the skeletal muscle mass is in the limbs (Snyder et al., 1984).

Prediction of Total Body Bone Mineral. Total body bone mineral (TBBM, g) affects body density (Bunt et al., 1990) and, therefore, it is included in four-component models based on density. TBBM, which is usually measured by dual energy x-ray absorptiometry (DXA), is the sum of the osseous and non-osseous mineral, but the latter is a small near-constant proportion of the total mineral. The validity of TBBM from DXA and dual photon absorptiometry has been established by comparison with total body calcium (Heymsfield et al., 1989; Mazess et al., 1981).

Anthropometric values, in combination with age, gender, and ethnicity, may be useful in predicting TBBM. During infancy and childhood, TBBM is highly correlated with weight and stature ($r = 0.9$) (Chan, 1992; Katzman, Bachrach, Carter, & Marcus, 1991), but the corresponding correlations in adulthood are only moderate ($r = 0.3$ to 0.7) (Rico et al., 1991; Wang et al., 1988). Adams, Deck-Côté, and Winters (1992) reported ethnic-specific equations developed from small samples of young women (26 black, 26 white) that predict TBBM from combinations of limb muscle plus bone cross-sectional areas, chest and head size, and joint breadths. These equations have RMSE of about 143 g for blacks and 187 g for whites, which are equivalent to about 6% of the means of the measured values. These equations have not been cross-validated, but it was shown that a general equation for both ethnic groups combined had larger RMSE than the ethnic-specific equations.

Estimation of Changes in Body Composition

The main interest in estimating changes in body composition relates to the effects of intervention in the obese. There are considerable errors in all body composition measures; these errors may be larger in the obese and they are necessarily larger for predicted values than for observed values. Therefore, anthropometry is unlikely to provide accurate measures of changes in body composition. The observed changes in body composition with weight loss in the obese, calculated from body density, may be inaccurate if a two-component model is used, because of changes in the density of FFM (Scherf et al., 1986; Seip, Snead, & Weltman, 1993). An alternative is to use a method that is equally valid in the obese and non-obese; serial CT scans meet this requirement but few can obtain them. It is generally agreed that efforts to estimate the changes in body composition with weight loss in the obese should be based on equations that use circumferences rather than skinfold thicknesses because the changes in circumferences are larger, with the possible exception of subscapular skinfold thickness (Bradfield, Schultz, & Lechtig, 1979; Bray et al., 1978).

All the analyses reported, discussed below, were based on two-component body density models.

The difficulties of evaluating changes in body composition were shown by Ballor and Katch (1989), who reported that in obese women with a mean loss of 2.7% BF, none of 10 common predictive equations accurately estimated the changes calculated from body density. The equations that performed best were the skinfold equation of Jackson et al. (1980) and the circumference equation of Katch and McArdle (1973), but even these were not recommended by Ballor and Katch. Others have reported that the equations of Jackson et al. (1980), Jackson and Pollock (1978), and Durnin and Womersley (1974) performed poorly after weight loss in the obese (Scherf et al., 1986; Teran et al., 1991) and that the equation of Teran et al. (1991) for obese women provided only fair predictions of the change in body fatness (PE = 2.9% BF) with weight loss.

Relationships Between Anthropometric Variables and Regional Body Composition

In relation to regional body composition, anthropometric data are used to describe the distribution of subcutaneous adipose tissue. They are also used to predict the amount of deep adipose tissue and the composition of the limbs.

Subcutaneous Adipose Tissue Distribution. The major interest in regional body composition concerns the distribution of adipose tissue. Following Bouchard (1988), the term *adipose tissue distribution* will be used in reference to the absolute and relative amounts of adipose tissue in body regions. When interpreting the relevant literature, it is important to distinguish between fat and adipose tissue. Most methods that provide regional data measure or estimate adipose tissue. They do not measure fat, which is a chemical term. The term *fat pattern*, which is in common use, is misleading since it usually refers to adipose tissue distribution. Furthermore, the word *pattern* implies a relative configuration or design that can be described only if many variables are measured. A ratio between two skinfold thicknesses cannot define a pattern or adequately describe the distribution of SAT, although some ratios between skinfolds are related to the prevalence of diseases.

Principal component analysis has been applied to skinfold thicknesses to describe the distribution of SAT. The results of such analyses depend on the skinfold thicknesses measured; these should include sites on the upper and lower limbs, the chest, and the abdomen. In principal component

analysis, orthogonal components are extracted from an intercorrelation matrix (Mueller & Reid, 1979). Each component is the linear weighted combination of the recorded variables that describes the maximum proportion of the variance remaining after earlier components have been extracted. These components are interpreted from the coefficients given to the individual variables. The first principal component from a set of skinfold thicknesses is usually interpreted as a measure of the mass of SAT or body fatness leading to the conclusion that later components are independent of the mass of SAT or body fatness. This is inaccurate. Rather, the first component reflects the general level of the skinfold thicknesses that were measured and the later components are independent of this general level, but are not necessarily independent of the mass of SAT or body fatness. Additionally, the loadings on the elements within the components are related to the general level of the skinfold thicknesses that were measured (Deutsch, Mueller, & Malina, 1985; Mueller & Reid, 1979). Typically, the second principal component contrasts trunk and extremity skinfold thicknesses while the third component may contrast upper and lower body SAT (e.g., subscapular and triceps skinfold thicknesses vs suprailiac and medial calf skinfold thicknesses). The subscapular site may, however, behave statistically like an arm site and chin skinfold thicknesses may be the dominant factor in the second component (Norgan & Ferro-Luzzi, 1986; Shephard et al., 1969).

Two studies (Mueller & Malina, 1987; Mueller et al., 1989) used canonical correlations between multiple skinfold thicknesses and circumferences to select the set of circumferences that best described the distribution of skinfold thicknesses with the assumption that skinfold thicknesses provide valid measures of the distribution of SAT. There were only low canonical correlations between the skinfold thicknesses and circumferences indicating that these sets of measures are not interchangeable.

Some have used ratios of skinfold thicknesses, or of their logs, or of the thickness at one site relative to the sum of the thicknesses at several sites, as indices of the distribution of SAT (Baumgartner et al., 1990). Commonly, these ratios are correlated with total body fatness, making it difficult to determine the independent effects of SAT distribution, but these correlations are low for ratios between skinfold thickness z-scores (Norgan & Ferro-Luzzi, 1986; Ramirez, 1993).

In the literature, the terms *upper (lower) body obesity* and *upper (lower) segment obesity* are used interchangeably without clear definitions of the anatomical limits of the upper body or the upper segment. These terms have been based on various indirect criteria, including (a) the waist/hip circumference ratio (WHR), (b) the ratio between triceps and subscapular skinfold thicknesses, and (c) the ratio between anthropometric cross-sectional areas of adipose tissue in the upper and lower limbs relative to the corresponding cross-sectional areas of muscle plus bone (Haffner et al., 1987; Kissebah et al., 1982). The distinction between upper and lower body obesity based on WHR is problematic since both waist and hip circumferences include many tissues and organs in addition to adipose tissue, and it has not been demonstrated that the circumferences at these levels predict the levels of fatness in the upper and lower body segments.

Interpretation of the literature concerning the WHR is difficult because waist and hip circumferences have been measured at various levels in different studies. When a waist is absent, as is common in the obese, another level must be chosen. Various levels have been recommended including: (a) the level of the umbilicus, (b) the level of the maximum anterior protrusion of the abdomen, and (c) a level midway between the costal margin and the iliac crest. There are difficulties with each of these. The level of the umbilicus relative to vertebrae is altered in the obese, the maximum anterior protrusion of the abdomen may be difficult to identify in the non-obese, and identification of the costal margin and the iliac crest may be difficult in the obese (Lohman et al., 1988; Seidell et al., 1988a). The choice of level for the measurement of waist circumference is important because it alters the recorded values, the organs represented in them, and the calculated relationships between waist circumference and abdominal adipose tissue (Seidell et al., 1987).

Further research is needed to establish the best anthropometric description of SAT distribution taking into account relationships with risk factors for selected cardiovascular and metabolic diseases and the functional characteristics of adipocytes at different locations.

Deep Adipose Tissue.   Recent interest in DAT has led to a literature that is confusing, particularly in the use of terms. By definition, DAT is all the adipose tissue deep to the deep fascia; it is not synonymous with visceral adipose tissue. A considerable proportion of the deep abdominal adipose tissue is extraperitoneal and is placed between the muscle walls of the abdomen and the peritoneum. The visceral adipose tissue of the abdomen occurs within peritoneal folds (omentum and mesentery). The deep abdominal adipose tissue that is extraperitoneal may differ functionally from the visceral abdominal adipose tissue partly because the latter has direct venous drainage to the liver by the portal system. Consequently, free fatty acids from omental and mesenteric adipocytes, which are very active metabolically (Bolinder, Kager, Ostman, & Arner, 1983), pass directly to the liver leading to increased risk of cardiac diseases and noninsulin dependent diabetes mellitus (Björntorp, 1990). In the statements that follow, the omental and mesenteric adipose tissue will be referred to as *portal adipose tissue*, following Björntorp.

In most studies based on CT or MRI images the extraperitoneal and portal adipose tissue have been combined and called deep abdominal adipose tissue or *visceral adipose tissue*. The area and volume of this adipose tissue has been calculated as the difference between total adipose tissue and SAT in single or serial CT or MRI scans of the abdomen. The volume of deep abdominal adipose tissue, obtained from serial CT scans, was 7.3 L ($SD = 4.5$ L) in men and 2.5 L ($SD = 1.9$ L) in women in the study by Kvist et al. (1988), but a lower value for men (4.1 L; $SD = 2.2$ L) was reported by Ross et al. (1992). A few have delineated the approximate area in which extraperitoneal deep adipose tissue occurs by drawing straight lines on abdominal scans from the midline between the aorta and inferior vera cava to the centers of the ascending and descending parts of the colon. About 60 to 75% of the deep abdominal adipose tissue is anterior to these lines and is considered portal adipose tissue (Ashwell et al., 1987; Rössner et al., 1990).

Reports of the areas of DAT in abdominal scans vary markedly among studies (Table 9.4). Much of the literature is based on scans at L4-5 where the deep adipose tissue occupies about 18% of the total cross-sectional area (Borkan et al., 1983; Bosello, Zamboni, Armellini, & Todesco, 1993). Since this is a relatively small percentage of the total area, it is not surprising that it is difficult, if not impossible, to predict the area of DAT in a CT scan from external abdominal dimensions or skinfold thicknesses at the same level. Furthermore, for reasons given earlier, it is desirable to predict portal adipose tissue, which would be more difficult since the portal adipose tissue area is even smaller (Ashwell et al., 1985; Baumgartner et al., 1988).

At L4-5, the reported mean SAT areas for men vary from 90 to 316 cm² and those for women vary from 134 to 391 cm². The corresponding mean areas of DAT at the same level vary from 79 to 173 cm² for men and from 77 to 139 cm² for women. The

Table 9.4   Selected Data for Adipose Tissue Areas (cm², *SD* in Parentheses) in Abdominal Scans

	Men		Women	
Author	SAT	DAT	SAT	DAT
Level L1				
Grauer et al., 1984	95	148	146	86
Level L3				
Grauer et al., 1984	150	148	202	113
Level L3-4				
Baumgartner et al., 1988	76 (72)	105	108 (71)	49
Level L4-5				
Baumgartner et al., 1988	98 (90)	131	134 (79)	77
Ashwell et al., 1985	176 (82)	91	278 (122)	86
Després et al., 1991	214 (124)	101 (57)	—	—
Koester et al., 1992	90 (67)	79 (59)	—	—
Ross et al., 1992	—	118 (62)	—	—
van der Kooy et al., 1993	316 (78)	156 (43)	391 (100)	108 (47)
Baumgartner et al., 1993	199 (58)	173 (57)	256 (103)	139 (33)
Level L5				
Grauer et al., 1984	170	88	312	110

Abbreviations: SAT, subcutaneous adipose tissue; DAT, deep adipose tissue.

lowest values for both SAT and DAT areas were reported by Koester et al. (1992) for men and Baumgartner et al. (1988) for women. The groups studied by these workers had mean BMI values of about 24 kg/m². The highest mean DAT areas were reported by Baumgartner et al. (1993) in an elderly group (mean age about 79 years) with a mean BMI of about 24 kg/m². This suggests that DAT areas are markedly larger in the elderly than in young adults at the same BMI. The highest mean SAT areas were reported by van der Kooy et al. (1993) for each gender in groups with mean BMI values of about 31 kg/m².

With some notable exceptions, the reported studies have been restricted to small samples and based on single abdominal scans. One scan may be sufficient since the total adipose tissue area in a scan predicts the total abdominal adipose tissue volume with a *CV* of 10%; also total abdominal adipose tissue volume can be predicted from weight/stature with a *CV* of about 8% (Borkan et al., 1983; Kvist et al., 1988). More importantly for the present context, the area of DAT in a scan at L4-5 is highly correlated with the total volume of deep abdominal adipose tissue (*r* = 0.95 to 0.99) (Kvist et al., 1988; Ross et al., 1992).

In attempts to develop equations for the prediction of DAT in the abdomen, the anthropometric variables have usually been obtained from CT images with the subjects supine. Supine values are affected by pressure on the posterior aspect of the trunk and buttocks, inability to measure buttocks circumference where it is maximal, and the movement of viscera between supine and erect positions. Nevertheless, there are close relationships between abdominal depths and the circumferences of the waist and hips measured standing and those measured on CT images, although the CT measures tend to be smaller for abdominal circumferences. The latter differences are greater for circumferences just superior to the iliac crest than for those at the waist (Koester et al., 1992; Kvist et al., 1988).

Després et al. (1991) reported an equation to predict the area of DAT at L4-5 from abdominal depth and WHR that had a RMSE equivalent to 28% of the mean with similar results on cross-validation (Koester et al., 1992; van der Kooy et al., 1993). The equations of Seidell et al. (1988b) and of Weits, van der Bek, Wedel, and ter Haar Romeny (1988) are even less accurate. Kvist et al. (1988) have reported equations to predict deep abdominal adipose tissue volume from abdominal depth, waist circumference, and BMI that have RMSE equal to 15% of the mean. None of these equations can be recommended. Others have investigated the ratio between waist circumference and thigh circumference as an index of deep abdominal adipose tissue, but this ratio is less closely related to abdominal adipose tissue area at L4-5 than is the WHR (Ashwell et al., 1985; Seidell et al., 1987).

Limb Composition.   The composition of the leg, particularly muscle mass, is important in the elderly because it is related to the prevalence of falls and fractures. In addition, arm muscle circumference from anthropometry, despite its inaccuracy, is related to longevity in middle-aged men (Roche, 1994), perhaps due to its associations with FFM and habitual physical activity. Furthermore, judgments of total body composition in sick or disabled individuals are commonly made using anthropometric data from the arm. Since limb muscle mass changes in response to physical exercise, accurate estimates of regional muscle areas or volumes would have widespread application although the functional capacity of skeletal muscle can vary independently of its volume, as occurs when its water content increases in severe protein-caloric malnutrition (Heymsfield et al., 1982).

Anthropometric indices of limb composition assume that (a) cross-sections of the limbs are circular, (b) that skinfold thicknesses are equal to the thickness of SAT at the site, and (c) that SAT in a cross-section of a limb is of constant thickness. These assumptions are incorrect. The anthropometric approach overestimates muscle plus bone cross-sectional areas in the limbs although the muscle plus bone areas from CT or MRI include some adipose tissue and connective tissue that is within muscles. This overestimation is larger in the elderly, particularly women, and in the obese (Baumgartner et al., 1992; Forbes, Brown, & Griffiths, 1988) partly due to increases in intra- and intermuscular adipose tissue, which are not related to the amounts of SAT (Frantzell & Ingelmark, 1951; Forsberg et al., 1991).

Skinfold thicknesses, used alone, are unlikely to be effective in the prediction of limb muscle mass since the thicknesses of adipose tissue and of muscle in the limbs are essentially independent (Hewitt, 1958; Malina, 1969). In overview, anthropometry alone does not provide accurate predictions of regional muscle mass; the more appropriate techniques are CT, MRI, or DXA. Additionally high frequency energy absorption may prove effective, but further developmental work is needed (Roche et al., in press).

Measures of bone mineral content (BMC) for a bone or part of the skeleton are indices of calcium stores and, by inference, they are indices of TBBM (Chestnut, Manske, Baylink, & Nelp, 1973). The validity of regional BMC values from DXA has been evaluated by comparison with the ash weight of excised bones. Most reports agree that DXA values are too high by 5 to 13% with a RMSE equal to about 8% of the mean (Braillon et al., 1992; Chan, 1992).

Anthropometric variables are related to regional BMC values. In children aged 5 to 14 years, combinations of stature, wrist breadth, biceps skinfold thickness, and limb circumferences are related to BMC of the radius, lumbar spine, and regions near the hip with $r = 0.9$ (Miller et al., 1991). Equations for adults are less effective with r values ranging from 0.3 to 0.5 (Dawson-Hughes, Shipp, Sadowski, & Dallal, 1987; Slemenda et al., 1990). The RMSE and PE of these equations have not been reported.

Ultrasound

Ultrasound was introduced for the measurement of SAT thicknesses by Booth, Goddard, and Paton (1966). This method uses high frequency sound waves that are produced by a piezoelectric crystal in a transducer (probe). These waves are introduced through the skin and reflected from interfaces (mainly deep fascia) to the transducer where they cause a pressure stress that is converted to an electric signal. At first, A-mode instruments (now obsolete) were used to measure the delay while a signal passed from a transducer on the skin to an interface (deep fascia) and returned. The distance from the skin to the fascia that is deep to the SAT was calculated with the assumption that the speed of transmission through the intervening tissues was 1,500 m/sec. Measurements with A-mode instruments are only moderately precise (Volz & Ostrove, 1984). A common source of error is the occurrence of multiple echoes from connective tissue layers within the SAT, particularly over the abdomen (Booth et al.; Volz & Ostrove).

During the past two decades, B-mode instruments have been introduced that construct cross-sectional images of tissues from reflected ultrasound waves. These instruments can measure the thicknesses of SAT and muscle, muscle cross-sectional areas, and abdominal depth. For SAT measurements, a frequency of 5 MHz is used, with a wavelength of 0.3 to 1.5 mm, and an 85 mm transducer. Cross-sectional images are obtained at the rate of 15 to 60/sec. These can be "frozen" to allow close inspection and measurement with electronic calipers to the nearest 1.0 mm. It is helpful to use a monitor that enlarges the images and to make hard copies. The operator can vary the brightness of the image and can increase its depth, which may be needed in the obese. When the depth of the image is increased, the resolution is reduced.

B-mode ultrasound and caliper measurements of SAT are about equal in precision, but ultrasound has the advantages of hard copies and little or no compression, although the latter may be less important than is generally considered. Furthermore, ultrasound measurements can be made in obese subjects and at some sites where calipers cannot be applied (e.g., sacral, paraspinal). The disadvantages of ultrasound, in comparison with calipers, are its greater expense and lesser portability.

Ultrasound measurements of SAT thicknesses have been reported for extremity sites (triceps, biceps, lateral forearm, anterior and posterior thigh, anterior and posterior calf, mid-thigh, calf) and trunk sites (suprailiac, sacral, epigastric, subscapular, waist). The paraspinal site is on the back 2 cm superior to the iliac crest and 2 cm to the left of the midline. The sacral site is in the midline posteriorly just superior to the lumbar fossae. The precision of ultrasound measurements of SAT is excellent with technical errors less than 0.2 mm with the exception of the triceps site in females (Table 9.5). Also the coefficients of reliability (CR) are high (91 to 98%) except at the paraspinal site, for which the CR is 86% for intraobserver data and 82% for interobserver data (Abe, Kondo, Kawakami, & Fukunaga, 1994; Bellisari, Roche, & Siervogel, 1993).

Table 9.5 Precision of Ultrasonic Measurements of Subcutaneous Adipose Tissue

Sites	Intraobserver		Interobserver	
	TE (mm)	CR (%)	TE (mm)	CR (%)
Suprailiac	0.14	91.07	0.15	89.77
Paraspinal	0.13	86.35	0.15	81.56
Sacral	0.08	94.34	0.09	94.06
Epigastric	0.09	95.06	0.08	96.25
Mid-thigh	0.08	97.69	0.13	93.66
Triceps	0.09	95.61	0.62	98.01

Abbreviations: TE, technical error; CR, coefficient of reliability.
Adapted from "Reliability of B-Mode Ultrasonic Measurements of Subcutaneous and Intra-Abdominal Adipose Tissue," by A. Bellisari, A.F. Roche, and R.M. Siervogel, 1993, *International Journal of Obesity, 17*, pp. 475-480. Copyright 1993 by Stockton Press. Adapted with permission.

Examples of B-mode ultrasound images at the triceps, suprailiac, and anterior mid-thigh sites are shown in Figures 9.1 through 9.3. In each of these figures, a line has been added to indicate the SAT thickness that was marked by thin electronic "cross-hatches" in the original images. In each figure, there are short white bands within the SAT that are parallel to the skin, but these are easily distinguished from the continuous white layer due to the deep fascia. Some of these discontinuous layers may be thick enough to cause an echo leading to spurious results with A-mode ultrasound. The figures indicate the need for careful site location. In Figures 9.1 and 9.2, measurements on the left sides of the images would result in larger values.

For B-mode measurements of SAT thicknesses, ultrasound gel is applied liberally to the skin, to the transducer, and to a bag of gel placed on the skin to separate the transducer from the skin. More gel should be applied if there are dark shadows or irregularly spaced narrow lines in the image.

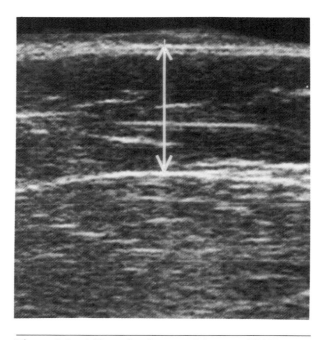

Figure 9.1 A B-mode ultrasound image of SAT at the triceps site with a gray scale on the right. The thickness of this layer (27 mm) was measured between the electronic caliper marks on the superficial surfaces of the skin and deep fascia. Here, and in Figures 9.2 and 9.3, lines have been added to show the planes of measurement and the limits of the SAT. Photo courtesy of Anna W. Bellisari. From "Sonographic Measurement of Adipose Tissue," by A. Bellisari, 1993, *Journal of Diagnostic Medical Sonography, 19*(1), p. 15. Reprinted with permission of J.B. Lippincott Company.

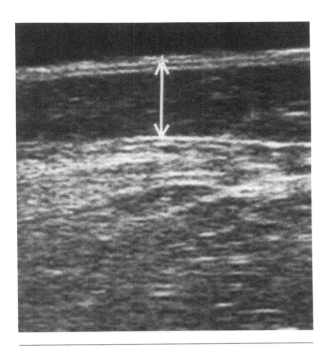

Figure 9.2 A B-mode ultrasound image of SAT at the suprailiac site (thickness 16 mm).
Photo courtesy of Anna W. Bellisari.

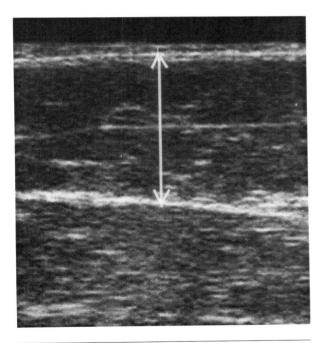

Figure 9.3 A B-mode ultrasound image of SAT at the anterior mid-thigh site (thickness 32 mm). The corresponding skinfold was too thick to be measured with skinfold calipers. Note a dense connective tissue layer within the SAT that could reflect ultrasonic waves, leading to spurious results with A-mode equipment.
Photo courtesy of Anna W. Bellisari.

The transducer is kept at right angles to the skin with only enough pressure to ensure contact between the transducer, the bag of gel, and the skin. If the transducer is not at right angles to the skin, the image will be blurred. To measure SAT thickness, the left and right sides of the transducer are aligned with the corresponding sides of the subject, except that measurements in the limbs and at the paraspinal site are made with the long axis of the transducer parallel to that of the limbs or the trunk, and suprailiac measurements are made with the long axis of the transducer directed towards the pubic symphysis. These variations in transducer alignment are made to match the directions of skinfolds elevated for caliper measurements. The precision of the measurements is increased when the skin is included in the measurements, but this may reduce their validity.

The relationships with body composition are similar for caliper and ultrasound measures of SAT in some studies (Fanelli & Kuczmarski, 1984), but others have reported closer associations for ultrasound values (Abe et al., 1994). Equations to predict body density from ultrasound SAT thicknesses that were reported by Abe et al. had RMSE of about 0.006 g/cc for men and women. On cross-validation, these equations tended to overpredict in men but not women. These workers also developed equations to predict FFM from muscle thicknesses measured by ultrasound at two sites (abdomen and anterior calf in men, abdomen and anterior thigh in women). These equations had RMSE of 4.4 kg for men and 2.5 kg for women. On cross-validation, in each gender, the predicted values for FFM were too low when the observed values were small and too high when the observed values were large.

Ultrasound has been employed to measure abdominal depth from the linea alba, and from the deep surface of the anterior abdominal SAT, to the posterior surface of the abdominal aorta (Armellini et al., 1990). These measurements are made near the midline 5 cm proximal to the umbilicus at a frequency of 3.5 MHz using a 100 mm transducer. Ultrasound gel is applied liberally to the skin and to the transducer; a "stand-off" is omitted to make the image sharper and because recognition of the skin surface is not necessary. Good precision with mean observer differences equal to 4.5% of the mean has been reported (Armellini et al., 1990), but others have failed to replicate these findings and have reported that the aorta is not always visible (Bellisari et al., 1993). Armellini et al. (1993) reported equations to predict DAT area at L4-5 in women from abdominal depth and SAT thickness measured with ultrasound, WHR, and age. The R^2 was 0.78, but the RMSE was not reported and the equations were not cross-validated.

Muscle thicknesses in the trunk and limbs measured with B-mode ultrasound using a 5 MHz transducer are highly precise (CR > 92%) and accurate (Fried, Coughlin, & Griffen, 1986; Ishida et al., 1992). In addition, B-mode ultrasound at 2.5 MHz with a water-based offset can be used to measure the cross-sectional areas of limb muscles. The transducer is mounted in a gantry that keeps it at 90° to the skin as it is swept around the limb. Stokes and Young (1986) state that considerable practice is needed to obtain a good image and that the measurements are more difficult in lean subjects because the muscle boundaries are poorly defined due to smaller amounts of intermuscular adipose tissue. With practice, however, the precision of measurements on successive days is excellent. Similar measurements can be made on CT images (Hudash et al., 1985).

Specialized ultrasonic equipment can measure the velocity of transmission through a bone and the attenuation of the signal at specific frequencies. The values obtained are closely related to bone mineral density (g/cm) (Tavakoli & Evans, 1991; Waud, Lew, & Baran, 1992). These applications of ultrasound are limited to a few bones and are only marginally relevant to body composition.

Overview

As new methods are introduced, anthropometry may be considered old-fashioned since it has been used for a long time, but it is far from obsolete. This chapter has addressed its utility when used alone in relation to the provision of indices and predicted values for total body composition and the measurement and prediction of regional body composition. While anthropometry is important in these contexts, it has many limitations when used alone. Anthropometry is particularly important in predictive equations that include values from bioelectric impedance.

B-mode ultrasound has been used to measure regional body composition for about 20 years. Its advantages over the measurement of skinfold thickness in the obese are now recognized more widely. This, and continual improvements in ultrasound equipment, are likely to lead to the increased use of ultrasound to measure SAT thicknesses in the obese and to measure the thicknesses and cross-sectional areas of muscles in the elderly and during rehabilitation.

Acknowledgment

This work was supported by the National Institutes of Health (Grant HD-12252). Gratitude is expressed to Anna W. Bellisari, Teresa Graham, and Joan Hunter for their generous help.

References

Abdel-Malek, A.K., Mukherjee, D., & Roche, A.F. (1985). A method of constructing an index of obesity. *Human Biology*, **57**, 415-430.

Abe, T., Kondo, M., Kawakami, Y., & Fukunaga, T. (1994). Prediction equations for body composition of Japanese adults by B-mode ultrasound. *American Journal of Human Biology*, **6**, 161-170.

Adams, W.C., Deck-Côté, K., & Winters, K.M. (1992). Anthropometric estimation of bone mineral content in young adult females. *American Journal of Human Biology*, **4**, 767-774.

Armellini, F., Zamboni, M., Rigo, L., et al. (1990). The contribution of sonography to the measurement of intra-abdominal fat. *Journal of Clinical Ultrasound*, **18**, 563-567.

Armellini, F., Zamboni, M., Rigo, L., et al. (1993). Measurements of intra-abdominal fat by ultrasound and computed tomography: Predictive equations in women. In K.L. Ellis & J.D. Eastman (Eds.), *Human body composition* (pp. 75-77). New York: Plenum.

Ashwell, M., Cole, T.J., & Dixon, A.K. (1985). Obesity: New insight into the anthropometric classification of fat distribution shown by computed tomography. *British Medical Journal*, **290**, 1692-1694.

Ashwell, M., McCall, S.A., Cole, T.J., et al. (1987). Fat distribution and its metabolic complications: Interpretations. In N.G. Norgan (Ed.), *Human body composition and fat distribution. Report of an EC workshop* (pp. 227-243). The Hague: CIP-gegenvens Koninklijke Bibliothekl. (Euro-Nut Conference Series).

Baker, G.L. (1969). Human adipose tissue composition and age. *American Journal of Clinical Nutrition*, **22**, 829-835.

Bakker, H.K., & Struikenkamp, R.S. (1977). Biological variability and lean body mass estimates. *Human Biology*, **49**, 187-202.

Ballor, D.L., & Katch, V.L. (1989). Validity of anthropometric regression equations for predicting changes in body fat of obese females. *American Journal of Human Biology*, **1**, 97-101.

Baumgartner, R.N., Heymsfield, S.B., Lichtman, S., et al. (1991). Body composition in elderly people: Effect of criterion estimates on predictive equations. *American Journal of Clinical Nutrition,* **53,** 1345-1349.

Baumgartner, R.N., Heymsfield, S.B., Roche, A.F., & Bernadino, M. (1988). Quantification of abdominal composition by computed tomography. *American Journal of Clinical Nutrition,* **48,** 936-945.

Baumgartner, R.N., Rhyne, R.L., Garry, P.J., et al. (1993). Body composition in the elderly from magnetic resonance imaging: Associations with cardiovascular disease risk factors. In K.J. Ellis and J.D. Eastman (Eds.), *Human body composition* (pp. 35-38). New York: Plenum.

Baumgartner, R.N., Rhyne, R.L., Troup, C., et al. (1992). Appendicular skeletal muscle areas assessed by magnetic resonance imaging in older persons. *Journal of Gerontology,* **47,** M67-M72.

Baumgartner, R.N., Roche, A.F., Guo, S., et al. (1990). Fat patterning and centralized obesity in Mexican-American children in the Hispanic Health and Nutrition Examination Survey (HHANES 1982-1984). *American Journal of Clinical Nutrition,* **51,** 936S-943S.

Bellisari, A. (1993). Sonographic measurement of adipose tissue. *Journal of Diagnostic Medical Sonography,* **9,** 11-18.

Bellisari, A., Roche, A.F., & Siervogel, R.M. (1993). Reliability of B-mode ultrasonic measurements of subcutaneous and intra-abdominal adipose tissue. *International Journal of Obesity,* **17,** 475-480.

Björntorp, P. (1990). "Portal" adipose tissue as a generator of risk factors for cardiovascular disease and diabetes. *Arteriosclerosis,* **10,** 493-496.

Bliznak, J., & Staple, T.W. (1975). Roentgenographic measurement of skin thickness in normal individuals. *Radiology,* **118,** 55-60.

Boileau, R.A., Lohman, T.G., Slaughter, M.H., et al. (1984). Hydration of the fat-free body in children during maturation. *Human Biology,* **56,** 651-666.

Boileau, R.A., Wilmore, J.H., Lohman, T.G., et al. (1981). Estimation of body density from skinfold thicknesses, body circumferences and skeletal widths in boys aged 8 to 11 years: Comparison of two samples. *Human Biology,* **53,** 575-592.

Bolinder, J., Kager, L., Ostman, J., & Arner, P. (1983). Differences at the receptor and post receptor levels between human omental and subcutaneous adipose tissue in the action of insulin on lipolysis. *Diabetes,* **32,** 117-123.

Booth, R.A.D., Goddard, B.A., & Paton, A. (1966). Measurement of fat thickness in man: A comparison of ultrasound, Harpenden calipers and electrical conductivity. *British Journal of Nutrition,* **20,** 719-725.

Borkan, G.A., Hults, D.E., Gerzof, S.G., et al. (1983). Relationships between computed tomograpy tissue areas, thicknesses and total body composition. *Annals of Human Biology,* **10,** 537-546.

Bosello, O., Zamboni, M., Armellini, F., & Todesco, T. (1993). Biological and clinical aspects of regional body fat distribution. *Diabetes Nutrition and Metabolism, Clinical and Experimental,* **6,** 163-171.

Bouchard, C., (1988). Introductory notes on the topic of fat distribution. In C. Bouchard & F.E. Johnston (Eds.), *Fat distribution during growth and later health outcomes* (pp. 1-8). New York: Alan R. Liss.

Bradfield, R.B., Schultz, Y., & Lechtig, A. (1979). Skinfold changes with weight loss. *American Journal of Clinical Nutrition,* **32,** 1756.

Braillon, P.M., Salle, B.L., Brunet, J., et al. (1992). Dual energy x-ray absorptiometry measurement of bone mineral content in newborns: Validation of the technique. *Pediatric Research,* **32,** 77-89.

Brans, Y.W., Sumners, J.E., Dweck, H.S., & Cassady, G. (1974). A noninvasive approach to body composition in the neonate: Dynamic skinfold measurements. *Pediatric Research,* **8,** 215-222.

Bray, G.A., Greenway, F.L., Molitch, M.E., et al. (1978). Use of anthropometric measures to assess weight loss. *American Journal of Clinical Nutrition,* **31,** 769-773.

Bunt, J.C., Going, S.B., Lohman, T.G., et al. (1990). Variation in bone mineral content and estimated body fat in young adult females. *Medicine and Science in Sports and Exercise,* **22,** 564-569.

Bunt, J.C., Lohman, T.G., & Boileau, R.A. (1989). Impact of total body water fluctuation on estimating of body fat from body density. *Medicine and Science in Sports and Exercise,* **21,** 96-100.

Chan, G.M. (1992). Performance of dual-energy x-ray absorptiometry in evaluating bone, lean body mass, and fat in pediatric subjects. *Journal of Bone Mineral Research,* **7,** 369-374.

Chestnut, C.H., III., Manske, E., Baylink, D., & Nelp, W.B. (1973). Preliminary report: Correlation of total body calcium (bone mass), as determined by neutron activation analysis with regional bone mass as determined by photon absorption. In R.B. Mazess (Ed.), *International conference on bone mineral measurement* (NIH Publication No. 75-683, pp. 34-38). Washington, DC: U.S. Department of Health, Education, and Welfare.

Chinn, K.S.K., & Allen, T.H. (1960). *Body fat in men from two skinfolds, weight, height, and age* (U.S. Army Medical Research and Nutrition Laboratory, Report No. 248). Washington, DC: Government Printing Office.

Chumlea, W.C., Roche, A.F., Steinbaugh, M.L. (1985b). Estimating stature from knee height for persons 60 to 90 years of age. *Journal of American Geriatric Society*, **33**, 116-120.

Chumlea, W.C., Steinbaugh, M.L., Roche, A.F., et al. (1985a). Nutritional anthropometric assessment in elderly persons 65 to 90 years of age. *Journal of Nutrition for the Elderly*, **4**, 39-51.

Cohn, S.H., Ellis, K.J., Vartsky, D., et al. (1981). Comparison of methods of estimating body fat in normal subjects and cancer patients. *American Journal of Clinical Nutrition*, **34**, 2839-2847.

Côté, K.D., & Adams, W.C. (1993). Effect of bone density on body composition estimates in young adult black and white women. *Medicine and Science in Sports and Exercise*, **25**, 290-296.

Crenier, E.J. (1966). La prédiction du poids corporel "normal" [The prediction of normal body weight]. *Revue de la Société de Biométrie Humaine*, **1**, 10-24.

Dawson-Hughes, B., Shipp, C., Sadowski, L., & Dallal, G. (1987). Bone density of the radius, spine, and hip in relation to percent of ideal body weight in postmenopausal women. *Calcified Tissue International*, **40**, 310-314.

Després, J. P., Prud'Homme, D., Pouilot, M.C., et al. (1991). Estimation of deep abdominal adipose tissue accumulation from simple anthropometric measurements in men. *American Journal of Clinical Nutrition*, **54**, 471-477.

Deurenberg, P., van der Kooy, K., & Hautvast, J.G.A.J. (1990). The assessment of the body composition in the elderly by densitometry, anthropometry and bioelectrical impedance. In S. Yasumura, J.E. Harrison, K.G. McNeill, A.D. Woodhead, & F.A. Dilmanian (Eds.), *In vivo body composition studies. Recent advances* (pp. 391-393). New York: Plenum.

Deurenberg, P., van der Kooy, K., Hulshof, T., & Evers, P. (1989). Body mass index as a measure of body fatness in the elderly. *European Journal of Clinical Nutrition*, **43**, 231-236.

Deutsch, M.I., Mueller, W.H., & Malina, R.M. (1985). Androgyny in fat patterning is associated with obesity in adolescents and young adults. *Annals of Human Biology*, **12**, 275-286.

Durnin, J., & Womersley, J. (1974). Body fat assessed from total body density and its estimation from skinfold thickness: Measurements on 481 men and women aged from 16 to 72 years. *British Journal of Nutrition*, **32**, 77-97.

Edholm, O.G., Adam, J.M., & Best, T.W. (1974). Day-to-day weight changes in young men. *Annals of Human Biology*, **3**, 3-12.

Edwards, D.A.W., Hammond, W.H., Healy, M.J.R., et al. (1955). Design and accuracy of calipers for measuring subcutaneous tissue thickness. *British Journal of Nutrition*, **2**, 133-143.

Fanelli, M.T., & Kuczmarski, R.J. (1984). Ultrasound as an approach to assessing body composition. *American Journal of Clinical Nutrition*, **39**, 703-709.

Fanelli, M.T., Kuczmarski, R.J., & Hirsch, M. (1988). Estimation of body fat from ultrasound measures of subcutaneous fat and circumferences in obese women. *International Journal of Obesity*, **12**, 125-132.

Forbes, G.B. (1974). Stature and lean body mass. *American Journal of Clinical Nutrition*, **27**, 595-602.

Forbes, G.B., Brown, M.R., & Griffiths, H.J.L. (1988). Arm muscle plus bone area: Anthropometry and CAT scan compared. *American Journal of Clinical Nutrition*, **47**, 929-931.

Forsberg, A.M., Nilsson, E., Werneman, J., et al. (1991). Muscle composition in relation to age and sex. *Clinical Science*, **81**, 249-256.

Frantzell, A. & Ingelmark, B.E. (1951). Occurrence and distribution of fat in human muscles at various age levels: A morphologic and roentgenologic investigation. *Acta Societatis Medicorum Upsaliensis*, **56**, 59-87.

Frerichs, R.R., Harsha, D.W., & Berenson, G.S. (1979). Equations for estimating percentage of body fat in children 10-14 years old. *Pediatric Research*, **13**, 170-174.

Fried, A.M., Coughlin, K., & Griffen, W.O. (1986). The sonographic fat/muscle ratio. *Investigative Radiology*, **21**, 71-75.

Fuchs, R.J., Theis, C.F., & Lancaster, M.C. (1978). A nomogram to predict lean body mass in men. *American Journal of Clinical Nutrition*, **31**, 673-678.

Fukagawa, N.K., Bandini, L.G., & Young, J.B. (1990). Effect of age on body composition and resting metabolic rate. *American Journal of Physiology*, **259**, E233-E238.

Fülöp, T., Jr, Worum, I., Csongor, J., et al. (1985). Body composition in elderly people. *Gerontology*, **31**, 150-157.

Grauer, W.O., Moss, A.A., Cann, C.E., et al. (1984). Quantification of body fat distribution in the abdomen using computed tomography. *American Journal of Clinical Nutrition*, **39**, 631-637.

Guo, S., Roche, A.F., & Houtkooper, L. (1989). Fat-free mass in children and young adults predicted from bioelectric impedance and anthropometric variables. *American Journal of Clinical Nutrition*, **50**, 435-443.

Haffner, S.M., Stern, M.P., Hazuda, H.P., et al. (1987). Do upper-body and centralized adiposity measure different aspects of regional body-fat distribution? Relationship to non-insulin-dependent diabetes mellitus, lipids, and lipoproteins. *Diabetes,* **36,** 43-51.

Haisman, M.F. (1970). The assessment of body fat content in young men from measurements of body density and skinfold thickness. *Human Biology,* **42,** 679-688.

Hammer, L.D., Wilson, D.M., Litt, I.F., et al. (1991). Impact of pubertal development on body fat distribution among white, Hispanic, and Asian female adolescents. *Journal of Pediatrics,* **118,** 975-980.

Harsha, D.W., Frerichs, R.R., & Berenson, G.S. (1978). Densitometry and anthropometry of black and white children. *Human Biology,* **50,** 261-280.

Harsha, D.W., Voors, A.W., & Berenson, G.S. (1980). Racial differences in subcutaneous fat patterns in children aged 7-15 years. *American Journal of Physical Anthropology,* **53,** 333-337.

Hewitt, D. (1958). Sib resemblance in bone, muscle and fat measurements of the human calf. *Annals of Human Genetics,* **22,** 213-221.

Heymsfield, S.B., Arteaga, C., McManus, C., et al. (1983). Measurement of muscle mass in humans: Validity of the 24-hour urinary creatinine method. *American Journal of Clinical Nutrition,* **37,** 478-494.

Heymsfield, S.B., McManus, C., & Smith, J., et al. (1982). Anthropometric measurement of muscle mass: Revised equations for calculating bone-free arm muscle area. *American Journal of Clinical Nutrition,* **36,** 680-690.

Heymsfield, S.B., Smith, R., Aulet, M., et al. (1990). Appendicular skeletal muscle mass: Measurement by dual-photon absorptiometry. *American Journal of Clinical Nutrition,* **52,** 214-218.

Heymsfield, S.B., Wang, J., Lichtman, S., et al. (1989). Body composition in elderly subjects: A critical appraisal of clinical methodology. *American Journal of Clinical Nutrition,* **50,** 1167-1175.

Himes, J.H. (1991). Considering frame size in nutritional assessment. In J.H. Himes (Ed.), *Anthropometric assessment of nutritional status* (pp. 141-150). New York: Wiley-Liss.

Himes, J.H., & Bouchard, C. (1989). Validity of anthropometry in classifying youths as obese. *International Journal of Obesity,* **13,** 183-193.

Himes, J.H., Roche, A.F., & Webb, P. (1980). Fat areas as estimates of total body fat. *American Journal of Clinical Nutrition,* **33,** 2093-2100.

Hudash, G., Albright, J.P., McAuley, E., et al. (1985). Cross-sectional thigh components: Computerized tomographic assessment. *Medicine and Science in Sports and Exercise,* **17,** 417-421.

Ishida, V., Carroll, M.L., Pollock, J.E., et al. (1992). Reliability of B-mode ultrasound for the measurement of body fat thickness. *American Journal of Human Biology,* **4,** 511-520.

Jackson, A.S., & Pollock, M.L. (1976). Factor analysis and multivariate scaling of anthropometric variables for the assessment of body composition. *Medicine and Science in Sports and Exercise,* **8,** 196-203.

Jackson, A.S., & Pollock, M.L. (1978). Generalized equations for predicting body density of men. *British Journal of Nutrition,* **40,** 497-504.

Jackson, A.S., Pollock, M.L., & Ward, A. (1980). Generalized equations for predicting body density of women. *Medicine and Science in Sports and Exercise,* **12,** 175-182.

Kabir, N., & Forsum, E. (1993). Estimation of total body fat and subcutaneous adipose tissue in full-term infants less than 3 months old. *Pediatric Research,* **34,** 448-454.

Katch, F.I., & McArdle, W.D. (1973). Prediction of body density from simple anthropometric measurements in college-age men and women. *Human Biology,* **45,** 445-454.

Katch, F.I., & Michael, E.D., Jr. (1968). Prediction of body density from skin-fold and girth measurements of college females. *Journal of Applied Physiology,* **25,** 92-94.

Katch, V.L., & Freedson, P.S. (1982). Body size and shape: derivation of the "HAT" frame size model. *American Journal of Clinical Nutrition,* **36,** 669-675.

Katzman, D.K., Bachrach, L.K., Carter, D.R., & Marcus, R. (1991). Clinical and anthropometric correlates of bone mineral acquisition in healthy adolescent girls. *Journal of Clinical Endocrinology and Metabolism,* **73,** 1332-1339.

Kissebah, A.H., Vydelingum, N., Murray, R., et al. (1982). Relation of body fat distribution to metabolic complications of obesity. *Journal of Clinical Endocrinology and Metabolism,* **54,** 254-260.

Koester, R.S., Hunter, G.R., Snyder, S., et al. (1992). Estimation of computerized tomography derived abdominal fat distribution. *International Journal of Obesity,* **16,** 543-554.

Kral, J.G., Mazariegos, M., McKeon, E.W., et al. (1993). Body composition studies in severe obesity. In J.G. Kral & T.B. Van Itallie (Eds.), *Recent developments in body composition analysis: Methods and applications* (pp. 137-146). London: Smith-Gordon.

Kuczmarksi, R.J., Fanelli, M.T., & Koch, G.G. (1987). Ultrasonic assessment of body composition in obese adults: Overcoming the limitations of the skinfold caliper. *American Journal of Clinical Nutrition, 45,* 717-724.

Kvist, H., Chowdhury, B., Grangard, U., et al. (1988). Total and visceral adipose-tissue volumes derived from measurements with computed tomography in adult men and women: Predictive equations. *American Journal of Clinical Nutrition, 48,* 1351-1361.

Kwok, T., & Whitelaw, M.N. (1991). The use of armspan in nutritional assessment of the elderly. *Journal of the American Geriatric Society, 39,* 492-496.

Lohman, T.G. (1981). Skinfolds and body density and their relation to body fatness: A review. *Human Biology, 53,* 181-225.

Lohman, T.G. (1988). Anthropometry and body composition. In T.G. Lohman, A.F. Roche, & R. Martorell (Eds.), *Anthropometric standardization reference manual* (pp. 125-129). Champaign, IL: Human Kinetics.

Lohman, T.G. (1991). Anthropometric assessment of fat-free body mass. In J.H. Himes (Ed.), *Anthropometric assessment of nutritional status* (pp. 173-183). New York: Wiley-Liss.

Lohman, T.G. (1992). *Advances in body composition assessment.* Current Issues in Exercise Science. Monograph No. 3. Champaign, IL: Human Kinetics.

Lohman, T.G., Boileau, R.A., & Massey, B.H. (1975). Prediction of lean body weight in young boys from skinfold thickness and body weight. *Human Biology, 47,* 245-262.

Lohman, T.G., Pollock, M.L., Slaughter, M.H., et al., (1984). Methodological factors and the prediction of body fat in female athletes. *Medicine and Science in Sports and Exercise, 16,* 92-96.

Lohman, T.G., Roche, A.F., & Martorell, R., (Eds.). (1988). *Anthropometric standardization reference manual.* Champaign, IL: Human Kinetics.

Malina, R.M. (1969). Quantification of fat, muscle and bone in man. *Clinical Orthopaedics and Related Research, 65,* 9-38.

Malina, R.M. (1986). Growth of muscle tissue and muscle mass. In F. Falkner & J.M. Tanner (Eds.), *Human growth: A comprehensive treatise* (2nd ed.) (Vol. 2: *Postnatal growth neurobiology*) (pp. 77-99). New York: Plenum.

Malina, R.M., Brown, K.H., & Zavaleta, A.N. (1987). Relative lower extremity length in Mexican American and in American black and white youth. *American Journal of Physical Anthropology, 72,* 89-94.

Martin, A.D., Ross, W.D., Drinkwater, D.T., & Clarys, J.P. (1985). Prediction of body fat by skinfold caliper: Assumptions and cadaver evidence. *International Journal of Obesity, 9,* 31-39.

Mayhew, J.L., Clark, B.A., McKeown, B.C., & Montaldi, D.H. (1985). Accuracy of anthropometric equations for estimating body composition of female athletes. *Journal of Sports Medicine and Physical Fitness, 25,* 120-126.

Mazess, R.B., Peppler, W.W., Chestnut, C.H., III, et al. (1981). Total body bone mineral and lean body mass by dual-photon absorptiometry, II: Comparison with total body calcium by neutron activation analysis. *Calcified Tissue International, 33,* 361-363.

Miller, J.Z., Slemenda, C.W., Meaney, F.J., et al. (1991). The relationship of bone mineral density and anthropometric variables in healthy male and female children. *Bone Mineral, 14,* 137-152.

Mueller, W.H., & Malina, R.M. (1987). Relative reliability of circumferences and skinfolds as measures of body fat distribution. *American Journal of Physical Anthropology, 72,* 437-439.

Mueller, W.H., Marbella, A., Harrist, R.B., et al. (1989). Body circumferences as alternatives to skinfold measures of body fat distribution in children. *Annals of Human Biology, 16,* 495-506.

Mueller, W., & Reid, R. (1979). A multivariate analysis of fatness and relative fat patterning. *American Journal of Physical Anthropology, 50,* 199-208.

Mueller, W.H., Wear, M.L., Hanis, et al. (1987). Body circumferences as alternatives to skinfold measurements of body fat distribution in Mexican Americans. *International Journal of Obesity, 11,* 309-318.

Nagamine, S., & Suzuki, S. (1964). Anthropometry and body composition of Japanese young men and women. *Human Biology, 36,* 8-15.

Najjar, M.F., & Rowland, M. (1987). *Anthropometric reference data and prevalence of overweight. United States, 1976-1980.* Vital and Health Statistics, Series 11, No. 238, National Center for Health Statistics. Washington, DC: U.S. Government Printing Office.

Norgan, N.G., & Ferro-Luzzi, A. (1985). The estimation of body density in men: Are general equations general? *Annals of Human Biology, 12,* 1-15.

Norgan, N.G., & Ferro-Luzzi, A. (1986). Simple indices of subcutaneous fat patterning. *Ecology of Food and Nutrition, 18,* 117-123.

Parízková, J. (1977). *Body fat and physical fitness.* The Hague: Martinus Nijhoff.

Pawan, G.E.S., & Clode, M. (1960). The gross chemical composition of subcutaneous adipose tissue in the lean and obese human subject. *Journal of Biochemistry, 74,* 9p.

Pollock, M.L., Hickman, T., Kendrick, Z., et al. (1976). Prediction of body density in young and middle-aged men. *Journal of Applied Physiology*, **40**, 300-304.

Pollock, M.L., Laughridge, E.E., Coleman, B., et al. (1975). Prediction of body density in young and middle-aged women. *Journal of Applied Physiology*, **38**, 745-749.

Ramirez, M.E. (1993). Subcutaneous fat distribution in adolescents. *Human Biology*, **65**, 771-782.

Rasmussen, M.H., Andersen, T., Breum, L., et al. (1993). Observer variation in measurements of waist-hip ratio and the abdominal sagittal diameter. *International Journal of Obesity*, **17**, 323-327.

Reid, I.R., Evans, M.C., & Ames, R. (1992). Relationships between upper-arm anthropometry and soft-tissue composition in postmenopausal women. *American Journal of Clinical Nutrition*, **56**, 463-466.

Rico, H., Revilla, M., Hernandez, E.R., et al. (1991). Age-related and weight-related changes in total body bone mineral in men. *Mineral and Electrolyte Metabolism*, **17**, 321-323.

Roche, A.F. (1994). Sarcopenia: A critical review of its measurement and health-related significance in the middle-aged and elderly. *American Journal of Human Biology*, **6**, 33-42.

Roche, A.F., Siervogel, R.M., Chumlea, W.C., & Webb, P. (1981). Grading body fatness from limited anthropometric data. *American Journal of Clinical Nutrition*, **34**, 2831-2838.

Roche, A.F., Wellens, W., Guo, S., et al. (in press). High frequency energy absorption and the measurement of muscle mass. Proceedings of Satellite Meeting to XV International Congress of Nutrition. Appropriate Technology in Body Composition. *Asia Pacific Journal of Clinical Nutrition*.

Ross, R., Léger, L., Marliss, E.B., et al. (1992). Quantification of adipose tissue by MRI: Relationship with anthropometric variables. *Journal of Applied Physiology*, **72**, 787-795.

Rössner, S., Bo, W.J., Hiltbrandt, E., et al. (1990). Adipose tissue determinations in cadavers: A comparison between cross-sectional planimetry and computed tomography. *International Journal of Obesity*, **14**, 893-902.

Ruiz, L., Colley, J.R.T., & Hamilton, P.J.S. (1971). Measurement of triceps skinfold thickness. An investigation of sources of variation. *British Journal of Preventive and Social Medicine*, **25**, 165-167.

Russell-Aulet, M., Wang, J., Thornton, J.C., et al. (1991). Bone mineral density and mass by total-body dual-photon absorptiometry in normal white and Asian men. *Journal of Bone Mineral Research*, **6**, 1109-1113.

Russell-Aulet, M., Wang, J., Thornton, J.C., et al. (1993). Bone mineral density and mass in a cross-sectional study of white and Asian women. *Journal of Bone Mineral Research*, **8**, 575-582.

Satwanti, K., Bharadwaj, H., & Singh, I.P. (1977). Relationship of body density to body measurements in young Punjabi women: Applicability of body composition prediction equations developed for women of European descent. *Human Biology*, **49**, 203-213.

Scherf, J., Franklin, B.A., Lucas, C.P., et al. (1986). Validity of skinfold thickness measures of formerly obese adults. *American Journal of Clinical Nutrition*, **43**, 128-135.

Schlemmer, A., Hassager, C., Haarbo, J., & Christiansen, C. (1990). Direct measurement of abdominal fat by dual photon absorptiometry. *International Journal of Obesity*, **14**, 603-611.

Segal, K.R., Van Loan, M., Fitzgerald, P.I., et al. (1988). Lean body mass estimation by bioelectrical impedance analysis: A four-site cross-validation study. *American Journal of Clinical Nutrition*, **47**, 7-14.

Seidell, J.C., Cigolini, M., Charzewski, J., et al. (1988a). Measurement of regional distribution of adipose tissue. In P. Björntorp & S. Rössner (Eds.), *Obesity in Europe* (pp. 351-357). London: John Libbey.

Seidell, J.C., Oosterlee, A., Deurenberg, P., et al. (1988b). Abdominal fat depots measured with computed tomography: Effects of degree of obesity, sex and age. *European Journal of Clinical Nutrition*, **42**, 805-815.

Seidell, J., Oosterlee, A., Thijssen, M.A.O., et al. (1987). Assessment of intraabdominal and subcutaneous abdominal fat: Relation between anthropometry and computed tomography. *American Journal of Clinical Nutrition*, **45**, 7-13.

Seip, R.L., Snead, D., & Weltman, A. (1993). Validity of anthropometric techniques for estimating percentage of body fat in obese females before and after sizable weight loss. *American Journal of Human Biology*, **5**, 549-557.

Shephard, R.J., Jones, J., Ishii, K., et al. (1969). Factors affecting body density and thickness of subcutaneous fat: Data on 518 Canadian city dwellers. *American Journal of Clinical Nutrition*, **22**, 1175-1189.

Singer, D.B., Sung, C.J., & Wigglesworth, J.S. (1991). Fetal growth and maturation: With standards for body and organ development. In J. Wigglesworth & D. Singer (Eds.), *Textbook of Fetal and Perinatal Pathology* (pp. 11-47). Chicago: Blackwell Scientific.

Sinning, W.E., Dolny, D.G., Little, K.D., et al. (1985). Validity of "generalized" equations for body composition analysis in male athletes. *Medicine and Science in Sports and Exercise, 17*, 124-130.

Sinning, W.E., & Wilson, J.R. (1984). Validity of "generalized" equations for body composition analysis in women athletes. *Research Quarterly for Exercise and Sport, 55*, 153-160.

Siri, W.E. (1956). The gross composition of the body. *Advances in Biological and Medical Physics, 4*, 239-280.

Sjöström, L. (1987). New aspects of weight-for-height indices and adipose tissue distribution in relation to cardiovascular risk and total adipose tissue volume. In E. Berry, S. Blondheim, H. Elihau, et al. (Eds.), *Recent advances in obesity research, V: Proceedings of the 5th International Congress on Obesity* (pp. 66-76). London: John Libbey.

Slaughter, M., & Lohman, T. (1980). An objective method for measurement of the musculoskeletal size to characterize body physique with application to the athletic population. *Medicine and Science in Sports and Exercise, 12*, 170-174.

Slemenda, C.W., Hui, S.L., Longcope, C., et al. (1990). Predictors of bone mass in perimenopausal women. A prospective study of clinical data using photon absorptiometry. *Annals of Internal Medicine, 112*, 96-101.

Sloan, A.W. (1967). Estimation of body fat in young men. *Journal of Applied Physiology, 23*, 311-315.

Sloan, A.W., Burt, J.J., & Blyth, C.S. (1962). Estimation of body fat in young women. *Journal of Applied Physiology, 17*, 967-970.

Snyder, W.S., Cook, M.J., Nasset, E.S., et al. (1984). *Report no. 23 of the task group on reference man.* Oxford, England: International Commission on Radiological Protection.

Steinkamp, R.C., Cohen, N.L., Gaffey, W.R., et al. (1965). Measures of body fat and related factors in normal adults, II: A simple clinical method to estimate body fat and lean body mass. *Journal of Chronic Diseases, 18*, 1291-1307.

Stokes, M., & Young, A. (1986). Measurement of quadriceps cross-sectional area by ultrasonography: A description of the technique and its applications in physiotherapy. *Physiotherapy Practice, 2*, 31-36.

Tavakoli, M.B., & Evans, J.A. (1991). Dependence of the velocity and attenuation of ultrasound in bone on the mineral content. *Physics in Medicine and Biology, 36*, 1529-1537.

Teran, J.C., Sparks, K.E., Quinn, L.M., et al. (1991). Percent body fat in obese white females predicted by anthropometric measurements. *American Journal of Clinical Nutrition, 53*, 7-13.

Thomas, L.W. (1962). The chemical composition of adipose tissue of man and mice. *Quarterly Journal of Experimental Physiology, 47*, 179-188.

Thorland, W.G., Johnson, G.O., Tharp, G.D., et al. (1984). Validity of anthropometric equations for the estimation of body density in adolescent athletes. *Medicine and Science in Sports and Exercise, 16*, 77-81.

van der Kooy, K., Leenen, R., Seidell, J.C., et al. (1993). Abdominal diameters as indicators of visceral fat: Comparison between magnetic resonance imaging and anthropometry. *British Journal of Nutrition, 70*, 47-58.

Volz, P.A., & Ostrove, S.M. (1984). Evaluation of a portable ultrasonoscope in assessing the body composition of college-age women. *Medicine and Science in Sports and Exercise, 16*, 97-102.

Vu Tran, Z., & Weltman, A. (1988). Predicting body composition of men from girth measurements. *Human Biology, 60*, 167-175.

Wang, J., Robinowitz, D., Aulet, M., et al. (1988). Bone density is a function of age, sex, race and body weight, but not of height, water, fat, or body cell mass in normals. *American Journal of Clinical Nutrition, 47*, 773.

Waud, C.E., Lew, R., & Baran, D.T. (1992). The relationship between ultrasound and densitometric measurements of bone mass at the calcaneus in women. *Calcified Tissue International, 51*, 415-418.

Weiss, L.W., & Clark, F.C. (1987). Three protocols for measuring subcutaneous fat thickness on the upper extremities. *European Journal of Applied Physiology, 56*, 217-221.

Weits, T., van der Bek, E.J., Wedel, M., & ter Haar Romeny, B.M. (1988). Computed tomography measurement of abdominal fat deposition in relation to anthropometry. *International Journal of Obesity, 23*, 217-225.

Wilmore, J.H., & Behnke, A.R. (1969). An anthropometric estimation of body density and lean body weight in young men. *Journal of Applied Physiology, 27*, 25-31.

Wilmore, J.H., & Behnke, A.R. (1970). An anthropometric estimation of body density and lean body weight in young women. *American Journal of Clinical Nutrition, 23*, 267-274.

Withers, R.T., Norton, K.I., Craig, N.P., et al. (1987). The relative body fat and anthropometric prediction of body density of South Australian females aged 17-35 years. *European Journal of Applied Physiology, 56*, 181-190.

Womersley, J., & Durnin, J.V.G.A. (1973). An experimental study of variability of measurements of skinfold thicknesses in young adults. *Human Biology, 45,* 281-292.

Womersley, J., & Durnin, J.V.G.A. (1977). A comparison of the skinfold method with extent of overweight and various weight-height relation-

ships in the assessment of obesity. *British Journal of Nutrition, 38,* 271-284.

Young, C.M., & Tensuan, R.S. (1963). Estimating the lean body mass of young women. *Journal of the American Dietetic Association, 42,* 46-51.

10

Statistical Methods for the Development and Testing of Predictive Equations

Shumei S. Guo and Wm. Cameron Chumlea

This chapter discusses the statistical methods for the development and application of predictive equations for body composition. The study of human body composition includes the quantification and distribution of fat and fat-free mass (FFM) and their variation as a function of age, race, and sex. The quantification of body composition into its fat and fat-free components is important in order to describe excesses or deficiencies of fat and FFM that have significant associations with the risk or onset of disease. The sophisticated "direct" methods for the measurement of body composition are time-consuming, expensive, and require fixed dedicated equipment and support in a laboratory setting. In epidemiological and clinical settings, it is frequently necessary to predict body composition (for groups or individuals) because the application of sophisticated direct methods is not practical.

Epidemiological investigations of cardiovascular and other chronic diseases require large sample sizes that necessitate simple, reliable, and portable procedures such as anthropometry, bioelectric impedance, and ultrasound, although these methods provide only indices of body composition. Bioelectric impedance measures body resistance, which

is proportional to the volume of total body water. Skinfold calipers and ultrasound can measure subcutaneous adipose tissue thickness, but the information is site-specific. Circumferences, which measure combinations of adipose tissue and fat-free tissues, are also site-specific. Body mass index (weight/stature^2; kg/m^2), which adjusts weight for stature, is another index of the level of body fatness. The utility of these indirect methods in epidemiological studies is reduced by the limited specificity of the recorded values and by the imprecision of their individual correlations with measures of total body composition. A practical solution is to use combinations of values from these indirect methods in predictive equations that can estimate body composition measures for the sample to be studied (Guo et al., 1993).

The prediction of body composition requires the formulation of a regression equation using indirect measures (typically bioelectric impedance and selected anthropometry) as predictor variables and percent body fat (% BF) or FFM from a sophisticated laboratory method as a response or dependent variable. The predictive equation is subsequently applied in epidemiological studies or field studies in which only the predictor variables are measured. The precision of the predicted values that are obtained during the development of the equation should be incorporated into the analysis and interpretation of the results. In longitudinal studies of body composition, some variables may not be measured throughout the course of investigation. In such studies, predictive equations can be applied retrospectively to predict variables of interest from the data that are available (Conlisk et al., 1992).

In the application of any predictive equation, it is most important to consider the accuracy of the predictions. An equation derived from a least squares method performs better than any other in the sample from which it was derived. The accuracy of an equation is reduced when it is applied to other samples, and this reduction may be substantial. Consequently, it is necessary to consider the factors that influence the accuracy of a predictive equation when applied to independent samples, ways in which this accuracy can be maximized, and the criteria by which the performance (accuracy) of predictive equations should be evaluated.

Accuracy of Predictive Equations

In accordance with common statistical usage, *accuracy* will be used to refer to the performance of a predictive equation when it is applied to an independent sample (cross-validation), whereas precision will be used to refer to the performance of the equation within the sample from which it was derived. The variable to be predicted by an equation is known as the *response variable*, and the variables used to achieve the prediction are referred to as *predictor variables*. The factors that can affect the accuracy of a predictive equation include:

- validity of the response variable,
- precision of the measured values of the predictor variables,
- biological and statistical relationships among the predictor variables and between the predictor variables and the response variable,
- statistical methods employed to formulate the equation, and
- size and the nature of the sample.

We will first address the aspects that can affect the development of a predictive equation and its subsequent accuracy.

Validity of the Response Variable

In using predictive equations, it should be recognized that a significant factor affecting the precision of the estimate is the validity of the response variable. If the method used to measure the response variable is prone to error, and/or has limited validity, the subsequent equation will perform poorly when applied to independent samples.

Body composition is frequently calculated from body density derived from underwater weights corrected for residual volume. The precision of underwater weighing is sensitive to the compliance of the subjects, and children and the elderly may find it difficult to perform the procedures. A two-component model is commonly used to calculate body composition values from body density (Conlisk et al., 1992; Deurenberg et al., 1989a, 1989b, 1990a, 1990b). The two-component model divides the body into fat and FFM components with an assumption that the density of FFM is a constant for all ages and both sexes (Lohman, 1986). This assumption is incorrect and limits the utility of the two-component model. Multicomponent models have been developed that include, for example, measures of body density, bone mineral, and total body water (Lohman). Such models can be applied to all normal subjects. Multicomponent models require several measurements to obtain the response variable. Consequently, there is an accumulation of measurement errors which inflates the errors in the calculated values for percent body fat (% BF) or FFM (Heymsfield et al., 1990). The validity of body composition measures from densitometry and from multicomponent models is discussed more fully in chapters 1 and 7.

Recently, dual energy x-ray absorptiometry (DXA), originally designed to measure bone mineral density, has been extended to measure body composition, as described in chapter 4. DXA measures are precise, and little subject compliance is required. However, the estimation of soft tissue from DXA relies on computer software and little is known of the algorithms that are employed (Roubenoff et al., 1993). Few published predictive equations have used DXA estimates of body composition as response variables.

Precision of the Predictor Variables

The measurement of the predictor variables from anthropometry and impedance should be as precise as possible. This will be achieved only if close attention is given to the selection and calibration of instruments, measurement procedures, and quality control.

Relationships Between Predictor Variables and Response Variables

Potential predictor variables for body composition measures include weight, stature, body circumferences, skinfold thicknesses, and measures of bioelectric impedance. These variables can be obtained easily in a variety of research or clinical settings at low cost and with high precision (Chumlea et al., 1991). The importance of a predictor variable in an equation depends on its biological and statistical relationships to the chosen response variable. Important predictor variables for % BF are primarily measures or indices of subcutaneous adipose tissue. These are easily obtained from skinfold thicknesses, or ultrasound, and body circumferences. It is important to include adipose tissue thicknesses at sites on the limbs and on the trunk because of sex- and age-specific patterns of subcutaneous adipose tissue distribution. Circumferences are indices of the cross-sectional area of FFM and adipose tissue present at a particular anatomical level. Arm circumference adjusted for skinfold thickness, in combination with other variables, has been used to predict FFM in children and young adults (Guo, Roche, & Houtkooper, 1989).

Measures of the skeleton are also possible predictor variables for FFM. Stature is positively correlated with FFM and with total body fat. Measures of bioelectric impedance are important predictor variables for FFM. The resistance index,

$$S^2 / R, \qquad (10.1)$$

where S is stature in centimeters and R is resistance in ohms, is the most significant single predictor of FFM (Guo et al., 1989, 1993). Consequently, when resistance is included as a predictor variable, FFM is the appropriate response variable. The resistance of the body depends on the electrical conductivity of FFM and the length and cross-sectional area of the conductor (FFM). Limb circumferences adjusted for subcutaneous adipose tissue thicknesses may act as indices of this cross-sectional area.

Some studies, relying on statistical associations only, have used biologically inappropriate predictor variables to estimate body composition measures. Skinfold thicknesses have been used to predict FFM, despite the low correlations between these variables. Bioelectric impedance has been used to predict % BF, although there are only weak biological and statistical relationships between these measures. The inclusion in an equation of a predictor variable, or set of predictor variables, that has strong direct biological and statistical relationships to the response variable will increase the probability that the resultant predictive equation will have a high degree of accuracy.

Statistical Methods

The correct choice of statistical methods is essential for the development of predictive equations that will be accurate when applied to independent samples. Computer programs for expediting regression analysis, which is the standard analytical method used to develop a predictive equation, are readily available in statistical packages including BMDP, SAS, SPSS, and others. Regression analysis depends upon several assumptions regarding the distributions of the response variable and its bivariate relationships with the predictor variables. The relationship between the response variable and each predictor variable has to be linear (i.e., the relationship between the values for each predictor variable and the response variable can be described by a straight line). If the relationships between the predictor and the response variables are nonlinear, the subsequent equations will have large errors of prediction, and their performance will be poor when they are applied to independent samples. This can be avoided by transforming the predictor variables so that these relationships become linear. A scatter plot of the response variable versus each predictor variable can indicate if the relationship is linear.

When there are multiple predictor variables, as is usual, the relationship between the response variable and any single predictor variable may be distorted, if there are high correlations among the predictor variables (multicollinearity). For example, if several skinfold thicknesses and circumferences are used to predict % BF, there will be interrelationships among these predictor variables. In this case, a partial regression leverage plot will reveal the true relationship between the response variable and the particular predictor variable. This is a plot of the response variable versus the predictor variable, after both these variables have been adjusted for the other predictor variables in the equation (Myers, 1986). In this procedure, the residuals for the response variable, obtained from regressing the response variable against a particular predictor variable, are plotted against the residuals from the regression of this predictor variable on the remaining predictor variables. An evaluation of their independent relationships with this response variable will aid the selection of the best set of predictor variables.

Homogeneity of the response variable should be tested. Under the assumption of homogeneity, the variance of the response variable is constant for all values of the predictor variable(s). The assumption of homogeneity is violated when the residual plot shows a pattern or trend in the residuals. There are several possible reasons for this. The relationship between the response variable and the predictor variable may be nonlinear. In this case, some other predictor variables should be included in the equation. A trend in the residuals may also be caused by highly influential observations or outliers in the data. When the relationship between the predicted values for the response variable and the predictor variables is nonlinear, or when the variance of the predicted response value is heterogeneous, a transformation of the data is needed. Several excellent descriptions of data transformation methods are available (Chatterjee & Price, 1979; Myers, 1986; Tukey, 1977).

In regression analysis, it is also assumed that the response variable is normally distributed in order to allow statistical inferences about the significance of the regression parameters. Normality of the response variable can be judged by the Shapiro and Wilks test (1965). Typically, % BF is not normally distributed and a transformation may be needed. The assumption of normality of the response variable is not as important as the absence of multicollinearity of the predictor variables and homogeneity of the response variable, if the main purpose of the equation is to predict the response variable.

Selection of Predictor Variables

There are several statistical methods to select the predictor variables and to determine the appropriate number of predictor variables to be included in an equation. To choose predictor variables, forward selection, stepwise regression, and backward elimination procedures work well. A forward selection regression procedure selects the predictor variable that has the highest correlation with the response variable to formulate a one-predictor variable equation. A second predictor variable is then selected that has the highest R^2 with the response variable among all the remaining predictor variables. This second predictor variable is incorporated into the one-predictor variable equation

and the significance of its contribution to the resulting two-predictor variable equation is evaluated by a partial F-test. This procedure is continued until the inclusion of any of the remaining predictor variables does not significantly improve the equation. Stepwise regression is similar to the forward selection method, but when each predictor variable is selected, the significance of its contribution to the R^2 of the equation is evaluated. The predictor variable is included only if its contribution to the relationship between the set of predictor variables and the response variable is statistically significant.

The backward elimination procedure begins by including all the possible predictor variables in the tentative equation. The predictor variables that do not yield statistically significant contributions to explain the variation in the response variable are deleted. Usually the significance level chosen for retention is 0.05. These methods are used commonly, especially when few variables are considered for inclusion; however, they should not be used if the predictor variables are interrelated (multicollinearity).

Multicollinearity can be detected by calculating the variance inflation factor (VIF) or by performing ridge regression (Belsley, Kuh, & Welsch, 1980; Hoerl & Kennard, 1968). The VIF is defined as

$$1 / (1 - R^2) \qquad (10.2)$$

where R^2 is derived from the regression of a particular predictor variable on the other predictor variables. Ridge regression is discussed later in the section on estimation procedures. Multicollinearity affects the precision of the regression coefficients and, thus, the accuracy of the prediction when the equation is applied to other samples. Multicollinearity can be reduced by screening the set of predictor variables for ones that are highly interrelated. Considerable multicollinearity may persist after highly intercorrelated predictor variables have been omitted.

When multicollinearity is present, a maximum R^2, or an all-possible subsets of regression, procedure is a more appropriate analytical choice. The maximum R^2 procedure starts by finding the one-predictor variable equation that yields the highest R^2. A two-predictor variable equation is then formulated by adding another variable selected from those remaining that results in the largest increase in R^2 from the one-predictor variable equation. The second variable is selected by pairing each possible predictor variable with the first predictor variable until the highest R^2 is found. This process is repeated—to select the best trio of predictor variables given the best pair—and is continued until increase of the predictor variable does not cause significant increases in the R^2 values.

An all-possible subsets of regression analysis evaluates every possible combination of predictor variables. This procedure results in the best predictive equation for the predictor and response variables in the population from which the equation is to be developed. If there are p predictor variables, the total number of possible equations evaluated is $2^p + 1$. If there are more than a few predictor variables, the number of possible equations can be large. In such cases, it is important to prescreen the possible predictor variables and to eliminate those that have low correlations with the response variable. This will reduce the number of equations generated and will usually reduce the chance of multicollinearity.

Estimation Procedure

Least squares estimation is commonly used in linear regression. By definition, this is the estimation of regression parameters through the minimization of the sum of squares of the deviations of the predicted values from the observed values. The square root of the sum of the squares of the deviations of the predicted values from the observed values, divided by the total number of observations minus the number of parameters, is the root mean square error (RMSE). That is,

$$\text{RMSE} = \sqrt{\frac{\Sigma \ (\text{observed} - \text{predicted})^2}{(n - p - 1)}}$$

(10.3)

where n is the number of observations and p is the number of predictor variables. The RMSE value is used as a measure of the goodness of fit of the equation.

When the predictor variables are interrelated (multicollinearity), the variance of the least squares estimators for the regression coefficients will be inflated and the precision and accuracy of the predictions will be poor (Montgomery & Peck, 1981). Ridge regression, which is an alternative to least squares estimation, is preferable when there is multicollinearity among the predictor variables. Ridge regression reduces the effects of multicollinearity by adding a small constant to the diagonal of the variance-covariance matrix of the predictor variables. The RMSE of a ridge regression is the summation of the residual sum of squares of the least squares regression and the value of the squared distance between the ridge estimator and the least squares estimator. Consequently, a ridge estimator is biased and does not provide the best fit to the data in the validation sample in the sense of minimum variance. Nevertheless, ridge regression performs better than least squares regression on cross-validation because it is less sample-specific.

Robust regression is used to circumvent influential observations (or outliers) that can cause large residuals from the regression. In robust regression, a weight function is incorporated into the analysis and the observations with large residuals are down-weighted. The two most common weight functions are Huber's weight and Tukey's bi-weight functions (Beaton & Tukey, 1979; Huber, 1964). Robust regression should improve the accuracy of the equation when applied to other samples because the influence of outliers in the validation sample is reduced.

Measures of Goodness of Fit

A predictive equation should fit well to the data from which the equation was generated. The coefficient of determination, or R^2, represents the proportion of the total variance in the response variable that is explained by the predictor variables in an equation. The larger the R^2 value, the better the equation fits the data. The RMSE is a measure of the precision of a predictive equation. When equations are compared, the one with the smallest RMSE value has the highest precision. The RMSE value can be standardized for the mean value of the response variable. This standardized value is called the coefficient of variation (CV). The CV is useful in comparing predictive equations with different response variables and, presumably, different units.

Parsimony

As the number of predictor variables in an equation increases, there is an increase in the R^2 value, which approaches 1.0, and a concurrent decrease in the RMSE values. The rates of improvement in the R^2 and RMSE values decelerate as the number of predictor variables increases. If there are too few predictor variables in an equation, prediction bias will result. When an equation is applied to a large number of independent samples, a mean prediction for the response variable in each sample can be obtained. In the presence of prediction bias, the distribution of these means will have a central tendency (mean) that differs from the mean of the true values. If there are too many predictors, the likelihood of severe multicollinearity is increased. There are several ways to select the appropriate number of predictor variables. Mallows' C_p statistic (1973) is an index of the appropriate number of predictor variables in the equation. Ideally, one would choose the equation with the minimum C_p value because this equation will have the maximum R^2 value and the minimum RMSE values and, therefore, a minimum of bias and of multicollinearity.

Cross-Validation

Cross-validation is the application of a predictive equation to a sample independent from the one used to construct the equation. The pure error, which is used to measure the performance of a predictive equation on cross-validation, is calculated as the square root of the sum of squared differences between the observed and the predicted values divided by the number of subjects in the cross-validation sample. Consequently, the pure error and the RMSE are conceptually similar but they differ numerically. The smaller the pure error, the greater the accuracy of the equation when applied to the independent sample. A criterion value for the pure error that would denote successful cross-validation has not been set. A general rule is that the value of the pure error should be similar to the RMSE of the same equation for the sample used in its development (validation sample). A large value for the pure error indicates that the prediction was poor when the equation was applied to the cross-validation group. Such a result reflects differences between the validation and cross-validation samples. These differences may be in ethnicity, age, and sex, or in the predictor and response variables, or in the relationships among these variables. For example, it is likely that an equation developed from a particular ethnic group will be applicable only to other samples from the same ethnic group, as shown by Zillikens and Conway (1990). Furthermore, an equation that performs well in males may perform poorly in females. There are differences between men and women in the relationships between skinfold thicknesses and total body fatness. In comparison

with men, women have less subcutaneous adipose tissue over the abdomen but more over the thighs. Therefore, skinfold thicknesses in these areas have sex-specific relationships with total body fatness. There are also sex-associated differences that are related to age. The triceps skinfold thickness decreases during adolescence in boys in association with increasing arm muscularity. This does not occur in girls. Consequently, the use of triceps skinfold thickness to predict body fatness in girls must be based on a relationship that differs from that for boys.

Cross-validation can be performed by the jackknife method, the PRESS procedure, or by applying the developed equation to an independent sample (Ducan, 1978; Geisser, 1974; Miller, 1974; Stone, 1974). In the jackknife method, the subjects are placed randomly into ten groups of equal size. The data for the first group are excluded when the equation is being developed and the residuals (the differences between pairs of observed values and those predicted from the equation) are calculated for the first group. The procedure is repeated for all ten groups, one at a time. The smaller the sums of squares of the residuals for each group, the more accurate the equation. In the PRESS procedure (Prediction of Sum of Squares), each subject in the total data set is excluded, one at a time, and regression analysis is performed. The value for each omitted subject is predicted and the difference from the observed value is called a PRESS residual. The sum of squares of the PRESS residuals yields the PRESS statistic (Belsley et al., 1980; Mason & Gunst, 1985). The jackknife and PRESS procedures are conceptually similar to data-splitting approaches in which, for example, two-thirds of the available sample are used to develop an equation and the remaining one-third is used to cross-validate it. Ideally, cross-validation is performed using an independent sample; this matches more closely the circumstances in which the equation is likely to be applied. The data for the predictor and response variables must be obtained in the independent sample using the same instruments and procedures that were used to record data in the sample from which the equation was derived.

Size and Nature of the Sample

It is not possible to determine, in advance, the sample size necessary to derive an accurate predictive equation. In general, the larger the sample size, the more precise and accurate the predictive equation. The sample size required to achieve accuracy of an equation on cross-validation depends on the relationships between the response variable and the predictor variables, the number of predictor variables, and the variance of the response variable. If the response variable and the predictor variables are highly correlated, only a small sample will be needed to develop a stable equation.

Figure 10.1 illustrates the relationship between sample size and statistical power for the increase in R^2 when a predictor variable is added during the development of an equation. The sample sizes considered range from 30 to 100 because most reported predictive equations have been developed from samples of this size. Statistical power, in this context, refers to the probability that the increase in R^2 due to the addition of another variable is significant. For example, the lowest curve in Figure 10.1 relates to an increase in the R^2 value from 0.85 to 0.86 when an additional predictor variable is added to an equation. If this occurs with a sample size of 30, the probability of significance (statistical power) is about 0.3, but for a sample size of 100, the probability of significance would be about 0.74. For increases of 0.02 in the R^2 value (0.85 to 0.87) the statistical power is only 0.53 for a sample of 30 but is 0.96 for a sample of 100. This illustrates one limitation that results from a small sample size—uncertainty about the significance of the predictor variables that are included in the equation. A sample of 100 is needed to achieve a significant 1% increase in R^2 precision or accuracy of a predictive equation (e.g., from $R^2 = 0.90$ to $R^2 = 0.91$) with a statistical power of 90%.

Published Predictive Equations

Equations to predict body composition from bioelectric impedance and selected anthropometry that were published between 1985 and 1992 have been reviewed (Table 10.1). Equations developed from samples of fewer than 30 subjects have been excluded. The focus of this review is on the characteristics of the study samples, the response and the predictor variables, the statistical methods used to formulate the equations, and the performance of these equations.

In a surprisingly large number of studies, data from the sexes were combined, and in some studies the age ranges were as large as 67 years (Deurenberg et al., 1991). The pooling of data from the two sexes and for many ages increases the sample size

and simplifies the application of the equation, but these advantages are more than offset by the loss of accuracy due to heterogeneity. Furthermore, such equations assume that the same set of predictor variables is appropriate for each sex and for a wide range of ages. The sample sizes for the selected studies range from 33 to 1069, but most are in the range from 60 to 140. For a surprisingly large number of the samples, ethnicity was not reported. In Table 10.1, ethnicity has been assigned when the source of the subjects (e.g., Denmark) makes the ethnicity almost certain even though it was not reported.

Most of the selected studies used fat-free mass (FFM) as the response variable and usually this was calculated from the two-component model of Siri (1961). This model is applied commonly in studies of children, although it is well established that this will lead to large systematic errors (Guo et al., 1989; Lohman, 1986). The predictor variables used most often in these equations were S^2/R and weight, followed by stature, sex, and age.

Most studies used predetermined sets of predictor variables in the regression analysis to formulate the equations. The majority of the reported predictive equations are parsimonious and include no more than five predictor variables. In only a few studies has the multicollinearity of the predictor variables in the equations been examined (Guo et al., 1989). Most of the equations were not cross-validated, and when cross-validation was performed, only a few investigators calculated the pure errors (Conlisk et al., 1992; Guo et al., 1989). Some have reported correlation coefficients between the observed and predicted values (Segal et al., 1985, 1988), but these coefficients are insufficient to evaluate the accuracy of a predictive equation.

In examining the published predictive equations, it appears that sample specificity is, to some extent, inevitable. For the few cross-validations of these equations that have been reported, the pure errors tend to be larger than the corresponding RMSE except for males in the study by Conlisk et al. (1992). Therefore, caution is necessary in the application of predictive equations in epidemiological or field studies. The best approach is to derive an equation from a random subset of the study population and apply this equation to the total sample. In this way, differences in the characteristics of samples, measuring techniques, and study protocols will be minimized.

Inaccuracy is to be expected when a predictive equation is applied to an individual. The errors of the individual predicted values are larger than

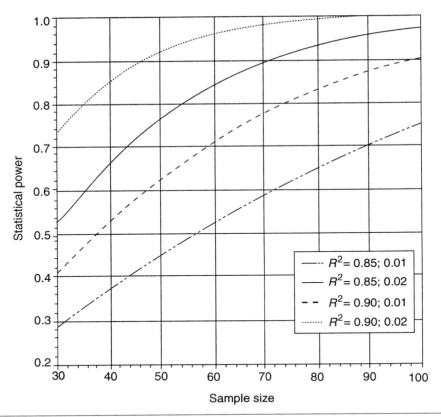

Figure 10.1   Statistical power in relation to sample size when R^2 of 0.85 and 0.90 increase significantly (0.01 and 0.02), resulting from the addition of a predictor variable.

those for the groups. These errors should be reported when predicting individuals.

Some equations that predict FFM were applied to data from the Fels longitudinal study; the results are summarized in Table 10.2. This table includes the R^2 and RMSE values from the validation samples as reported by the authors. The procedure included the following steps: Step 1. Fat-free mass was predicted for the Fels sample using the published equations. The pure errors (PE; kg) were calculated as

$$PE = \sqrt{\sum \frac{(\hat{Y} - Y)^2}{n}} \qquad (10.4)$$

where $\hat{Y}$ is the predicted FFM, Y is the observed FFM, and n is the number of subjects. Step 2. Multiple regression equations were calculated for the Fels sample, forcing in the variables used by each author with a new set of regression coefficients. If a predictor variable had an insignificant effect on the equation (P value > 0.10), the regression was calculated again without that variable. The coefficient of variation, R^2, and the RMSE values from

the Fels regression were compared with those reported by the author for the validation group.

The pure errors were consistently larger than those reported for the validation groups; the increases in these values ranged from 8.1 to 172.7% with a median value of 77.0%. This indicates that the level of accuracy was poor. For sex-specific equations derived by all possible subsets of regression, the pure errors exceeded the RMSE in an independent sample by only 12.5% for males and by 10.3% for females (Guo et al., 1989). When the Fels data were used to generate equations selected from those in Table 10.1 (Step 2), with retention of the same predictor variables but the calculation of new coefficients, the RMSE were larger (+4 to 104%) than those for the original equations when applied to the validation sample except for the equation reported by Deurenberg et al. (1990a). This indicates that for almost all these equations both the models and the coefficients were not well suited to the Fels data. To some extent, these findings reflect the specificity and size of the validation sample, but the statistical processes used to develop these equations are also important.

Table 10.1 Summary of Equations Published Between 1985 and 1993

Author	Sex	Ethnic group	Age (y)	N	Response variable	RMSE	CV (%)	Predictors	PE (kg)	CV (%)
									Cross-validation	
Chumlea et al., 1990	M	White	18-63	63	FFM from body density (2C model)	4.10 kg	6.7	S^2/R	NA	NA
	F	White	18-58	72		2.80 kg	6.7	S^2/R	NA	NA
Conlisk et al., 1992	M	Hispanic	11-25	79	FFM from body density (2C model)	1.82 kg	4.0	Note A	1.59 kg	4.2
	F	Hispanic	11-25	76		1.32 kg	4.8	Note B	1.64 kg	5.0
Deurenberg et al., 1989a	M & F	Dutch	8-11	64	FFM from body density (2C model)	1.31 kg	NA	S^2/R, W	NA	NA
Deurenberg et al., 1989b	M & F	Dutch	11-16	100	FFM from body density (2C model)	2.06 kg	5.0	S^2/R, W, S	NA	NA
Deurenberg et al., 1990a	M & F	Dutch	7-25	246	FFM from body density (2C model)	2.39 kg	5.9	Note C	NA	NA
Deurenberg et al., 1990b	M & F	Dutch	60-83	72	FFM from body density (2C model)	3.1 kg	6.0	S^2/R, S, W, thigh circ.	NA	NA
Deurenberg et al., 1991	M & F	Dutch	16-83	661	FFM from body density (2C model adjusted for age & fatness)	2.63 kg 1.68 kg	5.0 4.9	A, W, S, S^2/R, sex	NA	NA
Deurenberg et al., 1991	M & F	Dutch	7-15	165	FFM from body density (2C model adjusted for age)	1.68 kg	4.9	W, S^2/R, S, sex	NA	NA
Fredrix et al., 1990	M & F	Elderly	66	33	TBW	2.41 L	6.7	S^2/R	NA	NA
Guo et al., 1989	M	White	7-25	140	FFM from body density (multi-component model)	2.31 kg	5.02	S^2/R, W, lateral calf and midax. skinfolds	2.61	7.3
	F	White	7-25	110		2.23 kg	5.80		2.46	7.0
Hassager et al., 1986	M	Danes	20-72	98	FFM from DXA	2.3 kg	2.9	W, S, A	NA	NA
	F	Danes	20-72	130		2.2 kg	3.6	W, S, A	NA	NA
Heitmann, 1990	M & F	Danes	36-65	72	FFM from TBK and TBW	3.61 kg	NA	S^2/R, W · sex, S, A	NA	NA
Heitmann, 1990	M & F	Danes	35-65	139	TBW (isotope dilution)	3.47 L	NA	S^2/R, W · sex, S, W	NA	NA
Lukaski et al., 1986	M & F	NA	18-50	113	FFM from body density (2C model)	2.06 kg		S^2/R, W, reactance	NA	NA
Segal et al., 1985	M & F	NA	17-59	75	FFM from body density (2C model)	3.06 kg	NA	S^2/R, S, sex	NA	NA
Segal et al., 1988	M	NA	17-62	1,069	FFM from body density (2C model)	3.61 kg	NA	S^2/R, W, A	NA	NA
	F	NA	17-62	498		2.43 kg	NA	S^2/R, W, A	NA	NA

Abbreviations: A, age; DXA, dual-energy x-ray absorptiometry; LBM, lean body mass; NA, not available; PE, pure error; S, stature; S^2/R, stature²/resistance; TBK, total body potassium; TBW, total body water; 2C, two component; W, weight.

Note A: S^2/R, biiliac diameter, abdominal circumference, W. *Note B:* Suprailiac skinfold thickness, S^2/R, W. *Note C:* S^2/R, W, sex, S.

Table 10.2   Results From the Application of Selected Equations That Predict FFM to the Fels Longitudinal Study

Author	Sex	Validation by author		Fels cross-validation		Fels validation of model	
		R^2	RMSE (kg)	Pure error (kg)	R^2	RMSE (kg)	Insignificant predictors
Conlisk et al., 1992	M	0.97	1.82	4.05	0.97	2.62	Bicristal breadth
	F	0.95	1.32	3.60	0.89	2.69	—
Deurenberg et al., 1989a	M & F	0.89	1.31	2.98	0.82	1.97	Sex
Deurenberg et al., 1989b	M & F	0.97	2.06	3.05	0.94	2.76	—
Deurenberg et al., 1990a	M & F	0.99	2.39	4.10	0.95	2.06	Sex
Lukaski et al., 1986	M & F	0.98	2.06	4.06	0.89	3.68	—
Segal et al., 1985	M & F	0.96	3.06	4.79	0.90	3.64	—
Segal et al., 1988	M	0.9	3.61	3.90	0.80	3.67	—
	F	0.89	2.43	3.07	0.76	2.85	—

Summary and Future Directions

Equations that predict body composition variables have a long history. Stepwise regression is the most widely used method for their development, but a large set of possible predictor variables should first be screened so that some can be eliminated based on their statistical and biological relationship with the response variable and with each other. This will reduce the potential inaccuracy of the developed equation resulting from interrelationships among the predictor variables. All possible subsets of regressions should be applied in the development of an equation because, unlike stepwise regression, this procedure evaluates every combination of the potential predictor variables and their relationships with the response variable. Cross-validation of predictive equations is needed to assesses their generalizability. In both validation and cross-validation studies, the measures of precision (RMSE) and of accuracy (PE) should be standardized for the mean of the response variable.

In recent years, several important techniques have been introduced that provide accurate measures of FFM, which is the most common response variable. These include computed tomography, magnetic resonance imaging, and neutron activation, but these are very expensive and not readily accessible to research workers. They are still important as criterion methods, but the use of computed tomography and neutron activation is likely to be restricted to adults because of the ionizing radiation associated with these procedures. Dual energy x-ray absorptiometry (DXA) and bioelectric impedance have also been introduced, and these are more generally available. As a result, future predictive equations should be more accurate than those developed in the past, given the opportunity for more accurate measurements of the response variable using DXA in combination with densitometry and the probable inclusion of impedance measures with the predictor variables. Few published predictive equations have used response variables obtained from DXA, either alone or in combination with other procedures. This number is likely to increase because DXA can provide reasonably accurate measures of body composition in special populations such as children, the handicapped, and the elderly, for whom densitometry is difficult or impossible.

The use of bioelectric impedance to predict measures of body composition has focused on a single frequency (50 kHz), which provides an index of total body water. The possible inclusion of reactance and the phase angle as predictor variables deserves further attention. These values may facilitate the prediction of FFM in populations with wide ranges of body fatness.

Future improvements should occur in both the response and predictor variables, and there should be greater knowledge of the effects of sample characteristics (size, homogeneity) on the development of predictive equations and increased realization of the need for independent cross-validation. Better appreciation of the sources and extent of the errors when predictive equations are applied to individuals or to groups is expected. As a result of these changes, it is likely that in the future well developed predictive equations that are accurate on cross-validation will be applied more commonly in epidemiological and clinical studies. It is recommended, however, that direct measures of body composition be obtained in intervention studies where it is necessary to document changes within individuals as accurately as possible.

Acknowledgment

This work was supported by Grants HD-27063 and HD-12252 from the National Institutes of Health.

References

Beaton, A.E., & Tukey, J.W. (1979). The fitting of power series, mean polynomials, illustrated on band spectroscopic data. *Technometrics*, **21**, 215-223.

Belsley, D.A., Kuh, E., & Welsch, R.E. (1980). *Regression diagnostics: Identifying influential data and sources of collinearity*. New York: Wiley.

Chatterjee, S., & Price, B. (1979). *Regression analysis by example*. New York: Wiley.

Chumlea, W.C., Baumgartner, R.N., & Mitchell, C.O. (1990). The use of segmental bioelectrical impedance in estimating body composition. *Basic Life Sciences*, **55**, 375-385.

Chumlea, W.C., Guo, S., Kuczmarski, R.J., et al. (1991). Reliability for anthropometry in the Hispanic Health and Nutrition Examination Survey (HHANES). *American Journal of Clinical Nutrition*, **51**, 902-907.

Conlisk, E.A., Haas, J.D., Martinez, E.J., et al. (1992). Predicting body composition from anthropometry and bioimpedance in marginally undernourished adolescents and young adults. *American Journal of Clinical Nutrition*, **55**, 1051-1059.

Davies, P., Jagger, S., & Reilly, J.A. (1990). A relationship between bioelectrical impedance and total body water in young adults. *Annals of Human Biology*, **17**, 445-448.

Deurenberg, P., Kusters, C.S.L., & Smit, H.E. (1990a). Assessment of body composition by bioelectrical impedance in children and young adults is strongly age-dependent. *European Journal of Clinical Nutrition*, **44**, 261-268.

Deurenberg, P., Smit, H.E., & Kusters, C.S.L. (1989b). Is the bioelectric impedance method suitable for epidemiologic field studies? *European Journal of Clinical Nutrition*, **43**, 647-654.

Deurenberg, P., van der Kooy, K., Evers, P., & Hulshof, T. (1990b). Assessment of body composition by bioelectrical impedance in a population aged > 60 y. *American Journal of Clinical Nutrition*, **51**, 3-6.

Deurenberg, P., van der Kooy, K., Leenen, R., et al. (1991). Sex and age specific predication formulas for estimating body composition from bioelectrical impedance: A cross-validation study. *International Journal of Obesity*, **15**, 17-25.

Deurenberg, P., van der Kooy, K., Paling A., et al. (1989a). Assessment of body composition in 8-11 year old children by bioelectrical impedance. *European Journal of Clinical Nutrition*, **43**, 623-629.

Ducan, G.T. (1978). An empirical study of jackknife constructed confidence regions in non-linear regression. *Technometrics*, **20**, 123-129.

Fredrix, E.W.H.M., Saris, W.H.M., Soeters, P.B., et al. (1990). Estimation of body composition by bioelectrical impedance in cancer patients. *European Journal of Clinical Nutrition*, **44**, 749-752.

Geisser, S. (1974). A predictive approach to the random effect model. *Biometrica*, **61**, 101-107.

Guo, S., Khoury, P.R., Specker, B., et al. (1993). Prediction of fat-free mass from anthropometry and impedance in black and white pre-adolescent and adolescent girls. *American Journal of Human Biology*, **5**, 735-745.

Guo, S., Roche, A.F., & Houtkooper, L. (1989). Fat-free mass in children and young adults predicted from bioelectric impedance and anthropometric variables. *American Journal of Clinical Nutrition*, **50**, 435-443.

Hassager, C., Gotfredsen, A., Jensen, J., et al. (1986). Prediction of body composition by age, height, weight, and skinfold thickness in normal adults. *Metabolism*, **35**, 1081-1084.

Heitmann, B.L. (1990). Prediction of body water and fat in adult Danes from measurement of electrical impedance: A validation study. *International Journal of Obesity*, **14**, 789-802.

Heymsfield, S.B., Lichtman, S., Baumgartner, R.N., et al. (1990). Body composition of humans: Comparison of two improved four-compartment models that differ in expense, technical complexity and radiation exposure. *American Journal of Clinical Nutrition*, **52**, 52-58.

Hoerl, A.E., & Kennard, R.W. (1968). On regression analysis and biased estimation. *Technometrics*, **10**, 422-423.

Huber, P.J. (1964). Robust estimation of a location parameter. *Annals of Mathematical Statistics*, **35**, 73-101.

Lohman, T.G. (1986). Applicability of body composition techniques and constants for children and youths. *Exercise and Sport Science Reviews*, **14**, 25-27.

Lukaski, H.C., Bolonchuk, W.W., Hall, C.B., et al. (1986). Validation of tetrapolar bioelectrical impedance method to assess human body composition. *Journal of Applied Physiology*, **60**, 1327-1332.

Mallows, C.L. (1973). Some comments on C_p. *Technometrics*, **15**, 661-675.

Mason, R.L., & Gunst, R.F. (1985). Outlier-induced collinearities. *Technometrics*, **27**, 401-407.

Miller, R.G. (1974). The jackknife, a review. *Biometrika*, **61**, 1-15.

Montgomery, D.C., & Peck, E.A. (1981). *Introduction to linear regression analysis*. New York: Wiley.

Myers, R.H. (1986). *Classical and modern regression with applications*. Boston: Duxbury.

Roubenoff, R., Kehayias, J.J., Dawson-Hughes, B., et al. (1993). Use of dual-energy x-ray absorptiometry in body-composition studies: Not yet a "gold standard." *American Journal of Clinical Nutrition*, **58**, 589-591.

Segal, K.R., Gutin, B., Presta, E., et al. (1985). Estimation of human body composition by electrical impedance methods: A comparative study. *Journal of Applied Physiology*, **58**, 1565-1571.

Segal, K.R., Van Loan, M., Fitzgerald, P.I., et al. (1988). Lean body mass estimation by bioelectrical impedance analysis: A four-site cross-validation study. *American Journal of Clinical Nutrition*, **47**, 7-14.

Shapiro, S.S., & Wilks, M.B. (1965). An analysis of variance test for normality (complete samples). *Biometrika*, **52**, 115-124.

Siri, W.E. (1961) Body composition from fluid spaces and density: Analysis of methods. In J. Brožek & A. Henschel (Eds.), *Techniques for measuring body composition* (pp. 223-224). Washington, DC: National Academy of Sciences, National Research Council.

Stone, M. (1974). Cross-validitory choice and assessment of statistical predictions. *Journal of the Royal Statistical Society*, **36**, 111-133.

Tukey, J.W. (1977). *Exploratory data analysis*. Reading, MA: Addison-Wesley.

Zillikens, M.C., & Conway, J.M. (1990). Anthropometry in blacks: Applicability of generalized skinfold equations and differences in fat patterning between blacks and whites. *American Journal of Clinical Nutrition*, **52**, 45-51.

II

Findings

11

Total Body Composition: Birth to Old Age

Marta D. Van Loan

An understanding or basic knowledge of body composition is relevant to many disciplines including health and medicine, nutrition, exercise science, human performance, and other biological sciences. Nutritional status assessment, charting the course of diseases from diagnosis to recovery, growth and development, aging, and conditions of physical work are a few examples of situations and topics for which measurements of body composition can add to the understanding of physiological processes and aid in the treatment of diseases like obesity and anorexia.

Regardless of the area of interest, some basic information, such as stature, weight, body fatness, and fat-free mass (FFM), is usually needed by practitioners, researchers, clinicians, and others in health- and fitness-related professions. In other settings, physicians may be interested in specific information about body fluid compartments, body cell mass, or bone mineral density. All of these are part of a thorough understanding of body composition assessment.

The human body is a complex organism composed of a variety of tissues that change as the body develops, matures, and ages. It is important to recognize how these body compartments may be affected by age, gender, and ethnicity. This chapter attempts to provide the requisite information regarding the multiple components of the body that constitute total body composition and, when data are available, to discuss the effects of age, gender, and ethnicity on body composition. The focus will be on the major components of the body—FFM, fat mass (FM), percent body fat (% BF), total body water (TBW), bone mineral content, and fluid compartments—and on the changes observed from birth to maturation and through senescence. Where appropriate, the text will indicate if results are from data collected cross-sectionally rather than longitudinally.

Newborns and Infants to One Year of Age

Much of our information on muscle mass, TBW, bone, and other body components for newborns comes from studies of animals that have provided valuable data on changes in water, Cl, Na, and K. Vernadakis and Woodbury (1964) provided interesting data for changes in Cl, Na, K, N, and water during the first 45 days of life for the rat. The Cl, Na, and K electrolytes were about 59, 65, and 69 mM/kg wet weight of muscle one day after birth. The extracellular (ECF) to intracellular fluid (ICF) and the potassium to nitrogen (K/N) ratios were 1.7 and 4.5 mEq K/g N, respectively. Similar results have been observed in other species (e.g., pig, chicken, and human). In newborn human beings, Widdowson and Dickerson (1964) found that of the body's N, K, and water, 27%, 33%, and 28%, respectively, were in muscle tissue. A separate study revealed that skeletal muscle constituted about 25% of the body mass (Dickerson and Widdowson, 1960). Relatively speaking, the newborn infant has a much smaller muscle mass than the adult, about 25% versus 40% of body weight. At birth approximately 11% of the infant's weight is fat and about 89% is FFM with the constituents of FFM being about 11% protein, 75% water, 2.5% other minerals, carbohydrate, and nonprotein nitrogenous compounds (Fomon, 1967). Fomon and colleagues (1982) reported that, at birth, boys and girls did not differ in water, fat, protein, and osseous and non-osseous mineral contents. About 61% of the TBW is ECF and about 39% is ICF, giving an ECF/ICF ratio of about 1.5 for newborn boys and girls. As a percentage of FFM, however, TBW accounts for about 79 to 80%, with protein being 15 to 16% and minerals 4 to 5%.

During the early months of post-natal life, body weight and recumbent length increase progressively with almost a three-fold increase in weight and a 1.5-fold increase in recumbent length by the age of one year. According to Guo et al. (1991) the rate of weight gain is greatest in the first two months of life with an average increase of 33 g per day for boys and 28 g per day for girls. Similarly, the increase in recumbent length of infants is about 1 mm per day for both boys and girls during the first two months, decreasing to about 0.4 mm per day by one year of age. Corresponding changes in body components include an 8 to 9% increase in fat mass to a level of 22 to 24% at one year of age and a more than two-fold increase in FFM. The most notable change in the constituents of FFM is a large shift of water between the ECF and ICF compartments, although there is only a slight increase in TBW (1 to 2%). Generally, ECF decreases from about 50% of FFM to almost 42%, while ICF increases from about 30% to 37% of FFM. These changes are similar for boys and girls. The results of Fomon et al. (1982) are supported by the work of Friis-Hansen and colleagues (1961), who observed that TBW values ranged from 70 to 83% of body weight in newborn babies. In line with the increase in ICF, there is a corresponding increase in total body potassium (TBK) from 49 mEq/kg FFM to

almost 57 mEq/kg FFM and about a 2% increase in protein (Fomon et al.).

Other data related to body potassium, which is almost completely intracellular and, therefore, an indicator of FFM and of active cell mass, were reported by Maresh and Groome (1966), who showed that in a group of 9 infants TBK increased from about 7 g at one month of age to slightly more than 15 g at one year of age. These results are in general agreement with the findings of Novak and coworkers (1970) from whole-body ^{40}K counting. In a group of 31 male and 33 female infants, 31 days old, Novak et al. found the mean absolute amounts of TBK were 7.2 g and 7.6 g for males and females, respectively. Relative amounts for the males were 46 mEq/kg and 47 mEq/kg for the females. These data indicate marked similarity between males and females at one month of age.

Childhood, Puberty, and Adolescence

Before a discussion of body composition changes during childhood and adolescence, some terms need to be defined. Webster's dictionary defines childhood as "the period from infancy to puberty" (it is commonly agreed that infancy ends at one year of age) while puberty is "the state of physical development when sexual reproduction first becomes possible." Childhood, by definition, may span a decade or more while puberty is a theoretical point in time determined by the ability to reproduce. Like childhood, adolescence may last almost a decade and is a bridge between childhood and adulthood. Adolescence includes puberty and the years that follow until sexual maturation is complete. During this period, adult body composition characteristics and patterns of adipose tissue distribution are developing. Clearly, chronological ages cannot be used as precise points of demarcation for these developmental periods. Nevertheless, chronological age is important since there are numerous major differences between children and adolescents in body composition values and in the rates at which these values change.

Gradual changes in body composition occur throughout childhood such that, by two years of age, the proportion of ECF has dropped another 2% with an equal increase in the proportion of TBW that is intracellular. As would be expected, TBK and protein increase during this period while osseous mineral remains at the same level as at birth. By the age of five years, bone mineral has

Table 11.1 Body Composition Changes for Infants and Children

Age	Weight (kg)	Fat (%)	Components of fat-free mass			
			TBK (mEq/kg)	TBW (%FFM)	Protein (%FFM)	Mineral (%FFM)
Birth	3.5	14.0	49	80.6	15.0	3.7
1 month	4.2	15.5	50	80.5	15.1	3.7
6 month	7.7	26.0	54.5	79.5	16.0	3.7
1 year	10.1	23.0	57	79.0	16.6	3.7
5 year	18.1	15.6	63	77.0	18.2	4.0
10 year	32.0	16.5	66	76.0	19.0	4.3

Note: Averages based on Fomon et al. (1982) for boys and girls. From 6 months to 1 year, girls are lighter than boys by about 0.5 to 1.0 kg. At 5 years of age the values given for body fat and for mineral as a percentage of FFM are averages for boys and girls, but girls are about 1% fatter and have less mineral than boys at that age. At 10 years, girls are slightly heavier and almost 6% fatter than boys. See text for details regarding other components.

increased from 3.0% to 3.6% of FFM in boys, but not in girls. This appears to be the age at which differences between males and females in the bone mineral content of FFM are first observed.

Other gender differences appear in the distribution of TBW (Fomon et al., 1982). As a percentage of FFM, TBW declines slowly from the value observed at one year (79%) to about 77% by five years of age (Table 11.1). The values for TBW in Table 11.1 do not take into account the overestimation of approximately 4% when deuterium oxide distribution is used (see chapter 2). During this period, the decrease in ECF and the increase in ICF, proportionate to TBW, is larger in boys than girls. This change is indicative of a larger cell mass in the boys compared to the girls; this is supported by larger values for TBK and the protein content and density of FFM (1.078 g/cc for boys, 1.073 g/cc for girls). There are associated gender differences in the relative size of the fat mass. Even at the age of five years, % BF tends to be lower in boys (14.6%) than in girls (16.7%).

Similar changes in the various body components continue during the next five years. Increases in the gender differences between boys and girls are observed in fat mass (Chumlea et al., 1983), which continues to increase to almost 6% by the age of 10 years. Chumlea et al. also observed little or no change in % BF for girls from 10 to 18 years, although total fat mass increased at an annual rate of 1.14 kg per year. For the boys, % BF fat decreased annually by 1.15% across the age range. This decrease in % BF for boys was attributed to an annual increase in FFM of 4.38 kg per year without a large change in total fat mass. By 10 years of age, almost 20% of FFM is protein in boys while the corresponding value for girls is less than 19% (Fomon et al., 1982). The water content of FFM is about 75% and 77% for boys and girls, respectively. Boys continue to increase more rapidly than girls in ICF, osseous mineral, and TBK. Osseous mineral is 1% higher and TBK about 3 mEq/kg FFM higher for boys than girls (Fomon et al.).

Young, Sipin, and Roe (1968), in a sample of 102 girls demonstrated that from the ages of 9 and 10 years to 16 years skinfold thicknesses increased by 51% and body density decreased by 0.7%. Chumlea et al. (1983) reported annual increments from 10 to 18 years of age in % BF, fat mass, and FFM for boys and girls. The mean increments did not differ significantly between the genders for % BF, but the increments in fat mass were significantly larger in girls than in boys with an opposite gender difference in FFM. The annual increments in FFM decreased with age for girls but not for boys.

Hunt and Heald (1963) examined body constituents in adolescent boys 12 to 18 years of age. TBW was estimated by deuterium dilution and expressed as a percentage of body weight. Using regression analysis, they determined that mature hydration was attained about 11 years of age. Haschke (1983) found that TBW/weight decreased in boys at 10 to 11 years of age but then continued to increase through the age of 14 years (Table 11.2). Similarly, Boileau et al. (1984), in a study of black and white children and adults, found that TBW/weight was higher in males (61.6%) than females (55.8%) with the largest differences in the pubertal,

Table 11.2   Percentage Composition of FFM in Children and Youth

Author	Age (y)	Maturation	Ethnicity	Males TBW	Males Mineral*	Males Protein	Females TBW	Females Mineral*	Females Protein
Boileau et al., 1984		Prepubescent	Black	74.7	—	—	75.4	—	—
		Prepubescent	White	75.1	—	—	76.0	—	—
		Pubescent	Black	74.5	—	—	74.6	—	—
		Pubescent	White	75.0	—	—	74.6	—	—
		Postpubescent	Black	73.3	—	—	74.1	—	—
		Postpubescent	White	73.2	—	—	73.3	—	—
Haschke, 1983	10.5		White	75.2	4.9	19.3	74.9	5.0	19.6
	12.5		White	75.0	4.9	19.5	74.4	5.3	19.6
	14.5		White	74.5	5.0	19.8	74.0	7.0	19.7
	16.5		White	73.9	5.3	20.1	73.6	7.2	19.8
	18.5		White	73.6	5.5	20.3	73.5	7.2	19.8
Hewitt et al., 1993		Prepubescent	White	75.8	—	—	74.8	—	—
Lohman et al., 1984		Prepubescent	Black	—	5.2	—	—	5.1	—
		Prepubescent	White	—	5.2	—	—	5.2	—
		Pubescent	Black	—	5.7	—	—	5.3	—
		Pubescent	White	—	5.5	—	—	5.4	—
		Postpubescent	Black	—	6.3	—	—	5.9	—
		Postpubescent	White	—	6.2	—	—	5.7	—

*Mineral = osseous + non-osseous mineral.
Results for females were compiled from Young et al. (1968), Forbes (1987), and Haschke (1987).

postpubertal, and adult groups. Additionally, TBW/FFM decreased from prepubescence (75% boys, 76% girls) to adulthood (72% males, 73% females) by 0.38% annually, resulting in an overall decline of 2.8% in each gender.

Haschke (1983) reported that in a group of adolescents TBW decreased from about 75% FFM at 10 years to about 73% FFM at age 16 years. Other changes included a slight increase in protein, but the most notable change was an increase in mineral. More recently Hewitt et al. (1993) examined the effects of hydration level on the estimation of fat mass in children (5 to 10 years), young adults (22 to 39 years), and older adults (65 to 84 years). They used a multicomponent model that included regional bone mineral density, TBW, and body density to estimate FFM. Comparisons were made between the traditional two-component model and the multicomponent model to determine the extent to which estimates of fat mass are influenced by variation in the TBW/FFM ratio. Prepubescent children had significantly higher TBW/FFM values than the young adults; the mean values for % BF were 20% from the two-component model and 13.8% from the multicomponent model. Differences in mean % BF values for the young adults,

however, were smaller, being 14.0% to 16.4% for the two-component and multicomponent models, respectively. These authors concluded that variations in the hydration of FFM were significantly related to differences in estimates of fat mass and that prepubescent children had a significantly higher TBW/FFM ratio than did young adults.

Clearly, major changes in body composition occur during the adolescent period. These changes include a decrease in the water fraction of the FFM. There is also an increase in the calcium content of FFM that is faster than the increase in K and, therefore, suggestive of faster growth in the skeleton than in nonskeletal FFM (Forbes, 1962). The gender differences in the timing of the increases in total body calcium (TBCa) suggest that these changes are related to the timing of pubescence. Garn (1970) and Christiansen, Rödbro, and Thöger Nielson (1975) reported increases in cortical thickness and TBCa from preadolescence through adulthood, but differences between measurement techniques and in the nationality of the samples make it difficult to estimate the rate of Ca accretion during adolescence. Christiansen's data indicate that the largest increases in TBCa occurred between the ages of 11 and 12 years for the girls, a

Table 11.3 Mean Total Body Calcium in Children and Adolescents (g)

Age (y)	Males	Females
7	313	237
8	356	280
9	361	280
10	332	291
11	356	305
12	394	426
13	386	466
14	520	496
15	652	534
16	674	531
17	768	572
18	816	631
19	857	623
20	898	685

Reprinted from "Bone Mineral Content and Estimated Total Body Calcium in Normal Children and Adolescents," by C. Christiansen, P. Rödbro, and C. Thöger Nielson from *Scandinavian Journal of Clinical and Laboratory Investigations* (1975), **35**, pp. 507-510, by permission of Scandinavian University Press.

40% increase, but later for the boys with a 35% increase between the ages of 13 and 14 years (Table 11.3). Both Garn and Christiansen found markedly larger absolute amounts of Ca for boys than for girls.

Mazess and Cameron (1971), using single photon absorptiometry, measured bone mineral content (BMC) of the distal radius in 322 white children 6 to 14 years of age. There was an increase in BMC of about 8.5% per year. Because of these changes in BMC, Lohman et al. (1984) hypothesized that BMC of the distal radius and ulna would be associated with body density in children because this regional measure of mineral content probably reflected total body bone mineral. Therefore, differences in BMC might influence the density of FFM, and adjustments for this effect would reduce the errors in the densitometric estimation of fat mass. To explore this hypothesis, they made BMC measurements of the distal radius on 292 black and white males and females in four maturation groups from prepubescence to adulthood. Despite the large sample, some of the subgroups were small. Their results showed a significant interaction among gender, ethnic group, and maturation level for measurements of BMC. BMC values were larger for the males than for females; these gender differences were largest in the postpubescent and

adult groups of whites. Among blacks, the pubescent, postpubescent and adult groups differed little in the extent of the gender differences. The significant ethnic effect indicated that blacks had a greater BMC than whites by 0.054 g/cm or 6.1%. The ethnic effect was marked in the pubescent and postpubescent groups, but the black and white groups did not differ in BMC during prepubescence and adulthood. Lohman and co-workers also found that BMC measures were positively correlated with body density values. Adjusting for fat mass, about 16% of the variation in body density was explained by the variation in BMC.

Using the results of this investigation, Lohman and colleagues (1984) calculated the mineral content of the FFM as 5.27% in the prepubescent child, increasing to 6.0% in women and 6.66% in men. They also concluded that FFM in the prepubescent child contained 76.6% water and 5.4% mineral, yielding a density of 1.084 g/cc for FFM. Similar estimates were determined by Haschke (1983), using TBCa results from Christiansen et al. (1975). He concluded the osseous mineral fraction of FFM was 4.0% and the non-osseous mineral fraction was 1% for a total mineral fraction of 5%. Haschke's estimate of the water content of FFM was similar to that of Lohman et al. In children, Slaughter et al. (1990) found differences among black and white males and females in bone width (BW) and BMC. They observed larger BW in black males than in white males and slightly larger BW in black females than in white females. When the data were expressed per unit of stature, black males had larger BW/S than white males (mean difference 0.75). In females, however, an ethnic difference in BW/S was not noted. When BMC was expressed per unit of stature, black and white males had similar values (0.64 and 0.60, respectively), but black females had a significantly higher mean value than the white females (0.65 for blacks, 0.60 for whites).

There are gender differences during adolescence in the growth of FFM. According to Forbes (1987), from 10 to 20 years of age FFM increases by 33 kg in boys, but the increase in girls during the same period is only 16 kg. At 15 years of age, the male/female ratio in FFM is 1.23:1, but at 20 years of age it is 1.45:1. The increase in FFM continues for a longer period in males than in females; adult levels are reached at 18 years in females but not until about 20 years in males.

Boileau and colleagues (1984) noted that the major changes in the composition of FFM from pubescence to adulthood occur in the water and mineral portions. The data presented in Table 11.2

document these changes and show that a multi-component model is necessary in children and adolescents for the estimation of body composition from body density.

Young, Middle-Aged, and Older Adults

In 1923, Moulton suggested, primarily on the basis of animal research, that chemical maturity was reached at 4.4% of the life expectancy. Using a life expectancy of 80 years for human beings, Moulton concluded that chemical maturation was reached at about 3.5 years of age. The data discussed earlier in this chapter show this estimated age is much too young. Nonetheless, animal research can provide valuable information about the composition of mature species. For example, Pace and Rathbun (1945), using guinea pigs, determined that the water content of FFM was 72.4% and the N/FFM ratio was 3.5%. Similar results were observed in the rat, rabbit, cat, dog, and monkey.

As for the chemical growth of male human beings, Forbes (1962) observed that changes in Na, K, and water from mid-fetal life to young adulthood followed a differential curve. He calculated that in young adulthood 54% of body weight was water with 42 mEq/kg Na and 45 mEq/kg K. But this still does not answer the question: When is physical or chemical maturity attained in human beings? Brožek (1952) stated that from 20 to 55 years of age changes in body composition are slower compared with those during childhood, adolescence, or senescence. He indicated, from cross-sectional data that the notion of a "steady state" during this period was an illusion. Brožek noted that middle-aged men, ages 48 to 52 years, differed in body composition from young men, ages 23 to 29 years, in having larger values for % BF (24.0% vs 14.4%) and body weight (75.9 kg vs 70.6 kg). Men 53 to 57 years of age, however, differed little from the men aged 48 to 52 years in either % BF or body weight (25.2% and 76.0 kg). Brožek concluded that weight increments in adulthood and, therefore at a fixed stature, were associated with an increase in absolute and relative fat mass. In a cross-sectional study comparing body density in black and white males, Vickery, Cureton, and Collins (1988) found that mean body density was significantly higher in black men (1.075 g/cc) than in white men (1.065 g/cc); the mean of the sum of seven skinfolds was not significantly different between these groups, suggesting that the difference in the relationship

of skinfolds to body density in black and white men was due to variation in the composition of FFM. Roche (in press), in a review of ethnic influences on % BF, found that for the three ethnic groups compared, black men have the lowest values, Mexican-Americans intermediate levels, and whites the highest values. Because of uncertainties in sampling, there is a lack of agreement in the research literature about ethnic differences in % BF for middle-aged and older men, but Roche suggests that differences between white and black men in % BF decreases with age.

The differences in % BF between black and white girls, young women, and middle-aged women are smaller than the corresponding differences for males. Although results differ among studies, due to differences in sample characteristics and study design, it appears that % BF increases with age in women. Young et al. (1963) analyzed cross-sectional data from women 30 to 70 years of age. They found that body weight began to increase in the 40 to 50 year decade and remained stable thereafter. Until about 40 years, % BF was stable at about 28 to 29%, but by 40 to 50 years had increased to 35%. Sparling and Millard-Stafford (1990) examined differences in body density in a cross-sectional sample of black and white women, 17 to 40 years of age. The two ethnic groups had similar values for stature, weight, the sum of seven skinfolds, and selected limb girths, but significant differences were observed in body density. Black women had a higher mean density (1.0485 g/cc) than the white women (1.0435 g/cc). These data suggest the existence of ethnic differences between women in body composition.

Côté and Adams (1993), in a study of young black and white women, did not find significant differences in % BF when a multicomponent model was used; however, the black women had significantly higher BMC and BMD values than the white women. They found that in the women with the highest and lowest BMD values, % BF was substantially under- or over-predicted, respectively, by the Siri equation (1961). These authors concluded there is a wide range of BMD in young women. TBW reached a maximum at 40 to 50 years with a mean of about 30 L, after which there was a gradual decrease of about 2 L through ages 60 to 70 years. Lesser, Kumar, and Steele (1963) used inert gases and isotope tracer techniques to calculate TBW, FFM, and fat mass in a cross-sectional study of men and women aged 19 to 68 years. These investigators noted a decrease in the TBW/FFM ratio with age; the means for groups of young, middle-aged, and older men and women combined were

71.4, 70.7, and 70.5%, respectively. In addition, they noted a decrease in the ICF fraction with aging and a corresponding increase in the ECF fraction.

Mazess and Cameron (1971, 1975) measured BMC of the radius in large samples to determine average values for a variety of age groups. The radial bone mineral measurements were made at the junction of the middle and distal thirds of a line from the ulna styloid process to the olecranon. From these cross-sectional data, they concluded that BMC increases by about 8% per year until adolescence. After adolescence the rate of increase in BMC is slower in girls than in boys but continues until a peak BMC of 1000 g is attained by women at 30 to 39 years. In women aged 50 to 99 years, BMC decreases at a rate of 6 to 7% per decade. Males achieve adult mineralization by the age of 20 years with an average BMC of 1307 g, which remains constant from 50 to 60 years. A decrease in BMC in males begins between 60 and 70 years; the rate of decrease is about 10% from 70 to 85 years. These findings for the distal radius approximately parallel reported data for total body calcium (Fehling et al., 1992).

In a group of Alaskan Eskimos, Mazess and Mather (1974) found that the peak BMC for males is at a similar level and occurs at about the same age as for white males in the Mazess and Cameron studies. In male Eskimos, a decrease with a rate of about 5% per year begins at the age of 30 years, three decades sooner than for the white males. For Eskimo women, peak bone mass is achieved at about 35 years. This is later than for white women, but the values are similar. The rate of decrease, however, is more rapid in Eskimo women than in white women (13.6% vs 6%). These accelerated annual rates of BMC loss for the Eskimo women are independent of body size or bone size. The authors hypothesized that the rapid loss may be due to vitamin D deficiencies and decreased calcium absorption, reflecting effects of a long dark winter. Russell-Aulet et al. (1991) measured total body bone mineral (TBBM) in a group of Asian-American men ranging in age from 22 to 94 years. The Asian-American men had significantly lower TBBM than a comparison group of white men, but the TBBM values were similar in the two groups after adjustments were made for body weight, stature, and age.

In the late 1960s and early 1970s total body neutron activation analysis (NAA) was developed for medical research, particularly for measurements of TBCa. Since that time NAA has been extended to measure other elements. This has been a major advancement in body composition assessment. An investigation by Cohn et al. (1976) included the measurement of TBCa and total body phosphorus (TBP) in 39 men and 40 women ranging in age from 20 to 89 years (Tables 11.4 and 11.5). In addition, total body potassium (TBK) was measured by natural gamma radiation. The TBCa and TBK values were used to calculate lean body mass (LBM) and body cell mass (BCM). These investigators examined the elemental data based on parameters such as age, gender, and body size and expressed the results as ratios measured/normal (standard) values for the respective elements. These cross-sectional data suggest that the peak TBCa and TBK values for women are achieved between 40 and 49 years of age while the corresponding peak values for the men are attained between 30 and 39 years. These data clearly demonstrate a loss in TBCa and TBK for men and women with age. The TBCa/TBK ratio remains constant across all age groups, indicating that for women and men up to 70 years of age calcium and potassium are lost proportionally. In men older than 70 years, the TBCa/TBK ratio is higher, indicating a greater loss of muscle mass than of bone mineral content.

Individual variability for TBCa and TBK, in absolute terms, is large for all age groups and for men and women. The coefficients of variation for each age group of women range from about 8.5% to 9.8% for those younger than 70 years but are 6.2% for those older than 70 years. Variability among groups of men ranges from 5.4% to 9.0% between 30 to 69 years of age. Men older than 70 years have a coefficient of variation greater than 11%, which is about twice that of the women.

Cohn and colleagues (1980), in a cross-sectional study of 72 men and 62 women, demonstrated age-related changes in muscle mass and its protein content. They measured total body nitrogen (TBN) and TBCa by NAA, obtained TBK from total body counting, and calculated TBW from tritium dilution. Fat mass was calculated as the difference between body weight and the sum of the measured elements or calculated components. Cohn observed that, for men, skeletal muscle mass was 45% less for the age group 70 to 79 years than for the group aged 20 to 29 years. The means were 13.3 kg and 24.2 kg, respectively. The nonmuscle lean mass, mainly vital organs, did not change with age; total body protein (TBP) decreased 17% between 20 and 79 years of age. Based on TBW and TBK measurements, they estimated that BCM decreased in men by 23% between the group aged 20 to 29 years and the group aged 70 to 79 years. In similar fashion, the total body bone mineral

Table 11.4   Changes With Age in Body Composition of Men (White U.S. Unless Otherwise Noted)

Author	Age (y)	TBW (L)	TBN (g)	TBCa (g)	TBK (g)	LBM (kg)	BCM (kg)
Cohn et al., 1980, 1985	20-29	46.9	2060	1220	155	63.3	46.4
	30-39	41.0	1880	1135	139	56.7	31.1
	40-49	44.7	1950	1119	141	63.3	36.6
	50-59	45.2	1900	1083	131	58.5	32.7
	60-69	41.0	1910	1093	130	57.2	30.8
	70-79	43.0	1780	1093	112	55.8	29.2
	80-89	—	—	1006	94	—	—
Ellis et al., 1982	20-29	—	2023	—	155	—	—
	30-39	—	1813	—	139	—	—
	40-49	—	1825	—	140	—	—
	50-59	—	1818	—	141	—	—
	60-69	—	1696	—	130	—	—
	70-79	—	1549	—	118	—	—
Fehling et al., 1992	18-29	—	—	2978*	—	—	—
	30-39	—	—	2839*	—	—	—
	40-49	—	—	2846*	—	—	—
	50-59	—	—	2876*	—	—	—
	60-69	—	—	3022*	—	—	—
	70-80	—	—	2821*	—	—	—
Russell-Aulet et al., 1991	22-94	—	—	3040*	—	—	—
Asian-American	20-81	—	—	2697*	—	—	—

Abbreviations: BCM, body cell mass; LBM, lean body mass; TBN, total body nitrogen; TBCa, total body calcium; TBK, total body potassium; TBW, total body water.

*TBBM from dual photon absorptiometry.

(TBBM) decreased about 10% from 25 to 75 years (5.87 kg to 5.30 kg). During this same age range, % BF increased in men from 18.1 to 29.9%.

In the women studied by Cohn et al. (1980), TBK and TBN decreased between 30 and 80 years of age for a total loss of about 25% in these elements. Muscle mass for these women at 20 to 29 years was less than 50% of that for men the same age (9.9 kg) and decreased to 5.9 kg by the age of 79 years. Similarly, nonmuscle mass was lower in the women than in the men (32 kg vs 37 kg) and decreased about 15% between 30 and 80 years of age. TBBM was smaller (4.44 kg vs 5.87 kg) in the women than in the men at 20 to 29 years. These cross-sectional data indicate that, in women, after age 20 to 29 years, TBBM decreases 28% from a mean of 4.44 kg to 3.2 kg. Cohn and co-workers (1980) have clearly demonstrated gender and age differences in the body composition of adults and that muscle mass is particularly susceptible to the aging process. These studies are limited because of the small number of subjects in each age group, especially at older ages.

Some of these estimates have been questioned by Heymsfield et al. (1991), and they are considerably lower than those reported by Fehling et al. (1992).

Ellis et al. (1982) have also used NAA techniques for elemental and component analysis of the body. In 136 healthy adults studied cross-sectionally, these authors determined that TBN decreases during a 50 year age range by 21% in women and 14% in men while TBK decreases about 25% in each gender. These data were adjusted for age, gender, and body size and then compared with corresponding data from cancer patients and obese individuals. In comparison with the healthy subjects, the mean TBN was 10% less for the cancer patients but was the same or slightly higher for obese individuals.

Cohn et al. (1985), from a cross-sectional study of 123 healthy adults, concluded that FFM decreases between 20 and 79 years of age by about 12% and 19% for men and women, respectively. There are associated decreases in TBCa of 11% and 26% and in BCM of 19% and 24% for men

Table 11.5   Changes With Age in Body Composition of White U.S. Women

Author	Age (y)	TBW (L)	TBN (g)	TBCa (g)	TBK (g)	LBM (kg)	BCM (kg)
Cohn et al., 1980, 1985	20-29	32.2	2450	924	95	45.5	24.3
	30-39	33.1	1430	848	88	45.8	23.9
	40-49	31.5	1360	870	90	42.9	21.9
	50-59	32.0	1270	804	85	42.6	22.3
	60-69	28.5	1200	715	75	38.2	19.1
	70-79	26.6	1150	655	70	37.0	18.6
Ellis et al., 1982	20-29	—	1454	—	95	—	—
	30-39	—	1402	—	100	—	—
	40-49	—	1339	—	91	—	—
	50-59	—	1243	—	90	—	—
	60-69	—	1145	—	76	—	—
	70-79	—	1089	—	73	—	—
Fehling et al., 1992	18-29	—	—	2269*	—	—	—
	30-39	—	—	2274*	—	—	—
	40-49	—	—	2406*	—	—	—
	50-59	—	—	2268*	—	—	—
	60-69	—	—	2057*	—	—	—
	70-80	—	—	1901*	—	—	—

Abbreviations: BCM, body cell mass; LBM, lean body mass; TBN, total body nitrogen; TBCa, total body calcium; TBK, total body potassium; TBW, total body water.
*TBBM from dual photon absorptiometry.

and women, respectively. Total body water also decreases with age by about 6 L for each gender; this is equivalent to a decrease of 17% in men and 12% in women. Body weight was smaller in the older age groups; mean peak weight for men was in the 40 to 49 year group at about 85 kg and decreased to about 80 kg for the 70 to 79 year age group. For the women, peak weight was attained a decade earlier in the 30 to 39 year group at about 69 kg, and mean weight decreased to about 58 kg by the age of 79 years. This represents a 5% decrease in weight for men but a decrease of 15% for women.

Baumgartner et al. (1991) demonstrated a change in TBW in elderly people. In a cross-sectional study of men and women aged 65 to 94 years, these authors found that significant differences in FFM and % BF using a four-component model versus values from the Siri two-component model. The estimates of % BF from the four-component model were less than those obtained from the Siri equation. The authors measured TBW and TBBM and determined that the differences in the estimates of % BF were due to the variation in the hydration of FFM, whereas the mineral fraction of FFM did not have a significant impact on the differences

between paired estimates. Schoeller (1989) concluded from a literature review that TBW decreases with age. The decrease in women is small until 60 years but then is rapid. For men, however, the decrease in TBW starts in middle-age and continues through old age. Schoeller found that despite the decrease in TBW, the average hydration of FFM remained constant, indicating a decrease in FFM with age.

In summary, adults, like children and adolescents, change in body composition, but the changes during adulthood are slower. Some of these changes affect the composition of FFM and thereby alter its density. There is a lack of research literature concerning assessments of body composition by multiple component models among ethnic groups. As noted in chapter 12, there are data for regional measurements, such as skinfold thicknesses, from white, black, and Hispanic Americans and from studies of ethnic groups in other countries, but more investigations of total body composition in these groups are needed. Most of our knowledge of changes in total body composition has been inferred from cross-sectional data, which can show the mean changes but not individual variation.

References

Baumgartner, R.N., Heymsfield, S.B., Lichtman, S., et al. (1991). Body composition in elderly people: Effect of criterion estimates on predictive equations. *American Journal of Clinical Nutrition, 53*, 1345-1353.

Boileau, R.A., Lohman, T.G., Slaughter, M.H., et al. (1984). Hydration of the fat-free body in children during maturation. *Human Biology, 56*, 651-666.

Brožek, J. (1952). Changes of body composition in man during maturity and their nutritional implications. *Federation Proceedings, 11*, 784-793.

Christiansen, C., Rödbro, P., Thöger Nielson, C. (1975). Bone mineral content and estimated total body calcium in normal children and adolescents. *Scandanavian Journal of Clinical and Laboratory Investigations, 35*, 507-510.

Chumlea, W.C., Siervogel, R.M., Roche, A.F., et al. (1983). Increments across age in body composition for children 10-18 years of age. *Human Biology, 55*, 845-852.

Cohn, S.H., Vartsky, D., Yasumura, S., et al. (1980). Compartmental body composition based on total-body nitrogen, potassium, and calcium. *American Journal of Physiology, 239*, E524-E530.

Cohn, S.H., Vaswani, A., Yasumura, S., et al. (1985). Assessment of cellular mass and lean body mass by noninvasive nuclear techniques. *Journal of Laboratory and Clinical Medicine, 105*, 305-311.

Cohn, S.H., Vaswani, A., Zanzi, I., et al. (1976). Changes in body chemical composition with age measured by total-body neutron activation. *Metabolism, 25*, 85-95.

Côté, K.D., & Adams, W.C. (1993). Effect of bone density on body composition estimates in young adult black and white women. *Medicine and Science in Sports and Exercise, 25*, 290-296.

Dickerson, J.W.T., & Widdowson, E.M. (1960). Chemical changes in skeletal muscle during development. *Biochemical Journal, 74*, 247-257.

Ellis, K.J., Yasumura, S., Vartsky, D., et al. (1982). Total body nitrogen in health and disease: Effects of age, weight, height, and sex. *Journal of Laboratory and Clinical Medicine, 99*, 917-926.

Fehling, P.C., Stillman, R.J., Boileau, R.A., et al. (1992). Total body bone mineral content and density in males and females aged 10-80 years. *Medicine and Science in Sports and Exercise, 24*, S11.

Fomon, S.J. (1967). Body composition of the male reference infant during the first year of life. *Pediatrics, 40*, 863-870.

Fomon, S.J., Haschke, F., Ziegler, E.E., et al. (1982). Body composition of reference children from birth to age 10 years. *American Journal of Clinical Nutrition, 35*, 1169-1175.

Forbes, G.B. (1962). Methods for determining composition of the human body. *Pediatrics, 29*, 477-494.

Forbes, G.B. (1987). *Human body composition: Growth, aging, nutrition, and physical activity.* New York: Springer-Verlag.

Friis-Hansen, B. (1961). Body water compartments in children: Changes during growth and related changes in body composition. *Pediatrics, 28*, 169-181.

Garn, S.M. (1970). *The early gain and later loss of cortical bone in nutritional perspective.* Springfield, IL: Charles C. Thomas.

Guo, S., Roche, A.F., Fomon, S.J., et al. (1991). Reference data on gains in weight and length during the first two years of life. *Journal of Pediatrics, 119*, 355-362.

Haschke, F. (1983). Body composition of adolescent males. Part I: Total body water in normal adolescent males. Part II: Body composition of the male reference adolescent. *Acta Pediatrica Scandanavica, Suppl. 307*, 1-23.

Haschke, F. (1987). Body composition during adolescence. In N.W. J. Klish & N. Kretchmer (Eds.), *Body composition measurements in infants and children* (pp. 76-83). Report of the 98th Ross Conference. Columbus, OH: Ross Laboratories.

Hewitt, M.J., Going, S.B., Williams, D.P., et al. (1993). Hydration of fat-free body mass in children and adults: Implications for body composition assessment. *American Journal of Physiology, 265*, E88-E95.

Heymsfield, S.B., Waki, M., Kehayias, J., et al. (1991). Chemical and elemental analysis of humans in vivo using improved body composition models. *American Journal of Physiology, 261*, E190-E198.

Hunt, E.E., & Heald, F.P. (1963). Physique, body composition, and sexual maturation in adolescent boys. *Annals of the New York Academy of Science, 110*, 532-544.

Lesser, G.T., Kumar, I., Steele, J.M. (1963). Changes in body composition with age. *Annals of the New York Academy of Science, 110*, 576-588.

Lohman, T.G., Slaughter, M.H., Boileau, R.A., et al. (1984). Bone mineral measurements and their relation to body density in children, youth and adults. *Human Biology, 56*, 667-679.

Maresh, M., & Groome, D.S. (1966). Potassium-40: Serial determinations in infants. *Pediatrics, 38*, 642-646.

Mazess, R.B., & Cameron, J.R. (1971). Skeletal growth in school children: Maturation and bone mass. *American Journal of Physical Anthropology,* **35**, 399-408.

Mazess, R.B., & Cameron, J.R. (1975). Bone mineral content in normal U.S. whites. In R.B. Mazess (Ed.), *International conference on bone mineral measurement* (NIH Publication No. 75-863, pp. 228-238). Washington, DC: Government Printing Office.

Mazess, R.B., & Mather, W. (1974). Bone mineral content of North American Eskimos. *American Journal of Clinical Nutrition, 27,* 916-925.

Moulton, C.R. (1923). Age and chemical development in mammals. *Journal of Biological Science,* **57**, 79-97.

Novak, L.P., Hamamoto, K., Orvis, A.L., et al. (1970). Total body potassium in infants. *American Journal of Diseases in Children,* **119**, 419-423.

Pace, N., & Rathbun, E.N. (1945). Studies on body composition, III: The body water and chemically combined nitrogen content in relation to fat content. *Journal of Biological Chemistry,* **158**, 685-691.

Roche, A.F. (In press). Body composition of ethnic groups in the U.S. *Asia Pacific Journal of Clinical Nutrition.*

Russell-Aulet, M., Wang, J., Thornton, J., et al. (1991). Bone mineral density and mass by total-body dual-photon absorptiometry in normal white and Asian men. *Journal of Bone Mineral Research,* **6**, 1109-1113.

Schoeller, D.A. (1989). Changes in total body water with age. *American Journal of Clinical Nutrition,* **50**, 1176-1181.

Siri, W.E. (1961) Body composition from fluid spaces and density. In J. Brožek & A. Henschel (Eds.), *Techniques for measuring body composition* (pp. 223-244). Washington, DC: National Academy of Sciences.

Slaughter, M.H., Lohman, T.G., Boileau, R.A., et al. (1990). Differences in the subcomponents of fat-free body in relation to height between black and white children. *American Journal of Human Biology,* **2**, 209-217.

Sparling, P.B., & Millard-Stafford, M. (1990). Higher body density in black women. *Medicine and Science in Sports and Exercise,* **22**, S127.

Vernadakis, A., & Woodbury, D.M. (1964). Electrolyte and nitrogen changes in skeletal muscle of developing rats. *American Journal of Physiology,* **206**, 1365-1368.

Vickery, S.R., Cureton, K.J., & Collins, M.A. (1988). Prediction of body density from skinfolds in black and white young men. *Human Biology,* **60**, 135-149.

Widdowson, E.M. (1981). The demands of the fetal and maternal tissues for nutrients, and the bearing of these on the needs of mothers to "eat for two." In J. Dobbing (Ed.), *Maternal nutrition and pregnancy: Eating for two?* (pp. 1-41). New York: Academic.

Widdowson, E.M., & Dickerson, J.W.T. (1964). Chemical composition of the body. In C.L. Comar & F. Bronner (Eds.), *Mineral metabolism (2), Part A* (pp. 2-247). New York: Academic.

Young, C.M., Blondin, J., Tensuan, R., et al. (1963). Body composition studies of "older" women, thirty to seventy years of age. *Annals of the New York Academy of Science,* **110**, 589-607.

Young, C.M., Sipin, S.S., & Roe, D.A. (1968). Body composition of pre-adolescent and adolescent girls, I: Density and skinfolds. *Journal of the American Dietetic Association,* **53**, 25-31.

12

Regional Body Composition: Age, Sex, and Ethnic Variation

Robert M. Malina

Regional body composition refers to variation in the anatomical distribution of the major components of the body mass—adipose, skeletal muscle, and skeletal tissues. The term *distribution* refers to the absolute or relative amount of a tissue in different regions or compartments of the body. The term *patterning* is also used in discussions of regional body composition. It is ordinarily used in a relative sense to characterize a specific pattern of tissue distribution. For example, a relatively greater accumulation of subcutaneous adipose tissue on the trunk compared to the extremities is often described as a central or truncal pattern; a relatively greater accumulation of adipose tissue over the abdomen compared to that over the hips is described as an android pattern, while the reverse is labeled a gynoid pattern.

Understanding of regional variation in body composition must be set in the context of gross body composition, in which the body mass is often partitioned into fat-free mass (FFM) and fat mass (FM). Gross estimates of FFM and FM indicate little about the anatomical distribution or regional development of adipose, skeletal muscle, and skeletal tissues. All three are characterized by sig-

nificant variation associated with age, sex, and ethnicity. Individual differences in the timing and tempo of sexual maturation and the growth spurt are additional sources of variation.

Most of the emphasis in the study of regional body composition has focused on the distribution of adipose and skeletal tissues primarily in a clinical context. Abdominal fatness is often indicated as a significant determinant of the relationship between obesity and morbidity and as an independent risk factor for several degenerative diseases of adulthood, most notably some cardiovascular diseases and non-insulin-dependent diabetes (Bouchard, Després, & Mauriege, 1993; Vague et al., 1988). Ethnic variation in the amount and distribution of bone mineral suggests local metabolic differences and is implicated as a significant factor in the etiology of hip fractures (Malina, 1973; Pollitzer & Anderson, 1989). Population differences in body proportions and physique imply differences in the absolute and relative distributions of the underlying tissues. Thus, knowledge of age-, sex-, maturity-, and ethnicity-associated variation in regional body composition should contribute to the understanding of human variability. A major portion of the variability in body composition has its origins during the years of growth and maturation.

Adipose Tissue

Adipose tissue can be differentiated into that which is visceral (internal or deep) and that which is subcutaneous (external or outer). Information on the contribution of visceral adipose tissue (VAT) and subcutaneous adipose tissue (SAT) to FM during growth is limited, while that on changes during adulthood and with aging is more available. Most of the literature on age, sex, and ethnic variation in adipose tissue distribution is based upon skinfold thicknesses, usually in terms of the relative sizes of trunk (central) versus extremity (peripheral) skinfold thicknesses.

There is no consensus as to which methods best define and describe adipose tissue distribution. For example, Reynolds (1950) used measures of SAT thicknesses at six trunk (T) and extremity (E) sites on standardized radiographs. From age 6 to 17 years, the relative contribution of T SAT thicknesses to the sum of six SAT thicknesses increased, and the increase was greater in males than in females. Hammond (1955) analyzed several skinfold thicknesses in children and youth 2 to 18 years and identified a factor which differentiated T and E skinfold thicknesses. In addition, he reported different age-associated changes in E and T skinfold thicknesses during adolescence in males but not in females.

Subsequently, two major approaches have been used to describe changes in relative SAT distribution through the life cycle: principal components analysis of skinfold thicknesses, and ratios of skinfold thicknesses and/or circumferences. After controlling for the overall amount of SAT through the use of residuals of the regression of specific skinfold thicknesses on the mean skinfold thickness (usually log-transformed), the resulting principal components distinguish between T and E skinfold thicknesses, or between upper and lower T, or arm and leg, or upper and lower body, depending upon the skinfold thicknesses included in the analysis (Baumgartner et al., 1986, 1990; Deutsch, Mueller, & Malina, 1985; Mueller, 1982).

Ratios of skinfold thicknesses at various T and E sites also describe relative adipose tissue distribution. The use of several T and E skinfold thicknesses provides a better overall differentiation of

SAT distribution than a measurement at single T and E sites. The ratio of waist-to-hip circumferences (WHR) is widely used to differentiate a central (high WHR, upper body, android) and peripheral (low WHR, lower body, gynoid) distribution of adipose tissue. Although ratios have limitations (e.g., they assume linear relationships), they are relatively simple and are useful in surveys.

As described in detail in chapter 8, computerized tomography (CT) is the primary tool in the study of VAT and SAT, most often in the abdominal region. Since it requires a radiation dose, application of CT procedures to large samples and to clinically normal children is unlikely. Limited data based upon magnetic resonance imaging (MRI) provide some information on VAT and SAT in children and youth.

Age and Sex Differences

Changes in the ratio of T to E skinfold thicknesses (T/E ratio) from one month to 21 years are summarized in Figure 12.1. The ratio is based upon the sums of the subscapular and suprailiac (T) and of the triceps and biceps (E) skinfold thicknesses for a mixed-longitudinal French sample (Rolland-Cachera et al., 1990). Shortly after birth, infants have almost equal thicknesses of SAT on the T and E (i.e., the ratio is about 1.0). Subsequently, the ratio decreases through early childhood, reaching a low point at about 5 years. This suggests proportionally greater accumulation of SAT on the E than on the T. The sex difference in the ratio is negligible. After 5 years, the ratio increases gradually to 13 years in each sex, and the difference between the sexes is small. During adolescence and into young adulthood, males gain proportionally more SAT on the T than E, while females gain relatively similar amounts of SAT on the T and E. The increasing ratio in males is a function of a reduction in the thickness of E skinfolds and an increase in the thickness of T skinfolds during the growth spurt (see later). Qualitatively similar age- and sex-associated trends are apparent in T/E ratios calculated from half-yearly medians for five T and five E skinfolds for a mixed-longitudinal sample of children and youth 4 to 18 years of age from the Denver area enrolled in the Child Research Council growth study (Malina & Bouchard, 1988, 1991).

T/E ratios based on the sums of the subscapular, suprailiac, and abdominal skinfold thicknesses (T) and of the triceps, biceps, and medial calf skinfold thicknesses (E) for a cross-sectional sample from the Quebec area, of French Canadian ancestry, 9

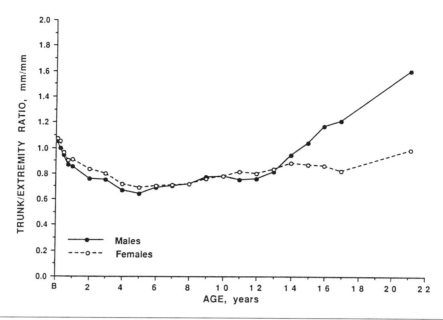

Figure 12.1 Trunk/extremity ratios [(subscapular + suprailiac)/(triceps + biceps skinfold thicknesses)] in French infants, children, adolescents, and young adults. Drawn from data reported by Rolland-Cachera et al. (1990).

to 60 years, are shown in Figure 12.2. The decrease in E skinfold thicknesses during adolescence in males is clear. After young adulthood, T skinfold thicknesses increase more than E skinfold thicknesses in males, while both T and E skinfold thicknesses increase by similar amounts through the fourth decade in females; subsequently, T increases more than E in females (Figure 12.2a & b). The T/E ratio (Figure 12.2c) does not differ between the sexes from late childhood into early adolescence; subsequently, the ratio is rather stable in females, but increases considerably in males during adolescence and more slowly through the fifth decade. Thus, males have proportionally more SAT on the T than E during adolescence and into adulthood.

Longitudinal data on the tracking of various T/E ratios or indices during childhood and adolescence are not extensive and are limited to samples of European (White) ancestry. Interage correlations for annual intervals between 2 and 18 years for the T/E component derived from a principal components analysis of four skinfold thicknesses (subscapular, suprailiac, triceps, biceps) of participants in the London Longitudinal Growth Study vary between the sexes. Correlations increase gradually with age in boys from 2 to 12 years, from < 0.2 to 0.6; they decline during adolescence (12 to 15 years) and then increase. Interage correlations for the T/E component are higher in girls, about 0.4 to 0.6, and increase only slightly with age (Kaplowitz et al., 1988). A similar pattern of low to moderate

interage correlations for two ratios (subscapular/triceps, suprailiac/triceps) at 14 years of age and earlier ages (beginning at age 4) is apparent in data from the Melbourne Growth Study (Baumgartner & Roche, 1988). Most of the correlations vary between 0.2 and 0.4. In the Leuven Growth Study of Belgian Boys, correlations between data at annual intervals for a T/E component derived from principal components analysis (triceps, subscapular, suprailiac, and medial calf skinfold thicknesses) approximate 0.1 between 13 and 18 years of age (Beunen et al., 1986).

The tracking of SAT distribution from childhood into adolescence is thus moderate at best. SAT distribution changes during sexual maturation and the growth spurt, particularly in males. The instability of the T/E component during male adolescence indicates that the relative distribution of SAT changes significantly in individual boys at this time (Roche & Baumgartner, 1988) and probably relates to variation in individual skinfold thicknesses.

Information on the tracking of SAT distribution in adults is limited. Correlations from one study are generally similar to those observed in children and youth. Interage correlations for the T/E ratio (subscapular + abdominal)/(triceps + biceps skinfold thicknesses) are 0.32 and 0.36 across 23 years in men seen initially at 42 to 50 and 51 to 62 years, respectively (Carmelli, McElroy, & Rosenman, 1991).

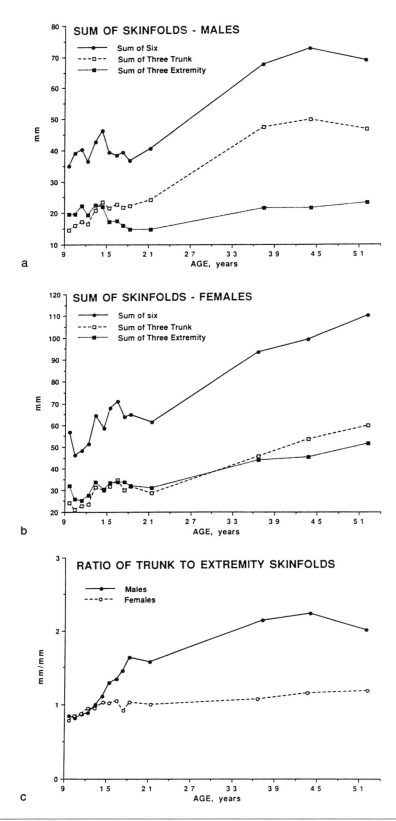

Figure 12.2   Trunk/extremity ratios [(subscapular + suprailiac + abdominal)/(triceps + biceps + medial calf skin-fold thicknesses)] in French Canadian children, adolescents, and adults: (a) sums of skinfold thicknesses in males, (b) sums of skinfold thicknesses in females, and (c) T/E ratio (Malina & Bouchard, 1988 and 1992).

Ethnic Variation

Data for a variety of T and E skinfold thicknesses for representative samples from different ethnic groups are not available. T/E ratios based on the subscapular (T) and triceps (E) skinfold thicknesses in Americans of European (White), African (Black), and Mexican (Mex Am) ancestry are shown in Figures 12.3 and 12.4 for males and females, respectively. The data are derived from the second Health and Nutrition Examination Survey (HANES II) and the Hispanic Health and Nutrition Examination Survey (HHANES), and the ratios were calculated from age- and sex-specific medians (Najjar & Kuczmarski, 1989; Najjar & Rowland, 1987; Ryan et al., 1990). The use of only two skinfold thicknesses provides, however, a limited view of relative SAT distribution. This ratio is also fat-dependent to some extent in children 6 to 10 years and adults (Garn, Ryan, & Robson, 1982); therefore, the median skinfold thicknesses are also indicated in the figures.

Among males, the T/E ratio does not consistently differ between White and Mexican American children and adolescents. Subsequently, it is consistently larger in Mexican Americans through adulthood. In contrast, the ratio is slightly but consistently larger in American Blacks during childhood and adolescence. It is also larger in Blacks than in Whites during adulthood, but slightly smaller in Blacks than Mexican Americans from the third through fifth decades (Figure 12.3a). The ratio decreases in all three groups of males in the seventh decade. This suggests that, among males, American Blacks have proportionally more SAT on the T than E during childhood through young adulthood than Whites and Mexican Americans. This is mainly due to the absolutely thinner triceps skinfold thicknesses in Blacks from childhood through the fourth decade (Figure 12.3b). In contrast, the subscapular skinfold thickness does not differ consistently among the three groups of males during childhood and adolescence (Figure 12.3c). During adolescence and through the fourth decade, however, Mexican American males gain more at the subscapular site, thus contributing to the large T/E ratio in this group. In the sixth and seventh decades, the triceps and subscapular skinfold thicknesses decrease more in Blacks and do not consistently differ between Mexican Americans and Whites. The T/E ratio is thus, on average, consistently larger in Black and Mexican American males than in White males throughout adulthood.

Beginning in late childhood and continuing through adulthood, the T/E ratio based on the subscapular and triceps skinfold thicknesses is similar in Black and Mexican American females, and the ratios for each of these groups are larger than those for White females (Figure 12.4a). During childhood and adolescence, the larger T/E ratio in Black girls is due to a smaller triceps skinfold thickness, as in males, while the larger T/E ratio in Mexican American girls is due to larger subscapular skinfold thicknesses after about 9 years of age (Figure 12.4b and 12.4c). Thus, Black girls and Mexican American girls have proportionally more SAT on the T than E compared to White girls. During adulthood, Black women and Mexican American women increase in both skinfold thicknesses more than White women, and these increases are larger at the subscapular site than at the triceps site. Hence, the T/E ratio is consistently larger in women from these two ethnic groups, indicating proportionally more SAT on the T.

Results of a principal components analysis of four skinfold thicknesses (triceps, subscapular, suprailiac, medial calf) in girls 12 to 17 years of age, of the San Diego area, from four ethnic groups (Mexican, $n = 327$; European [White], $n = 81$; Asian, $n = 63$; and African [Black], $n = 27$) are summarized in Figure 12.5. The first principal component, which differentiates between T and E skinfold thicknesses, differs significantly among the four groups and indicates a more central pattern of SAT distribution in adolescent girls of Asian or Mexican ancestry compared to those of European or African ancestry (Figure 12.5a). The same trend is apparent in the T/E ratio based on the sums of the two T and two E skinfold thicknesses (Figure 12.5b). The ratio is significantly larger in the girls of Asian ancestry than in those of Mexican, African, or European ancestry. The second and third principal components in this sample differentiate between upper and lower E skinfold thicknesses and between skinfold thicknesses on the upper (subscapular) and lower (suprailiac) trunk. The second component does not differ among the four ethnic groups, but the third component suggests greater lower trunk SAT in those of Asian, African, or Mexican American descent compared to White adolescent girls. Generally similar results are apparent in other principal components analyses of Black, White, and Mexican adolescent females (Mueller, Shoup, & Malina, 1982) and of young Japanese women (Hattori, 1987).

Using bivariate plots of median skinfold thicknesses, Mueller (1988) demonstrated similar patterns of ethnic variation in SAT distribution—that is, a more central distribution of SAT in American

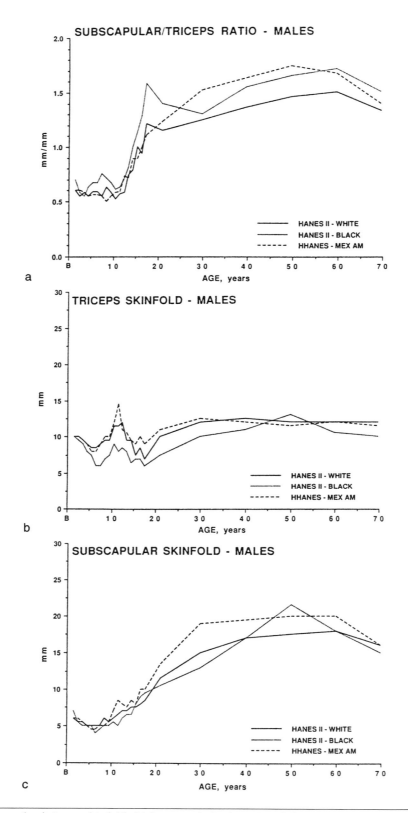

Figure 12.3 Subscapular/triceps skinfold thickness ratio in American White, American Black, and Mexican American males: (a) ratio, (b) triceps skinfold, and (c) subscapular skinfold. Calculated from data reported in the second Health and Nutrition Examination Survey (HANES II) by Najjar & Kuczmarski (1989), and Najjar & Rowland (1987), and in the Hispanic Health and Nutrition Examination Survey (HHANES) by Ryan et al. (1990).

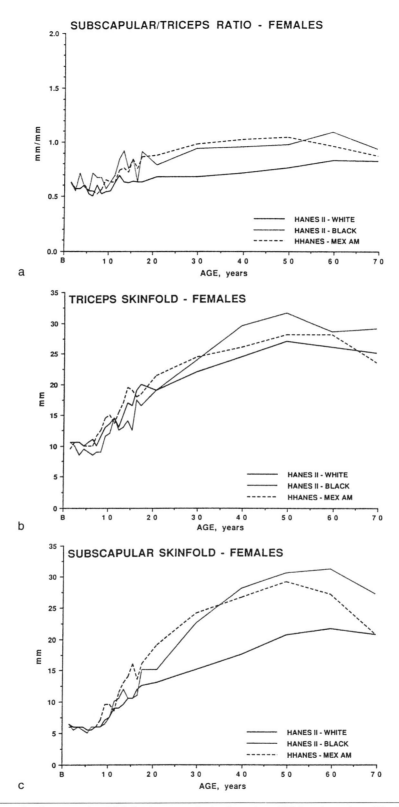

Figure 12.4 Subscapular/triceps skinfold thickness ratio in American White, American Black, and Mexican American females: (a) ratio, (b) triceps skinfold, and (c) subscapular skinfold. Calculated from data reported in the second Health and Nutrition Examination Survey (HANES II) by Najjar & Kuczmarski (1989), and Najjar & Rowland (1987), and in the Hispanic Health and Nutrition Examination Survey (HHANES) by Ryan et al. (1990).

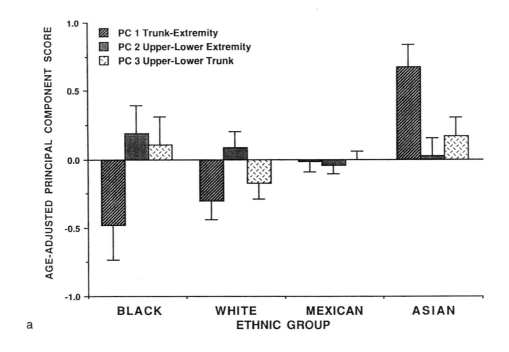

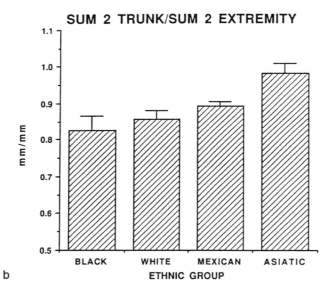

Figure 12.5 Subcutaneous adipose tissue distribution in adolescent girls from four ethnic groups: (a) age-adjusted principal component scores based on an analysis of four skinfold thicknesses (triceps, subscapular, suprailiac, medial calf); (b) trunk/extremity ratio [(subscapular + suprailiac)/(triceps + medial calf skinfold thicknesses)]. Malina, Huang, & Brown, 1995.

children and youth of Black, Mexican, and Japanese ancestry compared to American Whites, who had a more peripheral pattern. In a principal components analysis of nine skinfold thicknesses in American Blacks and Whites 6 to 30 years of age, controlling for stage of sexual maturation, Baumgartner et al. (1986) noted a tendency to accumulate proportionally more SAT on the T during sexual

maturation in males of both ethnic groups but not in females, and for Black males and females, respectively, to have a more central distribution of SAT than White males and females.

Similar trends are apparent in Mexican American and White adults from San Antonio (Table 12.1). Three T/E ratios of skinfold thicknesses are considered:

Table 12.1 Three Trunk/Extremity Skinfold Ratios (mm/mm) in American Whites and Mexicans in San Antonio, Texas

Age (y)	Mexican Americans			American Whites		
	n	M	SD	n	M	SD
Ratio 1: subscapular/triceps						
Men						
25-34	236	1.75	0.52	90	1.52	0.58
35-44	208	1.96	0.68	115	1.63	0.52
45-54	144	1.85	0.54	88	1.77	0.68
55-69	123	1.83	0.60	79	1.74	0.58
Women						
25-34	288	1.18	0.30	115	0.96	0.31
35-44	292	1.18	0.31	158	0.94	0.30
45-54	215	1.15	0.27	89	0.95	0.27
55-69	157	1.13	0.33	86	0.96	0.31
Ratio 2: (subscapular + suprailiac)/(triceps + biceps)						
Men						
25-34		2.16	0.54		2.00	0.64
35-44		2.37	0.64		2.11	0.56
45-54		2.27	0.62		2.22	0.61
55-69		2.20	0.62		2.24	0.57
Women						
25-34		1.54	0.34		1.39	0.39
35-44		1.55	0.35		1.38	0.35
45-54		1.55	0.35		1.44	0.37
55-69		1.52	0.39		1.43	0.42
Ratio 3: (subscapular + suprailiac)/(triceps + medial calf)						
Men						
25-34		1.88	0.50		1.69	0.55
35-44		2.09	0.54		1.80	0.49
45-54		2.05	0.57		1.98	0.63
55-69		2.01	0.65		2.00	0.60
Women						
25-34		1.31	0.29		1.12	0.35
35-44		1.35	0.34		1.13	0.35
45-54		1.38	0.34		1.19	0.32
55-69		1.34	0.33		1.20	0.40

Malina and Stern (1992).

- subscapular/triceps,
- (subscapular + suprailiac)/(triceps + biceps), and
- (subscapular + suprailiac)/(triceps + medial calf).

The three ratios are consistently higher in Mexican Americans, except in the oldest age group of males, which shows variation by ratio. The ethnic difference is greater in females than in males due especially to larger trunk skinfold thicknesses in Mexican American women. Moreover, the standard deviations of the three ratios are greater in males than in females within each ethnic group but do not consistently differ between ethnic groups within each sex.

Waist/Hip Ratio

The ratio between waist circumference and hip circumference is often used as an index of the distribution of adipose tissue, although this ratio is influenced by some other body tissues.

Age and Sex Differences

The utility of the waist/hip ratio (WHR) as an indicator of relative adipose tissue distribution in children and youth is not established, but it is useful in adults. Percentiles for the WHR in a large French sample (8,646 males; 9,747 females) 17 to 60 years of age (Tichet et al., 1993) and a large Danish sample (1,527 males; 1,467 females) 35 to 65 years of age (Heitmann, 1991) are shown in Figure 12.6. The overlap between the sexes is only 33% in the French sample. Medians in both samples are similar among males. In French females the medians and extreme percentiles increase gradually with age; in contrast, the medians and 10th percentiles in Danish women are rather constant from 35 to 65 years. At each age the corresponding percentiles are larger in males than in females.

WHRs of middle-aged women are influenced by menopausal status. Mean ratios change slightly from premenopause (0.73 ± 0.05, $n = 550$, 43.4 ± 3.9 years) to perimenopause (0.74 ± 0.06, $n = 168$, 49.2 ± 3.8 years) but increase significantly after menopause (0.78 ± 0.06, $n = 1133$, 58.6 ± 4.7 years) (Sonnenschein, Kim, Pasternack, & Toniolo, 1993).

An elevated WHR is usually accepted as an indication of proportionally more abdominal adipose tissue, but the accuracy of the WHR in distinguishing abdominal VAT from SAT needs further study. In obese individuals, changes in VAT after weight loss are not related to changes in the WHR (van der Kooy et al., 1993).

Ethnic Variation

Mean WHRs do not differ consistently among American White, Hispanic, and Asian adolescent girls from northern California, 10 to 16 years of

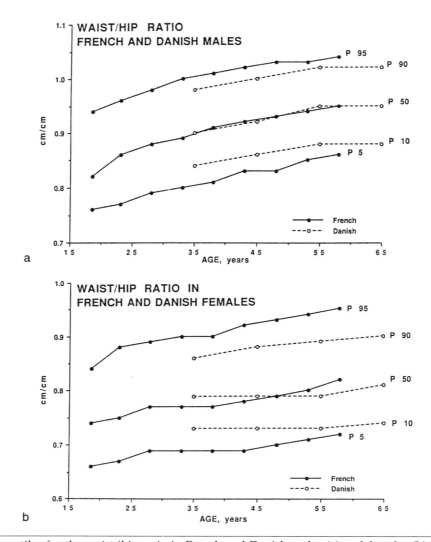

Figure 12.6 Percentiles for the waist/hip ratio in French and Danish males (a) and females (b). Drawn from data reported by Tichet et al. (1993) and Heitmann (1991).

age, grouped by self-reported stage of sexual maturation (Hammer et al., 1991). Estimated WHRs, calculated from mean abdominal and buttocks circumferences also do not consistently differ among American adolescent males and females of White, Black, or Asian ancestry (Hampton, Huenemann, & Shapiro, 1966). Among adults, mean WHRs are larger in Mexican American than in White females from San Antonio, Texas, but are slightly larger in White than in Mexican American males (Figure 12.7). Compared to the percentiles in a French population, mean WHRs in the San Antonio samples are larger than the respective French medians at most ages. The five samples of 38-year-old women from the European Fat Distribution Study (Seidell et al., 1990) have mean WHRs that are slightly larger than the French medians. WHRs

of young adult Black and White women and men in the U.S. differ only slightly (Kaye et al., 1993; Slattery et al., 1992), but mean WHRs for these young adult samples (about 24 to 25 years) are less than the respective French medians. Among older American Blacks (35 years), the mean WHR of males approaches the French median, while that for females is markedly larger than the French median (Croft et al., 1993).

In the San Antonio sample, there is a significant social class difference in the WHR among Mexican American males but not among females. The age-adjusted ratio in males increases from 0.92 in barrio residents (low SES) to 0.94 in residents from a transitional neighborhood to 0.95 in suburban residents (high SES). Corresponding age-adjusted means in Mexican American females are, respectively, 0.84,

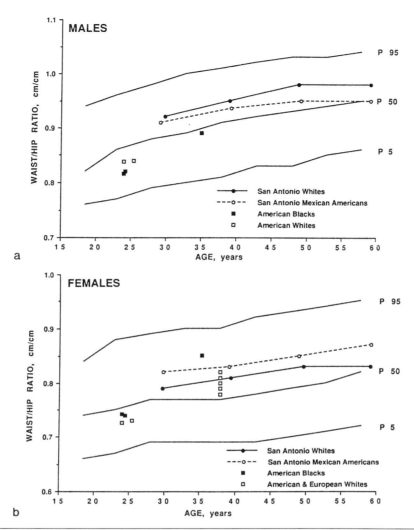

Figure 12.7 Waist/hip ratios in American Whites and Mexican Americans from San Antonio, Texas (Malina & Stern, 1992), American Blacks (Croft et al., 1993; Kaye et al., 1993; Slattery et al., 1992) and Whites (Kaye et al., 1993; Slattery et al., 1992), and European women (Seidell et al., 1990) compared to percentiles for a French population (Tichet et al., 1993).

0.83, and 0.84. In contrast, the WHR does not show a significant social class difference among White males and females in San Antonio (Malina and Stern, 1992).

Fat Mass and Subcutaneous Adipose Tissue

The ratio of the sum of several skinfold thicknesses to densitometrically estimated FM provides an indirect estimate of the contribution of SAT to FM and, by inference, changes in VAT during growth and aging. To this end, the ratio of the sum of six skinfold thicknesses to FM (SAT/

FM) was calculated for the cross-sectional sample of French Canadian ancestry, 9 to 60 years, described earlier. The densities were converted to % BF using the procedures of Lohman (1986) to allow for differences in the chemical composition of the FFM during growth and between sexes. The ratio was the same in the two sexes from 9 to 15 years (Figure 12.8a). The ratio temporarily increases in males into late adolescence and then linearly declines with age through the 50s. Thus, after adolescence, males have proportionally less SAT per unit FM and the ratio declines with age, suggesting that males accumulate more VAT with advancing age. Among females, however, the SAT/FM ratio decreases through adolescence into young adulthood, suggesting that females

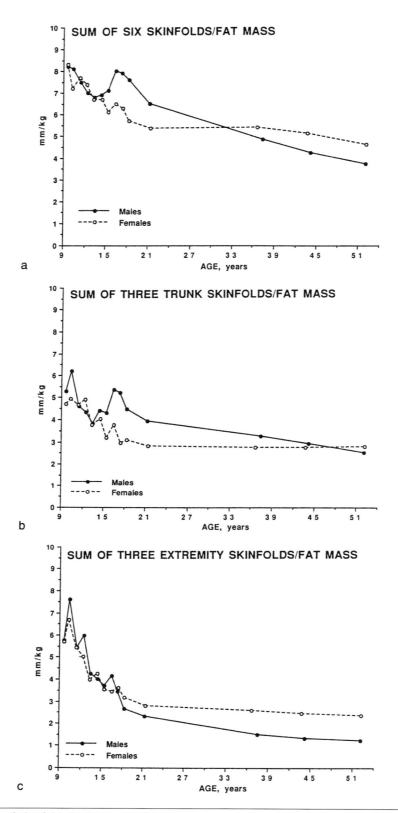

Figure 12.8 Ratios of skinfold thicknesses to fat mass in French Canadian children, adolescents, and adults: (a) ratio of the sum of six skinfold thicknesses to fat mass (SAT/FM ratio), (b) ratio of the sum of three trunk skinfold thicknesses to fat mass (T SAT/FM ratio), and (c) ratio of the sum of three extremity skinfold thicknesses to fat mass (E SAT/FM ratio). Malina & Bouchard (1988 and 1992).

accumulate proportionally more VAT during sexual maturation. After maturity is attained, the ratio is reasonably stable through the age range considered. In the fourth through sixth decades, however, the SAT/FM ratio is higher in females than in males (Figure 12.8a), suggesting slower accumulation of VAT with age in females. The sex difference in the SAT/FM ratio during adolescence is due to the greater accumulation of SAT on the T at this time. The T SAT/FM ratio increases at this time (Figure 12.8b), while the E SAT/FM ratio decreases (Figure 12.8c). In females, both ratios decrease through adolescence and are stable through adulthood, while in males both ratios decrease slightly with age. The T SAT/FM ratio is larger in males than in females from adolescence through the fourth decade but does not differ between the sexes in the 40s and 50s. The E SAT/FM ratio is larger in females from late adolescence through adulthood.

Subcutaneous and Internal Fat Mass

Two studies have attempted to partition FM into its subcutaneous and internal (visceral) components using anthropometric procedures (Hattori et al., 1991; Komiya, Muraoka, Zhang, & Masuda, 1992). Subcutaneous fat mass (SFM) was derived from 15 skinfold thicknesses, estimated segmental surface areas, and the density and proportion of fat in adipose tissue in young adult Japanese males and females 18 to 23 years (Hattori et al.), and from 14 skinfolds, body surface area, skin weight, and the density of adipose tissue in Japanese adults 40 to 77 years of age (Komiya et al.). Total FM was derived from body density in the former and from total body water in the latter. Internal fat mass (IFM) was derived by subtraction. Although the results of the two studies are not directly comparable, they indicate trends in the components of total FM with age and sex (Table 12.2). SFM comprises a greater percentage of total FM in females than males at all ages; by inference, males have proportionally more IFM. With increasing age, SFM contributes proportionally less to total FM in each sex. However, among men 40 to 77 years of age, estimated SFM decreases with age while estimated IFM is, on average, rather constant. The trend with age in SFM is similar in females, while IFM increases slightly.

Though not differentiating between SAT and VAT, estimates of android (upper body segment, trunk) and gynoid (hip and thigh region) distributions of adipose tissue (AT) from total body DXA scans indicate the sex difference and changes in relative AT distribution associated with menopause (Figure 12.9). The proportion of android AT is greater in postmenopausal women, while the proportion of gynoid AT is greater in premenopausal women. In both groups of women, however, the proportion of android fat is less than in men. Thus, with the transition to menopause, the relative AT distribution of women changes in the direction of that observed in men (Ley, Lees, & Stevenson, 1992).

Increasing attention is being directed to abdominal VAT, which is also called intra-abdominal or internal AT. Estimates of abdominal VAT and SAT areas from several studies are summarized in Table 12.3. Among 11-year-old boys and girls, sex differences in abdominal fatness are minimal. In this sample, abdominal VAT area is not related to densitometrically estimated FM ($r = 0.04$), while abdominal SAT is moderately correlated with FM ($r = 0.75$) (Peters et al., 1994). Early and late pubertal girls do not differ in abdominal VAT area, but the former have a significantly larger SAT area. Estimates of VAT from magnetic resonance imaging in the two studies of early adolescent girls are quite consistent, though SAT varies considerably. Compared to women 20 to 40 years, young adolescent girls have relatively little abdominal VAT, which suggests that abdominal VAT accumulates in later adolescence. During adulthood, abdominal VAT increases with age in each sex, more so in males than in females. Abdominal SAT also increases with age to about 60 years, and then decreases in each sex; females have, on average, more SAT than males. Males have proportionally more abdominal VAT than females and the sex difference increases with age. Women gain relatively more abdominal VAT after menopause, as indicated in SAT/VAT ratios of 2.81 ± 0.25 and 1.73 ± 0.28 in pre- and postmenopausal women, respectively (Enzi et al., 1986).

Estimates of abdominal VAT and SAT areas in men and women grouped by body mass index (BMI) are summarized in Table 12.4. Overweight individuals (BMI > 26.1 kg/m^2) have absolutely more SAT and VAT than normal weight subjects (BMI $\leq$ 26.0 kg/m^2). The two groups of men, however, do not differ in the relative distribution of SAT and VAT, but both groups increase proportionally more in VAT with age. Overweight women have proportionally more SAT than normal weight females until about 60 years of age, after which they have proportionally more VAT. The latter reflects, in part, the postmenopausal increase in abdominal VAT (Enzi et al., 1986).

Table 12.2   Anthropometric Estimates of Total Fat Mass (FM), Subcutaneous Fat Mass (SFM), and Internal Fat Mass (IFM) in Japanese Adults

Age	Sex	n	FM (kg)		SFM (kg)		IFM (kg)		% SFM	
			M	SD	M	SD	M	SD	M	SD
Hattori et al., 1991										
18-23	M	121	7.7	3.6	4.1	1.9	3.6	2.1	53.7	11.2
18-23	F	93	11.4	3.5	6.9	1.6	4.5	2.4	62.6	9.8
Komiya et al., 1992										
≤ 60 (47 ± 5)	M	42	19.7	6.2	8.8	4.5	10.9	3.1	42.8	12.9
≤ 60 (49 ± 6)	F	25	22.2	4.9	12.0	3.8	10.1	2.2	53.5	7.9
≥ 61 (67 ± 5)	M	23	14.9	4.4	5.1	2.0	9.8	3.2	33.7	8.8
≥ 61 (65 ± 4)	F	14	20.0	5.6	9.4	11.1	10.6	2.8	45.2	10.0

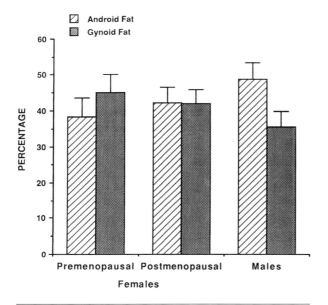

Figure 12.9 Proportion of android and gynoid adipose tissue in White premenopausal women ($n = 61$, 32 ± 6 years), postmenopausal women ($n = 70$, 53 ± 5 years), and men ($n = 103$, 51 ± 13 years). Drawn from data reported by Ley et al. (1992).

Comparisons of abdominal VAT and SAT (umbilical level) in Japanese Americans, classified on the basis of a cluster analysis using skinfold thicknesses as having an android or gynoid pattern of SAT distribution (Newell-Morris, Moceri, & Fujimoto, 1989), are summarized in Table 12.5. Women and men with an android pattern of SAT have greater absolute areas of abdominal VAT and SAT and proportionally more VAT. Among those with an android pattern of SAT, women have absolutely greater areas of VAT and SAT than men, but the

latter have proportionally more VAT. Women with a gynoid pattern of SAT have more abdominal SAT than men with a similar pattern; in contrast, gynoid men have absolutely and relatively more abdominal VAT (Fujimoto et al., 1990).

Maturity-Associated Variation in Adipose Tissue Distribution During Growth

Absolute and relative adipose tissue distributions change considerably during adolescence. The extent of these changes, however, is influenced somewhat by the individuality of timing and tempo of the adolescent growth spurt and sexual maturation. Hence, it is necessary to consider maturity-associated variations in indicators of adipose tissue distribution.

Individuals of Contrasting Maturity Status

As indicated earlier, the T-E principal component increases with stage of sexual maturation in males but not in females (Baumgartner et al., 1986). This trend reflects the simultaneous decrease in E skinfold thicknesses and increase in T skinfold thicknesses as males progress through sexual maturation. These results provide only an overview of changes in SAT distribution associated with sexual maturation. Given the wide age range of the subjects (7 to 30 years), variation among individuals of contrasting maturity status within a chronological age group could not be evaluated.

Table 12.3 Estimates of Visceral (V) and Subcutaneous (S) Abdominal Fat Areas (cm²) by Age and Sex

Reference	Method	Sex	n	Age (y) M	Age (y) SD	Visceral M	Visceral SD	Subcutaneous M	Subcutaneous SD	V/S Ratio M	V/S Ratio SD
Fox et al., 1993	MRI L4	M	25	11.5	—	17.8	10.1	78.1	48.5	0.31	0.28
		F	25	11.5	—	24.8	8.8	81.0	42.9	0.37	0.17
de Ridder et al., 1992	MRI minimal waist	F	13*	11.5	—	24.1	4.1	44.1	6.2	0.54	—
		F	11*	14.0	—	25.7	4.1	63.3	13.7	0.41	—
Seidell et al., 1988	CT L4-5	M	14	31.3	5.5	73.4	44.2	129.7	79.6	0.66	0.27
		F	7	34.0	3.9	58.3	46.4	209.6	132.3	0.32	0.28
		M	35	51.9	6.9	96.0	47.2	147.2	75.9	0.74	0.36
		F	19	52.7	8.2	93.5	49.1	244.3	104.9	0.40	0.19
		M	17	74.1	6.1	108.8	63.3	105.2	56.8	1.06	0.39
		F	8	68.0	2.0	114.5	58.9	198.6	147.7	0.40	0.14
Weits et al., 1988	CT L4	M	14	29.7	6.9	52.3	39.6	97.3	59.4	0.50	0.20
		F	12	33.7	6.1	55.5	22.6	186.5	78.3	0.35	0.20
		M	25	52.0	6.1	125.7	69.6	157.3	63.1	0.77	0.33
		F	27	52.0	5.0	86.9	52.5	242.6	108.7	0.35	0.13
		M	29	69.0	5.1	120.5	70.6	143.6	68.3	0.84	0.39
		F	23	67.4	5.8	88.6	59.7	222.4	93.9	0.37	0.18
Lemieux et al., 1993	CT L4-5	M	89	36.1	3.3	122.9	49.0	254.0	100.8	0.48	—
		F	75	35.4	4.9	103.7	53.8	427.9	200.5	0.24	—
Schwartz et al., 1990	CT umbilicus	M	16	28.1	2.4	72.6	38.2	232.6	112.8	0.33	0.16
		M	16	67.6	5.4	143.6	56.2	176.5	43.1	0.83	0.33
Ross et al., 1992	MRI L4-5	M	27	40.8	14.5	117.9	62.1	252.8	132.9	0.47	—
Borkan et al., 1983	CT umbilicus	M	21	46.3	2.6	125.6	49.8	205.7	95.6	0.61	—
		M	20	69.4	4.1	158.3	56.9	171.7	39.8	0.92	—

Note. When a standard deviation is not reported, the ratio is based on the group means.

*Early pubertal (breast stage 2) and late pubertal (breast stage 4) respectively.

This is relevant because individuals of the same maturity status but of different chronological age differ in size, physique, and body composition (Malina & Bouchard, 1991). For example, a 14-year-old girl in stage 2 of breast development differs from a 10-year-old girl in stage 2, and a 14-year-old premenarcheal girl differs from a 10-year-old premenarcheal girl.

Among 12-year-old girls from the U.S. Health Examination Survey (1966-1970), early and late maturing girls (defined by either skeletal age or stage of sexual maturation) differ only in overall fatness (the former have larger skinfold thicknesses at five sites) but not in relative SAT distribution. The same trend is apparent in 17-year-old girls classified as early maturing or late maturing on the basis of recalled ages at menarche. Thus, early maturation in girls is associated with greater levels of fatness and not with a distinctive distribution of SAT. In contrast, among 14-year-old boys, early maturers (defined by either skeletal age or

stage of sexual maturation) have proportionally more T fat than late maturers. In a subsequent principal components analysis, sexual and skeletal maturity status accounted for 20% of the variance in the T-E component in 14-year-old boys, while skeletal maturity accounted for only 5% of the variance in this component in 17-year-old boys. In contrast, none of the variance in the T-E component in 12- and 17-year-old girls was explained by indicators of maturity status (Deutsch et al., 1985). In a similar analysis, Tanner-Whitehouse skeletal age accounted for about 4%, 18%, and 8% of the variance in the T-E component in 12-, 14-, and 17-year-old Belgian boys, respectively, but only 2% to 3% of the corresponding T-E component variance in 9- and 10-year-old Belgian girls and none of the variance in 12- and 17-year-old girls (Beunen et al., 1992).

In a sample of Belgian males studied longitudinally from 13 to 18 years and then observed at 30 years of age, early maturers (age at peak height

Table 12.4   Visceral (V) and Subcutaneous (S) Abdominal Adipose Tissue Areas (cm²) by Age and Sex in Normal Weight and Overweight Individuals

| | Men | | | | Women | | | |
| | BMI ≤ 26 (kg/m²) | | BMI > 26.1 (kg/m²) | | BMI ≤ 26 (kg/m²) | | BMI > 26.1 (kg/m²) | |
Age	M	SD	M	SD	M	SD	M	SD
Visceral adipose tissue								
20-39	56.1	35	112.8	52	37.2	19	82.0	69
40-59	74.0	13	185.2	84	38.9	17	93.6	40
>60	93.7	76	180.1	64	56.9	32	124.5	37
Subcutaneous adipose tissue								
20-39	52.2	20	97.4	18	87.9	47	207.0	116
40-59	54.9	17	126.2	28	90.2	39	266.6	111
> 60	55.5	37	100.5	49	84.8	36	180.0	25
S/V ratio								
20-39	1.23	0.6	1.13	0.7	2.23	0.9	3.21	1.1
40-59	0.74	0.2	0.95	0.9	2.32	0.3	3.14	1.3
> 60	0.69	0.3	0.57	0.2	2.17	1.5	1.33	0.3

Note. Adapted from Enzi et al. (1986). CT scan at level of upper renal pole. Total *n* = 130, 62 men and 68 women, at least 10 subjects per group.

Table 12.5   Visceral (V) and Subcutaneous (S) Abdominal Adipose Tissue (cm²) in Japanese American Men and Women Classified as Having Android and Gynoid Patterns of Subcutaneous Fat Distribution

| | Women | | | | Men | | | |
| | Android (n = 15) | | Gynoid (n = 12) | | Android (n = 23) | | Gynoid (n = 16) | |
	M	SD	M	SD	M	SD	M	SD
Age	62.6	1.4	61.7	1.9	61.8	1.3	63.2	1.2
BMI, kg/m²	24.7	0.7	22.1	0.6	24.0	0.5	23.1	0.7
V, cm²	128.2	13.0	52.7	6.3	105.0	11.9	72.9	14.2
S, cm²	198.9	12.7	125.3	15.9	112.3	9.3	93.5	12.5

Note. Adapted from Fujimoto, Newell-Morris, & Shuman (1990). All subjects were second generation (Nisei). All women were postmenopausal and not taking estrogen, hypolipedemic agents, or insulin. Groups were defined by cluster analysis of seven skinfold thicknesses. [The android group had relatively more adipose tissue on the trunk and less on extremities, while the gynoid group had relatively less adipose tissue on the trunk and more on the extremities (Newell-Morris et al., 1989).]

velocity [**PHV**] < 13.4 years, *n* = 35) had thicker subscapular and suprailiac skinfolds at all ages during adolescence and at 30 years than average maturers (age at **PHV** 13.9 to 14.8 years, *n* = 56) and late maturers (age at **PHV** > 15.3 years, *n* = 24). The three contrasting maturity groups did not consistently differ in the triceps and medial calf skinfold thicknesses (Beunen et al., 1994), but they differed in the T/E ratio: early > average > late

during adolescence and at 30 years (Figure 12.10). Thus, early maturing males have relatively more SAT on the T than average and late maturing males not only during adolescence but also in adulthood, which suggests persistence of maturity-associated variation into adulthood. The central pattern of relative SAT distribution associated with early maturation in males is of additional interest because the three contrasting maturity groups did

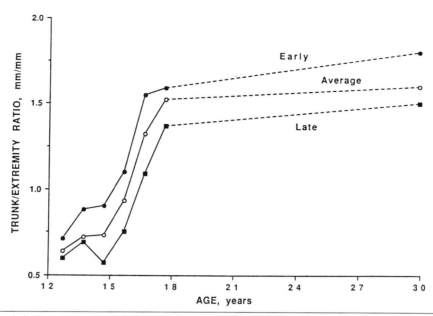

Figure 12.10   Trunk/extremity ratios [(subscapular + suprailiac)/(triceps + calf skinfold thicknesses)] in early, average, and late maturing males followed longitudinally during adolescence and at 30 years of age. Drawn from data of Beunen et al. (1994).

not significantly differ in stature, weight, and the BMI at 30 years of age. Thus, for the same size and mass, early maturing males have proportionally more T SAT as adults (Beunen et al., 1994).

Changes Relative to Age at Peak Height Velocity

A factor that influences T/E ratios during adolescence is the behavior of specific skinfold thicknesses relative to the age at peak height velocity (PHV). In mixed-longitudinal samples of southwestern Ohio children (about 29 of each sex), the triceps and subscapular skinfold thicknesses decrease 0.25 years before to 0.25 years after PHV in girls. Among boys, both these skinfold thicknesses decrease 0.25 years before PHV; however, triceps velocities show greater changes and remain, on average, negative through 1.75 years after PHV, while subscapular velocities become positive by 0.5 years after PHV (Cronk, Mukherjee, & Roche, 1983).

Four skinfold thicknesses show generally similar trends in a longitudinal sample of approximately 280 Belgian boys (Figure 12.11). Velocities of the triceps skinfold are positive until 1.0 years before PHV and then become negative, reaching a maximum negative velocity 1.5 years after PHV. The velocities remain negative until 2.5 years after PHV. In contrast to Ohio boys, estimated velocities

for the subscapular skinfold thickness in Belgian boys remain positive through the growth spurt and do not vary relative to PHV. Velocities of the suprailiac skinfold thickness are positive through the growth spurt and become negative 2.5 years after PHV. The estimated velocities for the medial calf skinfold thickness, though declining prior to PHV, approach zero at PHV and then become negative, reaching a maximum negative velocity about 3 years after PHV (Beunen & Malina, 1988; Beunen et al., 1988).

Similar trends are apparent in arm and calf SAT measured on standardized radiographs in a mixed-longitudinal sample of British children (Tanner, Hughes, & Whitehouse, 1981). Among boys, velocities of mid-arm SAT (anterior + posterior adipose tissue widths) become negative one year before PHV, reach maximum negative velocity coincident with PHV, and remain negative until one year after PHV. Velocities of calf SAT (medial + lateral adipose tissue widths at the level of maximum diameter) become negative about 0.5 years before PHV and remain negative until 2.5 years after PHV. Among British girls, velocities of mid-arm SAT are also negative from 0.5 years before to 0.5 years after PHV, while velocities of calf SAT remain positive through the growth spurt.

Skinfold thicknesses at different sites thus change variably relative to PHV. This is indicative of the significant changes that occur in the absolute

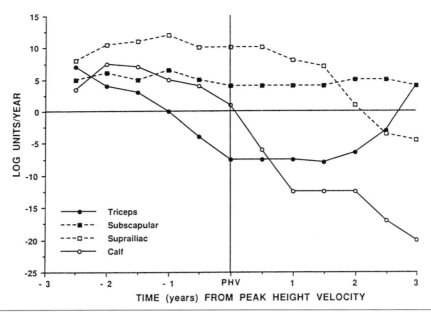

Figure 12.11   Changes in four skinfold thicknesses relative to the time of peak height velocity in a longitudinal sample of Belgian boys. Drawn from data of Beunen et al. (1988).

and relative distribution of SAT, especially during male adolescence. Since individual SAT sites behave differently, estimates of relative SAT distribution based on single T and E skinfold thicknesses must be viewed with caution.

Changes Relative to Sexual Maturation in Girls

Relative fatness has been implicated as an important factor in the sexual maturation of girls, specifically menarche (Frisch, 1976, 1988). This hypothesis has been criticized on the basis of methodological, statistical, and experimental considerations; in addition, available evidence does not support the specificity of fatness, or of a threshold level, as a critical variable for menarche (Bronson & Manning, 1991; Malina, 1991).

Early (breast stage 2, n = 13) and late (breast stage 4, n = 11) pubertal girls do not differ in VAT areas at the waist (Table 12.3). Only about one-half of the late pubertal girls had reached menarche. The late pubertal girls had more SAT, particularly at the levels of the waist and greater trochanter. This is consistent in changes in the WHR as girls mature sexually (Hammer et al., 1991) with broadening of the pelvis and the accumulation of SAT over the hips; in contrast, waist circumference shows proportionally less change.

The relationship between menarcheal status and relative AT distribution in a cross-sectional sample

of French Canadian girls is summarized in Table 12. 6 (upper part). Girls were grouped as pre- and postmenarcheal, and within each group they were subdivided as younger or older. It was assumed that the older premenarcheal girls (12.3 years) and younger postmenarcheal girls (13.6 years, age at menarche 12.2 years) were closer to menarche than the younger premenarcheal girls (10.2 years) and older postmenarcheal girls (16.4 years, age at menarche 13.1 years). Body density was converted to % BF using the procedures of Lohman (1986) to allow for age and sex differences in the chemical composition of the FFM. Although the data are cross-sectional, several trends are suggested. First, the decline in the median SAT/FM ratio from younger to older premenarcheal girls suggests a relatively greater accumulation of VAT as menarche approaches. SAT (sum of six skinfold thicknesses) does not differ between the two groups, while FM increases, thus implying a gain in VAT at this time. Second, comparison of older premenarcheal and younger postmenarcheal girls indicates little difference in median SAT/FM ratios, but greater FM and SAT in the latter. Thus, there appears to be a gain in overall fatness and SAT during the transition from the premenarcheal to the postmenarcheal state. Proportionally more SAT is accumulated on the T than on E at this time. Third, after menarche is attained, the SAT/FM ratio decreases while the T/E ratio is quite similar in younger and older postmenarcheal girls. Thus,

Table 12.6 Estimated Changes in Fatness and Adipose Tissue Distribution in Prepubertal, Pubertal, and Postpubertal Girls

	Fat mass (kg)	Sum of 6 SFT (mm)	Sum of 6 SFT/fat mass (mm/kg)	Sum of 3 trunk SFT (mm)	Sum of 3 extremity SFT (mm)	T/E ratio (mm/mm)
Quebec sample						
Premenarcheal						
Younger (n = 50, 10.2 y)	4.8	48.9	10.9	21.9	26.9	0.77
Older (n = 32, 12.3 y)	5.5	46.3	8.8	20.7	25.5	0.83
Postmenarcheal						
Younger (n = 36, 13.6 y)	7.7	61.5	8.0	29.6	30.8	0.94
Older (n = 96, 16.4 y)	10.0	66.6	6.8	32.7	34.9	0.96
New York Sample						
Prepubertal (n = 41, 10.8 y)	7.0	69.0	9.9	30.1	38.9	0.77
Pubertal, premenarcheal (n = 15, 12.9 y)	9.9	79.5	8.0	35.8	43.7	0.82
Postmenarcheal (n = 46, 14.6 y)	13.0	90.7	7.0	40.7	50.0	0.81

Note. SFT = skinfold thickness. The Quebec sample is from Malina and Bouchard (1988 and 1992). The New York sample was calculated from medians reported by Young, Sipin, and Roe (1968).

after menarche, proportionally more VAT is accumulated (lower SAT/FM ratio), while the relative distribution of SAT is unchanged (similar T/E ratios).

A similar analysis was made of data reported by Young, Sipin, & Roe (1968). The girls were classified as prepubertal (no or minimal breast and/or pubic hair development), pubertal (advanced breast and/or pubic hair development but had not reached menarche), or postpubertal (already attained menarche). Among the pubertal group, 12 of the 15 girls attained menarche within six months after the body composition assessments. Median body densities were converted to % BF using the age adjustments for FFM density suggested by Lohman (1986); FM was obtained from median body weights. Median skinfold thicknesses for six sites were combined: subscapular, umbilicus, and suprailiac on the T and triceps, mid-thigh, and suprapatellar on the E. The results are summarized in Table 12.6 (lower part). The general trends are similar to those observed in the Quebec sample. The SAT/FM ratio decreases as girls approach menarche and continues to decrease after menarche is attained, implying a greater accumulation of VAT.

Skeletal Tissue

Historically, one of the major obstacles to estimates of body composition was the lack of a verified in

vivo method for quantifying skeletal tissue. Earlier studies were based on analyses of the whole skeleton (e.g., the dry, fat-free skeletal weight as a percentage of body weight or percentage ash weight) and on bone sections (e.g., the ratio of ash to dry weight) (Malina, 1969). These studies suggest there is variability in local bone mineralization and mass. Radiographic densitometry and radiogrammetric anthropometry were widely used to study localized bone changes during growth and aging (Garn, 1961; Malina, 1969). These studies generally focused on periosteal, cortical, and medullary widths at specific skeletal sites. Subsequently, the development of new techniques has provided noninvasive methods to assess skeletal mineral status either locally or for the total body. These methods include single and dual photon absorptiometry (SPA, DPA) and dual energy x-ray absorptiometry (DXA).

The Skeleton and Its Parts

The lengths of body segments relative to the total length of the skeleton or stature vary among individuals. The net result is differences in proportions that vary with age, sex, and ethnicity. Data are most numerous for the ratio of sitting height to stature, which is an index of the relative contribution of the trunk, neck, and head (as a unit) to stature, and, by subtraction, for the relative contribution of the lower extremities, specifically subischial length to stature. The ratio is highest in infancy and decreases through childhood into adolescence. The ratio reaches its nadir during the early part of the adolescent growth spurt because spurts occur in the legs before they occur in other parts of the skeleton. When the spurt occurs in the trunk, the ratio increases into young adulthood at a time when elongation of the lower extremities is decelerating or has ceased. After about 30 to 35 years of age, sitting height begins to decrease, due largely to the compression and eventual loss of elasticity of the intervertebral discs with advancing age. Thus, the lower extremities contribute proportionally more to stature with advancing age; however, accumulation of SAT over the buttocks with advancing age, particularly in females, may offset to some extent the decline in measured sitting height.

Sex differences in the sitting height/stature ratio are not apparent during childhood. By about 10 to 12 years of age, the ratio becomes slightly higher in girls and remains so through adolescence into adulthood. Thus, during adolescence and adulthood, females have, on average, relatively shorter lower extremities than males for the same stature (Malina & Bouchard, 1991).

Ethnic variation in the sitting height/stature ratio is apparent throughout the life cycle. The ratio is consistently lower in Blacks from infancy through adulthood, whereas the ratios of American Whites and Mexicans differ slightly but consistently. The ratio should be viewed in the context of stature. American Black and White children, adolescents, and adults, on average, differ only slightly in stature; in contrast, Mexican Americans are shorter. American Blacks have shorter trunks and longer lower extremities than American Whites, while Mexican Americans have absolutely shorter trunks and lower extremities. Thus, for the same stature, Blacks have relatively short trunks, or conversely, relatively long lower extremities compared to American Whites and Mexicans. The relative proportions of the trunk or lower extremity lengths to stature do not differ markedly between American Whites and Mexicans, although the latter are absolutely smaller in both segments. Data for stature, sitting height, estimated leg length (stature minus sitting height, subischial length), and the sitting height/stature ratio for American children and youth of White, Black, and Mexican ancestry, 2 to 17 years of age, from NHANES II and HHANES are reported in Martorell, Malina, & Castillo (1988). Corresponding data for stature and sitting height

in adults 18 to 74 years of age from the same surveys have also been reported (Najjar & Kuczmarski, 1989; Najjar & Rowland, 1987).

Americans of Asian ancestry also tend to be shorter than American Whites and Blacks and differ in the proportional contribution of the lower extremities and trunk to stature. Shorter lower extremities account for the difference. Sitting height does not differ between U.S. groups of White and Japanese children and youth, but it is smaller in American Blacks. The absolute differences in stature and estimated leg length translate into proportional differences (Malina & Bouchard, 1991).

Data for specific segment or bone lengths are not extensive for groups other than American Blacks and Whites. The longer lower extremities of Blacks include an especially longer lower leg, while the longer upper extremities of Blacks include an especially longer forearm. The pelvis of Blacks is also, on average, more slender than that of Whites (i.e., smaller bicristal and bitrochanteric breadths) (Malina, 1973).

The dry, defatted skeleton weighs, on average, about 95 g in infant boys and slightly less in girls. In young adulthood, the skeleton weighs about 4.0 kg in men and 2.8 kg in women. As a percentage of body weight, the dry, fat-free skeleton comprises about 3% of body weight in the fetus and newborn and about 6 to 7% of body weight in the adult. Bone mineral, estimated from ash weight, comprises about 2% of body weight in infants and 4 to 5% of body weight in adults. These estimates are reasonably similar to measures of total body bone mineral (TBBM) derived from DXA (see below). The skeleton is consistently heavier (Table 12.7) and has more mineral in American Blacks than in Whites from infancy through adulthood (Malina, 1969; Trotter & Hixon, 1974; Trotter & Peterson, 1970).

Table 12.7   Mean Age-Adjusted Weights of the Dry, Fat-Free Skeleton of American Blacks and Whites (n = 30 per group)

Group	Weight (g)
Black men	3,899
White men	3,446
Black women	2,846
White women	2,335

Adapted from Trotter and Hixon (1974). Skeletal weights were adjusted to an age of 63.0 years by analysis of covariance.

The most comprehensive analysis of the whole skeleton and its parts has come from the work of Trotter and colleagues (Trotter & Hixon, 1974; Trotter & Peterson, 1962, 1970; Trotter, Broman, & Peterson, 1959, 1960). Variation in the densities of skeletal components associated with sex and ethnicity are summarized in (Table 12.8). Several trends are apparent:

1. Long bones (limbs and ribs) are more dense than vertebrae.
2. Cervical vertebrae are more dense than the other vertebrae in males but not significantly so in females.
3. Bones of males are more dense than those of females.
4. Bones of American Blacks are more dense than those of American Whites.
5. Densities of individual bones in males and females of both ethnic groups decrease with age.

The fat-free skeleton is a composite of bone mineral and organic bone matrix, and the ratio of ash weight to the weight of the dry, fat-free bone (% ash weight) provides an estimate of mineral content. In the studies of Trotter and colleagues (Trotter & Hixon, 1974; Trotter & Peterson, 1970), bone densities decrease with age, but % ash weight is variable among bones. Within each sex and ethnic group, the mandible has the highest and the sternum the lowest % ash weight. The cranium and long bones of the limbs rank closest to the mandible, while the vertebrae, ribs, and bones of the pelvis rank closest to the sternum. Males generally show higher % ash weights than females, which suggests that sex differences in density are related to bone mineral. Significant differences in % ash weight between Blacks and Whites are limited to the clavicles, scapulae, bones of the hand, ribs, thoracic vertebrae, lumbar vertebrae, sacrum, and sternum, but the major long bones do not show significantly greater % ash weights in American Blacks.

Radiogrammetric Studies

Radiogrammetric studies of regional variation in bone tissue from childhood into young adulthood have included the humerus, tibia, tibia plus fibula, second metacarpal, and combined widths of several long bones (Garn, 1970; Malina, 1969; Tanner et al., 1981). The earlier studies emphasized periosteal diameters measured at specific levels (e.g., mid-length) or level of maximum calf width, while later studies included cortical diameters and estimated areas. Changes in periosteal and cortical widths across the life span have focused largely on the second metacarpal (Garn, 1970).

Periosteal and cortical widths or areas of individual bones have a growth curve similar to that

Table 12.8 Densities (g/cm³) of Specific Bones and Bone Series in American Blacks and Whites (n = 20 per group)

| | Men | | | | | | Women | | | | | |
| | Black | | | White | | | Black | | | White | | |
	M	SD	AM	M	SD	AM	M	SD	AM	M	SD	AM
Humerus	.72	.10	.70	.64	.13	.65	.64	.14	.63	.57	.11	.59
Radius	.79	.10	.77	.73	.12	.74	.71	.15	.69	.62	.15	.65
Ulna	.85	.10	.84	.78	.12	.79	.72	.13	.73	.64	.13	.66
Femur	.70	.09	.69	.63	.11	.63	.65	.13	.64	.60	.12	.62
Tibia	.80	.13	.78	.74	.18	.75	.66	.17	.65	.64	.17	.66
Vertebrae:												
Cervical	.58	.09	.57	.52	.07	.52	.53	.12	.53	.44	.10	.45
Thoracic	.48	.08	.47	.42	.08	.42	.44	.11	.44	.39	.10	.39
Lumbar	.48	.10	.47	.42	.10	.42	.46	.14	.45	.38	.08	.39
Sacrum	.48	.09	.47	.40	.10	.39	.45	.15	.45	.36	.09	.37
Ribs	.68	.15	.67	.61	.14	.62	.67	.27	.66	.64	.13	.66

Note: AM = age-adjusted mean (to a mean age of 62.8 years) by analysis of covariance. Density is based on the gravimetric method, weight of dry, fat-free bone (g/volume) within its external surface (cm³). Adapted from Trotter et al. (1960) and Trotter and Hixon (1974).

for weight and stature. Based on data for the second metacarpal, humerus, and tibia, periosteal and cortical widths increase with age from early childhood into young adulthood in males and from early childhood through about 15 to 16 years in females. Sex differences are negligible prior to adolescence, when they favor males. Cortical widths do not differ between boys and girls during childhood; girls have wider cortical diameters during early adolescence (reflecting their earlier adolescent spurt), and it is only in late adolescence that cortical widths become larger in males (Malina & Bouchard, 1991). Estimated velocities of growth in humerus and tibial widths from a mixed-longitudinal sample of British children indicate that the velocities do not differ between the sexes during childhood. Boys have well defined spurts in both bones and the spurt occurs earlier in the tibia than in the humerus. Girls do not have clearly defined adolescent spurts in the periosteal widths of these bones, reflecting a lack of change in medullary cavity widths during female adolescence. When velocities are estimated for cortical widths of the humerus, however, both sexes show adolescent spurts, and that for girls occurs about two years earlier than in boys (Tanner et al., 1981).

The bone studied most extensively across the life span is the second metacarpal (MII). Results of these studies (Garn, 1964, 1970; Garn, Miller, & Larson, 1976) can be summarized as follows:

1. Sex differences in cortical thickness of MII are negligible during childhood through mid-adolescence.
2. There is a marked increase in the cortical thickness of MII from late adolescence (15+ years) into the mid-20s, and males gain more than females.
3. The sex difference in cortical thickness persists throughout adulthood.
4. Males and females experience decreases in cortical thickness after the fifth decade, but the rate of decrease is more marked in females.
5. Cortical thickness, as a percentage of total volume or cross-sectional area of MII, is greater in females prior to menopause.

Cortical area of MII is greater in American Blacks than in Whites by about 10% (Garn, Nagy, & Sandusky, 1972), and that in Whites is about 5% larger than that in Mexican Americans (Garn et al., 1976). Cortical bone of MII is also less per unit length in Chinese and Japanese than in American Whites (Garn, Pao, & Rihl, 1964). The onset and magnitude

of cortical bone loss with advancing age is similar in well nourished and undernourished populations, although MII dimensions are smaller in the latter. For example, the relative loss in MII cortical thickness from 30 to 80 years in American Whites and Blacks and in Guatemalans, El Salvadorans, and Costa Ricans varies between 11% and 17% in males and 36% and 41% in females (Garn, Rohman, & Wagner, 1967).

Single and Dual Photon Absorptiometry and Dual Energy X-Ray Absorptiometry

Bone mineral content (BMC) and bone mineral density (BMD) in the total body (total body bone mineral, TBBM; total body bone mineral density, TBMD) and several regions based on dual energy x-ray absorptiometry (DXA) measurements from childhood through young adulthood are summarized in Figure 12.12. The data from 8 to 16 years are largely for single year categories (Faulkner et al., 1993), while those for late adolescence and young adulthood are for five-year age groups between 15 and 29 years (Rico et al., 1992). Some of the variation is due to differences in delineating regions on the DXA scans. Though not shown in the figure, similar trends in age- and sex-associated variation are apparent in broader age groups of children and youth (i.e., 3 to 9, 10 to 15, 16 to 20, and 21 to 25 years) using dual photon absorptiometry (DPA) (Geusens et al., 1991). There is an absence of sex differences in BMC and BMD from childhood through mid-adolescence, except that the density of the upper limbs tends to be slightly larger in males. In later adolescence, and especially in young adulthood, however, males have a greater BMC and BMD. These trends persist into adulthood. There is also an absence of sex differences in BMC and BMD of the pelvis during childhood and early adolescence (not shown), although the pelvis in females has a greater density at 15 to 16 years (Faulkner et al.). The young adult data do not delineate the pelvis (Rico et al.), while DPA measures in older adults indicate larger BMC and BMD values for males than for females (Mazess, Peppler, & Chesney, 1984).

BMC and BMD in the total body and several regions based on DPA measurements in younger men and women and in older women are summarized in Table 12.9. Men have greater TBBM and TBMD and especially greater mineral content and density of the appendicular skeleton. Sex differences in the other areas of the skeleton are small, except that mineral density of the head is higher

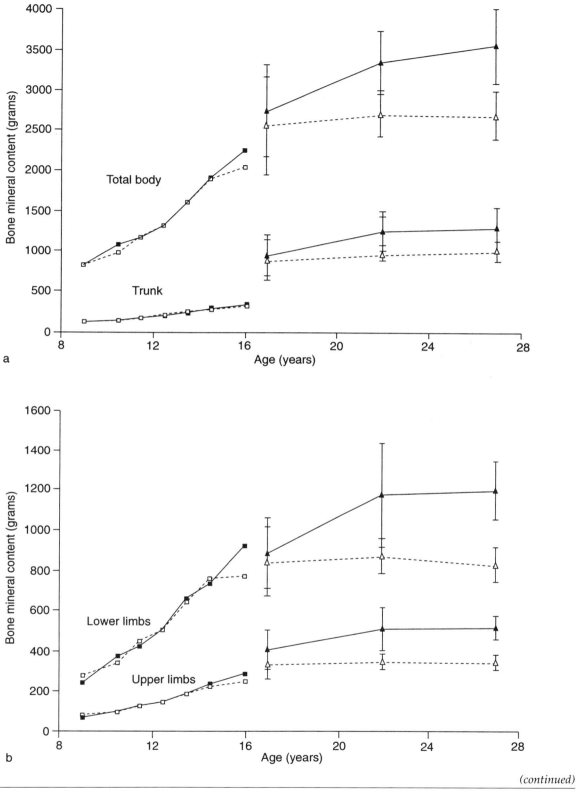

a

b

(continued)

Figure 12.12 Age changes and sex differences in bone mineral content (a and b) and bone mineral density (c and d) in males (solid line) and females (dashed line). Drawn from data of Faulkner et al. (1993) for ages 8 to 16 years and from data of Rico et al. (1992) for 15 to 29 years.

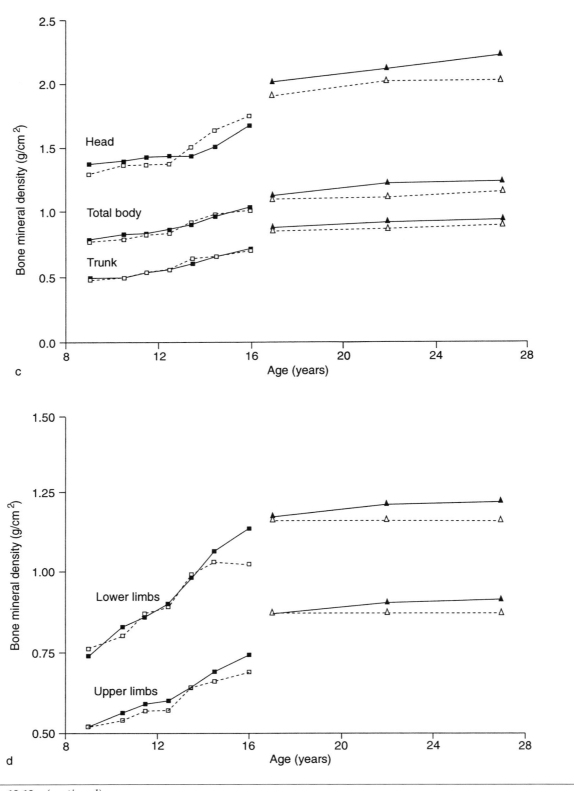

Figure 12.12 *(continued)*

Table 12.9 Bone Mineral Content (g) and Bone Mineral Density (g/cm²) From Dual Photon Absorptiometry in the Total Body and Several Regions in Clinically Normal Adults

	Men (n = 13) 34.2 ± 12.3 years				Women (n = 24) 34.5 ± 10.5 years				Women (n = 48) 57.6 ± 6.1 years			
	BMC		BMD		BMC		BMD		BMC		BMD	
	M	SD	M	SD	M	SD	M	SD	M	SD	M	SD
Total	3369	595	1.21	.11	2731	372	1.14	.08	2525	350	1.07	.08
Head	559	83	2.14	.34	562	66	2.39	.32	521	79	2.21	.29
Arms	495	86	1.04	.08	326	62	.90	.08	295	47	.85	.08
Legs	1300	245	1.39	.14	936	160	1.20	.09	880	133	1.11	.09
Trunk	940	350	.92	.13	906	147	.89	.07	851	226	.84	.07
Ribs	338	103	.71	.09	287	55	.67	.05	253	63	.63	.06
Pelvis	325	95	1.14	.20	258	54	1.11	.12	242	50	1.04	.10
Spine	354	93	1.02	.18	361	60	1.02	.10	343	57	.95	.09

Adapted from Mazess et al. (1984).

in females. The comparison of younger and normal older women indicates lower TBBM and TBMD in the latter and generally lower BMC and BMD in specific areas of the skeleton (Mazess et al., 1984). Using the means in Table 12.9, BMC and BMD of the normal older women are about 7% and 6%, respectively, less than in younger women, with relatively little variation among the different regions/segments of the skeleton (except for the ribs, about 12% less bone mineral in older women).

If the mean values for regional measures of BMC in Figure 12.12 are expressed as a percentage of TBBM, the following trends occur between 8 to 9 and 15 to 16 years of age: (1) the relative contribution of BMC of the head to TBBM declines from about 33% to about 20% of TBBM in each sex; (2) the relative contribution of the trunk to TBBM is rather stable at about 14 to 15%; and (3) the relative contribution of BMC of the limbs and pelvis to TBBM increases from childhood through mid-adolescence: upper limbs, 9 to 12% in each sex; lower limbs, 33 to 38% in females and 29 to 41% in males; pelvis, 10 to 13% in each sex. Corresponding estimates from 15-19 years to 25-29 years indicate small changes in the relative contributions of BMC of the trunk (34%-37%), upper limbs (12%-15%), and lower limbs (31%-35%) to TBBM, while the relative contribution of BMC of the head to TBBM is rather stable at about 19% in females, but declines in males to about 16%. The relative contributions of BMC of the upper and lower limbs to TBBM are slightly greater (1 to 2%) in males, while there is an absence of sex differences in the relative

contribution of BMC of the trunk. The variation in estimates from the two studies is due to differences in delineating segments on the DXA scans. Comparisons of estimates for older adults (Table 12.9) indicate similar relative contributions of BMC in different regions of the body to TBBM in younger and older women: head, 21%; upper limbs, 12%; lower limbs, 34%; and trunk, 33%. Among males, the corresponding percentages are: head, 17%; upper limbs, 15%; lower limbs, 39%; and trunk, 28%. Thus, the appendicular skeleton contributes relatively more to TBBM in men than in women.

Changes in TBBM are most apparent later in adolescence (Figure 12.12). TBBM does not significantly differ between boys and girls in early puberty but is considerably higher in boys in later puberty when sex differences are significant (Figure 12.13). Most other studies using DXA or DPA are limited to specific sections of a long bone or to specific vertebrae, and trends from childhood through adolescence are generally similar. In youth 10 to 15 years of age, BMD of L1-4 (DXA) does not show a rapid increase until late puberty (stage 5) (Glastre et al., 1990). Logistic curves fitted to cross-sectional data for BMC and BMD of L2-4 (DPA) indicate spurts in each measure (Gordon et al., 1991). The spurt is more intense in females, however, accounting for about 50% of peak bone mass, while that for males is more gradual and accounts for only about 15% of peak bone mass. Females show little change in lumbar BMD and BMC after about 14 years, while males gain steadily through the 20s (Gordon et al.). Measures of

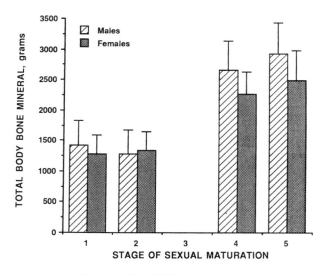

Figure 12.13 Total body bone mineral in boys and girls by stage of sexual maturation. Children at stage 3 were not included in the study. Drawn from data of Rico et al. (1993).

BMD and BMC of L2-4 and the neck and mid-shaft of the femur (DXA) in cross-sectional samples of boys and girls 9 to 18 years suggest that peak bone mass (young adult reference values, 20 to 35 years) is achieved in 14- to 15-year-old females and 17- to 18-year-old-males (Bonjour et al., 1991). Major increases in BMD and BMC occur during the first two years after menarche and to a lesser extent for the next two years. One year longitudinal observations of BMD and BMC (DXA) at the same sites indicate substantial increments between 11 to 14 years in females and 13 to 17 years in males. These appear to coincide with the adolescent growth spurt and sexual maturation. After 16 years in females, the increments are not significant, while those in males are significant, though small, from 17 to 20 years (Theintz et al., 1992).

Cross-sectional analysis of BMD at mid- and distal radius using single photon absorptiometry (SPA) and L1-4 (using DPA) indicate significant regional and sex differences in clinically normal men and women 20 to 89 years of age (Riggs et al., 1981). Vertebral BMD begins to decrease in young adulthood, and this decrease continues linearly with age, while reduction of radial BMD does not occur until 50 years of age, after which the rate of loss accelerates. The estimated decline in BMD is greater in females than males at each site: −0.0092 g/cm²/yr vs −0.0021 g/cm²/yr in L1-4, −0.0056 g/cm²/yr vs −0.0005 g/cm²/yr at mid-radius, and −0.0065 g/cm²/yr vs −0.0032 g/cm²/yr at distal radius, respectively. Overall, the decline in BMD is about 47% in L1-4, 39% for the distal radius, and 30% for mid-radius in females (Riggs et al., 1981). The decrease in BMC with age is similar in Japanese residents in Hawaii. The estimated decrease in BMC (SPA) during a 15-year period, from about 60-64 to 75-80 years, is approximately two to four times greater in Japanese women than in men, but the relative decline varies by skeletal site: distal radius, 12% in males, 29% in females; proximal radius, 7% in males, 22% in females; distal ulna, 12% in males, 31% in females; proximal ulna, 6% in males, 22% in females; and os calcis, 8% in males, 32% in females (Yano et al., 1984).

Short-term (0.8 to 3.4 years) longitudinal observations indicate an absence of changes in BMD at the mid-radius (SPA) prior to menopause but a significant decrease after menopause and a systematic decrease in BMD of the lumbar spine (DPA) before and after menopause (Riggs, Wahner, & Melton, 1986). In an 8 year longitudinal study, BMC of the distal radius (SPA) decreased linearly by about 1 to 2% per year after menopause, and the decline was independent of calcium intake (van Beresteijn et al., 1990).

TBBM and TBMD estimates for several samples of adults are given in Table 12.10. The samples of American Blacks and Whites are similar in age and body size. Subjects were matched for age, weight, and stature in two studies (Gerace et al., 1994; Ortiz et al., 1992), and females were matched for menstrual status (Ortiz et al.). Subjects in the third study were also similar in subcutaneous fatness (Adams, Deck-Côté, & Winters, 1992). Black and White adults differ significantly in TBBM and TBBD, the relative differences between the two samples of women reaching about 10% and 12% in TBBM and 7% in TBMD with the corresponding differences in males reaching about 9% in TBBM and 4% in TBMD. In the study of Ortiz et al., the ethnic difference in BMC is more marked in the upper extremities (about 19% greater in Blacks) than in the lower extremities (about 12% greater in Blacks). The available data thus indicate a significantly larger appendicular skeletal mass in Blacks.

Estimates of TBMD of U.S.-born Japanese American women overlap those for Black and White U.S. women and are generally greater than for Japan-born immigrant Japanese American women (Table 12.10). After adjustment for age, stature and weight, however, TBMD does not differ between U.S-born and Japan-born Japanese American women (Kin et al., 1993). However, some evidence suggests that TBMD and TBBM do not differ between men of Asian ancestry (77 of 84 were Chinese, primarily foreign born) and American Whites

Table 12.10   Ethnic Variation in Total Body Bone Mineral Content (TBBM) and Total Body Bone Mineral Density (TBMD)

	Age (y)			TBBM (g)		TBMD (g/cm^2)	
	n	M	SD	M	SD	M	SD
Adams et al. (1992), DXA							
Black women	26	22.5	3.6	3021	305	1.25	0.05
White women	26	23.6	2.8	2718	321	1.16	0.07
Ortiz et al. (1992), DPA							
Black women	28	44.2	15.2	2640	490	1.18	0.14
White women	28	43.6	15.3	2320	330	1.09	0.09
Gerace et al. (1994), DPA							
Black men	24	39.8	10.3	3430	476	1.28	0.11
White men	24	39.7	10.3	3156	513	1.23	0.11
Russell-Aulet et al. (1991), DPA							
White men	154	50.0	16.0	3040	532	1.19	0.12
Asian men*	84	51.0	17.0	2697	421	1.15	0.10
Tsunenari et al. (1993), DXA							
Japanese men	8	19.5	1.7	2540	410	—	—
	15	42.8	2.5	2450	250	—	—
	11	65.5	5.5	2370	950	—	—
Japanese women	10	21.4	0.5	2310	190	—	—
	10	43.4	3.2	2320	310	—	—
	14	66.0	3.7	1610	220	—	—
Kin et al. (1993), DXA							
Japanese American women, U.S. born	19	20-29				1.12	0.10
	30	30-39				1.12	0.07
	26	40-49				1.10	0.07
	11	50-59				1.06	0.10
	39	60-69				1.00	0.09
	20	70-79				0.93	0.05
	151	18-84				1.05	0.11
	151	18-84				1.04[†]	—
Japanese women, Japan born	10	30-39				1.09	0.06
	31	40-49				1.10	0.06
	48	50-59				1.03	0.09
	42	60-69				0.95	0.07
	137	19-89				1.03	0.10
	137	19-89				1.04[†]	—

*77 of the 84 subjects were of Chinese ancestry.

[†]Adjusted for age, stature, and weight.

after adjustment for age, stature, and weight (Russell-Aulet et al., 1991). Other data suggest TBBM of Japanese men and women is less than that of American Blacks and Whites, even allowing for smaller body size (Tsunenari et al., 1993). TBBM declines, on average, slightly across the three age groups of Japanese men. In contrast, the young and middle-age Japanese women do not differ in TBBM, but it is considerably less in older women (Tsunenari et al.). Comparisons across generations must be tempered, of course, due to possible cohort effects associated with secular changes in diet, health status, physical activity, and perhaps other variables.

Data for specific bone sites yield generally similar results in comparisons of American Black and White children, adolescents, and adults. BMC and bone width of the distal radius (SPA) are significantly greater in Black (n = 35 males, 43 females) than in White (n = 29 males, 24 females) children

1 to 6 years of age (Li et al., 1989) and in Black (*n* = 45 males, 46 females) than in White (*n* = 85 males, 63 females) children and youth 8 to 19 years of age (Slaughter et al., 1990). Similarly, BMD of L2-4 (DPA) is significantly greater in Black (*n* = 91) than in White (*n* = 155) children and adolescents 5 to 19 years of age (McCormick, Ponder, Fawcett, & Palmer, 1991). BMD of L2-4 in Hispanic children and youth (*n* = 66, most likely Mexican Americans) is also less than in Blacks but does not differ from that of Whites (McCormick et al.). Corresponding data for samples of children and adolescents of Asian ancestry are not available.

In premenopausal, non-obese subjects of similar body weight (mean age 35 years), Blacks (*n* = 51) have significantly greater BMD (SPA, DPA) at the mid-radius, L2-4, trochanter, and femoral neck than Whites (*n* = 89), the differences between means ranging from 4 to 8% (Liel, Edwards, & Shary, 1988). Among women 24 to 65 years, L2-4 BMD (DPA) and distal radius BMC (SPA) are higher in Blacks (*n* = 105) than in Whites (*n* = 114) by about 6.5% after adjusting for age and the BMI (Luckey et al., 1989). The estimated rate of decrease in vertebral BMD is similar in both ethnic groups. In premenopausal women (< 46 years), however, radial BMC increases in Blacks (3.8%/decade) but decreases in Whites (3.2%/decade); after 46 years, radial BMC decreases in both groups, but at a lesser rate in Blacks than in Whites, 5.2%/decade vs 8.9%/decade, respectively (Luckey et al.). BMC (SPA) at the mid-radius is greater in American Black (*n* = 36) than in White (*n* = 99) women of the same mean age (56.5 years), after adjusting for differences in body weight, and the estimated rate of BMC loss with age is greater in the White women (Nelson, Kleerekoper, & Parfitt, 1988). BMC is not apparently related to skin color (skin reflectance) in either sample. Measures of BMD (SPA, DPA) at seven sites in Black (*n* = 109 to 114) and White (*n* = 44 to 47) women 22 to 80 years are summarized in Table 12.11. BMD at each site is higher in Black women even after adjusting for age and the BMI (Nelson, Feingold, Bolin, & Parfitt, 1991).

In an insured population of adults 20 to 69 years, American Blacks generally have larger BMC of the distal radius (SPA) and larger BMD than American Whites and Asians, while differences between Whites and Asians are inconsistent (Goldsmith, Johnston, Picetti, & Garcia, 1973). Japanese residents in Hawaii, men 61 to 81 years and women 43 to 80 years, have generally less BMC of the distal and proximal radius (SPA) than American Whites (Yano et al., 1984). In a comparison of BMC

(SPA) at the proximal radius in Japanese and Japanese American men and women, the Japanese Americans have greater BMC (6 to 10%) and BMD (16 to 17%), but adjusting for weight and stature reduces the differences by about one-half (Ross et al., 1989). BMDs in several regions of the body of American White and Asian (largely Chinese) men are summarized in Table 12.12. BMDs are significantly higher in Whites for all regions of the body (4.0 to 6.5%) except the arms (difference only 2.0%); however, after controlling for age, stature, and weight, none of the differences is significant (Russell-Aulet et al.).

Within Asian samples, U.S.-born Japanese American women have slightly greater BMD at L2-4, femoral neck, Ward's triangle, and the greater trochanter than Japan-born Japanese American women after adjustment for age, stature, and weight (Kin et al., 1993). Note, however, TBMD does not differ between the two groups of Japanese American women after age, stature, and weight are controlled. Other data show relatively small differences in BMD at L2-4 and the femoral neck among cross-sectional samples of Japanese (*n* = 259), Korean (*n* = 62), and Taiwanese (*n* = 77) women and between Japanese (*n* = 81) and Korean (*n* = 48) men 20 to 90 years of age, but suggest ethnic variation among Asian populations in the loss of bone mineral with age (Sugimoto et al., 1992).

Skeletal Muscle Tissue

Although skeletal muscle is the work-producing tissue of the body, it is the component of body composition that is, perhaps, the most difficult to quantify in vivo. Estimated muscle mass, derived from creatinine excretion or potassium concentration, shows a growth pattern like that for body weight. Sex differences are small prior to the adolescent growth spurt, but males gain considerably more muscle mass than females during adolescence and the sex difference persists throughout the life span (Malina, 1969, 1986).

Body regions contribute differentially to total muscle mass during growth. Early dissection studies indicate that the head and trunk account for about 40% of the total weight of the musculature at birth but only 25 to 30% at maturity. Muscles of the lower extremities increase their relative contribution from about 40% at birth to 55% of the total weight of the musculature at maturity, while muscles of the upper extremities have a relatively

Table 12.11   Bone Mineral Densities (g/cm²) at Several Sites in Black and White Women

| Site | Bone mineral density | | | | Differences between Blacks and Whites | |
| | Blacks | | Whites | | | Adjusted for age & BMI |
	M	SD	M	SD	Unadjusted	
Midshaft radius	0.72	0.10	0.66	0.10	0.06	0.03
Radius/ulna	0.34	0.07	0.30	0.07	0.04	0.02
Distal radius	0.46	0.08	0.41	0.08	0.05	0.02
L2-4	1.15	0.19	1.06	0.20	0.09	0.06
Femoral neck	0.90	0.18	0.80	0.16	0.10	0.05
Ward's triangle	0.84	0.21	0.74	0.17	0.10	0.05
Greater trochanter	0.79	0.18	0.72	0.12	0.07	0.04

Adapted from Nelson et al. (1991). Mean ages: Blacks 56.4 ± 14.6, Whites 61.7 ± 14.2. Numbers vary: Blacks, *n* = 109 to 114; Whites, *n* = 44 to 47.

Table 12.12   Bone Mineral Density (g/cm²), From Dual Photon Absorptiometry, in White and Asian Males, 22-94 Years of Age

| | White (*n* = 154) | | Asian (*n* = 84) | |
	M	SD	M	SD
Total	1.188	.117	1.146	.100
Head	2.233	.319	2.131	.280
Trunk	0.977	.118	0.929	.103
Spine	1.160	.170	1.114	.161
Arms	0.881	.107	0.864	.101
Ribs	0.725	.082	0.678	.062
Legs	1.303	.146	1.220	.130
Pelvis	1.175	.172	1.111	.151

Adapted from Russell-Aulet et al. (1991). The Asian sample is primarily Chinese.

constant contribution of about 18 to 20% (Scammon, 1923). Other studies of regional variation in skeletal muscle tissue are based on radiography, while more recent approaches use many of the same methods as in studies of abdominal VAT and SAT.

Radiogrammetric Studies

Regional data for skeletal muscle development are limited largely to the arm and calf, but several have combined radiographic measures of muscle widths from different regions to provide an indication of "total muscle width" (Malina, 1969). Widths of muscle tissue in the calf (anteroposterior view, level of maximal muscle diameter) and arm (lateral view, midway between acromial process and head of the radius) during growth are shown in Figure 12.14. Muscles of the extremities increase in size during childhood and adolescence and have a growth pattern similar to that for body weight and estimates of muscle mass. Sex differences, although apparent, are small during childhood, boys having slightly wider muscles. By about 11 years of age, girls are in their adolescent spurt and have a temporary size advantage in calf muscle width but not in arm muscle width. Boys then have their adolescent spurt and develop considerably larger muscle widths of the arm and calf. Sex differences in muscle widths, established during adolescence, are more apparent in the upper than in the lower extremities. During adolescence, about 10 to 16 years in females and 12 to 18 years in males, each sex gains about 30% in calf muscle width, but males gain significantly more in arm muscle width, 40% compared to 28% in females. Thus by 18 years of age, arm musculature of males is about 25% larger than of females, while the corresponding difference in calf musculature is only about 10%. Radiographic data for the calf do not show a significant age-associated loss in muscle width in either sex, at least through the mid-40s (Garn & Saalberg, 1953; Reynolds & Grote, 1948).

The genesis of sex differences in arm and calf muscle widths is clearly apparent in estimated velocities of growth. Males show well defined spurts in both the arm and calf musculature. Females do

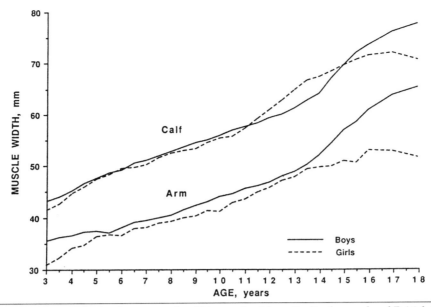

Figure 12.14 Mean muscle widths in the arm and calf in a mixed-longitudinal sample of British boys and girls. Drawn from data of Tanner et al. (1981).

not show a clearly defined spurt; rather they show a slight increase in rate of muscle growth followed by a plateau that persists for 4 to 5 years (Malina, 1986; Tanner et al., 1981). When the velocity data are aligned on the age at PHV, thus reducing the time spread along the chronological age axis, each sex shows peak gains in arm muscle width after PHV. The spurt in boys is approximately twice the magnitude of that in girls. In the calf, however, boys show a clear spurt after PHV while girls do not; rather, gains in calf muscle width are more or less constant from 1.0 year before to 1.5 years after PHV in girls. Gains in calf muscle width in males are only slightly greater than in females from about 1.0 year before to 2.0 years after PHV (Tanner et al.).

Muscle widths of the arm and calf also show maturity-associated variation within chronological age groups. Children advanced in skeletal or sexual maturity during childhood and adolescence have significantly wider arm and calf muscles, the differences reflecting the larger overall body size of early maturing children (Malina & Bouchard, 1991). Data on maturity-associated differences in regional development of muscle tissue are not available.

Radiographic data on ethnic variation in limb muscle are limited to athletes. Among world class athletes, Blacks have slightly wider muscles in the arm and thigh but smaller calf muscle widths than White athletes. Black athletes thus have substantially smaller calf muscles relative to muscle development in the arm and thigh (Tanner, 1964).

Anthropometric Estimates

Limb circumferences corrected for skinfold thicknesses are used to estimate muscular development. Mid-arm circumference adjusted for the thickness of the triceps skinfold is most often used, although occasionally adjustments are made for both the triceps and biceps skinfold thicknesses. In addition, calf circumference is sometimes adjusted for the thicknesses of the lateral and medial calf skinfold thicknesses. Formulas for converting limb circumferences to estimates of muscle circumferences or areas vary (Forbes, 1986; Heymsfield et al., 1982). Anthropometric estimates of limb musculature, however, consistently yield overestimates compared to CT measures (Baumgartner et al., 1992; de Koning, Binkhorst, Kauer, & Thijssen, 1986; Forbes, Brown, & Griffiths, 1988; Rice, Cunningham, Paterson, & Lefcoe, 1990).

Allowing for the limitations of anthropometric procedures, the pattern of age- and sex-associated variation in anthropometric estimates of limb musculature is similar to that for radiographic measures. Estimates of mid-arm muscle area (based on arm circumference adjusted for the triceps skinfold thickness) in nationally representative samples of American Black and White children do not consistently differ (Figure 12.15). The estimates are slightly larger for Blacks in later adolescence, and the apparent difference between Blacks and Whites persists through adulthood. Since American Blacks and Whites do not differ, on average, in stature,

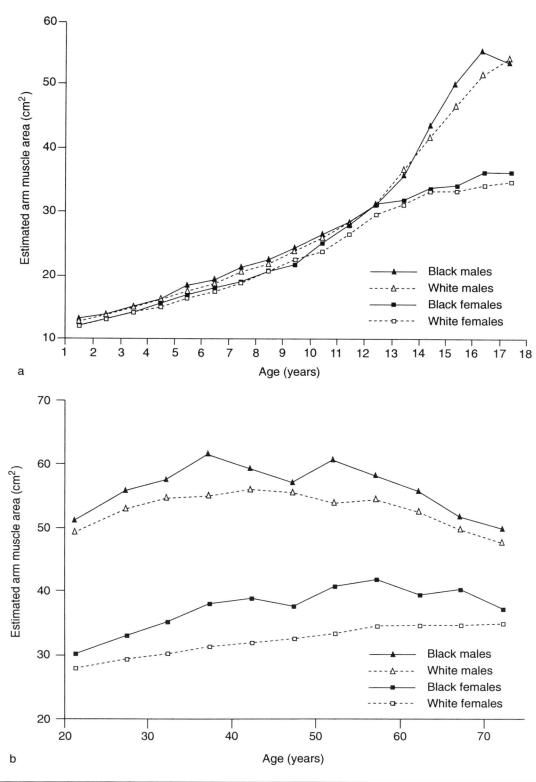

Figure 12.15 Median estimated mid-arm muscle areas in nationally representative samples of American Blacks and Whites: (a) children and adolescents; (b) adults. The values for adults have been adjusted for bone area by subtracting 10.0 cm^2 and 6.5 cm^2 from the calculated muscle areas for males and females, respectively. Drawn from data reported by Frisancho (1990).

the trends may suggest ethnic variation in muscle tissue distribution. The possible role of occupational variation in manual activities in the ethnic differences cannot be addressed in the data. Males of each group show a greater age-associated decrease in estimated muscularity of the arm than females.

Estimated mid-arm muscles areas of Mexican American children, 6 to 17 years, tend to be smaller than U.S. reference data, especially during adolescence, but expressing muscle areas relative to stature, thus allowing for size differences, virtually eliminates the apparent difference (Zavaleta & Malina, 1980). There are small differences in estimated mid-arm muscle circumference (arm circumference corrected for the triceps and biceps skinfolds) and calf muscle (calf circumference corrected for the medial and lateral calf skinfold thicknesses) of American Whites and Mexican Americans in San Antonio, Texas (Table 12.13). Allowing for stature differences between the samples (Mexican Americans are, on average, shorter), ratios of estimated arm and calf muscle circumferences per unit stature are identical in males from the two ethnic groups. The same is true for estimated calf muscle in women, but estimated arm muscle per unit stature is slightly greater in Mexican American women than in American Whites. Changes in mean estimated limb circumferences across the four age groups are small, as are social class differences within each ethnic group. The only exception is consistently smaller estimated mid-arm muscle circumferences in upper socioeconomic women in each ethnic group, which may reflect differences in occupational physical activity (Malina & Stern, 1992).

Computerized Tomography, Magnetic Resonance Imaging, Ultrasound, and Dual Photon Absorptiometry

Applications of these newer methods to the assessment of skeletal musculature are based primarily on small samples of adults of European ancestry. With few exceptions, estimates are limited to the arm and thigh, and results with the different methods are not directly comparable. For example, the cross-sectional area of the quadriceps is about 30% larger with CT than with ultrasound (Sipila & Suominen, 1993).

Estimates of cross-sectional areas (CSA) of the arm, thigh, and specific muscles or muscle groups are summarized in Table 12.14. Arm and thigh CSAs include muscle and bone, although Borkan

et al. (1983) simply refer to "lean" CSA. Sex differences are greater in the arm than in the thigh, but the magnitude of the differences varies among studies. The sex difference in the arm persists after adjustment for stature, while that for the thigh becomes nonsignificant (Schantz et al., 1983). CSAs decrease with age in each sex. The magnitude of the age-associated decrease varies with the age groups compared and muscle groups. For example, differences between younger and older men are about 25% for quadriceps CSA (25 and 75 years; Young, Stokes, & Crowe, 1985), about 24% for arm CSA, and 13% for calf CSA (31 and 75 years; Rice et al., 1990), and 12% for the "lean" CSAs of both the arm and thigh (46 and 69 years; Borkan et al.). A corresponding difference between younger and older women in quadriceps CSA is about 33% (24 and 74 years; Young, Stokes, & Crowe, 1984). Longitudinal observations on 14 subjects during eight years (from mid-70s to early 80s) indicate a median decrease in quadriceps CSA of 0.8%/yr (Greig, Botella, & Young, 1993). In a sample of 10 frail elderly (90 years; 6 females, 4 males), muscle CSA of the mid-thigh was only 31% of total CSA (Fiatarone et al., 1990), which is less than estimates from younger ages (e.g., 70% in "lean" thigh CSA in 69-year-old men; Borkan et al.), or 70% and 46% in mid-thigh CSA in 77-year-old men and 80-year-old women, respectively (Baumgartner et al., 1992). This would suggest that the atrophy of muscle tissue accelerates with advancing age into the ninth decade. However, eight weeks of resistance weight training in seven of the frail elderly resulted in a 9% increase in mid-thigh muscle CSA (Fiatarone et al.).

Asymmetry in quadriceps CSA is greater in older (mid-70s) than in younger (mid-20s) subjects. The relative differences between dominant and nondominant limbs is about 4 to 5% in young men and women and about 9% in older men and women (Young et al., 1984, 1985). Similar differences are apparent in muscle volumes between dominant and nondominant forearms (about 4%) of young adults of each sex (Maughan, Watson, & Weir, 1984).

The pattern of sex differences in the musculature of the upper and lower extremities based on CT, MRI, and ultrasound is replicated in estimates of muscle mass based on DPA (Heymsfield et al., 1990). Among males ($n = 18$) and females ($n = 16$), age 52 ± 20 years, the sex difference in the upper extremities (41%) is greater than in the lower extremities (22%). Males have proportionally more upper than lower extremity skeletal muscle than

Table 12.13 Estimated Mid-Arm and Calf Muscle Circumferences (cm) in Mexican Americans and American Whites in San Antonio, Texas

Age	n	Arm M	Arm SD	Calf M	Calf SD	n	Arm M	Arm SD	Calf M	Calf SD
		Mexican Americans					American Whites			
Men										
25-34	236	27.6	2.7	32.4	3.0	90	28.1	2.5	33.7	2.8
35-44	208	28.2	2.7	32.9	3.2	115	28.6	2.8	34.2	3.6
45-54	144	27.9	2.4	32.8	2.9	88	28.7	2.2	34.3	3.0
55-69	123	26.9	2.7	32.0	2.8	79	27.8	2.4	33.1	3.1
Women										
25-34	288	22.6	3.1	28.2	2.9	115	22.2	2.6	28.9	2.4
35-44	292	22.9	2.9	28.5	2.7	158	22.5	2.6	29.5	2.7
45-54	215	23.7	3.5	28.6	2.9	89	22.7	2.5	28.9	2.5
55-69	157	23.6	3.0	28.1	2.4	86	22.8	2.7	28.6	2.5

Malina and Stern (1992). Arm circumference is corrected for the thicknesses of the triceps and biceps skinfolds. Calf circumference is corrected for the thicknesses of the medial and lateral calf skinfolds.

females. Ratios of upper to lower extremity muscle mass are 0.57 in males and 0.44 in females.

Data are limited to one study, based on DPA, of 28 pairs of American Black and White females matched for age (44.2 and 43.6 years, respectively), weight (62.3 and 62.0 kg), stature (161 and 162 cm), and the BMI (23.0 and 23.6 kg/m²). Black women have 10 to 15% more appendicular skeletal muscle, and the ethnic difference is more marked in the upper (Blacks 21% greater) than in the lower extremity (Blacks 8% greater) (Ortiz et al., 1992). The differences need to be evaluated in the context of the longer limbs and more slender calves in Blacks (Malina, 1973).

Muscle thicknesses based on ultrasound measurements at upper extremity (forearm, biceps, triceps), trunk (subscapular, abdomen), and lower extremity (quadriceps, hamstrings, posterior calf) sites are greater in American White (N = 42) than in Japanese women 20 to 30 years of age (N = 42) (Ishida et al., 1992, 1994). The ethnic difference persists when muscle thicknesses are adjusted for FFM/stature² and when subjects are matched for the BMI. Ratios of upper extremity/trunk (2.5 vs 2.2) and lower extremity/trunk (6.7 vs 5.7) muscle thicknesses are greater in the Japanese American women, but the ratios of upper to lower extremity muscle thicknesses do not differ between the groups (0.4 vs 0.4) (Ishida et al., 1992).

Summary

Among the three tissues that constitute the body's composition, variation in regional distribution is best documented for adipose tissue and then for skeletal (bone) tissue. Regional variation in the distribution of skeletal muscle tissue is less well documented, but the situation should be improved in the future with the development of new noninvasive techniques. In the context of the available data, there is variation in the regional distribution of adipose, skeletal, and skeletal muscle tissues associated with age, sex, and ethnicity. Individuality in the timing and tempo of sexual maturation and the adolescent growth spurt adds to the variation. Several approaches have been used to express regional variation in the distribution of specific tissues. Further research is necessary to identify which are the most appropriate methods. For example, what is the most appropriate ratio or index to express relative SAT distribution, or the proportions of abdominal VAT and SAT?

Most of the information on regional distribution of adipose, skeletal, and skeletal muscle tissues is based on cross-sectional data. Longitudinal data are most plentiful for SAT during childhood and adolescence and very limited for skeletal and skeletal muscle tissues. Longitudinal data on regional variation in tissue distribution are lacking for the

Table 12.14   Estimated Cross-Sectional Areas (cm²) of Lean Tissue in the Upper and Lower Extremities by Computerized Tomography (CT), Magnetic Resonance Imaging (MRI), and Ultrasound

Area	Men				Women			
	n	Age (SD)*	M	SD	n	Age (SD)*	M	SD
Schantz et al. (1983), CT								
Arm								
Triceps brachii	8	26	31.1	1.6	6	27	19.0	0.7
Biceps brachii			23.5	1.2			14.4	0.6
Thigh								
Medial extensors	11	26	32.9	1.0	10	27	24.1	1.4
Lateral extensors			55.4	2.2			42.4	1.8
Non-extensors			95.1	3.8			75.3	2.4
Rice et al. (1990), CT								
Arm MBA	7	31.4 (4.3)	59.7	6.9				
	13	74.8 (7.1)	45.4	4.9				
Calf MBA	7		97.6	8.6				
			84.8	10.3				
de Koning et al. (1986), CT								
Arm MBA	10	20-50	49.6	9.1	8	20-30	26.0	3.2
Borkan et al. (1983), CT								
Arm "lean"	21	46.3 (2.6)	54.6	8.7				
	20	69.4 (4.1)	48.2	8.2				
Mid-thigh "lean"			147.3	14.6				
			129.1	15.3				
Baumgartner et al. (1992), MRI								
Arm MBA	8	77.0 (3.8)	47.8		17	80.5 (6.2)	26.4	
Mid-thigh MBA			118.2				76.8	
Sipila and Suominen (1991, 1993), ultrasound, CT								
Quadriceps								
Ultrasound	11	73.4 (2.4)	48.4	11.1	15	73.6 (2.9)	29.4	6.8
CT							43.2	7.5
Young et al. (1984, 1985), ultrasound								
Quadriceps	12	21-28	70.8	5.6	25	20-29	57.1	6.6
	12	70-79	53.2	6.3	25	71-81	38.7	8.5

*Age is reported as means (SD) or ranges. *Abbreviation*: MBA, muscle-bone cross-sectional area.

transition from adolescence into adulthood and for the changes that occur during adulthood. Hence, the present state of knowledge of regional variation in body composition during the life span is based largely on differences between age groups and not on changes which accompany age.

References

Adams, W.C., Deck-Côté, K., & Winters, K.M. (1992). Anthropometric estimation of bone mineral content in young adult females. *American Journal of Human Biology, 4,* 767-774.

Baumgartner, R.N., Rhyne, R.L., Troup, C., et al. (1992). Appendicular skeletal muscle areas assessed by magnetic resonance imaging in older persons. *Journal of Gerontology , 47,* M67-M72.

Baumgartner, R.N., & Roche, A.F. (1988). Tracking of fat pattern indices in childhood: The Melbourne Growth Study. *Human Biology, 60,* 549-567.

Baumgartner, R.N., Roche, A.F., Guo, S., et al. (1986). Adipose tissue distribution: The stability of principal components by sex, ethnicity and maturation stage. *Human Biology, 58,* 719-735.

Baumgartner, R.N., Roche, A.F., Guo, S., et al. (1990). Fat patterning and centralized obesity in Mexican-American children in the Hispanic Health and Nutrition Examination Survey

(HHANES 1982-1984). *American Journal of Clinical Nutrition*, **51**, 936S-943S.

Beunen, G., Claessens, A., Ostyn, M., et al. (1986). *Stability of subcutaneous fat patterning in adolescent boys.* Paper presented at the Fifth Congress of the European Anthropological Association, Lisbon.

Beunen, G., Lefevre, J., Claessens, A.L., et al. (1992). *Association between skeletal maturity and adipose tissue distribution during growth.* Poster presented at the annual meeting of the American Association of Physical Anthropologists, Las Vegas, NV.

Beunen, G., & Malina, R.M. (1988). Growth and physical performance relative to the timing of the adolescent spurt. *Exercise and Sport Sciences Reviews*, **16**, 503-540.

Beunen, G., Malina, R.M., Lefevre, J., et al. (1994). Size, fatness and relative fat distribution of males of contrasting maturity status during adolescence and as adults. *International Journal of Obesity*, **18**, 670-678.

Beunen, G.P., Malina, R.M., Van't Hof, M.A., et al. (1988). *Adolescent growth and motor performance: A longitudinal study of Belgian boys.* Champaign, IL: Human Kinetics.

Bonjour, J-P., Theintz, G., Buchs, B., et al. (1991). Critical years and stages of puberty for spinal and femoral bone mass accumulation during adolescence. *Journal of Clinical Endocrinology and Metabolism*, **73**, 555-563.

Borkan, G.A., Hults, D.E., Gerzof, S.G., et al. (1983). Age changes in body composition revealed by computed tomography. *Journal of Gerontology*, **38**, 673-677.

Bouchard, C., Després, J-P., & Mauriege, P. (1993). Genetic and nongenetic determinants of regional fat distribution. *Endocrine Reviews*, **14**, 72-93.

Bronson, F.H., & Manning, J.M. (1991). The energetic regulation of ovulation: A realistic role for body fat. *Biology of Reproduction*, **44**, 945-950.

Carmelli, D., McElroy, M.R., & Rosenman, R.H. (1991). Longitudinal changes in fat distribution in the Western Collaborative Group Study: A 23-year follow-up. *International Journal of Obesity*, **15**, 67-74.

Croft, J.B., Strogatz, D.S., Keenan, N.L., et al. (1993). The independent effects of obesity and body fat distribution on blood pressure in Black adults: The Pitt County Study. *International Journal of Obesity*, **17**, 391-397.

Cronk, C.E., Mukherjee, D., & Roche, A.F. (1983). Changes in triceps and subscapular skinfold thickness during adolescence. *Human Biology*, **55**, 707-721.

de Koning, F.L., Binkhorst, R.A., Kauer, J.M.G., & Thijssen, H.O.M. (1986). Accuracy of an anthropometric estimate of the muscle and bone area in a transversal cross-section of the arm. *International Journal of Sports Medicine*, **7**, 246-249.

de Ridder, C.M., de Boer, R.W., Seidell, J.C., et al. (1992). Body fat distribution in pubertal girls quantified by magnetic resonance imaging. *International Journal of Obesity*, **16**, 443-449.

Deutsch, M.I., Mueller, W.H., & Malina, R.M. (1985). Androgyny in fat patterning is associated with obesity in adolescents and young adults. *Annals of Human Biology*, **12**, 275-286.

Enzi, G., Gasparo, M., Biondetti, P.R., et al. (1986). Subcutaneous and visceral fat distribution according to sex, age, and overweight, evaluated by computed tomography. *American Journal of Clinical Nutrition*, **44**, 739-746.

Faulkner, R.A., Bailey, D.A., Drinkwater, D.T., et al. (1993). Regional and total body bone mineral content, bone mineral density, and total body tissue composition in children 8-16 years of age. *Calcified Tissue International*, **53**, 7-12.

Fiatarone, M.A., Marks, E.C., Ryan, N.D., et al. (1990). High-intensity strength training in nonagenarians. *Journal of the American Medical Association*, **263**, 3029-3034.

Forbes, G.B. (1986). Body composition in adolescence. In F. Falkner & J.M. Tanner (Eds.), *Human growth. Volume 2: Postnatal growth, neurobiology* (pp. 119-145). New York: Plenum.

Forbes, G.B., Brown, M.R., & Griffiths, H.J.L. (1988). Arm muscle plus bone area, anthropometry and CAT compared. *American Journal of Clinical Nutrition*, **47**, 929-931.

Fox, K., Peters, D., Armstrong, N., & Bell, M. (1993). Abdominal fat deposition in 11-year-old children. *International Journal of Obesity*, **17**, 11-16.

Frisancho, A.R. (1990). *Anthropometric standards for the assessment of growth and nutritional status.* Ann Arbor: University of Michigan.

Frisch, R.E. (1976). Fatness of girls from menarche to age 18 years, with a nomogram. *Human Biology*, **48**, 353-359.

Frisch, R.E. (1988). Fatness and fertility. *Scientific American*, **258**, 88-95.

Fujimoto, W.Y., Newell-Morris, L.L., & Shuman, W.P. (1990). Intra-abdominal fat and risk variables for non-insulin dependent diabetes (NIDDM) and coronary heart disease in Japanese American women with android and gynoid fat patterning. In Y. Oomura, S. Tarui, S. Inoue, & T. Shimazu (Eds.), *Progress in obesity research* (pp. 317-322). London: John Libbey.

Garn, S.M. (1961). Radiographic analysis of body composition. In J. Brožek & A. Henschel (Eds.), *Techniques for measuring body composition* (pp. 36-58). Washington, DC: National Academy of Science/National Research Council.

Garn, S.M. (1964). The developmental nature of bone changes during aging. In J.E. Birren (Ed.), *Relations of development and aging* (pp. 41-61). Springfield, IL: C.C. Thomas.

Garn, S.M. (1970). *The earlier gain and the later loss of cortical bone.* Springfield, IL: C.C. Thomas.

Garn, S.M., Miller, R.L., & Larson, K.E. (1976). *Metacarpal lengths, cortical diameters and areas from the 10-State Nutrition Survey.* Ann Arbor: University of Michigan.

Garn, S.M., Nagy, J.M., & Sandusky, S.T. (1972). Differential sexual dimorphism in bone diameters of subjects of European and African ancestry. *American Journal of Physical Anthropology, 37,* 127-130.

Garn, S.M., Pao, E.M., & Rihl, M.E. (1964). Compact bone in Chinese and Japanese. *Science, 143,* 1439-1440.

Garn, S.M., Rohmann, C.G., & Wagner, B. (1967). Bone loss as a general phenomenon in man. *Federation Proceedings, 26,* 1729-1736.

Garn, S.M., Ryan, A.S., & Robson, J.K.R. (1982). Fatness-dependence and utility of the subscapular/triceps ratio. *Ecology of Food and Nutrition, 12,* 173-177.

Garn, S.M., & Saalberg, J.H. (1953). Sex and age differences in the composition of the adult leg. *Human Biology, 25,* 144-153.

Gerace, L., Aliprantis, A., Russell, M., et al. (1994). Skeletal differences between Black and White men and their relevance to body composition estimates. *American Journal of Human Biology, 6,* 255-262.

Geusens, P., Cantatore, F., Nijs, J., et al. (1991). Heterogeneity of growth of bone in children at the spine, radius and total skeleton. *Growth, Development, and Aging, 55,* 249-256.

Glastre, C., Braillon, P., David, L., et al. (1990). Measurement of bone mineral content of the lumbar spine by dual energy x-ray absorptiometry in normal children: Correlations with growth parameters. *Journal of Clinical Endocrinology and Metabolism, 70,* 1330-1333.

Goldsmith, N.F., Johnston, J.O., Picetti, G., & Garcia, C. (1973). Bone mineral in the radius and vertebral osteoporosis in an insured population: A correlative study using ^{125}I photon absorption and miniature roentgenography. *Journal of Bone and Joint Surgery, 55A,* 1276-1293.

Gordon, C.L., Halton, J.M., Atkinson, S.A., et al. (1991). The contributions of growth and puberty to peak bone mass. *Growth, development, and aging, 55,* 257-262.

Greig, C.A., Botella, J., & Young, A. (1993). The quadriceps strength of healthy, elderly people remeasured after eight years. *Muscle and Nerve, 16,* 6-10.

Hammer, L.D., Wilson, D.M., Litt, I.F., et al. (1991). Impact of pubertal development on body fat distribution among White, Hispanic, and Asian female adolescents. *Journal of Pediatrics, 118,* 975-980.

Hammond, W.H. (1955). Measurement and interpretation of subcutaneous fat, with norms for children and young adult males. *British Journal of Preventive and Social Medicine, 9,* 201-211.

Hampton, M.C., Huenemann, R.L., & Shapiro, L.R. (1966). A longitudinal study of gross body composition and body conformation and their association with food and activity in a teen-age population. *American Journal of Clinical Nutrition, 19,* 422-435.

Hattori, K. (1987). Subcutaneous fat distribution pattern in Japanese young adults. *Journal of the Anthropological Society of Nippon, 95,* 353-359.

Hattori, K., Numata, N., Ikoma, M., et. al. (1991). Sex differences in the distribution of subcutaneous and internal fat. *Human Biology, 63,* 53-63.

Heitmann, B.L. (1991). Body fat distribution in the adult Danish population aged 35-65 years: An epidemiological study. *International Journal of Obesity, 15,* 535-545.

Heymsfield, S.B., McManus, C., Smith, J., et. al. (1982). Anthropometric measurement of muscle mass: Revised equations for calculating bone-free arm muscle area. *American Journal of Clinical Nutrition, 36,* 680-690.

Heymsfield, S.B., Smith, R., Aulet, M., et al. (1990). Appendicular skeletal muscle mass: Measurement by dual-photon absorptiometry. *American Journal of Clinical Nutrition, 52,* 214-218.

Ishida, Y., Kanehisa, H., Fukunaga, T., & Pollock, M. L. (1992). A comparison of fat and muscle thickness in Japanese and American women. *Annals of Physiological Anthropology, 11,* 29-35.

Ishida, Y., Kanehisa, H., Kondo, M., et al. (1994). Body fat and muscle thickness in Japanese and Caucasian females. *American Journal of Human Biology, 6,* 711-718.

Kaplowitz, H.J., Wild, K.A., Mueller, W.H., et al. (1988). Serial and parent-child changes in components of body fat distribution and fatness in children from the London Longitudinal Growth Study, ages two to eighteen years. *Human Biology, 60,* 739-758.

Kaye, S.A., Folsom, A.R., Jacobs, D.R., Jr., et al. (1993). Psychosocial correlates of body fat distribution in Black and White young adults. *International Journal of Obesity, 17,* 271-277.

Kin, K., Lee, J.H.E., Kushida, K., et al. (1993). Bone density and body composition on the Pacific rim: A comparison between Japan-born and U.S.-born Japanese-American women. *Journal of Bone and Mineral Research, 8*, 861-869.

Komiya, S., Muraoka, Y., Zhang, F-S., & Masuda, T. (1992). Age-related changes in body fat distribution in middle-aged and elderly Japanese. *Journal of the Anthropological Society of Nippon, 100*, 161-169.

Lemieux, S., Prud'homme, D., & Bouchard, C. (1993). Sex differences in the relation of visceral adipose tissue accumulation to total body fatness. *American Journal of Clinical Nutrition, 58*, 463-467.

Ley, C.J., Lees, B., & Stevenson, J.C. (1992). Sex- and menopause-associated changes in body-fat distribution. *American Journal of Clinical Nutrition, 55*, 950-954.

Li, J-Y., Specker, B.L., Ho, M.L., et al. (1989). Bone mineral content in Black and White children 1 to 6 years of age. *American Journal of Diseases of Children, 143*, 1346-1349.

Liel, Y., Edwards, J., & Shary, J. (1988). The effects of race and body habitus on bone mineral density of the radius, hip, and spine in premenopausal women. *Journal of Clinical Endocrinology and Metabolism, 66*, 1247-1250.

Lohman, T.G. (1986). Applicability of body composition techniques and constants for children and youths. *Exercise and Sport Sciences Reviews, 14*, 325-357.

Luckey, M.M., Meier, D.E., Mandeli, J.P., et al. (1989). Radial and vertebral bone density in White and Black women: Evidence for racial differences in premenopausal bone homeostasis. *Journal of Clinical Endocrinology and Metabolism, 69*, 762-770.

Malina, R.M. (1969). Quantification of fat, muscle and bone in man. *Clinical Orthopaedics and Related Research, 65*, 9-38.

Malina, R.M. (1973). Biological substrata. In K.S. Miller & R.M. Dreger (Eds.), *Comparative studies of Blacks and Whites in the United States* (pp. 53-123). New York: Seminar.

Malina, R.M. (1986). Growth of muscle tissue and muscle mass. In F. Falkner & J.M. Tanner (Eds.), *Human growth. Volume 2: Postnatal growth, neurobiology* (pp. 77-99). New York: Plenum.

Malina, R.M. (1991). Darwinian fitness, physical fitness and physical activity. In C.G.N. Mascie-Taylor & G.W. Lasker (Eds.), *Applications of biological anthropology to human affairs* (pp. 143-184). Cambridge, England: Cambridge University.

Malina, R.M., & Bouchard, C. (1988). Subcutaneous fat distribution during growth. In C. Bouchard & F.E. Johnston (Eds.), *Fat distribution during growth and later health outcomes* (pp. 63-84). New York: Plenum.

Malina, R.M., & Bouchard, C. (1991). *Growth, maturation, and physical activity.* Champaign, IL: Human Kinetics.

Malina, R.M., & Bouchard, C. (1992). [The Quebec Family Study]. Unpublished raw data.

Malina, R.M., Huang, Y.-C., & Brown, K.H. (in press). Subcutaneous adipose tissue distribution in adolescent girls of four ethnic groups. *International Journal of Obesity.*

Malina, R.M., & Stern, M.P. (1992). [The San Antonio Heart Study]. Unpublished raw data.

Martorell, R., Malina, R.M., & Castillo, R.O. (1988). Body proportions in three ethnic groups: Children and youths 2-17 years in NHANES II and HHANES. *Human Biology, 60*, 205-222.

Maughan, R.J., Watson, J.S., & Weir, J. (1984). The relative proportions of fat, muscle and bone in the normal human forearm as determined by computed tomography. *Clinical Science, 66*, 683-689.

Mazess, R.B., Peppler, W.W., & Chesney, R.W. (1984). Total body and regional bone mineral by dual-photon absorptiometry in metabolic bone disease. *Calcified Tissue International, 36*, 8-13.

McCormick, D.P., Ponder, S.W., Fawcett, H.D., & Palmer, J. L. (1991). Spinal bone mineral density in 335 normal and obese children and adolescents: Evidence for ethnic and sex differences. *Journal of Bone and Mineral Research, 6*, 507-513.

Mueller, W.H. (1982). The changes with age of the anatomical distribution of fat. *Social Science Medicine, 16*, 191-196.

Mueller, W.H. (1988). Ethnic differences in fat distribution during growth. In C. Bouchard & F.E. Johnston (Eds.). *Fat distribution during growth and later health outcomes* (pp. 127-145). New York: Plenum.

Mueller, W.H., Shoup, R.F., & Malina, R.M. (1982). Fat patterning in athletes in relation to ethnic origin and sport. *Annals of Human Biology, 9*, 371-376.

Najjar, M.F., & Kuczmarski, R.J. (1989). *Anthropometric data and prevalence of overweight for Hispanics, 1982-1984* (Vital and Health Statistics, Series 11, No. 239). Washington, DC: Government Printing Office.

Najjar, M.F., & Rowland, M. (1987). *Anthropometric reference data and prevalence of overweight, United States, 1976-1980* (Vital and Health Statistics,

Series 11, No. 238). Washington, DC: Government Printing Office.

Nelson, D.A., Feingold, M., Bolin, F., & Parfitt, A.M. (1991). Principal components analysis of regional bone density in Black and White women: Relationship to body size and composition. *American Journal of Physical Anthropology*, **86**, 507-514.

Nelson, D.A., Kleerekoper, M., & Parfitt, A.M. (1988). Bone mass, skin color and body size among Black and White women. *Bone and Mineral*, **4**, 257-264.

Newell-Morris, L., Moceri, V., & Fujimoto, W. (1989). Gynoid and android fat patterning in Japanese-American men, body build and glucose metabolism. *American Journal of Human Biology*, **1**, 73-86.

Ortiz, O., Russell, M., & Daley, T.L. (1992). Differences in skeletal muscle and bone mineral mass between Black and White females and their relevance to estimates of body composition. *American Journal of Clinical Nutrition*, **55**, 8-13.

Peters D., Fox, K., Armstrong, N., et al. (1994). Estimation of body fat and body fat distribution in 11-year-old children using magnetic resonance imaging and hydrostatic weighing, skinfolds, and anthropometry. *American Journal of Human Biology*, **6**, 237-243.

Pollitzer, W.S., & Anderson, J.J.B. (1989). Ethnic and genetic differences in bone mass: A review with a hereditary vs environmental perspective. *American Journal of Clinical Nutrition*, **50**, 1244-1259.

Reynolds, E.L. (1950). The distribution of subcutaneous fat in childhood and adolescence. *Monographs of the Society for Research in Child Development*, **15** (Serial No. 50), 1-189.

Reynolds, E.L., & Grote, P. (1948). Sex differences in the distribution of tissue components in the human leg from birth to maturity. *Anatomical Record*, **102**, 45-53.

Rice, C.L., Cunningham, D.A., Paterson, D.H., & Lefcoe, M. S. (1990). A comparison of anthropometry with computed tomography in limbs of young and aged men. *Journal of Gerontology*, **45**, M174-M179.

Rico, H., Revilla, M., Hernandez, E.R., et al. (1992). Sex differences in the acquisition of total bone mineral mass peak assessed through dual-energy x-ray absorptiometry. *Calcified Tissue International*, **51**, 251-254.

Rico, H., Revilla, M., Villa, L.F., et al. (1993). Body composition in children and Tanner's stages: A study with dual-energy x-ray absorptiometry. *Metabolism*, **42**, 967-970.

Riggs, B.L., Wahner, H.W., Dunn, W.L., et al. (1981). Differential changes in bone mineral density of the appendicular and axial skeleton with aging. *Journal of Clinical Investigation*, **67**, 328-335.

Riggs, B.L., Wahner, H.W., & Melton, L.J. (1986). Rates of bone loss in the appendicular and axial skeletons of women. *Journal of Clinical Investigation*, **77**, 1487-1491.

Roche, A.F., & Baumgartner, R.N. (1988). Tracking in fat distribution during growth. In C. Bouchard & F.E. Johnston (Eds.), *Fat distribution during growth and later health outcomes* (pp. 147-162). New York: Plenum.

Rolland-Cachera, M.-F., Bellisle, F., Deheeger, M., et al. (1990). Influence of body fat distribution during childhood on body fat distribution in adulthood: A two-decade follow-up study. *International Journal of Obesity*, **14**, 473-481.

Ross, P.D., Orimo, H., Wasnich, R.D., et al. (1989). Methodological issues in comparing genetic and environmental influences on bone mass. *Bone and Mineral*, **7**, 67-77.

Ross, R., Leger, L., Morris, D., et al. (1992). Quantification of adipose tissue by MRI: Relationship with anthropometric variables. *Journal of Applied Physiology*, **72**, 787-795.

Russell-Aulet, M., Wang, J., Thornton, J., et al. (1991). Bone mineral density and mass by total-body dual-photon absorptiometry in normal White and Asian men. *Journal of Bone and Mineral Research*, **6**, 1109-1113.

Ryan, A.S., Martinez, G.A., Baumgartner, R.N., et al. (1990). Median skinfold thickness distributions and fat-wave patterns in Mexican-American children from the Hispanic Health and Nutrition Examination Survey (HHANES 1982-1984). *American Journal of Clinical Nutrition*, **51**, 925S-935S.

Scammon, R.E. (1923). A summary of the anatomy of the infant and child. In I.A. Abt (Ed.), *Pediatrics* (pp. 257-444). Philadelphia: Saunders.

Schantz, P., Randall-Fox, E., Hutchinson, W., et al. (1983). Muscle fiber type distribution, muscle cross-sectional area and maximal voluntary strength in humans. *Acta Physiologica Scandinavica*, **117**, 219-226.

Schwartz, R.S., Shuman, W.P., Bradbury, V.L., et al. (1990). Body fat distribution in healthy young and older men. *Journal of Gerontology*, **45**, M181-M185.

Seidell, J.C., Cigolini, M., Charzewska, J., et al. (1990). Androgenicity in relation to body fat distribution and metabolism in 38-year-old women: The European Fat Distribution Study. *Journal of Clinical Epidemiology*, **43**, 21-34.

Seidell, J.C., Oosterlee, A., Deurenberg, P., et al. (1988). Abdominal fat depots measured with computed tomography: Effects of degree of obesity, sex, and age. *European Journal of Clinical Nutrition, 42*, 805-815.

Sipila, S., & Suominen, H. (1991). Ultrasound imaging of the quadriceps muscle in elderly athletes and untrained men. *Muscle and Nerve, 14*, 527-533.

Sipila, S., & Suominen, H. (1993). Muscle ultrasonography and computed tomography in elderly trained and untrained women. *Muscle and Nerve, 16*, 294-300.

Slattery, M.L., McDonald, A., Bild, D.E., et al. (1992). Associations of body fat and its distribution with dietary intake, physical activity, alcohol, and smoking in Blacks and Whites. *American Journal of Clinical Nutrition, 55*, 943-949.

Slaughter, M.H., Lohman, T.G., Boileau, R.A., et al. (1990). Differences in the subcomponents of fat-free body in relation to height between Black and White children. *American Journal of Human Biology, 2*, 209-217.

Sonnenschein, E.G., Kim, M.Y., Pasternack, B.S., & Toniolo, P.G. (1993). Sources of variability in waist and hip measurements in middle-aged women. *American Journal of Epidemiology, 138*, 301-309.

Sugimoto, T., Tsutsumi, M., Fujii, Y., et al. (1992). Comparison of bone mineral content among Japanese, Koreans, and Taiwanese assessed by dual-photon absorptiometry. *Journal of Bone and Mineral Research, 7*, 153-159.

Tanner, J.M. (1964). *The physique of the olympic athlete.* London: George Allen and Unwin.

Tanner, J.M., Hughes, P.C.R., & Whitehouse, R.H. (1981). Radiographically determined widths of bone, muscle and fat in the upper arm and calf from age 3-18 years. *Annals of Human Biology, 8*, 495-517.

Theintz, G., Buchs, B., Rizzoli, R., et al. (1992). Longitudinal monitoring of bone mass accumulation in healthy adolescents: Evidence for a marked reduction after 16 years of age at the levels of lumbar spine and femoral neck in female subjects. *Journal of Clinical Endocrinology and Metabolism, 75*, 1060-1065.

Tichet, J., Vol, S., Balkau, B., et al. (1993). Android fat distribution by age and sex: The waist hip ratio. Diabete et Metabolisme, *19*, 273-276.

Trotter, M., Broman, G.E., & Peterson, R.R. (1959). Density of cervical vertebrae and comparisons with densities of other bones. *American Journal of Physical Anthropology, 17*, 19-25.

Trotter, M., Broman, G.E., & Peterson, R.R. (1960). Densities of bones of White and Negro skeletons. *Journal of Bone and Joint Surgery, 42A*, 50-58.

Trotter, M., & Hixon, B.B. (1974). Sequential changes in weight, density, and percentage ash weight of human skeletons from an early fetal period through old age. *Anatomical Record, 179*, 1-18.

Trotter, M., & Peterson, R.R. (1962). The relationship of ash weight and organic weight of human skeletons. *Journal of Bone and Joint Surgery, 44A*, 669-681.

Trotter, M., & Peterson, R.R. (1970). The density of bones in the fetal skeleton. *Growth, 34*, 283-292.

Tsunenari, T., Tsutsumi, M., Ohno, K., et al. (1993). Age- and gender-related changes in body composition in Japanese subjects. *Journal of Bone and Mineral Research, 8*, 397-402.

Vague, J., Vague, P., Jubelin, J., et al. (1988). Fat distribution, obesities and health: Evolution of concepts. In C. Bouchard, & F.E. Johnston (Eds.), *Fat distribution during growth and later health outcomes* (pp. 9-41). New York: Plenum.

van Beresteijn, E.C.H., van't Hof, M.A., Schaafsma, G., et al. (1990). Habitual dietary calcium intake and cortical bone loss in perimenopausal women: A longitudinal study. *Calcified Tissue International, 47*, 338-344.

van der Kooy, K., Leenen, R., Seidell, J.C., et al. (1993). Waist-hip ratio is a poor predictor of changes in visceral fat. *American Journal of Clinical Nutrition, 57*, 327-333.

Weits, T., van der Beek, E.J., & Wedel, M. (1988). Computed tomography measurement of abdominal fat deposition in relation to anthropometry. *International Journal of Obesity, 12*, 217-225.

Yano, K., Wasnich, R.D., & Vogel, J.M. (1984). Bone mineral measurements among middle-aged and elderly Japanese residents in Hawaii. *American Journal of Epidemiology, 119*, 751-764.

Young, A., Stokes, M., & Crowe, M. (1984). Size and strength of the quadriceps muscles of old and young women. *European Journal of Clinical Investigation, 14*, 282-287.

Young, A., Stokes, M., & Crowe, M. (1985). The size and strength of the quadriceps muscles of old and young men. *Clinical Physiology, 5*, 145-154.

Young, C.M., Sipin, S.S., & Roe, D.A. (1968). Body composition of pre-adolescent and adolescent girls, I: Density and skinfold measurements. *Journal of American Dietetic Association, 53*, 25-31.

Zavaleta, A.N., & Malina, R.M. (1980). Growth, fatness, and leanness in Mexican-American children. *American Journal of Clinical Nutrition, 33*, 2008-2020.

13

Body Composition in Athletes

Wayne E. Sinning

Specific uses of body composition analysis in athletes include the determination of appropriate weight for competition, particularly in sports such as gymnastics where appearance is important and in weight-limit sports such as wrestling. Concerns about eating disorders and over-training in these groups make knowledge of the athlete's body composition critical. The potential for eating disorders in athletes is a real issue (Brownell & Rodin, 1992). In women's sports, the combination of disordered eating patterns, amenorrhea, and osteoporosis, associated with reproductive dysfunction and very low body weights, has recently been labeled the female athlete triad (Yeager, Agostini, Nattiv, & Drinkwater, 1993). Storlie (1991) considers that the objective analysis of body weight is the first step in the nutritional counseling of athletes.

Minimum Weight of Athletes

The minimum weight (MW) of an athlete is defined here as the lowest weight that he or she can maintain indefinitely without adverse effects on health and performance. Unfortunately, there is no definitive answer to what a MW should be. Behnke (1969) proposed that the lean body mass (LBM)

and MW are the same in the male. The LBM contains the fat-free mass (FFM) plus essential lipid substances present in bone marrow, spinal cord, brain, and certain organs. The LBM is a theoretical in vivo entity while the FFM is an in vitro entity based on carcass analysis (Behnke, 1961). The FFM is a measurable quantity while the LBM is not. In males, Behnke (1961) suggested that MW is typified by the leanest males in a healthy population and contains 3% body fat (BF), while in females MW includes lipids in mammary and other sex-specific tissues and contains 14% BF (Behnke, 1969). Lohman (1992) suggests the LBM of males may be obtained by dividing the FFM by 0.97 or by dividing the MW by 0.95. For females, LBM may be obtained by dividing the FFM by 0.95 or by dividing the MW by 0.88.

Weight reduction for sports involves two problems. The first is the effect of maintaining a very low weight over a long period of time, even years, on health and performance. The second is the effect and safety of rapid dehydration and dietary restriction to "make weight" for a single competition, as occurs in wrestling.

Long-Term Weight Depletion

Weight reduction has been studied most extensively in wrestling due to the practices followed in this sport. Studies by Kelly, Gorney, and Kalm (1978) and Siders, Bolunchuk, and Lukaski (1991) showed significant decreases in weight and % BF during a wrestling season without changes in the FFM, but other studies have shown a loss of FFM with weight reduction (Horswill et al., 1990a; Roemmich, 1994; Roemmich, Sinning, & Roemmich, 1991; Sinning, Wilensky, & Myers, 1976; Widerman & Hagan, 1982).

A major concern is the potential effects of long-term weight reduction on nutrition and metabolism. Horswill, Park, and Roemmich (1990c) demonstrated adverse effects on indices of protein nutritional status during a season in adolescent wrestlers who decreased their energy intake to 35% below pre-season levels and lost 6.6% of their pre-season body weight. Steen, Oppliger, and Brownell (1988) found resting metabolic rates in adolescent wrestlers who weight cycled were 14% lower than in those who did not, which might predispose an individual to later obesity. These findings were not supported, however, by the studies of McCarger and Crawford (1992) and Schmidt, Corrigan, and Melby (1993).

Some studies have suggested that growth retardation occurs during the wrestling season (Sinning et al., 1976; Tcheng & Tipton, 1973), but Housh, Johnson, Stout, & Housh (1993) did not find any adverse effect on the growth of 477 high school wrestlers, although the weight increase per year was lower in the wrestlers than in a national sample. In adolescent wrestlers, Roemmich (1994) found a retardation of soft tissue growth and a reduction in FFM during a season but no effect on longitudinal skeletal growth or skeletal maturation.

The effects of the long-term maintenance of a low body weight on sports performance is also of interest. Kelly et al. (1978) found cardiovascular function was stable during a collegiate wrestling season and five weeks post-season, but muscular strength increased post-season. Eckerson, Housh, Housh, and Johnson (1994) found decreases in peak power and peak torque for several isokinetic measures of arm and leg flexion and extension during a high school wrestling season. These changes were not associated with a decrease in weight. Roemmich et al. (1991), however, found significant in-season decreases and post-season increases in arm strength and power, which became nonsignificant when covaried for changes in FFM.

There is an apparent interaction between low body weight and normal endocrine function that is not understood. In highly trained female athletes, low estrogen levels and secondary amenorrhea are not uncommon. The possible mechanisms

have been discussed elsewhere (Loucks, 1990; Warren, 1992). Amenorrheic athletes tend to be lean, but % BF is apparently not the causative factor. Carlberg, Buckman, Peake, and Riedesel (1983) found amenorrheic athletes have significantly lower % BF than eumenorrheic athletes, but other studies have provided contrary findings (Calabrese et al., 1983, Linnell et al., 1984). Warren (1992) noted that it is difficult to induce menstrual cycle dysfunction in normally cycling women without weight loss.

Altered reproductive function with leanness and endurance training is not limited to females. Low reproductive hormone levels have been found in lean, endurance-trained males by Hackney, Sinning, and Bruot (1988, 1990) and Wheeler, Wall, Belcastro, and Cumming (1984), but reproductive dysfunction in males has not been reported. Blood testosterone levels are reduced in college wrestlers who lose weight (Hackney & Sinning, 1986; Strauss, Lenase, & Malarkey, 1985). In an extensive study of the effects of weight reduction by adolescent wrestlers, Roemmich (1994) found in-season decreases in testosterone, free-testosterone, dihydroepiandrosterone-sulfate, insulin-like growth factor, and growth-hormone binding protein. Growth hormone and sex-hormone binding globulin increased, while changes did not occur in luteinizing hormone, estradiol, prolactin, cortisol, insulin, triiodothyronine (T3), thyroxine (T4), and insulin-like growth factor binding protein-3. All hormone concentrations returned to control levels within four months post-season.

A major concern relative to menstrual dysfunction in amenorrheic women athletes is the effect on bone mineral (Calabrese et al., 1983; Cann, Genant, Ettinger, & Gordon, 1980; Cann, Martin, & Jaffe, 1984; Drinkwater et al., 1984; Lindberg et al., 1984; Marcus et al., 1985). These women typically have low energy intakes and low body weight (Drinkwater et al., 1984; Drinkwater, Bruemner, & Chestnut, 1990; Marcus et al.; Nelson et al., 1986). Deuster et al. (1986) did not find differences in caloric intake between elite eumenorrheic and amenorrheic marathon runners but concluded, on the basis of dietary records, that low intakes of dietary fat and zinc as well as excess intakes of β-carotene may play a role in inducing amenorrhea. Women with low body weight but normal menstrual function do not show bone loss (Drinkwater et al., 1990). Recovery of bone mineral in previously amenorrheic athletes is associated with an increase of body weight (Drinkwater, Nilson, Ott, & Chestnut, 1986).

In summary, prolonged maintenance of an excessively low body weight may be associated with negative physiological changes. Whether body composition changes parallel or cause these changes is not yet known. Nevertheless, whether cause or effect, marked changes in body composition should alert the athletic trainer or coach to potential problems and the need for medical consultation. Regular, supervised measurements of weight with reviews of longitudinal records should be enough to identify adverse weight changes.

Rapid Weight Loss for Competition

Making weight, or reaching a weight limit, during a short time is attained primarily by dehydration. The most common method is food and fluid abstention combined with exercise and thermal dehydration. A few athletes may resort to extreme measures such as forced vomiting, laxatives, and diuretics (Steen & Brownell, 1990; Woods, Wilson, & Masland, 1988). Usually there is time for some rehydration before competition. College wrestlers may weigh-in a maximum of five hours and a minimum of one-half hour before quadrangular, triangular, and dual meets; for tournaments the maximum and minimum time limits are 24 hours and one-half hour, respectively, while high school rules stipulate a maximum of one hour and a minimum of one-half hour (National Collegiate Athletic Association, 1991).

Weight reduction decreases functional capacity, and this is not regained with short-term rehydration. Webster, Rutt, & Weltman (1990) demonstrated that an acute loss of 5% of body weight produced deleterious effects on strength, anaerobic power, anaerobic capacity, and lactate threshold. The loss of work capacity associated with a 4.8% weight reduction could not be recovered with five hours of rehydration (Herbert & Ribsl, 1972). Huston, Marin, Green, & Thompson (1981) found significant decreases in muscle glycogen and dynamic strength but no change in anaerobic work capacity with an 8% weight loss during four days. Three hours of rehydration did not improve muscle glycogen stores or strength. Horswill et al. (1990a) studied 12 wrestlers who reduced their weights by 6% during four days; six consumed a hypocaloric diet that was high in carbohydrate, the others consumed a low carbohydrate diet. Sprint arm work and blood lactate levels during exercise, an index of available glycogen, both decreased. The plasma volume of the low carbohydrate group decreased while that of the high carbohydrate group increased. Also, the confusion, depression, anger, and tension scores on a profile of mood states test increased while vigor decreased. Zambreski et al. (1974, 1975) found elevated specific gravity, creatinine, osmolality, and potassium and protein levels in two studies of state high school wrestling finalists. In the second study, urine samples collected at a morning weigh-in and after the second of two matches in one day showed that the athletes had not completely rehydrated. The review by Horswill (1992) is recommended for those who have further interest in this topic.

Whatever the effects of rapid dehydration, it is an accepted practice by coaches and participants in sports where the athlete must meet weight limits. Simple field tests of hydration status are not readily available, although bioimpedance analysis, which is based on the relationship between fluid volume and electrical resistance, may provide one (see chapter 5).

Setting a Minimum Weight

Wrestling is the only sport where there has been a concerted effort to establish a MW. Tcheng and Tipton (1973) developed the first equation to estimate MW using anthropometric values from 582 finalists in the Iowa High School Championship Tournament. Their study was important, not only for the equations that were defined, but also for establishing the conceptual model for subsequent research. On the basis of estimates from skinfold thicknesses and reports of the body composition of lean athletes in the literature, they assumed that the wrestlers had 5% BF and that this was the desirable amount for a MW in these athletes.

Subsequent studies evaluated these equations. Sinning (1974), using college athletes, found that the Tcheng-Tipton equations underestimated the MW measured by densitometry (i.e., FFM + 5% BF). Of more importance, the SEE of 4 kg for the equations was extremely large for predicting MW in wrestlers; the 95% confidence limits spanned four weight classes. Equations for the prediction of FFM using skinfold thicknesses alone or skinfold thicknesses with skeletal measures had SEEs from 2.1 to 2.3 kg. With exception of a study by Williford et al. (1986), who showed the Tcheng-Tipton equations to be superior to others, subsequent studies have confirmed these observations in high school wrestlers (Clark, Kuta, & Oppliger, 1992; Housh et al., 1989; Sinning et al., 1976; Thorland, Johnson, Cisar, & Housh, 1987; Thorland et al., 1991). The 1991 study by Thorland et al. is especially significant because it used 860 subjects in five states.

The equation that has consistently given superior results is one developed by Lohman (1981), which uses the sum of three skinfolds (3SF: triceps + subscapular + abdominal) to estimate body density (BD), from which the FFM and MW are computed as:

$$BD = 1.0982 - 0.000815 \, (3SF) - 0.00000084 \, (3SF)^2. \qquad (13.1)$$

Cross-validation studies of this equation typically have pure errors (PE, the square root of the mean square of the residuals) of 2.0 to 2.6 kg (Clark, Kuta, & Oppliger, 1992), which is within plus or minus one weight class in the 12-class system.

In 1976 the American College of Sports Medicine (ACSM) issued a position statement recommending that a MW containing 5% BF be determined for wrestlers several weeks before the season begins. The Wisconsin Interscholastic Athletic Association has established a program derived from the ACSM recommendation that is based on a 7% BF minimum (Clark et al., 1992) and use of the Lohman equation (1981).

Even though a program has been established for wrestlers, more information is needed about the effects of weight reduction on health, growth, hormone function, and metabolism and about the choice of the 5% BF criterion. Kelly et al. (1978) noted that collegiate wrestlers tend to have a relative fat content higher than the recommended 5% (Table 13.1). This reflects my experience; wrestlers tend to maintain a day to day weight that includes 6 to 10% BF and then dehydrate to attain weight limits.

More research is needed regarding MWs of male and female athletes. It is unlikely that the minimal weight is the same for everyone of a given gender. Lohman (1992), in his discussion of MW, notes that extensive investigation is needed on the relative fat levels associated with significant changes in physiological and metabolic function. I would add the importance of including the behavioral aspects of weight control, given the pychosomatic characteristics of eating disorders.

Body Composition Profiles of Athletes

Knowledge of the typical body composition of athletes in a sport is helpful in determining suitable target weights and in evaluating the effects of training programs. Unfortunately, the ideal weight and fat content of an athlete for optimum performance are not known precisely. The use of reference body composition values as standards for individual athletes requires two assumptions:

1. The average % BF of the reference group reflects the desirable physiological and biomechanical requirements of the sport as well as the appropriate genetic endowment.
2. These characteristics are best exemplified by the most elite athletes.

Sport by sport overviews of body composition have been presented by Wilmore (1983) and Fleck (1983). This summary is limited to studies where body density (BD), total body water (TBW), or total body potassium (TBK) was used to measure body composition. Most studies do not consider ethnic differences, even though it has been demonstrated that such differences may affect the accuracy of body composition measures (Hortobàgyi et al., 1992; Schutte et al., 1984).

Ballet

Ballet is not usually thought of as a sport, but many problems associated with amenorrhea and eating disorders in women athletes were found by Calabrese et al. (1983) in 29 professional ballet dancers and 5 advanced students. These subjects, like gymnasts, showed delayed menarche and menstrual irregularities. Clarkson et al. (1985), who studied advanced and adolescent students, found relatively low values for % BF (mean 16.4%).

Baseball and Softball

Even though males and females participate in baseball and softball, high school, collegiate, and international championships recognize softball as a sport for women and baseball as a sport for men. The mean % BF for the South Australian women's softball team reported by Withers et al. (1987b) is similar to that expected for nonathlete college women. The data of Wilmore (1976) for major league baseball players are included in Table 13.1. In collegiate baseball players means of 11.8, 9.8, and 14.2% BF, respectively, have been reported by Forsyth and Sinning (1973), Sinning et al. (1985), and Novak, Hyatt, and Alexander (1968).

Basketball

The study by Walsh, Heyward, and Schau (1984) of female basketball players is especially significant

Table 13.1   Selected Reports of Body Composition Characteristics of Athletes (Means ± SD)

Sport/specialty	Gender	N	Age (y)	Height (cm)	Weight (kg)	% BF	Source
Ballet							
	F	34	21.9 ±4.3	168.0 ±6.8	54.4 ±6.0	16.9 ±4.7	Calabrese et al., 1983
Baseball and softball							
Baseball	M		27.4	183.1	88.0	12.6	Wilmore, 1983
Softball	F	14	22.6 ±4.1	167.1 ±6.1	59.6 ±5.8	19.1 ±5.0	Withers et al., 1987b
Basketball							
	F	49	19.3 ±1.4	176.5 ±8.8	66.8 ±6.7	19.2 ±4.6	Walsh et al., 1984
	M	10	20.9 ±1.3	194.3 ±10.2	87.5 ±7.2	10.5 ±3.8	Siders et al., 1991
Bicycling							
	M	11	22.2 ±3.6	176.4 ±7.1	68.5 ±6.4	10.5 ±2.4	Withers et al., 1987a
Field events							
Decathlon	M	3	22.5 ±2.2	186.3 ±1.4	84.1 ±9.2	8.4 ±5.1	Withers et al., 1987a
Pentathlon	F	9	21.5 ±3.1	175.4 ±3.0	65.4 ±5.7	11.0 ±3.3	Krahenbuhl et al., 1979
Throwing	F	9	18.8 ±3.0	173.9 ±6.9	80.8 ±21.1	27.0 ±8.4	Wilmore et al., 1977
Discus	M	7	28.3 ±5.0	186.1 ±2.6	104.7 ±13.2	16.4 ±4.3	Fahey et al., 1975
Shot	M	5	27.0 ±3.9	188.2 ±3.6	112.5 ±7.3	16.5 ±4.3	Fahey et al., 1975
Jumping	F	13	17.4 ±0.9	173.6 ±8.0	57.1 ±6.0	12.9 ±2.5	Thorland et al., 1981
	M	16	17.6 ±0.8	181.7 ±6.1	69.2 ±7.2	8.5 ±2.1	Thorland et al., 1981
Field hockey							
	F	13	19.8 ±1.4	159.8 ±5.5	58.1 ±6.6	21.3 ±7.2	Sinning & Wilson, 1984
Football							
Defensive backs	M	26	24.5 ±3.2	182.5 ±4.5	84.8 ±5.2	9.6 ±4.2	Wilmore et al., 1976
Offensive backs and wide receivers	M	40	24.7 ±3.0	183.8 ±4.1	90.7 ±8.4	9.4 ±4.0	
Line backers	M	28	24.2 ±2.4	188.6 ±2.9	102.2 ±6.3	14.0 ±4.6	
Offensive line	M	38	24.7 ±3.2	193.0 ±3.5	112.6 ±6.8	15.6 ±3.8	
Defensive line	M	32	25.7 ±3.4	192.4 ±6.5	117.1 ±10.3	18.2 ±5.4	
Quarterbacks	M	16	24.1 ±2.7	185.0 ±5.4	90.1 ±11.3	14.4 ±6.5	
Gymnastics							
	F	44	19.4 ±1.1	160.6 ±4.4	53.7 ±5.9	15.3 ±4.0	Sinning, 1978
	M	19		168.7 ±6.7	65.8 ±4.3	6.5 ±2.4	Sinning et al., 1985

(continued)

Table 13.1 *(continued)*

Sport/specialty	Gender	N	Age (y)	Height (cm)	Weight (kg)	% BF	Source
Lacrosse							
	F	17	24.4 ±4.5	166.3 ±7.5	60.6 ±7.3	19.3 ±5.7	Withers et al., 1987b
	M	26	26.7 ±4.2	177.6 ±5.5	74.0 ±8.6	12.3 ±4.3	Withers et al., 1987a
Orienteering							
	M	7	25.9 ±8.5	176.2 ±6.8	64.7 ±5.0	10.7 ±2.9	Withers et al., 1987a
Racket sports							
Badminton	F	6	23.0 ±5.3	167.7 ±2.5	61.5 ±2.6	21.0 ±2.1	Withers et al., 1987b
	M	7	24.5 ±3.6	180.0 ±5.2	71.2 ±5.6	12.8 ±3.1	Withers et al., 1987a
Tennis	F	7	21.3 ±0.9	164.7 ±4.2	59.6 ±4.6	22.4 ±2.0	Sinning & Wilson, 1984
	M	9		179.1 ±4.5	73.8 ±7.3	11.3 ±5.2	Sinning et al., 1985
Squash	M	9	22.6 ±6.8	177.5 ±4.1	71.9 ±8.3	11.2 ±3.7	Withers et al., 1987a
Skating							
Ice hockey	M	27	24.9 ±3.6	182.9 ±6.1	85.6 ±7.1	9.2 ±4.6	Agre et al., 1988
Speed skating	F	9	19.7 ±3.0	165.0 ±6.0	61.2 ±6.9	16.5 ±4.1	Pollock et al., 1986
	M	6	22.2 ±4.1	178.0 ±7.1	73.3 ±7.1	7.4 ±2.5	Pollock et al., 1986
Skiing (Nordic)							
	F	5	23.5 ±4.7	164.5 ±3.3	56.9 ±1.1	16.1 ±1.6	Sinning et al., 1977
	M	11	22.8 ±1.9	179.0 ±5.0	71.8 ±5.4	7.2 ±1.9	Sinning et al., 1977
Soccer							
	F	11	22.1 ±4.1	164.9 ±5.6	61.2 ±8.6	22.0 ±6.8	Withers et al., 1987b
	M	19		176.8 ±6.6	72.4 ±8.9	9.5 ±4.9	Sinning et al., 1985
Swimming							
	F	9	13.5 ±0.9	164.5 ±7.4	53.3 ±5.3	17.2 ±3.6	Meleski et al., 1982
	F	13	16.4 ±0.9	168.8 ±7.1	57.9 ±5.5	15.6 ±4.0	
	F	19	19.2 ±0.8	169.6 ±4.7	56.0 ±3.1	16.1 ±3.7	
	M	27		178.3 ±6.4	71.0 ±5.9	8.8 ±3.2	Sinning et al., 1985
Channel swimmers	M	11	38.2 ±10.2	173.8 ±7.4	87.5 ±10.4	22.4 ±7.5	Pugh et al., 1955
Track events							
Distance runners	F	15	27	161.0 ±4.0	47.2 ±4.6	14.3 ±3.3	Graves et al., 1987
	M	20		177.0 ±6.0	63.1 ±4.8	4.7 ±3.1	Pollock et al., 1977

(continued)

Table 13.1 *(continued)*

Sport/specialty	Gender	N	Age (y)	Height (cm)	Weight (kg)	% BF	Source
Distance runners *(continued)*							
Masters and competitors	M	11	40-49	180.7	63.1	4.7	Pollock et al., 1974
		5	50-59	174.2	67.2	10.9	
		6	60-69	175.4	67.1	11.3	
		3	70.8	175.6	66.7	13.6	
Sprinters and hurdlers	F	8	15.8	166.5	54.0	10.9	Wilmore et al., 1977
			±2.7	±9.3	±8.4	±3.6	
	M	5	28.4	179.9	66.8	8.3	Withers et al., 1987a
			±0.1	±0.7	±0.9	±5.2	
Walkers	F	4	24.9	163.4	51.7	18.1	Withers et al., 1987b
			±6.3	±3.9	±4.8	±4.4	
	M	3	20.3	178.4	66.1	7.3	Withers et al., 1987a
			±2.0	±2.1	±1.8	±1.3	
Triathlon	F	16	24.2	162.1	55.2	16.5	Leake et al., 1991
			±4.3	±6.3	±4.6	±1.4	
	M	14	36.0	176.4	73.3	12.5	Lofton et al., 1988
			±9.9	±8.6	±8.6	±5.9	
Volleyball	F	14	21.6	178.3	70.5	17.9	Puhl et al., 1982
			±0.8	±4.2	±5.5	±3.6	
	M	11	20.9	185.3	78.3	9.8	Withers et al., 1987a
			±3.7	±10.2	±12.0	±2.9	
Weight lifting and body building							
Olympic lift	M	10	30.1	179.3	91.3	9.9	Spitler et al., 1980
			±8.1	±6.1	±8.9	±1.9	
Power lift	F	10	25.2	164.6	68.6	21.5	Johnson et al., 1990
			±6.0	±3.7	±3.6	±1.3	
	M	13	24.8	173.5	80.8	9.1	Katch et al., 1980
			±1.6	±2.8	±3.2	±1.2	
Body builders	F	10	30.4	165.2	56.5	13.5	Johnson et al., 1990
			±8.2	±5.6	±0.9	±1.5	
	M	18	27.8	177.1	82.4	9.3	Katch et al., 1980
			±1.8	±1.1	±1.0	±0.8	
Wrestling							
Adult	M	37	19.6	174.6	74.8	8.8	Sinning, 1974
			±1.34	±7.0	±12.2	±4.1	
Adolescent	M	409	16.2	171.0	63.2	11.0	Housh et al., 1989
			±1.0	±7.1	±10.0	±4.0	

Data rounded to 0.1. Reported *SEM*s converted to *SD* on the basis of sample size. *SD* reported when available. Information by sport extracted from data reported on female athletes in Sinning & Wilson (1984).

because of the size of the sample and the inclusion of athletes from four universities (Table 13.1). Other studies support their findings. Johnson and Nebelsick-Gullett (1989), Siders et al. (1991), Sinning (1973), and Withers et al. (1987b) found 20.1 to 20.8% BF in college women basketball players. The data for male basketball players are from a collegiate team (Siders et al.). Similar data were reported by Parr et al. (1978) for professional players who, with exception of a small sample of centers who were 7.1% BF, ranged from 9.0 to 10.6%

BF. Withers, Craig, Bourdon, and Norton (1987a) reported 10.3% BF in national caliber Australian basketball players.

Bicycling

Only limited data are available on cyclists. Withers et al. (1987a) studied members of a South Australian team preparing for national competition. The cyclists, at 10.5% BF, were similar in body fatness to athletes in other sports that involve prolonged endurance training.

Field Events

The decathlon and pentathlon are included as field events in Table 13.1, although they involve both track and field events. Both males and females are very lean at 8.4 and 11.0% BF, respectively.

The data of Wilmore, Brown, and Davis (1977) were selected to represent female throwers. In four collegiate throwers, Sinning and Wilson (1984) found an average of 24.0% BF. Behnke and Wilmore (1974) also found female javelin throwers to be leaner than female shot and discuss athletes. Thorland et al. (1981) found an average of 22.0% BF in 16 female Junior Olympic competitors. The examples from Fahey, Akka, and Ralph (1975) in Table 13.1 demonstrate the tendency for male discus and shot throwers to be large and lean. Thorland et al. (1981) found Junior Olympic throwers, who averaged 13.9% BF, were taller (184.1 cm) and heavier (87.3 kg) than other adolescent athletes.

Data on jumpers is limited. The examples of female and male jumpers given in Table 13.1 are from Junior Olympic athletes tested by Thorland et al. (1981). Sinning and Wilson (1984) found 17.1% BF in three female college jumpers.

Field Hockey

Data on female field hockey players reported in Table 13.1 are from a college team. They were similar in % BF to participants in soccer (field hockey 21.3% BF compared to soccer 22.0% BF), a sport that has similar metabolic requirements. However, the soccer players were taller (164.9 cm compared to 159.8 cm) and heavier (61.2 kg compared to 58.1 kg).

Football

The body composition characteristics of professional football players given in Table 13.1 represent 185 players from 14 teams in the National Football League (Wilmore et al., 1976). Samples of National Collegiate Athletic Association (U.S.) Division I (Smith & Mansfield, 1984) and Division II teams (White, Mayhew, & Piper, 1980) showed similar % BF values. Position-specific % BF values tend to be similar at all levels of competition, but professional athletes are larger than Division I players, and Division I players are larger than Division II

players. The higher % BF for some lineman positions may reflect a perceived need for a large body mass for these positions without regard to body composition.

Gymnastics

Data for female gymnasts in Table 13.1 were from members of two college teams. Other studies have reported similar values. Johnson and Nebelsick-Gullett (1989) found 14.5% BF in eight college competitors while Novak, Woodward, Bestit, and Mellerowicz (1977) reported 12.9% BF for Olympic contenders. Moffatt, Surina, Golden, and Ayres (1984) found 13.1% BF for a state championship high school team. It is unlikely that the profiles presented here are typical of the very young elite female gymnasts who compete for national and world championships. Claessens et al. (1991) studied the anthropometric characteristics of 201 females and 165 males at the Artistic Gymnastics World Championships. The mean age of the females was 16.5 ± 1.8 years with individuals ranging from 13.2 to 23.8 years, 39.8% having not yet attained menarche.

Like their female counterparts, the 19 collegiate male gymnasts reported by Sinning et al. (1985) were similar in % BF to national level competitors who averaged 7.9% BF (Withers et al., 1987a). Novak et al. (1968) found 4.6% BF for Olympic contenders.

Lacrosse

Representative data on lacrosse players on national teams were reported by Withers et al. (1987a, 1987b). Sinning et al. (1985) found male college players at 8.9% BF to be leaner than those reported by Withers et al., 1987a.

Orienteering

Orienteering is an endurance sport in which competitors race cross-country through unfamiliar territory using a map and compass. Although lean at 10.7% BF, the male participants reported in Table 13.1 were more similar to athletes in team sports such as basketball, lacrosse, volleyball, and soccer than distance runners.

Racket Sports

Relative fatness appears to be similar across racket sports, with females ranging from 21.0 to 22.4% BF while males range from 11.2 to 12.8% BF. Vodak, Savin, Haskell, and Wood (1980), in a study of older recreational players, found males, who averaged 42 years, had 16.3% BF while females, who averaged 39.0 years, were slightly leaner at 20.3% BF than the collegiate players studied by Withers et al. (1987b) and by Sinning and Wilson (1984).

Skating

The ice hockey data reported in Table 13.1 represent 27 National Hockey League players (Agre et al., 1988). By position, goalies were 8.7% BF, forwards 7.7% BF, and defensemen 12.2% BF. The speed skaters studied by Pollock, Pels, Foster, & Holum (1986) were competing for selection to the U.S. Olympic team. These athletes are similar to endurance athletes in % BF.

Nordic Skiing

Nordic skiers tend to be lean, much like distance runners, reflecting the endurance training required. In addition to the male Olympic team members studied by Sinning, Cunningham, Racaniello, and Sholes (1977), Sprynarová and Pařízková (1971) found 7.4% BF and Hanson (1973) 8.9% BF in other Olympic teams. Orvanová (1987), in a review of winter sport athletes, reported anthropometric estimated values ranged from 9.4 to 14.1% BF for male Alpine skiers and from 16.2 to 20.0% BF for females.

Soccer

The female soccer players reported by Withers et al. (1987b) at 22.0% BF were within normal ranges for women their age. The male collegiate players studied by Sinning et al. (1985) were comparable in % BF to a sample studied by Withers et al. (1987a), who reported 9.7% BF, but Farmosi, Apor, Mecseki, and Haàsz (1984) found only 6.9% BF in national level players.

Swimming

Representative data for female swimmers are from Meleski, Shoup, and Malina (1982), who did not find significant differences in % BF between age groups. The oldest group included national caliber swimmers. Studies by Novak et al. (1977) and by Sprynarová and Pařízková (1971) reported similar values of 18.9 and 19.2% BF for mature swimmers

while Thorland, Johnson, Housh, and Refsell (1983) reported 19.7% BF in adolescent swimmers who averaged 15.8 years. Studies on male swimmers show them to be quite lean. In addition to the 8.8% BF reported by Sinning et al. (1985) and shown in Table 13.1, Sprynarová and Pařízková (1971) reported 8.5% BF, Novak et al. (1968) 5.0% BF, and Withers et al. (1987a) 9.5% BF. However, Thorland et al. (1983) found 12.1% BF in Junior Olympic swimmers with an average age of 17.3 years. Thermoregulation is a serious problem in channel swimming because of the heat storage capacity and conductive characteristics of water. Consequently, the insulating effect of fat is important (Pugh et al., 1955). However, the best finishers of the subjects reviewed in Table 13.1 were among the leaner individuals.

Track Events

Examples for distance runners emphasize studies by Graves, Pollock, and Sparling (1987) on female and Pollock et al. (1977) on male elite performers, some holding national and world records. The female runners were slightly leaner than good college runners studied at the same time, who were 16.8% BF. The range for the elite runners was 9.8 to 20.8% BF. Wilmore et al. (1977) found 16.5% BF in 28 young distance runners (13.4 years) and 16.5% BF in 42 older runners (25.0 years). Thorland et al. (1981) found 12.5% BF in 41 young female Junior Olympic runners averaging 16.6 years. The range of relative fat content for the elite male runners ranged from 0.2 to 10.8% BF (Pollock et al., 1977). Thorland et al. (1981) found an average of 9.9% BF in male Junior Olympic distance and middle distance runners. The data on male Masters athletes by Pollock, Miller, and Wilmore (1974) are especially interesting because 24 of them were retested 10 years after the original study (Pollock et al., 1987). Both those who continued to compete and those who ceased competing and reduced training decreased slightly in weight but increased in % BF. Even though training maintained the aerobic capacity of the competitors, overall adiposity increased from 13.1 to 15.1% BF due to the loss of FFM.

The body composition of sprinters and hurdlers has not been studied as extensively as that of middle and long distance runners. Like distance runners, female hurdlers tend to be quite lean, averaging 10.9% BF (Table 13.1). Thorland et al. (1981) reported an average of 13.4% BF for young female sprinters. Male sprinters are also quite lean.

Thorland et al. (1981) found Junior Olympic sprinters and hurdlers averaged 8.3% BF, the same as shown for adults in Table 13.1.

Reported means (Table 13.1) for adult walkers were 18.1% BF (females) and 7.3% BF (males). Female Junior Olympic walkers (16.8 years) reported by Thorland et al. (1981) were slightly leaner at 15.1% BF while young males (17.5 years) were slightly fatter than the adults at 9.9% BF.

Triathlon

The triathlon requires proficiency in swimming, cycling, and running. Both males and females tend to be quite lean. Holly et al. (1986) reported lower % BF values for six males and three females who competed in the Hawaii Ironman Triathlon World Championship. Four males who finished in the top 10 averaged 7.1% BF, while the other two averaged 10.2% BF. The females, one of whom finished in the top 10, averaged 12.6% BF.

Volleyball

Both female and male volleyball players tend to be lean. Representative female volleyball players in Table 13.1 were members of a United States World University Games team (Puhl, Case, Fleck, & Van Handel, 1982). Withers et al. (1987b) reported 17.0% BF in national level Australian players while Kovaleski, Parr, Hornak, and Roitman (1980) reported 19.5% BF in collegiate players. The 9.8% BF reported by Withers et al. (1987a) was for national level male Australian players (Table 13.1). Puhl et al. reported 12.5% BF in University World Games players while Sinning et al. (1985) found 10.9% BF for 15 collegiate players.

Weightlifting and Bodybuilding

Both male and female body builders tend to be quite lean (Table 13.1). In another study of female body builders, Freedson, Mihvec, Loucks, and Girandola (1983) reported 13.2% BF. For male body builders, Fahey et al. (1975) reported 8.4% BF and Spitler, Diaz, Horvath, and Wright (1980) 9.9% BF. These values are more likely to represent body composition during routine training rather than during competition, when both men and women reduce subcutaneous fat to a minimum to optimize muscle definition. Freedson et al. reported that 9 of their 10 subjects were above competitive weight when body composition was measured. The % BF is less an issue with weight and power lifters than it is with body builders. The one report of female power lifters included in Table 13.1 shows a much higher fat content for the power lifters than for the body builders (21.5% vs 13.5%), but the male power lifters and Olympic lifters were similar in % BF to the body builders. In other studies, Katch, Katch, Moffatt, and Gittleson (1980) found 10.8% BF in Olympic lifters while Sprynarová and Pařízková (1971) reported a mean of 9.8% BF.

Wrestling

Extensive data are available on wrestlers due to research on weight reduction and the need to establish MW. Adolescent wrestlers are especially of concern because of potential effects of extreme weight loss on health and growth. The study by Sinning (1974) was the first to report % BF from body density for college wrestlers during the season (Table 13.1). Subsequent studies confirmed the leanness of these athletes, Sinning et al. (1985) reporting 8.3% BF and Kelly et al. (1978) reporting 10.4% BF. The data by Housh et al. (1989) were collected two weeks before the first competition (Table 13.1). Other studies of adolescent wrestlers have reported means ranging from 9.4 to 11.9% BF (Sinning et al., 1976; Thorland et al., 1981, 1987), which are higher than the 5% BF currently accepted as appropriate for a MW. However, Williford et al. (1986) reported 5.6% BF in high school wrestlers, and Sady, Thompson, Berg, and Savage (1984) found 12.9% BF in prepubescent wrestlers who averaged 11.0 years in age.

Measuring the Body Composition of Athletes

Body densitometry has been used more commonly than other methods in research on body composition in athletes, and it is usually used to validate other methods. Anthropometry, especially skinfold thicknesses, is most commonly used for field testing by trainers and coaches to determine target or minimum weights, but bioimpedance analysis (BIA) is being used more widely. The theories underlying this method are discussed in chapter 5. The major problem in applying any method to athletes is whether the assumptions of the method are met by the study. Issues include the physical and skeletal maturity of young athletes, variations in the density of FFM, differential effects of various training programs and sports, and ethnic differences.

Body Densitometry

Factors related to the accuracy of densitometry and the use of two-component models (assuming the body is composed of fat and FFM) versus multicomponent models that account for differences in components of the FFM (i.e., mineral, water, and protein) have been discussed in chapter 1. The equations of Brožek, Grande, Anderson, and Keys (1963) and Siri (1961), which are based on a two-component model to estimate % BF, have been used most frequently for research on athletes.

Research since the recent advent of dual photon and dual energy x-ray absorptiometry (DPA and DXA) suggests that training and nutritional practices of athletes may affect the mineral content and density of the FFM. Myburgh, Bachrach, Kent, and Marcus (1993), as well as Rutherford (1993), found significantly lower bone mineral content (BMC) in amenorrheic compared to eumenorrheic runners in both the axial and appendicular skeleton. Resistance exercise increases bone mineral mass in males (Conroy et al., 1993; Menkes et al., 1993) and females (Heinrich et al., 1990). Bernard et al. (1991) found higher BMC in competitive male athletes than in those in school and noncompetitive activities, but young competitive cyclists did not show increased bone mineral (Rico et al., 1993). Even though training may affect the BMC of athletes in some sports, it is not possible to establish a model that is characteristic of all athletes.

An important but often neglected issue is ethnic variation. It has long been known that the BMC of black males and females is greater than in whites (Merz, Trotter, & Peterson, 1956). Côté and Adams (1993) recently showed that young black females have higher BMC and BMC · FFM^{-1} than age-, stature-, and weight-matched white females. Schutte et al. (1984) found that the FFM calculated from body density (BD) was higher than that calculated from TBW or anthropometric estimates in black males, suggesting that the density of the FFM was higher than the assumed 1.1 g · cm^{-3}. Therefore, % BF values approaching zero or even negative values with densitometry in well trained black males is not uncommon when using conventional conversion equations. Schutte et al. presented a revised equation to use with black males that we have found useful:

$$\% \text{ BF} = 100 \; [(4.374 \cdot \text{BD}^{-1}) - 3.928]. \quad (13.2)$$

The effects of varying hydration states in athletes on densitometry have not been addressed in depth. Lohman has discussed this issue with respect to the effects of water content on body density (BD) relative to multicomponent models in adults (1992) and children (1986), and his recommendations can be applied to measuring the body composition of athletes. However, we do not know the extent to which specific responses to different training protocols, such as the plasma volume expansion with endurance training or the repeated dehydration by wrestlers to make weight limits, may affect the relative water content of the FFM.

How much do these variations in the composition and density of the FFM affect the accuracy of densitometric body composition analysis? Horswill et al. (1990b) found that alternate models using densitometry corrected for TBW and/or bone mineral did not significantly improve the estimates of % BF for adolescent males. Côté and Adams (1993) found within-group % BF was not significantly different when using two- or multicomponent models to calculate the body composition of black and white females, but individuals within the groups with the highest and lowest BMD were markedly over- or underestimated when bone mineral was not taken into account. Withers et al. (1992) used TBW, TBK, and DXA to measure body composition in young endurance athletes. Like Horswill et al. (1990b), they found there was no advantage to using multicomponent models over the traditional two-component model.

In summary, because of variation in mineral content and hydration status between and within athlete groups, it may be difficult to provide conversion constants by sport or for athletes in general. However, adjustments for chemical maturity in children (Lohman, 1986) appear to be advantageous when working with young athletes. The equation of Schutte et al. (1984) should be used when measuring black men. For studying group body composition characteristics, the two-component model apparently provides meaningful data. Nevertheless, when recommending target weights to individuals, it is important to use as much information as possible, interpreting the results within the limitations of the methods used.

Anthropometry

Forsyth and Sinning (1973) found that anthropometric equations developed on nonathlete populations to estimate % BF may not be accurate for male athletes. They developed new equations based on a sample of athletes. Sport-specific equations have also been developed by Sinning (1978) for women gymnasts and by Walsh et al. (1984) for women

Table 13.2   Anthropometric Equations Recommended for Estimating the Body Density of Athletes

Source	Gender	Equation
Jackson et al. (1980)	F	$BD = 1.096095 - 0.0006952\ X_1 + 0.0000011\ X_1^2 - 0.0000714\ X_2$
Withers et al. (1987b)	F	$BD = 1.18562 - 0.08258\ X_3$
Withers et al. (1987b)	F	$BD = 1.15726 - 0.05501\ X_3 - 0.00088\ X_4 + 0.00746\ X_5 - 0.001026\ X_6$
Jackson & Pollock (1978)	M	$BD = 1.112 - 0.00043499\ X_7 + 0.0000055\ X_7^2 - 0.00028826\ X_2$
Jackson & Pollock (1978)	M	$BD = 1.15737 - 0.02288\ X_8 - 0.00019\ X_2 - 0.0075\ X_9 + 0.0223\ X_{10}$

$X_1 = \Sigma$ triceps, abdominal, suprailiac, and thigh skinfolds (mm). X_2 = age (years). $X_3 = \lg (\Sigma$ triceps, subscapular, and calf skinfolds) (mm). X_4 = maximum thigh girth (cm). X_5 = elbow breadth (cm). X_6 = natural waist girth (cm). $X_7 = \Sigma$ triceps, subscapular, pectoral, mid-axillary, suprailiac, abdominal, and thigh skinfolds (mm). $X_8 = Ln (\Sigma$ pectoral, abdominal, and thigh skinfolds) (mm). X_9 = umbilical girth (cm). X_{10} = forearm girth (cm).

basketball players. Withers et al. (1987a, 1987b) developed equations for male and female athletes based on 205 male and 183 female athletes.

Although it may be desirable to have sport-specific equations, research suggests that existing equations developed from large populations ("generalized equations"), which account for the effects of age and the curvilinear relationship between % BF and skinfold thicknesses, are applicable for estimating % BF in athletes. Sinning and Wilson (1984) found that an equation developed by Jackson, Pollock, and Ward (1980) was more accurate than other equations for women athletes ($r = 0.79$; *SEE* ±3.27; *PE* = 3.23% BF) who ranged from 10.3 to 34.0% BF. Withers et al. (1987b) found similar accuracy ($r = 0.87$; *SEE* ± 3.6% BF) in 183 Australian women athletes. For men, Sinning et al. (1985) found generalized equations developed by Jackson and Pollock (1978) were more accurate than other selected equations ($r = 0.82$ to 0.84; *SEE* 2.38 to 2.51; *PE* 2.38 to 2.53% BF) for estimating % BF in 265 male athletes. There were similar findings by Hortobàgyi et al. (1992) from a study of 88 college football players, 55 of whom were black. Density was converted to % BF for the black subjects using the equation by Schutte et al. (1984).

It is not possible to summarize all the equations available to estimate the body composition of athletes from anthropometry. Table 13.2 presents selected equations by Jackson et al. (1978) that have been cross-validated using 79 female athletes (Sinning & Wilson, 1984) as well as equations by Jackson and Pollock (1978) that were cross-validated using 265 male athletes (Sinning et al., 1985). For this review, the equations developed by Withers et al. (1987b) for females were also cross-validated against the same 79 subjects used by Sinning and

Wilson. Regressions of the measured on the estimated % BF values showed them to be acceptably accurate over a wide range of % BF values. Equations that include girth measures have been included in Table 13.2, even though there is little evidence to suggest adding these variables improves the accuracy of the estimate.

Other Methods

Bioelectric impedance (BI) and near-infrared spectrophotometry (NIR) are frequently used to measure body composition in fitness and nutritional centers, although, the validity of these methods for athletes has not been studied extensively. Hortobàgyi et al. (1992) found NIR significantly underpredicted % BF in both black and white male athletes.

Lukaski, Bolunchuk, Siders, and Hall (1990) found BI was quite accurate for measuring the body composition of 48 male and 46 female athletes under controlled (eat 2 hours before, no recent exercise) and uncontrolled conditions. They used an equation that had been developed on subjects ranging in age from 18 to 74 years:

$$FFM = \frac{0.734 \cdot S^2}{R} + (0.116 \cdot W) + (0.96 \cdot Xc) + (0.878 \cdot G)$$

$$(13.3)$$

where FFM is in kg, S is stature in centimeters, R is resistance in ohms, W is weight in kg, Xc is reactance in ohms, and G is a multiplier for gender (male = 1, female = 0). The *SEE* was 2.81% BF with the controlled condition being the more accurate.

Hortobàgyi et al. (1992) found that the equations provided by the manufacturer for BI underestimated % BF by 5.4% in black football players and by 3.9% in white players, even though the correlation between estimated and measured values was 0.83. The difference between the results of Hortobàgyi et al. and Lukaski et al. (1990) illustrates the need to know the equations used and the population from which they were derived.

In summary, we lack a single body composition method that can provide acceptably accurate measurements for every athlete in every sport. The results must be interpreted within the limitations of the method or methods used. Consequently, it is important that the testers be experienced and understand the underlying concepts of the method, whether the tester is an athletic trainer, coach, team physician, or other specialist.

References

Agre, J.C., Casal, D.C., Leon, A.S., et al. (1988). Professional ice hockey players: Physiologic, anthropometric, and musculoskeletal characteristics. *Archives of Physical Medicine and Rehabilitation,* **69,** 188-192.

American College of Sports Medicine. (1976). Position statement on weight loss in wrestlers. *Sports Medicine Bulletin,* **22,** 2-3.

Behnke, A.R. (1961). Comment on the determination of whole body density and a résumé of body composition data. In J. Brožek & A. Henschel (Eds.), *Techniques for measuring body composition* (pp. 118-133). Washington, DC: National Academy of Sciences National Research Council.

Behnke, A.R. (1969). New concepts of height-weight relationships. In N.L. Wilson (Ed.), *Obesity* (pp. 25-53). Philadelphia: F.A. Davis.

Behnke, A.R., & Wilmore, J.H. (1974). *Evaluation and regulation of body build and body composition.* Englewood Cliffs, NJ: Prentice-Hall.

Bernard, J., Telmont, N., Benozet, J.F., et al. (1991). Étude par ostèodensitomètrie «corps entier» de 269 hommes de 17 à 21 ans. *Revue du Rhumatisme,* **58,** 467-470.

Brownell, K.D., & Rodin, J. (1992). Prevalence of eating disorders in athletes. In K.D. Brownell, J. Rodin, & J.H. Wilmore (Eds.), *Eating, body weight, and performance in athletes* (pp. 128-145). Philadelphia: Lea & Febiger.

Brožek, J.F., Grande, F., Anderson, J.T., & Keys, A. (1963). Densitometric analysis of body composition: Revision of some quantitative assumptions. *Annals of the New York Academy of Sciences,* **110,** 113-140.

Calabrese, L.H., Kirkendall, D.T., Floyd, M., et al. (1983). Menstrual abnormalities, nutrition patterns, and body composition in female classical ballet dancers. *The Physician and Sportsmedicine,* **11,** 86-89.

Cann, C.E., Genant, H.K., Ettinger, B., & Gordon, G.S. (1980). Spinal mineral loss in oophorectomized women. *Journal of the American Medical Association,* **244,** 2056-2059.

Cann, C.E., Martin, M.C., & Jaffe, R.B. (1984). Decreased spinal bone mineral content in amenorrheic women. *Journal of the American Medical Association,* **251,** 626-629.

Carlberg, K.A., Buckman, M.T., Peake, G.T., & Riedesel, M.L. (1983). Body composition of oligo/amenorrheic athletes. *Medicine and Science in Sports and Exercise,* **15,** 215-217.

Claessens, A.L., Veer, F.M., Stijnen, V., et al. (1991). Anthropometric characteristics of outstanding male and female gymnasts. *Journal of Sports Sciences,* **9,** 53-74.

Clark, R.R., Kuta, J.M., & Oppliger, R.A. (1992). The Wisconsin wrestling minimal weight project: Cross validation of prediction equations. *Pediatric Exercise Science,* **4,** 117-127.

Clarkson, P.M., Freedson, P.S., Keller, B. et al. (1985). Maximal oxygen uptake, nutritional patterns and body composition of adolescent female ballet dancers. *Research Quarterly for Exercise and Sport,* **56,** 180-184.

Conroy, B.P., Kraemer, W.J., Maresh, C.M., et al. (1993). Bone mineral density in elite junior Olympic weightlifters. *Medicine and Science in Sports and Exercise,* **25,** 1103-1109.

Côté, K.D., & Adams, W.C. (1993). Effect of bone density on body composition estimates in young adult black and white women. *Medicine and Science in Sports and Exercise,* **25,** 290-296.

Deuster, P.A., Kyle, S.B., Moser, P.B., et al. (1986). Nutritional intakes and status of highly trained amenorrheic and eumenorrheic women runners. *Fertility and Sterility,* **46,** 636-643.

Drinkwater, B.L., Bruemner, B., & Chestnut, C.H., III. (1990). Menstrual history as a determinant of current bone density in young athletes. *Journal of the American Medical Association,* **263,** 545-548.

Drinkwater, B.L., Nilson, K., Chestnut, C.H., III, et al. (1984). Bone mineral content of amenorrheic and eumenorrheic athletes. *New England Journal of Medicine,* **311,** 277-281.

Drinkwater, B.L., Nilson, K., Ott, S., & Chestnut, C.H., III. (1986). Bone mineral density after resumption of menses in amenorrheic athletes. *Journal of the American Medical Association,* **256,** 380-382.

Eckerson, J.M., Housh, D.J., Housh, T.J., & Johnson, G.O. (1994). Seasonal changes in body composition, strength, and muscular power in high school wrestlers. *Pediatric Exercise Science*, **6**, 39-52.

Fahey, T.D., Akka, L., & Ralph, R. (1975). Body composition and VO₂max of exceptional weight trained athletes. *Journal of Applied Physiology*, **39**, 559-561.

Farmosi, I., Apor, P., Mecseki, S., & Haàsz, S. (1984). Body composition of notable soccer players. *Sportorvosi Szembe. Hungarian Review of Sports Medicine*, **25**, 91-96.

Fleck, S.J. (1983). Percent of body fat of various groups of athletes. *NSCA Journal*, **5**, 46-50.

Forsyth, H.L., & Sinning, W.E. (1973). The anthropometric estimation of body density and lean body weight of male athletes. *Medicine and Science in Sports*, **5**, 174-180.

Freedson, P.S., Mihvec, P.M., Loucks, A.B., & Girandola, R.N. (1983). Physique, body composition, and psychological characteristics of competitive female body builders. *The Physician and Sportsmedicine*, **11**, 85-93.

Graves, J.E., Pollock, M.L., & Sparling, P.B. (1987). Body composition of elite female distance runners. *International Journal of Sports Medicine*, **8**, 96-102.

Hackney, A.C., & Sinning, W.E. (1986). The effects of wrestling training on reproductive hormones. *Medicine and Science in Sports and Exercise*, **18**, S40.

Hackney, A.C., Sinning, W.E., & Bruot, B.C. (1988). Reproductive hormonal profiles of endurance-trained and untrained males. *Medicine and Science in Sports and Exercise*, **20**, 60-65.

Hackney, A.C., Sinning, W.E., & Bruot, B.C. (1990). Hypothalamic-pituitary-testicular axis function in endurance trained males. *International Journal of Sports Medicine*, **11**, 298-303.

Hanson, J.S. (1973). Maximal exercise performance in members of the U.S. Nordic ski team. *Journal of Applied Physiology*, **35**, 592-595.

Heinrich, C.H., Going, S.B., Pamenter, R.W., et al. (1990). Bone mineral content of cyclicly menstruating female resistance and endurance trained athletes. *Medicine and Science in Sports and Exercise*, **22**, 558-563.

Herbert, W.G., & Ribsl, P.M. (1972). Effects of dehydration upon physical working capacity of wrestlers under competitive conditions. *Research Quarterly*, **43**, 416-422.

Holly, R.G., Barnard, R.J., & Rosenthal, M., et al. (1986). Triathlete characterization and response to prolonged strenuous competition. *Medicine and Science in Sports and Exercise*, **18**, 123-127.

Horswill, C.A. (1992). Applied physiology of amateur wrestling. *Sports Medicine*, **14**, 114-143.

Horswill, C.A., Hickner, R.C., Scott, J.R., et al. (1990a). Weight loss, dietary carbohydrate modifications, and high intensity physical performance. *Medicine and Science in Sports and Exercise*, **22**, 470-476.

Horswill, C.A., Lohman, T.G., Slaughter, M.H., et al. (1990b). Estimation of minimal weight of adolescent males using multicomponent models. *Medicine and Science in Sports and Exercise*, **22**, 528-532.

Horswill, C.A., Park, S.H., & Roemmich, J.N. (1990c). Changes in the protein nutritional status of adolescent wrestlers. *Medicine and Science in Sports and Exercise*, **22**, 599-604.

Hortobàgyi, T., Israel, R.G., Houmard, J.A., et al. (1992). Comparison of four methods to assess body composition in black and white athletes. *International Journal of Sport Nutrition*, **2**, 60-74.

Housh, T.J., Johnson, G.O., Kenney, K.B., et al. (1989). Validity of anthropometric estimations of body composition in high school wrestlers. *Research Quarterly for Exercise and Sport*, **60**, 239-245.

Housh, T.J., Johnson, G.O., Stout, J., & Housh, D.J. (1993). Anthropometric growth patterns of high school wrestlers. *Medicine and Science in Sports and Exercise*, **25**, 1141-1150.

Huston, M.E., Marin, D.A., Green, H.J., & Thompson, J.A. (1981). The effect of rapid weight loss on physiological function in wrestlers. *The Physician and Sportsmedicine*, **9**, 73-78.

Jackson, A.S., & Pollock, M.L. (1978). Generalized equations for predicting body density of men. *British Journal of Nutrition*, **40**, 497-504.

Jackson, A.S., Pollock, M.L., & Ward, A. (1980). Generalized equations for predicting body density of women. *Medicine and Science in Sports and Exercise*, **12**, 175-182.

Johnson, G.O., Housh, T.J., Powell, D.R., & Ansorge, C.J. (1990). A physiological profile comparison of female body builders and power lifters. *Journal of Sports Medicine and Physical Fitness*, **30**, 361-364.

Johnson, G.O., & Nebelsick-Gullett, L.I. (1989). The effect of a competitive season on the body composition of university female athletes. *Journal of Sports Medicine and Physical Fitness*, **29**, 314-320.

Katch, V.L., Katch, F.I., Moffatt, R., & Gittleson, M. (1980). Muscular development and lean body weight in body builders and weight lifters. *Medicine and Science in Sports*, **12**, 340-344.

Kelly, J.M., Gorney, B.A., & Kalm, K.K. (1978). The effects of a collegiate wrestling season on body composition, cardiovascular fitness and muscular strength and endurance. *Medicine and Science in Sports,* **10,** 119-124.

Kovaleski, J.E., Parr, R.B., Hornak, R.B., & Roitman, J.L. (1980). Athletic profile of women college volleyball players. *The Physician and Sportsmedicine,* **8,** 112-116.

Krahenbuhl, G.S., Wells, C.L., Brown, C.H., & Wood, P.E. (1979). Characteristics of national and world class female pentathletes. *Medicine and Science in Sports,* **11,** 20-23.

Leake, C.N., & Carter, J.E.L. (1991). Comparison of body composition and somatotype of trained female triathletes. *Journal of Sports Sciences,* **9,** 125-135.

Lindberg, J.S., Fears, W.B., Hunt, M.M., et al. (1984). Exercise-induced amenorrhea and bone density. *Annals of Internal Medicine,* **101,** 647-648.

Linnell, S.L., Stager, J.M., Blue, P.W., et al. (1984). Bone mineral content and menstrual regularity in female runners. *Medicine and Science in Sports and Exercise,* **16,** 343-348.

Lofton, M., Warren, B.L., Zingraf, S., et al. (1988). Peak physiological function and performance of recreational triathletes. *Journal of Sports Medicine and Physical Fitness,* **28,** 330-335.

Lohman, T.G. (1981). Skinfolds and body density and their relation to body fatness: A review. *Human Biology,* **53,** 181-225.

Lohman, T.G. (1986). Applicability of body composition techniques and constants for children and youths. *Exercise and Sports Science Reviews,* **11** 325-358.

Lohman, T.G. (1992). *Advances in body composition assessment* (pp. 109-118). Champaign IL: Human Kinetics.

Loucks, A.B. (1990). Effects of exercise training on the menstrual cycle: Existence and mechanisms. *Medicine and Science in Sports and Exercise,* **22,** 275-280.

Lukaski, H.C., Bolonchuk, W.W., Siders, W.A., & Hall, C.B. (1990). Body composition assessment of athletes using bioelectric impedance measurements. *Journal of Sports Medicine and Physical Fitness,* **30,** 434-440.

Marcus, R., Cann, C.E., Madvig, P., et al. (1985). Menstrual function and bone mass in elite women distance runners. *Annals of Internal Medicine,* **102,** 158-163.

McCargar, L.J., & Crawford, S.M. (1992). Metabolic and anthropometric changes with weight cutting in wrestlers. *Medicine and Science in Sports and Exercise,* **24,** 1270-1275.

Meleski, B.W., Shoup, R.F., & Malina, R.M. (1982). Size, physique and body composition of competitive female swimmers 11 through 20 years of age. *Human Biology,* **54,** 609-625.

Menkes, A., Mazel, S., Redmond, R.A., et al. (1993). Strength training increases regional bone mineral density and bone remodeling in middle-aged and adult men. *Journal of Applied Physiology,* **74,** 2478-2484.

Merz, A.L., Trotter, M., & Peterson, R.R. (1956). Estimation of skeletal weight in the living. *American Journal of Physical Anthropology,* **14,** 589-609.

Moffatt, R.J., Surina, B., Golden, B., & Ayres, N. (1984). Body composition and physiological characteristics of female high school gymnasts. *Research Quarterly for Exercise and Sports,* **55,** 80-84.

Myburgh, K.H., Bachrach, B.L., Kent, K., & Marcus, R. (1993). Low bone mineral density at axial and appendicular sites in amenorrheic athletes. *Medicine and Science in Sports and Exercise,* **25,** 1197-1201.

National Collegiate Athletic Association. (1991). *1992 NCAA wrestling: Rules and interpretations.* Overland Park, KS: National Collegiate Athletic Association.

Nelson, M.E., Fisher, E.C., Catsos, P.D., et al. (1986). Diet and bone status in amenorrheic runners. *American Journal of Clinical Nutrition,* **43,** 910-916.

Novak, L.P., Hyatt, R.E., & Alexander, J.F. (1968). Body composition and physiologic function of athletes. *Journal of the American Medical Association,* **205,** 764-770.

Novak, L.P., Woodward, W.A., Bestit, C., & Mellerowicz, H. (1977). Working capacity, body composition and anthropometry of Olympic female athletes. *Journal of Sports Medicine and Physical Fitness,* **17,** 275-283.

Orvanová, E. (1987). Physical structure of winter sports athletes. *Journal of Sports Sciences,* **5,** 197-248.

Parr, R.B., Wilmore, J.H., Hoover, D., et al. (1978). Professional basketball players: Athletic profiles. *The Physician and Sportsmedicine,* **7,** 77-84.

Pollock, M.L., Foster, C., Knapp, D., et al. (1987). Effects of age and training on aerobic capacity and body composition of master athletes. *Journal of Applied Physiology,* **62,** 725-731.

Pollock, M.L., Gettman, L.R., Jackson, A., et al. (1977). Body composition of elite class distance runners. *Annals of the New York Academy of Sciences,* **301,** 361-370.

Pollock, M.L., Miller, H.S., Jr., & Wilmore, J. (1974). Physiological characteristics of champion American track athletes 40 to 75 years of age. *Journal of Gerontology,* **29,** 645-649.

Pollock, M.L., Pels, A.E., III, Foster, C., & Holum, D. (1986). Comparison of male and female speedskating candidates. In D.M. Landers (Ed.), *Sports and elite performance* (pp. 143-152). Champaign, IL: Human Kinetics.

Pugh, L.G.C.E., Edholm, O.G., Fox, R.H., et al. (1955). A physiological study of channel swimming. *Clinical Science, 19*, 257-273.

Puhl, J., Case, S., Fleck, S., & Van Handel, P. (1982). Physical and physiological characteristics of elite volleyball players. *Research Quarterly for Exercise and Sport, 53*, 257-262.

Rico, H., Revilla, M., Villa, L.F., et al. (1993). Body composition in postpubertal boy cyclists. *Journal of Sports Medicine and Physical Fitness, 33*, 278-281.

Roemmich, J.N. (1994). *Weight loss effects on growth, maturation, growth related hormones, protein nutrition markers, and body composition of adolescent wrestlers.* Unpublished doctoral dissertation, Kent State University, Kent, OH.

Roemmich, J.N., Sinning, W.E., & Roemmich, S.R. (1991). Seasonal changes in anaerobic power, strength, and body composition of adolescent wrestlers. *Medicine and Science in Sports and Exercise, 23* (Suppl), S24.

Rutherford, D.M. (1993). Spine and total body bone mineral density in amenorrheic endurance athletes. *Journal of Applied Physiology, 74*, 2904-2908.

Sady, S.E., Thompson, W.H., Berg, K., & Savage, M. (1984). Physiological characteristics of high-ability prepubescent wrestlers. *Medicine and Science in Sports and Exercise, 16*, 72-78.

Schmidt, W.D., Corrigan, D., & Melby, C.L. (1993). Two seasons of weight cycling does not lower resting metabolic rate in college wrestlers. *Medicine and Science in Sports and Exercise, 25*, 613-619.

Schutte, J.E., Townsend, E.J., Hugg, J., et al. (1984). Density of lean body mass is greater in blacks than in whites. *Journal of Applied Physiology: Respiratory, Environmental and Exercise Physiology, 56*, 1647-1649.

Siders, W.A., Bolonchuk, W.A., & Lukaski, H.C. (1991). Effects of participation in a collegiate sport season on body composition. *Journal of Sports Medicine and Physical Fitness, 31*, 571-576.

Sinning, W.E. (1973). Body composition, cardiorespiratory function, and rule changes in women's basketball. *Research Quarterly, 44*, 313-321.

Sinning, W.E. (1974). Body composition assessment of college wrestlers. *Medicine and Science in Sports, 6*, 139-145.

Sinning, W.E. (1978). Anthropometric estimation of body density, fat, and lean body weight in women gymnasts. *Medicine and Science in Sports, 10*, 243-249.

Sinning, W.E., Cunningham, L.N., Racaniello, A.P., & Sholes, J.L. (1977). Body composition and somatotype of male and female Nordic skiers. *Research Quarterly, 48*, 741-749.

Sinning, W.E., Dolny, D.E., Little, K.D., et al. (1985). Validity of generalized equations for body composition analysis in male athletes. *Medicine and Science in Sports and Exercise, 17*, 124-130.

Sinning, W.E., Wilensky, N.F., & Meyers, E.J. (1976). Post-season body composition changes and weight estimation in high-school wrestlers. In J. Broekhoff (Ed.), *Physical education, sports, and the sports sciences* (pp. 137-153). Eugene, OR: Microform Publications.

Sinning, W.E., & Wilson, J.R. (1984). Validity of "generalized" equations for body composition analysis in women athletes. *Research Quarterly for Exercise and Sports, 55*, 153-160.

Siri, W.E. (1961) Body composition from fluid spaces and density: Analysis of methods. In J. Brožek & A. Henschel (Eds.), *Techniques for measuring body composition* (pp. 223-244). Washington, DC: National Academy of Sciences National Research Council.

Smith, J.F., & Mansfield, E.R. (1984). Body composition prediction in university football players. *Medicine and Science in Sports and Exercise, 16*, 398-405.

Spitler, D.L., Diaz, F.J., Horvath, S.M., & Wright, J.E. (1980). Body composition and maximal aerobic capacity of body builders. *Journal of Sports Medicine and Physical Fitness, 20*, 181-188.

Sprynarová, S., & Pařízková, J. (1971). Functional capacity and body composition in top weightlifters, swimmers, runners and skiers. *Internationale Zeitschrift fur Angewandte Physiologie Einschliessen Arbeitsphysiologie, 29*, 184-194.

Steen, S.N., & Brownell, K.D. (1990). Patterns of weight loss and regain in wrestlers: Has the tradition changed? *Medicine and Science in Sports and Exercise, 22*, 762-768.

Steen, S.N., Oppliger, R.A., & Brownell, K.D. (1988). Metabolic effects of repeated weight loss and regain in adolescent wrestlers. *Journal of the American Medical Association, 260*, 47-50.

Storlie, J. (1991). Nutrition assessment of athletes: A model for integrating nutrition and physical performance indicators. *International Journal of Sport Nutrition, 1*, 192-209.

Strauss, R.H., Lanese R.R., & Malarkey, W.B. (1985). Weight loss in wrestlers and its effect on serum testosterone levels. *Journal of the American Medical Association, 254*, 3337-3338.

Tcheng, T.K., & Tipton, C.M. (1973). Iowa wrestling study: Anthropometric measurements and the prediction of a "minimal" body weight for high school wrestlers. *Medicine and Science in Sports,* **5,** 1-10.

Thorland, W.G., Johnson, G.O., Cisar, C.J., & Housh, T.J. (1987). Estimation of minimal wrestling weight using measures of body build and body composition. *International Journal of Sports Medicine,* **8,** 365-370.

Thorland, W.G., Johnson, G.O., Fagot, T.G., et al. (1981). Body composition and somatotype characteristics of junior olympic athletes. *Medicine and Science in Sports and Exercise,* **13,** 332-338.

Thorland, W.G., Johnson, G.O., Housh, T.J., & Refsell, M.J. (1983). Anthropometric characteristics of elite adolescent competitive swimmers. *Human Biology,* **55,** 735-748.

Thorland, W.G., Tipton, C.M., Lohman, T.G., et al. (1991). Midwest Wrestling Study: Prediction of minimal weight for high school wrestlers. *Medicine and Science in Sports and Exercise,* **23,** 1102-1110.

Vodak, P.A., Savin, W.M., Haskell, W.L., & Wood, P.D. (1980). Physiological profiles of middle-aged male and female tennis players. *Medicine and Science in Sports and Exercise,* **12,** 159-163.

Walsh, F.K., Heyward, V.H., & Schau, C.G. (1984). Estimation of body composition of female intercollegiate basketball players. *Physician and Sportsmedicine,* **12** , 74-79.

Warren, M.P. (1992). Eating, body weight, and menstrual function. In K.D. Brownell, J. Rodin, & J.H. Wilmore (Eds.), *Eating, body weight, and performance in athletes* (pp. 222-234). Philadelphia: Lea & Febiger.

Webster, S., Rutt, R., & Weltman, A. (1990). Physiological effects of a weight loss regimen practiced by college wrestlers. *Medicine and Science in Sports and Exercise,* **22,** 229-234.

Wheeler, G.D., Wall, S., Belcastro, A.N., & Cumming, D.C. (1984). Reduced serum testosterone and prolactin levels in male distance runners. *Journal of the American Medical Association,* **252,** 514-516.

White, J., Mayhew, J.L., & Piper, F.C. (1980). Prediction of body composition in college football players. *Journal of Sports Medicine and Physical Fitness,* **20,** 317-324.

Widerman, P.M., & Hagan, R.D. (1982). Body weight loss in a wrestler preparing for competition: A case report. *Medicine and Science in Sports and Exercise,* **14,** 413-418.

Williford, H.N., Smith, J.F., Mansfield, E.R., et al. (1986). Validation of body composition models for high school wrestlers. *Medicine and Science in Sports and Exercise,* **18,** 216-224.

Wilmore, J.H. (1983). Body composition in sport and exercise: Directions for future research. *Medicine and Science in Sports and Exercise,* **15,** 21-31.

Wilmore, J.H., Brown, C.H., & Davis, J.A. (1977). Body physique and composition of the female distance runner. *Annals of the New York Academy of Sciences,* **301,** 764-776.

Wilmore, J.H., Parr, R.B., Haskell, W.L., et al. (1976). Football pro's strengths and CV weaknesses charted. *The Physician and Sportsmedicine,* **4,** 45-54.

Withers, R.T., Craig, N.P., Bourdon, P.C., & Norton, K.I. (1987a). Relative body fat and anthropometric prediction of body density of male athletes. *European Journal of Applied Physiology,* **56,** 191-200.

Withers, R.T., Smith, D.A., Chatterton, B.E., et al. (1992). A comparison of four methods of estimating the body composition of male endurance athletes. *European Journal of Clinical Nutrition,* **46,** 773-784.

Withers, R.T., Whittingham, N.O., Norton, K.I., et al. (1987b). Relative body fat and anthropometric prediction of body density of female athletes. *European Journal of Applied Physiology,* **56,** 169-180.

Woods, E.R., Wilson, C.D., & Masland, R.P., Jr. (1988). Weight control methods in high school wrestlers. *Journal of Adolescent Health Care,* **9,** 394-397.

Yeager, K.K., Agostini, R., Nattiv, A., & Drinkwater, B. (1993). The female athlete triad: Disordered eating, amenorrhea, osteoporosis. *Medicine and Science in Sports and Exercise,* **25,** 775-777.

Zambraski, E.J., Tipton, C.M., Jordon, H.R., et al. (1974). Iowa Wrestling Study: Urinary profiles of state finalists prior to competition. *Medicine and Science in Sports,* **6,** 129-132.

Zambraski, E.J., Tipton, C.M., Tcheng, T.K., et al. (1975). Iowa Wrestling Study: Changes in the urinary profiles of wrestlers prior to and after competition. *Medicine and Science in Sports,* **7,** 217-220.

14

Body Composition in Weight Loss and Pathological States

Khursheed N. Jeejeebhoy

Weight loss occurs because of an imbalance between nutrient intake and requirements. There are two main metabolic situations associated with weight loss: first, starvation or hypocaloric feeding resulting in a lack of nutrient intake and, second, pathological weight loss resulting from sepsis, trauma, cancer, or hypermetabolic states.

To understand the changes in body composition caused by malnutrition and disease, it is necessary to understand the various body components. Broadly the body is composed of fat and lean tissue. The lean tissue in turn is made up of cells, which are rich in potassium; consequently total body potassium is a measure of body cell mass. Moreover, cells and extracellular fluid both contain protein; since nitrogen is an essential component of protein, total body nitrogen (TBN) is a measure of body protein.

Physiological Basis of Weight Loss

Starvation will result in marked wasting unless compensatory mechanisms occur. These mechanisms result in progressive adaptation.

Starvation and Adaptation to Protein-Energy Deficit

Whenever there is a deficit between nutrient needs and intake, the balance must come from body stores. The predominant aim of adaptation to such a deficit is to supply glucose or ketones to the brain because these are mandatory to maintain brain function. The brain is injured rapidly in the absence of these nutrients. The secondary aim is to preserve the structural elements of the body, namely protein. To understand the availability of the body stores, it is necessary to know the nature of these stores and basal energy requirements.

Carbohydrates, mainly as glycogen, are insufficient to meet the energy requirements of the human body for more than 24 hours (Tables 14.1 and 14.2). In theory, protein stores can supply energy for about 30 days, but by then the whole body would disappear since all organs would be used up. Body proteins cannot provide energy without destroying the structure of organs. The only remaining source is body fat, which is an expendable source of substrate and is energy dense. Fat, however, cannot supply glucose, an essential substrate for the brain, which requires 72 g per day of glucose. In early stages of starvation, the requirement of the brain for glucose is met by gluconeogenesis from protein catabolism and glycerol derived from lipolysis. With a prolonged energy deficit, however, fatty acids being transported to the liver are converted to ketones, and the brain progressively uses these ketones for energy. Thus body protein is spared. Estimates of basal energy expenditure for some body organs or systems are given in Table 14.2. The values for percent of basal energy consumption in Table 14.2 sum to more than 100% because "muscle + other" overlaps viscera and the other organs listed.

It is important to understand how these energy substrates are stored, because the energy density of storage determines how much weight loss occurs when these stores are utilized. Fat as triglyceride (TG) is stored in adipose tissues as an oil with only small amounts of water, protein, and electrolytes. Pure TG has an energy density of 9 kcals/g, which is only slightly more than adipose tissue, which has an energy density of 8 kcals/g. In contrast carbohydrate (as glycogen) and proteins are stored

Table 14.1   Sources of Energy and Protein in a 75 kg Man

Source	Amount (kg)	Energy (kcal)
Triglycerides	12	110,000
Protein	12	50,000
Carbohydrate	0.62	2,480

Table 14.2   Basal Energy Consumption of a 75 kg Man

Organ	% of basal energy consumption	Energy consumed (kcal)
Brain	20	288
Heart	5	2
Kidneys	10	144
Viscera	30	480
Muscle + other	45	648

Basal energy consumption, 1 kcal/min = 1440 kcal/day.

in the cytosol with water and potassium at an energy density of 1 kcal/g, which is lower than the 4 kcal/g for pure glycogen or protein.

Early Effects of Starvation

Soon after the onset of starvation, there is a decrease in the level of insulin and an increase in the level of glucagon. These hormonal changes result in a breakdown of glycogen and a release of glucose for use by the brain. Unfortunately, the total glycogen stores can, at most, provide energy for 24 hours (Table 14.1); therefore it is necessary to mobilize and use alternative sources of energy. The most important sources are free fatty acids (FFA) from TG and glucose synthesized from lactate, amino acids, and glycerol (GY) by the process called gluconeogenesis. The decreased insulin levels activate hormone-sensitive lipase in the adipose tissue, which then hydrolyzes TG in adipose tissue to FFA and GY. FFA become a source of energy to muscle and liver, while GY is available for glucose synthesis.

The decrease in insulin levels results in protein hydrolysis in muscle and transamination of nitrogen from a variety of amino acids to pyruvate and α-ketoglutarate (α-KG), resulting in the formation of alanine and glutamine. Alanine is a precursor for gluconeogenesis by the liver. Glutamine carries nitrogen to the liver and is an energy substrate for the gut and lymphocytes and a substrate for the synthesis of ammonia by the kidney. Thus, this flow of amino acids from the muscles to the viscera maintains visceral and plasma protein synthesis despite wasting of muscle. Ultimately nitrogen that is not incorporated into visceral proteins is converted to urea and is excreted. The nitrogen lost as urea is equal to the nitrogen intake prior to the start of starvation or reduced protein intake. When the nitrogen intake is reduced, the nitrogen loss continues at the rate of the previous intake, and therefore there is an initial negative nitrogen balance. Later the losses of nitrogen decrease until equilibrium is restored. This pool of nitrogen that changes with intake is called the labile nitrogen pool (Munro, 1964). In summary, nitrogen losses are high at the start of protein-calorie malnutrition (PCM), but they decrease rapidly until the losses equal the intake.

As mentioned earlier, glycogen and protein are stored with water in a state of low energy density. Therefore, weight loss is rapid during early starvation, but the weight loss becomes slower as protein loss is reduced and body fat is used.

Prolonged Starvation

In prolonged starvation, the FFA levels increase and the FFA are converted to ketones by the liver. The reasons for the development of ketosis are:

1. increased availability of FFA to the liver (because low insulin levels promote lipolysis),
2. reduced glucose to form glycerol for re-esterification to TG, and
3. reduced fat oxidation in the liver (because the oxaloacetate needed by the liver for tricarboxylic cycle function is used in the increased gluconeogenesis resulting from the low insulin levels).

These ketones are used in the brain and other tissues as a source of energy instead of glucose. In this way, the body conserves protein and uses fat as a source of energy.

Trauma and Sepsis

Trauma and sepsis often occur together (for example, a person suffering a fractured pelvis and rupture of the bowel often develops peritonitis, and burn patients often develop septic wounds) and have similar effects on the metabolism of nutrients. Therefore it is useful to consider the metabolic effects of trauma and sepsis together.

Protein and Energy

Sir David Cuthbertson is credited with the first comprehensive observations of the effect of trauma on metabolism. He described patients after bone fracture and rats subjected to experimental fracture. In human beings, there is increased protein catabolism, mainly in muscle. The excretion of nitrogen as urea and of sulfate and phosphorus increases to a maximum between the third and eighth day after the injury and then decreases. Associated with the increase in protein catabolism is an increase in metabolic rate. However, excess catabolism is not seen in animals or human beings who were malnourished prior to the injury. It is believed that the increased catabolism is related to the mobilization of the labile nitrogen pool. Similarly, the increased metabolic rate is not seen in protein-depleted rats. Therefore, hypercatabolism appears to be related to the protein nutrition of the animal or man when trauma is present without sepsis.

Glucose and Lipid Metabolism

Gluconeogenesis, which is the production of glucose from lactate and alanine in the liver, is markedly enhanced in the presence of trauma and is not sensitive to insulin infusion. In normal individuals, the administration of small amounts of insulin results in complete suppression of gluconeogenesis. In trauma-septic patients, gluconeogenesis is not suppressed by insulin; this phenomenon is called insulin resistance. In addition, there is increased lipolysis because insulin resistance prevents insulin from suppressing lipolysis. The output of FFA increases and fat oxidation is increased. The net result is hyperglycemia and mild acidosis.

Hormonal and Neuroendocrine Responses

With trauma and sepsis, there is a marked increase in the counter-regulatory hormones that oppose the action of insulin. These hormones are cortisol, catecholamines, and glucagon (Table 14.3). Note that total parenteral nutrition (TPN) increases the levels of these hormones and that, despite high insulin levels, the glucose levels are high and FFA release from adipose tissue is not stopped. Cortisol increases protein catabolism, mobilizes amino acids from muscle, and increases hepatic glucose production. The increase in catecholamines (e.g., norepinephrine) increases the metabolic rate, increases liver glucose output, and increases lipolysis. The increases in cortisol and catecholamines are probably mediated by the central nervous system through the hypothalamic activation of the sympathetic nervous system and the release of corticotrophin releasing factor (CRF). CRF in turn increases adrenocorticotropic hormone (ACTH), which stimulates the adrenals to secrete cortisol.

Table 14.3 Hormone Levels in Trauma and Sepsis

Hormone	Control	Trauma and Sepsis 5% dextrose	TPN
Cortisol, μmol/L	0.4	0.7	1.0
Norepinephrine, μmol/L	1.8	3.8	8.0
Glucagon, pmol/L	43.0	73.0	90.0
Insulin, μmol/L	0.1	0.2	0.8
Plasma glucose, mmol/L	4.0	6.7	10.0
Plasma FFA, μmol/L	550.0	500.0	300.0

Abbreviations: FFA, free fatty acids; TPN, total parenteral nutrition.

Cytokines

Cytokines are peptides secreted by macrophages, lymphocytes, and endothelial cells in response to endotoxins and injury. They act on other organs to alter metabolism. The cytokines associated with trauma-sepsis are tumor necrosis factor alpha (TNF), interleukin-1 (IL-1), and interleukin-6 (IL-6). These cytokines cause anorexia and weight loss due to reduced intake of nutrients (Hoshino et al., 1991). If attempts are made to feed animals infused with TNF so as to promote weight gain, the animals develop multisystem organ failure; a corresponding phenomenon is seen in septic human patients. These patients have severe hyperglycemia, azotemia, and liver failure (Matsui, Cameron, & Kurian, 1993). Therefore feeding trauma-septic patients is not a simple matter of giving lots of nutrients to meet the metabolic requirements.

Summary of Metabolic Effects of Disease

Diseases can influence the intake and absorption of nutrients. Obstruction of the gastrointestinal (GI) tract, inflammatory bowel disease (IBD), celiac disease, pancreatitis, and bacterial overgrowth are examples of conditions in which changes in body composition reflect those seen in starvation. Contrariwise, in conditions such as cancer, trauma, and sepsis there are changes in the hormonal and cytokine profiles, and the net results are increased metabolic rate and increased mobilization of amino acids from muscle to viscera.

Despite these two contrasting profiles, it should be recognized that the changes in body composition seen clinically in association with diseases are due to the operation of both groups of changes. For example, weight loss in small cell lung cancer with hypermetabolism is due to relative anorexia (Russell et al., 1984). In patients with IBD, there are increased cytokine levels (MacDonald et al., 1990). Finally, the main mediator of wasting in animals receiving TNF is anorexia (Hoshino et al., 1991).

Keys et al. (1950) studied volunteers who were subjected to hypocaloric feeding. The changes in body composition during a 24 week period have been estimated from their data (Table 14.4). The data show that hypocaloric feeding results in a marked loss of body fat with relative preservation of body cell mass.

Table 14.4   Changes in Body Composition With Hypocaloric Feeding

Time	Body fat (kg)	Lean body mass (kg)
Baseline	9.7	60.3
After 24 weeks of hypocaloric feeding	2.6	50.2
% control	37	83

Table 14.5   Changes in Body Composition in Anorexia Nervosa on Refeeding

Groups	Body fat (kg)	TBK (mol)	TBN (kg)	K/N
Control	12.5	2.47	1.54	1.6
Baseline	5.5	1.59	1.21	1.3
% of control	44	64	78	81
4 weeks	6.8	1.9	1.33	1.4
8 weeks	7.9	2.1	1.37	1.53
% gain	44	32	13	—

Abbreviations: TBK, total body potassium; TBN, total body nitrogen.

Pure Nutrient Deprivation: Anorexia Nervosa

The effects of pure malnutrition are similar to those of starvation (Table 14.5). There is a massive loss of body fat with preservation of body nitrogen (Russell et al., 1983). The loss of body fat in proportion to the loss of total body potassium (TBK) or TBN, which corresponds to the lean tissue, is comparable to that seen in the study by Keys et al. (1950). Of interest is the fact that the TBK loss is greater than the TBN loss; the anorexic patient is relatively depleted of potassium. On refeeding, the changes in body fat and TBK are rapid and linear during an 8 week period. In contrast, TBN increases slowly until the K/N ratio approaches the normal value.

Gastrointestinal Disease: Crohn's Disease

Malnourished patients with Crohn's disease (Royall et al., 1994), unlike anorexics, lose body fat, TBK, and TBN to considerable extents, but there is a relative preservation of TBN as compared with TBK (Table 14.6). There is a greater loss of TBK and TBN relative to fat that may be due to the muscle catabolism that occurs in these patients resulting from corticosteroid treatment.

Acute Illness and Sepsis

Jeejeebhoy et al. (1982) found proportionate decreases in TBK and fat with relative preservation of TBN in 25 patients with clinical sepsis and positive blood cultures (Table 14.7). Compared with anorexic individuals, those with acute illness and sepsis have less loss of body fat in relation to TBK or TBN, but there is a larger decrease in TBK than in TBN.

Hypermetabolic Small Cell Cancer of the Lung

The cause of weight loss in cancer varies with the location and nature of the tumor. Hence it is necessary to control for the tumor type and nutritional

Table 14.6 Body Composition in Patients With Crohn's Disease

Groups	Body fat (kg)	TBK (mol)	TBN (kg)	K/N
Control*	14.2	3.28	1.72	1.9
Crohn's Disease	10.5	2.27	1.44	1.57
% control	74	69	84	—

Abbreviations: TBK, total body potassium; TBN, total body nitrogen.

*Estimated control values based on stature and sex.

Table 14.7 Body Composition in Acute Illness and Sepsis

Groups	Body fat (kg)	TBK (mol)	TBN (kg)	K/N
Control*	14.2	3.28	1.72	1.9
Acute illness + sepsis	10.1	2.32	1.42	1.63
% control	71	70	82	—

Abbreviations: TBK, total body potassium; TBN, total body nitrogen.

*Estimated control values based on stature and sex.

intake. In a controlled trial of nutritional support in metastatic small cell lung cancer associated with demonstrable hypermetabolism, it was possible to observe the effect of the tumor on body composition by comparison with a control group. Patients with metastatic small cell cancer of the lung were randomized to a control group that was allowed to eat a normal diet or to a group that, in addition, received 40 Kcal/kg intravenously by TPN. Both groups received chemotherapy. After four weeks, TPN was stopped and all the patients were studied for a further 28 weeks (Shike et al., 1984).

The controls lost an average of 16% of their body fat, 14.4% of TBK, and 12% of TBN during the 32 week period (Figure 14.1). As in the case of patients with acute illness and sepsis, the proportionate losses of body components were similar for fat, TBK, and TBN in the control group. The TPN patients gained 20% body fat and 8% TBK, but TBN was not statistically different from the value before TPN. After TPN was stopped, this group lost, on average, 20% body fat, 18% TBK, and 12% TBN. The major effect of the TPN appeared to be on body fat.

The disproportionate loss of potassium seen in anorexia, Crohn's disease, acute illness, and lung cancer can be interpreted in two ways. One interpretation is that since TBK represents body cell mass, the loss of cells is greater than that of total body protein. In other words, cell protein is lost to a greater relative extent than extracellular protein. Since both cellular and extracellular protein contribute to TBN, there is a smaller change in TBN than in TBK. This interpretation does not, however, explain the finding that TBK increases on refeeding but TBN does not change. If cell protein alone were being restored, as indicated by the increase in TBK, then TBN should increase proportionately. Another interpretation is that in malnutrition there is a specific loss of cellular potassium that is related to changes in cell energetics or permeability. This is considered in a later section on energetics of the Na-K ATPase pump.

Effect of Total Parenteral Nutrition and Enteral Nutrition on Body Composition in Malnourished Subjects

Yeung, Smith, and Hill (1979), in a study of patients with inflammatory bowel disease, showed that while TPN resulted in a gain of body weight, enteral nutrition for the same period did not change body composition. The weight gain with TPN was due to

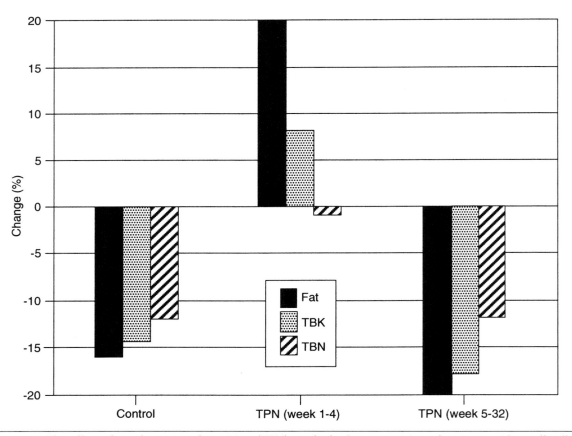

Figure 14.1 The effect of total parenteral nutrition (TPN) on the body composition of patients with small cell cancer of the lung receiving chemotherapy. A orally fed control group was studied (based on data from Shike et al., 1984).

a gain in body water and fat but not in TBN. Other reports from this research group have shown that TPN provides most of the energy as glucose and that with TPN therapy increases are observed in body fat and water but not in TBN (MacFie et al., 1981b). The one exception was in a study where a glucose-fat mixture was given (MacFie et al., 1981a). In studies by Jeejeebhoy et al. (1982) TPN resulted in significant increases in TBK but little change in TBN. Similar findings were obtained by Almond et al. (1989), who showed that patients who, on average, did not gain TBN gained an average of 250 mmol of TBK. On the other hand, in patients with Crohn's disease, we showed that enteral nutrition providing 35 kcal/kg per day resulted in greater increases in TBN than in TBK (Royall et al., 1994).

Changes in Body Composition in Weight Losing States

Taken as a whole, the findings considered earlier show that, with a reduction of food intake alone,

the change in body composition is as would be predicted for the metabolic effects of starvation and sepsis: namely, a major loss of body fat with relative preservation of TBN. In diseases where there is inflammation, cancer, or sepsis, the losses are similar for fat, TBN, and TBK. These observations are consistent with the metabolic effects of starvation versus those in trauma-sepsis. However, irrespective of the cause of weight loss, the loss of TBN is greater than that of TBK. Similarly, refeeding an anorexic individual a normal oral diet results in an enhanced gain of TBK. Therefore the increase in TBK seen in patients given TPN is not simply the result of the route of administering nutrients. The only exception is enteral feeding of Crohn's disease patients, which is associated with greater increases in TBN than in TBK.

The greater depletion of TBK with weight loss could be due to a loss of muscle. Since muscle is rich in potassium, wasting of muscle with preservation of nonmuscle nitrogen could result in relative sparing of TBN with loss of TBK. The alternative explanation is that there is a specific effect of malnutrition on cell energetics with altered transmembrane distribution of potassium. Animal studies have been performed to evaluate this possibility.

Studies of Intracellular Potassium, Phosphogens, Free ADP, Free Mg^{2+}, Free Energy Change of ATP Hydrolysis, and pH

Rats were randomly allocated to an ad libitum-fed control group or to a hypocaloric group fed 25% of the calories eaten by their pair-fed controls. All measurements were made after the hypocaloric animals had lost 20% of their initial weights. One group of hypocaloric animals was refed ad libitum for one week after having lost 20% of their initial weights.

If the fall in TBK with hypocaloric feeding was entirely due to muscle wasting, we would expect to find the intracellular potassium concentration to remain unchanged. In contrast, the mean intracellular potassium fell significantly from 139 to 107 mM/L in the soleus muscle ($p < 0.05$) (Pichard, Hoshino, & Allard, 1991). On refeeding, the muscle potassium increased to 124 mM/L . In this muscle, the mean membrane potential decreased significantly from −73.4 to −69.1 mV and the active intracellular potassium (aK$_i$) decreased significantly from 92.3 to 80.2 mM/L ($p < 0.05$ for both).

In an earlier study, Pichard et al. (1988) did not find any change in levels of muscle ATP (adenosine triphosphate, an energy-storing nucleotide) in hypocaloric rats, but there was a significant decrease in muscle creatine phosphate (CrP) and a small but significant decrease in pH. Free muscle magnesium remained unchanged. Free muscle ADP (the precursor of ATP) increased significantly and the free energy change of ATP hydrolysis decreased significantly. Refeeding restored these abnormalities (Table 14.8).

The body potassium to nitrogen ratio in the stable individual is comparable to that observed by carcass analysis, but severely malnourished anorexic patients are relatively depleted in potassium. Furthermore, on refeeding, there is a significant increase in body potassium without a corresponding change in nitrogen. The initial effects of refeeding appear to involve changes in ion distribution rather than increased protein synthesis, though it is not clear from total body measurements where the extra potassium is situated. Studies of rat muscle suggest

Table 14.8 Muscle ATP, Creatine Phosphate (CrP), Free Intracellular Mg^{2+}, Free ADP, and Free Energy Change of ATP Hydrolysis

Groups	ATP (mM)	CrP (mM)	Free Mg^{2+} (μM)	Free ADP (μM)	ΔG$_{atp}$ (kJ/M)
Control	8.0	30.1	532	39.2	−69
Hypocal	7.8	16.1	516	108.3	−66
Refed	7.7	26.2	628	41.9	−67

Data from Pichard et al. (1988).

ΔG$_{atp}$ = Free energy change of ATP hydrolysis; kJ/M = kilojoules/mole; Hypocal = hypocalorically fed; Refed = refed after a hypocaloric period (see text for details).

that, in part, there are changes in both free ionic potassium (as indicated by the change in aK$_i$) as well as in total intracellular potassium. It is important to determine the mechanisms responsible for these changes. Ion distribution is determined by either a change in the energetics of the Na-K ATPase pump and/or the permeability and selectivity of the cell membrane.

Energetics of the Na-K ATPase Pump

The muscle cell membrane maintains a gradient of high extracellular and low intracellular Na$^+$ and a high intracellular and a low extracelluar K$^+$. This gradient exerts an electrochemical force expressed as the *free energy change of ion movement*, which is counteracted by the *free energy change of ATP hydrolysis*. Since hypocaloric feeding of rats results in a decrease in the free energy change of ATP hydrolysis, on theoretical grounds there should be a change in the ion gradient (i.e., a decrease in intracellular potassium and an increase in intracellular sodium).

The free energy change of an ion (ΔG$_{ion}$) is calculated as

$$\Delta G_{ion} = R \cdot T \left(\ln \frac{Ci}{Ce} \right) + (Z \cdot F \cdot MP)$$

$$(14.1)$$

where R is the universal gas constant, T is the temperature in Kelvins, Ci is the intracellular concentration of an ion, Ce is the extracellular concentration of the ion, Z is its valence, F is the Faraday constant, and MP is the membrane potential in volts (Kammermeier, 1987). The ion gradient across a muscle cell membrane, with a high Na^+ on the outside and a high K^+ inside, is maintained by the operation of an Na-K ATPase "ion pump," which uses the energy of ATP hydrolysis to oppose the free energy change of the ion gradient. The effect of the free energy change of ATP hydrolysis on the change in the ratio of intra- to extracellular concentration of Na^+ can be calculated as follows:

$$\Delta G_{atp}(J/mol) = \Delta GK^+ = 3 \cdot R \cdot T \left(\ln \frac{Ci}{Ce} \right)$$
$$+ (Z \cdot F \cdot MP) \qquad (14.2)$$

because one mole of ATP is used to pump 3 moles of Na^+.

Rearranging the equation:

$$\frac{Ci}{Ce} = \exp^{\left(\frac{\Delta G_{atp} - (Z \cdot F \cdot MP)}{3RT} \right)}. \qquad (14.3)$$

$$\frac{\frac{Ci}{Ce} \text{ (control)}}{\frac{Ci}{Ce} \text{ (hypocaloric)}} = \frac{\exp^{\left(\frac{\Delta G_{atp} - (Z \cdot F \cdot MP)}{3RT_{control}} \right)}}{\exp^{\left(\frac{\Delta G_{atp} - (Z \cdot F \cdot MP)}{3RT_{hypocaloric}} \right)}. \qquad (14.4)$$

Using the mean values for ΔG_{atp} and the membrane potential given by Pichard et al. (1988) and Pichard, Hoshino, & Allard (1991) on p. 281, the control/hypocaloric ratio of Ci/Ce is 0.70. Since Ce is unchanged, the hypocaloric muscle will have about 42% more sodium. Since the normal intracellular sodium is about 15 mM/liter, it is likely that the hypocaloric muscle will have $15 \times 1.42 = 21$ mM/liter of sodium. Since Na/K exchange is in the ratio of 2 to 3, the outflow of potassium would be $(21 - 15) \times 3/2 = 9$ mM/liter. This value is close to the figure of 12 mM/liter obtained directly. Hence it is likely that the change of ΔG_{atp} may contribute significantly to the decrease in intracellular K^+.

Permeability and Selectivity

Increased permeability to potassium or chloride would cause the membrane potential to become more negative (Darnell, Lodish, & Baltimore, 1986), which is contrary to the observed change. However, if permeability to sodium were increased, then the membrane potential would become less negative. In this case, we would have

to postulate a selective conductance for Na^+. In conclusion, the effect of malnutrition and refeeding on body potassium is rapid and disproportionate to that of nitrogen. This difference is likely to be due to changes in cell energetics and/or selective permeability to Na^+ ions. The present evidence favors the former mechanism.

References

Almond, D.J., King, R.F.G.J., Burkinshaw, L., et al. (1989). Influence of energy source upon body composition in patients receiving intravenous nutrition. *Journal of Parenteral and Enteral Nutrition, 13*, 471-477.

Darnell, J., Lodish H., & Baltimore D. (1986). *Molecular cell biology*. New York: Scientific American.

Hoshino, E., Pichard, C., Greenwood, C.E., et al. (1991). Body composition and metabolic rate in rats during a continuous infusion of cachectin. *American Journal of Physiology, 260*, E27-E36.

Jeejeebhoy, K.N., Baker, J.P., Wolman, S.L., et al. (1982). Critical evaluation of the role of clinical assessment and body composition studies in patients with malnutrition and after total parenteral nutrition. *American Journal of Clinical Nutrition, 35*, (Suppl.), 1117-1127.

Kammermeier, H., (1987). Interrelationship between the free energy change of ATP-hydrolysis, cytosolic inorganic phosphate and cardiac performance during hypoxia and reoxygenation. *Biomedica Biochimica Acta, 8*, S499.

Keys, A., Brožek, J., Hanschel, A., et al . (1950). *The biology of human starvation*. Minneapolis: University of Minnesota Press.

MacDonald, T.T., Hutchings, P., Choy, M.Y., et al. (1990). Tumor necrosis factor-alpha and interferon-gamma production measured at the single cell level in normal and inflamed human intestine. *Clinical and Experimental Immunology, 81*, 301-305.

MacFie, J., Smith, R.C., & Hill, G.L. (1981a). Glucose or fat as a non-protein energy source? A controlled clinical trial in gastroenterological patients requiring intravenous nutrition. *Gastroenterology, 80*, 103-107.

MacFie, J., Yule, A.G., Hill, G.L. (1981b). Effect of added insulin on body composition of gastroenterological patients receiving intravenous nutrition: A controlled clinical trial. *Gastroenterology, 81*, 285-289.

Matsui, J., Cameron, R.G., & Kurian, R. (1993). Nutritional, hepatic and metabolic effects of cachectin/tumor necrosis factor in rats receiving total parenteral nutrition. *Gastroenterology, 104*, 235-243.

Munro, H.N. (1964). General aspects of the regulation of protein metabolism by diet and by hormones. In H.N. Munro & J.B. Allison (Eds.), *Mammalian protein metabolism, 1* (pp. 381-481). New York: Academic.

Pichard, C., Hoshino, E., & Allard, J.P. (1991) . Intracellular potassium and membrane potential in rat muscles during malnutrition and subsequent refeeding. *American Journal of Clinical Nutrition, 54*, 489-498.

Pichard, C., Vaughan, C., Struk, R., et al. (1988). The effect of dietary manipulations (fasting, hypocaloric feeding and subsequent refeeding) on rat muscle energetics as assessed by nuclear magnetic resonance spectroscopy. *Journal of Clinical Investigation, 82*, 895-901.

Royall, D., Jeejeebhoy, K.N., Baker, J.P., et al. (1994). Comparison of amino acid versus peptide based enteral diets in active Crohn's disease: Clinical and nutritional outcome. *Gut, 35*, 783-787.

Russell, D. McR., Prendergast, P.J., Darby, P.L., et al. (1983). A comparison between muscle function and body composition in anorexia nervosa: The effect of refeeding. *American Journal of Clinical Nutrition, 38*, 229-237.

Russell, D. McR., Shike, M., Marliss, E.B., et al. (1984). Effects of total parenteral nutrition and chemotherapy on the metabolic derangements in small cell lung cancer. *Cancer Research, 44*, 1706-1711.

Shike, M., Russell, D. McR., Detsky, A.S., et al. (1984). Changes in body composition in patients with small-cell lung cancer. *Annals of Internal Medicine, 101*, 303-309.

Yeung, C.K., Smith, R.C., & Hill, G.L. (1979). Effect of an elemental diet on body composition: A comparison with intravenous nutrition. *Gastroenterology, 77*, 652-657.

Influencing Factors
and
Relationships to Disease

15

Exercise Training and Body Composition Changes

Douglas L. Ballor

This chapter characterizes the changes that occur in body composition following various types of exercise training. This is a difficult task since adaptations to exercise training depend on many interrelated factors, including initial level of training, gender, body fat levels and distribution, age, and genetic makeup. The data are further confounded by the lack of definitive measures by which to assess exercise-induced changes in body composition. Finally, while the majority of studies investigating the effects of exercise training on body composition have been conducted over relatively short periods of time (i.e., 8 to 20 weeks), it is likely that the effects of exercise training on changes in body composition manifest themselves over an extended period of time. Using short-term exercise training studies to predict how long-term exercise training will affect body composition is fraught with problems since the changes are likely to be exponential in nature and eventually plateau. Cross-sectional comparisons between habitual exercisers and sedentary individuals provide some insight as to how long-term exercise training may affect body composition, but these comparisons suffer from self-selection bias.

Since exercise training-induced changes in body composition are dependent on various external factors (e.g., gender, age, genetic makeup), changes in body composition following an exercise training program vary greatly among individuals. Bouchard, Dionne, Simoneau, and Boulay (1992) at Laval University have added greatly to our knowledge in this area through a series of experiments that compared the responses of monozygotic twin to exercise training. Their data show much larger variation between twin pairs than within twin pairs with respect to adaptations consequent to exercise training. For example, Hamel et al. (1986) compared enzyme activity changes in the vastus lateralis muscle in six pairs of monozygotic twins who underwent a 15 week endurance training program. Variation between twin pairs, with respect to adaptations in skeletal muscle following exercise training, was 5 to 10 times higher than that within twin pairs. Similarly, Després and Bouchard (1984) present data which show that changes from basal lipolysis to maximal epinephrine-stimulated lipolysis in adipocytes following training are more closely correlated within rather than between pairs of monozygotic twins. Thus, the closer the genotypes of individuals are to each other, the more similar the adaptations in skeletal and adipose tissue following exercise training.

Thus, characterizing changes in body composition induced by exercise training is not a simple matter. Since there is a great deal of heterogeneity among study participants, changes induced by exercise training are also likely to be variable, making the exercise literature difficult to interpret. Indeed, conflicting findings regarding adaptation to exercise training are present in a number of areas. For example, recent reviews show there is not a consensus with respect to the effects of exercise training on

1. resting metabolic rate (RMR) during ad libitum feeding (Poehlman, 1989),
2. RMR during diet-induced weight loss (Mole, 1990),
3. the composition of diet-induced weight loss (Prentice et al., 1991), and
4. body weight, especially with respect to whether genders respond similarly (Keesey, 1988).

Because of the heterogeneity among individuals, exercise and body composition will be discussed in relation to other variables that might mitigate the effects of exercise training. The chapter is written in a teleological fashion, in which theoretical models and local adaptations are presented and discussed before addressing whole-body adaptations to exercise training. This approach should help the reader to understand the interindividual variations that may occur in response to exercise training.

Evaluation of Commonly Used Methods

Body composition of animals can be determined with a high degree of validity and reliability by using techniques such as ether fat extraction, nitrogen assays, and desiccation to determine body fat, protein, and water content, respectively. These techniques have a high degree of validity because they directly measure the variables of interest. However, these methods cannot be used with living human beings, and we must choose alternative less invasive methods. Body composition of human beings is commonly estimated from measures that are related to body composition. For example, body composition can be estimated from body density, skinfold thicknesses, and total body

water because each of these is related to body composition. While estimates from these various techniques intercorrelate fairly well (Pierson et al., 1991), they do not necessarily yield the same mean estimates. For example, Pierson et al. (1991) estimated percent body fat (% BF) in 389 Caucasians using eight methods of assessing body composition. The mean estimates of % BF for males ranged from a low of 17.2% to a high of 27.6%. For bioelectrical impedance (mean = 17.2%), the Durnin skinfold equation (Durnin & Womersley, 1974; mean = 19.9%), and densitometry (mean = 20.8%), three commonly available methods of assessing body composition, the mean % BF estimates were much closer to each other.

When selecting a technique to assess body composition changes following exercise training, the validity of the technique used to assess body composition must be considered and its validity for estimating body composition changes needs to be explored. The following discussion will briefly address these issues for three commonly used body composition techniques: densitometry (underwater weighing), skinfold predictive equations, and bioelectrical impedance. Other techniques, such as computed tomography and dual x-ray absorptiometry, hold promise for use in body composition assessment but are currently too expensive for general use.

Validity of Densitometry

Densitometry has been used for many years to estimate % BF via a two-compartment model (Siri, 1961) in which the body is considered to contain fat (specific gravity = 0.9 g/cc) and fat-free (specific gravity = 1.1 g/cc) subcomponents.

As discussed in chapters 1 and 7, there are several problems associated with using a two-component model to estimate body composition. This model assumes that the relative amounts of the constituents that make up the fat-free mass (FFM) are constant across race, gender, and age. Recent research suggests that there are racial and age differences in the density of fat-free mass that are associated with differences in bone mineral content. For example, African-American females have a larger bone mineral mass than white females (Ortiz et al., 1992), and losses of bone mineral mass with advancing age are well documented (Halioua & Anderson, 1989). Two-compartment models also assume a constant state of hydration. With over- or underhydration, % BF will be under- or overestimated, respectively. For example, Girandola, Wiswell, and Romero (1977) found that increasing body water mass by an average of 1.8 kg increased body density-estimated % BF by approximately 1.0% (i.e., from 12.3 to 13.3% BF), while reducing body water mass by 1.0 kg via dehydration resulted in body density-estimated % BF being reduced by 0.7%. Lohman (1981) estimates that, for the total population, the estimation of % BF from body density has a biological variation of ±3.8%.

Three-component (measuring body density and water mass) and four-component (measuring body density, water mass, and bone mineral mass) models have been developed that improve the validity with which % BF can be estimated from body density, thereby reducing errors due to racial and age differences. Heymsfield et al. (1990) estimate that the use of four-compartment models can reduce error in the estimation of % BF to approximately ±1%, but the equipment needed is relatively expensive.

Due to the high precision of body density measurements, changes in body density following exercise training are potentially useful for the estimation of associated changes in body composition. If the accuracy of the underlying assumptions of densitometry are not altered by training, one should be able to measure changes in body composition following training even if the actual % BF values are uncertain.

Aerobic exercise training results in a modest increase in muscle mass and a decrease in fat mass (Ballor & Keesey, 1991). In addition, aerobic exercise training sometimes, but not always, results in an increase in extracellular water mass (Saltin & Golnick, 1988). Taken collectively, these changes increase body density. When this greater body density is used to determine a new % BF via the Siri two-component equation, there will be a tendency to underestimate the increase in FFM and overestimate the decrease in fat mass. This error is likely to be small since the amount by which exercise training can elevate body water is limited (~1 to 2 L), and the greater the change in body composition with aerobic exercise training, the smaller the relative error in assessing changes in body composition.

Weight training generally results in modest reductions in fat mass and potentially large increases in muscle mass. In addition, extracellular water mass is less likely to be increased by weight training than by aerobic exercise. Thus, for changes in muscle and fat mass induced by modest weight training, the two-component densitometry model

should give reasonable estimates. Nevertheless, as muscle mass increases, it represents an increasingly larger portion of the fat-free mass. Depending on the subject's initial body density, this can lead to an over- or underestimation of % BF. The density of muscle tissue is ~1.06 g/cc. If the initial body density is less than 1.06 g/cc (a body density of 1.06 g/cc is equivalent to 17% BF using the Siri two-component equation), adding muscle mass will increase body density, leading to an appearance of reduced body fat. If the initial body density is more than 1.06 g/cc, increases in muscle mass will reduce body density, making it appear that body fat has increased. Despite these limitations, which have been discussed extensively by Lohman (1984), densitometry is probably better than skinfold predictive equations or bioelectrical impedance for ascertaining exercise-induced changes in body composition.

Validity of Skinfold Predictive Equations

Approximately one-half of the body fat is located subcutaneously, and regression equations that estimate % BF have been developed based upon this relationship. One can, therefore, measure the thickness of skinfolds in various locations on the body and use one of a variety of regression equations to estimate % BF (see chapters 9 and 10). These skinfold predictive equations make several assumptions about the relationships between skinfold thickness and adiposity:

1. A fixed relationship exists between subcutaneous and deep adipose tissue.
2. Selected skinfold thicknesses and adiposity change in proportion to each other.
3. FFM is relatively constant for a given body size and given skinfold thicknesses; FFM changes in some coordinated fashion with body size and skinfold thicknesses.

Unfortunately, the relationship between skinfold thicknesses and adiposity is dependent on gender, race, age, and exercise training status (Lohman, 1981). This has led to the development of many skinfold predictive equations in attempts to improve the validity of the estimates. Lohman posits that when the subject is similar to the population from which a given equation was developed, % BF can be estimated with an accuracy of 3 to 4%, compared to 2 to 3% for densitometry. Thus, care must be taken in the selection of a skinfold equation for application to a given individual. Even when properly used, the possible range of estimated values in relation to the true value is large for any predictive equation. It is recommended that skinfold equations be used only in combination with other procedures in the assessment of changes in body composition following exercise training.

Exercise training can increase the FFM and can result in skinfold thickness predictive equations overestimating % BF. For example, in 79 women athletes, Sinning and Wilson (1984) compared % BF from densitometry with values from a variety of skinfold predictive equations. Eight of the nine equations evaluated yielded estimates of % BF that were higher than those from densitometry. The Jackson, Pollock, and Ward (1980) and Durnin and Womersly (1974) equations yielded mean estimates of % BF that were 1% and 4%, respectively, larger than those from densitometry.

Several investigators have examined the validity of skinfold equations to assess body composition change. Scherf et al. (1986) reported that skinfold equations tended to overpredict % BF compared to densitometry in formerly obese adults with total errors ranging from ±4.4 to ±8.4% BF. Wilmore, Girandola, and Moody (1970) examined changes in body composition in 55 men following a jogging program. They reported correlations between body density changes from densitometry and from skinfold equations of $r = 0.43$ to 0.64. These findings are similar to those of Ballor and Katch (1989, p. 97) for obese women in weight loss or exercise programs. The latter workers also noted a tendency for skinfold equations to underpredict changes in % BF relative to those from densitometry. Given the relatively low correlations and the high total error associated with the changes in body composition, they concluded that "use of anthropometric prediction equations to estimate individual percent fat change scores results in large errors and is not recommended."

Validity of Bioelectrical Impedance

Bioelectrical impedance, which is considered in detail in chapter 5, is the measurement of the resistance and reactance of a conductor (the human body) to the flow of an alternating current. Since the resistance of the human body is closely related to total body water, which is in turn closely related to FFM, bioelectrical impedance methods for assessing body composition have become increasingly popular (Baumgartner, Chumlea, & Roche, 1990). The correlations between densitometric determinations of % BF and those from equations

including impedance are generally similar to those found using skinfold equations. For example, Pierson et al. (1991) found correlations between values from densitometry and either bioelectrical impedance or the Durnin and Womersly (1974) skinfold equation of $r = 0.72$ and $r = 0.77$, respectively, in a sample of 233 females. Baumgartner et al., p. 210, in their fine review on the use of bioelectrical impedance to assess body composition, noted that equations that estimate % BF from bioelectrical impedance "are not markedly better than those from anthropometry alone."

Since bioelectrical impedance is sensitive to changes in water mass, any exercise regimens (such as aerobic exercise training) that increase extracellular water volume may yield artificial increases in estimates of FFM from bioelectric impedance. Conversely, while changes in skinfold thicknesses may not accurately represent exercise-induced changes in FFM, bioelectrical impedance would be expected to estimate these changes more accurately since it measures a close correlate of FFM (i.e., total body water). Forbes, Simon, and Amatruda (1992) combined data from seven studies to compare changes in lean body mass (obtained from various criterion measures) and total body resistance (in ohms) following various diet and exercise interventions. They found a correlation of $r = -0.56$ between changes in lean body mass and resistance, which was similar to that found for skinfold equations. Forbes and colleagues also noted that weight change alone was a better predictor ($r = 0.69$) of lean mass change than was change in total body resistance. Ross, Léger, Martin, and Roy (1989) reported that two of the four bioelectrical impedance equations they examined provided mean % BF and lean mass values that were not statistically different from those estimated by densitometry before and after a 10 week program of dietary restriction and exercise. The variance associated with these measures was relatively high (SD ±3.8 to ±5.8% for % BF and ±5.4 to ±6.6 kg for lean mass), and it seems unlikely that correlations between these change scores would be higher than those reported by Forbes et al. Thus, as with skinfold equations, one should not use bioelectrical impedance as the only criterion to assess exercise training-induced changes in body composition.

Exercise and Body Weight

Body weight is dependent on the first and second laws of thermodynamics. Weight gain is inevitable when total energy intake exceeds total energy expenditure. Contrariwise, when total energy expenditure exceeds total energy intake, body weight will decrease. Thus, the energy balance equation (i.e., weight change = energy intake minus energy expenditure) governs change in weight. Exercise training, especially aerobic-type training, is commonly undertaken to promote weight loss since it can potentially increase energy expenditure without changing energy intake.

In a simplistic approach, exercise energy expenditure is sometimes used to predict body weight loss on the assumption that energy intake and other components of total energy expenditure do not change. For example, it can be calculated that increasing exercise energy expenditure by 100 kcal per day (without changing intake) should result in a weight loss of approximately 0.4 kg per month or 4.8 kg per year, but such extrapolations cannot be justified.

Aerobic exercise training has an inconsistent effect on body weight because body weight generally stabilizes at some level for all individuals; this level depends on many factors, including gender, exercise status, the distribution of muscle fiber types, percentage of fat in the diet, and number, type, and distribution of adipocytes. Thus, reductions in body weight with exercise training will not occur if the body weight is already at the minimum level for an individual. A comparison of the responses to similar training programs in genetically similar animals illustrates this point. Figure 15.1 depicts the effects that 9 to 11 weeks of treadmill exercise

training, 5 days per week, has on normal weight (lean) and obese Sprague-Dawley male and female rats (Ballor, 1991a, 1991b; Ballor et al., 1990c). The normal weight rats were 90 days old at the start of the experiment and were fed a low-fat chow (4 kcal/g) ad libitum. The obese rats (~175 days old at the beginning of the exercise training) were fed a high-fat chow (5.8 kcal/g) ad libitum for 12 weeks prior to and during the exercise training. Exercise training reduced the body weights (compared to sedentary controls) of obese males by 95 g (15%), normal weight males by 39 g (9%), and normal weight females by 3 g (1%).

These disparate changes in body weight in rats in response to similar exercise training regimens are caused by at least two factors. First, there were reductions in the dietary intakes of obese males (−9.3 kcal per day) and normal weight males (−4.8 kcal per day) while there was a modest increase in dietary intake for the female rats (1.2 kcal per day). Second, while exercise training increased daily relative energy expenditure by 7 to 10% (i.e., per kg$^{0.75}$) for males, it had no effect on the total daily relative energy expenditure of the females. These data suggest that rats can adjust intake and/ or nonexercising total daily energy expenditure in attempts to keep body weight within a desired range. They also expose the danger of simply counting exercise calories to predict body weight changes. Thus, the effects of exercise training on body weight must be examined within the context of a regulatory model. When this is done, much of the variation between studies with respect to

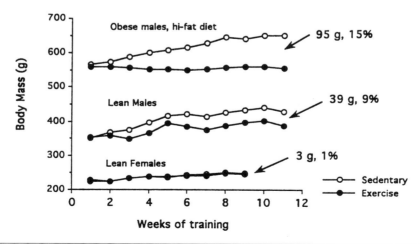

Figure 15.1 Mean body masses for sedentary and exercise-trained groups of Sprague-Dawley rats. Listed also are the mean differences between sedentary and exercise-trained groups in g and the percentage difference from the sedentary group. Note that exercise training did not differentially affect body mass for normal weight (lean) females; the sedentary and exercise trained mean data points overlap. Data from Ballor, 1991a, 1991b; Ballor et al., 1990c.

the effects of exercise training on body weight can be explained.

Currently it is not clear how, or whether, body weight is regulated, but there are at least two hypotheses for which supporting data are present. Flatt (1989) suggested that body weight is determined by total caloric intake and "settles" up or down with changes in total intake until caloric expenditure and intake are matched. He further suggests that the percentage of fat in the diet is a major determinant of body weight since body weight changes until the total fat intake equals fat oxidation. Using the energy balance equation in this fashion suggests that if exercise training increases total daily energy expenditure, body weight will decrease, with a concomitant reduction in resting energy expenditure (due to reduced metabolic mass), until energy expenditure and intake are in balance. This suggests there is a series of levels at which the weight of an individual might stabilize depending on the extent of the increase in exercise energy expenditure. This hypothesis assumes that non-exercising energy expenditure is unaffected by exercise training, but this is not always the case (Poehlman & Danforth, 1991). Recent research also suggests that exercise training can reduce the preference of rodents for high-fat foods (Gerado-Gettens et al., 1991). This might be one mechanism by which exercise training can alter body weight.

In contrast, other data are consistent with active regulation of body weight. When body weight is more or less than the physiologically desired level, resting metabolism may be altered to return body weight to the desired level (Keesey, 1988). Consistent with this hypothesis are the classic studies by Mayer and associates (Mayer et al., 1954; Mayer, Roy, & Mitra, 1956), which show that while exercise training or increased energy expenditure activity results in initial reductions in body weight, as activity increases dietary intake becomes greater, thus stabilizing the reduced body weight.

It is likely that both weight settling and weight regulation mechanisms participate in the determination of body weight in association with exercise training. In general, loss of body weight in an exercise program is more likely if the initial body weight is markedly greater than the desired level, the person is sedentary, and there is a high percentage of fat in the diet. The effect of aerobic exercise training on body weight is mostly manifested via changes in fat stores, as discussed later.

Ballor and Keesey (1991) published a meta-analysis of the effects of exercise training on changes in body weight and body composition. Meta-analysis treats mean data from various studies as individual data points and subjects them to parametric statistical analyses (McGaw, 1988). This procedure allows inferences about the extent to which different parameters may affect responses to exercise training. Figure 15.2 shows how weekly exercise energy expenditure and initial body weight affect the reductions in body weight with aerobic (run/walk and cycling) exercise training.

The upper portion of the figure shows the relationship between weekly energy expenditure and changes in body weight (mass). The regression line represents the data for males and females. As weekly energy expenditure increases so does the weight loss ($r = -0.58$), but the weight losses are generally modest even with relatively large weekly energy expenditures.

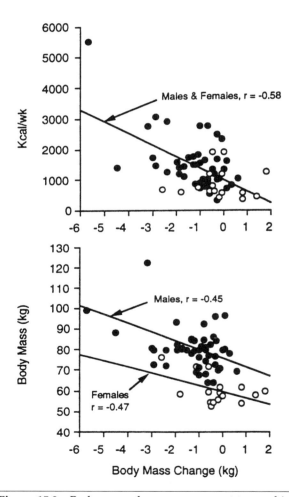

Figure 15.2 Body mass change consequent to aerobic exercise training relative to either weekly exercise energy expenditure (top panel) or initial body mass (bottom panel). Males are represented by solid circles and females by open circles. Data are drawn from Ballor and Keesey (1991).

The lower portion of the figure shows the relationships between initial body weight (mass) and body weight change for males and females. The change in weight for most of the groups is modest (male mean change = -1.2 kg, female mean change = -0.3 kg), and the regression lines relating loss of weight with exercise to initial body weight are similar for the two genders. In each gender, the larger the initial weight, the greater the loss of weight with exercise.

Frequency and Duration of Exercise and Body Weight Change

The meta-analysis of Ballor and Keesey (1991) indicates that males and females differ with respect to the effects of aerobic exercise on body weight. In males, exercise-induced changes in body weight are more closely correlated with weekly exercise energy expenditure ($r = -0.61$) than with either the number of exercise sessions per week ($r = -0.32$) or minutes per session ($r = -0.37$). For women, the correlations were much lower for all indices of energy expenditure (weekly exercise energy expenditure, $r = 0.03$; sessions per week, $r = -0.19$; minutes per session, $r = -0.16$) and were statistically nonsignificant ($p > 0.05$), suggesting that men and women respond differently to exercise training. On average, the males were slightly more fat (% BF ~20%) than the women (% BF ~27%) in comparison with general groups matching gender. This may be related to the gender differences in the responses to exercise training.

Exercise Intensity and Body Weight

Exercise intensity does not appear to affect the rate at which weight is lost. Three studies illustrate this point. Duncan, Gordon, and Scott (1991) examined the effects of walking 4.8 km five days per week at three different speeds (4.8, 6.4, and 8.0 kmh) for 24 weeks on body weight in 59 women aged 20 to 40 years with a mean % BF of about 26%. The low, medium, and high speed walkers gained 0.8, 0.1, and 1.1 kg, respectively. Gaesser and Rich (1984) compared high and low intensity cycle ergometry exercise in which young men (20 to 30 years) with moderate % BF (mean ~19%) expended approximately 300 kcal per session at either 85 to 90% or 45 to 50% of maximum oxygen uptake three days per week for 18 weeks. The high intensity group gained 0.6 kg of body weight while the low intensity group lost 0.3 kg. Finally, Tremblay et al. (1990) compared 2,600 men and women who participated

in the 1981 Canada Fitness Survey. They grouped individuals based upon the MET level (1 MET = 3.5 ml O_2/kg of body mass per minute) at which they habitually exercised. There were no statistical differences between MET groups for body weight; within gender, the mean weights differed by less than 1.1 kg.

Resistance Training and Body Weight

The recent large increases in the body weights of college and professional football linemen provide anecdotal evidence that resistance training can greatly increase body weight. Unfortunately, it is difficult to determine the extent to which these increases are due to exercise training alone or to other factors such as performance enhancing drugs. In addition, these changes are likely to extend over long periods, and few studies follow subjects for these lengths of time. Ballor and Keesey (1991) report that the mean weight increase for males in 11 different weight training studies was 1.2 kg during 11 weeks, but it is not known if this trend would continue with extended training. There is also a great deal of variety with respect to the number of exercises, sets, repetitions, and intensity (i.e., percentage of one repetition maximum) used by weight trainers.

Age, Exercise, and Body Weight

Aging is associated with increased body weight, most of which is fat. Because older adults are more likely to be overfat, they are also more likely to lose body weight in response to an aerobic exercise training program. Kohrt, Malley, Dalsky, and Halloszy (1992a) compared body weight and body composition from densitometry in young (18 to 31 years) and older (52 to 72 years), sedentary and aerobic exercise-trained, men and women. As shown in Figure 15.3, exercise-trained young men weigh about 7.0 kg less than their sedentary counterparts, but exercise-trained young women weigh about 2.5 kg less than their sedentary counterparts. In contrast, exercise-trained older men and women weigh 16 and 10 kg less, respectively, than their sedentary counterparts. These data are consistent with the following conclusions:

1. The loss of weight due to participation in an exercise training program is related to the degree to which one is overweight.
2. Older women may be more likely to lose weight in response to an exercise training program than younger women.

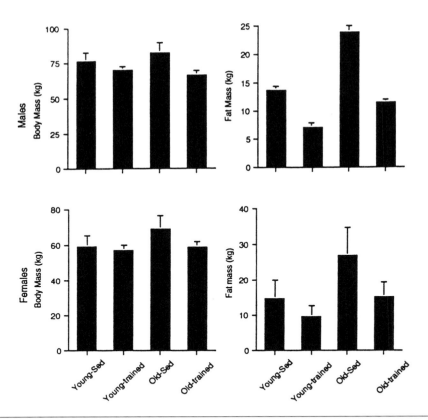

Figure 15.3   Effects of age and/or exercise training status on body mass and fat mass in males and females. Young = 18 to 31 years; Old = 52 to 72 years; Sed = sedentary; trained = exercise trained. Data are from Kohrt et al. (1992a).

3. A lifetime of regular physical activity can minimize weight gain, or, conversely, older adults who are overweight are likely to lose weight in response to exercise training.

These conclusions are tentative because the data are cross-sectional and selection bias may have influenced the results.

Summary

The responses of body weight to aerobic exercise training appear to be quite variable, with males more likely to lose weight in response to the initiation of an exercise training program than females. A loss of body weight is also more likely for individuals who are overfat. The loss of weight in response to an exercise training program appears to be more dependent on total energy expenditure than on the frequency, duration, and intensity of the exercise.

Exercise Training and Fat Mass

Most of the weight lost with aerobic exercise training is fat. In addition, most of the variability between subjects in exercise-induced changes in body weight are related to differences in the loss of fat. This may be due in part to differences among individuals with respect to the number, type, and distribution of adipocytes (Rebuffé-Scrive, 1988). For example, females are more likely than males to store fat in alpha-mediated adipocytes, especially in the thigh region. These adipocytes are less likely to release fat during adrenergic stimulation than beta-mediated cells. In comparison, males are more likely to store fat in beta-mediated adipocytes located in the abdominal area. In addition the volumes of adipocytes seem to be regulated or controlled in some fashion. For example, lipoprotein lipase activity, which facilitates fat storage, increases when adipocyte volumes are reduced (Kern, Ong, Saffari, & Carty, 1990). Adipocytes enlarge and become insulin-resistant in the obese; this reduces the ability of adipocytes to store fat (Craig, Garthwaite, & Halloszy, 1987). Thus, the response of body fat to exercise training depends, in part, on adipocyte morphology and function.

Exercise training seems able to induce reductions in adipocyte volumes to some "floor" level (Björntorp et al., 1972), and therefore body weight commonly stabilizes at a lower value after an exercise training program. This reduction in adipocyte volume may be passive, due to a decrease in body weight until energy expenditure and intake are equal, or active, due to increased resting metabolic rate or decreased appetite. An exercise training program will have only small effects on the total body fat of individuals in whom adipocyte volume is near the "floor" level at the initiation of the program.

Losses in body fat with exercise training may be proportional to the increase in exercise energy expenditure until adipocyte volumes are reduced to a threshold level. At this point, dietary intake will increase to maintain a constant adipocyte volume and body weight. Since the number of adipocytes varies among individuals, stabilization can occur at a variety of body weights and % BF levels. These reductions in fat mass with continued exercise training seem to occur over extended periods of time. For example, Wood et al. (1988) examined the effect of a one year aerobic exercise training program on changes in body composition in 47 men. Fat mass decreased by 3.0 kg during the first seven months of training and by 1.0 kg during the next five months of training.

If a relationship does exist between fat cell volumes and adaptations to exercise training, this suggests that obese individuals with enlarged adipocytes are more likely to lose body fat in response to exercise training than are those with an increased number of adipocytes of normal size. Consistent with this premise are data reported by Tremblay, Després, LaBlanc, and Bouchard (1984), who studied the effects of a 20 week aerobic exercise program on suprailiac adipocyte weight in 28 normal weight men and women. They ranked the subjects by initial adipocyte weight within gender-specific groups and divided them into subgroups with large or small adipocyte weights. Males with large initial adipocyte weights lost an average of 4.2 kg of body fat in response to exercise training, compared to a mean loss of 0.7 kg for men with small initial adipocyte weights. In contrast, females did not significantly reduce their fat mass or adipocyte weight in response to exercise training, and there were no statistically significant differences in weight loss between subgroups of females with large or small initial adipocyte weights. Similarly, Andersson et al. (1991) reported differential responses between males and females in exercise training-induced changes in fat mass. While slightly obese men and obese women lost fat mass during an aerobic exercise training program, slightly obese women did not. A study by Boileau

et al. (1971) also shows differential responses to exercise training. They compared fat mass change in groups of lean and obese men who expended 3,000 kcal per week by running or walking for nine weeks. The eight obese men (mean body mass = 122 kg) reduced their fat mass by 5.9 kg while the 15 lean men (mean body mass = 66.6 kg) reduced their fat mass by only 2.1 kg. Thus, the same total energy expenditure does not necessarily elicit the same reduction in fat mass.

With advancing age, women are more likely to be overfat and to deposit fat in adipocytes in which the fat is more labile, especially abdominal adipocytes. When this occurs, women are more likely to lose body fat with the onset of an exercise training program. The findings from two studies (Kohrt et al., 1992a; Kohrt, Obert, & Halloszy, 1992b) are consistent with this concept. Figure 15.3 (data from Kohrt et al., 1992a) compares fat mass between young and old adults who are sedentary or regularly participate in exercise training. Young men who regularly exercise have approximately 6.6 kg less fat mass than sedentary controls. Young women who regularly exercise have approximately 5.1 kg less fat mass than sedentary controls. In contrast, older men and women have 12.4 kg and 11.8 kg less fat mass, respectively, than sedentary counterparts. Kohrt et al. (1992b) compared the effects of a 9 to 12 month aerobic training program on fat mass and adipose tissue distribution in men and women 60 to 70 years old. Men reduced their fat mass, on average, by 3.1 kg and women by 1.6 kg. These gender differences in the changes in fat mass were not statistically significant when expressed as % BF (men = 3.7%, women = 2.3%). For both males and females, the greatest reduction in adipose tissue occurred in the truncal area, suggesting preferential loss of fat from this region.

Ballor and Keesey (1991), in a meta-analysis, examined the changes in body composition with short-term exercise interventions. The data base included studies that used a variety of methods to estimate % BF, including densitometry, skinfold thicknesses, and the measurement of total body potassium. The preponderance of the studies used densitometry, and most of the remainder used skinfold thicknesses. Tests were made to determine whether the changes in % BF from densitometry or skinfold thicknesses with aerobic exercise training differed for males and females. The two genders lost the same amount of weight (1.0 kg), and the changes in % BF were not statistically different between methods (densitometry: −1.8 ±1.1% BF; skinfold assessment: −1.6 ±2.0% BF). Thus, the ability of these methods to predict mean changes seems similar, which would be expected since estimates from them are highly intercorrelated (Pierson et al., 1991).

Figure 15.4 depicts changes in fat mass following short-term aerobic exercise training for groups of males and females included in the meta-analysis of Ballor and Keesey (1991). The upper portion of the figure shows the relationship between weekly energy expenditure and fat mass change. As one might expect, the greater the weekly energy expenditure, the larger the reduction in fat mass (males, $r = -0.69$; females, $r = -0.53$). Average weekly energy expenditures are lower for females, as is the average reduction in fat mass (males = -1.7 kg; females = -1.0 kg). The smaller changes in body fat mass for females may be related to lower exercise energy expenditure due to smaller body mass, lower levels of training, and/or physiologically

differing responses to exercise training. The lower panel shows the relationship between initial % BF and changes in fat mass with exercise training. For both males ($r = -0.58$) and females ($r = -0.56$) a correlation exists between initial levels of adiposity and the magnitude of reduction in fat mass with an aerobic exercise training regimen. This is consistent with the premise that the extent of obesity is directly related to the loss of body mass with exercise training.

Surprisingly, weight training exercise also seems to induce reductions in fat mass in males that are similar to those found with aerobic training, at least for brief periods after the training. Figure 15.5 shows mean fat mass change for the total period (lower panel) and the change per week (upper panel) with aerobic exercise and weight training for studies included in a recent meta-analysis (Ballor & Keesey, 1991). For the most part, weight training and aerobic exercise training both elicit reductions in fat mass. There is a great deal of variability in the data ($r = 0.12$) suggesting that the total changes in fat mass with training are not closely related to weeks of training. Fat mass may decrease with training to a certain level and remain stable.

The data in the upper panel suggest that weight training also reduces fat mass and are consistent with a plateauing of fat mass loss over time. Fat mass changes per week are similar with aerobic exercise (mean change = -0.12 kg) and with weight training exercise (mean change = -0.11 kg). The changes in fat mass per week for either aerobic or weight training exercise for a similar number of weeks are in good agreement. Furthermore, for aerobic training the average rate of change decreases as the number of weeks of training increases ($r = 0.44$). A corresponding analysis of weight training was not made because the reported studies differed little in the duration of training. (See the section on the validity of densitometry to assess changes in muscle and fat mass as a result of weight training exercises.)

Body Fat and Exercise Intensity

The intensity of exercise affects the mix of substrates used to supply energy. For example, Ballor, McCarthy, & Wilterdink (1990a) reported that women on a 1,200 kcal per day intake and exercising at work rates equivalent to 85% or 51% of peak oxygen uptake had respiratory exchange ratios of 0.92 and 0.80, respectively. This corresponds to obtaining either 33% or 74% of energy from fat

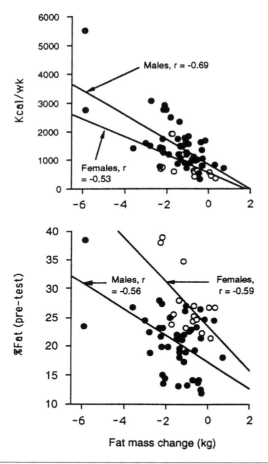

Figure 15.4 Effect of weekly exercise energy expenditure (top panel) and initial level of % BF (lower panel) on fat mass changes subsequent to aerobic exercise training. Males are represented by solid circles and females by open circles. Data are drawn from Ballor and Keesey (1991).

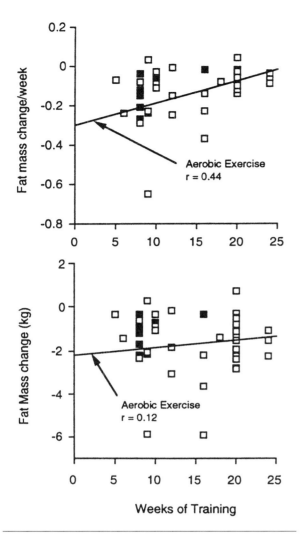

Figure 15.5 Effects of weeks of training on fat mass change per week (upper panel) and total fat mass change (lower panel) for males undergoing either aerobic exercise training (open squares) or weight exercise training (solid squares). Regression lines are drawn for aerobic exercise training only, due to the limited differences between the responses to weight training. Data are drawn from Ballor and Keesey (1991).

during the exercise training. It could be concluded from these data that low intensity exercise training is better for facilitating fat mass losses since more fat mass is being oxidized. It is, however, necessary to consider substrate interconversions or expenditures after the exercise period. In addition, fat stores, like carbohydrate stores, appear to be regulated.

The available data do not support the theory that low intensity exercise is better than vigorous exercise in promoting fat mass losses. For example,

in two studies (Ballor et al., 1990a; Ballor, Tommerup, Smith, & Thomas, 1990b) high and low intensity exercise training had similar effects on the percentage of weight lost as fat. Similar results have been reported by others (Duncan et al., 1991; Gaesser and Rich, 1984).

Body Fat and Duration or Frequency of Exercise

Findings from the meta-analysis of Ballor & Keesey (1991) indicate that fat mass reductions with aerobic exercise training are correlated with weekly energy expenditure for both men ($r = 0.69$) and women ($r = 0.53$). Since weekly energy expenditure is a function of the duration and frequency of exercise training, it is not surprising that both these variables are related to fat mass loss with exercise training. For example, Pollock, Miller, Linnerud, and Cooper (1975) examined the effects of 30 to 45 minutes running per session for two, three, or four days per week for 20 weeks on the sum of six skinfold thicknesses in 148 middle-aged men. The sums decreased by 7, 14, and 20%, respectively, for men training two, three, and four days per week. Meredith, Zackin, Frontera, and Evans (1987) examined the relationship between fat mass and number of hours per week of aerobic exercise training for young and middle-aged individuals who had been habitually exercising for at least two years. They found a fairly strong ($r = -0.82$) correlation between the number of hours per week of training and the amount of fat mass that was lost. Marti and Howald (1990) followed 27 former elite runners for 15 years and separated them into highly active, active, and formerly active groups based upon their current levels of training. During the 15 year period the mean changes in fat mass were -2.5 kg, +1.5 kg, and +8.8 kg for the highly active, active, and formerly active groups, respectively. Collectively, the preceding data suggest that fat mass is related to level of training (or weekly energy expenditure) and that regular training can greatly attenuate age-related gains in body fat.

Summary

Aerobic exercise training induces reductions in total fat mass, and the size of the reduction is related to the total weekly energy expenditure via exercise. Body fat is reduced with training until total energy expenditure and total energy intake are equal. Body fat levels are much more likely to be reduced following exercise training for those individuals with large adipocytes. Young men are more likely to lose fat mass with exercise training than are young women. Older women may be more likely to lose body fat with exercise training than younger women. The age-related increase in body fat during adulthood seems to be strongly related to reductions in exercise training volume. Older people are more likely to lose body fat with the onset of an exercise training program, mostly because they tend to have more body fat.

Exercise Training and Fat-Free Mass

Fat-free mass (FFM) consists of water, bone, muscle, connective tissue, and vital organs. While exercise training can increase bone density (see later section on bone mineral mass) and the strength of connective tissue (Fleck & Kramer, 1988), most people are interested in the effects of exercise training on FFM as it relates to muscle, and the following discussion will focus on this issue.

Aerobic exercise training is associated with moderate hypertrophy of skeletal muscle fibers with similar responses in males and females (Costill, 1986). In contrast to the changes in fat mass with aerobic training, which usually occur over extended time periods, skeletal muscle adaptations are more rapid. As described earlier, Marti and Howald (1990) studied former athletes who maintained different levels of training. Fat-free mass increased by 2.1 kg for the highly active former athletes, decreased slightly (−0.4 kg) for the active former athletes, and did not change for the inactive former athletes. Kohrt et al. (1992a) compared body composition between young and old men and women who were habitually active or sedentary. For young and older women, the means for FFM for the trained groups were 2.6 kg and 1.6 kg higher, respectively, than those for their sedentary counterparts. In men, exercise training did not enhance FFM, with young and older men having 0.3 kg less and 3.4 kg less FFM, respectively, than their sedentary counterparts. Again, this may be related to sampling bias.

Weight training can induce hypertrophy of muscle fibers in men and women (MacDougall, Sale, Elder, & Sutton, 1982; Staron et al., 1989). Other research suggests that, when considered relative to the baseline value, men and women respond similarly to weight training (Cureton, Collins, Hill, & McElhannon, 1988). Anecdotal evidence suggests that it takes several years of training for body builders to develop the massive amounts of

FFM that are common in these athletes. The need for long-term resistance training to induce increases in FFM may be related to hyperplasia of muscle fibers. Controversial data consistent with skeletal muscle hyperplasia in human beings have been reported (Antonio & Gonyea, 1993). For example, MacDougall et al. compared triceps brachii muscle fiber diameters between elite strength-trained individuals (powerlifters and body builders) and previously untrained subjects who had undergone six months of heavy resistance training. The size of the muscle fibers and other muscle fiber-related morphological characteristics were not different between the two groups. Despite this, the elite group had arm circumferences that were 26% larger than those of the previously untrained group and they were much stronger. In their interpretation of these findings, McDougall et al. suggested that the elite group was either genetically endowed with a greater number of muscle fibers or that the number of muscle fibers increased in response to training. These data also imply that there are theoretical upper limits to muscle fiber hypertrophy that could limit gains in FFM in the absence of hyperplasia.

As discussed earlier, gender-related differences with respect to adaptations of skeletal muscle to either aerobic exercise training or resistance training exercise do not appear to exist. Additionally, there do not appear to be age-related differences in the ability of skeletal muscle to adapt to aerobic or resistance training exercise. For example, Fiatarone et al. (1990) reported that seven 90 year old men increased their total mid-thigh muscle area (assessed via CT scan) by an average of 9% following an eight-week resistance training program. Charette et al. (1991) reported that the cross-sectional area of Type II vastus lateralis muscle fibers increased by 20% in 13 women with a mean age of 69 years following a 12 week resistance training program. Hagberg et al. (1989) have presented data that show that maximum oxygen uptake increased by 26% in 16 men and women 70 to 79 years old following a 26 week aerobic exercise training program.

Although age-related differences in adaptations to exercise training do not appear to exist on a regional level, it is likely that the overall effect on FFM is less in older than in younger adults. Lexell, Taylor, and Sjöström et al. (1988) counted the number of muscle fibers in cross-sections of vastus lateralis muscles from cadavers of previously healthy men ranging in age from 15 to 83 years. They found that muscle fiber number decreased by approximately 40% from age 20 to 80 years and that the rate of loss increased exponentially after 50 years. The effect of the training on muscle mass may be less in the elderly due to this reduction in the number of muscle fibers.

Short-Term Effects of Exercise Training on Fat-Free Mass

Figure 15.6 presents data from the meta-analysis of Ballor and Keesey (1991) on the effects of number of weeks of training and of weekly energy expenditure on change in FFM. The upper panel relates changes in FFM to weeks of training for males undergoing either aerobic exercise or weight training. For aerobic training, number of weeks of training correlates weakly and negatively ($r = -0.37$) with changes in FFM. With weight training, there is a consistent increase in FFM (mean = 2.2 kg) that is not closely related to the duration of training. Unfortunately, there are insufficient long-duration weight training studies to predict the time course of changes in FFM with resistance training exercises.

The lower panel shows the relationship between kcal expended via aerobic exercise per week and FFM change for males and females. Correlations between kcal per week and FFM change were higher for females ($r = 0.56$) than for males ($r = 0.25$, $p > 0.05$) although the slopes of the regression lines were similar. The lower correlation for men is seemingly due to the greater variety in weekly energy expenditure. High levels of weekly aerobic energy expenditure do not seem to translate into greater increases in FFM, which suggests that a "ceiling" may exist with respect to the ability of weekly energy expenditure to increase fat-free mass. Fat-free mass increased by an average of 0.8 kg for females for the 16 means shown in the lower panel of Figure 15.6. In contrast, FFM for males increased by an average of only 0.4 kg despite a weekly exercise energy expenditure almost twice that of the females. Costill (1986) noted similar findings with respect to changes in muscle fiber size following aerobic training (i.e., greater change in women compared to men) and postulated that it may reflect a lower level of fitness for women compared to men at the initiation of training.

Summary

Aerobic exercise training results in modest increases in FFM. Much larger increases are possible with weight training, but the time course of these changes has not been well studied. Neither age nor gender appears to differentially affect exercise training-induced changes in FFM, but the magnitude of the increases in FFM with training may be diminished with advancing age due to the concomitant reduction in the number of muscle fibers.

Exercise Training and Bone Mineral Mass

Advancing age is associated with reductions in bone mineral mass (Geusens, Dequeker, Verstraeten, & Nijs, 1986; Riggs et al., 1981). The loss begins earlier in women than in men, and the rate of loss is greater in women, especially during the 10 year period immediately following menopause (Geusens et al.). Since osteoporosis is related to increased risk of fractures, there is much current interest in procedures to reduce the rate of bone mineral loss and thereby reduce the incidence of osteoporosis in the elderly population. Exercise training and calcium intake are two areas of interest since each has the potential to enhance bone mineral mass and/or attenuate the rate of loss of bone mineral with advancing age (Halioua & Anderson, 1989; Marcus et al., 1992).

While there is much evidence suggestive of a positive relationship between exercise training and bone mineral density, the data do not allow definitive conclusions. The data are confounded by the fact that bone remodeling is a slow process and seems to be site-specific (i.e., localized to regions where stresses are imposed). Short-term intervention studies often lack sufficient statistical power to detect the small changes in bone mass that may occur with exercise training. In addition, if bone mineral densities are measured at sites that are not stressed by the exercise training, it is unlikely that changes in bone mineral density will be found. Cross-sectional studies examining the effects of exercise training on bone mineral mass, especially those that compare athletes to nonathletes, often show increased bone mineral mass for exercising individuals; however, self-selection limits the interpretation of these data in terms of an exercise effect. Due to these limitations, the possible effects of exercise intensity, duration, and frequency on changes in bone mineral mass will not be addressed in the following discussion. It is important also to note that while the data suggest a positive relationship between bone mineral mass and exercise training, the results of prospective exercise training studies on bone mass are mixed (Block, Smith, Friedlander, & Genant, 1989).

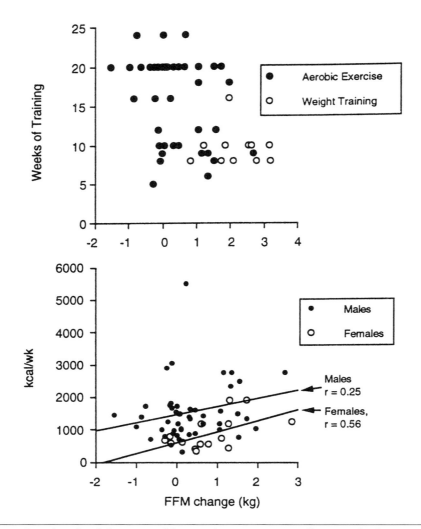

Figure 15.6 Effects of weeks of training or weekly exercise energy expenditure on fat-free mass. The upper panel compares changes subsequent to aerobic or weight training exercise in males as a function of the number of weeks of training. The lower panel compares changes subsequent to aerobic or weight training exercise for males and females. Data are drawn from Ballor and Keesey (1991).

Bone mass is dynamic; it increases and decreases in response to various stressors (Snow-Harter & Marcus, 1991). Although not proven conclusively, it appears that bone mineral mass increases in proportion to the magnitude of the strain placed upon it. For example, Rubin and Lanyon (1985) found a close relationship between the magnitude of strain imposed on turkey ulnae and the change in cross-sectional area of the bones. These data suggest that the magnitude of the strain, not the total amount of strain, determines the extent of the increase in bone mineral mass in response to exercise stresses. From this we can infer that weight bearing exercises would cause greater increases in bone mineral mass than non-weight bearing exercises. In addition, resistance weight training exercise may induce greater site-specific changes in bone mineral

mass than other forms of training since the localized stresses on bone are commonly five times greater than those for aerobic training exercises such as running, walking, and cycling. Cross-sectional data from Nilsson and Westlin (1971), who compared bone densities of the distal femur between groups of competitive athletes, illustrate this. The mean bone density of weight lifters (0.247 g/cc) was higher than that of runners (0.235 g/cc), which, in turn, was higher than that of competitive swimmers (0.226 g/cc).

As noted earlier, cross-sectional studies that compare habitual exercisers to sedentary counterparts commonly find that those who exercise regularly have greater levels of bone mineral mass. For example, Block et al. (1989) examined 10 cross-sectional studies in which bone mineral densities were compared between athletes and nonathletes. They reported that for 9 of the 14 site-specific comparisons in these studies, athletes had statistically significantly more bone mineral mass. Zylstra et al. (1989) reported that lumbar spine and femoral neck densities were greater in a large cohort of women (mean age = 50 years) who exercised regularly than in those who did not exercise. Femoral and lumbar spine densities were increased by 1.9% and 0.8%, respectively, for each hour of daily walking in these women. Similarly, Pocock et al. (1986) reported that peak oxygen uptake was positively correlated with femoral neck ($r = 0.60$), lumbar spine ($r = 0.54$), and forearm ($r = 0.42$) bone mineral densities in 46 postmenopausal women. Since peak oxygen uptake and exercise training are interrelated, this is suggestive of a relationship between bone mineral density and exercise training.

Relatively few long-term (i.e., > 1 year) studies have reported the effects of exercise training on bone mineral mass. Block et al. (1989) examined four studies (1 to 3 years duration) that compared exercising individuals to sedentary controls. Three of the four studies reported that bone mineral mass was higher in those who exercised regularly. A four year prospective study by Smith et al. (1989) reported changes that reflect those expected following an exercise training program and also show the variance associated with changes in bone mineral density. They followed 80 exercising women and 62 sedentary women (initial mean age = 50 years). The exercising group performed a variety of aerobic and resistance training activities three times per week for 45 minutes per session. The researchers measured bone mineral content and bone width bilaterally in the radius, ulna, and humerus 11 times during the four year period. The sedentary control group had less bone mineral content for all three bones. When compared to the sedentary group, the exercise-trained group had significantly lower rates of loss for 12 of the 18 bone-related variables measured. The largest effects of the exercise training were on the radius and ulna. For most of the sites evaluated, exercise training attenuated but did not stop or reverse the loss of bone mineral.

Dalsky et al. (1988) examined the effects of vigorous weight bearing exercise combined with calcium supplementation on lumbar bone mineral content in 15 postmenopausal women 55 to 70 years old. The subjects exercised for 50 to 60 minutes per session three times per week for 22 months. Lumbar bone mineral mass was assessed at the beginning and end of the training and 13 months following the completion of the training.

The 22 months of exercise training and calcium supplementation resulted in a 6% increase in the bone mineral mass of the lumbar spine. Following 13 months of detraining, while calcium supplementation was continued, lumbar bone mineral mass returned to baseline levels. This study indicates that bone mass is dynamic, although the rate of change is slow, and that exercise training can reverse the osteoporic process.

Summary

Bone mineral mass increases in response to specific stresses. The greater the stresses on a given bone, the greater the likelihood of an increase in bone mineral mass. Weight bearing and/or resistive training exercises are more likely to result in an increase in bone mineral mass since they induce greater stresses on bone than activities such as swimming or cycling. A review of the literature suggests that while exercise training is commonly associated with an increase in bone mineral density, the adaptations are site-specific. Long-term intervention studies, while few in number, suggest that exercise training can increase bone mineral mass and/or slow the rate of bone mineral loss associated with aging.

Recommendations

As discussed earlier, methodological problems limit the validity of the commonly used body composition assessment methods in estimating exercise-induced changes in body composition. It seems likely that a combination of densiometry, skinfold thicknesses, and total body water (bioelectrical impedance) would increase the accuracy of estimations of body composition status and body composition changes. Each of these methods focuses on different components of body composition. The more accurately each component of the body is measured, the more accurately body composition status and change can be estimated. Heymsfield et al. (1990) suggest that four-component models of estimating body composition, which involve the use of labeled water and dual photon absorptiometry, improve the accuracy of the estimate of body composition to ±1% BF. It seems that combining less sophisticated procedures, such as densitometry, skinfold thicknesses, and bioelectrical impedance, may also improve the accuracy with which % BF status and change are measured.

References

Andersson, B., Xu, X., Rebuffé-Scrive, M., et al. (1991). The effects of exercise training on body composition and metabolism in men and women. *International Journal of Obesity*, **15**, 75-81.

Antonio, J., & Gonyea, W.J. (1993). Skeletal muscle fiber hyperplasia. *Medicine and Science in Sports and Exercise*, **12**, 1333-1345.

Ballor, D.L. (1991a). Effect of dietary restriction and/or exercise on 23-h metabolic rate and body composition in female rats. *Journal of Applied Physiology*, **71**, 801-806.

Ballor, D.L. (1991b). Exercise training elevates RMR during moderate but not severe dietary restriction in obese male rats. *Journal of Applied Physiology*, **70**, 2303-2310.

Ballor, D.L., & Katch, V.L. (1989). Validity of anthropometric regression equations for predicting changes in body fat of obese females. *American Journal of Human Biology*, **1**, 97-101.

Ballor, D.L., & Keesey, R.E. (1991). A meta-analysis of the factors affecting exercise-induced changes in body mass, fat mass and fat-free mass in males and females. *International Journal of Obesity*, **15**, 717-726.

Ballor, D.L., McCarthy, J.P., & Wilterdink, E.J. (1990a). Exercise intensity does not affect the composition of diet- and exercise-induced body mass loss. *American Journal of Clinical Nutrition*, **51**, 142-146.

Ballor, D.L., Tommerup, L.J., Smith, D.B., & Thomas, D.P. (1990b). Body composition, muscle and fat pad changes following two levels of dietary restriction and/or exercise training in male rats. *International Journal of Obesity*, **14**, 711-722.

Ballor, D.L., Tommerup, L.J., Thomas, D.P., et al. (1990c). Exercise training attenuates diet-induced reduction in metabolic rate. *Journal of Applied Physiology*, **68**, 2612-2617.

Baumgartner, R.N., Chumlea, W.C., & Roche, A.F. (1990). Bioelectric impedance for body composition. *Exercise and Sport Sciences Reviews*, **18**, 193-224.

Björntorp, P., Grimby, G., Sanne, H., et al. (1972). Adipose tissue fat cell size in relation to metabolism in weight-stable physically active men. *Hormone and Metabolic Research*, **4**, 178-182.

Block, J.E., Smith, R., Friedlander, A., & Genant, H.K. (1989). Preventing osteoporosis with exercise: A review with emphasis on methodology. *Medical Hypotheses*, **30**, 9-19.

Boileau, R.A., Buskirk, E.R., Horstman, D.H., et al. (1971). Body composition changes in obese and lean men during physical conditioning. *Medicine and Science in Sports*, **3**, 183-189.

Bouchard, C., Dionne, F.T., Simoneau, J.A., & Boulay, M.R. (1992). Genetics of aerobic and anaerobic performances. *Exercise and Sport Sciences Reviews*, **20**, 27-58.

Charette, S.L., McEvoy, L., Pyka, G., et al. (1991). Muscle hypertrophy response to resistance training in older women. *Journal of Applied Physiology*, **70**, 1912-1916.

Costill, D.L. (1986). *Inside running: Basics of sports physiology*. Indianapolis, IN: Benchmark.

Craig, B.W., Garthwaite, S.M., & Holloszy, J.O. (1987). Adipocyte insulin resistance: Effects of aging, obesity, exercise, and food restriction. *Journal of Applied Physiology*, **62**, 95-100.

Cureton, K.J., Collins, M.A., Hill, D.W., & McElhannon, F.M. (1988). Muscle hypertrophy in men and women. *Medicine and Science in Sports and Exercise*, **20**, 338-344.

Dalsky, G.P., Stocke, K.S., Ehsani, A.A., et al. (1988). Weight-bearing exercise training and lumbar bone mineral content in postmenopausal women. *Annals of Internal Medicine*, **108**, 824-828.

Després, J.P., & Bouchard, C. (1984). Effects of aerobic training and heredity on body fatness and adipocyte lipolysis in humans. *Journal of Obesity and Weight Regulation*, **3**, 219-235.

Duncan, J.J., Gordon, N.F., & Scott, C.B. (1991). Women walking for health and fitness: How much is enough? *Journal of the American Medical Association*, **226**, 3295-3299.

Durnin, J.V.G.A., & Womersly, J. (1974). Body fat assessed from total body density and its estimation from skinfold thickness: Measurements on 481 men and women aged from 16-72 years. *British Journal of Nutrition*, **32**, 77-97.

Fiatarone, M.A., Marks, E.C., Ryan, N.D., et al. (1990). High-intensity strength training in nonagenarians: Effects on skeletal muscle. *Journal of the American Medical Association*, **263**, 3029-3034.

Flatt, J.P. (1989). Differences in the regulation of fat and carbohydrate metabolism and their implications for body weight regulation. In H.A. Lardy & F.W. Stratman (Eds.), *Hormones, thermogenesis and obesity* (pp. 3-9). New York: Elsevier.

Fleck, S.J., & Kraemer, W.J. (1988). Resistance training: Physiological responses and adaptations (part 2 of 4). *The Physician and Sportsmedicine*, **16**, 108-124.

Forbes, G.B., Simon, W., & Amatruda, J.M. (1992). Is bioimpedance a good predictor of body composition change? *American Journal of Clinical Nutrition*, **56**, 4-6.

Gaesser, G.A., & Rich, R.G. (1984). Effects of high- and low-intensity exercise training on aerobic capacity and blood lipids. *Medicine and Science in Sports and Exercise, 16*, 269-274.

Gerado-Gettens, T., Miller, G.D., Horwitz, B.A., et al. (1991). Exercise decreases fat selection in female rats during weight cycling. *American Journal of Physiology, 260*, R518-R524.

Geusens, P., Dequeker, J., Verstraeten, A., & Nijs, J. (1986). Age-, sex-, and menopause-related changes of vertebral and peripheral bone: Population study using dual and single photon absorptiometry and radiogrammetry. *Journal of Nuclear Medicine, 27*, 1540-1549.

Girandola, R.N., Wiswell, R.A., & Romero, R. (1977). Body composition changes resulting from fluid ingestion and dehydration. *Research Quarterly, 48*, 299-303.

Hagberg, J.M., Graves, J.E., Limacher, M., et al. (1989). Cardiovascular responses of 70- to 79-yr-old men and women to exercise training. *Journal of Applied Physiology, 66*, 2589-2594.

Halioua, L., & Anderson, J.J.B. (1989). Lifetime calcium intake and physical activity habits: Independent and combined effects on the radial bone of healthy premenopausal Caucasian women. *American Journal of Clinical Nutrition, 49*, 534-541.

Hamel, P., Simoneau, J.A., Lortie G., et al. (1986). Heredity and muscle adaptation to endurance training. *Medicine and Science in Sports and Exercise, 18*, 690-696.

Heymsfield, S.B., Lichtman, S., Baumgartner, R.N., et al. (1990). Body composition of humans: Comparison of two improved four-compartment models that differ in expense, technical complexity, and radiation exposure. *American Journal of Clinical Nutrition, 52*, 52-58.

Jackson, A.S., Pollock, M.L., & Ward, A. (1980). Generalized equations for predicting body density of women. *Medicine and Science in Sports and Exercise, 12*, 175-182.

Keesey, R.E. (1988). The relation between energy expenditure and the body weight set-point: Its significance to obesity. In G.D. Burrows, P.J.V. Beumont, & R.C. Casper (Eds.), *Handbook of eating disorders, Part 2* (pp. 87-102). New York: Elsevier.

Kern, P.A., Ong, J.M., Saffari, B., & Carty, J. (1990). The effects of weight loss on the activity and expression of adipose tissue lipoprotein lipase in very obese humans. *New England Journal of Medicine, 322*, 1053-1059.

Kohrt, W., Malley, M.T., Dalsky, G.P., & Holloszy, J.O. (1992a). Body composition of healthy sedentary and trained, young and older men and women. *Medicine and Science in Sports and Exercise, 24*, 832-837.

Kohrt, W.M., Obert, K.A., & Holloszy, J.O. (1992b). Exercise training improves fat distribution patterns in 60-70-year-old men and women. *Journal of Gerontology: Medical Sciences, 47*, M99-M105.

Lexell, J., Taylor, C.C., & Sjöström, M. (1988). What is the cause of the ageing atrophy? Total number, size and proportion of different fiber types studied in whole vastus lateralis muscle from 15- to 83-year-old men. *Journal of Neurological Science, 84*, 275-294.

Lohman, T.G. (1981). Skinfolds and body density and their relation to body fatness: A review. Human Biology, *53*, 181-225.

Lohman, T.G. (1984). Research progress in validation of laboratory methods of assessing body composition. *Medicine and Science in Sports and Exercise, 16*, 596-603.

MacDougall, J.D., Sale, D.G., Elder, G.C.B., & Sutton, J.R. (1982). Muscle ultrastructural characteristics of elite powerlifters and body builders. *European Journal of Applied Physiology, 48*, 117-126.

Marcus, R., Drinkwater, B., Dalsky, G., et al. (1992). Osteoporosis and exercise in women. *Medicine and Science in Sports and Exercise, 24*, S301-S307.

Marti, B., & Howald, H. (1990). Long-term effects of physical training on aerobic capacity: Controlled study of former elite athletes. *Journal of Applied Physiology, 69*, 1451-1459.

Mayer, J., Marshall, N.B., Vitale, J.J., et al. (1954). Exercise, food intake and body weight in normal rats and genetically obese adult mice. *American Journal of Physiology, 177*, 544-548.

Mayer, J., Roy, P., & Mitra, K.P. (1956). Relation between caloric intake, body weight and physical work: Studies in an industrial male population in West Bengal. *American Journal of Clinical Nutrition, 4*, 169-175.

McGaw, B. (1988). Meta-analysis. In J.P. Keeves (Ed.), *Educational research, methodology, and measurement: An international handbook* (pp. 678-685). New York: Pergamon.

Meredith, C., Zackin, M.J., Frontera, W.R., & Evans, W.J. (1987). Body composition and aerobic capacity in young and middle-aged endurance-trained men. *Medicine and Science in Sports and Exercise, 19*, 557-563.

Mole, P.A. (1990). Impact of energy intake and exercise on resting metabolic rate. *Sports Medicine, 10*, 72-87.

Nilsson, B.E., & Westlin, N.E. (1971). Bone density in athletes. *Clinical Orthopedics, 77*, 179-182.

Ortiz, O., Russell, M., Daley, T.L., et al. (1992). Differences in skeletal muscle mass and bone mineral mass between black and white females and their relevance to estimates of body composition. *American Journal of Clinical Nutrition, 55,* 8-13.

Pierson, R.N., Wang, J., Heymsfield, S.B., et al. (1991). Measuring body fat: Calibrating the rulers. Intermethod comparisons in 389 normal Caucasian subjects. *American Journal of Physiology, 261,* E103-E108.

Pocock, N.A., Eisman, J.A., Yeates, M.G., et al. (1986). Physical fitness is a major determinant of femoral neck and lumbar spine bone mineral density. *Journal of Clinical Investigation, 78,* 618-621.

Poehlman, E.T. (1989). A review: Exercise and its influence on resting energy metabolism in man. *Medicine and Science in Sports and Exercise, 21,* 515-525.

Poehlman, E.T., & Danforth, E. (1991). Endurance training increases resting energy expenditure and sympathetic nervous system activity in older individuals. *American Journal of Physiology, 261,* E233-E239.

Pollock, M.L., Miller, H.S., Linnerud, A.C., & Cooper, K.H. (1975). Frequency of training as a determinant for improvement in cardiovascular function and body composition of middle-aged men. *Archives of Physical and Medical Rehabilitation, 56,* 141-145.

Prentice, A.M., Goldberg, G.R., Jebb, S.A., et al. (1991). Physiological responses to slimming. *Proceedings of the Nutrition Society, 50,* 441-458.

Rebuffé-Scrive, M. (1988). Metabolic differences in fat depots. In C. Bouchard & F.E. Johnston (Eds.), *Fat distribution during growth and later health outcomes* (pp. 163-173). New York: Alan R. Liss.

Riggs, B.L., Wahner, H.W., Dann, W.L., et al. (1981). Differential changes in bone mineral density of the appendicular and axial skeleton with aging. *Journal of Clinical Investigation, 67,* 328-335.

Ross, R., Léger, L., Martin, P., & Roy, R. (1989). Sensitivity of bioelectrical impedance to detect changes in human body composition. *Journal of Applied Physiology, 67,* 1643-1648.

Rubin, C.T., & Lanyon, C.E. (1985). Regulation of bone mass by mechanical strain magnitude: The effect of peak strain magnitude. *Calcified Tissue International, 37,* 411-417.

Saltin, B., & Golnick, P.D. (1988). Fuel for muscular exercise: Role of carbohydrate. In E.S. Horton & R.L. Terjung (Eds.), *Exercise, nutrition and energy metabolism* (pp. 45-71). New York: Macmillan.

Scherf, J., Franklin, B.A., Lucas, C.P., et al. (1986). Validity of skinfold thickness measures of formerly obese adults. *American Journal of Clinical Nutrition, 43,* 128-135.

Sinning, W.E., & Wilson, J.R. (1984). Validity of "generalized" equations for body composition analysis in women athletes. *Research Quarterly for Exercise and Sport, 55,* 153-160.

Siri, W.E. (1961). Body composition from fluid spaces and density: Analysis of methods. In J. Brožek & A. Henschel (Eds.), *Techniques for measuring body composition* (pp. 223-224). Washington, DC: National Academy of Sciences.

Smith, E.L., Gilligan, C., McAdam, M., et al. (1989). Deterring bone loss by exercise intervention in premenopausal and postmenopausal women. *Calcified Tissue International, 44,* 312-321.

Snow-Harter, C., & Marcus, R. (1991). *Exercise, bone mineral density and osteoporosis. Exercise and Sport Sciences Reviews, 19,* 351-358.

Staron, R.S., Malicky, E.S., Leonardi, M.J., et al. (1989). Muscle hypertrophy and fast fiber type conversions in heavy resistance-trained women. *European Journal of Applied Physiology, 60,* 71-79.

Tremblay, A., Després, J.P., LeBlanc, C., & Bouchard, C. (1984). Sex dimorphism in fat loss in response to exercise training. *Journal of Obesity and Weight Regulation, 3,* 193-203.

Tremblay, A., Després, J.P., LeBlanc, C., et al. (1990). Effect of intensity of physical activity on body fatness and fat distribution. *American Journal of Clinical Nutrition, 51,* 153-157.

Wilmore, J.H., Girandola, R.N., & Moody, D.L. (1970). Validity of skinfold and girth assessment for predicting alterations in body composition. *Journal of Applied Physiology, 29,* 313-317.

Wood, P.D., Stefanick, M.L., Dreon, D.M., et al. (1988). Changes in plasma lipids and lipoproteins in overweight men during weight loss through dieting as compared with exercise. *New England Journal of Medicine, 319,* 1173-1179.

Zylstra, S., Hopkins, A., Erk, M., et al. (1989). Effect of physical activity on lumbar spine and femoral neck bone densities. *International Journal of Sports Medicine, 10,* 181-186.

16

Genetic Influences on Human Body Composition and Physique

Claude Bouchard

Human body composition and other somatic characteristics are known to be influenced by a variety of environmental agents and the lifestyle of the individual. They can also be altered by disease, and they change naturally with growth and aging. It is not surprising, given the large panel of phenotypes that has emerged from the research conducted on body composition and physique, and the availability of laboratory and field methods to measure these phenotypes, that there would be interest in asking questions about their genetic and nongenetic determinants.

Among the questions that have attracted the attention of scientists, the heritability of body dimensions and body composition has been the most frequently asked. Several reports have dealt with segregation patterns and the hypothesis of single-gene effects, but few body composition and physique phenotypes, other than body fat, have been investigated with the tools of molecular biology in the context of association and linkage studies, with cross-breeding animal experiments, or with the quantitative trait locus mapping approach.

This chapter provides an overview of the findings pertaining to the role of inherited variation and specific-gene polymorphism on body fat content, adipose tissue topography, skeletal muscle mass, skeletal characteristics, and physique. It begins with a brief examination of key concepts and the methods commonly used to study the genetic basis of complex multifactorial traits such as those considered here.

Basic Concepts

Human body composition and physique phenotypes are complex multifactorial traits that cannot readily be reduced to simple Mendelian phenotypes. These traits have evolved under the interactive influences of dozens of affectors from the social, behavioral, physiological, metabolic, cellular, and molecular domains. It is difficult to detect segregation of the genes that are involved in familial or pedigree studies, and, whatever the influence of the genotype, it is generally attenuated or exacerbated by nongenetic factors (Bouchard, 1991a).

Efforts to understand the genetic causes of such phenotypes can be successful only if they are based on an appropriate conceptual framework, adequate phenotype measurements, proper samples of unrelated persons and nuclear families or extended pedigrees, and extensive candidate gene typing and other molecular markers. In this context, the distinction between "necessary" genes and "susceptibility" genes proposed recently by Greenberg (1993) seems particularly relevant. A *susceptibility gene* is defined by Greenberg as one that increases susceptibility or risk for a disease but is not necessary for disease expression. An allele at a susceptibility gene may make it more likely that the carrier will become affected, but the presence of that allele is not sufficient by itself to explain the occurrence of the disease. It merely lowers the threshold for a person to develop the disease. The concept is also relevant to complex quantitative phenotypes such as those considered in this chapter. The concept implies that the true causes of variation in a quantitative phenotype may be nongenetic or genetic, including genetic variation at a gene other than the susceptibility gene or additive or interactive effects at several susceptibility loci. As proposed by Greenberg, if susceptibility genes are neither necessary nor sufficient for disease expression (or for a high or a low value for the phenotype), linkage analysis is likely to yield little more information than that obtained from association studies. This is particularly true when the deficient allele at the locus under consideration carries less than about 10 times the risk for the disease in comparison with the normal allele.

In contrast, a *necessary gene* is one that is sufficient to cause the disease if the deficient allele or alleles have been inherited. For a quantitative phenotype, a necessary gene would be one with a large effect on the phenotype. The distinction between susceptibility and necessary genes may sometimes be blurred for nondisease traits.

Another important issue is whether there are genotype-environment effects and/or gene-gene effects that influence the phenotype. They remain very difficult to investigate even with the present-day techniques. We have proposed (Bouchard et al., 1990) that one way to test for the presence of a genotype-environment (i.e., diet or exercise) effect in human beings is to challenge several genotypes in a similar manner by submitting both members of monozygotic (MZ) twin pairs to a standardized treatment and compare the within- and the between-pair variances of the response to the treatment. The finding of a significantly higher variance in the response between pairs than within pairs suggests that the changes induced by the treatment are more heterogeneous in genetically dissimilar individuals. In a series of experiments conducted on MZ twins during the last decade, we used either exercise training, with or without negative energy balance, or chronic overfeeding as treatments to investigate these effects. In general, these studies have revealed that genotype-environment interaction effects on body composition phenotypes seem to be ubiquitous (Bouchard et al., 1990; 1992c; 1994). Molecular markers can also be used in the MZ twin intervention design defined above to delineate both the quantitative importance of the genotype-treatment interaction effect and its molecular basis. The approach can be extended to several genes or molecular markers in order to seek evidence of gene-gene interaction effects.

In the search for genes associated with genotype-environment effects, one could also use the method proposed by Berg (1981, 1990). This method is less demanding from an experimental point of view since it can be applied to cross-sectional observations of pairs of MZ twins, but a relatively large number of pairs is required for the findings to be robust and conclusive. Briefly, since MZ brothers or sisters have the same genes, any difference in a multifactorial phenotype between two members of a given pair is caused by nongenetic factors. One can then compare the mean within-pair phenotypic difference between MZ pairs who have a given allele at a particular locus with those who have other alleles of the same gene. Berg has argued that if an allele has a permissive effect, the within-pair variance would be greater in those pairs with the allele than in those lacking the particular allele. The opposite would be true for an allele with a restrictive effect. This essentially amounts to a method that tests for genotype-environment interaction effect considering one gene at a time. Berg (1988) has applied this approach to plasma lipids and lipoproteins in a series of studies and has reported several cases of apolipoprotein genes having significant effects on phenotypic variability within MZ pairs. The method has not been used extensively in the investigation of other quantitative phenotypes.

Gene-gene interaction effects on body composition and physique phenotypes have not yet been mentioned. It seems that gene-gene interactions are ubiquitous in the field of body composition and physique. There is no doubt that they will attract considerable attention during the next decade. It is likely to be a complicated research area, however, in the sense that large sample sizes will be needed if several genes are to be considered in the same analysis. Innovative experimental designs will have to be developed, and the panel of the most important genes to investigate will probably emerge only when strong data become available from association, linkage, quantitative trait locus, positional cloning, or transgenic studies.

A schematic representation of these various genetic effects is depicted in Figure 16.1. The figure incorporates necessary gene effects, susceptibility gene effects, gene-gene interaction effects, and gene-environment interaction effects on body composition and physique phenotypes. It also allows for the contribution of nongenetic factors.

Methods

There are obvious individual differences in body composition and physique among human beings. Although most of the relevant phenotypes tend to aggregate in families, they do not seem to behave as simple Mendelian traits when segregation patterns across generations are considered. It should eventually become possible to reduce the genetic component of the physique and body composition phenotypes to a series of single-gene effects, but this stage has not yet been reached. Most of the current evidence on these continuously distributed multifactorial phenotypes has been obtained by the methods of genetic epidemiology, but there are increasing opportunities arising from the progress made over the last decade in the capacity to uncover DNA polymorphisms.

Two strategies have been traditionally used by geneticists to study the role of genes in continuously distributed phenotypes in human beings. As shown in Figure 16.2, they are referred to as the measured genotype and the unmeasured genotype approaches (Sing & Boerwinkle, 1987; Sing et al., 1988). The bottom-up and top-down approaches incorporate a large network of designs and techniques that are used by human geneticists in efforts to understand the genetic basis of complex multifactorial phenotypes and diseases.

The measured genotype approach is based on direct measurement of genetic variation at the protein or DNA levels in an effort to assess the impact of allelic variation on the phenotypic variation. Since inference about the role of genes is made from the gene to the phenotype, this approach is, at times, referred to as the bottom-up strategy (Sing et al., 1988). Direct measures of genetic variation may be obtained by studying gene products or, better still, DNA sequences. Advances in recombinant DNA techniques during the last two decades have made possible the measurement of genetic variation at the DNA level and have provided the impetus necessary for the extensive use of the measured genotype approach in human genetic studies. The unmeasured genotype approach attempts to estimate the contribution of genetic variation to the phenotypic variance and to find quantitative evidence for single genes with detectable (major) effects on the phenotype. As inferences about the contribution of genes are made from the phenotype, this approach is referred as to the top-down strategy. Here one uses various sampling designs (twins, nuclear families, families with adoptees,

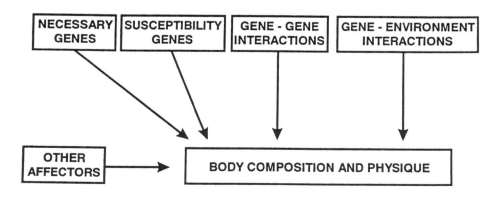

Figure 16.1   An overview of the four types of genetic effects.

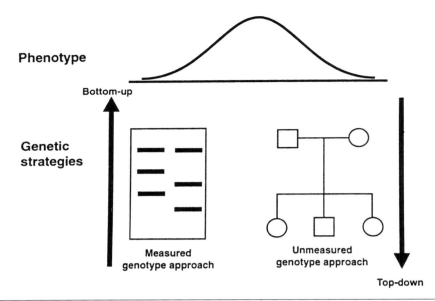

Figure 16.2 The two main strategies to study the role of genes in continuously distributed phenotypes (adapted from Sing & Boerwinkle, 1987).

extended pedigrees, etc.) in combination with statistical tools such as path analysis, variance component estimation, and complex segregation analysis.

Genetic Epidemiology

The field of genetic epidemiology is concerned with multifactorial phenotypes and, until recently, utilized almost exclusively the unmeasured genotype approach. Five strategies have been applied to physique and body composition phenotypes. First, inference on the role of inherited variation was commonly made on the basis of population differences, taking into account the within- and between-population variances and making assumptions about the similarity of the environmental conditions prevailing for each population. Second, familial aggregation was investigated, and spouse, parent-child, and sibling resemblance was computed. Total transmission (genetic and nongenetic) across generations was assessed and maternal versus paternal effects contrasted. Such studies were undertaken with a panel of nuclear families and, in a few cases, with extended pedigrees. Third, pairs of MZ and heterozygous (DZ) twins were used to estimate the heritability of complex multifactorial phenotypes. The method is based on the principle that MZ twins are genetically identical while DZ twins share only 50% of their genomes. The differences among pairs of MZ and DZ twins can then be ascribed to the genetic heterogeneity in DZ pairs, provided that both types of twins have experienced similar environments. MZ

twins reared apart have also been used to make inferences about the role of the genotype in multifactorial phenotypes.

Fourth, adoption studies have commonly been used either in a full adoption or a partial adoption design. In brief, variation among adoptees (foster parents with adopted children or siblings by adoption) is compared to the variation among the adoptees and their biologically related parents or siblings. Several designs can be derived from the basic adoption model to infer genetic and nongenetic effects. Fifth, segregation analyses have been performed to test whether single-gene effects can be inferred for a given phenotype. Here, nuclear families and/or extended pedigrees are used to verify whether a major effect compatible with Mendelian transmission or a major effect combined with a multifactorial effect (mixed model) best fits the data. Likelihood statistical tests are performed to identify the most likely model, and the parameters of the model are computed. Several computer programs are available to execute these analyses, to compute the parameters with maximum likelihood procedures, and to obtain the goodness of fit tests. The role of all these genetic epidemiology procedures, and of segregation analysis in particular, is to dissect the phenotype variance into components that can be studied subsequently at the gene level (MacCluer, 1992).

Association and Linkage Studies

The contribution of molecular biology to the study of human health and disease has increased steadily during the last few years. Even the most complex of human traits can now be investigated with molecular methods. Progress has reached a stage where it is now proposed that the field of epidemiology should move into the era of "molecular epidemiology" (Schulte & Perera, 1993). Of course, genetic epidemiology embarked on this path several years ago. Association and linkage studies with genetic polymorphisms have been a central focus of molecular genetic epidemiology for some time; these approaches are important for the delineation of the genetic basis of physique and body composition.

The terms *association* and *linkage* cannot be used interchangeably. The concept of association refers to a situation in which the correlation of a genetic polymorphism with a phenotype is investigated. Such studies are made of samples of unrelated individuals. They may take several forms, including comparison of cases versus controls (e.g., obese versus lean subjects), analysis of variance across genotypes for the locus under consideration, and comparison of carriers versus noncarriers of a given allele. If a significant association is observed with a polymorphism at a candidate gene locus, there are two likely explanations: Either the locus is causally related to the phenotype, or the locus is in linkage disequilibrium with another relevant polymorphism as a result of natural selection or chance. Association studies may provide important information on genes with a major or a minor contribution to a phenotype; the method is particularly useful for the identification of genes that make only minor contributions (Greenberg, 1993).

When a gene has a large influence on a given phenotype, both the gene and the phenotype will be transmitted together across generations. This concept is referred to as linkage. Linkage analysis can be performed with candidate gene markers or with a variety of other polymorphic markers such as microsatellites. Evidence for linkage becomes more apparent in studies of marker loci that are closer to the true locus and co-segregate with the phenotype. Linkage procedures can be applied to large pedigrees or to panels of nuclear families. They are commonly used for complex multifactorial phenotypes that are characterized by the presence of a segregating major gene, but it is not always appropriate to use a parametric linkage analysis procedure with LOD scores, which are obtained from the log of the odds for and against linkage.

An alternative and practical method is sib-pair linkage analysis, which can screen for potential linkage relationships between quantitative phenotypes and genetic markers (Haseman & Elston, 1972). The method is based on the notion that sibs who share a greater number of alleles (at a given locus) identical by descent at a linked locus will also share more alleles at the phenotype locus. Thus these sibs will have more similar phenotypes than pairs of sibs who share fewer marker alleles. Under these conditions, the slope of the regression of squared sib-pair phenotype differences on the proportion of genes identical by descent is expected to be negative when linkage is present. An important advantage of the method is that it is not necessary to specify the mode of inheritance for the phenotype being considered.

The merits and problems of association and linkage studies have been described recently as they apply to the genetics of common diseases (Cantor & Rotter, 1992; Sparkes, 1992), hypertension (Williams et al., 1994), and atherosclerosis and related risk factors (Mehrabian & Lusis, 1992). A more general exposé of the strengths and limitations of each research strategy has been published by Greenberg (1993).

Quantitative Trait Locus Mapping

The identification of genes contributing to individual differences in a human quantitative phenotype has traditionally been based on association and linkage studies with candidate genes. Another method originally developed for plant genetics is now commonly used with rodents to identify the loci that influence quantitative phenotypes. This is known as the quantitative trait locus mapping method or the QTL. The method was fully described recently by Warden et al. (1992), and it has been used to identify loci that are linked with body fat in rodents (Fisler, Warden, Pace, & Lusis, 1993; Warden et al., 1993).

Briefly, QTL mapping requires two key resources: two inbred strains and a detailed genetic map of the animal genome. The procedure requires the following steps (Warden et al., 1992):

1. Two inbred strains divergent for the phenotype under consideration are crossed to produce F1 and then F2 or backcross progeny.
2. The animals are individually genotyped for markers to span the entire genome at close intervals (the denser the panel of markers, the better).
3. The animals are appropriately phenotyped.

4. QTLs are located by an interval mapping approach such as that provided by the program Mapmaker (Lander & Botstein, 1989).

Mapmaker uses genetic markers and quantitative phenotypes to identify QTLs with a LOD score. Because of the density of the genetic map of the mouse genome, mice are at present the preferred species for QTL studies. Moreover, regions of homology between mouse and human chromosomes have been extensively defined, and this often allows the identification of the approximate location of a putative gene linked to the phenotype of interest on the human gene map. Nevertheless, the human genome currently contains even more mapped markers. The basic strategy used in the QTL mapping could also be adapted to identify loci contributing to quantitative phenotypes in human beings. This approach is becoming more feasible with the recognition of microsatellites as markers distributed throughout the human genome.

It is important to recognize that when a QTL on a given chromosome has been found with an acceptable LOD score, considerable work is needed before the true nature of the gene involved is identified. Positional cloning, DNA sequencing, development of congenic strains, and other tools are needed to define the gene implicated.

Transgenic Animals

Another area that will eventually contribute in a major way to our understanding of the genetic and molecular basis of human body composition and physique is that of the transgenic models (Jaenisch, 1988; Merlino, 1991; Metsäranta & Vuorio, 1992). Hundreds of studies are currently in progress with a variety of transgenes, and the reported data indicate that much will be learned about gene expression and dysfunction for a wide spectrum of phenotypes, including body composition. Indeed, it is progressively becoming apparent that dysregulation in the expression of an otherwise normal gene product, even in pathways that appear to be totally unrelated to the phenotype, has the potential to disrupt normal phenotypic variation.

Genetics and Body Fat Content

More is known on the genetics of body fat content than of any other body composition and physique phenotype. This section will review the evidence concerning heritability levels, segregation of a major gene, contribution of specific molecular markers, and other types of evidence emerging from experimental studies and animal genetic models.

Heritability of Body Fat Content

There is still some disagreement among researchers regarding the importance of genetic factors in the familial resemblance observed for body fat (Bouchard & Pérusse, 1988; Garn, Sullivan, & Hawthorne, 1989). Most studies used the body mass index (BMI) or skinfold thicknesses at a few sites as measures of body fat content. Heritability estimates ranging from almost zero to values as high as 90% have been reported for BMI (Bouchard & Pérusse, 1988; Stunkard, Foch, & Hrubec, 1986a). With the use of different designs (twin, family, and adoption studies), with large variation in age of subjects, and with only a few types of relatives and, very often, small sample sizes, such wide variation in the reported heritabilities within and between populations is not unexpected. With few exceptions, these studies could not separate the effects of genes from those of the environment shared by relatives living together in the same household. Moreover, few studies have included the full range of BMI values to ensure that the phenotype was adequately represented.

Twin and Adoption Data. The comparison of MZ twins reared apart with MZ twins reared together represents an interesting design to assess the role of heredity, with some control over the confounding influences of shared environment. The correlations of MZ twins reared apart are generally similar to those of MZ twins reared together (MacDonald & Stunkard, 1990; Price & Gottesman, 1991; Stunkard, Harris, Pederson, & McClearn, 1990), suggesting that shared familial environment is not a major contributor to the variation in BMI. The correlations of MZ twins reared apart provide a direct estimate of the genetic effect, if we assume that:

1. members of the same pair were not placed in similar environments,
2. the twins were not, for some undefined reasons, behaving similarly despite the fact that they were living apart, and
3. intrauterine factors did not influence long-term variation in BMI.

According to these studies, the heritability of BMI is in the range from 40% to 70%. Other twin study designs generate similar or even higher heritability estimates for BMI.

Table 16.1   Familial Correlations for Body Mass Index, Derived from Four Large Studies

Relationship	Framingham Heart Study	Canada Fitness Survey	Quebec Family Study	Norway
Spouses	.19 (1,163)	.12 (3,183)	.10 (248)	.12 (23,936)
Parent-offspring	.23 (4,027)	.20 (7,194)	.23 (1,239)	.20 (43,586)
Siblings	.28 (992)	.34 (3,924)	.26 (370)	.24 (19,157)
Uncle or aunt & nephew or niece	.08 (1,970)	−.11 (34)	.14 (88)	0 (1,146)
Grandparent grandchild	NA	.05 (32)	NA	.07 (1,251)
Dizygotic twins	NA	NA	.34 (69)	.20 (90)
Monozygotic twins	NA	NA	.88 (87)	.58 (79)

Numbers of pairs are given in parentheses. NA = No data available.

Data derived from Heller et al. (1984) for the Framingham Heart Study, Pérusse et al. (1988) for the Canada Fitness Survey, Bouchard et al. (1988b) for the Quebec Family Study, and Tambs et al. (1991) for Norway. Table reproduced from Bouchard (1994) with permission from CRC Press.

Five recent adoption studies (Price, Cadoret, Stunkard, & Troughton, 1987; Sorensen, Holst, & Stunkard, 1992a; Sorensen, Holst, Stunkard, & Thiel, 1992b; Sorensen, Price, Stunkard, & Schulsinger, 1989; Stunkard et al., 1986b), in which BMI data were available for both the biologic and adoptive relatives of the adoptees reported that the effects of shared family environment on BMI was negligible. In a recent review, Grilo and Pogue-Geile (1991) also concluded that experiences shared among family members appeared largely irrelevant in determining individual differences in body weight and obesity. These findings are somewhat at odds with the strong familiarity of some of the major affectors of energy balance and body fat content (e.g., energy intake, Pérusse & Bouchard, 1994; energy expenditure, Bouchard et al., 1993a). The whole issue deserves further investigation by genetic epidemiologists. The heritability estimates for BMI derived from the adoption studies tend to cluster around 30% or less.

Family Studies.   During the last 60 years or so, many authors have reported that the risk of having obese children is greater for obese parents than for lean parents (Bray, 1981). These investigations were complemented by studies comparing the resemblance in pairs of spouses, parents-children,

and brothers and sisters for body weight, BMI, and selected skinfold thicknesses. These studies have been reviewed by Mueller (1983) and Bouchard and Pérusse (1988, 1993).

Table 16.1 summarizes some of the correlations reported in four rather large family-based studies of BMI. These results were obtained from the Framingham Heart Study (Heller et al., 1984) the Canada Fitness Survey (Pérusse, Leblanc, & Bouchard, 1988), the Quebec Family Study (Bouchard et al., 1988b), and the Nord-Trondelag Norwegian National Health Screening Service Family Study (Tambs et al., 1991).

In the Framingham Heart Study, adult levels of BMI were used in both the parental and the offspring generations (Heller et al., 1984). The authors reported that their results provided little support for a genetic effect on BMI. In the more recent study of BMI obtained on 74,994 persons of both genders, 20 years of age and older, from the population of Nord-Trondelag, Norway, correlations were available for many types of relatives, some of which are summarized in Table 16.1. Fitting a path model for genetic and environmental transmission to the data, a broad heritability of about 40% was obtained. Tambs et al. (1991) concluded that a simple model with only an additive genetic effect and an individual environmental effect could be rejected.

Two of our studies considered the transmission effects and heritability of BMI and subcutaneous fat as assessed by the sum of several skinfold thicknesses. The first was based on a stratified sample of the Canadian population and included BMI and the sum of five skinfold thicknesses for 18,073 subjects living in thousands of households, yielding 4,825 pairs of spouses, 8,881 parent-child pairs, 3,929 pairs of siblings, 43 uncle or aunt and nephew or niece pairs, and 85 grandparent-grandchild pairs (Pérusse et al., 1988). The total transmission effect across generations for the age- and gender-adjusted phenotypes reached about 35%. The second study relied on 1,698 members of 409 families, which included nine types of relatives by descent or adoption (Bouchard et al., 1988b). Under these conditions, there was a total transmissible variance across generations for BMI and the sum of six skinfold thicknesses of about 35% but a genetic effect of only 5%.

Only one report has dealt with fat mass and percent body fat (% BF) measured with one of the commonly accepted direct methods for measuring body composition (Bouchard et al., 1988b). Underwater weighing measurements of body density were performed on a relatively large number of individuals representing nine kinds of relatives. About one-half of the variance, after adjustment for age and gender, in fat mass or % BF was associated with a transmissible effect, and 25% of the variance was compatible with an additive genetic effect (Figure 16.3).

Trends in Heritability Estimates.   The genetic epidemiology features of body fat content are summarized in Tables 16.2 and 16.3. Table 16.2 describes these trends in terms of the various designs used to generate the data. Thus, the heritability level is highest with twin studies, intermediate with nuclear family data, and lowest when derived from adoption data. When several types of relatives are used jointly in the same design, the heritability estimates typically cluster around 25 to 40% of the age- and gender-adjusted phenotype variance. Clear evidence for a specific maternal or paternal effect is lacking, and the common familial environmental effect is marginal. The presence of a nonadditive genetic effect is often suggested from these research.

Evidence for a Major Gene

Table 16.3 summarizes the trends in the complex segregation analysis results obtained on BMI,

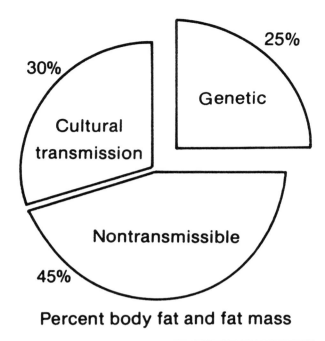

Percent body fat and fat mass

Figure 16.3   Total transmissible variance and its genetic component for body fat content phenotypes, derived from underwater weighing.
Adapted from "Inheritance of the Amount and Distribution of Human Body Fat," by C. Bouchard, L. Perusse, C. Leblanc, et al., 1988, *International Journal of Obesity*, **12**, pp. 205-215. Adapted with permission.

weight adjusted for stature, or % BF in various studies. All studies report evidence for a multifactorial component and a major genetic effect. Nevertheless in two reports the major effect was non-Mendelian. In a third paper, the major effect became Mendelian only when age and sex related variations in the major effect were considered. In five of the seven studies, the estimated gene frequency of the putative recessive gene ranged from about 0.2 to 0.3.

Molecular Markers

The investigation of the association between DNA sequence variation at specific genes and body fat phenotypes has just begun. Table 16.4 summarizes the results of the studies reported to date. Thus far, an association has not been found with molecular markers of GLUT-1, GLUT-4, insulin, insulin receptor, and glucocorticoid receptor. Contrariwise, statistically significant associations have been found with red blood cell acid phosphatase, LDL receptor, apo B, apo D, uncoupling protein, alpha 2 and beta genes of the Na K, ATPase pump, 3-beta-hydroxysteroid dehydrogenase, and alpha 2

Table 16.2   Overview of the Genetic Epidemiology of Human Body Fat Content

	Heritability/transmission (%)	Maternal/paternal	Familial environment
Nuclear families	30 to 50	No	Minor
Adoption studies	10 to 30	Mixed results	Minor
Twin studies	50 to 80	No	No
Combined strategies	25 to 40	No	Minor

Table reproduced from Bouchard (1994) with permission from CRC Press.

Table 16.3   Overview of Segregation Analysis Results for Body Mass Index or Body Fat Phenotypes

Study	Multifactorial transmission (%)	Major effect	Major gene	Gene frequency
Province et al., 1990	41	Yes, 20%	Yes	0.25
Price et al., 1990	34	Yes	Yes	0.21
Moll et al., 1991	42	Yes, 35%	Yes	0.25
Tiret et al., 1992*	39	Yes	No	Non-Mendelian
Rice et al. 1993a	42	Yes, 20%	No	Non-Mendelian
Borecki et al., 1993	Yes	Yes	Age- and sex-related	0.22
Rice et al., 1993b**	25	Yes, 45%	Yes	0.30

*Weight adjusted for stature.

**Percent body fat.

Table reproduced from Bouchard (1994) with permission from CRC Press.

adrenergic receptor genes. These findings are generally based on small sample sizes; consequently there may be false positive and false negative results.

The data on linkage between body fat phenotypes and candidate genes or other molecular markers are even less abundant. Significant linkage has been found with markers at the adenosine deaminase, Kell, esterase D, and alpha 2 and beta loci of the Na K, ATPase, and 3-beta-hydroxysteroid dehydrogenase genes. Lack of linkage has been reported for GLUT-1 and the alpha 1 locus of the Na K, ATPase. Conflicting results have been obtained for the adenylate kinase-1 (Bouchard, 1994).

Other Types of Evidence

The limited molecular marker studies that have been published suggest that several genes are associated and/or linked with human body fat content.

Different types of evidence indicate that other important loci may be involved. For instance, five mouse mutations causing obesity are encoded on five different mouse chromosomes. These mouse obesity genes are in coding regions that have human homologous equivalents that are also located on five different chromosomes (Chua & Leibel, 1994; Friedman, Leibel, & Bahary, 1991). Interestingly the mouse db gene may be homologous to the rat fa obesity gene (Truett, Bahary, Friedman, & Leibel, 1991), and each appears to have a human homologous coding region on human chromosome 1p31 (Friedman et al.).

A new mouse gene for body fat content may have been identified recently by use of the QTL procedure. Fisler et al. (1993) obtained a backcross between the strains Mus Spretus and C57BL/6J, which they called the BSB mouse. BSB exhibits a wide range of carcass lipid, from 1 to 50%. Based on the QTL approach with a large number of markers, Warden et al. (1993) reported that a locus on BSB

Table 16.4   Studies of Body Mass Index or Body Fat Association With Candidate Genes

Study	Gene	N cases	Association
Rajput-Williams et al., 1988	Apo B	232	Yes
Lucarini et al., 1990	RBC-ACP	75	Yes
Weaver et al., 1992a	GLUT-1	52	No
Weaver et al., 1992b	GLUT-4	48	No
	Insulin	35	No
	Insulin receptor	35	No
Weaver et al., 1992c	Glucocorticoid receptor	55	No
Zee et al., 1992	LDL receptor	84	Yes
Vijayaraghavan et al., 1993	Apo D	114	Yes
Oppert et al., 1993	Uncoupling protein	100	Yes
Dériaz et al., 1993	Na K, ATPase (α_2 and β)	113	Yes
Vohl et al., 1994	3β-HSD	132	Yes
Oppert et al., 1995	α_2 adrenergic receptor	280	Yes

Modified and enlarged from Bouchard, 1994.

chromosome 7 determines the lipid content of the carcass (LOD score of 3.8). Mouse chromosome 7 is also known to encode the Tubby and Adipose genes. Although the BSB locus seems to differ from these two other genes, further characterization is needed before a definitive conclusion can be reached. It is interesting to note that the percent carcass lipid locus on chromosome 7 contributes also to an elevated plasma cholesterol level (LOD score of 5.8) (Warden et al., 1993).

Results from transgenic mouse models also reveal that dysfunction in certain genes can cause obesity. For example, a transgenic mouse with impaired corticosteroid receptor function was created by a partial knock out of the type II glucocorticoid receptor with an antisense RNA transgene (Pépin, Pothier, & Barden, 1992). The transgenic animals had increased fat deposition with a body mass twice that of controls by six months of age. This was observed despite the fact that the transgenic animals ate about 15% less than the normal mice. More recently, it has been reported that a transgenic mouse that expresses GLUT-4 constitutively in the adipose tissue becomes quite fat with only a moderate elevation in body mass (Shepherd et al., 1993).

Genetic-Environmental Interactions

We recently tried to test whether differences in body fat content could be explained by genetic factors. We compared the intrapair (within genotype) and interpair (between genotypes) resemblances in the response of MZ twins to overfeeding and negative energy balance or, in other words, tested for the presence of genotype-environment interaction effects.

Response to Overfeeding. Two experiments were undertaken to study individual differences when subjects were exposed to a positive energy balance protocol. In both experiments, subjects ate a 4.2 MJ (1,000 kcal) per day caloric surplus during 22 days in a short-term overfeeding experiment (Bouchard et al., 1988c; Poehlman et al., 1986) and during 100 days in a long-term overfeeding experiment (Bouchard et al., 1990). Both experiments resulted in significant changes in the various body fat phenotypes, but considerable interindividual differences in the adaptation to the extra calories were observed. In the long-term overfeeding experiment, the mean body weight gain of the 24 subjects (12 pairs of MZ twins) was 8.1 kg, but the range of weight gain was from 4 to 13 kg (Bouchard et al., 1990). The variation observed was not randomly distributed; the variance in response to long-term overfeeding was about three times larger between pairs than within pairs for gains in body weight and fat mass (Bouchard et al., 1990). Figure 16.4 illustrates the within-pair resemblance in weight gain under the influence of the 100-day overfeeding protocol (left panel). The same pattern was observed for the changes in fat mass and other

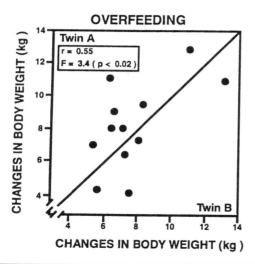
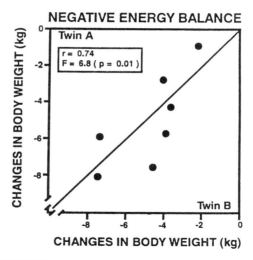

Figure 16.4 Intrapair resemblance in the response of identical twins to prolonged overfeeding (12 pairs of identical twins) or to prolonged negative energy balance (7 pairs of identical twins).
Adapted from "The Response to Long-Term Overfeeding in Identical Twins," by C. Bouchard, A. Tremblay, J.P. Després, et al., 1990, *New England Journal of Medicine,* **322**, pp. 1477-1482, and "The Response to Exercise With Constant Energy Intake in Identical Twins," by C. Bouchard, A. Tremblay, J.P. Despres, et al., 1994, *Obesity Research,* **2**, pp. 400-410. Adapted with permission.

indicators of body fat. These results suggest that the amount of weight gained or fat stored in response to a caloric surplus is significantly influenced by the genotype of the individual.

Response to Negative Energy Balance. In two other experiments, exercise was used to induce an energy deficit in MZ twins to test for the contribution of the genotype to the response to negative energy balance sustained for 22 days (Poehlman et al., 1987) or about 100 days (Bouchard et al., 1994). In both experiments, the energy deficit was obtained by exercising the twins on a cycle ergometer twice a day for about 50 minutes per session. The exercise prescription was designed to induce an additional energy expenditure of about 4.2 MJ (1,000 kcal) over resting metabolic rate, while maintaining energy intake at the baseline level throughout the study. Results from the long-term experiment revealed a significant within-pair resemblance for the reduction in body weight (right panel of Figure 16.4) and fat mass, while results from the short-term study revealed that only fat-free mass (FFM) changes were characterized by a significant MZ twin resemblance.

Thus results from both overfeeding and negative energy balance experiments generally suggest that undetermined genetic characteristics specific to each individual are associated with the response of body composition phenotypes to changes in energy balance. We have now reached the stage at which the measured genotype approach could

help identify some of the genes involved in determining variation in responsiveness.

Genetics and Adipose Tissue Topography

Regional adipose tissue distribution is an important determinant of the relationship between obesity and health and an independent risk factor for various morbid conditions, such as cardiovascular diseases or non-insulin-dependent diabetes. Elsewhere, we have reviewed more extensively the genetics of adipose tissue topography phenotypes (Bouchard, Després, & Mauriège, 1993b).

Truncal-Abdominal Subcutaneous Adipose Tissue

Upper body obesity is more prevalent in males than in females, and it increases in frequency with age in males and after menopause in females. Upper body obesity is moderately correlated with total body fat and appears to be more prevalent in individuals habitually exposed to stress and in females is moderately correlated with levels of plasma androgens and cortisol. In addition, the activity of abdominal adipose tissue lipoprotein lipase is elevated when there are high levels of truncal-abdominal adipose tissue (Bouchard et al., 1991).

Evidence for familial resemblance in adipose tissue distribution has been reported (Donahue, Prineas, Gomez, & Hong, 1992). Based on skinfold measurements of in 173 MZ and 178 DZ pairs of male twins, Selby et al. (1989) concluded that there was a significant genetic influence on central deposition of adipose tissue. Using data from the Canada Fitness Survey and the strategy of path analysis, we have shown that the transmissible effect across generations reached about 40% for trunk skinfold thicknesses (sum of subscapular and suprailiac skinfold thicknesses), limb skinfold thicknesses (sum of biceps, triceps, and medial calf skinfolds thicknesses), and the trunk-to-limb skinfold thickness ratio. The transmissible effect was 28% for the waist-to-hip circumference ratio (Pérusse et al., 1988). Assuming that all transmissible effects are genetic, these results suggest that heredity accounts for a maximum of 40% of the phenotypic variance for various indicators of adipose tissue topography.

The biological and cultural components of the transmission of regional adipose tissue distribution were further assessed with data from the Quebec Family Study (Bouchard et al., 1988b). Two indicators of regional adipose tissue distribution were considered. The trunk-to-limb skinfold thickness ratio and the subcutaneous adipose tissue to fat mass ratio, obtained by dividing the sum of the six skinfold thicknesses by fat mass derived from body density. Genetic effects of 25% to 30% were obtained. When the influence of total body adipose tissue was taken into account, the profile of subcutaneous adipose tissue deposition was found to be characterized by higher heritability estimates, reaching about 40% to 50% of the residual variance (Bouchard, 1988, 1990). These results imply that, for a given level of fatness, some individuals store more adipose tissue on the trunk or abdominal area than others.

Results from two studies suggest the influence of major genes for regional adipose tissue distribution phenotypes. Hasstedt, Ramirez, Kuida, & Williams (1989) reported a major gene effect explaining 42% of the variance in a relative adipose tissue pattern index defined as the ratio of the subscapular skinfold thickness to the sum of the subscapular and suprailiac skinfold thicknesses. Recent results from the Quebec Family Study suggest major gene effects for the trunk-to-extremity skinfold thickness ratio, adjusted for total fat mass, accounting for about 35% of the phenotypic variance (Borecki, Rice, Bouchard, & Rao, in press).

That the pattern of subcutaneous adipose tissue distribution is influenced by some genetically controlled mechanisms is not surprising, given the heritability levels of lipolysis in collagenase-isolated adipocytes and heparin-releasable lipoprotein lipase activity in adipose tissue from the suprailiac depot (Bouchard, 1985).

Abdominal Visceral Adipose Tissue

We know less about the causes of individual differences in the amounts of abdominal visceral adipose tissue compared to other fat depots. Visceral adipose tissue increases with age in each gender and in lean and obese individuals (Enzi et al., 1986). Males have, on average, more visceral adipose tissue than females, and the obese have more than lean persons. Nevertheless, the amount of visceral adipose tissue is only moderately correlated with total body fat, with a common variance level ranging from about 30 to 50% and perhaps lower (Bouchard et al., 1990; Ferland et al., 1989). In women, high plasma androgen and cortisol concentrations are commonly associated with augmented amounts of visceral adipose tissue. In addition, there are high lipoprotein lipase and lipolytic activities in the visceral adipose depot, but it is not known if these characteristics are causes or effects of visceral obesity. Data have not been reported on the heritability of the amounts of abdominal visceral adipose tissue. The population data needed to deal with this topic are difficult to generate with the methods that are available, as visceral adipose tissue can be assessed only by computerized tomography or nuclear magnetic resonance. Unpublished data from the Quebec Family Study indicate, however, that significant familial aggregation occurs beyond that seen for total body fat.

Genetic-Environmental Interactions

Further evidence that the genotype may be an important determinant of subcutaneous adipose tissue distribution and of the amount of abdominal visceral adipose tissue phenotypes comes from our overfeeding and negative energy balance studies with pairs of identical twins (Bouchard et al., 1990, 1994). We found about six times more variance between pairs than within pairs for the increases with overfeeding in subcutaneous adipose tissue distribution and in amounts of abdominal visceral adipose tissue from computerized tomography after controlling for the gains in total fat. Significant intrapair resemblance was also obtained in the negative energy balance experiment for the decrease in abdominal visceral adipose tissue.

These results are coherent with the significant identical twin intrapair resemblance in the response of adipose tissue lipolysis and lipoprotein lipase activity to challenge by overfeeding, acute exercise, or exercise training (Després et al., 1984; Mauriège et al., 1992; Poehlman et al., 1986; Savard & Bouchard, 1990). They imply that for a given level of fatness or fat mass gain or fat mass loss, some individuals store or mobilize fat on the trunk or in the visceral depot while others mainly store or mobilize fat on the lower body segments (Bouchard, 1990; Bouchard et al., 1990, 1994).

Genetics and Skeletal Muscle Mass

Sarcopenia, skeletal muscle atrophy, and skeletal muscle hypertrophy are examples of variation in muscle mass. Differences in skeletal muscle mass occur apart from these extreme conditions. Skeletal muscle mass is an important component of body composition and physique at all ages. Its direct health implications have not been considered extensively in relation to morbidity and mortality endpoints (Roche, 1994). Skeletal muscle mass is commonly approximated by measurements of FFM obtained by various procedures or is estimated from imaging techniques applied to specific sites or regions of the body. Few genetic studies have been performed on skeletal muscle mass phenotypes or on surrogate measurements.

Fat-Free Mass

In the Quebec Family Study, we showed that the heritability of FFM derived from underwater weighing estimates of body density reached about 30% of the age- and gender-adjusted phenotype variance (Bouchard et al., 1988b). A major gene effect was not identified by segregation analysis of the data from the nuclear families in the Quebec Family Study (Rice, Borecki, Bouchard, & Rao, 1993a). The latter finding was confirmed in a sample of Mexican-American subjects (Comuzzie et al., 1993).

Estimated Muscle Mass

Nutritional assessment of muscle mass is commonly attempted from anthropometric indicators such as limb circumferences corrected for skinfold thicknesses. Such data were available in the midparent-natural child and foster midparent-adopted child sets of the Quebec Family Study (Bouchard,

Table 16.5 Midparent-Child Interclass Correlations for Estimated Muscle Size

Diameter	Foster midparent-adopted child (N = 154 sets)	Midparent-natural child (N = 622 sets)
Upper arm muscle	.09	.30*
Calf muscle	.10	.29*

Scores were adjusted for age and gender by generation and normalized. Diameters defined as in Bouchard (1994). Reproduced with permission from Wiley-Liss.
*P < 0.001

1991b). We used the upper arm circumference corrected for the triceps skinfold thickness and the calf circumference corrected for the medial calf skinfold thickness, as described by Brožek (1961). The correlations for the estimated muscle diameters are presented in Table 16.5. These correlations are not significantly different from zero in the relatives by adoption, but they reached 0.3 in the biological relatives. These results are compatible with our observations on the heritability of FFM, which indicate that the genotype contributes significantly to variations in densitometrically estimated FFM and most likely to muscle size or mass.

Nutrient Partitioning

Nutrient partitioning can be defined in terms of the pattern of deposition of the ingested energy in the form of fat (lipid) or lean (protein) tissue. Nutrient partitioning can be visualized by following the processes of dietary carbon utilization in the body. In men and women, the prime metabolic fate of the ingested energy is to sustain ATP synthesis for the maintenance of cells, protein synthesis, tissue renewal, and a variety of essential functions. By some estimates, about 99% of the food energy serves to meet these needs, particularly in mature individuals (Reeds, Fiorotto, & Davis, 1992). In animal husbandry, it has been shown that nutrient partitioning can be altered by various factors, including diet and energy expenditure (Reeds et al.). It is also influenced by genetic differences.

All cells and tissues of the body are exposed to the same profile of blood substrates and humoral factors. One may entertain the notion that variation in nutrient partitioning characteristics is likely to depend upon end-organ sensitivity and responsiveness to a variety of circulating regulatory factors as well as gene expression. We are, however, particularly interested by the issue of the contribution of DNA sequence variation to individual differences in nutrient partitioning because it may influence the level of muscle mass. From the animal literature, we know that there are strain differences in nutrient partitioning characteristics that indicate that genes are important determinants of the phenotype. Only one report has dealt with the heritability of nutrient partitioning characteristics in human beings, and it is based on data from the Quebec Family Study (Bouchard et al., 1992b). A total transmission effect of about 50% was found with a genetic transmission of approximately 20% after adjustment for the proper concomitants.

Skeletal Muscle Characteristics

In human beings, as well as in most mammals, skeletal muscle contains varying proportions of two major categories of fibers exhibiting specific contractile properties. These skeletal muscle fiber categories have been commonly named slow-twitch (ST) and fast-twitch (FT) fibers because they differ in the time required to reach peak isometric tension in a single twitch. In human beings, ST and FT muscle fibers have an approximate mean time to peak tension of 90 and 45 msec, respectively (Gollnick, 1982; Saltin & Gollnick, 1983). The vastus lateralis muscle has a slightly greater percentage of type II fibers and higher enzyme activities of the anaerobic energy processes in sedentary subjects from Western and Central African countries than in sedentary white subjects, while enzyme markers of aerobic-oxidative metabolism are similar for both groups (Ama et al., 1986). Gender differences are also noted between mean values for histochemical, morphological, and biochemical characteristics of human skeletal muscle. Thus women exhibit, on average, a slightly higher proportion of type I fibers, smaller fiber areas, and lower glycolytic potential than men (Simoneau & Bouchard, 1989).

An important topic is the extent to which human skeletal muscle characteristics are under the control of genetic factors. Few data are available, and the results are widely divergent. In 1977, Komi et al. reported heritability coefficients of 0.995 in male subjects and of 0.928 in female subjects for the proportion of muscle fibers on the basis of the data derived from a small sample of DZ and MZ twins. Such high heritability coefficients suggest that the fiber type proportion phenotype is almost exclusively genotype-dependent and is not affected by any error variance or by nongenetic factors, which is, of course, hard to accept. For instance, the determination of the skeletal muscle fiber type proportion in human subjects is influenced by tissue sampling and technical errors. Repeated measurements within the same muscle, such as the vastus lateralis, reveal that sampling and technical error combined (standard deviation for repeated measurements) represents from 5 to 10% of the mean value of each fiber type category (Blomstrand & Ekblom, 1982; Gollnick et al., 1973; Simoneau et al., 1986).

Two studies of interest have appeared on this topic in recent years. Nimmo, Wilson, & Snow (1985), using inbred strains of mice, showed that genetic factors accounted for about 75% of the variation in the proportion of type I fiber of the soleus muscle with 95% confidence intervals ranging from 55% to 89%. Our own study, based on a sample of brothers (n = 32 pairs), DZ twins (n = 26 pairs), and MZ twins (n = 35 pairs), indicated that the heritability of muscle fiber type proportion was much lower than previous estimates (Bouchard et al., 1986). Intraclass correlations for the percentage of type I fibers were significant, being 0.33 in brothers, 0.52 in DZ twins, and 0.55 in MZ twins. Broad heritability estimates can be obtained from twice the biological sib correlation (66%), from twice the difference between MZ and DZ correlations (6%), or directly from the MZ twin sibship correlation (55%) (Falconer, 1960). Although brothers and DZ twins share about one-half of their genome by descent, comparison of the correlations for these groups suggests that increased environmental similarity (i.e., DZ twins experience more similar environmental circumstances than regular brothers) is associated with increased phenotypic resemblance for the proportion of type I skeletal muscle fibers. From the preceding, it is clear that the heritability level of skeletal muscle fiber type proportion in human beings is not well established. Currently available values range from a low of 6% to a high of almost 100% (Bouchard et al., 1992a). Further work on this issue is clearly warranted.

The large interindividual variability in the enzyme activity profile of human skeletal muscle confirms that the catabolism of different substrates in the skeletal muscle of healthy sedentary and moderately active individuals of both genders will vary (Simoneau & Bouchard, 1989). Numerous factors are undoubtedly involved in accounting for the large interindividual catabolic variations observed. Only one study has dealt with the heritability of different enzyme markers of human skeletal

Table 16.6 Summary of Current Data on Familial Resemblance and Heritability of Skeletal Muscle Mass and Other Muscle Characteristics

	Familial resemblance	Estimated heritability (%)
Fat-free mass	Yes	30
Estimated muscle mass	Yes	40
Nutrient partitioning	Yes	20
Muscle fiber type proportion	Yes	6 to 100*
Muscle oxidative potential	Yes	< 50

Heritability expressed as a percentage of the age- and gender-adjusted phenotypic variance.

*See text.

muscle energy metabolism during the last decade. Maximal enzyme activity of creatine kinase, hexokinase, phosphofructokinase (PFK), lactate dehydrogenase, malate dehydrogenase, 3-hydroxyacyl CoA dehydrogenase, and oxoglutarate dehydrogenase (OGDH) were determined in brother, DZ twin, and MZ twin sibships (Bouchard et al., 1986). Genetic factors appeared to be responsible for about 25 to 50% of the total phenotypic variation in the activities of the regulatory enzymes of the glycolytic (PFK) and citric acid cycle (OGDH) pathways and in the variation of the glycolytic to oxidative activity ratio (PFK/OGDH ratio), when the data were adjusted for age and gender differences (Bouchard et al., 1986). These results indicate that variation in the key enzyme activity of human skeletal muscle appears to be inherited to a significant extent. Such a genetic effect could not be accounted for by chance variation in the enzyme molecules (Bouchard et al., 1988a; Marcotte, Chagnon, Côté, Thibault, Boulay, & Bouchard, 1987). The trends in the data available for FFM and skeletal muscle phenotypes are summarized in Table 16.6.

Genetics and Bone Characteristics

Three main phenotypes will be considered: bone length, bone breadth, and bone mass.

Bone Length

Segmental and bone lengths are apparently under a significant degree of genotypic control, probably more so than other morphological measurements (Howells, 1953; Schreider, 1969; Tanner, 1953). In an early review of twin studies, Vandenberg (1962) reported significant F-ratios (variance of within-DZ pairs over variance of within-MZ pairs) for suprasternal height, sitting height, leg length, total arm length, forearm length, foot length, and hand length measurements; only one out of 24 reported F-ratios was not statistically significant.

Heritability coefficients from 12 twin samples were computed from the published variances, correlations, or F-ratios (Bouchard, 1991b). Total arm length had a coefficient of 0.84 (±0.04), while foot length reached a mean value of 0.82 (±0.02). The most significant results from this survey were probably those concerning the two direct measurements of single long bones (i.e., upper arm length and forearm length). The mean values were in reasonable agreement with each other and had a rather narrow range (0.62 ± 0.01 and 0.71 ± 0.09) of heritability estimates.

Parent-child and full-sib data have also been summarized (Bouchard & Lortie, 1984). Mean full-sib weighted correlations reached 0.56 for total leg length ($n = 355$ pairs) and 0.47 for total arm length ($n = 332$ pairs). Using the length of the tibia as the dependent variable, Ikoma and Murotani (1976) submitted familial data to quantitative genetic analysis to estimate additive and dominance components. They concluded that the dominance effect was very small (0.01) for tibial length, in contrast to the additive genetic effect (0.80).

Table 16.7 summarizes some Quebec Family Study results for upper arm length (essentially length of the humerus bone) and tibial height measured from the floor. The midparent-child coefficients are about twice as high for individuals sharing genes by descent and home environment than for those sharing only home environment (foster midparent-adopted child). These data strongly support the hypothesis of a significant genetic effect determining the length of individual long bones.

There is also some statistical support in favor of a genetic pleiotropic effect on bone length. Using eight indicators of bone length measured in 208 pairs of 10 year old sibs, we demonstrated that one factor accounted for 92% of the variation in skeletal length measurements, after adjustment for environment and familial indices (Bouchard, Demirjian, & Malina, 1980). This study suggested that skeletal lengths were likely influenced by a single genetic system.

Table 16.7 Midparent-Child Interclass Correlations for Selected Bone Dimensions

Variable	Foster midparent-adopted child (N = 154 sets)	Midparent-natural child (N = 622 sets)
Upper arm length	0.20**	0.39**
Tibial height	0.29**	0.54**
Femur breadth	0.15*	0.53**
Ankle breadth	0.08	0.49**
Humerus breadth	0.25**	0.62**
Wrist breadth	−0.03	0.44*
Biacromial breadth	0.01	0.43**
Biiliac breadth	0.13	0.42**

*$P < 0.05$. **$P < 0.01$.

Scores were adjusted for age and gender by generation and normalized.
Reprinted from "Genetic Aspects of Anthropometric Dimensions Relevant to Assessment of Nutritional Status," by C. Bouchard. In *Anthropometric Assessment of Nutritional Status* (pp. 213-231) by J. Himes (Ed.), 1991, New York: Wiley-Liss. Copyright 1991 by John Wiley & Sons. Reprinted by permission of John Wiley & Sons, Inc.

Bone Breadth

Although it is commonly thought that there is more stringent genetic regulation of linear skeletal dimensions than of breadth and mass of the skeleton (Osborne & DeGeorge, 1959; Schreider, 1969), the latter are not without a substantial genetic variance. The genetic determination of skeletal breadth has been studied primarily through anthropometric data. After pooling data reported in nine twin studies (Clark, 1956; Dahlberg, 1926; Osborne & DeGeorge, 1959; Vandenberg & Strandskov, 1964; Venerando & Milani-Comparetti, 1973; Vogel & Wendt, 1956; Von Verschuer, 1954), we obtained mean heritability coefficients for biacromial and biiliac diameters of 0.64 (± 0.22) and 0.60 (± 0.13), respectively (Bouchard, 1991b). A few twin studies have been reported on wrist breadth, ankle breadth, and bicondylar diameters of humerus and of femur, and the available data indicate a fairly high degree of heritability ($0.61 \leq H_B \leq 0.82$). Overall, the mean heritability coefficients for these skeletal phenotypes reached 0.60 (±0.18) (Bouchard, 1991b).

Parent-child and full-sib correlations have also been published for skeletal breadths. On the basis of approximately 1,000 parent-child pairs, mean weighted correlations of 0.34 and 0.41 have been computed for biacromial and biiliac diameters, respectively (Bouchard, 1991b). For the same two variables, the average sib-sib correlations were 0.44 and 0.46. Average parent-child correlations reached 0.32 for the bicondylar diameter of the humerus and 0.34 for bicondylar diameter of the femur. Full-sib coefficients for these skeletal breadths were 0.35 and 0.52, respectively. The data reviewed did not provide evidence of a clear sex-linked genetic effect (Bouchard & Lortie, 1984).

In the Quebec Family Study, several indicators of skeletal breadths were obtained in 150 foster midparent-adopted child sets and 622 midparent-natural child sets. The correlations were essentially zero for four of the six measurements in the foster midparent-adopted child sets but consistently larger than 0.4 in the biological midparent-natural child sets. These results suggest the presence of a rather strong genetic effect on skeletal breadths, an effect that seems to be even stronger than that for skeletal lengths in the same subjects (Table 16.7).

An earlier study had suggested that the pleiotropic effect of a single genetic system was evident across a series of skeletal breadths (Bouchard et al., 1980). Moreover, it has been suggested, at least in one study, that the same genes were contributing to some extent to both skeletal lengths and breadths as revealed by a bivariate path analysis of twin data for stature and biiliac breadth (Kramer et al., 1986).

Bone Mass

Because of its role in the etiology of fractures and osteoporosis, bone mass has received much attention during the last two decades. Peak bone mass in young adults, decrease in bone mass with the advent of menopause, and the reduction in bone mass with age in vertebrae and long bones have been considered in many epidemiological and intervention studies, as well as in familial and twin studies. Bone mass is known to be affected by race, hormonal status (particularly estrogen levels in women), dietary calcium intake, level of physical activity, body mass and body composition, smoking behavior, and perhaps alcohol and caffeine intake (Sowers & Galuska, 1993).

The role of these factors on bone mass may vary as a function of undetermined genetic characteristics. In a MZ twin study of females, ages 27 to 73 years, in which bone mineral density was compared between members of pairs who were discordant for smoking behavior, Hopper and Seeman

(1994) found the smoking twins had less bone mineral density at all three sites considered compared to the sisters who smoked less or not at all. The deficit was about 1% when the difference in smoking behavior was slight, but it reached 4.0% and more when the discordance in smoking behavior between the twin sisters was more pronounced. These results suggest that smoking has a negative effect on bone mineral density irrespective of the genotype of the person. Studies of a possible genotype-environment interaction effect on bone mass have not been reported.

The familial resemblance and the heritability levels for bone mass have been studied primarily with nuclear families and the classical twin study design. The results of these studies have been summarized by Pollitzer and Anderson (1989) and by Kelly, Eisman, and Sambrook (1990). In brief, the results suggest that the heritability of bone mass at commonly measured sites is high. Garn (1962), for example, suggested that the bone-related mineral mass of the human body could be under significant genetic control in each sex, as illustrated by the higher mineralisation of African Americans than of U.S. whites. Another line of evidence submitted by Garn (1962) was that 12 year old male MZ twins are more alike than male DZ twins in cortical and medullary thicknesses of the tibia at the mid-shaft level. Hewitt (1957) has shown that radiographic bone breadths in the calf in sib pairs, 6 months to 5 years of age, tend to exhibit a higher genetic determination than other tissues. Smith et al. (1973) have reported on the bone mineral density and width of the radius from photon absorptiometry in 71 juvenile and 70 adult twin pairs. In both the juveniles and the adults, the intrapair variance of MZ twins was significantly lower than that of the DZ twins for both bone mineral density and radius width. The intrapair variance for the 23 juvenile DZ pairs reached $0.0052 \, \text{g/cm}^2$ for bone mineral density and $0.0011 \, \text{cm}$ for the radius width, while the variance in 48 MZ pairs attained only $0.0013 \, \text{g/cm}^2$ ($p < 0.001$) and $0.0006 \, \text{cm}$ ($p < 0.05$) for bone mineral density and bone width, respectively. The genetic effect seems to be more pronounced during growth and early adulthood. With the decline in bone mineral density in the middle-aged and elderly, the environment component of the phenotypic variance appears to increase, particularly in women after menopause. It has also been reported that daughters of postmenopausal women with osteoporosis have reduced bone mass, even before they attain menopause (Seeman et al., 1989). A report based on photon absorptiometry in DZ and MZ twins also found evidence

for genetic determinants of bone mass and concluded that a single gene or set of genes determines bone mass at all sites assessed in the study, namely, one forearm site, one lumbar spine site, and three femoral sites (Pocock et al., 1987).

To our knowledge, evidence for a major gene through segregation analysis has not been reported for bone mass. It has been shown, however, that allelic variation at the gene encoding the vitamin D receptor was predictive of up to 75% of the total genetic effect on bone mineral density in healthy individuals (Morrison et al., 1994). The allele for the low bone density caused a decrease in bone mineral density that was equivalent to about 10 years of aging when homozygotes for the high bone density allele were compared to homozygotes for the low bone density allele. The same authors report that about 16% of Australian women are homozygotes for the low bone density allele (Hopkin, 1994).

Genetics and Physique

Physique characteristics are often assessed with the somatotyping techniques. Parnell (1958) was apparently the first to compare somatotypes of children and their parents. Since then many studies of somatotypes based on family or twin data have been reported. These have been reviewed by Carter and Heath (1990), Song, Malina, and Bouchard (1993), and Song, Pérusse, Malina, and Bouchard (1994). In general, these studies suggest that all three somatotype components are characterized by a significant genetic effect when considered individually, but there is a trend for mesomorphy to exhibit a higher level of heritability than ectomorphy or endomorphy in both family and twin studies.

Recently the notion that each somatotype component should be analyzed with statistical control over the other two components was developed (Song et al., 1993, 1994). When somatotype data are analyzed in this manner, parent-child correlations are significant for all three components, with mesomorphy again exhibiting a higher degree of covariation than the other two components. The same trend is found in full sibling correlations. Adjusting the phenotypes for level of activity and energy intake did not influence the results in any significant manner (Song et al., 1993). The same analytical strategy was used in a study in which pairs of MZ and DZ twins, ages 9 to 23 years, were compared. The intraclass correlations were

Table 16.8   Midparent-Child Interclass Correlations for Somatotype Components

Variable	Foster midparent-adopted child (N = 154 sets)		Midparent-natural child (N = 622 sets)	
Endomorphy	0.37**[1]	0.19*[2]	0.35**[1]	0.41**[2]
Mesomorphy	0.19*	0.02	0.41**	0.41**
Ectomorphy	0.26**	0.02	0.33**	0.32**

*$P < 0.05$. **$P < 0.001$.

[1]Scores adjusted for age and sex effects by generation and normalized (column 1 and 3).

[2]Scores adjusted for age and sex effects and for the other two somatotypes components by generation and normalized (column 2 and 4).

marginally reduced in both female MZ and DZ twins when the analyses were performed with statistical control over the other two components (Song et al., 1994). In the male twins, however, there was some indication that the genetic effect was dramatically reduced by this procedure.

Somatotype data were obtained from foster parents and adopted children in the 1980 data collection phase of the Quebec Family Study. The findings from comparisons of the adoption versus biological dyads are summarized in Table 16.8. The correlations were markedly higher in the midparent-natural child sets than in the foster midparent-adopted child sets for mesomorphy. The difference between the two sets persisted and was even increased when mesomorphy was statistically adjusted for endomorphy and ectomorphy. The other two components maintained their level of correlation at 0.3 to 0.4 when each component was adjusted for the other two in the biological relatives, but it decreased in the relatives by adoption. These results appear to imply that the level of heritability is highest for mesomorphy.

Conclusions

Understanding the causes of human variation in body composition and physique has been a goal of human biological disciplines for a long time. Population genetic and quantitative genetic studies have revealed that a significant portion of within-population variation in body composition and physique, and perhaps some of the variability across populations, can be accounted for by inherited differences. In the last decade or so, genetic epidemiology research has shown that body fat and adipose tissue topography phenotypes are generally characterized by the contribution of a multifactorial transmitted component as well as a major recessive gene effect. A major gene effect has been detected for FFM. Corresponding analyses are apparently lacking for skeletal characteristics and physique components.

Association and linkage studies with molecular markers have begun to appear. There is growing evidence that the genetic component of body composition and physique phenotypes will eventually be defined in terms of a series of contributing and interacting genes. Although much remains to be done, the techniques and study designs that have the potential to generate such information are now available and are routinely employed in many laboratories. The availability of these investigative tools along with the new imaging techniques should allow us to progress more rapidly in the study of the genetic basis of body composition and physique as well as organ size (Mahaney, Williams-Blangero, Blangero, & Leland, 1993), an area that has been largely neglected.

References

Ama, P.F.M., Simoneau, J.A., Boulay, M.R., et al. (1986). Skeletal muscle characteristics in sedentary Black and Caucasian males. *Journal of Applied Physiology*, **61**, 1758-1761.

Berg, K. (1981). Twin research in coronary heart disease. In L. Gedda, P. Parisi, & W.E. Nance (Eds.), *Twin research 3, part C: Epidemiological and clinical studies* (pp. 117-130). New York: Alan R. Liss.

Berg, K. (1988). Variability gene effect on cholesterol at the Kidd blood group locus. *Clinical Genetics*, **33**, 102-107.

Berg, K. (1990). Molecular genetics and nutrition. In A.P. Simopoulos & B. Childs (Eds.), *Genetic variation and nutrition* (pp. 49-59). Basel: Karger.

Blomstrand, E., & Ekblom, B. (1982). The needle biopsy technique for fiber type determination in human skeletal muscle: A methodological study. *Acta Physiologica Scandinavica*, **116**, 437-442.

Borecki, I.B., Bonney, G.E., Rice, T., et al. (1993). Influence of genotype-dependent effects of covariates on the outcome of segregation analysis of the body mass index. *American Journal of Human Genetics*, **53**, 676-687.

Borecki, I.B., Rice, T., Pérusse, L., Bouchard, C., & Rao, D.C. (1995). Major gene influence on the propensity to store fat in trunk versus extremity depots: Evidence from the Quebec Family Study. *Obesity Research, 3,* 1-8.

Bouchard, C. (1985). Inheritance of human fat distribution and adipose tissue metabolism. In J. Vague, P. Björntorp, B. Guy-Grand, et al. (Eds.), *Metabolic complications of human obesities* (pp. 87-96). Amsterdam: Elsevier.

Bouchard, C. (1988). Inheritance of human fat distribution. In C. Bouchard & F.E. Johnson (Eds.), *Fat distribution during growth and later health outcomes* (pp. 103-125). New York: Alan R. Liss.

Bouchard, C. (1990). Variation in human body fat: The contribution of the genotype. In G.A. Bray, D. Ricquier, & B.M. Spiegelman (Eds.), *Obesity: Towards a molecular approach* (pp. 17-28). New York: Alan R. Liss.

Bouchard, C. (1991a). Current understanding of the etiology of obesity: Genetic and nongenetic factors. *American Journal of Clinical Nutrition, 53,* 1561S-1565S.

Bouchard, C. (1991b). Genetic aspects of anthropometric dimensions relevant to assessment of nutritional status. In J. Himes (Ed.), *Anthropometric assessment of nutritional status* (pp. 213-231). New York: Alan R. Liss.

Bouchard, C. (1994). Genetics of obesity: Overview and research directions. In C. Bouchard (Ed.), *The genetics of obesity* (pp. 223-233). Boca Raton, FL: CRC.

Bouchard, C., Chagnon, M., Thibault, M.C., et al. (1988a). Absence of charge variants in human skeletal muscle enzymes of the glycolytic pathways. *Human Genetics, 78,* 100.

Bouchard, C., Demirjian, A., & Malina, R.M. (1980). Genetic pleiotropism in skeletal lengths and breadths. In M. Ostyn, G. Beunen, & J. Simons (Eds.), *Kinanthropometry II.* Vol. 9, International Series on Sport Sciences (pp. 78-87). Baltimore: University Park.

Bouchard, C., Després, J.P., Mauriège, P., et al. (1991). The genes in the constellation of determinants of regional fat distribution. *International Journal of Obesity, 15,* 9-18.

Bouchard, C., Després, J.P., & Mauriège, P. (1993b). Genetic and nongenetic determinants of regional fat distribution. *Endocrine Reviews, 14,* 72-93.

Bouchard, C., Dionne, F.T., Simoneau, J.A., et al. (1992a). Genetics of aerobic and anaerobic performances. In J.O. Holloszy (Ed.), *Exercise and sport sciences reviews* (pp. 27-58). Baltimore: William & Wilkins.

Bouchard, C., & Lortie, G. (1984). Heredity and endurance performance. *Sports Medicine, 1,* 38-64.

Bouchard, C., & Pérusse, L. (1988). Heredity and body fat. *Annual Review of Nutrition, 8,* 259-277.

Bouchard, C., & Pérusse, L. (1993). Genetics of obesity. *Annual Review of Nutrition, 13,* 337-354.

Bouchard, C., Pérusse, L., Dériaz, O., et al. (1993a). Genetic influences on energy expenditure in humans. *Critical Reviews in Food Science and Nutrition, 33,* 345-350.

Bouchard, C., Pérusse, L., Leblanc, C., et al. (1988b). Inheritance of the amount and distribution of human body fat. *International Journal of Obesity, 12,* 205-215.

Bouchard, C., Simoneau, J.A., Lortie, G. et al. (1986). Genetic effects in human skeletal muscle fiber type distribution and enzyme activities. *Canadian Journal of Physiology and Pharmacology, 64,* 1245-1251.

Bouchard, C., Tremblay, A., Després, J.P., et al. (1988c). Sensitivity to overfeeding: The Quebec experiment with identical twins. *Progress in Food and Nutrition Science, 12,* 45-72.

Bouchard, C., Tremblay, A., Després, J.P., et al. (1990). The response to long-term overfeeding in identical twins. *New England Journal of Medicine, 322,* 1477-1482.

Bouchard, C., Tremblay, A., Després, J.P., et al. (1992b). The genetics of body energy content and energy balance: An overview. In G.A. Bray & D.H. Ryan (Eds.), *The science of food regulation: Food intake, taste, nutrient partitioning and energy expenditure* (pp. 3-21). Baton Rouge: Louisiana State University Press.

Bouchard, C., Tremblay, A., Després, J.P., et al. (1992c). The response to exercise with constant energy intake in identical twins. *FASEB Journal, 6,* A1647.

Bouchard, C., Tremblay, A., Després, J.P., et al. (1994). The response to exercise with constant energy intake in identical twins. *Obesity Research, 2,* 400-410.

Bray, G.A. (1981). The inheritance of corpulence. In L.A. Cioffi, W.P.T. James, & T.B. VanItallie (Eds.), *The body weight regulatory system: Normal and disturbed mechanisms* (pp. 185-195). New York: Raven.

Brožek, J. (1961). Body measurements including skinfold thickness, as indicators of body composition. In J. Brožek & A. Henschel (Eds.), *Techniques for measuring body composition* (pp. 3-35). Washington, DC: National Research Council.

Cantor, R.M., & Rotter, J.I. (1992). Analysis of genetic data: Methods and interpretation. In R.A.

King, J.I. Rotter, & A.G. Motulsky (Eds.), *The genetic basis of common diseases* (pp. 49-70). Oxford: Oxford University Press.

Carter, J.E.L., & Heath, B.H. (1990). *Somatotyping: Development and applications.* Cambridge, England: Cambridge University Press.

Chua, S.C., & Leibel, R.L. (1994). Molecular genetic approaches to obesity. In C. Bouchard (Ed.), *The genetics of obesity* (pp. 213-222). Boca Raton, FL: CRC.

Clark, P.J. (1956). The heritability of certain anthropometric characters as ascertained from measurements of twins. *American Journal of Human Genetics, 8,* 49-54.

Comuzzie, A.G., Blangero, J., Mitchell, B.D., et al. (1993). Segregation analysis of fat mass and fat free mass. *Genetic Epidemiology, 10,* 340.

Dahlberg, G. (1926). *Twin births and twins from a hereditary point of view.* Stockholm: Tidems Tsyckeri.

Dériaz, O., Dionne, F.T., Pérusse, L., et al. (1994). DNA variation in the genes of the NA, K-Adenosine triphosphatase and its relation with resting metabolic rate, respiratory quotient, and body fat. *Journal of Clinical Investigation, 93,* 838-843.

Després, J.P., Bouchard, C., Savard, R., et al. (1984). Adaptive changes to training in adipose tissue lipolysis are genotype dependent. *International Journal of Obesity, 8,* 87-95.

Donahue, R.P., Prineas, R.J., Gomez, O., & Hong, C.P. (1992). Familial resemblance of body fat distribution: The Minneapolis Children's blood pressure study. *International Journal of Obesity, 16,* 161-167.

Enzi, G., Gasparo, M., Biondetti, P.R., et al. (1986). Subcutaneous and visceral fat distribution according to sex, age, and overweight, evaluated by computed tomography. *American Journal of Clinical Nutrition, 44,* 739-746.

Falconer, D.S. (1960). *Introduction to quantitative genetics.* New York: Ronald.

Ferland, M., Després, J.P., Tremblay, A., et al. (1989). Assessment of adipose tissue distribution by computed axial tomography in obese women: Association with body density and anthropometric measurements. *British Journal of Nutrition, 61,* 139-148.

Fisler, J.S., Warden, C.H., Pace, M.J., & Lusis, A.J. (1993). BSB: A new mouse model of multigenic obesity. *Obesity Research, 1,* 271-280.

Friedman, J.M., Leibel, R.L., & Bahary, N. (1991). Molecular mapping of obesity genes. *Mammalian Genome, 1,* 130-144.

Garn, S.M. (1962). The genetics of normal human growth. In Gedda, L. (Ed.), *De genetica medica,* Vol. 2 (pp. 415-434). Rome: Mendel Institute.

Garn, S.M., Sullivan, T.V., & Hawthorne, V.M. (1989). Fatness and obesity of the parents of obese individuals. *American Journal of Clinical Nutrition, 50,* 1308-1313.

Gollnick, P.D. (1982). Relationship of strength and endurance with skeletal muscle structure and metabolic potential. *International Journal of Sports Medicine, 3,* 26-32.

Gollnick, P.D., Armstrong, R.B., Saltin, B., et al. (1973). Effect of training on enzyme activity and fiber type composition of human skeletal muscle. *Journal of Applied Physiology, 34,* 107-111.

Greenberg, D.A. (1993). Linkage analysis of "necessary" disease loci versus "susceptibility" loci. *American Journal of Human Genetics, 52,* 135-143.

Grilo, C.M., & Pogue-Geile, M.F. (1991). The nature of environmental influences on weight and obesity: A behavior genetic analysis. *Psychology Bulletin, 110,* 520-537.

Haseman, J.K., & Elston, R.C. (1972): The investigation of linkage between a quantitative trait and a marker locus. *Behavior Genetics, 2,* 3-19.

Hasstedt, S.J., Ramirez, M.E., Kuida, H., & Williams, R.R. (1989). Recessive inheritance of a relative fat pattern. *American Journal of Human Genetics, 45,* 917-925.

Heller, R., Garrison, R.J., Havlik, R.J., et al. (1984). Family resemblances in height and relative weight in the Framingham Heart Study. *International Journal of Obesity, 8,* 399-405.

Hewitt, D. (1957). Sib resemblance in bone, muscle and fat measurements of the human calf. *Annals of Human Genetics, 22,* 213-221.

Hopkin, K. (1994). Osteoporosis: A simpler pincture emerges. *Journal of NIH Research, 6,* 27-29.

Hopper, J.L., & Seeman, E. (1994). The bone density of female twins discordant for tobacco use. *New England Journal of Medicine, 330,* 387-392.

Howells, W.W. (1953). Correlations of brothers in factor scores. *American Journal of Physiology and Anthropology, 11,* 121-140.

Ikoma, E., & Murotani, N. (1976). A genetic study on the length of tibia. *Annals of Human Genetics, 39,* 475-483.

Jaenisch, R. (1988). Transgenic animals. *Science, 240,* 1468-1474.

Kelly, P.J., Eisman, J.A., & Sambrook, P.N. (1990). Interaction of genetic and enrivonmental influences on peak bone density. *Osteoporosis International, 1,* 56-60.

Komi, P.V., Viitasalo, J.H.T., Havu, M., et al. (1977). Skeletal muscle fibres and muscle enzyme activities in monozygous and dizygous twins of both sexes. *Acta Physiological Scandinavica, 100,* 385-392.

Kramer, A.A., Green, I.J., Croghan, I.T., et al. (1986). Bivariate path analysis of twin children for stature and biiliac diameter: Estimation of genetic variation and co-variation. *Human Biology*, **58**, 517-525.

Lander, E.S., & Botstein, D. (1989). Mapping Mendelian factors underlying quantitative traits using RFLP linkage maps. *Genetics*, **121**, 185-199.

Lucarini, N., Finocchi, G., Gloria-Bottini, F., Macioce, M., et al. (1990). A possible genetic component of obesity in childhood: Observations on acid phosphatase polymorphism. *Experientia*, **46**, 90-91.

MacCluer, J.W. (1992). Biometrical studies to detect new genes with major effects on quantitative risk factors for atherosclerosis. *Current Opinion in Lipidology*, **3**, 114-121.

MacDonald, A., & Stunkard, A.J. (1990). Body mass indexes of British separated twins. *New England Journal of Medicine*, **322**, 1530.

Mahaney, M.C., Williams-Blangero, S., Blangero, J., & Leland, M.M. (1993). Quantitative genetics of relative organ weight variation in captive baboons. *Human Biology*, **65**, 991-1003.

Marcotte, M., Chagnon, M., Côté, C., Thibault, M.C., Boulay, M.R., & Bouchard, C. (1987). Lack of genetic polymorphism in human skeletal muscle enzymes of the tricarboxilic acid cycle. *Human Genetics*, **77**, 200.

Mauriège, P., Després, J.P., Marcotte, M., et al. (1992). Adipose tissue lipolysis after long-term overfeeding in identical twins. *International Journal of Obesity*, **16**, 219-225.

Mehrabian, M., & Lusis, A.J. (1992). Genetic markers for studies of atherosclerosis and related risk factors. In A.J. Lusis, J.I. Rotter, & R.S. Sparkes (Eds.), *Molecular genetics of coronary artery disease* (pp. 363-418) (Monographs in Human Genetics, No. 14). Basel: Karger.

Merlino, G.T. (1991). Transgenic animals in biomedical research. *FASEB Journal*, **5**, 2996-3001.

Metsäranta, M., & Vuorio, E. (1992). Transgenic mice as models for heritable diseases. *Annals of Medicine*, **24**, 117-120.

Moll, P.P., Burns, T.L., & Lauer, R.M. (1991). The genetic and environmental sources of body mass index variability: The Muscatine Ponderosity Family Study. *American Journal of Human Genetics*, **49**, 1243-1255.

Morrison, N.A., Cheng, J., Tokita, A., et al. (1994). Prediction of bone density from vitamin D receptor alleles. *Nature*, **367**, 284-287.

Mueller, W.H. (1983). The genetics of human fatness. *Yearbook of Physiology and Anthropology*, **26**, 215-230.

Nimmo, M.A., Wilson, R.H., & Snow, D.H. (1985). The inheritance of skeletal muscle fibre composition in mice. *Comparative Biochemistry and Physiology*, **81A**, 109-115.

Oppert, J.M., Tourville, J., Chagnon, M., et al. (1995). DNA polymorphisms in the a_2^- and b_2^- adrenoceptor genes and regional fat distribution in humans: Association and linkage studies. *Obesity Research*, **3**, 249-255.

Oppert, J.M., Vohl, M.C., Chagnon, M., et al. (1994). DNA polymorphism in the uncoupling protein (UCP) gene and human body fat. *International Journal of Obesity*, **18**, 526-531.

Osborne, R.H., & DeGeorge, F.V. (1959). *Genetic basis of morphological variation*. Cambridge, MA: Harvard University Press.

Parnell, R.W. (1958). *Behaviour and physique: An introduction to practical and applied somatometry*. London: Edward Arnold.

Pépin, M.C., Pothier, F., & Barden, N. (1992). Impaired type II glucocorticoid-receptor function in mice bearing antisense RNA transgene. *Nature*, **235**, 725-728.

Pérusse, L., & Bouchard, C. (1994). Genetics of energy intake and food preferences. In C. Bouchard (Ed.), *The genetics of obesity* (pp. 125-134). Boca Raton, FL: CRC.

Pérusse, L., Leblanc, C., & Bouchard, C. (1988). Inter-generation transmission of physical fitness in the Canadian population. *Canadian Journal of Sport Sciences*, **13**, 8-14.

Pocock, N.A., Eisman, J.A., Hopper, J.L., et al. (1987). Genetic determinants of bone mass in adults: A twin study. *Journal of Clinical Investigation*, **80**, 706-710.

Poehlman, E.T., Després, J.P., Marcotte, M., et al. (1986). Genotype dependency of adaptation in adipose tissue metabolism after short-term overfeeding. *American Journal of Physiology*, **250**, E480-E485.

Poehlman, E.T., Tremblay, A., Marcotte, M., et al. (1987). Heredity and changes in body composition and adipose tissue metabolism after short-term exercise training. *European Journal of Applied Physiology*, **56**, 398-402.

Pollitzer, W.S., & Anderson, J.J.B. (1989). Ethnic and genetic differences in bone mass: A review with a hereditary vs environmental perspective. *American Journal of Clinical Nutrition*, **50**, 1244-1259.

Price, R.A., Cadoret, R.J., Stunkard, A.J., & Troughton, E. (1987). Genetic contributions to human fatness: An adoption study. *American Journal of Psychiatry*, **144**, 1003-1008.

Price, R.A., & Gottesman, I.I. (1991). Body fat in identical twins reared apart: Roles for genes and environment. *Behavioral Genetics, 21*, 1-7.

Price, R.A., Ness, R., & Laskarzewski, P. (1990). Common major gene inheritance of extreme overweight. *Human Biology, 62*, 747-765.

Province, M.A., Amqvist, P., Keller, J., et al. (1990). Strong evidence for a major gene for obesity in the large, unselected, total Community Health Study of Tecumseh. *American Journal of Human Genetics, 47*, A143.

Rajput-Williams, J., Wallis, S.C., Yarnell, J., et al. (1988). Variation of apolipoprotein-B gene is associated with obesity, high blood cholesterol levels, and increased risk of coronary heart disease. *The Lancet, 2*, 1442-1446.

Reeds, P.J., Fiorotto, M.L., & Davis, T.A. (1992). Nutrient partitioning: An overview. In G.A. Bray & D.H. Ryan (Eds.), *The science of food regulation: Food intake, taste, nutrient partitioning, and energy expenditure* (pp. 103-120). Baton Rouge: Louisiana State University Press.

Rice, T., Borecki, I.B., Bouchard, C., & Rao, D.C. (1993a). Segregation analysis of fat mass and other body composition measures derived from underwater weighing. *American Journal of Human Genetics, 52*, 967-973.

Rice, T., Borecki, I.B., Bouchard, C., & Rao, D.C. (1993b). Segregation analysis of body mass index in an unselected French-Canadian sample: The Québec Family Study. *Obesity Research, 1*, 288-294.

Roche, A.F. (1994). Sarcopenia: A critical review of its measurement and health-related significance in the middle-aged and elderly. *American Journal of Human Biology, 6*, 33-42.

Saltin, B., & Gollnick, P.D. (1983). Skeletal muscle adaptability: Significance for metabolism and performance. In L.D. Peachy, R.H. Adrian, & S.R. Geiger (Eds.), *Handbook of physiology*, Section 10 (pp. 555-631). Bethesda, MD: American Physiological Society.

Savard, R., & Bouchard, C. (1990). Genetic effects in the response of adipose tissue lipoprotein lipase activity to prolonged exercise: A twin study. *International Journal of Obesity, 14*, 771-777.

Schreider, E. (1969). Biométrie et génétique [Biometry and genetic]. *Biométrie Humaine, 4*, 65-85.

Schulte, P.A., & Perera, F.P. (1993). Validation. In P.A. Schulte & F.P. Perera (Eds.), *Molecular epidemiology: Principles and practices* (pp. 81-107). San Diego: Academic.

Seeman, E., Hopper, J.L., Bach, L.A., et al. (1989). Reduced bone mass in daughters of women with osteoporosis. *New England Journal of Medicine, 320*, 554-558.

Selby, J.V., Newman, B., Quesenberry, C.P., Jr., et al. (1989). Evidence of genetic influence on central body fat in middle-aged twins. *Human Biology, 61*, 179-193.

Shepherd, P.R., Gnudi, L., Tozzo, E., et al. (1993). Enhanced glucose disposal and obesity in transgenic mice overexpressing Glut 4 selectively in fat. *Diabetes 42* (Abstract No. 239), 53rd Annual Meeting, Las Vegas.

Simoneau, J.A., & Bouchard, C. (1989). Human variation in skeletal muscle fiber-type proportion and enzyme activities. *American Journal of Physiology, 257*, E567-E572.

Simoneau, J.A., Lortie, G., Boulay, M.R., et al. (1986). Repeatability of fiber type and enzyme activity measurements in human skeletal muscle. *Clinical Physiology, 6*, 347-356.

Sing, C.F., & Boerwinkle, E.A. (1987). Genetic architecture of inter-individual variability in apolipoprotein, lipoprotein and lipid phenotypes. In D. Weatherall (Ed.), *Molecular approaches to human polygenic disease* (pp. 99-127). New York: John Wiley.

Sing, C.F., Boerwinkle, E., Moll, P.P., & Templeton, A.R. (1988). Characterization of genes affecting quantitative traits in humans. In B.S. Weir, E.J. Eisen, M.M. Goddman, & G. Namkoong (Eds.), *Proceedings of the second international conference on quantitative genetics* (pp.250-269). Sunderland, MA: Sinauer.

Smith, D.M., Nance, W.E., Kang, K.W., et al. (1973). Genetic factors in determining bone mass. *Journal of Clinical Investigation, 52*, 2800-2808.

Song, T.M.K., Malina, R.M., & Bouchard, C. (1993). Familial resemblance in somatotype. *American Journal of Human Biology, 5*, 265-272.

Song, T.M.K., Pérusse, L., Malina, R.M., & Bouchard, C. (1994). Twin resemblance in somatotype and comparisons with other twin studies. *Human Biology, 66*, 453-464.

Sorensen, T.I.A., Holst, C., & Stunkard, A.J. (1992a). Childhood body mass index: Genetic and familial environmental influences assessed in a longitudinal adoption study. *International Journal of Obesity, 16*, 705-714.

Sorensen, T.I.A., Holst, C., Stunkard, A.J., & Theil, L. (1992b). Correlations of body mass index of adult adoptees and their biological relatives. *International Journal of Obesity, 16*, 227-236.

Sorensen, T.I.A., Price, R.A., Stunkard, A.J., & Schulsinger, F. (1989). Genetics of obesity in adult adoptees and their biological siblings. *British Journal of Medicine, 298*, 87-90.

Sowers, M.R., & Galuska, D.A. (1993). Epidemiology of bone mass in premenopausal women. *Epidemiologic Reviews, 15*, 374-398.

Sparkes, R.S. (1992). Human gene mapping, linkage, and association. In R.A. King, J.I. Rotter, & A.G. Motulsky (Eds.), *The genetic basis of common diseases* (pp. 34-48). Oxford: Oxford University Press.

Stunkard, A.J., Foch, T.T., & Hrubec, Z. (1986a). A twin study of human obesity. *Journal of the American Medical Association, 256*, 51-54.

Stunkard, A.J., Harris, J.R., Pedersen, N.L., & McClearn, G.E. (1990). The body-mass index of twins who have been reared apart. *New England Journal of Medicine, 322*, 1483-1487.

Stunkard, A.J., Sorensen, T.I.A., Hannis, C., et al. (1986b). An adoption study of human obesity. *New England Journal of Medicine, 314*, 193-198.

Tambs, K., Moum, T., Eaves, L., et al. (1991). Genetic and environmental contributions to the variance of the body mass index in a Norwegian sample of first and second-degree relatives. *American Journal of Human Biology, 3*, 257-267.

Tanner, J.M. (1953). Inheritance of morphological and physiological traits. In A. Sorsby (Ed.), *Clinical genetics* (pp. 155-174). St Louis: Mosby.

Tiret, L., André, J.L., Ducimetière, P., et al. (1992). Segregation analysis of height-adjusted weight with generation- and age-dependent effects: The Nancy Family Study. *Genetic Epidemiology, 9*, 389-403.

Truett, G.E., Bahary, N., Friedman, J.M., & Leibel, R.L. (1991). Rat obesity gene fatty (fa) maps to chromosome 5: Evidence for homology with the mouse gene diabetes (db). *Proceedings of the National Academy of Sciences, 88*, 7806-7809.

Vandenberg, S.G. (1962). How stable are heritability estimates? A comparison of heritability estimates from six anthropometric studies. *American Journal of Physiology and Anthropology, 20*, 331-338.

Vandenberg, S.G., & Strandskov, H.H. (1964). A comparison of identical and fraternal twins on some anthropometric measures. *Human Biology, 36*, 45-52.

Venerando, A., & Milani-Comparetti, M. (1973). Heredity versus environment in biomechanics. In S. Cerquiglini, A. Venerando, & J. Wartenweiler (Eds.), *Biomechanics III* (pp. 151-155). Basel: Karger.

Vijayaraghavan, S., Hitman, G.A., Weaver, J.U., & Kopelman, P.G. (1993). Apolipoprotein D polymorphism: A shared genetic determinant between obesity and NIDDM. *International Journal of Obesity, 17*, 107.

Vogel, F., & Wendt, G.G. (1956). Zwillingsuntursuchung über die erblichkeit einiger anthropologischer masse und konstitutionsindices [Twin studies on the role of heredity in anthropological measures and constitutions]. *Zeitschrift für Menschliche Verebung Konstitutionslehere, 33*, 425-446.

Vohl, M.C., Dionne, F.T., Pérusse, L., et al. (1994). Relation between BglII polymorphism in 3β-hydroxysteroid dehydrogenase gene and adipose tissue distribution in humans. *Obesity Research, 2*, 444-449.

Von Verschuer, O. (1954). *Wirksame faktoren im leben des menachen* [Important factors in human life]. Wiesbaden: F. Steiner.

Warden, C.H., Daluiski, A., & Lusis, A.J. (1992). Identification of new genes contributing to atherosclerosis: The mapping of genes contributing to complex disorders in animal models. In A.J. Lusis, J.I. Rotter, & R.S. Sparkes (Eds.), *Molecular genetics of coronary artery disease* (pp. 419-441) (Monographs in Human Genetics, No. 14). Basel: Karger.

Warden, C.H., Fisler, J.S., Pace, M.J., et al. (1993). Coincidence of genetic loci for plasma cholesterol levels and obesity in a multifactorial mouse model. *Journal of Clinical Investigation, 92*, 773-779.

Weaver, J.U., Hitman, G.A., & Kopelman, P.G. (1992c). An association between a BcII restriction fragment length polymorphism of the glucocorticoid receptor locus and hyperinsulinaemia in obese women. *Journal of Molecular Endocrinology, 9*, 295-300.

Weaver, J.U., Kopelman, P.G., & Hitman, G.A. (1992a). Glucose transporter (Glut 1) as a possible candidate gene for obesity. In G. Ailhaud, B. Guy-Grand, M. Lafontan, & C. Ricquier (Eds.), *Proceedings of the 3rd European Congress on Obesity* (pp. 89-93). Paris: John Libbey.

Weaver, J.U., Kopelman, P.G., & Hitman, G.A. (1992b). Central obesity and hyperinsulinaemia in women are associated with polymorphism in the 5' flanking region of the human insulin gene. *European Journal of Clinical Investigation, 22*, 265-270.

Williams, R.R., Hunt, S.C., Hopkins, P.N., et al. (1994). Tabulations and expectations regarding the genetics of human hypertension. *Kidney International, 45*, 557-564.

Zee, R.Y.L., Griffiths, L.R., & Morris, B.J. (1992). Marked association of a RFLP for the low density lipoprotein receptor gene with obesity in essential hypertensives. *Biochemical and Biophysical Research Communications, 189*, 965-971.

17

Hormonal Influences on Human Body Composition

Per Björntorp and Staffan Edén

Hormones exert major, determining effects on body composition. Extreme examples may be found in clinical entities such as acromegaly, dwarfism, eunuchism, Cushing's disease, and hyperthyroidism. Both peptide and steroid hormones, alone or in combination, exert profound changes on both the lean and fat compartments of body composition. It is impossible to review this large field comprehensively within a limited number of pages. Therefore, the present review is restricted to a summary of recent advances in selected areas with emphasis on the effects of physiological steroid hormones and their interactions with insulin and growth hormone (GH). With the recent recognition of the importance of the regional distribution of body fat in relation to serious and prevalent diseases, the focus has been placed on the effects of the main physiological steroid hormones—cortisol, testosterone (T), and 17-beta-estradiol—on muscle mass as well as adipose tissue and its distribution, because these hormones are probably involved as pathogenetic factors. The effects of these steroid hormones are dependent on the interactions of GH and insulin. GH has been the subject of particular attention due to the recent, rapid developments in this area.

There are striking age- and sex-dependent changes in body composition. During infancy, the child accumulates fat during the first year of life (Faust, 1986; Knittle et al., 1979). During childhood, the total number of adipocytes increases relatively slowly until a second increase occurs before puberty (Knittle et al.). In adult life, adipocyte number does not vary greatly, and changes in adipose tissue mass are believed to reflect changes mainly in the size of existing adipocytes. During puberty, there is also a marked increase in muscle mass in boys, and the distribution of adipose tissue changes (Malina, 1986). Thereafter there is a steady increase in body weight, depending upon an increase in body fat, up to age 70 (Bruce, Andersson, Arvidsson, & Isaksson, 1980). From age 70, body weight seems to decrease, but the relative amount of body fat still increases (Steen, 1988).

Cortisol

Excess cortisol secretion and its consequences are clearly seen in Cushing's syndrome as a wasting of lean body mass, particularly muscle. Body fat mass and distribution are also changed. Clinical anecdotal evidence suggests that the changes in adipose tissue are dependent on the prevailing insulin concentrations. These in turn are determined by the insulin resistance, commonly seen in Cushing's syndrome, created by the glucocorticoid excess. With insufficiency of the compensatory secretion of insulin, the condition will become diabetes, with its well known lack of the anabolic effects of insulin on both protein sparing in muscle and on maintaining storage fat mass in adipose tissue. Therefore the interactions of insulin become important for the net effect of glucocorticoids on muscle mass as well as on adipose tissue mass and distribution.

Glucocorticoids probably exert direct effects on the insulin sensitivity of both liver and muscle (Baxter & Rosseau, 1979; McMahon, Gerich, & Rizza, 1988). A recent study has suggested that to a great extent these effects are mediated via free fatty acids (FFA) (Guillaume-Gentil, Assimacopoulos-Jeannet, & Jeanrenaud, 1993). In that study, rats were subjected to a slight excess of glucocorticoids, such as seen during stress. The consequences were insulin resistance of hepatic gluconeogenesis as well as of glucose metabolism in muscles. These perturbations were obliterated by the administration of etomoxir, an inhibitor of fatty acid oxidation. These results suggest that the effects of glucocorticoids on the mobilization of FFA from adipose tissue are of primary importance for the insulin resistance of that condition in the integrated system.

Studies on the mechanism for the effects of glucocorticoids on adipose tissue have given conflicting results. Effects on both the mechanisms for triglyceride uptake and for mobilization have been reported, and there is strong evidence that these effects vary in intensity in different regions of the adipose tissue organ. The main enzymatic regulator of triglyceride uptake, lipoprotein lipase (LPL), is influenced by glucocorticoids. The reports in literature on this subject are not congruent, some showing inhibitory, others stimulatory, effects (De Gasquet, Pequignot-Planchy, Tomm, & Diaby, 1975; Krotkiewski, Björntorp, & Smith, 1976a). Some of these controversies may well be due to the well known species differences in the regulation of adipose tissue metabolism. Recent studies on human adipose tissue, under fully controlled tissue-culture conditions, seem to have resolved at least some of these controversies. Cortisol alone seems to exert limited effects on LPL expression in human adipose tissue; the presence of insulin is critically important (Appel & Fried, 1992; Cigolini & Smith, 1979; Ottosson et al., 1994). The effects are exerted at the levels of gene expression, apparently in combination with a post-translatory interaction by insulin, leading to a stabilization of

enzyme activity. GH obliterates the expression of LPL activity by cortisol and insulin (Ottosson et al.). These results may explain the previous controversies in this topic area. In some studies these hormones and their interactions have not been controlled. For example, in vivo interrelationships between the secretion of cortisol, insulin, and GH may be expected. The effects of cortisol on insulin sensitivity, mentioned above, will result in compensatory increase of insulin secretion. Furthermore, cortisol and insulin are known to inhibit GH secretion (Chrousos & Gold, 1992). In the integrated physiological situation, cortisol excess will be followed by hyperinsulinemia and blunted GH secretion. The net effects in vivo then would indeed be expected to be a stimulation of LPL activity in adipose tissue, at least as long as insulin resistance can be compensated for by hyperinsulinemia.

The results of these studies illustrate the complex interactions between steroid and peptide hormones in the regulation of adipose tissue metabolism and its subsequent effects on body fat mass. The situation is, however, probably even more complex. The sex steroid hormones interact with cortisol in their specific ways, as will be reviewed in a subsequent section. In the condition of excess cortisol secretion of central origin, sex steroid secretion is, however, probably inhibited through interactions by corticotropin releasing factor (CRF) on gonadotropin releasing hormone (Olsen & Ferin, 1987). Therefore the net effects will mainly be those of cortisol and insulin, whereas the effects of GH and sex steroid hormones are lacking, which contributes to the total effects of cortisol excess on body fat due to central inhibitory mechanisms.

Glucocorticoids also exert marked effects on lipid mobilization in adipose tissue, again with interactive effects by other hormones. The original observation by Fain, Kovacev, and Scow (1965) that glucocorticoids, particularly in the presence of GH, act by increasing lipid mobilization in vitro in adipose tissue from rats has, in essence, held true. It should be noted that in these experiments the effects were more marked at the end of a 4 hour incubation period, suggesting that early transcriptional or translational effects on the system were observed. Again it is important to interpret the results in relation to the species studied. In human adipose tissue, the acute short-term effects of cortisol seem to be essentially absent. In long-term (days) experiments under fully controlled conditions, the effects are easier to detect. In the presence of insulin, cortisol by itself has a rather weak inhibitory effect on catecholamine-induced lipolysis, but cortisol induces a marked "permissive" effect by GH on lipolysis (Cigolini & Smith, 1979; Ottosson, Lönnroth, Björntorp, & Edén, 1995). The integrated effect of cortisol on lipolysis in vivo would not be expected to increase lipolysis because, with cortisol excess, GH secretion is blunted, as described above. Furthermore, insulin secretion is elevated, with its consequences for lipid mobilization.

The interaction of insulin in the system of cortisol-regulation of lipolysis is complex. After the long-term presence of cortisol and insulin, the insulin effect on lipolysis-regulation may well be stimulatory, as described previously in similar systems (Björntorp & Smith, 1976). Insulin also exerts an acute inhibitory effect on lipolysis, which is apparently independent of the long-term induction of lipolysis (Björntorp & Smith). The nature of both these effects is unknown. It is interesting, however, that after long-term exposure of adipose tissue to both cortisol and insulin, the acute inhibitory effect of insulin has been described to be blunted (Cigolini & Smith, 1979). The important regulatory effects of insulin would therefore, in conditions with cortisol excess in vivo, be expected to be, in general terms, a balance between a slight inhibition of lipolysis and a blunted antilipolytic effect of insulin.

Mobilization of triglycerides from adipose tissue is, however, dependent not only on lipolysis but also on the capacity of the adipocyte to re-esterify FFA produced by the lipolytic process. There is evidence that glucocorticoids may inhibit this process by interactions with glucose transport into adipocytes (Carter-Su & Okamoto, 1987), glucose being obligatory for re-esterification.

The net effects of glucocorticoids on lipid mobilization in vivo have been found to result in marked increases of circulating FFA both in man (Divertie, Jensen, & Miles, 1991) and rats (Guillaume-Gentil et al., 1993). Studies in vitro of adipose tissue from patients suffering from Cushing's syndrome with hyperinsulinemia have shown that the lipolytic sensitivity to catecholamine is unchanged or inhibited (Rebuffé-Scrive, Krotkiewski, Elfverson, & Björntorp, 1988). The elevated FFA concentrations after cortisol excess may therefore be due either to a weak antilipolytic effect of insulin or an inhibited glucose transport, leading to diminished fatty acid re-esterification in adipose tissue, or a combination of both. Again, as with LPL regulation, sex steroid hormones may interfere with several of these regulatory steps of FFA mobilization. In states of hypercortisolemia, however, the secretion of sex steroid hormones is decreased, minimizing such effects,

which, however, probably play important roles in the normal situation, particularly in young adults with intact sex steroid hormone secretion.

Steroid hormones usually exert their effects via interaction with specific receptors for subsequent interactions of the hormone-receptor complex at the level of the appropriate genes. A glucocorticoid receptor (GR) has been described in adipose tissue from rats (Feldman & Loose, 1977) and human beings (Rebuffé-Scrive, Lundholm, & Björntorp, 1985b). The density of this receptor seems to vary in different regions of adipose tissue, and there is evidence that the density is higher in intra-abdominal (visceral) than in subcutaneous adipose tissues in studies with ligand binding in cytosol preparations in man (Rebuffé-Scrive et al., 1985b) and in intact cells in rats (Sjögren, Weck, & Björntorp, 1993). Furthermore, the steady state GR mRNA levels have been reported to be higher in visceral than subcutaneous adipose tissue in man (Rebuffé-Scrive et al., 1990). This increase in mRNA seems to be accompanied by an increase in the GR protein (Peeke et al., 1993).

Obviously the effects of glucocorticoids on the metabolic regulation of adipose tissue metabolism, mass, and distribution are dependent on the density of the GR, mediating the glucocorticoid effects. The GR density is regulated by glucocorticoids, which exert down-regulatory effects (McDonald & Goldfine, 1988). In conditions with hypercortisolemia such consequences will therefore be expected. Interestingly, however, the rank order of GR density in different adipose tissue regions seems to remain after down-regulation (Peeke et al., 1993).

There are, however, some major regulators of adipose tissue metabolism other than those exerted by direct hormonal actions on adipocytes. The density of fat cells (in other words, the number of cells per unit tissue mass), blood flow, and innervation are such factors. The number of adipocytes will determine the active cellular mass of an adipose tissue and therefore the tissue density of, for example, regulatory enzymes for lipid accumulation and mobilization. Blood flow determines the delivery of substrate for the lipid uptake process in adipocytes and is essential for the efficient removal of products of lipolysis, whereas FFA have been shown to cause a feedback inhibition on the lipolytic process (Rosell & Belfrage, 1979). At least in human adipose tissue, the acute lipolytic effects of catecholamines are probably regulated by direct effects of the sympathetic nervous system (Björntorp & Östman, 1971). In summary, the basis for the integrated metabolic regulation depends on the sensitivity and capacity of the individual adipocytes to assimilate and mobilize lipids. The number of such cells per unit mass is of obvious importance. Furthermore, the circulation determines the access to steroid and peptide hormones, as well as delivery of triglyceride for uptake and removal of lipolytic products. The potential influence of hormones on the latter factors is essentially unknown.

The effects of glucocorticoids on adipose tissue are clearly regionally specific. The most dramatic evidence for this statement is found in Cushing's syndrome, with its marked redistribution of storage fat from the periphery to central, mainly intra-abdominal, depots. The reason for this is most likely a combination of several factors. There is a high density of the GR in this depot (Rebuffé-Scrive et al., 1985b, 1990; Sjögren et al., 1993). In the normal condition the cellular density of visceral fat depots (Salans, Cushman, & Weissmann, 1973), as well as blood flow (West, Prinz, & Greenwood, 1989) and innervation (Rebuffé-Scrive, 1991), are probably higher than in other adipose tissues, further exaggerating the effects of hypercortisolemia on these adipose tissues. In the integrated system in vivo, hypercortisolemia will be followed by elevated insulin concentrations and inhibited GH secretion. The combined metabolic effects in the adipocytes of these hormonal changes will be expected to be an augmented LPL expression by cortisol plus insulin with lack of effects of GH, and perhaps a diminished lipolytic potential for the same reason. Such aberrations have also been observed, with a regional difference, in patients with Cushing's syndrome (Rebuffé-Scrive et al., 1988), suggesting that the interpretation is correct. Nevertheless, FFA concentrations are elevated, perhaps due to a combination of a re-esterification defect or a blunted antilipolytic effect of insulin, or both. Increased concentration of FFA would tend to diminish adipose tissue mass. It might be considered that these effects are also regionally different, sparing central adipose tissue, or that the effects on the balance between lipid accumulation and mobilization are disturbed, with more pronounced effects on the former.

Cushing's syndrome is the clinical condition where the net effects of increased cortisol secretion are most clearly seen, but other conditions with long-term exposure to excess glucocorticoids are followed by redistribution of adipose tissue, as in treatment with glucocorticoids of bronchial asthma and rheumatoid arthritis (Krotkiewski, Blohmé, Lindholm, & Björntorp, 1976b). Furthermore, recent evidence strongly suggests that obesity, with disproportional increase of visceral fat depots, is a condition with increased cortisol secretion due to a high sensitivity of the hypothalamo-adrenal axis to different forms of stress (Mårin et al., 1992). The accumulation of excess depot fat in visceral depots may be a consequence of periodic hypercortisolemia through the mechanisms suggested above. Thus, the excessive changes of body fat distribution and metabolism seen in Cushing's syndrome may have clear relevance for our understanding of the pathophysiological mechanisms involved in the condition of visceral obesity.

Testosterone

The effects of testosterone (T) on lean body mass are well established. Castrated animals accumulate nitrogen and muscular mass after substitution with T (Kochakian & Endahl, 1959; Papanicolaou & Falk, 1938). The elevation of muscle mass with puberty in boys is well known. In boys with delayed puberty, administration of T is followed by an increased velocity of growth of lean body mass and stature (Gregory et al., 1992). In normal men, large doses of T seem to be required to obtain similar effects, probably due to the inhibition of endogenous T-secretion (Friedl, Hannan, Jones, & Plymate, 1990; Friedl, Dettori, Hannon, & Plymate, 1991). T administration to aging men has also recently been reported to be followed by increases of lean body mass (Tenover, 1992). Large doses of androgens are frequently used by power athletes with the hope of improving performance, but this is followed by a number of unwanted effects (Friedl, 1990; Wade, 1972), including insulin resistance (Cohen & Hickman, 1987; Holmäng & Björntorp, 1992). The effects of androgen administration on muscle seem to include protein synthesis in muscle (Alen, Hakkinen, & Komi, 1994; Hervey et al., 1981), but the precise mechanism is not known. This area has been reviewed previously (Forbes, 1987).

The effects of T on total adipose tissue mass are apparently not very marked in normal adults (Friedl et al., 1990, 1991) or in aging men (Tenover, 1992). Adipose tissue distribution is, however, probably regulated by T. T-deficiency has been suggested to be associated with centralization of body fat mass (Björntorp, 1993a). This might be the explanation for the well known tendency of aging men with decreased T-secretion to develop central fat accumulation. Furthermore, middle-aged men tend to store excess body fat in visceral depots, parallel to a decrease in circulating T concentrations (Haffner, Waldez, Stern, & Katz, 1993;

Khaw, Chir, & Barrett-Connor, 1992; Seidell et al., 1990; Simon et al., 1992). The accumulation of visceral fat can, at least partly, be reversed by T-treatment (Mårin et al., 1993a).

The cellular effects of T on adipocytes have been surprisingly little studied. Recent work has, however, provided a basis for the understanding of some of these effects. Starting with lipid accumulation, the activity of LPL and other enzymes of importance for triglyceride synthesis are apparently inhibited (Xu & Björntorp, 1994). Furthermore, the cortisol-induced stimulation of LPL is prevented by T (Ottosson & Björntorp, 1994). Also, LPL activity in vivo is clearly inhibited in abdominal but not in femoral adipose tissue in men after T-administration (Mårin, Gustafsson, Odén, & Björntorp, 1995a; Rebuffé-Scrive, 1991). Furthermore, triglyceride uptake, measured in serial biopsies of adipose tissue in men after oral administration of labeled triglycerides, is clearly inhibited by T-administration, this effect again being more pronounced in abdominal than femoral adipose tissue (Mårin et al., 1994).

Available evidence is thus consistent. Both in the total integrated system, with physiological, oral administration of triglyceride, and in measurements of LPL activity in adipose tissue, as well as in fully controlled studies at the cellular level, T inhibits lipid uptake and LPL activity. The precise cellular mechanisms have not yet been studied. It is thus not known, for example, if the T effects are mainly expressed as opposing those of glucocorticoids, described earlier.

An additional feature of these observations is the consistent findings of differences in the expression of effects in different adipose tissue regions. The expression is mainly confined to the abdominal subcutaneous adipose tissue. Recent studies have shown that the inhibitory effect of T on lipid uptake, measured in the integrated system with the method of oral labeled triglyceride, is clearly more pronounced in the visceral than subcutaneous depots (Mårin et al., 1995b). This observation is consistent with the findings of an apparently specific decrease of visceral fat mass, measured with computerized tomography (CT), after T-treatment (Mårin et al., 1993a).

The lipolytic machinery is also regulated by T, and these effects are clearly dependent on GH in a synergistic manner. In adipocytes from castrated male rats, or in recently differentiated adipocytes under fully controlled conditions in tissue culture, T enhances the lipolytic cascade at several levels, including the density of beta-adrenergic receptors, as well as the activities of the adenylate cyclase

and protein kinase A and/or the hormone-sensitive lipase (Pecquery, Leneveau, & Guidicelli, 1988; Xu, De Pergola, & Björntorp, 1990a). The entire lipolytic chain, with the exception of the G-proteins, thus seems to be involved. These findings can be reproduced in hypophysectomized rats given replacement therapy with glucocorticoids and thyroxin. In this model, essentially the same effects of T are seen, but they are critically dependent upon the presence of GH. In fact, testosterone alone has only minor or no effects at the mentioned levels of the lipolytic cascade (Yang, Björntorp, Edén, 1995).

The congruence with the results of cortisol without or with GH, as reviewed above, is quite striking. It is thus apparent that, in addition to cortisol, T also exerts a "permissive" role on the acute regulation by catecholamines of lipolysis and that these effects are dependent on GH. Whether the cellular and molecular mechanisms of both the steroid hormones are similar is not yet known.

These observations at the cellular and molecular level are in line with results obtained in the intact organism. In men, T-substitution is followed by a shorter half-life of labeled triglyceride in adipose tissue, again with specific effects on abdominal rather than femoral subcutaneous adipose tissue (Mårin et al., 1994). Such measurements require serial adipose tissue biopsies and therefore cannot be performed in visceral adipose tissue in men. However, CT scan measurements after T-substitution suggest specific effects of T on visceral fat mass, compatible with effects of T on either the lipid accumulation (inhibitory) or lipid mobilization (stimulatory) systems or on both.

The androgen effects on adipose tissue are most likely mediated via a specific androgen receptor (AR), which is present in human adipose tissue (Miller, Kral, Strain, & Zumoff, 1989) as well as in rat adipocytes (Xu, De Pergola, & Björntorp, 1991). The AR has the interesting characteristic that its density is apparently up-regulated by androgens (De Pergola et al., 1990b). In this way T might amplify its own effects by increasing the density of AR.

Direct information is not currently available on the density of the AR in different adipose tissue regions. However, indirect evidence suggests that the density may be higher in visceral adipose tissue than in nonvisceral adipose tissue because beta-adrenergic sensitivity, an effect regulated by androgens through the AR, is higher in men than women and higher in young than older men, in parallel with the expected T concentrations in these conditions (Rebuffé-Scrive, Andersson, Olbe, &

Björntorp, 1989). The rat AR density is apparently higher in intraabdominal than subcutaneous adipose tissue, measured as nuclear binding (Sjögren, Li, & Björntorp, 1995). Direct measurements in human adipose tissue are, however, required to resolve this important issue, because the more marked effects on visceral than other adipose tissue masses might be explained by differences in AR density. As discussed above with respect to cortisol, the marked effect of androgens on visceral fat depots may also be due to the higher cellular density of these depots or to effects via innervation and/or blood flow.

Androgens are also produced by women, albeit in much smaller amounts. The studies of effects of androgens on adipose tissue have, for natural reasons, so far been concentrated on adipocytes from males. In females, the effects of T on adipose tissue might be weaker, due to the lower concentrations of T, or be different, as suggested by T effects on adipose tissue metabolism in oophorectomized female rats (De Pergola et al., 1990a). Furthermore, estrogens seem to down regulate AR density in adipose tissue of female rats, and thus perhaps may be protective against androgen effects (Li & Björntorp, 1995). This is an important issue for further research because of the distribution of depot fat to central visceral adipose tissue in hyperandrogenic conditions in women, including the polycystic ovarian syndrome (Rebuffé-Scrive et al., 1989), visceral obesity (Vague et al., 1985), and non-insulin-dependent diabetes mellitus (Andersson et al., 1994). Very recent studies have now also been reported where T-administration to transsexual women is followed by visceral fat accumulation (Elbers et al., 1995).

Growth Hormone

Pituitary growth hormone (GH) is obviously a major regulator of body composition. Recent data also suggest that this hormone may be important in the regulation of adipose tissue distribution. GH has marked effects on tissue growth, on protein, carbohydrate, lipid, mineral, and on water metabolism.

Effects on Body Composition

In man, the growth promoting effects of GH were first revealed when the species specificity of the hormone was clarified in the early 1960s (Raben, 1962). In summary, GH excess, as in acromegaly or in transgenic animals, results in an increased body cell mass, reflecting increases in muscle mass and in visceral organs other than the spleen and brain (Ebert et al., 1988; Wieghart et al., 1988). It also results in increases in extracellular water volume and in a marked decrease in body fat (Bengtsson, Brummer, Edén, & Brosaeus, 1989). GH deficiency in children (Parra et al., 1979; Tanner & Whitehouse, 1967) and in adults (Rosén et al., 1993) is associated with increased body fat, which is reversed by GH treatment (Bengtsson et al., 1993; Jørgensen et al., 1989a; Parra et al., 1979; Salomon, Cuneo, Hesp, & Sönksen, 1989; Tanner & Whitehouse, 1967). Interestingly, the effect of GH seems to be more pronounced in visceral than in peripheral fat depots both in children (Collipp et al., 1973; Parra et al., 1979; Rosenbaum, Gertner, & Leibel, 1989) and adults (Bengtsson et al., 1993).

Effects on Cell Differentiation

GH affects adipose tissue growth and metabolism in different ways. An important observation was that GH seems to promote the conversion of preadipocytes to fully differentiated adipocytes, at least in clonal preadipocyte cell lines (Hauner, 1992; Morikawa, Nixon, & Green, 1982). This observation was the basis for the "dual effector theory of GH action" proposed by Green, Morikawa, and Nixon (1985) and Isaksson, Lindahl, Nilsson, and Isgaard (1987). According to this hypothesis, GH stimulates stem cells (prechondrocytes, preadipocytes) to differentiate. During this process, IGF-I is expressed and produced, which contributes to clonal expansion, growth, and terminal differentiation. In line with this hypothesis, it has been reported that children with GH deficiency have fewer adipocytes than normal children and that GH treatment increases the number of adipocytes. The changes in body fat observed in GH-deficient children are, therefore, due to increases in fat cell size, and GH reduces body fat mainly by reducing fat cell size (Bonnet, Vanderscheuren-Lodeweyckx, Beckel, & Malvaux, 1974). However, it is unclear if this growth promoting effect of GH on preadipocytes is important in human beings after puberty, since effects of GH on preadipocyte conversion to adipocytes have not been observed (Hauner, 1992), indicating that these cells may be already "committed" in adult life.

Effects on Adipose Tissue Metabolism

The long-term effects of GH on adipose tissue metabolism are undoubtedly a stimulation of lipolysis and inhibition of lipogenesis, reflected in the marked changes in body composition with GH excess or deficiency. There is, however, still some controversy as to whether GH alone has any direct lipolytic effects on adipose tissue. GH receptors are found in both rat and human adipocytes (DiGirolamo et al., 1986; Fagin, Lackey, Reagan, DiGirolamo, 1980), and GH receptor mRNA is expressed in adipose tissue (Vikman, Carlsson, Billig, & Edén, 1991a). In long-term culture, GH has an inhibitory effect on lipogenesis and a moderate lipolytic effect on both the 3T3 adipocyte cell line (Schwartz, Foster, & Satin, 1985) and human adipose tissue (Ottosson, Lönnroth, Björntorp, & Edén, 1995), indicating that indeed GH exerts its effect directly on the adipocyte. It has been proposed that this effect is partly due to inhibition of glucose transport via a decrease in glucose carriers (Silverman et al., 1989), in line with the findings that GH must exert its insulin antagonistic effect distal to the insulin receptor (Dietz & Schwartz, 1991).

The mechanism by which GH induces its metabolic effects is still unclear. Recent studies in the 3T3 adipocyte cell line have partly clarified the way GH interacts with its receptor, resulting in dimerization of the receptor and tyrosine phosphorylation of several intracellular proteins, including the receptor itself. This process, which shares many aspects of receptor activation with other members of this cytokine receptor family, seems to involve a specific tyrosine phosphoralase named JAK 2, which has been reviewed recently by Stahl and Yancopoulos (1993). It remains to be established if these processes are involved in the metabolic effects of GH on adipose tissue.

Certainly, other signaling mechanisms may be involved. GH has previously been shown to interfere with the cAMP system and has been shown to further elevate cAMP levels stimulated by theophylline, epinephrine, and glucagon (Davidsson, 1987). Consistent effects of GH on basal cAMP levels have not been observed (Davidsson), but incubation of the rat diaphragm for a prolonged period of time has been shown to increase the release of cAMP into the medium (Kostyo, Gimpel, & Isaksson, 1975), indicating that GH increases a free pool of cAMP in the cells. Other indications of interactions between the adenylate cyclase system and GH are in the regulation of hepatic mRNA for IGF-I. In cultured primary rat hepatocytes, GH induces IGF-I mRNA. The cAMP analogues, forskolin, and glucagon were also able to induce this mRNA and were additive to the effect of GH (Tollet, Legraverend, Gustafsson, & Mode, 1991). It has been proposed that this effect of GH and the cAMP

system may involve effects on the cytoskeleton resulting in changes in the cellular distribution of G-proteins, which results in a relative decrease in the tonic inhibitory influence of Gi on adenylyl cyclase (Yip & Goodman, 1993). Such a mechanism is in line with the effect of GH on lipolysis.

Interactions With Other Hormones

The hypophysectomized rat model has been used extensively to elucidate the role of the pituitary and pituitary-dependent hormones in the regulation of lipolysis. It was established early that hypophysectomy resulted in impaired fat mobilization in response to fasting and catecholamines (Goodman & Schwartz, 1974). It was also established that glucocorticoids, thyroid hormones, and GH were all important for the ability of adipose tissue to respond to lipolytic stimuli (Goodman & Schwartz). Several previous studies have shown that GH can modify the lipolytic effects of other hormones. Most consistently, GH has been shown to enhance the lipolytic effect of adrenaline in animal models (Vernon & Flint, 1989). Similarly, GH treatment of GH-deficient adults for six months resulted in an increased lipolytic response to adrenaline and isoproterenol, whereas changes in the response to a selective alpha-2-receptor agonist were not found, indicating that GH acted by increasing the efficiency of the beta-adrenergic pathway (Beauville et al., 1992). In line with these studies, it has previously been shown that there is an increase in the number of β-adrenergic receptors in adipocytes cultured in the presence of GH (Vernon & Flint). Thus, the effect of GH on lipolysis may be due to increased responsiveness to stimulation of lipolysis by other hormones. This may explain why there does not seem to be an increase in the basal lipolytic activity in adipocytes obtained after GH treatment of normal or GH-deficient individuals (Gertner, 1992). Obviously, GH has effects on β-adrenergic receptors, which seems to be of great relevance to the physiological effects of the hormone, including the lipokinetic effect and the stimulation of lipid oxidation. In this context, it is important to point out that GH also seems to interfere with thyroid hormone homeostasis and stimulates the conversion of T4 and T3 in the periphery (Grunfeld, Sherman, & Cavalieri, 1988; Jørgensen et al., 1989b).

The metabolic effects of GH are also dependent on insulin and glucocorticoids (Vernon & Flint, 1989). GH has no growth promoting effect in the absence of insulin (Cheek & Hill, 1974), and the metabolic effects of GH in adipose tissue also seem to be dependent on the presence of insulin. In fact, insulin increases GH binding to adipocytes (Gause & Edén, 1985), which may be important for the ability of GH to interact with target tissues, apart from the obvious importance of insulin in maintaining the intracellular metabolic machinery intact. Moreover, GH seems to directly stimulate insulin secretion from the pancreatic B-cells (Nielsen, 1982), complicating the hormonal interactions even further. As discussed above, glucocorticoids seem to enhance the effects of both insulin and GH on adipose tissue metabolism.

The role of the gonadal steroids in this regulation has been studied much less extensively. In preliminary experiments, in which thyroid hormone and glucocorticoids were given in replacement doses to hypophysectomized rats previously shown to be "physiological" (Jansson et al., 1982), we have demonstrated an additive or synergistic effect of T and GH on the regulation of lipolysis. In fact, when GH and T were given together, the lipolytic responsiveness of the adipocytes was fully restored, an effect that, at least in part, seemed to be explained by an additive effect of the two hormones on β-adrenergic receptors (Yang, Björntorp, & Edén, 1995). As mentioned previously, it seems as if the effects of T on adipose tissue are dependent upon the presence of GH. Indeed, some of the effects of GH may also be dependent of androgens. For example, we found, in a follow-up study of treated acromegalic patients that body cell mass was less than expected in male patients with gonadal insufficiency despite persisting high levels of GH (Bengtsson et al., 1989).

Insulin-like growth factor-I is an important mediator of many of the effects of GH. This growth factor is supposed to act as an autocrine or paracrine factor to promote tissue growth and also as an endocrine factor. It is of importance for the growth-promoting effects of GH, as discussed in detail by Isaksson et al. (1987). IGF-I is expressed and synthesized in many tissues in response to GH, including cartilage, liver, muscle (Isaksson et al., 1987), and adipose tissue (Vikman, Isgaard, & Edén, 1991b). However, the effects of GH on lipid metabolism do not seem to be mediated via IGF-I (Goodman, Schwartz, Tai, & Gorin, 1990). In preliminary studies, we have also found that IGF-I and GH have quite different effects on lipoprotein metabolism in the rat (Sjöberg, Oscarsson, Olofsson, & Edén, 1994).

Regulation of Growth Hormone Secretion

GH is secreted in a pulsatile fashion in all species so far studied (Edén, 1978; Jansson, Edén, & Isaksson,

1985). The physiological importance of this pulsatile secretion of GH has been studied mainly in experimental animals, in which the secretory pattern has been shown to be of importance for growth, but also in the regulation of hepatic steroid metabolism, plasma proteins, and lipoproteins (Edén, 1978; Jansson et al., 1985; Oscarsson, Olofsson, Bondjers, & Edén, 1989; Oscarsson, Olofsson, Vikman, & Edén, 1991). In man, GH secretion is dependent upon age and gonadal function (Iranmanesh, Lizarralde, & Veldhuis, 1991). Changes in GH secretion are also observed in physiological and pathophysiological states such as fasting, uncontrolled diabetes, hypothyroidism, and Cushing's syndrome (Asplin et al., 1989; Hartman et al., 1992; Jørgensen et al., 1989b; Wiedemann, 1981). Apart from the effects of GH on growth, the physiological importance of differences in the secretory pattern of GH in man has only been studied in GH-deficient patients in short-term studies lasting 1 to 4 days (Jørgensen, Möller, Lauritzen, & Christiansen, 1990; Tamborlane, Genel, Gianfredi, & Gertner, 1984).

Sex differences in the secretory pattern of GH in the rat may be of importance for the regulation of sex differences in lipid metabolism in this species (Oscarsson et al., 1989, 1991). It has been demonstrated that the higher concentrations of serum high density lipoprotein (HDL) cholesterol and apolipoprotein E in female rats may be ascribed to the more continuous secretion of GH in the female rat. The effect of the female-type secretory pattern of GH seems to be exerted at several different levels. Thus, a continuous administration of GH results in marked increases in hepatic triglyceride secretion (Elam, Solomon, Wilcox, & Heimberg, 1992). Whether such effects of changes in the secretory pattern of GH have any relevance for the metabolic effects of GH in humans remains to be established.

Thus there is the possibility that many of the effects of hormones, such as thyroid hormones and sex steroids, on metabolism and body composition are mediated in part via the effects of these hormones on the hypothalamus and pituitary (e.g., GH secretion). Another important observation is the consistent decrease in GH secretion in obesity (Iranmanesh et al., 1991). Since GH secretion is restored in obese subjects who lose weight (Kelijman & Frohman, 1988), the impaired GH secretion in obesity seems to be secondary rather than primary. However, this observation indicates that GH secretion is also under important metabolic regulation. The impaired GH secretion is more pronounced in visceral than peripheral obesity (Mårin et al., 1993b), suggesting that additional factors contribute in this subgroup of obesity. The relationship between a decrease in GH secretion and changes in body composition with aging is in agreement with this concept. Since this subject has been recently reviewed (Corpas, Harman, & Blackman, 1993), it will not be discussed further here.

Female Sex Steroid Hormones

Female sex steroid hormone concentrations also regulate adipose tissue mass, although it is not clear whether these effects are direct or mediated via energy intake and/or expenditure (Wade & Gray, 1979). It is clear that these hormones affect body fat distribution in women. With menopause, visceral fat mass increases, but this is preventable by hormonal replacement therapy (Haarbo, Marskew, Gottfredsen, & Christiansen, 1991). Furthermore, the specific female enlargement of femoral subcutaneous adipocytes disappears with menopause. This enlargement is paralleled by an elevated LPL activity and a low sensitivity to lipolytic agents, which might be responsible for the adipocyte enlargement in this depot. This metabolic pattern is reversed during late pregnancy and lactation, suggesting that this depot might be reserved for these conditions and the survival of the fetus and newborn child (Rebuffé-Scrive et al., 1985a). The typical functional characteristics suggest lipid retention decreases with menopause but can be restored, at least partially, by hormonal replacement therapy in postmenopausal women (Rebuffé-Scrive, Eldh, Hafström, & Björntorp, 1986).

Thus, there is a considerable body of evidence suggesting that female sex steroid hormones exert important effects on adipose tissue distribution. The observation that normal premenopausal women have less visceral fat mass than men supports this view (Kvist et al., 1988). The mechanisms in women are, however, unclear. In contrast to female rats (Wade & Gray, 1979), adipose tissue from women does not seem to contain estrogen or progesterone receptors. This conclusion is based on studies utilizing various ligand binding assays, protein determinations with antibodies, or mRNA measurements with solution hybridization assays or PCR (Brönnegård et al., 1993; Rebuffé-Scrive et al., 1990). Progesterone competes with the GR (Rebuffé-Scrive et al., 1985b; Xu, Hoebeke, & Björntorp, 1990b) and may protect from glucocorticoid effects during the late luteal phase of the menstrual cycle and particularly during pregnancy. It seems likely, however, that the effects of female sex steroid hormones on adipose tissue metabolism might be mediated via indirect mechanisms. As mentioned previously, the GH secretion pattern is dependent on estrogen. GH exposure mimicking male or female secretion patterns influences LPL activity differently at the level of the transcription of the LPL gene (Vikman et al., 1994). Such effects seem to be less dependent on concomitant direct cellular effects of the female sex steroid hormones than of the androgens, because they are found without sex steroid replacement in hypophysectomized female rats (Vikman et al., 1994), while androgen replacement is required for full T effects (Yang, Björtorp, & Edén, 1995). Further studies are clearly needed to explore this important area.

Combination of Effects

As mentioned earlier, there are clearly interactions between the effects of the steroid and the peptide hormones, insulin and GH, as well as the catecholamines. In addition, there are most likely interactions between the corticosteroid and sex steroid hormones. Normally, cortisol is always present and is necessary for survival. The sex steroid hormones, however, vary in concentration with age, menopausal status, and within the menstrual cycle of women. The sex steroid hormone effects would therefore be expected to modify the basal effects of the corticosteroids. Very little is known about such interactions, but the homology of the promotor areas of several genes where the steroid hormone-receptor complex interacts (Carson-Jurica, Schrader, & O'Malley, 1990) suggests possibilities for interactions. Furthermore, the homology of the receptor family, not least the DNA-binding domain, also suggests gene interactions for expression of effects.

From a physiological aspect, it is interesting to compare the mechanisms of action of, particularly, cortisol and T and the interaction of insulin and GH on adipose tissue. As reviewed earlier, the net effect of cortisol in combination with insulin seems to be lipid accumulation both by induction of LPL activity and by inhibition of lipolysis. It is clear that this is efficiently reversed by GH. T, however, decreases lipid accumulation by inhibition of LPL and stimulation of lipid mobilization, this effect again being critically dependent on GH. Taken together, these observations seem to indicate that cortisol and insulin are mainly promoting lipid accumulation and retention of triglycerides in the adipocytes, while T and GH oppose this effect. The dual interaction by GH in these processes is particularly interesting, but the mechanism is largely unknown.

It should be observed that these effects seem to be particularly pronounced in the visceral fat depot, as observed mainly in clinical cross-sectional and intervention studies. The mechanisms for these regionally specific effects are only partially known, as reviewed earlier.

It is interesting to compare the experimental results just summarized above with body fat distribution in clinical situations characterized by changes in the secretion of these hormones. In Cushing's syndrome cortisol and insulin concentrations are elevated while T and GH secretions are blunted. This might explain the dramatic accumulation of visceral fat, with cortisol and insulin shifting the balance towards visceral fat accumulation with little counteraction of T and GH. Aging and menopause are associated with essentially normal cortisol and insulin values, but decreases occur for T and GH in men and for estrogens and GH in women. This would make the hormonal balance tip towards visceral fat accumulation because of the relative lack of the presumed counterbalancing effects of the sex steroids in combination with GH. In GH deficiency in human beings after hypophysectomy, with normal concentrations of cortisol and sex steroid hormones after substitution, the balance will again be towards visceral fat accumulation due to the lack of GH effects. These are reversed by GH substitution, and exaggerated in acromegaly. Finally, in visceral obesity, characterized by an elevated cortisol secretion, hyperinsulinemia, and diminished secretion of sex steroid hormones and GH, a marked accumulation of visceral fat mass would be expected and is indeed observed. Taken together, observations in clinically well defined endocrinological disturbances of cortisol, insulin, sex steroid hormones, and GH strongly suggest that the balance between cortisol and insulin on the one hand and sex steroid hormones and GH on the other are important factors in the regulation of body fat distribution, particularly visceral fat accumulation.

Recently the importance of visceral fat accumulation in relation to the prevalence of selected diseases has evoked considerable interest (Björntorp, 1993b). This condition is associated with abnormalities in the secretion of those hormones that, as discussed in this review, are expected to cause visceral fat accumulation (elevated cortisol and insulin as well as low sex steroid hormones and GH). Visceral fat accumulation in this syndrome may thus be an index of the underlying endocrine dysbalance. This disturbance may, in turn, exert direct effects on muscular regulation of insulin sensitivity and may also influence hepatic metabolism via portal FFA, leading to a Metabolic Syndrome, which is a precursor state to non-insulin-dependent diabetes mellitus, cardiovascular disease, and stroke (Björntorp, 1990). Further exploration of this syndrome, including the consequences of its endocrine abnormalities on body composition and metabolic regulations, is an area of considerable importance.

Summary and Conclusions

In this review, the effects of physiological steroid hormones alone and in combination with insulin and GH on the mass and function of muscle and adipose tissue masses and distribution have been reviewed, with an emphasis on recently obtained information. T, insulin, and GH have anabolic effects on muscle mass, while cortisol exerts opposite activities. Cortisol, in combination with insulin, seems to have positive effects on the balance of adipose tissue triglyceride accumulation and retention, mediated via stimulatory effects on the lipid uptake system and via inhibitory effects on lipid mobilization. These consequences are reversed by GH. Female sex steroid hormones and T probably have negative effects, amplified by GH, on adipose tissue triglyceride accumulation and retention. The mechanisms have been partially elucidated by observations at the clinical, interventional, cellular, and molecular levels in studies in man and experimental animals and are probably most pronounced in visceral adipose tissue. The reasons for this local preponderance of effects are not clear, but a high density of adipocytes and their specific steroid hormone receptors, in combination with blood flow and innervation, may well be responsible.

The importance of this area of research is emphasized by observations of associations between the prevalence of some diseases and visceral fat accumulation. This redistribution of body fat stores might be a consequence of multiple endocrine abnormalities, perhaps leading directly, or via visceral fat accumulation, to the generation of metabolic risk factors and triggers for non-insulin-dependent diabetes mellitus, cardiovascular disease, and stroke.

References

Alen, M., Hakkinen, A., & Komi, P. (1994). Changes in neuromuscular performance and muscle fiber characteristics of elite power athletes self-administering androgen and anabolic steroids. *Acta Physiologica Scandinavica*, **122**, 535-544.

Andersson, B., Mårin, P., Lissner, L., et al. (in press). Testosterone concentrations in women and men with non-insulin dependent diabetes mellitus. *Diabetes Care*.

Appel, B., & Fried, S. (1992). Effects of insulin and dexamethasone on lipoprotein lipase in human adipose tissue. *American Journal of Physiology*, **262**, E695-E699.

Asplin, C., Faria, A., Carlsen, E., et al. (1989). Alterations in the pulsatile mode of growth hormone release in men and women with insulin-dependent diabetes mellitus. *Journal of Clinical Endocrinology and Metabolism*, **69**, 239-245.

Baxter, J.D., & Rosseau, G.G. (1979). Glucocorticoid hormone action. *Endocrinology*, **12**, 1-26.

Beauville, M., Harant, I., Crampes, F., et al. (1992). Effect of long-term rhGH administration in GH-deficient adults on fat cell epinephrine response. *American Journal of Physiology*, **263**, E467-E472.

Bengtsson, B.-Å., Brummer, R., Edén, S., & Bosaeus, I. (1989). Body composition in acromegaly. *Clinical Endocrinology*, **30**, 121-130.

Bengtsson, B.-Å., Edén, S., Lönn, L., et al. (1993). Treatment of adults with growth hormone deficiency with recombinant human growth hormone. *Journal of Clinical Endocrinology and Metabolism*, **76**, 309-317.

Björntorp, P. (1990). "Portal" adipose tissue as a generator of risk factors for cardiovascular disease and diabetes. *Arteriosclerosis*, **10**, 493-496.

Björntorp, P. (1993a). Androgens, the Metabolic Syndrome and non-insulin dependent diabetes mellitus. *Annals of the New York Academy of Science*, **676**, 242-252.

Björntorp, P. (1993b). Visceral obesity: A "Civilization Syndrome." *Obesity Research*, **1**, 206-222.

Björntorp, P., & Östman, J. (1971). Human adipose tissue: Dynamics and regulation. *Advances in Metabolic Disorders*, **5**, 277-327.

Björntorp, P., & Smith, U. (1976). The effect of fat cell size on subcutaneous adipose tissue metabolism. *Frontiers of Matrix Biology*, **2**, 37-47.

Bonnet, F., Vanderscheuren-Lodeweyckx, M., Beckel, R., & Malvaux, P. (1974). Subcutaneous adipose tissue and lipids in blood in growth hormone deficiency before and after treatment with human growth hormone. *Pediatric Research*, **8**, 800-805.

Brönnegård, M., Ottosson, M., Böös, J., Marcus, C., & Björntorp, P. (1994). Lack of evidence for estrogen and progesterone receptors in human adipose tissue. *Journal of Steroid Biochemistry and Molecular Biology*, **51**, 275-281.

Bruce, A., Andersson, M., Arvidsson, B., & Isaksson, B. (1980). Body composition. Prediction of normal body potassium, body water and body fat in adults on the basis of body height, body weight and age. *Scandinavian Journal of Clinical & Laboratory Investigation*, **40**, 461-473.

Carson-Jurica, M., Schrader, T., & O'Malley, B. (1990). Steroid receptor family: Structure and functions. *Endocrine Reviews*, **11**, 201-220.

Carter-Su, C., & Okamoto, K. (1987). Effect of insulin and glucocorticoids on glucose transporters in rat adipocytes. *American Journal of Physiology*, **252**, E441-E453.

Cheek, D., & Hill, D. (1974). Effect of growth hormone on cell and somatic growth. In R. Greep & E. Astwood (Eds.), *Handbook of Physiology* (pp. 159-185). Washington, DC: American Physiological Society.

Chrousos, G., & Gold, P. (1992). The concept of stress and stress system disorders. *Journal of the American Medical Association*, **267**, 1244-1252.

Cigolini, M., & Smith, U. (1979). Human adipose tissue in culture, VIII: Studies on the insulin-antagonistic effect of glucocorticoids. *Metabolism*, **28**, 502-510.

Cohen, J.C., & Hickman, R. (1987). Insulin resistance and diminished glucose tolerance in power lifters ingesting anabolic steroids. *Journal of Clinical Endocrinology and Metabolism*, **64**, 960-963.

Collipp, P., Curti, V., Thomas, J., et al. (1973). Body composition changes in children receiving human growth hormone. *Metabolism*, **22**, 589-595.

Corpas, E., Harman, S., & Blackman, M. (1993). Human growth hormone and human aging. *Endocrine Reviews*, **14**, 20-39.

Davidsson, M. (1987). Effect of growth hormone on carbohydrate and lipid metabolism. *Endocrine Reviews*, **8**, 115-131.

De Gasquet, P., Pequignot-Planche, E., Tomm, N., & Diaby, F. (1975). Effect of glucocorticoids on lipoprotein lipase activity in rat heart and adipose tissue. *Hormone and Metabolic Research*, **7**, 152-157.

De Pergola, G., Holmäng, A., Svedberg, J., et al. (1990a). Testosterone treatment of ovariectomized rats: Effects on lipolysis regulation in adipocytes. *Acta Endocrinologica (Copenh)*, **123**, 61-66.

De Pergola, G., Xu, X., Yang, S., et al. (1990b). Up-regulation of androgen receptor binding in male rat fat pad adipose precursor cells exposed to testosterone: Study in a whole cell assay system. *Journal of Steroid Biochemistry and Molecular Biology, 4,* 553-558.

Dietz, J., & Schwartz, J. (1991). Growth hormone alters lipolysis and hormone sensitive lipase activity in 3T3-F442A adipocytes. *Metabolism, 40,* 800-806.

DiGirolamo, M., Edén, S., Enberg, G., et al. (1986). Specific binding of human growth hormone but not insulin-like growth factors by human adipocytes. *Febs Letters: Federation of European Biochemical Societies, 205,* 15-19.

Divertie, G., Jensen, M., & Miles, J. (1991). Stimulation of lipolysis in humans by physiological hypercortisolemia. *Diabetes, 40,* 1228-1232.

Ebert, K., Low, M., Overstrom, E., et al. (1988). A moloney MLV-rat somatotropin fusion gene produces biologically active somatotropin in a transgenic pig. *Molecular Endocrinology, 2,* 277-283.

Edén, S. (1978). The secretory pattern of growth hormone. *Acta Physiologica Scandinavica, 458* (Suppl. 1), 1-54.

Elam, M.B., Solomon, S.S., Wilcox, H.G., & Heimberg, M. (1992). In vivo growth hormone treatment stimulates secretion of very low density lipoproteins by the perfused rat liver. *Endocrinology, 131,* 2717-2722.

Elbers, J.M.H., Asscheman, H., Seidell, J.C., & Gooren, L.J.G. (1995). Increased accumulation of visceral fat after long-term androgen administration in women. *International Journal of Obesity, 19* (Suppl. 2), 25 (Abstract).

Fagin, K., Lackey, S., Reagan, C., & DiGirolamo, M. (1980). Specific binding of growth hormone by rat adipocytes. *Endocrinology, 107,* 608-615.

Fain, J.N., Kovacev, V.P., & Scow, R.O. (1965). Effect of growth hormone and dexamethason on lipolysis and metabolism in isolated fat cells of the rat. *Journal of Biological Chemistry, 240,* 3522-3529.

Faust, I.M. (1986). Adipose tissue growth and obesity. In F. Falkner & J.M. Tanner (Eds.), *Human growth* (pp. 61-75). New York: Plenum.

Feldman, D., & Loose, G. (1977). Glucocorticoid receptors in adipose tissue. *Endocrinology, 100,* 389-405.

Forbes, G. (1987). *Human body composition.* New York: Springer-Verlag.

Friedl, K. (1990). Reappraisal of the health risks associated with the use of high doses of oral and injectable androgenic steroids. In G. Lin & L. Erinoff (Eds.), *Anabolic steroid abuse* (pp. 142-177). Washington, DC: Department of Health and Human Services.

Friedl, K., Dettori, J., Hannan, C., Jr., & Plymate, S. (1991). Comparison of the effects of high dose testosterone and 19-nortestosterone to a replacement dose of testosterone on strength and body composition in normal men. *Journal of Steroid Biochemistry and Molecular Biology, 40,* 607-612.

Friedl, K., Hannan, C., Jones, R., & Plymate, S. (1990). High-density lipoprotein cholesterol is not decreased if an aromatizable androgen is administered. *Metabolism, 39,* 69-74.

Gause, I., & Edén, S. (1985). Hormonal regulation of growth hormone binding and responsiveness in adipose tissue and adipocytes of hypophysectomized rats. *Journal of Endocrinology, 105,* 331-337.

Gertner, J. (1992). Growth hormone actions on fat distribution and metabolism. *Hormone Research, 38* (Suppl. 2), 41-43.

Goodman, H., & Schwartz, J. (1974). Growth hormone and lipid metabolism. In E. Knobil & W. Sawyer (Eds.), *Handbook of physiology,* IV, part 2 (pp. 211-232). Washington, DC: American Physiological Society.

Goodman, H., Schwartz, Y., Tai, L., & Gorin, E. (1990). Actions of growth hormone on adipose tissue: Possible involvement of autocrine and paracrine factors. *Acta Paediatrica Scandinavica, 367* (Suppl.), 132-136.

Green, H., Morikawa, M., & Nixon, T. (1985). A dual effector theory of growth hormone action. *Differentiation, 29,* 195-198.

Gregory, J., Greene, S., Thompson, J., et al. (1992). Effects of oral testosterone undecanoate on growth, body composition, strength and energy expenditure of adolescent boys. *Journal of Clinical Endocrinology, 37,* 207-213.

Grunfeld, C., Sherman, B., & Cavalieri, R. (1988). The acute effects of human growth hormone administration on thyroid function in normal men. *Journal of Clinical Endocrinology and Metabolism, 67,* 1111-1114.

Guillaume-Gentil, C., Assimacopoulos-Jeannet, F., & Jeanrenaud, B. (1993). Involvement of non-esterified fatty acid oxidation in glucocorticoid-induced peripheral insulin resistance in vivo in rats. *Diabetologia, 36,* 899-906.

Haarbo, J., Marskew, U., Gottfredsen, A., & Christiansen, C. (1991). Postmenopausal hormone replacement therapy prevents central distribution of body fat after menopause. *Metabolism, 40,* 323-326.

Haffner, S.H., Waldez, R.A., Stern, M.P., & Katz, M.S. (1993). Obesity, body fat distribution and sex hormones in men. *International Journal of Obesity, 17*, 643-650.

Hartman, M., Veldhuis, J., Johnson, M., et al. (1992). Augmented growth hormone (GH) secretory burst frequency and amplitude mediate enhanced GH secretion during a two-day fast in normal men. *Journal of Clinical Endocrinology and Metabolism, 74*, 757-765.

Hauner, H. (1992). Physiology of the fat cell, with emphasis on the role of growth hormone. *Acta Paediatrica Scandinavica, 383* (Suppl.), 47-51.

Hervey, G., Knibbs, A., Burkinshaw, L., et al. (1987). Effects of methandienone on the performance and body composition of men undergoing athletic training. *Clinical Science, 60*, 457-461.

Holmäng, A., & Björntorp, P. (1992). The effects of testosterone on insulin sensitivity in male rats. *Acta Physiologica Scandinavica, 146*, 505-510.

Iranmanesh, A., Lizarralde, G., & Veldhuis, J. (1991). Age and relative adiposity are specific negative determinants of the frequency and amplitude of growth hormone (GH) secretory bursts and the half-life of endogenous GH in healthy men. *Journal of Clinical Endocrinology and Metabolism, 73*, 1081-1088.

Isaksson, O.G.P., Lindahl, A., Nilsson, A., Isgaard, J. (1987). The mechanism of the stimulatory effect of growth hormone on longitudinal bone growth. *Endocrine Reviews, 8*, 426-438.

Jansson, J.-O., Albertsson-Wikland, K., Edén, S., et al. (1982). Circumstantial evidence for a role of the secretory pattern of growth hormone in control of body growth. *Acta Endocrinologica* (Cbh), *99*, 24-30.

Jansson, J.O., Edén, S., & Isaksson, O. (1985). Sexual dimorphism in the control of growth hormone secretion. *Endocrine Reviews, 6*, 128-150.

Jørgensen, J., Möller, N., Lauritzen, T., & Christiansen, J. (1990). Pulsatile versus continuous intravenous administration of growth hormone (GH) in GH-deficient patients: Effects on circulating insulin-like growth factor-I and metabolic indices. *Journal of Clinical Endocrinology and Metabolism, 70*, 1616-1623.

Jørgensen, J., Pedersen, S., Laurberg, P., et al. (1989b). Effects of growth hormone therapy on thyroid function of growth hormone-deficient adults with and without concomitant thyroxine-substituted central hypothyroidism. *Journal of Clinical Endocrinology and Metabolism, 69*, 1127-1132.

Jørgensen, J., Thuesen, L., Ingemann-Hansen, T., et al. (1989a). Beneficial effects of growth hormone treatment in GH-deficient adults. *Lancet, 2*, 1221-1225.

Kelijman, M., & Frohman, L. (1988). Enhanced growth hormone (GH) responsiveness to GH-releasing hormone after dietary manipulation in obese and non-obese subjects. *Journal of Clinical Endocrinology and Metabolism, 66*, 489-494.

Khaw, K., Chir, B., & Barrett-Connor, E. (1992). Lower endogenous androgens predict central adiposity in men. *American Journal of Epidemiology, 2*, 675-682.

Knittle, J., Timmers, K., Ginsburg-Fellner, F., et al. (1979). The growth of adipose tissue in children and adolescents: Cross-sectional and longitudinal studies of adipose cell number and size. *Journal of Clinical Investigation, 63*, 929-941.

Kochakian, C., & Endahl, B. (1959). Changes in body weight of normal and castrated rats by different doses of testosterone propionate. *Proceedings of the Society for Experimental Biology and Medicine, 100*, 520-527.

Kostyo, J., Gimpel, L., & Isaksson, O. (1975). In vitro effects of growth hormone on cyclic AMP metabolism in the isolated rat diaphragm. In R. Luft & K. Hall (Eds.), *Advances in metabolic disorders, somatomedins and some other growth factors* (pp. 249-262). New York: Academic.

Krotkiewski, M., Björntorp, P., & Smith, U. (1976a). The effect of long-term dexamethasone treatment on lipoprotein lipase activity in rat fat cells. *Hormone and Metabolic Research, 8*, 245-246.

Krotkiewski, M., Blohmé, B., Lindholm, N., & Björntorp, P. (1976b). The effects of adrenal corticosteroids on regional adipocyte size in man. *Journal of Clinical Endocrinology and Metabolism, 42*, 91-97.

Kvist, H., Chowdhury, B., Grangård, U., et al. (1988). Total and visceral adipose-tissue volumes derived from measurements with computed tomography in adult men and women: Predictive equations. *American Journal of Clinical Nutrition, 48*, 1351-1361.

Li, M., & Björntorp, P. (1995). [Estrogens and AR density in adipose tissue of female rats]. Unpublished raw data.

Malina, R.M. (1986). Growth of muscle tissue and muscle mass. In F. Falkner & J.M. Tanner (Eds.), *Human growth* (pp. 77-99). New York: Plenum.

Mårin, P., Darin, N., Amemiya, T., et al. (1992). Cortisol secretion in relation to body fat distribution in obese premenopausal women. *Metabolism, 41*, 882-886.

Mårin, P., Gustafsson, C., Odén, B., & Björntorp, P. (1995a). Assimilation and mobilization of triglycerides in subcutaneous abdominal and femoral adipose tissue in vivo in men: Effects of androgens. *Journal of Clinical Endocrinology and Metabolism, 80*, 239-243.

Mårin, P., Holmäng, S., Gustafsson, C., et al. (1993a). Androgen treatment of abdominally obese men. *Obesity Research, 1*, 245-251.

Mårin, P., Kvist, H., Lindstedt, G., et al. (1993b). Low concentrations of insulin-like growth factor I in abdominal obesity. *International Journal of Obesity, 17*, 83-89.

Mårin, P., Lönn, L., Andersson, B., Odén, B., Olbe, L., Bengtsson, B.Å., & Björntorp, P. (1995b). *Assimilation of triglycerides in subcutaneous and intraabdominal adipose tissue in vivo in men: Effect of testosterone.* Manuscript submitted for publication.

McDonald, A., & Goldfine, J. (1988). Glucocorticoid regulation of insulin receptor gene transcription in IM-9 cultured lymphocytes. *Journal of Clinical Investigation, 81*, 499-504.

McMahon, M., Gerich, J., & Rizza, J. (1988). Effects of glucocorticoids on carbohydrate metabolism. *Diabetes and Metabolic Reviews, 4*, 17-30.

Miller, L.K., Kral, J.G., Strain, G.W., & Zumoff, B. (1989). *Androgen binding to human adipose tissue.* Paper presented at the 6th Annual Meeting of the North American Association for the Study of Obesity, Bethesda, MD.

Morikawa, M., Nixon, T., & Green, H. (1982). Growth hormone and the adipose conversion of 3T3 cells. *Cell, 29*, 783-789.

Nielsen, J. (1982). Effects of growth hormone, prolactin, and placental lactogen on insulin content and release, and deoxyribonucleic acid synthesis in cultured pancreatic islets. *Endocrinology, 110*, 600-606.

Olsen, D., & Ferin, M. (1987). Corticotropin-releasing hormone inhibits gonadotropin secretion in ovariectomized Rhesus monkey. *Journal of Clinical Endocrinology and Metabolism, 65*, 262-267.

Oscarsson, J., Olofsson, S.O., Bondjers, G., & Edén, S. (1989). Differential effects of continuous versus intermittent administration of growth hormone to hypophysectomized female rats on serum lipoproteins and their apoproteins. *Endocrinology, 125*, 1638-1649.

Oscarsson, J., Olofsson, S.O., Vikman, K., & Edén, S. (1991). Growth hormone regulation of serum lipoproteins in the rat: Different growth hormone regulatory principles for apolipoprotein (apo) B and the sexually dimorphic apo E concentrations. *Metabolism, 40*, 1191-1198.

Ottosson, M., & Björntorp, P. (1994). [Cortisol-induced stimulation of LPL and T]. Unpublished raw data.

Ottosson, M., Lönnroth, P., Björntorp, P., & Edén, S. (1995). *Differential effects of cortisol and growth hormone on lipolysis in human adipose tissue.* Manuscript submitted for publication.

Ottosson, M., Vikman-Adolfsson, K., Enerbäck, S., et al. (1994). The effects of cortisol on the regulation of lipoprotein lipase activity in human adipose tissue. *Journal of Clinical Endocrinology and Metabolism, 79*, 820-825.

Papanicolaou, G., & Falk, E. (1938). General muscular hypertrophy induced by androgenic hormone. *Science, 87*, 238-239.

Parra, A., Argote, R., Garcia, G., et al. (1979). Body composition in hypopituitary dwarfs before and during human growth hormone therapy. *Metabolism, 28*, 851-857.

Pecquery, R., Leneveau, M.C., & Guidicelli, Y. (1988). Influence of androgenic status on the alfa-2/beta-adrenergic control of lipolysis in isolated fat cells, predominant alfa-2-antilipolytic response in testosterone treated castrated hamsters. *Endocrinology, 122*, 2590-2598.

Peeke, P., Oldfield, E., Alexander, R., et al. (1993). Glucocorticoid receptor protein in omental and subcutaneous adipose tissue of patients with Cushing syndrome prior to and after surgical cure. *Obesity Research, 1*, Supp. 2, Abstract No. 49.

Raben, M. (1962). Clinical use of human growth hormone. *New England Journal of Medicine, 266*, 82-86.

Rebuffé-Scrive, M. (1991). Neuroregulation of adipose tissue: Molecular and hormonal mechanisms. *International Journal of Obesity, 15*, 83-86.

Rebuffé-Scrive, M., Andersson, B., Olbe, L., & Björntorp, P. (1989). Metabolism of adipose tissue in intraabdominal depots of non obese men and women. *Metabolism, 38*, 453-458.

Rebuffé-Scrive, M., Brönnegård, M., Nilsson, A., et al. (1990). Steroid hormone receptors in human adipose tissues. *Journal of Clinical Endocrinology and Metabolism, 71*, 1215-1219.

Rebuffé-Scrive, M., Eldh, J., Hafström, L.-O., & Björntorp, P. (1986). Metabolism of mammary, abdominal and femoral adipocytes in women before and after menopause. *Metabolism, 35*, 792-797.

Rebuffé-Scrive, M., Enk, L., Crona, N., et al. (1985a). Fat cell metabolism in different regions in women: Effect of menstrual cycle, pregnancy, and lactation. *Journal of Clinical Investigation, 75*, 1973-1976.

Rebuffé-Scrive, M., Krotkiewski, M., Elfverson, J., & Björntorp, P. (1988). Muscle and adipose tissue morphology and metabolism in Cushings syndrome. *Journal of Clinical Endocrinology and Metabolism,* **67,** 1122-1128.

Rebuffé-Scrive, M., Lundholm, K., & Björntorp, P. (1985b). Glucocorticoid hormone binding to human adipose tissue. *European Journal of Clinical Investigation,* **15,** 267-272.

Rebuffé-Scrive, M., Mårin, P., & Björntorp, P. (1991). Effect of testosterone on abdominal adipose tissue in men. *International Journal of Obesity,* **15,** 791-795.

Rosell, S., & Belfrage, E. (1979). Blood circulation in adipose tissue. *Physiological Reviews,* **59,** 1078-1104.

Rosén, T., Bosaeus, I., Tölli, J., et al. (1993). Increased body fat and decreased extracellular fluid volume in adults with growth hormone deficiency. *Clinical Endocrinology,* **38,** 63-71.

Rosenbaum, M., Gertner, J., & Leibel, R. (1989). Effects of systemic growth hormone (GH) administration on regional adipose tissue distribution and metabolism in growth hormone deficient children. *Journal of Clinical Endocrinology and Metabolism,* **69,** 1274-1281.

Salans, L.B., Cushman, S.W., & Weismann, R.E. (1973). Studies of human adipose tissue: Adipose cell size and number in non-obese and obese patients. *Metabolism,* **52,** 929-941.

Salomon, F., Cuneo, R., Hesp, R., & Sönksen, P. (1989). The effects of treatment with recombinant human growth hormone on body composition and metabolism in adults with growth hormone deficiency. *New England Journal of Medicine,* **321,** 1797-1803.

Schwartz, J., Foster, C., & Satin, M. (1985). Growth hormone and insulin-like growth factors-I and II produce distinct alterations in glucose metabolism in STS-F442A adipocytes. *Proceedings of the National Academy of Science, U.S.A.* **82,** 8724-8728.

Seidell, J.C., Björntorp, P., Sjöström, L., et al. (1990). Visceral fat accumulation in men is positively associated with insulin, glucose and C-peptide levels, but negatively with testosterone levels. *Metabolism,* **39,** 897-901.

Silverman, M., Mynarcik, D., Corin, R., et al. (1989). Antagonism by growth hormone of insulin sensitive hexose transport in 3T3-F442A adipocytes. *Endocrinology,* **125,** 2600-2604.

Simon, D., Preziosi, P., Barrett-Connor, E., et al. (1992). Interrelation between plasma testosterone and plasma insulin in healthy adult men: The Telecom Study. *Diabetologia,* **35,** 173-177.

Sjöberg, A., Oscarrson, J., Olofsson, S-O, & Edén, S. (1994). Insulin-like growth factor-I and growth hormone treatment have different effects on serum lipoproteins and secretion of lipoproteins from cultured rat hepatocytes. *Endocrinology,* **135,** 1415-1421.

Sjögren, J., Li, M., & Björntorp, P. (1995). Androgen hormone binding to adipose tissue in rats. *Biochimica Biophysica Acta,* **1244,** 117-120.

Sjögren, J., Weck, M., Nilsson, A., Ottosson, M., & Björntorp, P. (1994). Glucocorticoid binding to rat adipocytes. *Biochimica et Biophysica Acta,* **1224,** 17-21.

Stahl, N., & Yancopoulos, G. (1993). The alphas, betas and kinases of cytokine receptor complexes. *Cell,* **74,** 587-590.

Steen, B. (1988). Body composition and aging. *Nutrition Reviews,* **46,** 45-51.

Tamborlane, W., Genel, M., Gianfredi, M., & Gertner, J. (1984). The effect of small but sustained elevations in circulating growth hormone on fuel metabolism in growth hormone deficiency. *Pediatric Research,* **18,** 212-215.

Tanner, J.M., & Whitehouse, R.H. (1967). The effect of human growth hormone on subcutaneous fat thickness in hyposomatotrophic and panhypopituitary dwarfs. *Journal of Endocrinology,* **39,** 263-275.

Tenover, J. (1992). Effects of testosterone supplementation in the aging male. *Journal of Clinical Endocrinology and Metabolism,* **75,** 1092-1098.

Tollet, P., Legraverend, C., Gustafsson, J.-A., & Mode, A. (1991). A role for protein kinases in the growth hormone regulation of cytochrome P4502C12 and insulin-like growth factor-1 messenger RNA expression in primary adult rat hepatocytes. *Molecular Endocrinology,* **5,** 1351-1358.

Vague, J., Meignen, J.M., Negrin, J.F., et al. (1985). Le diabète de la femme androide: Trente-cinq ans après [Diabetes in the android woman: Thirty-five years after]. *Semaine des Hopitaux de Paris,* **61,** 1015-1025.

Vernon, R., & Flint, D. (1989). Role of growth hormone in the regulation of adipocyte growth and function. In R. Heap, C. Prosser, & G. Lamming (Eds.), *Biotechnology in growth regulation* (pp. 57-71). London: Butterworths.

Vikman, K., Carlsson, B., Billig, H., & Edén, S. (1991a). Expression and regulation of growth hormone (GH) receptor messenger ribonucleic acid (mRNA) in rat adipose tissue, adipocytes and adipose precursor cells: GH regulation of GH receptor mRNA. *Endocrinology,* **129,** 1155-1161.

Vikman, K., Isgaard, J., & Edén, S. (1991b). Growth hormone regulation of insulin-like growth factor I mRNA in rat adipose tissue and isolated rat adipocytes. *Journal of Endocrinology,* **131,** 139-145.

Vikman, K., Oscarsson, J., Nilsson-Ehle, P., & Edén, S. (1994). Growth hormone but not gonadal steroids influence lipoprotein lipase and hepatic lipase activity in hypophysectomized rats. *Endocrinology*, **140**, 203-209.

Wade, G.N., & Gray, J.M. (1979). Gonadal effects on food intake and adiposity: A metabolic hypothesis. *Physiology and Behavior*, **22**, 583-593.

Wade, N. (1972). Anabolic steroids: Doctors denounce them, but athletes aren't listening. *Science*, **176**, 1399-1403.

West, D.B., Prinz, W.A., & Greenwood, M.R.C. (1989). Regional changes in adipose tissue, blood flow and metabolism in rats after a meal. *American Journal of Physiology*, **257**, R711-R716.

Wiedemann, E. (1981). Adrenal and gonadal steroids. In W.H. Daughaday (Ed.), *Endocrine control of growth* (pp. 67-119). New York: Elsevier Science.

Wieghart, M., Hoover, J., Choe, S., et al. (1988). Genetic engineering of livestock: Transgenic pigs containing a chimeric bovine growth hormone (PEPCK/bGH) gene. *Journal of Animal Science*, **66** (Suppl. 1), 261.

Xu, X. & Björntorp, P. (1994). [Activity of LPL and other enzymes for triglyceride synthesis]. Unpublished raw data.

Xu, X., De Pergola, G., & Björntorp, P. (1990a). The effects of androgens on the regulation of lipolysis in adipose precursor cells. *Endocrinology*, **126**, 1229-1234.

Xu, X., De Pergola, G., & Björntorp, P. (1991). Testosterone increases lipolysis and the number of adrenoceptors in male rat adipocytes. *Endocrinology*, **128**, 379-382.

Xu, X., Hoebeke, J., & Björntorp, P. (1990b). Progestin binds to the glucocorticoid receptor and mediates antiglucocorticoid effect in rat adipose precursor cells. *Journal of Steroid Biochemistry*, **36**, 465-471.

Yang, S., Björntorp, P., & Edén, S. (1995). *Additive effects of growth hormone and testosterone on lipolysis in adipocytes of hypophysectomized rats*. Manuscript submitted for publication.

Yip, R., & Goodman, H. (1993). *Growth hormone (GH) increases lipolysis in rat adipocytes by a mechanism that involves the cytoskeleton*. The Endocrine Society, 75th Annual Meeting, Las Vegas, Abstract No. 1878.

18

Relationships of Total and Regional Body Composition to Morbidity and Mortality

Jacob C. Seidell

The relationships between body composition and the risks of disease and death are complex because they can be modulated by many factors. Such modulating factors may change over time and complicate general statements about the relationships between body composition and diseases. For instance, in a population in which the majority of deaths can be attributed to infectious diseases at a relatively early age and in which relatively high levels of fatness are associated with affluence, the relationship between overweight and mortality may be inverse to that in developed countries. In countries where most people live beyond their fifties, and in which cardiovascular disease is the predominant cause of death and relatively high levels of fatness are associated with low socioeconomic status, the relationship between overweight and mortality will most probably be positive.

In a single society, such very different relationships between disease and body composition may co-exist simultaneously. For instance, even in racially homogeneous populations in Europe, the older cohorts will have been born in the 1930s or earlier when relationships between socioeconomic factors and body composition, as well as disease patterns, were markedly different from those for cohorts born after the 1950s. Such complexities become even more pronounced when there is an inflow of migrants from cultures at different stages of socioeconomic transition and with different genetic predispositions for certain disorders.

In addition, in most studies only simple anthropometric variables, such as stature and weight, are available to study the relationships between body composition and disease. The relationships between such anthropometric variables and body composition may differ depending on racial/ethnic factors and long-term socioeconomic conditions. For instance, in undernourished populations where stunting is common, body proportions (such as the relationship of sitting height to leg length) may differ from those in well nourished populations, and identical body mass indices may have different implications compared to those in nonstunted populations. Furthermore, loss of stature with aging and other aging-related phenomena may affect body composition and the body mass index (BMI: weight in kg/stature in m^2) even when body weight remains constant. Finally, indicators of body composition, such as BMI, do not allow for differences in fat distribution, which may be particularly important in determining the health risks associated with different levels of overweight.

Table 18.1 shows some of the factors that may affect the relationships between body composition and disease. In the remainder of this chapter, primarily findings of studies performed in European or United States (U.S.) populations will be discussed, commonly with the BMI as the sole indicator of body composition. It is clear that conclusions based on these studies may not necessarily apply to other populations and circumstances.

Especially in populations undergoing rapid cultural and lifestyle changes there is some evidence that individuals may be vulnerable to development of high levels of fatness and abdominal fat distribution and its complications. Such examples are manyfold and include Japanese immigrants to the U.S., native Americans, and inhabitants of Polynesia and Micronesia. The cultural changes in countries such as China may be predictive of such physiological changes with huge public health implications.

As mentioned previously, much of the current evidence on the relationships between total and regional body composition and health depends on studies in which the BMI and the abdomen to hip circumference ratio (waist/hip ratio) have been interpreted as indicators of fatness and abdominal fatness. Body mass index is, however, an indicator of total body mass (weight) independent of stature and includes, besides fat mass, contributions of muscle, organs, bone, and body water. The relationships between these latter components and indicators of health have rarely been studied. There are a few exceptions. The relationship between bone mass and osteoporosis is well documented. The relation between fat-free mass and health has primarily been studied with regard to energy deficiency and the prevalence of falls and fractures. As will be discussed in more detail in the section on body composition and mortality, a critical level of fat-free mass is necessary for sustaining life. Levels of the BMI lower than 18.5 kg/m^2 indicate thinness, and further decreases are increasingly likely to reflect chronic deficiency of energy intake.

Relationships of Body Composition to Risk Factors for Disease

Body composition is related to many diseases. Research usually focuses on the relationships between high levels of fatness and diseases, such as cardiovascular disease, type II diabetes mellitus, and specific types of cancer (e.g., colon and breast cancer), of affluent societies.

Body Composition and Cardiovascular Risk Factors

Among all relationships studied between body composition and metabolic risk factors those between BMI and serum lipids and glucose tolerance

---

Table 18.1   Factors That May Affect the Relationships Between Anthropometric Indicators and Risk of Disease and Death

Sociocultural and demographic factors
- age (menopause)
- sex
- race (ethnicity)
- income and education
- socioeconomic conditions and hygiene

Lifestyle factors
- smoking habits (including past smoking habits)
- dietary intake (e.g., amount and type of fat, antioxidants)
- alcohol consumption
- physical activity

Health-related factors
- background prevalence of disease
- genetic predisposition to diseases
- presence of diseases
- presence of other risk factors

Biometric factors
- stature (including history of stunting and wasting)
- fat distribution
- body proportions (leg length/sitting height)
- history of large fluctuations in weight

Table 18.2   Risk Factors for Cardiovascular Disease Associated With a High Body Mass Index and High Waist/ Hip Ratio

Elevated concentrations
- very low density lipoproteins, triglycerides
- glucose and insulin (glucose intolerance and insulin resistance)
- uric acid

Normal concentrations
- total and LDL cholesterol but the particles are smaller and more dense (richer in apolipoprotein B and cholesterol)

Reduced concentrations
- high density lipoprotein (especially HDL_2)

Other risk factors
- increased blood pressure (hypertension)
- alteration in cardiac structure (e.g., eccentric left ventricular hypertrophy)
- sleeping disturbances (snoring, sleep apnea)
- electrophysiological abnormalities (e.g., prolonged QT interval on electrocardiogram)
- increased blood viscosity and decreased fibrinolytic capacity

have been most extensively reported. More recently, hundreds of publications have appeared on the relationships between fat distribution indexed by the waist/hip ratio and indicators of lipid and glucose metabolism.

Table 18.2 gives an overview of the cardiovascular risk factors associated with increased BMI and increased waist/hip ratio. Many of these risk factors are interrelated, and some are part of the so-called insulin resistance syndrome or syndrome X (Ferrannini, 1993), which probably includes increased abdominal fatness. The causality of the relationships is not firmly established in all cases. The best evidence for causal relationships is for those between increased BMI and altered serum lipid levels, hypertension, and glucose intolerance. Analyses of the prospective Framingham Heart Study showed that weight changes corresponded to changes in serum cholesterol, systolic blood pressure, blood glucose, and uric acid (Ashley & Kannel, 1974). A recent meta-analysis of 70 studies showed that weight loss is associated with decreases in all lipid levels, except high density lipoprotein cholesterol (HDL-C), which increases with weight loss (Datillo & Kris-Etherton, 1992). A limitation of most studies is that they do not allow discrimination between the effects of weight loss per se and the changes in dietary composition to which treated obese subjects are usually subjected. A recent study by Leenen et al. (1993) showed that there is an effect of weight loss on serum lipid levels independent of dietary changes. Meta-analyses have also shown clear effects of weight loss on blood pressure (Staessen, Fagard, & Amery, 1988). Experimental obesity in normal young men induces insulin resistance that is reversible with weight loss (Sims et al., 1973).

A potential mechanism for the relationship between increased fatness and dyslipidemia, insulin resistance, glucose intolerance, and hypertension, as proposed by Björntorp (1990), is shown in Figure 18.1.

A crucial role is proposed for increased visceral fat, or, more specifically, the mesenteric and omental fat stores, which are also called "portal" adipose tissues. Adipocytes in these visceral depots are two to four times more sensitive to lipolytic stimuli than subcutaneous adipocytes, which implies that they release more fatty acids into the bloodstream. In addition, these visceral adipocytes are less sensitive to the antilipolytic effects of insulin. This is important because insulin levels tend to be increased in those with an increased accumulation of visceral fat.

Perhaps more importantly, the fatty acids released from the mesenteric and omental adipose tissue pass directly into the portal vein (Björntorp, 1990). The potentially increased portal concentrations of free fatty acids may give rise to metabolic derangements. The liver will be exposed to an elevated inflow of fatty acids, which may stimulate gluconeogenesis and reduce insulin clearance (Björntorp). This, in turn, may lead to hyperinsulinemia and, consequently, to insulin resistance in muscle. Insulin resistance may be a contributing factor to the development of hypertension (Reaven & Hoffman, 1987). Increased exposure of the liver to free fatty acids may also lead to increased synthesis of triglycerides and secretion of very low density lipoprotein cholesterol (VLDL-C) (Després, 1991). As suggested by Després, the high circulating VLDL-C levels may lead to a triglyceride enrichment of low density lipoprotein cholesterol (LDL-C) and of high density lipoprotein cholesterol (HDL-C) and result in reduced plasma HDL-C and the formation of atherogenic, small "dense" LDL. Després also proposed that the

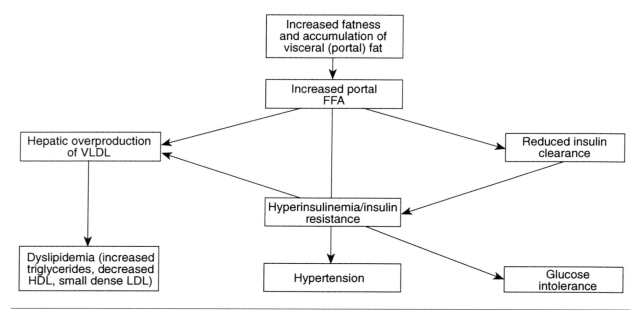

Figure 18.1 Potential mechanism underlying the association between general and abdominal fatness and cardiovascular risk factors (adapted from Björntorp, 1990).

slow catabolism of VLDL-C and the high activity of hepatic triglyceride lipase activity may contribute to a further lowering of HDL-C levels. The mechanisms responsible for the association between visceral fat and lipoproteins may also include effects of glucocorticosteroids and androgens, which are related to the accumulation of fat in the abdominal cavity as well as to disturbances in glucose and lipid metabolism.

Body Composition and Morbidity

Despite the clear association of BMI and the waist/hip ratio with a large number of risk factors for coronary heart disease, the relationship between BMI and the incidence of coronary heart disease has been disputed. In some reviews, predominantly covering studies of middle-aged men, it was concluded that in most such studies BMI and coronary heart disease were not clearly associated or such an association was noted only in certain countries or only in the younger age groups (Barrett-Connor, 1985; Pooling Project Research Group, 1978).

It was suggested by Sjöström (1992) that many of these studies had insufficient statistical power because of limited sample size or short follow-up. In addition (as will be discussed in the section dealing with BMI and mortality), there were methodological problems in most studies, such as inadequate control for the effects of cigarette smoking,

inappropriate control for intermediates in the relationships (such as hypertension, dyslipidemia, and glucose intolerance), and failure to correct for the presence of other diseases (Manson, Stampfer, Hennekens, & Willett, 1987). More recently, studies with sufficient statistical power and with adequate statistical analyses showed a continuous increase of the risk of coronary heart disease with increasing BMI values (Lindsted et al., 1991; Manson et al., 1990). Interestingly, in the large Nurses Health Study, it was clearly shown that overweight in the presence of hypertension, smoking, hypercholesterolemia, or diabetes mellitus was much more clearly related to the prevalence of coronary heart disease than when such additional risk factors were not present (Manson et al., 1990). It has not been demonstrated, however, in a major epidemiological study, that weight loss is associated with a reduction in the prevalence of coronary heart disease.

Furthermore, it has been observed that the relationships between BMI and coronary heart disease may be less pronounced among some U.S. minority populations compared to those in white Americans (Kumanyika, 1993). The phenomena described in the introduction of this chapter may be partly responsible for the racial/ethnic differences in health consequences. For instance, Kumanyika noted that U.S. African Americans have higher prevalences of overweight, particularly among women, and also considerably higher rates of infectious diseases, accidents, and homicide compared to white Americans and argued that these competing causes of death may partially mask the association between BMI and coronary heart disease mortality.

Fat distribution, as assessed by the waist/hip ratio or ratios between skinfold thicknesses, is positively associated with coronary heart disease independent of the degree of overweight (Larsson, 1988). A Swedish study showed that sex differences in fat distribution may account for the higher incidence of coronary heart disease among men compared to women (Larsson et al., 1992). Because the methods for assessing fat distribution, as well as the definition of cut-off points, vary greatly among studies, and because the sample size is limited in most studies, it seems premature to define cut-off points for classification into low and high risk groups.

For many decades obesity has been recognized as an important risk factor for non-insulin-dependent diabetes mellitus (NIDDM). Barrett-Connor (1985, 1989) suggested that the duration of obesity and previous overweight may be more important than current overweight, perhaps because weight loss often precedes the diagnosis of NIDDM. Data from the Nurses Health Study showed that more than 90% of the prevalence of NIDDM could be attributed to a BMI greater than 22 kg/m^2 (Colditz et al., 1990). Although weight loss clearly improves glucose tolerance and insulin resistance, it has not been clearly shown that weight loss prevents NIDDM or reduces the risk of complications. An increased waist/hip ratio has been shown to be associated with an increased risk for the development of NIDDM, independently of the degree of overweight, in several prospective studies (Björntorp, 1990). The risk of increased abdominal fatness for the development of NIDDM seems to be race-dependent (Dowling & Pi-Sunyer, 1993).

An increased BMI and increased waist/hip ratio have been shown to be associated with diseases other than coronary heart disease and NIDDM (Table 18.3). The associations between these other conditions and BMI, or an index of abdominal obesity, are sometimes primarily the result of mechanical effects of excess fat storage (e.g., osteoarthritis and pulmonary insufficiency) and are sometimes primarily the result of metabolic aberrations in glucose and lipid metabolism (e.g., gall bladder disease). Some of these associations are discussed below.

The relationships between overweight and a reduced risk of osteoporosis in postmenopausal women is thought to be due to the aromatization of androgens to estrogens in adipose tissue, leading to increased estrogen levels. The risk of osteoporosis is obviously strongly affected by other aspects of body composition such as total body bone mineral and regional measures of bone mineral density and bone mineral content (Godfredsen, Hassager, & Christiansen, 1990).

The relatively high estrogen levels in obese postmenopausal women are, on the other hand, thought to be partly responsible for an increased risk of breast cancer. In addition, relatively high androgen levels may be involved in the mechanisms underlying this association, which may partly explain the relationship that is sometimes observed between abdominal fatness and breast cancer (Den Tonkelaar, Seidell, & Collette, 1995).

Although the pathogenesis and risk factors for osteoarthritis are not well understood, there is increasing evidence that obesity is associated with an increased prevalence of osteoarthritis of the knee. The mechanical stress induced by carrying excess weight may be particularly harmful to the knee joints. The relationships between overweight and osteoarthritis of nonweightbearing joints remain obscure and may reflect other intermediate metabolic consequences of obesity. Davis (1988) has suggested that obesity-related conditions, such as NIDDM, hyperuricemia, or hypercholesterolemia, that may influence cartilage degradation, may act together with excessive wear and tear from the mechanical stress on the joints to produce osteoarthritis. The association between obesity and osteoarthritis has important public health implications, as illustrated by a Finnish study that showed that overweight contributed significantly to the number of disability pensions because of arthritis of the knee and hip (Rissanen et al., 1990).

Body Composition and Respiratory Function

The associations between severe obesity and the clinically obvious obesity-hypoventilation syndrome (or Pickwickian syndrome) is well known (Kopelman, 1992). It is increasingly recognized, in addition, that disordered breathing in sleep may constitute a major and often undiagnosed public health problem (Young et al., 1993). The prevalence of disordered breathing in sleep, defined as a relative high apnea-hypopnea score, is as high as 9% in U.S. women and 24% in U.S. men. High BMI values and high waist/hip ratios are strongly associated with these breathing disorders. An increase of one standard deviation in BMI is associated with

Table 18.3   Diseases Associated With a High Body Mass Index (BMI) or a High Waist/Hip Ratio (WHR)

Disease	Associated with BMI	WHR	Comments
Stroke	+ / ?	+ / ?	Despite clear association with hypertension.
Varicose veins	+	–	No prospective studies.
Breast cancer	+ / ?	+ / ?	In postmenopausal women; clearer in case-control than in prospective studies.
Endometrial cancer	+	+	
Gall bladder disease	+	+	Increased risk of stones containing cholesterol; dieting may increase short-term risk.
Osteoarthritis	+	– / ?	Large mechanical, but also present in nonweightbearing joints.
Gout	+	?	Via increased uric acid levels.
Osteoporosis	–	?	In postmenopausal women.
Pulmonary insufficiency	+	+ / ?	Especially pronounced in severe overweight.
Psycho-social problems	+	+ / ?	Causality not clear.

+ positive association; – negative association; ? uncertain association.

a more than four-fold risk of such problems (Young et al., 1993).

For a more thorough discussion of the relationships between overweight and disease the reader is referred to some specialized monographs (Björntorp & Brodoff, 1992; Garrow, 1988).

Body Composition and Mortality Rates

It seems well established that there is a curvilinear relationship between BMI and total or all-cause mortality (Kushner, 1993). From such U-shaped or J-shaped associations, attempts have been made to establish ranges of BMI that are "optimal" for longevity (i.e., those associated with the lowest mortality rates). The "recommended BMI ranges" from the U.S. Department of Agriculture and Health and Human Services are one example (National Research Council, 1989). These ranges, which have been the subject of considerable discussion, are 19 to 25 kg/m² for people aged 19 to 34 years and 21 to 27 kg/m² for those aged 35 years and older. The World Health Organization (in press) has more recently recommended the following classification based on BMI values.

< 18.5 kg/m², thin
18.5 to 24.99 kg/m², acceptable
25.0 to 29.99 kg/m², grade I overweight
30.0 to 39.99 kg/m², grade II overweight
≥ 40.0 kg/m², grade III overweight

Earlier in this chapter it was noted that a relationship between BMI and coronary heart disease was not noted in all studies. This is true also for the relationship between BMI and mortality rates. Sjöström (1992) showed that such studies often suffer of one or more of the following shortcomings:

1. insufficient sample size (less than 7,000 subjects),
2. insufficient follow-up time (less than five years),
3. failure to control for smoking,
4. failure to eliminate early mortality or presence of (sub)clinical disease from the analysis,
5. inappropriate control for intermediate cardiovascular risk factors, and
6. failure to take into account the effects of different types of fat distribution.

The increased mortality at the higher end of the range of BMI values can be readily explained by an increased risk of dying from cardiovascular diseases, NIDDM, and cancers of the breast, endometrium, and prostate (Kushner, 1993). Consideration of the increased mortality rates at the lower end of the range of BMI values is much more complex. Some attribute this largely to the effects of smoking and the presence of diseases at baseline or during follow-up. Subjects who later develop lung cancer, for instance, may already involuntarily lose weight some years before the disease is diagnosed. Indeed, it was shown in two prospective studies that mortality among very lean males was exceptionally high during the first two to five years of follow-up (Sidney, Friedman, & Siegelaub, 1987; Wannamethee & Shaper, 1989). A 26 year follow-up study of 8,828 nonsmoking Seventh Day Adventist men who did not drink alcohol showed that the mortality rate was lowest in the leanest group (BMI < 20 kg/m²). The leanest men were also the most strict with regard to the practice of vegetarianism and avoidance of coffee. The authors suggest that leanness associated with healthy lifestyles is not associated with increased mortality (Lindsted et al., 1991). On the other hand, a low BMI may reflect recurrent infections or relative energy deficiency or imply impaired immuno-competence (Shetty & James, 1994).

As discussed earlier, in some countries BMI is as much a measure of lean tissue mass as it is a measure of fat mass. This is commonly the case in developing countries. A low BMI may be associated with both low lean tissue mass and low fat mass. After reviewing the literature, Shetty and James (1994) proposed that in developed countries thinness (BMI < 18.5 kg/m²) is associated with decreases in work output, productivity, and income-generating ability, which may jeopardize long-term survival.

As mentioned previously, the relationship of BMI to all-causes mortality rates can be affected by many factors, such as race/ethnicity (Kumanyika, 1993). The relationship between BMI and mortality seems, however, to be quite similar in Japanese adults and in white populations (Tokunaga et al., 1991). It also seems that the risks of overweight and excess abdominal fat may be less pronounced among elderly compared to younger adults, although the implications for public policy recommendations are unclear (Andres et al., 1985; Seidell, Andres, Sorkin, & Muller, 1994). There may be several reasons for a diminishing impact of obesity on survival with aging. They include selective survival of relatively healthy obese individuals and increased competition of factors determining death or survival in the elderly. In addition, abdominal adipose tissue may be less hazardous in older compared to younger people. Engfeldt and Arner (1988) showed, for instance, that the response of omental adipocytes to lipolytic stimuli is greatly reduced in older compared to younger adults.

Overview

A high BMI and, in particular, a high waist/hip ratio, which indicate overweight and abdominal

fatness, respectively, are important health risk factors for some severe and potentially disabling conditions. It must be recognized, however, that a high BMI and a high waist/hip ratio may reflect heterogeneous underlying genetic, socioeconomic, and lifestyle factors that may substantially affect their health implications. Weight loss seems to have at least short-term beneficial results for almost all overweight subjects, regardless of their race/ethnicity, sex, or age, who tend to suffer, partly as a result of their overweight, from conditions such as coronary heart disease, hyperlipidemia, NIDDM, hypertension, or mechanical problems of overweight (Pi-Sunyer, 1993). Strategies to characterize and approach different subgroups that differ in the causes and consequences of overweight and abdominal fatness have yet be developed. Because therapies for the attainment of "optimal" weights are commonly unsuccessful, the concept of "reasonable" weight and weight loss goals should be further developed (St. Jeor et al., 1993), and a focus on the maintenance of attained "reasonable" weights is necessary. From a public health viewpoint, it is desirable that emphasis be placed on the prevention of overweight, but preventive strategies are mainly theoretical. None has been proven to be successful.

Acknowledgment

Expert secretarial assistance by R.M.O.M. Wouters is gratefully acknowledged.

References

Andres, R., Elahi, D., Tobin, J.D., et al. (1985). Impact of age on weight goals. *Annals of Internal Medicine, 103*, 1030-1033.

Ashley, F.W., Jr, & Kannel, W.B. (1974). Relation of weight change to changes in atherogenic traits: The Framingham Study. *Journal of Chronic Diseases, 27*, 103-114.

Barrett-Connor, E.L. (1985). Obesity, atherosclerosis, and coronary artery disease. *Annals of Internal Medicine, 103*, 1010-1019.

Barrett-Connor, E. (1989). Epidemiology, obesity, and non-insulin dependent diabetes mellitus. *Epidemiology Reviews, 11*, 172-181.

Björntorp, P. (1990). "Portal" adipose tissue as a generator of risk factors for cardiovascular disease and diabetes. *Arteriosclerosis, 10*, 493-496.

Björntorp, P., & Brodoff, B.N. (Eds.) (1992). *Obesity.* Philadelphia: J. B. Lippincott.

Colditz, G.A., Willett, W.C., Stampfer, M.J., et al. (1990). Weight as a risk factor for clinical diabetes in women. *American Journal of Epidemiology,* **132,** 501-513.

Datillo, A.M., & Kris-Etherton, P.M. (1992). Effects of weight reduction on blood lipids and lipoproteins: A meta-analysis. *American Journal of Clinical Nutrition,* **56,** 320-328.

Davis, M.A. (1988). Epidemiology of osteoarthritis. *Clinics in Geriatric Medicine,* **4,** 241-255.

Den Tonkelaar, I., Seidell, J.C., & Collette, H.J.A. (1995). Body fat distribution in relation to breast cancer in women participating in the DOM project. *Breast Cancer Research & Treatment,* **34,** 55-61.

Després, J.-P. (1991). Obesity and lipid metabolism: Relevance of body fat distribution. *Current Opinions in Lipidology,* **2,** 5-15.

Dowling, H.J., & Pi-Sunyer, F.X. (1993). Race-dependent health risks of upper body obesity. *Diabetes,* **42,** 537-543.

Engfeldt, P., & Arner, P. (1988). Lipolysis in human adipocytes: Effects of cell size, age and regional differences. *Hormone and Metabolic Research,* **19** (Suppl.), 26-31.

Ferrannini, E. (1993). Syndrome X. *Hormone Research,* **39** (Suppl.), 107-111.

Garrow, J.S. (1988). *Obesity and related diseases.* New York: Churchill Livingstone.

Godfredsen, A., Hassager, C., & Christiansen, C. (1990). Total and regional bone mass in healthy and osteoporotic women. In S. Yasumura, J.E. Harrison, K.C. McNeill, et al. (Eds.), *Advances in in vivo body composition studies* (pp.101-106). New York: Plenum.

James, W.P.T., & Ralph, A. (1994). The functional significance of low body mass index (BMI). *European Journal of Clinical Nutrition,* **48** (Suppl. 3), S1-S202.

Kopelman, P.G. (1992). Altered respiratory function in obesity: Sleep disordered breathing and the Pickwickian syndrome. In P. Björntorp & B.N. Brodoff (Eds.), *Obesity* (pp. 568-575). Philadelphia: J.B. Lippincott.

Kumanyika, S.K. (1993). Special issues regarding obesity in minority populations. *Annals of Internal Medicine,* **119,** 650-654.

Kushner, R.F. (1993). Body weight and mortality. *Nutrition Reviews,* **51,** 127-136.

Larsson, B. (1988). Fat distribution and risk of death, myocardial infarction and stroke. In C. Bouchard & F.E. Johnston (Eds.), *Fat distribution during growth and later health outcomes* (pp. 193-201). New York: Alan R. Liss.

Larsson, B., Bengtsson, C., Björntorp, P., et al. (1992). Is abdominal body fat distribution a major explanation for the sex difference in the incidence of myocardial infarction? *American Journal of Epidemiology,* **135,** 266-273.

Leenen, R., van der Kooy, K., Meyboom, S., et al. (1993). Relative effects of weight loss and dietary fat modification on serum lipid levels in the dietary treatment of obesity. *Journal of Lipid Research,* **34,** 2183-2191.

Lindsted, K., Tonstad, S., Kuzma, J.W., et al. (1991). Body mass index and patterns of mortality among Seventh-day Adventist men. *International Journal of Obesity,* **15,** 397-406.

Manson, J.E., Colditz, G.A., Stampfer, M.J., et al. (1990). A prospective study of obesity and risk of coronary heart disease in women. *New England Journal of Medicine,* **322,** 882-889.

Manson, J.E., Stampfer, M.J., Hennekens, C.H., & Willett, W.C. (1987). Body weight and longevity: A reassessment. *Journal of the American Medical Association,* **257,** 353-358.

National Research Council (U.S.), Committee on Diet and Health. (1989). *Diet and health: Implications for reducing chronic disease.* Washington, DC: National Academy.

Pi-Sunyer, F.X. (1993). Short-term medical benefits and adverse effects of weight loss. *Annals of Internal Medicine,* **119,** 722-726.

Pooling Project Research Group. (1978). Relationship of blood pressure, serum cholesterol, smoking habit, relative weight and ECG abnormalities to incidence of major coronary events: Final report of the Pooling Project. *Journal of Chronic Diseases,* **31,** 201-235.

Reaven, G.R., & Hoffman, B.B. (1987). A role for insulin in the aetiology and course of hypertension? *Lancet,* **2,** 435-436.

Rissanen, A., Heliovaara, M., Knekt, P., et al. (1990). Risk of disability and mortality due to overweight in a Finnish population. *British Medical Journal,* **301,** 835-837.

Seidell, J.C., Andres, R., Sorkin, J.D., & Muller, D.C. (1994). The sagittal diameter and mortality in men: The Baltimore Longitudinal Study on Aging. *International Journal of Obesity,* **18,** 61-67.

Shetty, P.S., & James, W.P.T. (1994). *Body mass index: A measure of chronic energy deficiency in adults.* Food and Agriculture Organization, United Nations, Rome.

Sidney, S., Friedman, G.D., & Siegelaub, A.B. (1987). Thinness and mortality. *American Journal of Public Health,* **77,** 317-322.

Sims, E.A.H., Danforth, E., Horton, E.S., et al. (1973). Endocrine and metabolic effects of experimental obesity in man. *Recent Progress in Hormone Research,* **29**:457-496.

Sjöström, L.V. (1992). Mortality of severely obese subjects. *American Journal of Clinical Nutrition,* **55**, 516S-523S.

Staessen, J., Fagard, R., & Amery, A. (1988). The relationship between body weight and blood pressure. *Journal of Human Hypertension,* **2**, 207-217.

St. Jeor, S.T., Brownell, K.D., Atkinson, R.L., et al. (1993). Obesity, workshop III. *Circulation,* **88**, 1391-1396.

Tokunaga, K., Matsuzawa, Y., Kotani, K., et al. (1991). Ideal body weight estimated from the body mass index with the lowest morbidity. *International Journal of Obesity,* **15**, 1-5.

Wannamethee, G., & Shaper, A.G. (1989). Body weight and mortality in middle aged British men: Impact of smoking. *British Medical Journal,* **299**, 1497-1502.

World Health Organization. (in press). Physical status: Use and interpretation of anthropometry. Technical Report Series.

Young, T., Palta, M., Dempsey, J., et al. (1993). The occurrence of sleep disordered breathing among middle-aged adults. *New England Journal of Medicine,* **328**, 1230-1235.

Equipment and Suppliers

EQUIPMENT

Densitometry

Poolside underwater weighing system
Novel Products, Inc.

Force transducers/load cells
IC Sensors
Interface, Inc.
Sensotech, Inc.
T-Hydronics

Autopsy scales
Novel Products, Inc.
Yagami Company

Spirometers and breathing valves
Hans Rudolph, Inc.
Vacmed
Warren E. Collins, Inc.

Gas analyzers
FITCO
Hans Rudolph, Inc.
Medical Graphics Corporation
Sensor Medics

Telethermometers/temperature probes
Yellow Springs Instrument Co., Inc.

Hydrometry

Isotope ratio mass spectrometers
Europa Scientific
Finnigan MAT
PATCO

Stable isotopes
Cambridge Isotope Labs
Euriso-top
Isotec, Inc.

Electrical impedance

Single frequency analyzers
Body Composition Analyzers, Inc.

RJL Systems, Inc. (several models)
SEAC Labs Health Care Services
Tanita Corporation
Valhalla Scientific, Inc.

Multiple frequency analyzers
Dietosystem s.r.l.
UniQuest Limited
Xitron Technologies, Inc.

Dual energy x-ray absorptiometers

Hologic, Inc.
Lunar Corporation
Norland Company

Anthropometry

Sliding and spreading calipers
Best Priced Products, Inc.
Dietosystem s.r.l.
Lafayette Instrument
Mediform
Pfister Import-Export, Inc.
Takei Kiki Kogyo

Skinfold calipers
Best Priced Products, Inc.
British Indicators Ltd.
Cambridge Scientific Industries
Country Technology, Inc.
Cramer Products
Creative Health Products
Dietosystem s.r.l.
H.E. Morse Co.
Human Performance Systems, Inc.
Lafayette Instrument
McGaw Laboratories
Pfister Import-Export, Inc.
Rosscraft Ltd.
Seritex, Inc.
Takei Kiki Kogyo
Yagami Company

Stadiometers
    CMS Weighing Equipment, Ltd.
    Holtain, Ltd.
    Pfister Import-Export, Inc.
    Raven Equipment, Inc.

Tape measures
    Lafayette Instrument
    Medline Industries

Weighing scales
    CMS Weighing Equipment, Ltd.
    Continental Scale Corporation
    Detecto Scales, Inc.
    John Chatillon & Sons
    Marsden Weighing Machine Group, Ltd.
    Rasmussen, Webb & Company
    Salter International Measurement, Ltd.
    Toledo Scale

B-mode ultrasound
    Biosound
    Esaote Biomedica s.p.a.
    Shimadzu Corporation
    Toshiba

SUPPLIERS

Akern s.r.l.
Via Panciatichi 56/13
Firenze, Italy

Best Priced Products, Inc.
Box 1174
White Plains, New York 10602 USA
Phone: 800-824-2939
FAX: 800-356-8587

Biosound
Castleway Drive
Box 50858
Indianapolis, IN 45250-0858 USA
Phone: 317-849-1793

Body Composition Analyzers, Inc.
West Schaumburg Ave.
Schaumburg, IL 60194 USA
Phone: 708-980-3793

British Indicators, Ltd.
Sutton Road
St. Albans, Herts., UK

Cambridge Iostope Labs.
20 Commerce Way
Woburn, MA 01801 USA
Phone: 617-938-0067

Cambridge Scientific Industries
P.O. Box 265
Cambridge, MD 21613 USA
Phone: 800-638-9566
        302-228-5111

CMS Weighing Equipment, Ltd.
18 Camden High Street
London, NWI OJH, UK

Continental Scale Corporation
7400 West 100th Place
Bridgeview, IL 60455 USA
Phone: 708-598-9100

Country Technology, Inc.
P.O. Box 87
Gays Mills, WI 54631 USA
Phone: 608-735-4718

Cramer Products
P.O. Box 1001
Gardner, KS 66030 USA
Phone: 913-884-7511

Creative Health Products
5148 Saddle Ridge Road
Plymouth, MI 48170 USA
Phone: 313-453-5309
        313-455-0177

Detecto Scales, Inc.
Detecto International
240 Grand Avenue
Leonia, NJ 07605-2013 USA
Phone: 201-944-3888

Dietosystem s.r.l.
Via Teddosio, 74
Milano, Italy
Phone: 02-26-82-16-68
FAX: 02-26-82-12-75

Esaote Biomedica s.p.a.
Ansaldo Elettronica Biomedicale
Via Ariosto 22
Padova, Italy
Phone: 49-77-66-99
FAX: 49-80-700-45

Euriso-top
Parc des Algorithmes-Batiment Homere
Route de l'Orme
91194 Saint Aubin Cedix, France
Phone: 33 1 69.41.95.96

Europa Scientific
Europa House
Electra Way
Crewe, CW1 1ZA, UK
Phone: 44-270-589398

Finnigan MAT
355 River Oaks Parkway
San Jose, CA 95134 USA
Phone: 408-433-4800

FITCO
Route 110
Farmingdale, NY 11735 USA
Phone: 516-694-6550
FAX: 516-694-6604

H.E. Morse Co.
455 Douglas Avenue
Holland, MI 49423 USA
Phone: 616-396-4604

Hans Rudolph, Inc.
Wyandotte St.
Kansas City, MO 64114 USA
Phone: 800-456-6695
FAX: 816-822-1414

Hologic, Inc.
590 Lincoln Street
Waltham, MA 02154 USA
Phone: 617-890-2300
FAX: 617-890-8031

Holtain, Ltd.
Crosswell, Crymmych, Dyfed
Wales, UK

Human Performance Systems, Inc.
P.O. Drawer 1324
Fayetteville, AR 72701 USA
Phone: 501-521-3180

IC Sensors
1701 McCarthy Blvd.
Milpitas, CA 94035 USA
Phone: 800-767-1888

Interface, Inc.
7401 E. Butherus Dr.
Scottsdale, AZ 85260 USA
Phone: 602-948-5555

Isotec, Inc.
3858 Benner Rd.
Miamisburg, OH 45342 USA
Phone: 513-859-1808

John Chatillon & Sons
83-30 Kew Gardens Road
Kew Gardens, NY 11415 USA
Phone: 718-847-5000

Lafayette Instrument
Sagamore Parkway N.
Box 5729
Lafayette, IN 47903 USA
Phone: 800-428-7545
Phone: 317-423-1505
FAX: 317-423-4111

Life Measurement Instruments
Box 4456
Davis, CA 95617-2146
Phone: 916-757-2146
FAX: 916-757-2140

Lunar Corporation
313 W. Beltline Highway
Madison, WI 53713 USA
Phone: 800-445-8627
FAX: 608-274-5374

Marsden Weighing Machine Group, Ltd.
388 Harrow Road
London W9 2HU, UK
Phone: 44-71-289-1066
FAX: 44-71-286-6349

McGaw Laboratories
Division of American Hospital Supply
Irvine, CA 92714 USA

Medical Graphics Corporation
350 Oak Grove Parkway
St. Paul, MN 55127 USA
Phone: 800-950-5597

Mediform
5150 S.W. Griffith Drive
Beaverton, OR 97005 USA
Phone: 800-633-3676
          503-643-1670

Medline Industries
1825 Shermer Road
Northbrook, IL 60062 USA
Phone: 800-323-5886

Norland Company
W. 6340 Hackbarth Rd.
Fort Atkinson, WI 53538-8999 USA
Phone: 414-563-8456
FAX: 414-563-9501

Novel Products, Inc.
Box 408
Rockton, IL 61072 USA
Phone: 800-323-5143

PATCO
1155 Zion Rd.
Bellefonte, PA 16823 USA
Phone: 814-353-0603

Pfister Import-Export, Inc.
450 Barell Avenue
Carlstadt, NJ 07072 USA
Phone: 201-939-4606

Rasmussen, Webb & Company
First Floor
12116 Laystall Street
London ECIR 4UB, UK

Raven Equipment, Ltd.
Little Easton
Dunmow, Essex, CM6 2ES, UK

RJL Systems, Inc.
Harper Avenue
Clinton Township, MI 48035 USA
Phone: 800-528-4513
FAX: 810-790-0205

Rosscraft Ltd.
14732 16-A Avenue
Surrey, B.C. V4A 5M7
Canada
Phone: 604-531-5049

Salter International Measurement, Ltd.
George Street
West Bromwich, Staffs, UK

SEAC Labs Health Care Services
Sandon Street
Graceville, Queensland
Australia 4075
Phone: 07-2781092

Sensor Medics
Savi Ranch Parkway
Yorba Linda, CA 92687 USA
Phone: 800-231-2468
FAX: 714-283-8439

Sensotech, Inc.
Chesapeake Ave.
Columbus, OH 43212 USA
Phone: 800-848-6564
FAX: 614-486-0606

Seritex, Inc.
Barell Avenue
Carlstadt, NJ 07072 USA
Phone: 201-939-4606
FAX: 201-939-3468

Shimadzu Corporation
Kanda-Nishikicho
1-Chome, Chiyoda-Ku
Tokyo 101, Japan
Phone: 03-219-5641
FAX: 201-939-3468

Space Labs Health Care Services
150th Ave., N.E.
Box 97013
Redmond, WA 98073-9713 USA
Phone: 206-882-3700

Takei Kiki Kogyo
Shihaga Wa-Ku
Hatonodai 1-6-18
Tokyo 142, Japan
Phone: 03-786-4111
FAX: 03-787-8673

Tanita Corporation
Church Street
Skokie, IL 60077 USA
Phone: 708-581-0250
FAX: 708-581-0268

T-Hydronics
Stelzer Court
Sunbury, OH 43074 USA
Phone: 614-965-9340
FAX: 614-965-9438

Toledo Scale
431 Ohio Pike
Suite 302, Way Cross Office Park
Toledo, OH 43611 USA
Phone: 513-528-2300

Toshiba
Michelle Drive
Tustin, CA 92680 USA
Phone: 800-421-1968
Phone: 714-730-5000

UniQuest Limited
Box 69
St. Lucia, Queensland
Australia 4072
Phone: 61-7-365-4037
FAX: 61-7-365-4433

Vacmed, Inc.
5770 Nicolle St.
Ventura, CA 93003, USA
Phone: 800-235-3333
        805-644-7461

Valhalla Scientific, Inc.
9955 Mesa Rim Road
San Diego, CA 92121 USA
Phone: 800-395-4565
FAX: 619-536-9879

Warren E. Collins, Inc.
Wood Road
Braintree, MA 02184 USA
Phone: 617-843-0610

Xitron Technologies, Inc.
10225 Barnes Canyon Rd., Suite A102
San Diego, CA 92121 USA
Phone: 619-458-9852
FAX: 619-458-9213

Yagami Company
Naka-Ku Marunoucho
3-2.29 Japan
Phone: 052-951-9251
FAX: 052-951-6173

Yellow Springs Instrument Company, Inc.
Box 279
Yellow Springs, OH 45387 USA
Phone: 800-343-4357
FAX: 513--767-9353

Index

About the Editors

Alex F. Roche, MD, PhD, DSc, is Fels Professor of Community Health and Pediatrics at Wright State University School of Medicine in Yellow Springs, Ohio. He has been involved in body composition as a researcher, teacher, speaker, and author for more than 35 years.

A prolific writer, Dr. Roche has contributed to more than 690 publications. He is one of the editors of the *Anthropometric Standardization Reference Manual*, published by Human Kinetics. Since 1993 he has served as editor-in-chief of the *Journal of Human Ecology*. He also has served on the editorial boards of several prestigious journals, including *Annals of Human Biology, American Journal of Human Biology, American Journal of Clinical Nutrition, Human Biology,* and *Monographs of the Society for Research in Child Development*.

Throughout his career, Dr. Roche has participated in national and international conferences and associations related to body composition and child health. An active member of the Human Biology Association, Dr. Roche was named a fellow in 1976 and served as president from 1980 to 1982. He is also a council member of the International Association of Human Biologists, the vice president of the Centre Oncologique et Biologique de Recherche Appliqueé, a member of the American Society of Clinical Nutrition, and a fellow of the Indian Society for Human Ecology.

Steven B. Heymsfield, MD, brings a broad range of experience in research to the writing of this book. He is the deputy director of the Obesity Research Center at St. Luke's-Roosevelt Hospital and professor of medicine at the Columbia University, New York, College of Physicians and Surgeons.

In addition to holding a patent on a radiometric digital caliper, Dr. Heymsfield has conducted national and international presentations and made many contributions to publications in the field. He is on the editorial board of the *Nutrition International* journal, *Journal of Parenteral and Enteral Nutrition*, and the *American Journal of Human Biology*.

Dr. Heymsfield is an active member of the American Society of Clinical Nutrition, the American Institute of Nutrition, American Federation of Clinical Research, and the North American Association for the Study of Obesity. He is president-elect of the American Society of Parenteral and Enteral Nutrition.

Timothy G. Lohman, PhD, is a leading scientist in the field of body composition assessment. A respected researcher, he explores body composition methodology and changes in body composition with growth and development, exercise, and aging. His leadership in standardization of body composition methodology is well recognized.

Dr. Lohman is a professor in the Department of Exercise Science at the University of Arizona. He is the author of many research articles and an editor of the *Anthropometric Standardization Reference Manual*, published by Human Kinetics. Dr. Lohman is also author of *Advances in Body Composition Assessment*.

Dr. Lohman is a fellow of the American Academy of Physical Edcuation, a member of the American College of Sports Medicine, and a member of the Youth Fitness Advisory Committee of the Cooper Institute for Aerobics Research in Dallas, Texas. He serves as a reviewer for many scholarly publications, including *Journal of Applied Physiology, International Journal of Obesity, American Journal of Human Biology, Medicine and Science in Sports and Exercise,* and *Research Quarterly for Exercise and Sport*.